Under Siege: Four African Cities

Documenta11_Platform4

**Under Siege: Four African Cities
Freetown, Johannesburg, Kinshasa, Lagos**

Documenta11_Platform4

Edited by
Okwui Enwezor
Carlos Basualdo
Ute Meta Bauer
Susanne Ghez
Sarat Maharaj
Mark Nash
Octavio Zaya

Hatje Cantz

This volume contains all contributions to Documenta11_Platform4, "Under Siege: Four African Cities – Freetown, Johannesburg, Kinshasa, Lagos," a conference and workshop held in Lagos, Goethe-Institut Inter Nationes, March 16–20, 2002.

Managing Editor: Gerti Fietzek

Editing: Philomena Mariani

Translations: Miranda Robbins

Visual Concept and Typography: Ecke Bonk

Typesetting: Weyhing digital, Ostfildern-Ruit

Printed by Dr. Cantz'sche Druckerei, Ostfildern-Ruit

© 2002 documenta und Museum Fridericianum-Veranstaltungs GmbH, Kassel, Hatje Cantz Publishers, and authors

Photo Credits:
pp. 155–171 Lindsay J. Bremner; pp. 174, 176, 178–180, 183 Rem Koolhaas; pp. 240–241 Courtesy Koku Konu; pp. 244–285 © Marie-Françoise Plissart; p. 288 © 2000 newafrica.com.

Published by
Hatje Cantz Publishers
Senefelderstrasse 12
73760 Ostfildern-Ruit, Germany
www.hatjecantz.de

Distribution in the USA
D.A.P., Distributed Art Publishers, Inc.
155 Avenue of the Americas, 2nd Floor
New York, NY 10013, USA
www.artbook.com

ISBN 3-7757-9090-X

Printed in Germany

Die Deutsche Bibliothek – CIP-Einheitsaufnahme
A catalogue record for this book is available from Die Deutsche Bibliothek.

Platform4 was organized in collaboration with the Goethe-Institut Inter Nationes, Munich and Lagos, and CODESRIA (Council for the Development of Social Science Research in Africa), Dakar, Senegal.

Project Advisor: AbdouMaliq Simone

Research: Chika Okeke, Nadja Rottner

Organization: Markus Müller, Christian Rattemeyer, Christina Werner

Coordination: Chika Okeke
Assistants: Jahman Anikulapo, Uche Edochie, Uche Nwosu, Nkechi Nwosu-Igbo

Thanks to:
Mahmood Mamdani, President, CODESRIA
Adebayo Olukoshi, Executive Secretary, CODESRIA
Sheila Bunwaree, Head of Research and Documentation Department, CODESRIA
Bruno Sonko, Program Assistant, Research and Documentation Department, CODESRIA
Damien Pwono, Program Officer, Media, Arts, and Culture, The Ford Foundation, New York
Michael Müller-Verweyen, Director, Goethe-Institut Inter Nationes, Kyoto
Heiko Sievers, Head of Program Department, Goethe-Institut Inter Nationes, Munich
Annesusanne Fackler-Kabisch, Head of Fine Arts Section, Goethe-Institut Inter Nationes, Munich
Karin Uwaje, Program Officer, Goethe-Institut Inter Nationes, Lagos
Sunday Umweni, Assistant Program Officer, Goethe-Institut Inter Nationes, Lagos
Ursel Olupitan, Acting Director and Head of Administration, Goethe-Institut Inter Nationes, Lagos
Monday Osegbe, technical support, Goethe-Institut Inter Nationes, Lagos
Ado Abana, technical support, Goethe-Institut Inter Nationes, Lagos
Rasaki Oseni, driver, Goethe-Institut Inter Nationes, Lagos
Dickson Begusa, security, Goethe-Institut Inter Nationes, Lagos

Platform4 was realized with the generous support of
The Ford Foundation, New York
Goethe-Institut Inter Nationes, Munich and Lagos
and with the assistance of CODESRIA, Dakar.

Contents

Preface   9

Introduction   13

Cities in Transition: The Fate of African Urban Systems

AbdouMaliq Simone
The Visible and Invisible: Remaking Cities in Africa   23

Carole Rakodi
Order and Disorder in African Cities:
Governance, Politics, and Urban Land Development Processes   45

Antoine Bouillon
Between Euphemism and Informalism: Inventing the City   81

Achille Mbembe and Janet Roitman
Figures of the Subject in Times of Crisis   99

From Obsolescence to Dynamism: Reinterpreting African Urban Futures

Babatunde A. Ahonsi
Popular Shaping of Metropolitan Forms and Processes in Nigeria:
Glimpses and Interpretations from an Informed Lagosian   129

Lindsay J. Bremner
Closure, Simulation, and "Making Do" in the
Contemporary Johannesburg Landscape   153

Rem Koolhaas
Fragments of a Lecture on Lagos 173

Thierry Nlandu
Kinshasa: Beyond Chaos 185

Ibrahim Abdullah
**Space, Culture, and Agency in Contemporary Freetown:
The Making and Remaking of a Postcolonial City** 201

Exploring the Rift/Shift in the African Urban Paradigm

Maxine Reitzes
**"There's Space for Africa in the New South Africa (?)":
African Migrants and Urban Governance in Johannesburg** 215

Koku Konu
Regenerating Downtown Lagos 239

Filip De Boeck
With photographs by Marie-Françoise Plissart
Kinshasa: Tales of the "Invisible City" and the Second World 243

Alfred B. Zack-Williams
**Freetown: From the "Athens of West Africa" to a City Under Siege:
The Rise and Fall of Sub-Saharan First Municipality** 287

Onookome Okome
**Writing the Anxious City:
Images of Lagos in Nigerian Home Video Films** 315

Urban Processes and Change in Africa

Mohamadou Abdoul
**The Production of the City and Urban Informalities:
The Borough of Thiaroye-sur-mer in the City of Pikine, Senegal** 337

Victor A. O. Adetula
Welfare Associations and the Dynamics of City Politics in Nigeria: Jos Metropolis as Case Study   359

Mohammed Gheris
Housing in Marrakech: The Contradictions of Public Interventions   381

Jean Omasombo Tshonda
Kisangani and the Curve of Destiny   401

Mohammed-Bello Yunusa
Environment and Inhabitants of an Unplanned Area of Zaria, Nigeria   417

Bahru Zewde
The City Center: A Shifting Concept in the History of Addis Ababa   431

Contributors   449

Preface

It is now commonplace to declare that the world changed with the spectacular and traumatizing events of September 11, 2001. What the change represents, however, is still hard to define, given how deeply such change is also seen to be caught in the proliferating processes of globalization. A teleological reading of September 11 positions it in a sort of flawed cause-and-effect representation. That it marks a deep cleavage in the ways one thinks of political Islam is certain, but whether this should mean that all responses to it should be understood from the point of view of the pre- and post-syndrome that has overtaken all discussions around it, especially in the United States, is quite another matter.

Even if we cannot deny that the events of September 11 and its aftermath in the war in Afghanistan have significantly widened the political horizon of democratic and juridical discourses of our time, they could hardly be pronounced the central ground on which the struggle to overcome Westernism and imperialism is being waged. September 11 represents one of the most radical and terrible visions of the conflict of values that has attended the slow dismantling of imperialism. It is also a sanguine lesson for late modernity, and has launched debates worldwide – from Palestine, Pakistan, Saudi Arabia, Iran, and the rest of the Islamic world to the United States, France, England, the North Atlantic Treaty Organisation alliance, and Russia – on themes of fundamentalism (religious and secular), concepts of governance and political participation, juridical interpretations of civil society, ethical principles of terrorism as a tool of radical political struggle, peace, security, and other secular and theocratic themes. Whatever the outcome of these debates, the commonplaces we all share are to be found in the very features of global instability and insecurity that explode the triumphalist conceit of "a new world order." Not since the end of World War II and then the collapse of communism in the Soviet Union have there been such demands for such radical rearticulations and reinterpretions of the basic principles of universal political rights.

What is to be done? This popular refrain, heard so often in these tense times, is a measure of the incertitudes that have suddenly arisen to make deeper demands on the sunny projections of globalist progress. Such incertitudes mark another kind of critical procedure, namely the analogous idea that globalization and the political discourse of terrorism have a common root in fundamentalism, whether secular or theocratic, in that they respectively hegemonize the markets and religion with limited participation from other sources.

The series of conferences, public debates, and film and video projects from which the first four books of Documenta11's five Platforms are drawn were planned and begun more than two years before the events of September 11 brought a new urgency to the political and philosophical debates that form the focus of our wider project – debates on democracy, justice, cultural and religious difference, and new spatial arrangements. Nonetheless, the contributions to these volumes share a common assumption in the fact that each is an attempt by the author to illuminate the epistemological texture and complexity of the present political and cultural climate.

Beginning in Vienna on March 15, 2001, and ending in Kassel on September 15, 2002, the Platforms, based on the conceptual initiative of Documenta11, unfolded over the course of eighteen months. The first four Platforms were constituted as collaborations between Documenta11 and the Prince Claus Fund for Culture and Development, The Hague; the India Habitat Centre, New Delhi; the Academy of Fine Arts Vienna; the House of World Cultures, Berlin; DAAD (Deutscher Akademischer Austauschdienst – German Academic Exchange Service), Berlin; CODESRIA (Council for the Development of Social Science Research in Africa), Dakar; and the Goethe-Institut Inter Nationes, Munich and Lagos. For the present volume, Documenta11, CODESRIA, and the Goethe-Institut have worked closely at every stage of the realization of the Lagos conference and workshop.

These collaborations not only highlight the larger scope of Documenta11's intellectual project based on the principle of shared research interests, they inscribe within Documenta11's exhibition project a critical interdisciplinary methodology that is to be distinguished from interdisciplinarity as a form of exhibitionism. The interdisciplinary dimension that forms part of our common association is also a manifestation of a central concern of Documenta11 from the very beginning, namely the idea that the space of contemporary art, and the mechanisms that bring it to a wider public domain, require radical rethinking and enlargement.

Such an enlargement has both spatial and temporal consequences. In a kind of counterprocedure, it represents a limit and a horizon. The limit specifies the point of Documenta11's beginning, that is, the articulation of the exhibition dimension of the project; while the horizon points to the intellectual and artistic circuits that make up aspects of the exhibition project's drive toward the production of knowledge, through a gesture of open contestation, debate, and transparent processes of research. The framework within which this takes place has both political and aesthetic objectives. But rather than subsume the concerns of art and artists into the narrow terrain of Western institutional aesthetic discourses that are part of the current crisis, we have conceived of this project as part of the production of a common public sphere. Such a public sphere, we believe, creates a space whereby the critical models of artists, theorists, philosophers, historians, activists, urbanists, writers, and others working within other intellectual traditions and artistic positions could productively be represented and discussed. The public sphere imagined by these collaborations is to be understood, then, as a constellation of multifaceted Platforms in which artists, intellectuals, communities, audiences, practices, voices, situations, actions come together to examine and analyze the predicaments and transformations that form part of the deeply inflected historical procedures and processes of our time.

If there is a politics of any kind to be deduced from the above, it is a politics of nonambiguity, and the idea that all discourses, all critical models (be they artistic or social, intellectual or pragmatic, interpretive or historical), emerge from a location or situation, even when they are not defined or restricted by it. In proposing the five Platforms that make up our common public sphere, we have above all else been attentive to how contemporary artists and intellectuals begin from the location and situation of their practice. The objective of all five Platforms has been to bring all the forces emanating from these disciplinary departures and conjunctions into an enabling space of productive intellectual and artistic activity.

Okwui Enwezor
Artistic Director, Documenta11

Adebayo Olukoshi
Executive Secretary, CODESRIA, Dakar

Heiko Sievers
Head of Program Department, Goethe-Institut Inter Nationes, Munich

Introduction

The contemporary African city has often been characterized as a territory of intense social and spatial claims to postcolonial citizenship and modernity. This characterization subtends a more enduring image – that of the African city as chaotic and disorderly, and therefore always outside the category of order of modern urban planning and procedures of rational spatial organization. With decolonization and globalization, the discourse of African urban systems has also been expressed through the paradigms of development and modernization. The development argument pushes African urban systems to reform themselves into new vectors of political and mercantile liberalism, while the modernization argument stresses the importance of retooling outdated and neglected infrastructure and policy sectors in order to make urban economies more efficient and conducive to the generation of wealth and social dividends. However, deeply embedded in these discourses – between postcolonial citizenship and modernity, chaos and disorder, development and modernization – is the clear recognition that postcolonial African cities have long been understood only in relation to a range of spectral binary oppositions and spatial and temporal distortions. Even though urban geographers and social scientists still employ these oppositions and distinctions to study contemporary African urban conditions, there has also been a clear recognition of the change in the urban paradigm when old colonial spatial designs slowly began to lose their decisive functionalist parameters and became subordinated to the mutations wrought by new civic and urban cultures. The question then is: How do today's African urban discourses respond affirmatively and critically to the changes in the colonial city, as postcolonial urban imagination – wittingly and unwittingly – continues to overwrite the hard-edged colonial formalist distinctions that established an epistemological division between urban and rural, tradition and modernity, formal and informal, village and city, authentic and inauthentic, chaotic and orderly?

Whatever the descriptive labels social scientists, urbanists, architects, political demographers, and development institutions append to contemporary African urban conditions, a singular tension defines and animates the spatial character of most African cities today. The tension is to be found in the difficulty in ameliorating the conflicting paradigms of the colonial and postcolonial heritage of African spatial designs. If the formal logic of colonial urban systems codified the use of space along a highly legalistic grid of urban regimes that were discriminatory, and as such produced a limited notion of urban citizenship, recent postcolonial attempts to redraw the old colonial boundaries – between distinctly designated systems of habitat and use – for a less rigidly codified, and thus more imaginative, experiential and democratic design of urban life have further exacerbated this tension.

Yet for all its imaginative and creative exuberance, the contemporary African city is today in crisis. Recently, many African cities have experienced serious spatial entropy, a decline in infrastructure, the unraveling of traditional institutional and social networks, the erosion of state capacity to provide adequate social amenities, inequality of access to economic and political capacities, etc. All of these pose serious challenges to urban stability and sustainability. Moreover, they have contributed to alarming reductions in quality of life for the average urban resident, and have produced governance and management pressures that require careful analytical study. Obviously, given their individual histories and complexity, no one can speak of *the* African city in a generic sense. Nor should we pursue its analysis from an overdetermined position and impose a unified meaning on its content. Any study of the contemporary African city must respond to the unique situation (historical as well as contemporary) of each city, assessing differences, complexities, distinctiveness, horizons, and limits.

The implications for this project are threefold. The first layer situates the positions and research that emerged from the conference and workshop within the context of an African urban ethic, living arrangements, creativity, and vitality. Therefore, rather than a generalized and diffuse discussion on the contemporary city as a phenomenon of globalizing tendencies, this project takes its challenge from and focuses on the African urban situation. Given the impact of processes of urbanization on the shaping of contemporary urban forms in the African city, we wish to ask a number of questions, namely: Can a distinction be made between the idea of a global city and the postcolonial city? What are the impact of global capitalism, development and modernization theories on emergent forms of urban governance and new civic associations in shaping the critical agency of the African urban dweller, especially in light of the disastrous effects of the structural adjustment programs of the 1980s?

A second layer to the debate is to be found in discussions that analyze the relationship between the state and civil society. These include a perspicacious study of the production of citizenship based on affiliations and multiple relations to new semi-institutional regimes such as NGOs and social movements, markets, neighborhoods, industries, and professions, many of which describe and identify a range of agents, actors, networks, and mediators in the urban landscape. The evolving attitude of the state to movements toward the development of an independent civil society is best described in relation to the dialectical and normative tension that exists between the formal and informal sectors of the urban economy.

The third layer describes the evolving nature of African urban paradigms caught in the grip of two paradoxes. The first paradox insists upon the idea that the postcolonial African city is a series of spatio-socio-temporal sites ruled simultaneously by exuberance and dynamism on the one hand, and baseness and obsolescence on the other. The second paradox sees the postcolonial African city alternating between hope and hopelessness, haunted by its orderly colonial past and liberated by the creative potential of its newfound postcolonial essence.

Whatever conclusions may be drawn from the foregoing, what is readily discernable is the need for a rethinking of African urban space. This becomes evermore obvious when viewed from the perspective and effects of a dichotomizing globalism, which constructs a neat cleavage between cities that are linked to the new circuits of global capital, labor, information, technology, knowledge, and trade, and those that are chronically dependent economies which serve both as new markets for global capital expansion and sources of cheap labor. In such cases, large urban agglomerations come to define both the sources and quests for new kinds of global citizenship.

The Nation-State, the City, and the Locations of Citizenship Many would argue today that the old star of the nation-state as the engine of the modern economy and the guarantor of citizenship is a dimming meteor. The former, stalwart coordinates of the state no longer guarantee security and stability, especially in the wake of the rise of networked global institutions that constantly breach the boundary-defining character of the nation-state. Today, the State in Africa is in crisis. Declining per capita productivity, increasing dependence on foreign aid, lack of transparency in governance and democratic participation by citizens, weakened legal institutions, along with decades of conflict have contributed to the perception of crisis and the erosion of the state's capacity to act independently. Nonetheless, there is an increasing awareness among civil society movements of the necessity of a properly functioning state in Africa. In places like Democratic Republic of Congo or Sierra Leone, the inability of the state to sustain itself has been a great deficit to the context of citizenship. However, in concert with the state, civil society organizations are redefining the very model of the state and the state's claim to sovereignty invested in the idea of citizenship.

Several questions may be asked in the context of urban studies: What are the forms of civil society in Africa? And what is citizenship? What binds the production of these highly incommensurable denominations to the creative intercourse of cultural, political, and social processes? We would like to think that, while the idea of nation-state remains, to reconceptualize the axes around which such questions revolve, it would be necessary to tease out their evolution in postcolonial Africa where arbitrary colonial map making radically displaced a range of political and cultural identities. The point, however, is that it is through the study of the micropolitics of cities, as the primary locations of modern state identification, that we witness how civil society and citizenship are fused in the postcolonial context.

The relationship of the state and the city has come to define the range of experiences often attributed to modern life. The consequence of this has meant that for quite some time agglomerations of people, histories, languages, identities, religions, commodities, cultures in cities have generated increasing tensions and demands for more appropriate definitions of citizenship, for example, the attempts to define migrants and residents, or the distinction between settler and native, permanence and impermanence. The relationship between the nation-state, citizenship, and the city is most strikingly troubling in the case of migrants traversing old colonial borders. The colonial city was especially adroit in exacerbating and exploiting these divisions in the crafting of its laws. Because many of these laws still remain as functioning legal codes, the spatial dynamics of cities now call for more efficient management. New theories of the rise in urban formations and the pressure points of expanding populations as witnessed in the last half century have seen many cities transformed, their social fabric recut, yet unable to reconcile the changes that make urban spaces dynamic and volatile at the same time. This tension continues to be one of the challenging features of urban life in Africa.

Global Urbanism and the Urban Economies of the "Third World" If the exploding urban context of the last fifty years has been predicated on the precarious – between chaos and sustainability – calling for the suture of dynamism and volatility, nowhere is the sense of precariousness more apparent than in the cities of the "developing world." The processes of industrialization and rapid urbanization in the developing economies have contributed to the principal shifts which can be seen not only through the decline of the rural, largely agrarian economies, but are clearly linked and exacerbated through patterns of migration and relocation to cities, which have radically altered cultural patterns. With little coherent socioeconomic policy in place to meet the demands of skyrocketing urban populations, most cities end up creating conditions for the development of slums. On the next level, social and political upheavals have produced another kind of test for policy makers. Since many contemporary African cities have for some time been susceptible to constant political transition, analysts tend to produce doomsday scenarios of urban life based on narratives of civic, systemic, and institutional destabilization.

But the cities of Africa are hardly unique in essaying the kinds of social upheavals we witness across many global cities, where competing claims of national and cultural uniqueness and migration have produced endemic conflicts. Migration, relocation, dislocation, destabilization have become the main features of cities everywhere. In turn, they have produced new theories and cartographies of space, forms and iconographies of living and dwelling, strategies of survival, concepts of citizenship, typologies of difference, demographics of identity and community, and a situational aesthetics which throw into relief dislocutions in the syntax of the cities' urban narrative and iconography. Whether in Asia, Europe, or Africa, the move to reverse the trends that now threaten the foundation of civil society in these regions has spurred considerations of how new imaginative processes might be used to intervene in the unstable spaces of global cities.

Urban Density and Population Explosion   In the early 1950s, close to 300 million people, or 16 percent of the "Third World's" total population, lived in cities; ten years ago it had reached 1.5 billion, or close to 30 percent. And today, more than a third of urban residents live in some 300 cities comprising more than one million population each.

Within this picture, some assert that Africa is becoming an increasingly urban continent. But to say that urbanization is taking place at an accelerating speed in Africa is an understatement. Between 1950 and 1985, the world population trebled, and in cities like São Paulo, Istanbul, Mexico City, and New Delhi quadrupled. Today, in many African cities, such as Lagos, Nairobi, Dar es Salaam, Lusaka, or Kinshasa, the population has multiplied sevenfold. Today, forty percent of the African population live in cities, an explosion that is dangerously approaching a cataclysmic crisis.

Because of profound historical discontinuity and rupture, and as a consequence of their colonial legacy, many African cities still remain administrative systems disconnected from urban dynamics. Many of these cities are collision points between tradition and modernity, between African development and external pressures; new sites for the reformulation of old and new influences, and an opportunity for the symbolic production of postcolonial identities. They reflect the unstable confluence of divergent paths and agendas (political, social, economic, cultural, infrastructural, institutional, etc.). In any case, the syntax of these cities today is not defined by the "modern" grammar inherited from colonialism, nor by the assumption of an organic connection between individual and collective memory, of testimonies and beliefs. In these cities, there is a great deal of experimentation in the production of space and habitat. The resilience and inventiveness of urban dwellers have kept many cities functional. Everything is translated and reprocessed to fit new modalities of living. Urban life, far from being dystopic, is outlined by the apparent exuberance of the everyday, where forms of self-organizing, parallel and informal economies continue to produce new interpretations of urban cultures and modes of transmitting their efficacy to the city polity at large.

The Mottled Screen: Africa's Urban Vision Because Africa's political scene has been branded in the larger imagination almost exclusively through media representations of civil wars, military coups, and disorders of every sort, many observers fail to see the complexity and creativity with which cities in Africa have been able to cope with dwindling resources and human capital. But the issue is not to question whether or not these simplifications have a basis in reality. Indeed, Africa – East, West, North, and South – is beleaguered by one conflict or another, but this should be seen within, rather than outside of the pressure politics of a larger, albeit brutal globalizing process. Clearly, African urban and social fabrics are under severe strain and the continuous human flow from the countryside to the city has virtually shifted poverty and environmental degradation to urban areas. Some analysts point to this shift as an example of the increasing urbanization of poverty. And they also argue that the high unemployment, housing shortages, inadequate sanitation, lack of planning and investment in social services are partly the result of the "structural adjustment" measures imposed by the World Bank during the 1980s as part of debt repayment schedules.

As in any other urban space around the world, African cities are centers for the migration and refuge of increasing numbers of people. As such, they are also the meeting place and battleground for two conflicting worlds of power and impotence, wealth and poverty, corruption and hope, center and periphery. But the issue we want to emphasize is that African cities are not conditioned by these troubling bifurcations alone. Nor do we wish to reproduce only the image of cities riddled with crime, grinding poverty, overcrowded suburbs and shanty towns, congested living spaces which usually lack essential services and are breeding grounds of disease, ethnic violence, high mortality rates, or the degradation of the environment. These are certainly important issues which need addressing. Yet, our attention is persistently called to also focus on the ethical accounting of these cities' dynamism as hosts of great potentials which challenge the often gloomy pictures painted by the popular media.

Conclusion By more than a few accounts, the African city is the site for the challenge to the political and at the same time the location for negotiations and agreements where new organizations and services, freedoms and autonomous spaces are emerging and developing. This emergence and development simultaneously proposes a modernizing cultural revision and a rearrangement of many of the essential elements of familial identification and authority. Out of these transformations, many of which are improvisatory, new types of relations and exchanges, development and subsistence, forms of solidarity and resistance are produced. On different levels, they reflect the expansion of the so-called informal economy, with its small traders, black markets, recycling, and all the numerous forms of urban survival which emerge as radical restructurings of the organizational forms of economic activity. With unemployment and underemployment rates of 70 percent the norm for most African cities, the ways in which income is generated require constant provisionality and innovation. And it is in the polymorphous and apparently chaotic logic of the postcolonial city that we may find the signs and new codes of expression of urban identities in formation.

While there is no question that African cities are remarkably different, the web of histories, styles, cultural productions, aesthetic vocabularies, and identifications that distinguish each urban center is clearly being unraveled by globalization. New forms of urban street culture, music, fashion, media (the video film industry in Lagos, for example), associations, cultural and mercantile networks have reshuffled and reinvented this web from city to city. One important example is the phenomenon and the rise of charismatic Christianity that has flourished in West, East, Central, and southern African cities. In many of these cities, the proliferation of religious associations is significant. Some analysts consider religious expression and organization to be the predominant local initiative in urban Africa in the last two decades. In some cities, within the heterogeneous and multi-ethnic context, ethnic and group identification resembles the fluid and shifting options offered by the informal economy. And yet in other cities, old institutions and local associations are reassembled to suit the needs of the neighborhood, the *quartier*, or *cité*.

What can be gleaned from the foregoing is that there can be no neat histories of urban dwelling in Africa, nor in any other region of the world for that matter.

Cities in their present context are modern inventions, and as the new electronic pathways that crisscross the globe circulate and readapt images of the modern city, they also produce a desire for tourism that fuels new contacts and movements within already clogged global travel circuits, unraveling the strict hegemonic tendencies that have always made it difficult to read the map of spatial difference. To this end, Freetown, Johannesburg, Kinshasa, and Lagos are good examples of these kinds of unraveling, reformulation, and innovation. *Under Siege: Four African Cities – Freetown, Johannesburg, Kinshasa, Lagos* proposes to examine the roots of this unraveling and social undoing. Equally it will aim to shine a bright critical light on the approaches in these four cities that open up new paths of agency, creative reappropriations of resources, and the new subjectivities they produce. We must take new measures to articulate the reductionism of afro-pessimism which often interprets these new series of operations primarily as emanations or reactions to the West. We must ask ourselves whether there are modernities outside the reactive "alternatives" to the West; modernities that emerge out of postcolonial histories and global phenomena, but which also engage different kinds of understanding of wealth, subjectivity, and the social sphere so often taken for granted when approaching modernity and globalization.

The focus and subject of this conference and book are a direct response to questions posed by the emerging narratives of contemporary African urban conditions within a global context. There are three distinct areas that define the theme of the book: the first is constituted by a broad theoretical analysis of urbanism in Africa. The second part, which is the core of the project, is based on a series of case studies that identify cities that are seen to be under siege. These case studies focus on Freetown, Johannesburg, Kinshasa, and Lagos. The third part, "Urban Processes and Change in Africa," is an initiative developed and supported by the Council for the Development of Social Science Research in Africa (CODESRIA) based in Dakar. More importantly, the essays collected in this volume respond to broader disciplinary quests in African studies. The quests are inimitably shaped, also, by theoretical perspectives concerned with the discursive elaboration of the state of the global public sphere.

Okwui Enwezor
Carlos Basualdo
Ute Meta Bauer
Susanne Ghez
Sarat Maharaj
Mark Nash
Octavio Zaya

Cities in Transition:
The Fate of African Urban Systems

The Visible and Invisible: Remaking Cities in Africa

AbdouMaliq Simone

Part One: A Practicing Urban Politics

The Ghost in the (Political) Machine   Lagos is situated on a brackish, shallow lagoon drained by four major rivers and interlaced with a series of canals to evacuate overflows and waste. At the end of January 2002, nearly 2,000 people perished in the Isolo Canal at Oke-Afa, Ikotun-Egbe, and Ejigbo, as well as the Ajao Estate Canal in Mafoluku. People were fleeing massive fireballs, which to them at the time were of unknown origin, but later were determined to be thousands of pounds of exploding armaments stored in the nearby Ikeja Military Cantonment, themselves set off by a mysterious fire.

Even as mass panic took hold, there was general wonder why so many rushed into the canals – since most could not swim, what made them believe, even in their panic, that they could reach the other side? The general conclusion was that, as the canals were covered in water hyacinth, most believed that the vegetation provided a sound footing on which to cross. At the same time, even for those able to swim, death could have come from the extreme toxicity of certain industrial pollutants.

Water hyacinth is one of the most productive plants on earth, as well as one of the most problematic. The glossy green, leathery leaf blades grow to 20 centimeters long and 5–15 centimeters wide, and are attached to petiole that are often spongy-inflated. The plant can form impenetrable mats of floating vegetation, and numerous dark, branched, fibrous roots dangle in the water from the underside. It reproduces by seeds and by daughter plants that form on rhizomes. Individual plants break off the mat and can be dispersed by winds and water currents. As many as 5,000 seeds can be produced by a single plant. Low oxygen conditions develop beneath hyacinth mats, impeding water flow and creating breeding grounds for mosquitoes.

It is the very productivity of the water hyacinth – its rhizomatic structure that seemingly impedes any limiting effort based on cutting it off from the "roots" – that accounts for the mixture of fascination and alarm through which it is usually approached. For the mats are a surface that is both inclusive and structuring of new and open-ended relationships, providing a series of connections, switches, relays, and circuits for activating matter and information.

Rescue efforts proved exceedingly difficult as rescuers had to cut their way through the dense entanglement that had already encompassed individual bodies. It is perhaps ironic that morphology so capable of spreading itself rapidly across a fluid surface can so impede another's mobility. As the reputed criminals, to whom these canals have been conceded by local residents, pointed out in the aftermath of the tragedy, it is not a matter of trying to run across the matted vegetation. Rather, the key is rolling over, gliding along the surface, allowing the body to do things that it never thought it was capable of doing.

As one "area boy" told a reporter from the *Vanguard* newspaper, the canals had long been haunted – after all, these are conduits to a different world. The question is: What is this different world whose passageways are supervised by ghosts? What are the invisible circuits of navigation that haunt the city in its present form?

For, there is a ghostly order in the city. In many cities, trucks come and go in the middle of the night, and it is not clear what they carry or bring in, despite constant police checks.[1] At the end of 2000, it was reported that there were 2,177 religious sects newly constituted in Kinshasa, many who meet during all-night prayer sessions, where bodies, money, and capacity appear and disappear to discordant logics.[2] Urban quarters throughout the continent whisper to themselves, if at all, where did "so and so" go, having difficulty keeping track of the disappeared, while also barely accounting for a wide range of events that appear to have no responsible agent.

Yes, cities are full of the material. There is the materiality of fetching water, riding on overcrowded taxis, negotiating hard for a good price for tomatoes, avoiding the downpour seeping through a weathered tin roof, fighting off malarial fever, ignoring the stench of overflowing sewage drains, or taking apart an engine block in the hot sun. But across these activities, there is a large swathe of the ephemeral attempting to enroll the sweat and passion of hardworking urban bodies into networks of concrete becoming that go beyond the artifice of citizenship.

Residents along the Isolo-Oshidi axis poured from their "indented" quarters, Shogunle, Jakande Estate, Ejigbo, and converged on the canals because the lay-

---

1 See Poul Ove Pedersen, "The Changing Structure of Transport under Trade Liberalization and Globalization and Its Impact on African Development," *Working Paper Subseries on Globalization and Economic Restructuring in Africa*, no. 7 (Copenhagen: Centre for Development Research, 2000).
2 See Panafrican News Agency, October 27, 2000.

out of their quarters meant that escape necessarily led them in this direction. People ran into each other after years of not being in contact; acquaintances discovered that they were virtual neighbors; people extended help and support on this day and even in the months after. But additionally, there was also the uncanny ability of apparent strangers to identify precisely where the dead or where rescuers actually lived. An invisible architecture of connections, in the wake of this tragedy, has found various visible forms. Children have been returned to families on the basis of "hunches." Mutual assistance is now connecting quarters that may be in close proximity, but due to the topography of the city can be connected only through highly circuitous navigation. There are hundreds of stories of people rediscovering each other, of a basis for connection in a city whose fragmenting pulls were substantially intensified in the wake of the disaster.

Every city has its "wild topographies." For practicing everyday urban survival always generates "ghostly correlates of unactualized possibilities" that collapse the difference between near and far.[3] In this spirit, cities like Lagos and Kinshasa, Freetown and Johannesburg, usually marked with great historical, economic, and cultural distance from each other, find ways of circling in the same orbit. It is usually the underside that wins the claim on visibility in terms of these connections between cities. Nigerian drug dealers in Johannesburg; Executive Outcome mercenaries and diamond dealers in Freetown; South African shady business in Kinshasa, and so forth. But if this canalization of illegality is the most visible architecture through which otherwise "distant" cities converge, what else might have happened? What other economies might have ensued; what other exchanges and collaborations might still be possible if the conventional maps of regionalization and urban economic development would, on the surface, seem to move them further from each other?

Urban theory now tells us that heterogeneous forces, surfaces, and spaces constitute each urban condition that exists as a structuring context. All cities are places of multiple intensities and layers. These layers and intensities pass through, settle, consolidate, and disperse across the diverse spaces to which their various intersections themselves give rise. These intensities include populations, sounds, machines, roads, discourses, buildings, grids of water and electricity, organizational forms and sites, nurturing and dispossession, as well as the emanations of nature, to name a few. The uses and implications of these intensities hurtle along vast circuits of connectivity. Identities and actions are situated in multiple loops of causation, opportunity, and constraint.[4]

---

3 Nigel Thrift, "Afterwords," *Environment and Planning D: Society and Space* 18 (2000), pp. 213–255.
4 Ibid.

The intersection of intensities is not that of fixed objects and identities with clear boundaries. Rather, it is an intersection which "frees" pieces of objects and identities from specific constitutive enclosures, opening them up to new layers and formations. Since there is no "real" difference between multiple formations and the criss-crossing of intensities – dividing up or connecting with other intensities – the multiplicities only grow by changing their nature.[5] For the "event" of this convergence of multiple intensities expresses itself only as that which is subject to variation.[6] A series of these variations is held together and set apart momentarily from a larger environment through enfolding connections and implications. The convergence of exteriors that do not belong together at a paradoxical element is an intensity opened to both increasing stratification, ordering, and dispersion. So at this intersection or coexistence of intensities in urban Africa, the discernible decline of living standards, the incessant politics of emergency and social dissipation, AND the emergence of singular capacities, of social cohabitation and general intellect take on and configure new conditions of possibility. As Deleuze would remind us, in the midst of every city, there is a substantial and groundless complexity of arrangements and interactions – among people, objects, territories, climates – which take that city outside of its confines. To draw upon this capacity is not an act of a particular remembering. It is not an act of repositioning or relinking an observer to a more perspicacious line of sight.[7]

Rather, such complexity is revealed in the moments in which a place is "blown apart" – the convergence of trajectories – movements, unfoldings, expulsions, gatherings – linked in an apparent impossibility – and thus redistributing what has come before and opening up to what is yet to come. Jean-Luc Nancy has stated that contemporary political existence is one of intersection – i.e., an incessant process of acting without a model, and is thus an environment also in the making. Instead of consolidating clearly discernible and bounded territories as platforms of action and interaction, there is a process of "spacing out," of generating, enfolding, and extending space in which mapping is always behind, struggling to "catch up."[8]

---

5 See Deepak Narang Sawhney, "Palimpsest: Towards a Minor Literature in Monstrosity," in *Deleuze and Philosophy: The Difference Engineer*, ed. Keith Ansell-Pearson (London: Routledge, 1997).
6 Peter Canning, "The Crack of Time and the Ideal Game," in *Gilles Deleuze and the Theater of Philosophy*, ed. Constantin V. Boundas and Dorothea Olkowski (New York: Routledge, 1994).
7 John Rajchman, *Constructions* (Cambridge, Mass.: MIT Press, 1998).
8 Jean-Luc Nancy, "War, Right, Sovereignty–Technè," in *Being Singular Plural* (Stanford: Stanford University Press, 2000).

The Politics of Invisibility   Indeed, across Africa there is a greater preoccupation with death. Death not so much as the termination of life – although the intensifying difficulties faced by people in proliferating conflict, economic debilitation, and HIV/AIDs do amplify such a connotation. But more powerful is the sense of death related to the capacity for sudden transformation, of being able to completely transform oneself into something else, to go somewhere else. Cities are full of stories of sudden and inexplicable transformations and resurrections – of people who have nothing suddenly accumulating massive amounts of wealth only to lose it overnight and then have it "resurrected" at a later time. These oscillations are embedded in a context where the horizons of a reasonably attainable future and the capacity to imagine them have disappeared for many youth – now the region's largest population group. Urban Africans also appear increasingly uncertain how to spatialize an assessment of their life chances – i.e., where will they secure livelihood, where can they feel protected and looked after, where will they acquire the critical skills and capacities.

Given the heightened mobility of African populations among locations marked by ever-increasing disparities in economic capacity, the pressures for maintaining functional cohesion within the framework of extended family systems and the practices of resource distribution that go with it are enormous. There is a preoccupation on the part of many residents in African cities with the extent to which they are tied to the fates of others whom they witness "sinking" all around them. At the same time, they hope that the ties around them are sufficiently strong to rescue them if need be.

The very acts of mooring and unmooring social ties become the locus of intense contestation and concern – i.e., who can do what with whom under what circumstances becomes a domain so fraught with tension and even violence that clear demarcations are deferred and made undecidable. In other words, it is not clear just what is taking place. This ambiguity is a reality that urban residents not only must face but also seem to weave themselves. In the city of Douala, this process of obscuring is called *mapan*. The word refers to architectures of movement and dwelling where the layout of the quarter is meant to always confound and unhinge clear assessments about what is going on in the face of the overwhelming threats of disappearance posed by both state and "mystical" authorities.

Perhaps the overarching framework precipitating these concerns in African cities has been structural adjustment. Briefly, adjustment has been materialized in five areas of reform. There is the determination of prices by "free markets"; the reduction of state control on prices; the divestiture of state resources into the private sector; the absolute reduction of the state budget; and a reorientation of public bureaucracy toward support of the private sector.

But adjustment not only refers to policies that restructure the economy. It also refers to the restructuring of the time and space of African lives as well, with an adjustment in the economy of language itself – i.e., the instrument through which it becomes possible to construct subject positions and discernible relationships between things and value, the real and the symbolic. Out of the crises in the political field occasioned by floating currencies, financial fluxes at high velocities, and insurmountable debt emerges the concentration of value in hyperreal finance that comes to embody all the limits of what is imaginable.

In other words, seemingly the entirety of a nation's material resources is owed to foreign interests and, in the process, becomes owned by them as well. Spaces of transaction are effectively eroded, as whatever a nation possesses – its material, human, and cultural resources – is consumed in a spectral conception of value – i.e., the values of virtual financial capital. The spectral is channeled through the calculus of submitting the volatility of postcolonial societies in the making to the volatility of price fluctuations which constitute the standard through which derivatives, the primary instrument through which African resources are leveraged to an indeterminable future, are priced. In this mechanism aimed at objectifying all risk, the particularities and contingencies of locales are subsumed to a restructuring of the relationship between discourse and experience, words and things, in such a way as everything disappears in the face of this spectrality of value that mirrors the world as a totality.

This era of structural adjustment, then, frames the intense preoccupation across the region with a *politics of invisibility*. If a discernible future and a life outside of incessant immiseration have become unthinkable, then Africans must operate through the spectral in order to proffer some counter-reality. Invisibility as a practice does not reflect some intrinsic cultural predilection or capacity. Rather, invisibility is a political construction – a means of both configuring and managing particular resources and the medium through which specific instantiations of the political are deployed. In cities where livelihood, mobility, and opportunity are produced and enacted through the very agglomeration of different bodies marked and situated in diverse ways, how can permutations in the intersection of their given physical existence, their stories, networks, and inclinations, produce specific value and capacity? If the city is a huge intersection of bodies in need and with desires in part propelled by the sheer number of them, how can larger numbers of bodies sustain themselves by imposing themselves in critical junctures, whether these junctures are discrete spaces, life events, sites of consumption or production?

Invisibility is not simply an intrinsic condition of some unyielding tradition or alternative modernity. It is not the cloak of the clandestine adorned in order to carry out specific agendas, or to sneak through the surveillance of prevailing administrations, authorities, or "conceptual fields." It is not the articulation of a pragmatics which foregrounds the relative incapacity and marginality of African urban functions, residents, and places as a means to divert external attention away from a more "authentic" and efficacious version of urban life. Invisibility is both product and practice. Invisibility ensues from collisions among what are, on the surface, divergent trajectories. On the one hand, there are trajectories of resource disposition, trade, cultural recognition, and political power where African spaces seem excluded from active participation in flows and transactions at various larger scales.

On the other, there are trajectories where these spaces become frontiers in an often very deliberate experimentation of extending and reordering space. In these latter trajectories, African cities are engaged as openings onto the possibilities of the unconventional and the unrecorded – where urban dynamics are shifted away from actual cities to murky borderlands, and where new formulations of sovereignty, belonging, and nationhood are provisionally concretized. Exclusion and incorporation, marginality and experimentation, then, converge in ways that are not easily discernible to any kind of actor operating in this interstice.

These "collisions" are also of the infiltration among "inconsistent" temporalities.[9] What looks to be stasis, when nothing appears to have been accomplished, may actually be the highly intricate engineering of interactions among different events, actors, and situations. In such occurrences, events, actors, and situations may "pass through" each other and take notice of each other without discernible conditions actually changing. It is just these possibilities – of different actors and situations dealing with each other without apparent ramification – which make African cities appear dynamic and static at the same time. On the other hand, things can happen very fast, and where seemingly nothing has been brought to bear on a particular setting. In other words, sometimes conditions change with remarkable speed – e.g., the structures of authority, the alignments of loyalty and collaboration, the mobilization of money and resources – where it is not apparent just what is going on and who is contributing what to these changes.

Still, we must recognize that larger numbers of urban Africans are disconnected from both the postindependence narratives of national development and the collective social memories that had established an interweaving of individual life histories with the prospective and "eternal" return of ancestral knowledge. As stated earlier, possibilities of social reproduction are foreclosed for increasing numbers of youth. As such, the actions, identities, and social composition

---

9 Michael Rowlands, "Inconsistent Temporalities in a Nation-Space," in *Worlds Apart: Modernity through the Prism of the Local*, ed. Daniel Miller (London: Routledge, 1995).

through which individuals attempt to eke out daily survival are incessantly provisional, positioning them in a proliferation of seemingly diffuse and discordant times. Without structured responsibilities and certainties, the places they inhabit and the movements they undertake become instances of disjointed geographies – i.e., subsuming places into mystical, subterranean, or sorceral orders, prophetic or eschatological universes, highly localized myths that "capture" the allegiances of large social bodies, or daily reinvented routines that have little relationship to anything.

At the extreme, as the material underpinnings of the confidence in once reliable local institutions dissipates, larger numbers of Africans "disappear" very visibly into a receding interior space – a kind of collective hallucination moving "away" from the world. This can be a highly volatile space, for even if marked by intricate geographies of spirit worlds, it can upend "civil life" in an inchoate mix of cruelty and tenderness, indifference and generosity. At the same time, new relational webs are pieced together with different cultural strands and references. These webs promote a capacity for residents to be conversant with sites, institutions, and transactions at different scales – in other words, a capacity to know what to do in order to gain access to various kinds of instrumental resources.

The African urban environment is increasingly one where it is difficult to ascertain just what social practices, alliances, and knowledge can be mobilized sufficient enough to produce outcomes conceptualized in advance. Similarly, the rapidity through which impressions can be fixed in the popular imagination, unanticipated resourcefulness organized, and the dispositions of behavior transformed often does not permit any certainty as to the identities of the ingredients or processes involved.

At the same time, the survival of these cities is increasingly predicated on the extent of their connections to a broad range of international organizations, bilateral and multilateral agreements that provide the funds for many of the basic urban services that are delivered. Thus, cities remain, at least "officially," inscribed in a narrative of development. But development, as a specific modality of temporality, is not simply about meeting the needs of citizens. It is also about capturing residents to a life-aesthetic defined by the state so that they can be citizens. It is about making ethical beings; about holding people in relations that make them governable. As such, development is about assisting residents to meet their needs in a "good" way or a "moral" way.[10] Yet, within African cities, the sustainability of communities largely means sustaining ways of associating

---

10 Ivor Chipkin, "'Functional' and 'Dysfunctional' Communities: Development's Normative Presuppositions," paper prepared for the Community Development Department, City of Cape Town, 2000.

and moving that are not conducive to such citizenship nor to the production of the moral beings of the type needed by states and other "supervisory" and/or donor entities.

The investment in a politics of invisibility – i.e., of trying to navigate a difficult and often oppressive urban world with stealth, inversion, and guile – may enable daily survival, but it does not get around the need to create new cities even if the old ones are being dismantled. And so the visibility of collective action remains critical. How do people collaborate, on what basis, and with what objectives and tools? How are these collaborations nurtured and extended, both in space and time? What will be recognized as useful and salient? People must still determine what information, experiences, and resources can be used to get by, or do more than get by. They must still establish a means of recognizing what can be used to create more opportunities, find out more things, and expand possibilities for better livelihoods, both in the short term and over the long run.

The Return of Sight There is a need to talk about urban politics in the broad sense: about things in the making. Too many of the sounds emerging from African cities are rendered inaudible or inexplicable. Speech is often violently foreclosed or relentless in its mimicry, its promises, or its desperate fear of taking pause. Politics thus concerns the invention of a platform or scene on which the cacophony of urban voices are audible and become understood, and on which speakers are made visible. What is given as an objective status is put into question through making visible that which has not, under the optics of a given perceptive field, been visible.[11] It is given a "name," not necessarily a "right name," but a designation nevertheless, a technique, an instrument that allows something to effect and be affected. This instrument, and thus politics, cannot be traced back to embodying or representing specific social realities or organizations. It comes from the "outside," possessing, taking hold of a community in order for it to recognize itself, but always already steering it away from itself.[12]

So here I am concerned with forms of spectral instrumentality potentially capable of revitalizing an affective glue, a desire for social interchange and cooperation that might contain the seeds of social economies that extend themselves through scale, time, and reach. But this is not about civil society organizations and NGOs, micro-credit associations or people's associations. Rather, I am

---

11 Jacques Rancière, "Ten Theses on Politics," *Theory and Event* 5, no. 3 (2001).
12 Pheng Cheah, "Spectral Nationality: The Living On [*sur-vie*] of the Postcolonial Nation in Neocolonial Globalization,"*Boundary 2* 26, no. 3 (1999), pp. 225–252.

interested here in more diffuse but no less concrete ways in which diverse urban actors are assembled and act. What are some of the ways in which urban residents are building a particular emotional field in the city, trying to restore a very physical sense of connection to one another? This is a micropolitics of alignment, interdependency, and exuberance. This is not the work of detailed ethnographic examinations of new social movements, new living arrangements, or new forms of urban productivity. It is a practice of being attuned to faint signals, flashes of important creativity in otherwise desperate maneuvers, small eruptions in the social fabric which provide new texture, small but important platforms from which to access new views.

In recent years, the development business has been replete with references to the importance of knowledge, knowledge management, and knowledge practices. The United Nations Development Program (UNDP), for example, is now officially a knowledge practice network. But knowledge is a tricky thing. In part because some 90 percent of our human ability to know what to do in any particular situation is tacit, outside the domain of cognition that centers on conscious reflection. Rather, most human knowledge is a kind of perception-in-movement, an ability to act based on how the body is positioned in specific situations, how it is concretely located in a heterogeneous network of other persons, information fields, physical forces, and so forth. Knowledgeable action is largely a practical activity involving the construction of new relations in the gaps that always open up in the process of conducting existing relations – of acting, gesturing, moving, and aligning. This is why the otherwise excluded, meaningless, nonsensical, or disturbing dimensions of urban life become critical perturbances, in that they provoke elaborate and potentially effective social relations and rituals.[13]

So, urban collaboration does not simply reflect and institutionalize clearly identifiable social processes and forms. There are gaps and openings, room for collaboration and provocation, and this collaboration can take many forms. Sometimes people coalesce in organizations that have names, but where it is unclear to almost everyone what precisely the organization is and what it does. At other times, an event may trigger an entire neighborhood into apparently unfamiliar courses of action, but with a synchronicity that makes it appear as if some deep-seated logic of social mobilization is being unleashed. Still at other times, the arduous interplay of local social change and resistance, planned development and arbitrary decisions construct tentative platforms for people to collaborate in "silent" but powerful ways which have the potential of substantially altering the position of the locality within the larger urban system.

13 Michel Serres, *The Parasite*, trans. Lawrence R. Schehr (Baltimore: Johns Hopkins University Press, 1982).

One must situate this focus in what has been a predominant emphasis in African urban development on reintensifying efforts to configure appropriate modalities of urban governance. Such emphasis includes not only the evolution of effective public municipal institutions but also the rationalization of land markets, investment in infrastructure, and more coherent laws, taxation, and planning. Particularly important is the ongoing entrenchment of specific norms of good governance capable of guiding institutional behaviors and decision making. A hard-won consensus within the international community specifies norms that appear to have general applicability to governance issues across the world. These norms include sustainability, decentralization or subsidiarity, equity, efficiency, transparency and accountability, civic engagement and citizenship, and security. Such norms purportedly enable practitioners, politicians, and residents to better compare heterogeneous urban contexts and work together to bring diverse resources, experiences, and skills to bear on the improvement of life in distinct cities. More important, these norms are to lay the foundations for viable urban citizenship, a sense that the city belongs to its inhabitants, with a framework of rights and responsibilities.

Despite the past decade of concentrated reform, African urban politics remains a rough-and-tumble world. Cities are not generating, nor have other access to, the kinds of finance necessary to pull off the sweeping restructuring necessary to substantially increase the number of jobs, opportunities, and services. As national and local states have long regulated urban spaces with such unreality and arbitrariness, this inability to provide at least a basic framework for sustainable urban livelihoods means that public authority is rarely taken seriously, as public authority rarely takes a sense of urban citizenship seriously.

Despite emerging notions of governance, which at least cursorily point to the importance of mutual belonging – through the emphasis on partnerships – the status of the urban citizen largely remains a solitary one. Not only have formal public institutions largely "abandoned" urban residents, visible collective actions that might provide some alternative measures of belonging and provisioning are impeded. As African states must adhere to "disciplinary measures" enforced by the North and multilateral institutions, and as the North depends on displays of the apparent sovereignty and coherence of these states, the space for effective and visible alternatives for organizing urban life is often constrained.

At the heart of the challenge about governing cities is the issue of the political management of complex and incessant trade-offs that must be made by all cities in a context of sometimes painful global exposure. The trade-offs concern to what extent, for example, fiscal soundness takes precedence over the equitable delivery of urban services, or the extent to which managerial proficiency supercedes expanded popular participation in decision making.

The critical issue is how these trade-offs are defined. Who is involved in negotiating them? What are the appropriate forms of community organization and mobilization in a context where urban government is increasingly less capable of meeting the demands of all citizens? How does one combine, relate, and balance different forms of participation, negotiation, contestation, and partnership to ensure vibrant politics and constructive collaboration to solve real problems? How can forms of political community be reimagined, especially in a temporal period where the contradictions of expanding global capitalism are more extensively interwoven in local urban life? How can such political community be reimagined in a context where formerly valued modalities and practices of social cohesion dissipate, as do the territorial parameters through which cohesion is recognized and performed?[14]

So while citizenship may be a necessary aspect of ensuring the long-term sustainability of African cities, it is not a sufficient condition in and of itself. Again, if the very constructs of sociality are increasingly scrutinized, challenged, and fragmented, the passions generated by issues of belonging cannot be adequately addressed simply by constitutional guarantees, particularly in political contexts which have limited resources and little will to enforce them. Notions of citizenship are important not because they impose an abstract framework of identity in which prior modalities of belonging and affective connection are subsumed. Nor are they important because they can institutionalize those modalities of belonging in a calculus of obligations, freedoms, and responsibilities vis-à-vis others who do not share them. Rather, citizenship is the acknowledgment of the artificial and contingent character of the rules that constitute social collaboration and cohabitation, allowing for the combination of perspectives and histories that are otherwise antinomies.[15] It is the question of how to remain oneself and not be inferior, even if unequal, when compared to others, and thus, the right not to be rooted, not to belong.

Struggles over which identities have legitimate access to and rights over specific places and resources are, indeed, on the increase. To whom does a particular place belong? Who belongs to a particular place? In part, the trend toward subsidiarity in governance amplifies such questions of belonging. Proponents of decentralization and the "new localism" argue that it is difficult to engage in the kinds of sustained behaviors and cooperation needed over the long term to ensure effective planning and implementation of economic projects. Yet, the

---

14 Bob Jessop, "The Crisis of the National Spatio-Temporal Fix and the Tendential Ecological Dominance of Globalizing Capitalism," *International Journal of Urban and Regional Research* 24, no. 2 (2000), pp. 323–360.

15 Augusto Illuminati, "Unrepresentable Citizenship," in *Radical Thought in Italy*, ed. Paolo Virno and Michael Hardt (Minneapolis: Minnesota University Press, 1996).

proliferation of disputes concerning belonging all reinforce the need to secure and consolidate particularistic identities, which would seem to limit maneuverability and reach. This dynamic can be seen from the contested citizenship of Kuanda in Zambia and Ouattara in Côte d'Ivoire so as to eliminate their presidential candidacies, to the expulsion of "migrants" in Gabon, to intensified ethnic claims of particular regions in Cameroon, to the fight over whether *sharīʿa* belongs in Nigeria.

The restrictive emphasis on contests about belonging tends to underplay the ways in which African societies display a remarkable capacity to operate in the interstices of stability and instability, individuation and forms of social solidarity, the material and spiritual. It underplays a substantial history where many African societies elaborated intricate relations between the rural and the urban, colonial zones of domination and spaces of relative autonomy, among highly diverse localities and social practices, as well as between home and nonhome. How are various African actors and social ensembles using this period of scalar recomposition, emerging from the rearticulation of capitalist expansion and political regulation, to configure new modalities for pursuing economic opportunity, expand the scope and reach of trade and mobility, and activate new forms of political coordination?

For example, religious brotherhoods and fraternities, ethnically based trading regimes, syndicates, and even community-based and multi-association operations are functioning with increasing scope. Urban quarters not only serve as platforms for popular initiatives – e.g., waste management, micro-enterprise development, and shelter provision – but readapt local modalities of cohesion and sociality to more regional and global frameworks. Some localities, such as Nima (Accra), Obalende (Lagos), Texas-Adjame (Abidjan), and Grand Yoff (Dakar), reflect a strong relationship between the elaboration of local associations and the generation of new economic activities and resources. Here, associations become important in configuring new divisions of labor. They help coordinate the cross-border, small and medium-scale trade of individual entrepreneurs. They pool and reinvest the proceeds of this trade to access larger quantities of tradable goods, diversify collective holdings, and reach new markets. The mechanisms through which local economies expand in scale are, albeit, often murky and problematic. They can entail highly tenuous and frequently clandestine articulations among, for example, religious and fraternal networks, public officials operating in private capacities, clientelist networks mobilizing very cheap labor, foreign political parties, and large transnational corporations operating outside of conventional procedures.

Through this lens, to what extent are conflicts about belonging only fights over the disposition of particular places for their own sake – i.e., about what can be drawn to and developed within a specific place on the basis of controlling key natural resources? Rather, to what extent are fights about belonging and the rights incumbent to belonging for access to resources more about what the control of these resources means to enhancing the possibilities for actors to operate on the level of the larger world? Here, the focus is not so much on how place is brought under the singular control of a particular force, but how place is linked to a plurality of allegiances and opportunities. The question is, rather, how can local actors feel that their operations in localized spaces are also conduits to or extensions of a much larger world? To what extent are such struggles, then, not so much over the terms of territorial encompassment or closure, but rather maintaining a sense of the open-ended?

However, citizenship, even if it encompasses the interface between heterogeneous systems and directions, does not itself make up its own desire. The desire for citizenship is the desire for a space of maneuverability and becoming for the kinds of collaborations, the kinds of being-with others – in work, residence, movement, worship, and so forth – that one wants. The issue becomes, quite simply, what kinds of political assemblages most effectively embody the urban worlds that Africans seek to conjure on the basis of their memories, skills, and aspirations? What kinds of political mechanisms best facilitate the capacity of urban residents to act, and act with the autonomy necessary to make best use of the particular resources present within a given city?

From the vantage point of various histories of urban youth associations, from the Leopards of Léopoldville to the *garçons du forêt* of Bandalwunga (Kinshasa), of the Tsotsi of Kliptown to the *kole se koko* boys of Hospital Hill (Johannesburg), from the area boys of Oshu-Elegba to the Dankasas of Mushin (Lagos), from the Rarray Boys to the West End Boys in Freetown, what are the conduits that can lead them to each other? If youth without anticipation now constitute the majority of African cities – perpetually exposed to political manipulation, proliferating spaces of criminal activity, and the disconnection from extended family – what ghostly leadership is coordinating action on the fronts of these cities?

What ghosts say about the city, what they speak about themselves, is that the past is not really past. What is thrown away has not really been disposed of, and as such, it stands outside any knowable sequence of events, pointing to the possibility that what could have happened but did not can still take place – i.e., where actuality and possibility become indistinct. There is autonomy from the maps imposed and autonomy from the dominant systems of representation, that is, the dominant paradigms of city making. As such, it is in the apparent ruins of the city, its places of marginalization, and the interfaces where the most mundane activities are unsettled or disrupted that these ghosts command.

Impoverished urban youth fight off their disappearance in very desperate gestures. They intervene into those urban practices and gestures most taken for granted – a husband greeting his wife at the door; a merchant opening his shop in the morning; a businessman placing a letter in the post; a congregation commencing to kneel in prayer. They turn these everyday events into a ruin, or, at least, unsettle them, open them out to unanticipated implications.

Whatever wear and tear is placed on the social fabric by these disruptions, they open the terrain of the urban to a compulsion to imagine differently; to place the stories of decades upon decades of urban settlement at the "disposal" of those barely making it day after day. Traders emerge with air tickets to China and empty suitcases. There are those who walk for months from city to city in search of a different life; those who wait hours at the few Internet cafes in Kinshasa, having practiced a particularly difficult combination of numbers to be sent to bewitch a distant European with a good apartment. There are those who piece together extended family networks from years circulating various Mano River Union refugee camps, with each "member" placed strategically in small towns and cities across the region, talking to each other constantly.

Part Two: Douala, Cameroon

The Disappeared President Paul Biya established Operation Command on February 20, 2000 as a means of rectifying the alarming increase in violent crime in Douala. At first residents across the city applauded this military operation, as they had become increasingly frightened of venturing anywhere in public, even during daylight hours. It was common for people from all walks of life and in all quarters to tell stories of being held up at work, on the street, or in their homes. Equipped with vast powers of search and seizure, as well as arbitrary detention, Operation Command quickly zeroed in on a huge network of warehouses harboring stolen goods, as well as illicit acquisitions of cars, houses, and consumer goods.

As the net widened, almost everyone came under suspicion. During raids on homes, if the residents were unable to immediately provide receipts for items like televisions or refrigerators, they would be confiscated. Increasingly, Operation Command appeared to Doualaise as organized military theft. There were also reports about large-scale extrajudicial killings, of detainees disappearing from prisons. Bodies of suspected criminals were often found in the streets with signs of torture and bullet wounds.

On January 23, 2001, nine youths from the Bapenda quarter were picked up after a neighbor had reported them as having stolen a gas canister. They were taken to a gendarme station in Bonanjo, on the other side of the city, where they were allowed to visit their families and correspond with them, although they reported being physically tortured. On January 28, they were transferred to an Operation Command post whereupon all communication from them stopped. The parents were unable to find out any information as to the location of their children. Following the disappearance of the "Bapenda 9," Douala witnessed the first in a series of marches and demonstrations which were brutally suppressed by the police.

During this time, there were many reputed sightings of the disappeared, usually at night and usually in quarters considered highly dangerous. The sightings would describe the boys as beaten and emaciated, but desperate to hide from the expected onslaught of Operation Command from which they inexplicably slipped. There was widespread concern that if there were any validity to these sightings, that all should be done to keep the boys alive as testimonials to what was assumed to be a practice killing thousands. As Marc Etaha, Frederic Ngouffo, Chatry Kuete, Eric Chia, Jean Roger Tchiwan, Charles Kouatou, Chia Effician, Elysee Kouatou, and Fabrice Kuate – the Bapenda 9[16] – served as a kind of "last straw" for public patience with Operation Command, there was an uneasy mixture of guilt, anger, impotence, and mysticism wrapped up in the larger public response to their disappearance.

Whether or not people actually believed the reputed sightings of the disappeared, in some quarters of the city a ritual developed where efforts were made to feed the disappeared. Because the sightings were most frequently in very dangerous parts of the city, households would send their girl domestics, often great distances, to deliver food. It is common in Douala to take in young girls from the rural areas as unpaid servants. Many rural households can no longer provide for their children and so either throw them out of the home or sell them to intermediaries. These girls remain the "property" of the households they work for and are usually badly mistreated and have little freedom of mobility. From one sighting of the disappeared to the next, from one part of the city to the other, these girls took the risk of their own disappearance on the feeding expeditions. In the process, they crossed Douala at night in ways that at the time were without precedent. Sometimes they would meet up with other girls they had met on previous journeys and share what they had seen, as well as embellish stories and invent new ones. The danger entailed was secondary to the flush of this sudden and usually daily freedom, for soon they would meet up in particular spots and go where they wanted, never mind whether it corresponded with the destination they were instructed to seek out.

16 From reports of Christian Action Against Torture, Douala, March 3, 2001.

They would leave ciphers and other marks on cars and household walls, on store windows and security grates, or pile up empty pots and pans at key intersections. They would then tell their respective employers that the disappeared were attempting to leave messages, to communicate with the residents of the city about what was really taking place. Word spread that these girls had become interlocutors between the disappeared and the city and not merely deliverers of food. Their capacities were greatly inflated in a city where the reputations of those able to navigate the world of the night were already inflated. And so several of the girls began to be sought out by various officials, businesspersons, and even top personnel of Operation Command itself. They came not so much for direct information about the disappeared themselves nor to interpret their supposed conveyances. Rather, they wanted interpretations of their dreams, advice on new ventures, insights on the wheeling and dealing of colleagues and competitors.

Girls of thirteen who not long before had gone hungry in rural areas experiencing thorough economic and social decline, bought and sold to fetch water, now suddenly found 10,000 CFA notes pressed in their hands, and started demanding more. Stories spread how one of the girls, Sally, would hold court by the pool at the Meridien Hotel, cellphone in hand and surrounded by her entourage of body guards.

Illuminating Nkongmondo   Nkongmondo is set back from the intersection of two major roads, one leading into Douala, the other to Yaounde. During the rains, the area floods easily and is traversed with great difficulty. It is a quarter with a reputation for thieves, killers, and malaria. What success these neighborhood "emissaries" have had in the past has not been necessarily attributed to deft skill or astute planning. Instead, twenty guys will show up somewhere completely improbable – a formal luncheon for ambassadors' wives, payday at the bank – during times where places are either crowded or full of security and simply bully their way to some relatively modest cash, usually taking significant casualties on the way. Sometimes the ruthlessness will result in a big score. But the brutal intrusiveness and take-no-prisoners attitude is what has earned the quarter its characterization as a sullen dump of thuggery and its young male criminals the name "head-bangers." Few attempts at quarter "improvement" are initiated, though both the police and security command have repeatedly tried to clean out the growing criminal element.

Given the number of schemes, syndicates, and confidence games that often have occasion to make use of such "blind determination," one might think there would be safer and more lucrative opportunities for the young men here. But there is a seeming insistence to stand apart, as very few are willing to work as brute force for more sophisticated networks or ringleaders. Detention and death are also not persuasive deterrents to the endless supply of youth from the area purportedly identified as assailants and perpetrators.

Not two minutes from the western entrance to the quarter stand the remains of what was once Douala's largest cinema, now closed for the past several years. Next door stands a four-story building that once housed one of the city's better Catholic high schools, now moved to another, more suburban location. The demise of both has a lot to do with the relationship between them. The school kids would skip out of classes and crowd matinee showings of an endless fare of cheap kung fu movies. The kids would barely pay attention to the films; it was more a place to smoke marijuana and have sex. Some efforts were made to get the authority to at least close the place during school hours. But this was to no avail, especially as the very popular soft-porn showings on the weekends drew crowds of functionaries already disappointed that they hadn't attained the positions which would entitle them to the special twice-monthly strip shows and beyond featuring Parisian women held in Bonanjo.

While over the years the cinema had been stripped clean of seats, carpet, even major sections of the roof, the locked projection booth strangely remained intact. Given its proximity to Nkongmondo, the cinema was a convenient hangout for neighborhood youth, a beguiling place of refuge given how, despite its present locked-down fortress appearance, its status as a gathering spot of criminals was well known to the police. But as far as I could make out, there were no raids, no arrests. Unlike the high school kids, these youth actually came to watch cinema, perhaps as a respite from just how much their lives had become clumsy imitations of grade C movies. The thing was that there were no movies per se to watch. Rather, they had managed to attach the projector to a small generator to simply get it running and would then sit, often for hours, watching the rays of light as they reached the surface of the screen. Afterwards, they would get beers and have long discussions about what they had seen, arguing over plot lines and characters. But what was clear was that an important way of life was being depicted. The landscape and composition of this life, imposed on the screen from their imaginations, was discussed in great detail following these "showings."

Like most Doualaise, they were fascinated with this specter of distant lands, and also like most, they were determined to save money any way they could in order to buy tickets and secure visas. But unlike these others, they never could identify the name of the destination or figure out how far away it really was, or conversely, the name and distance would change all the time, as would the relevant authorities and the ways of getting there. So it would never be clear just how much money they needed, what the cost would be. As it was always difficult to hide money or to keep from spending it either to be left alone or buy one's way out of trouble, the problems seemed endless.

In the summer of 2001, a new organization, Forum for Inhabitants, made a preliminary effort to organize some form of community association in Nkongmondo. It consulted the village chief and with his assistance put together an initial assembly of over fifty residents to talk about what they could do about the insalubrious conditions that prevailed. Unlike most such meetings across the city, and across most cities in the region today, the complaints about present conditions were muted. Sure there was flooding and the lack of basic services, but the community had long been able to get by with being what they were; their aspirations were neither great, nor did they think that, whatever they might do, anything significant would likely ensue. When asked if the large numbers of criminals who reputedly operated from the community and subjected the community to harassment and a bad name put a damper on their motivation, a gray bearded man of about seventy forcefully responded, "no, not at all, they are invisible to us."

How does one locate this invisibility and to what ends? Within cities, the process of making individuals strangers to each other has been critical to incorporating their bodies and energies as labor for production of increasingly ephemeral commodities without referenced value, and the consumption of which grows more frenetic and dissociated from the stabilization of place or livelihood. Even across the impoverished quarters of Douala, there is an obsession with eating well, and neighborhoods become identified through the particularities of the foods cooked and the ways in which they are presented. From fried plantains served on images of the President's bare ass in specific humorous newspapers to the specific colors of plastic forks which must be used to eat certain stews on specific days, this incorporation of bits and pieces of quotidian objects into a complex economy of consuming basic meals makes the act of eating something potentially fractal – spacing out in all directions without clear aleatory channels or implications.

On the other hand, the unleashing of signifiers also is deployed as an excessive marker of belonging; excessive evidence of narrow genealogies cited to explain just where residents should be fixed. Fixed in the sense of specifying clearly eligible domains where the "broken" nature that characterizes most residents lives can be "repaired." But also fixed in the sense of being able to be pinned down and summed up, even as kin and communitarian relationships have become increasingly murky and fragmented in how they actually operate. Autochthony increasingly becomes a vehicle through which claims on resources can be made and legitimated.

But between the estrangement of labor and the reparation of belonging is the space of remembrance. Between embellishing anticipation of the next meal with traces of the "news" of yesterday and the undoing of the news of yesterday with the conviction that one has not yet "eaten well," there remains the collective process of sitting down to eat. Increasing numbers of youth are forced to float across the city in search of livelihood or run in a constant cat-and-mouse game, chasing those who owe them money, running from those whose money they have stolen. To locate someone, then, is often to speculate about when and where they will eat. In the midst of this speculation, and the uncertainty as to who is allied with whom, who knows what in an economy of appropriation and theft, sudden accumulation and loss, those who stop to eat must be careful about what they say. They may inevitably share their food, but they will make sure to say nothing to give themselves away. Sitting down to eat is then engineered with a complex toolbox of declensions, fragmented words, smirks, tongue clicks, and grunts.

Pinned down by the oozing appearance of identity markers, yet footloose in the pursuit of those from whom one is escaping, there is little to be presented, and achievement is not based on the figuration of a more comprehensive narrative. The circulation of communication's materiality "clears the bush for the bush to return," as the Sawa residents would say. In other words, as Agamben points out in his notion of *decreation*, what could have been and was becomes indistinguishable from what could have been but was not.[17]

The Doualaise know that they cannot go it alone, but who exactly to go with is another matter. For we have seen the pulling apart of conventional social ties. This is the place, then, of remembrance. There are no maps, no grand visions for a viable future, as in turn, there is nothing intact from the "archive" to be returned to life or to be reinvented. Rather, the boundary between the actual and the possible is effaced, as that which never happened but could is remembered as if it were about to happen now. The flickering projection in the cinema, the punctuation of meals by unnecessary language, the feeding of the disappeared and subsequent valorization of domestic girls – all point to a repositioning to call upon possibilities that have been there all along. It is a repositioning that releases a multiplicity of active forces to be in play, rather than assigned to reiterate existing values and differentials.[18]

---

17 Giorgio Agamben, *Potentialities: Collected Essays in Philosophy*, ed. and trans. Daniel Heller-Roazen (Stanford: Stanford University Press, 1999).
18 Michel Serres, *Angels: A Modern Myth*, trans. Francis Cowper (Paris: Flammarion, 1995).

Concluding Note

New trajectories of urban mobility and mobilization are taking place in the interstices of complex urban politics. Distinct groups and capacities are provisionally assembled into surprising, yet often dynamic, intersections outside of any formal opportunity the city presents for the interaction of diverse identities and situations.

Across urban Africa, there is a persistent tension as to what is possible to do within the city and the appropriate forms of social connections through which such possibilities can be pursued. Increasingly, more ephemeral forms of social collaboration are coming to the fore, and more effective formal governance partnerships often succeed to the degree to which they can draw on them. This emergence is a means of circumventing the intensifying contestation as to what kinds of social modalities and identities can legitimately mobilize resources and people's energies. Throughout these efforts lingers the question as to how urban residents reach a "larger world" of operations. What happens within the domain of the city itself that allows urban actors, often deeply rooted in specific places and ascriptions, to operate outside these confines? How are apparent realities of social coherence and cohesion maintained while opportunities, that would seemingly require behaviors and attitudes antithetical to the sustainability of such cohesion, are pursued?

Urban Africans are on the move, and the ability to move, through their quarters or cities or among cities, must draw on a capacity to see themselves as more than just marginal to prevalent global urban processes. Residents must see that deteriorating urban conditions do not simply mean that they become further removed from where the real power or opportunities lie, and that access to expanded domains of operation is not fixed to specific "development trajectories," institutional memberships, or transportation circuits. There are multiple geographies pieced together and navigated through the particular ways in which urban residents constitute the connections among themselves and the ways in which these connections are folded along a series of other daily interactions.

Order and Disorder in African Cities:
Governance, Politics, and Urban Land Development Processes

Carole Rakodi

> The postcolonial city ... [represents] a chaotic clash between old and new, power and impotence, poverty and ease. ... The chaos ... is also a source of fear and danger.[1]

The above conclusion emerges from a review of postcolonial novels in Kenya, but such a portrayal of African cities as having descended into chaos is not uncommon. The collapse of effective governance in states riven by conflict and warlordism is reflected in an absence of city government and often accompanied by an influx of refugees from rural insecurity – cities like Mogadishu, Kinshasa, Luanda, or Freetown are mirrors for the fears of other African countries as well as foreigners, including international development agencies. More generally, African cities are often seen as threatened by chaos: parasitic on the economy and thus antidevelopmental; characterized by excessively rapid demographic growth, sucking the most active and qualified people from the rural areas; unplanned and sprawling; unhealthy because of the inability of infrastructure providers to keep pace with growth and the exacerbating effects of density on the transmission of infectious disease; and characterized by incompetent and corrupt government structures. The fear is epitomized by the reactions of the rich and powerful: the colonial settlers of South Africa or Zimbabwe created enclaves modeled on the towns and cities of the European countries from which they or their ancestors came; today, the elites of cities from Nairobi to Lagos to Johannesburg fortify their houses, support massive unproductive private security industries, and create gated communities which insulate them from the supposedly chaotic life of the city beyond and reduce their motivation to hold public service providers to account.

Perceptions of urban chaos and fear of disorder have two historical roots. The first is the experience of unregulated urbanization in other parts of the world, especially 19th-century Europe. The unsatisfactory urban growth patterns, mixed land use, and unsanitary living conditions which resulted led to concerted efforts to develop municipal infrastructure technology and to plan and regulate urban development. Colonial administrators' dismay at the appar-

---

1 J. Roger Kurtz, *Urban Obsessions, Urban Fears: The Postcolonial Kenyan Novel* (Trenton, N.J.: Africa World Press, 1998), p. 84.

ent squalor and disorder of indigenous urban settlements stemmed, therefore, from their ideas about the form that orderly urban development should take, as well as their lack of understanding of the social and political organization of indigenous societies. Second, the fragility of the colonial military, political, and administrative apparatus fueled fears that they might not be able to maintain control over large and politically volatile urban populations. Such fears have not receded with the demise of colonialism: postindependence governments have been unable to keep pace with the demands of rapid urban growth, and the need to maintain social and political control over urban populations has strongly influenced their political and economic strategies.

Both colonial and postindependence governments have, therefore, attempted to impose "order" on towns and cities, in particular with respect to politico-administrative systems for urban management and the development of urban land. This paper will, first, explore the form which these attempts to achieve orderly urban development have taken, and second, assess the extent to which they have succeeded. We will see that their influence on urban development has been limited, with the result that most political activity and land development do not comply with the rules of the formal political and land administration systems. The common view that cities are, as a result, chaotic will, however, be challenged. It will be asserted that, far from behaving in an anarchic fashion, actors in urban politics and land development base their behavior on widely understood and accepted, if informal, rules for social interaction. As a result, the appropriateness of the concepts of order underlying attempts to institutionalize particular forms of political and physical order is questionable. Finally, some pointers for the future will be identified.

The urban experience on which this paper draws is largely that of the medium-sized cities of African states which have not been embroiled in civil war. These are cities in which relatively few people are, literally, homeless; some services and utilities continue to function, however inadequate their coverage and unreliable the provision; and social and political relationships between city governments and their citizens and between residents themselves are not, generally speaking, anarchic, although dysfunctional political relationships, social malaise, and poor urban governance are widespread.[2] Most of the examples are

---

2 See J. Campbell, J. Mwami, and M. Ntukula, "Urban Social Organization: An Exploration of Kinship, Social Networks, Gender Relations and Household and Community in Dar es Salaam," in *Gender, Family and Household in Tanzania*, ed. Colin Creighton and Cuthbert K. Omari (Aldershot: Avebury, 1995), pp. 221–252; Carole Rakodi, ed., *The Urban Challenge in Africa: Growth and Management of Its Largest Cities* (Tokyo: United Nations University Press, 1997); Arne Tostensen, Inge Tvedten, and Mariken Vaa, eds. *Associational Life in African Cities: Popular Responses to the Urban Crisis* (Uppsala: Nordiska Afrikainstitutet, 2001).

drawn neither from collapsed states nor from urban settlements at the extremes of the size continuum. This paper therefore complements the in-depth analyses of the cities on which this volume focuses, although the generalizations it contains should, of course, be treated with caution.

I. Imposing Order on Unruly Urban Development

In trying to achieve political control over growing urban populations, regulate urban growth, and improve health and efficiency, decision makers have imposed their own ideas of what constitutes order and systems by which that order is to be achieved. Here, colonial and postcolonial attempts to impose political and physical order will be outlined.

Colonial and Settler Approaches to Towns and Cities The political systems introduced by colonial administrators reflected both the political philosophies and systems of their home countries and the means adopted to secure control over the resources required by colonial trade and enterprise. Both of the principal colonial powers – Britain and France – had liberal democratic political systems in formation. However, their legal systems, degree of centralization, and view of the political relationship of their colonies to the mother state differed. As a result, the political system instituted in the urban settlements established alongside indigenous towns or in areas of agriculture or mining enterprise reflected both the characteristics of and differences between their home countries, and the differing approaches to colonial rule adopted in different parts of Africa. Where the new towns were established by mining companies (as in the Copperbelt of Zambia), democratic structures were absent or weak. Elsewhere in anglophone countries, local councils were established based on ward-level elections and the enfranchisement (as in the UK at the time) of property owners, which conveniently restricted representation and decision-making power to male settlers, businesspeople, and colonial administrators.

Gradually, as independence approached, the representation of previously excluded groups improved: initially tokenistic, by the time of independence the scene was set for representative local councils with a degree of autonomy (if often apparent rather than real), although often the preexisting indigenous settlements (especially in countries under indirect rule) were not fully part of this political system, and in the settler colonies, the parts of urban settlements reserved for African occupation were separately administered. Unlike anglophone colonies, francophone colonies' status and the centralized political and administrative structure of the French state resulted in a top-down system of urban administration which persisted long after independence.

Capitalist development in Europe and North America was accompanied by the individualization and formalization of land and property rights, with legal systems designed to protect the interests of owners. Following rapid uncontrolled urbanization during the industrial revolution and the early years of the 20th century, systems for planning and regulating urban development were gradually introduced. These were underpinned by conceptualizations of the nature of property rights and the legitimate role of the state, and were influenced by the principles on which the legal and political systems were based in the countries concerned, their differing historical experiences and geographical characteristics, and the constellations of interests dominant in particular historical periods. As noted above, the primacy of individual rights to the enjoyment of property in perpetuity and to dispose of it freely was the basis of a liberal capitalist economic system. Moreover, it was believed, on the basis of economic theory, that given accessibility constraints, the most efficient urban land use patterns would emerge if owners were free to sell their property to the highest bidder, leading to a concentration of uses capable of paying the highest rents and using land most intensively at the most accessible nodes of the urban area, usually the city center. Only where one rightsholder's enjoyment of his or her property interferes with the ability of others to do the same is state intervention, in theory, legitimate. Although in practice state intervention may be extended based on additional goals that are also considered legitimate, in principle, the rights of property holders are primary and the state can only curtail these rights with their consent.

One of the purposes of state intervention is therefore to protect and guarantee the rights of property owners and occupiers by registering those rights and enforcing contracts for their transfer. Land registration is also needed for property to be used as collateral for raising investment funds. To this minimum, historical experience has added a series of other state roles which are, to a greater or lesser extent, accepted as legitimate.

First, action to provide (or ensure the provision of) physical infrastructure and regulate standards of development in order to protect public health was accepted, not least because many of the diseases related to deficient utilities or poor waste management affect all income groups (e.g., air pollution, cholera), even if they have the greatest impact on the poor. Municipal engineering technologies and standards, therefore, were developed initially to deal with rapid urbanization associated with industrialization in the North. When the colonial powers began to develop urban enclaves to accommodate their businesses, officials, and other nationals, as well as their local employees, they applied the same engineering technologies and standards, although often adjusted in line with perceptions of their new environment. Thus colonial appropriation of large tracts of land for urban development was underlaid by a failure to recognize existing land rights and a perception that land was abundant,[3] leading to the adoption of lower densities than in Europe.

Second, the European experience of unregulated urban expansion resulted in cities where the juxtaposition of residential areas with industries spewing uncontrolled emissions of waste and pollution, as well as a shortage of sites for public facilities, adversely affected health and quality of life. It also resulted in the conversion of large swathes of agricultural land for urban use, a danger brought home to high-density countries such as the Netherlands and the UK by food shortages during and after World War II. Such experiences led to the institution of effective systems of planning and development control. It was accepted that the state had the right and capacity to curtail the interests of property owners in the wider social interest. The common experience of the adverse consequences of unregulated urban development and belief in an efficacious and well-meaning state generated such wide public support that commercial developers and investors were forced to accept the limitations on their freedom to operate. Although the restrictions also affected individuals, increasing home ownership led more and more urban households to recognize that the restrictions were outweighed by the degree of protection thereby afforded their living environments and property values.

The legal basis of land use planning and development control varied according to the principles on which the legal systems were based in particular countries, especially the distinction between systems based on common and codified law (the UK and Ireland and the rest of Europe respectively).[4] The legal basis of the system influenced the nature and status of land use plans; the training and professional status of practitioners; and the relationship in law and practice between the allocation of land for particular uses in development plans, the regulation of subdivision for urban uses, and control over the standards, form, and appearance of buildings. Inextricably linked to the regulatory system were ideas on what constituted a "good urban built environment," which were embodied

---

3 See also Donald A. Krueckeberg, "Private Property in Africa: Creation Stories of Economy, State, and Culture," *Journal of Planning Education and Research* 19, no. 2 (1999), pp. 176–182.

4 The fossilized political systems of Spain and Portugal meant that they were not part of the European mainstream in this respect. The rights of private property owners continued to be paramount, subject only to a degree of building control for public health and safety reasons. Land use planning, subdivision, and development control were ineffective until democratization and subsequent accession to the European Union led to pressure to comply with European standards in order to qualify for development assistance funds.

in plan proposals and implemented through public investment and development control decisions. Perhaps the most influential of these was the desirability of separating uses, but other important ideas included the concept of a (self-contained) neighborhood and the necessity of planning for increased vehicle ownership.

In the colonial era, therefore, the political control necessary to ensure the viability of colonial enterprises, the financial self-sufficiency of (especially British) colonial administrations, and the safety of colonial and settler populations were inextricably linked to claims on land and property as well as the European tenure and land administration systems considered necessary to promote enterprise, safeguard the interests of business, and protect the health and living standards of European urban residents. The use of land policy and planning as an instrument of social control was demonstrated most starkly in the settler economies of countries such as South Africa and Zimbabwe. The refusal to extend political and property ownership rights to other population groups, especially indigenous rural-urban migrants, however, was strongly contested throughout the colonial period, and especially from the mid-1940s onward.

Postindependence Politics and Land Administration In the years leading up to independence, efforts had already been made, especially in the British colonies, to prepare the ground for representative democratic political systems at the urban level. The structures of broader-based democracy were, therefore, already in place, with administrative structures staffed largely by expatriate professionals capable of managing the (generally small) cities which were the capitals, ports, mining towns, and agricultural service centers of the newly independent states. In theory, the extension of the franchise and abolition of separate administrative arrangements for the European and African sectors of cities created conditions for continued orderly development of the inherited urban fabric. In practice, the imperatives of state formation, the pursuit of national economic development goals, the desire to fulfill political promises made to the peasantry, conflicts between factions (often along ethnic lines), and a desire to hold onto power invariably led to centralization of political and administrative power and the imposition of authoritarian political systems.

In most countries, a military ruler or executive president emerged who was able to stand above and manipulate factions or bypass parties and place the bureaucracy under his own control (e.g., Zambia, Tanzania, Senegal, Cameroon, Kenya). Representative institutions such as parties, parliament, local government, and trade unions were downgraded or abolished. Although many of the regimes instituted mechanisms for allowing the expression of political voice, generally through the machinery of the dominant party ("participatory democracy"), the scope for freedom of expression was rapidly eroded and the machinery used predominantly for information giving, mobilization, and eventually repression. Single-party or military rule at the national level was reproduced at local government levels, although elections were, in some cases, retained. In some of the more populist single-party systems, political stability and developmental progress were achieved until, from the mid-1970s onward, economic crisis, growing authoritarianism, and decreasing accountability undermined the regime. Elsewhere, periods of military rule alternated with shaky civilian regimes, opening the way for extreme clientelist spoils politics (e.g., Nigeria, Sierra Leone, Liberia) and sometimes complete breakdown. In such systems, the winner (the dominant faction) takes all, looting an economy dominated by the black market, general economic crisis, pervasive corruption, and the use of communalism to mobilize political support, resulting in widespread instability and the erosion of authority.[5]

Everywhere, in the 1980s, economic crisis followed by structural adjustment depleted the resource base not only for achieving economic growth but also for the patronage resources on which both civilian and military regimes depended to manufacture consent. Eventually, by the later 1980s, domestic movements for political change, reinforced by external pressures, aid conditionality, and the changing geopolitical order, resulted in a widespread process of (re)democratization. The core areas of political reform in the 1990s have been those associated with liberal democracy: political plurality, fair elections, and decentralization.[6] Thus processes of political change at the national level have been reproduced at local government levels: where elected single-party local councils had survived, local elections were increasingly contested on party political lines, and where they had not, local elections were reintroduced. The processes leading to redemocratization differed, and the constitutional outcomes and subsequent experience vary as well. However, the vast majority of Africa's democracies today are fragile and unconsolidated. The key problems are identified by some as primarily external but by others as essentially internal. Rita Abrahamsen, for example, argues that democratization is unsustainable in societies dependent on externally controlled resources which are also subject to conditionality based on neoliberal economic theory.[7] The pressure for democratization, she suggests,

---

5 See Patrick Chabal and Jean-Pascal Daloz, *Africa Works: Disorder as Political Instrument* (London and Bloomington: James Currey and Indiana University Press, 1999).
6 See Yusuf Bangura, "Democratization, Equity, and Stability: African Politics and Societies in the 1990s," in *Renewing Social and Economic Progress in Africa*, ed. Dharam P. Ghai (Basingstoke: Macmillan/UNRISD, 2000), pp. 167–198.
7 Rita Abrahamsen, *Disciplining Democracy: Development Discourse and Good Governance in Africa* (London: Zed Books, 2000).

was first and foremost a demand for socioeconomic change and, although political rights may be valued, the new regimes were expected to restore mass prosperity. Unable to do this because of their lack of control over policy and resources, they are "exclusionary democracies: they allow for political parties and elections but cannot respond to the demands of the majority or incorporate the masses in any meaningful way"[8] and are therefore unlikely to become consolidated. Yusuf Bangura, in contrast, attributes failures of democratic consolidation to an inability to maintain elite cohesion (resulting in factional struggles to gain political power and control over state spoils), failure to hold the bureaucracy and the armed forces to account, constraints on the expression of political voice, and lack of respect for some of the key assumptions of a liberal democratic model (e.g., fair elections, peaceful alternation of power, separation of the bureaucracy from the ruling political party).[9]

Both in the independence settlements of most ex-colonies and in the late 1980s, therefore, the dominant ideology of political order has been liberal representative democracy, in which

> liberalism determines the nature of the state (formal, abstract), its structure (separate from the autonomous civil society, a clear separation between public and private), its rationale (protection of the basic rights of its citizens) and its basic units (individuals rather than groups or communities). Democracy specifies who constitutes the legitimate government and wields the authority inherent in the state (the elected representatives), how they acquire authority (free elections, choice between parties) and how they are to exercise it (in broad harmony with public opinion).[10]

The concern of liberal democratic theory is therefore not with the rightful place of active citizens in the life of a political community, but with the legitimate pursuit by individuals of their interests and with government as a means of enhancing those interests.[11] The state can only govern by consent, which can be withdrawn if individuals believe their rights (to liberty, prosperity, or freedom of expression) have been violated.

Prosperity is to be achieved through the operations of a capitalist economy based on the matching principles of economic liberalism. In theory, therefore, the state should not pursue large-scale economic and social goals, since property

---

8 Ibid., p. 134.
9 Bangura, "Democratization, Equity, and Stability."
10 Bhikhu Parekh, "The Cultural Particularity of Liberal Democracy," in *Prospects for Democracy: North, South, East, West*, ed. David Held (Cambridge: Polity Press, 1993), p. 165.
11 See ibid.

is privately owned, economic functions operate through the market, and government interference is deemed counterproductive. But in practice the boundary between the public and private spheres is contested and views on the legitimate role of government vary. Thus the compacts between colonial powers and early nationalist leaders during the transition to independence instituted liberal democratic political systems, but coupled these with a strongly interventionist role for the state in the economy. In comparison, the move toward liberal democracy in the 1990s, again resulting from a combination of internal and external pressures, was associated with a neoliberal approach to economic policy.

Based on the assumptions of economic and political liberalism, much of the longstanding debate about democracy has, therefore, taken the form of attempting to identify the most suitable mechanisms for selecting rulers who will ensure that the rights of individuals are protected and can be held accountable in this respect. In its consolidated late 20th-century form, representative democracy is organized around a general cluster of rules and institutions, which include those identified by Bhikhu Parekh above and also political competition based on the principle of alternation of power and organized through political parties which embody different political platforms and ensure pluralism; associational autonomy in order, *inter alia*, to enable government to manage conflicting interests, to disperse power between them (organized as interest groups or political parties) without any becoming dominant, and to ensure accountability; and institutional separation of powers between the executive, the legislature, and the judiciary, in order to ensure the rule of law and the subordination of officials of the state to the law and accountability of the executive to the legislature.

By adopting these mechanisms of democracy, it was expected, relations between state and people would be satisfactorily regulated, competing interests would be balanced and reconciled, development objectives of economic growth and basic needs satisfaction would be achieved, and elected representatives and the bureaucracies which implement their decisions would be held to account. Moreover, citizens would be willing to pay taxes and comply with regulatory systems, since the transparency of resource allocation and decision making would give them confidence in the ability of decision makers to respond to their needs and demands, and avenues of redress would be available through either voice in the political process or resort to the legal system.

With respect to the administration of private property and physical order, little has changed. The conceptions of physical order, and the planning and regulatory systems designed to ensure that the urban built environment fitted these conceptions, have persisted. Exported to Africa by the colonial powers, they have been perpetuated by legislation and practice, and reinforced by the continued export of Northern ideas and technology through models of professional training, the use of international consultants and contractors, and the preconceptions and practices of international development agencies and their staff. These ideas and practices relate to tenure and administration of land and property, planning for urban development and infrastructure provision, and systems for development regulation. The belief persists that individual title, underpinned by administrative and legal systems to protect and reinforce property rights, is the most appropriate land tenure system. It is accompanied by a belief that engineering efficiency is best achieved through installing infrastructure in straight lines; a supply-driven approach to urban water provision which downplays the real costs and discourages demand management; and the notion that universal road access and water-borne sewerage are desirable. The latter led to excessive width standards for roads, and human waste-disposal methods which are costly in terms of finance and water use. With respect to regulation, notions of physical order based on land use segregation reinforce attempts to universalize zoning and land use control and formalize informal activities. In addition, there is also a belief that detailed control over the construction of individual houses is essential in order to protect urban dwellers against builders of substandard housing, rapacious landlords, fire, infectious disease, and other health hazards.

II. Politics and Land Development in African Cities

As is clearly evident in African cities, attempts to base urban political organization on liberal democracy and land administration on individual property title and land use control have been problematic. An important question, therefore, is whether the problems arise from the assumptions on which the models are based – assumptions about what characteristics political and physical order should have and how it should be achieved – or from shortcomings in the way the political and land administration systems have been designed and operationalized.

Liberal Representative Democracy Restored? In Africa, despite progress in restoring civil and political rights and democracy in the 1990s, political instability is endemic, and some multiparty democratic reforms have been reversed. There are clearly a number of problems, in practice and principle, in applying the liberal democratic model to Africa:

- Liberal/representative democracy defines the individual as an essentially self-contained person. However, in practice, the boundary between an individual and society is drawn differently in every society. Ascriptive membership of a social group implies that such membership is an integral part of the person's social identity and determines his or her rights and duties.[12] Where individuals are defined in communal terms, freedom, equality, property, justice, loyalty, power, and authority may be conceived differently and groups believe that their members' individual rights can and should be restricted. Liberalism, which places the individual above the community, may, in such circumstances, be seen as a threat to the shared body of ideas and values.[13] In Africa, it is argued, the notion of a discrete, autonomous individual is mistaken: representation is communal and legitimacy rests on, first, embodying the identity and qualities of the community and, second, the ability to discharge obligations – to distribute resources, even if illegally. Only when redistribution stops, Chabal and Daloz assert, do illegal practices come to be regarded as illegitimate and labeled corrupt or criminal.[14]

- The winner/loser system is thought to sit badly with a culture of consensus, in which people see themselves as part of a community that has a moral authority over them, share in the articulation of group interests, and in return are obliged to follow the ensuing consensus.[15]
- In a competitive multiparty system, elections are costly, potentially divisive, encourage corruption, and pose particular dangers in multicommunal societies. The latter is especially true in a simple majoritarian system.[16] Recent democratization has increased competing demands at a time when the weakened state can manage neither social conflict nor economic recovery.[17] Parties are often based on elite factions rather than ideology, and it is relatively easy for the ruling group to rig elections using the resources of the state.[18] Because parties lack policy, electoral discourse is forced back on local identity, ethnicity, personal characteristics, and often unrealistic promises. In the absence of loyalties other than those associated with an ethnic group, ethnicity is used to mobilize political support and divert attention from the ruling party's own accumulation and abuse of power, leading Goran Hyden to hypothesize that "the more competitive elections

---

12 See ibid.
13 See ibid.
14 Chabal and Daloz, *Africa Works: Disorder as Political Instrument*.
15 See Richard Hodder-Williams, "The Bases of Political Systems Which Are Both Democratic and African," paper presented at the SCUSA Colloquium, University of East Anglia, September 5–8, 1999.
16 See Bangura, "Democratization, Equity, and Stability."
17 See Parekh, "The Cultural Particularity of Liberal Democracy."
18 See Geoffrey Hawthorn, "Sub-Saharan Africa," in *Prospects for Democracy*, ed. Held, pp. 330–354.

are, the greater the risk of falling back on ascriptive criteria for conducting politics."[19]
- Formal democratic systems are not necessarily equitable,[20] although there is scope for improving their representativeness and equity by adapting their design. However, political participation by lower-income groups is inhibited for practical reasons (especially preoccupation with making a living) and because of elite resistance.
- Organized civil society, one of the roles of which is supposedly to safeguard democratic rights and the concerns of society vis-à-vis the state, is either weak or not autonomous from the state.[21]
- In a state-centered development model, access to state resources is key to economic advancement and so the stakes of winning or losing in the electoral game are very high. Exacerbating this, the state is seen as having access to resources inherited from a colonial regime or attracted from overseas, and so politics comes to be perceived as a competition for a fixed pool of resources, especially in stagnant economies.[22]
- The relationship of democratic institutions to other authority structures and the influence of the latter on state-society relations are often problematic.

These problems, and the last in particular, lead to the question of whether, if competitive liberal democracy is so hard to institutionalize in Africa, the conception of politics on which it rests and the assumptions of the model itself are appropriate to the African context.

Although democratic theory holds that democratic local governance will increase political participation, resulting in the more adequate representation and empowerment of varied political interests, in turn leading to more widespread policy benefits such as poverty reduction,[23] liberal representative democracy is no less problematic, if less studied, at the urban level. At this level, the first key issue is the division of resources and functions between central and urban levels of government, the political and operational framework at each level, and the relations between them. A second set of issues relates to the design and operation of the electoral system, and a third to questions of accountability.

19 Goran Hyden, "The Governance Challenge in Africa," in *African Perspectives on Governance*, ed. Goran Hyden, Dele Olowu, and Hastings W. O. Okoth Ogendo (Trenton, N.J.: Africa World Press, 2000), p. 23.
20 See Bangura, "Democratization, Equity, and Stability."
21 See Dwayne Woods, "Civil Society in Europe and Africa: Limiting State Power through a Public Sphere," *African Studies Review* 35, no. 2 (1992), pp. 77–100.
22 See Hyden, "The Governance Challenge in Africa."
23 See Harry Blair, "Participation and Accountability at the Periphery: Democratic Local Governance in Six Countries," *World Development* 28, no. 1 (2000), pp. 21–39.

1. Central-Local Relations. Except to some extent in federal systems, where local autonomy is enshrined in a constitution, the degree of local autonomy depends primarily on central government motives, which are supposedly to share power and achieve economic efficiency.[24] In theory, devolution is intended to enhance local responsiveness and accountability and to provide a check on the power of higher levels of government. In reality, a national regime's motive for power sharing is generally to enhance political stability and its own hold on power, by providing opportunities for the expression of preferences at the local level and the representation of local groups and minorities in decision making, and by reducing the extent to which central government can be blamed for poor performance. In practice, local representative political organization has more often been seen as a challenge to both political stability and the ruling party, by providing sectional interests or opposition parties with a political platform. Even in democratic periods, poor performance has often been used as an excuse to suspend elected city councils when a political impasse is reached, e.g., in Dar es Salaam in 1996. In the 1990s, as elsewhere in the world, it was common for the majority party in city councils to be an opposition party, leading to political tensions with the national government and failure to provide a satisfactory financial resource base. Consequently, autonomous decision making is limited and, in part as a result, it is difficult to attract good-quality candidates to stand for political office at the municipal level.

The economic efficiency argument for devolution rests on an assumption that local spending decisions will result in more cost-effective provision of services, especially when the financial resources are locally generated and there is local accountability. In practice, central government's motives may have more to do with reducing demands on national revenue. Moreover, the greater efficiency (or pro-poor) allocation of resources by local government remains a hypothesis: the extent to which it is realized will depend on the local political system and the capacity of the administrative arm of local government to deliver.[25] The limited administrative and financial capacity of African municipalities in a situation of rapid urban growth and the disruptive effect of successive reform attempts has resulted in severe infrastructure and service deficiencies, particularly for poor residents.

2. The Electoral System. The second key aspect of the formal urban political system is the electoral arrangements. Even within the general framework of representative democracy, various systems are possible, featuring different arrange-

---

24 See Kenneth Davey, "The Structure and Functions of Urban Government," in Kenneth Davey et al., *Urban Management: The Challenge of Growth* (Aldershot: Avebury, 1996), pp. 47–102.
25 See ibid.

ments for the election of representatives, executive control, the role of parties, and arrangements for city-wide and sub-city-level decision making and administration.

Election of representatives can be ward-based or at-large; first-past-the-post, proportional representation, or a mixture of the two. In a ward-based system, councillors are more likely to identify with and represent the interests of their constituents.[26] However, this is by no means assured. Their motives for seeking political office may be power and status, to advance a political career or to personally benefit from access to public-sector resources. The latter may not involve grand corruption, but derive from privileged access to information (on property development, infrastructure routes, contracts), allowances/salaries, or patronage resources such as municipal jobs, public housing, or trade licenses. Urban wards are likely to contain a mixture of income groups and residential and economic interests, and even when they are predominantly poor, councillors themselves may not share the socioeconomic characteristics of voters, and levels of voter turnout may be low. In addition, ward councillors are likely to advance particularistic arguments, reducing the attention given to strategic issues and city-wide redistribution needs. Ward-based elections tend to be associated with a first-past-the-post system, in which many representatives may be elected with only minority support, while other minorities are unrepresented in the political system. While ward-based systems predominate in anglophone countries, party list systems are more common elsewhere. Closed party list systems reduce the choice available to voters.[27] Difficulties arising from the single list electoral system led some of the ten municipalities in Abidjan to introduce neighborhood management councils or committees to ensure more participatory management of local services.[28] Elections at-large, based on a proportional representation system, may reduce the extent to which councillors identify with the interests of their constituents but also make it more likely that strategic objectives can be addressed and minorities and small parties adequately represented. In terms of the design of the electoral system, therefore, some of the disadvantages of majoritarian competitive democracy can be overcome by combining first-past-the-post and proportional representation elements, as in the design of the new electoral system for Johannesburg.[29]

---

26 See Nick Devas et al., *Urban Governance and Poverty: Lessons from a Study of Ten Cities in the South* (Birmingham: International Development Department, School of Public Policy, University of Birmingham, 2001).
27 See Koffi Attahi, "Decentralization and Urban Participatory Governance in Francophone Africa," in *Governing Africa's Cities*, ed. Mark Swilling (Johannesburg: Witwatersrand University Press, 1997), pp. 161–209.
28 See Koffi Attahi, *Metropolitan Governance in Abidjan*, Seminar on Development and Urban Africa (Barcelona: Centre d'Estudis Africans, 1999).

Executive control. There is relatively little variation in the structure and roles of legislatures at city level, but considerable differences in the way executive bodies are structured and their functions performed, with implications for representativeness, accountability, and effectiveness. These differences relate to whether the executive is single (a mayor) or plural (a committee or cabinet), whether it is elected or appointed, whether it has political or managerial powers and how clearly these are separated, and the system for appointing senior staff and rules on terms of office.[30] For example, following the political settlement in Mozambique in 1994, a municipalities law was passed which provides for an elected administrator and local assembly, from which a municipal council is appointed by the administrator. Subsequent research detected concerns about whether elected administrators could successfully combine executive and legislative roles, especially given the inherited experience of a coercive and militarized state.[31] Central appointment of the executive reduces autonomy and accountability to the local legislature. This is seen clearly in Ghanaian cities, especially Kumasi,[32] although it may result in benefits if the appointee is able to use his or her position to secure a larger flow of central funds than might otherwise be available. An executive (and councillors) with managerial powers tends to become closely engaged in day-to-day operations, opening the door to political favoritism, inefficiency, and corruption. If senior staff are centrally appointed, as in Kenya,[33] accountability to local councillors is reduced. If locally appointed, they may be unable to uphold bureaucratic norms against dubious political practices and less competent because of the lack of a good career structure, although they may also be more committed to local development objectives. Rules that restrict elected representatives to a single term may exacerbate the tendency to favor politically visible short-term projects over long-term solutions to problems.

The role of parties. Democratic theory suggests that individual interests can be aggregated and represented most adequately through a party system. Political

---

29 See Jo Beall, Owen Crankshaw, and Susan Parnell, *Towards Inclusive Urban Governance in Johannesburg*, Urban Governance, Partnership and Poverty Working Paper 24 (Birmingham: International Development Department, School of Public Policy, University of Birmingham, 2001).

30 See David Pasteur, "Internal Organisation and Management Process," in Kenneth Davey et al., *Urban Management: The Challenge of Growth* (Aldershot: Avebury, 1996), pp. 103–160.

31 See Jocelyn Alexander, "The Local State in Post-war Mozambique: Political Practice and Ideas about Authority," *Africa* 67, no. 1 (1997), pp. 1–26.

32 See Nick Devas and David Korboe, "City Governance and Poverty: The Case of Kumasi," *Environment and Urbanization* 12, no. 1 (2000), pp. 123–136; Rudith King, Dan Inkoom, and Kokjo Mensah Abrampah, *Urban Governance in Kumasi: Poverty and Exclusion*, Urban Governance, Partnership and Poverty Working Paper 23 (Birmingham: International Development Department, School of Public Policy, University of Birmingham, 2001).

33 See Carole Rakodi, Rose Gatabaki-Kamau, and Nick Devas, "Poverty and Political Conflict in Mombasa," *Environment and Urbanization* 12, no. 1 (2000), pp. 153–170.

parties, it is argued, sharpen accountability by presenting voters with policy choices, which on election representatives have a remit and responsibility to implement. However, David Pasteur concludes that in practice there is no obvious correlation between multiparty competition and the responsiveness and integrity of urban management in developing countries.[34] Partisan interests may well be put before either overall city development objectives or the needs of supporters of other parties. Moreover, it is rare for political parties in Africa to have a coherent policy platform or to aggregate and articulate local interests, in part because they lack funds and also because they are not themselves democratic institutions. Pluralism may instead encourage destructive competition between factions, levels of government, and neighboring jurisdictions, without giving voters policy choices. The strategies parties pursue to widen their political base include coopton or camouflaging party political activity as grassroots (community-level) organization. Moreover, parties do not command loyalty, because they are seen merely as a means to attaining power. Politicians often change parties to improve their electoral chances or gain access to the resources of the ruling party. Also parties and politicians have to raise funds for campaigning and patronage, so they are obligated to both their sponsors and supporters, resulting in clientelistic and particularistic practices. All of these features are seen in, for example, Kenya's political system.

City-wide and local decision making and implementation. City governments with comprehensive boundaries and functions and a strong financial base are probably best placed to manage urban growth.[35] However, on the one hand, metropolitan governments are often administratively fragmented and, on the other, city-level government is remote from residents, adversely affecting access and accountability, unless there is a ward-based electoral system. Possible solutions to the former problem (amalgamation of adjacent municipalities, extension of the core municipality, or directly elected metropolitan government) may face political resistance. Alternative solutions include voluntary cooperation between municipalities, the establishment of metropolitan bodies for specific functions, or an indirectly elected metropolitan body. A possible solution to the latter problem is the establishment of sub-city political and administrative structures. In Abidjan, for example, the metropolitan area (current population 3.5 million) was divided into ten municipalities in 1980. Each elects five councillors and a mayor who, together with a metropolitan mayor, are also members of the supra-metropolitan body, Ville d'Abidjan. The eleven mayors form an executive committee. This federal system has not, however, solved all the problems

---

34 Pasteur, "Internal Organisation and Management Process."
35 See Davey, "The Structure and Functions of Urban Government."

of lack of clarity in the allocation and overlapping of responsibilities, reluctance to devolve authority, lack of coordination between local and central government, difficulties in coordinating municipalities with very different levels of wealth, lack of municipal capacity, and weakness of metropolitan leadership.[36] A similar system was established in Greater Dakar in 1996, with an additional layer at the city level. In Pikine (population one million), AbdouMaliq Simone identifies severe fiscal shortfalls and conflicting interests within and between the sixteen wards as hindrances to a serious attempt to develop ward action plans and a city strategic development plan. The lack of legitimacy which results from arbitrary administrative boundaries and failure to deliver services gives rise, he suggests, to a sense of disconnection between residents and the city administration.[37]

The ability of elected sub-municipal governments to represent and respond to the interests of residents depends on their relationships with municipal councillors as well as the resources available to them. For example, in Kumasi, sub-metro assemblies, town councils, and unit committees have never become effective, largely because the resources made available to them by the chief executive and municipal assembly have been insufficient.[38] In both authoritarian and some ostensibly democratic systems, sub-municipal structures may have administrative responsibilities but in practice be merely tools for political control from above. Kenya's chiefs and sub-chiefs, who are appointed by the administrative/security apparatus of the central government, are a case in point.[39] In contrast, local representative organizations (and NGOs) may be outside the hierarchical structure of government or party but nevertheless recognized for consultation purposes (e.g., Bulawayo Residents' Associations[40]).

3. Accountability. A third important aspect of urban politics is accountability.[41] In theory, a democratic system, through periodic elections and other arrangements, ensures both external and internal accountability. Elected municipal government is, in theory, open to the public gaze: it is relatively accessible compared to national government, local politicians are relatively active and numerous, there are likely to be local media, and residents have political rights.

---

36 See Attahi, *Metropolitan Governance in Abidjan.*
37 AbdouMaliq Simone, "Constructing an Interface: On the Emergence of 'Small' Collaborations in Pikine, Senegal," paper presented at the Nordic Africa Institute conference "The Formal and Informal City – What Happens at the Interface?," Copenhagen, June 15–18, 2000.
38 See King et al., *Urban Governance in Kumasi: Poverty and Exclusion*; Devas and Korboe, "City Governance and Poverty."
39 See Rakodi et al., "Poverty and Political Conflict in Mombasa."
40 See Pasteur, "Internal Organisation and Management Process."
41 See Dele Olowu, "Accountability and Transparency," in *Public Administration in Africa*, ed. Ladipo Adamolekun (Boulder, Colo.: Westview Press, 1999), pp. 139–158.

This does not mean that those with the greatest influence are the poor, and even if they are, the need to ensure electoral support does not ensure integrity. Mechanisms to enhance external accountability may include executive, judicial, and legislative controls, central government regulation, the exercise of political voice, and independent scrutiny bodies.

The first of these mechanisms implies that the bureaucratic and political executive are separate. However, in practice, politicians and officials exchange mutual favors, and the ability of the legislature to ensure accountability is limited because of its political weakness. In addition, in British-model systems, because the elected council has executive functions, it is not an independent accountability mechanism, especially if it is dominated by a single party. Where there is a strong opposition party, it can encourage accountability, but these rarely exist in Africa's fragmented and unstable party systems.[42] According to Dele Olowu, the effectiveness of judicial remedy is only medium-low in Africa, while independent scrutiny bodies are rare.[43] Central government has control and regulatory powers but is ineffective in holding local government to account when local politicians and the ruling party or employees in the field offices of central government have forged an alliance for mutual benefit.

In theory, the electoral system allows voters to register their general approval or disapproval of an incumbent's performance and to select new representatives. However, electoral politics may only legitimize the power of the local elite. Middle-class residents tend to have interests in common with the bureaucracy and either manage to secure services for themselves or insulate themselves by self-provision or the purchase of private services (from gated communities and private health care to individual septic tanks and generators). They do not, therefore, try to hold local government to account for its failure to tackle environmental health problems. In addition, elections are occasional, only address the broadest issues, and the system is affected by the ratio of citizens to councillors, the timing of municipal vis-à-vis national elections, and the voter registration process. Under-representation is common in the largest cities (either because the redrawing of boundaries lags behind population growth or because the ruling party is reluctant to provide opposition supporters with greater representation) and where voter registration is voluntary. Furthermore, timing municipal to coincide with national elections reduces them to a sideshow and may rob them of the most able candidates.

Democratic pragmatists suggest that limitations on the accountability provided by the electoral system can be offset by the use of public meetings or hear-

---

42 See Blair, "Participation and Accountability at the Periphery."
43 Olowu, "Accountability and Transparency."

ings, opinion surveys on the extent of citizen satisfaction with municipal services, as well as a watchdog role for the media and civil society organizations. Although greater freedom of expression accompanied democratization and has increased the role of the media in improving accountability in the 1990s, investigative journalism is still hindered by intimidation, repression, and lack of resources. There is much ambivalence about the political salience of NGOs, grassroots and other membership organizations. Seen by liberal democracy theorists as a means of increasing accountability, others regard them as, in effect, a parallel administration: a para-political structure linking the official political apparatus to residents.[44] The functions and motives of NGOs and the political space available to them vary, influencing their political behavior. Some undertake developmental activities or provide services, typically to residents underserved by public agencies. Others act as intermediaries between residents and public-sector agencies or create structures to coordinate unorganized interests and increase their political influence at the city or community level. Sometimes NGOs develop positive relationships with residents, politicians, and local government, as in the Nairobi Informal Settlements Coordinating Committee. However, governments often regard them as a political or security threat, or view them merely as useful instruments to advance government aims or counter public-sector deficiencies.[45] The former view leads to NGOs being ignored, regulated, or oppressed; the latter to corruption or establishment of government-oriented NGOs. NGOs may support communities or they may encourage dependent relationships. They are accountable only to their boards, or perhaps to donors. This accountability gap results in failure to monitor their own performance and even to fraud, as seen in some particularly dysfunctional "briefcase" NGOs.

Membership organizations include religious associations, trade unions, and business associations. Although religious organizations have proliferated and their membership has grown, most, especially the newer churches, do not take on a political role at the urban level.[46] In contrast, although the proportion of urban workers who are trade union members has fallen to insignificant levels in most cities, unions are still an important political force in some countries. Supposedly nonpolitical in their aims are business associations. However, in Tanzania, Aili Mari Tripp asserts, these are hooked into the patronage system, depend

---

44 See Attahi, *Metropolitan Governance in Abidjan*.
45 See Charles Polidano and David Hulme, "No Magic Wands: Accountability and Governance in Developing Countries," *Regional Development Dialogue* 18, no. 2 (1997), pp. 1–16.
46 But see Michael Watts, "Islamic Modernities? Citizenship, Civil Society and Islamism in a Nigerian City," in *Cities and Citizenship*, ed. James Holston (Durham, N.C.: Duke University Press, 1999), pp. 67–102.

on contacts and kickbacks, and may exert both formal and informal influence on urban politics and policies.[47] Christie Gombay's study of the vendors' association in Owino Market, Kampala illustrates its contradictory relations with the city council.[48] It is more likely that such associations link existing powerful groups to the power structure than that they give voice to previously under-represented interests.[49]

Grassroots membership organizations are most widespread in residential communities of the poor, although where they have been formed in high-income areas they can be important in both the provision of services (especially security) and in the exercise of political voice (e.g., the Sandton Residents Association whose rates boycott has created a financial crisis for Johannesburg Metro Council[50]). Most of the social groups important to the lives of residents are informal associations, only some of which are engaged in political activity. Many are ethnically based, including cultural and burial groups and hometown associations. In Tanzania, hometown associations, previously banned as a potential source of ethnic divisiveness, have been tolerated again since the 1980s.[51] In Lagos, landlords manipulated their ties with both patrons and clients so astutely that their leaders came to be recognized as traditional chiefs.[52] Landlord and tenant associations for matters (such as service provision) where the interests of these two groups do not conflict are important in some neighborhoods.[53] In the 1980s, new voluntary associations emerged, partly to cope with economic and governmental crisis and partly out of a concern with the wider interests of society. In Tanzania, the new groups included local defense teams (*sungusungu*) which formed from about 1987 onward to deal with the absence of state-provided security, and were formalized in Dar es Salaam in 1990, leading to an immediate drop in crime rates. Women's associations are among the fastest

---

47 Aili Mari Tripp, "Local Organizations, Participation and the State in Urban Tanzania," in *Governance and Politics in Africa*, ed. Goran Hyden and Michael Bratton (Boulder, Colo.: Lynne Rienner, 1992), pp. 221–242; idem, *Changing the Rules: The Politics of Liberalization and the Urban Informal Economy in Tanzania* (Berkeley: University of California Press, 1997).

48 Christie Gombay, "Eating and Meeting in Owino: Market Vendors, City Government, and the World Bank in Kampala, Uganda," in *Street-level Democracy: Political Settings at the Margins of Global Power*, ed. Jonathan Barker and Anne-Marie Cwikowski (Hartford, Conn.: Kumarian, 1999), pp. 150–182.

49 See Richard Batley, "Political Control of Urban Planning and Management," in *Managing Fast Growing Cities*, ed. Nick Devas and Carole Rakodi (Harlow: Longman, 1993), pp. 176–206.

50 See Beall et al., *Towards Inclusive Urban Governance in Johannesburg*.

51 See Aili Mari Tripp, "Gender, Political Participation and the Transformation of Associational Life in Uganda and Tanzania," *African Studies Review* 37, no. 1 (1994), pp. 107–132; idem, "Local Organizations, Participation and the State in Urban Tanzania"; and idem, *Changing the Rules*.

52 See Sandra T. Barnes, *Patrons and Power: Creating a Political Community in Metropolitan Lagos* (Manchester: Manchester University Press, 1986).

53 See Akin L. Mabogunje, *Perspective on Urban Land and Urban Management Policies in Sub-Saharan Africa* (Washington D.C.: World Bank, 1992).

growing new associations. Most organizations emphasize self-reliance and the development of solutions to everyday problems.[54]

However, civil society organizations are generally only weakly developed, often emerge to compensate for state failure, and do not have a clear role in enhancing the accountability of the formal political system in most African cities.

Both earlier and recent attempts to base urban political systems on liberal representative democracy have, therefore, encountered problems. As at the national level, urban political systems are typically fragile and unconsolidated. However, the democratic systems under consideration are not alone in this: the authoritarian political regimes of the 1970s and 1980s also experienced problems. Despite some early achievements, lack of accountability and economic crisis ultimately undermined those in power at both national and city levels. Extensive patronage systems favored the better off over the poor and some ethnic groups over others. As local government's efficacy and legitimacy declined, residents without access to patron-client networks increasingly adopted the political strategies of exit (as seen in the growth of mutual support organizations noted above), noncompliance, or "agitational practices."[55] In Dar es Salaam, for example, widespread noncompliance with government regulations on construction and informal-sector activity have led to political responses, notably partial retreats by the government from many of its past heavy-handed interventions.[56] Mamadou Diouf describes young people in Dakar as having abandoned both government-constituted youth organizations and party politics for confrontations with the state, parents, and educators, targeting symbols of the state in election-related riots, or attempting to reclaim authority over urban districts by establishing militias, engaging in punitive expeditions against addicts, drunks, and thieves, challenging service providers, and organizing neighborhood clean-up operations.[57] Whether the prevalence of patronage, exit, and noncompliance despite the formal trappings of democracy constitutes chaos will be further discussed in the next section. First, however, the experience of formal land administration will be briefly analyzed.

---

54 See Tripp, "Local Organizations, Participation and the State in Urban Tanzania"; and *idem, Changing the Rules.*
55 See Mamadou Diouf, "Urban Youth and Senegalese Politics: Dakar 1988–1994," in *Cities and Citizenship*, ed. James Holston (Durham, N.C.: Duke University Press, 1998), pp. 42–66.
56 See Tripp, "Local Organizations, Participation and the State in Urban Tanzania"; *idem*, "Gender, Political Participation and the Transformation of Associational Life in Uganda and Tanzania"; and *idem, Changing the Rules.*
57 Diouf, "Urban Youth and Senegalese Politics."

Planning Urban Expansion and Controlling Development   As noted above, the form of tenure considered suitable for urban areas is individual, based on the issue of formal title, and intermediate rights of occupancy are considered inferior or incomplete. To administer a system of formal title, a full cadastre and efficient registration system are needed as a minimum, resting on the one hand on recognition of individual ownership rights and on the other on technical requirements for mapping, plot survey, registration, and conveyancing. Shortages of qualified professionals and finance, coupled with rapid urban growth, mean that mapping has lagged further and further behind urban expansion, and the cumbersome procedures and centralized administration for registration and transfer have been unable to respond to increased demand. Moreover, on the outskirts of many urban areas, the claims of indigenous residents to land were regulated under customary tenure systems. Even if these systems are recognized in law, the relationship between them and formal land administration in the urban context has often been problematic. Generally, either the contradictions have not been resolved or formal land law supposedly takes precedence, a position which those with indigenous claims are not prepared to accept.

In addition, urban planning systems based on the preparation of comprehensive land use plans implemented by means of public investment in infrastructure and development, accompanied by detailed development and building control over private subdivision and construction, have proved unable to cope with the demands of rapid urban growth. Limited professional and financial resources have restricted investment in new infrastructure, and insufficient resources for and attention to maintenance have resulted in the rapid deterioration of those roads and utilities that were installed. During the heyday of state-led development, a desire to control urban development and, on the part of some leaders, to restrict speculation and profiteering or modernize land administration, led to land nationalization. However, the state machinery, predictably, lacked the capacity to make the land in its ownership available for development sufficiently rapidly to keep pace with demand, or to approve transactions between private leaseholders. Instead, public land subdivision, allocation, and regulation provided extensive opportunities for rent seeking and patronage, produced bottlenecks in the supply of land for urban use, and resulted in extensive evasion. Reversal of this legislation in the 1990s in most countries has produced few improvements.

The result is that the formal land administration system has only ever succeeded in meeting the demands of a few – typically between a third and half of the urban population.[58] In practice, much land is occupied without formal title,

---

58 See Alain Durand-Lasserve and Valerie Clerc, *Regulation and Integration of Irregular Settlements: Lessons from Experience* (Washington, D.C.: World Bank/UNDP/UNCHS, 1996).

much development takes place in areas which are not designated for urban use in development plans (or is mixed use in areas zoned for sole residential or other use), and the majority of residents live in areas which are inadequately served or unserved by road access and publicly provided water, sanitation, electricity, and social facilities.

III. The African Urban Experience: A Disorderly Reality?

Attempts to impose order on political practice and urban development, to regulate the activities of private enterprises and citizens, and to outlaw systems and practices regarded as unsuitable and undesirable have, therefore, largely failed. Patron-clientelistic politics, exit, and noncompliance with regulatory requirements are prevalent. The question is whether the current situation in African cities is correctly characterized as chaotic, or whether systems of social rule are operating which are different from those of the formal systems but which are either more effective or command greater legitimacy.

Sociocultural Bases for Politics   As noted above, liberal democratic political systems are based on an individualistic exchange view of politics[59] and political practices which do not fit into formal systems of electoral representation and decision making are often regarded as undesirable and disorderly. However, there is another view of politics which regards political actors as culturally dependent and socially constructed, and political action, therefore, as embedded in social rules and institutions. Such institutions define the behavioral and social bases of the terms of political exchange and provide a framework of roles, identities, and rules (of which self-interested calculation is only one). In practice, some argue that in the African context, many of the formal institutions of governance, including (but not confined to) a liberal democratic political system, are not rooted in local culture: the shared meanings, representations, and values underlying the social system, and expressed in social relationships and practices.

The disconnect, Mamadou Dia suggests, is seen in political institutions that lack moral and political legitimacy. Indigenous institutions, on the contrary, he argues, are anchored in local culture and values, and so are legitimate and enforceable.[60] Dia suggests that traditional government in Africa was hierarchi-

---

59 See James G. March and Johan P. Olsen, "Institutional Perspectives on Political Institutions," *Governance* 9, no. 3 (1996), pp. 247–264.
60 Mamadou Dia, *Africa's Management in the 1990s and Beyond: Reconciling Indigenous and Transplanted Institutions* (Washington, D.C.: World Bank, 1996).

cal but broadly representative and that most societies were governed by consensus: rulers had authority but shared power. They were often selected by a specific body, whose choice then had to be approved; failure of rulers to discharge their functions led to retribution, usually deposition. The abuse of power was checked by rotating office, imposing fixed terms, or creating positions for individuals who would not be removable by the leader. The checks and balances operating in the system were expressed in moral concepts and axioms. Decision making was generally consensual rather than authoritarian and, although the acquisition of wealth by leaders was considered legitimate, they were expected to share this wealth by guaranteeing the welfare of their followers and by assisting those who were in need. The central values were, therefore, sharing (because of the need for security), deference to rank, the sanctity of group commitment, a regard for compromise and consensus (win-win solutions), and economic, social, and personal relations based on trust. Dia's is an essentially positive view, although he admits that traditional institutions can harbor undesirable practices, such as discrimination on the basis of gender and age, and may find it difficult to change to accommodate present-day demands (including, I would add, those associated with urbanization). However, others have a less positive view, pointing to the links between chiefly structures and patronage systems of politics and the practice of calling on "culture" to justify political practices in which ethnic rivalry is deliberately mobilized as a means of retaining or gaining power.

The result of colonial ideologies which encouraged Africans to view government as a source of benefits is that now, Francis Enemuo suggests, there are two public spheres: an amoral civic public sphere from which benefits are expected but which is unimportant in the definition of duties, and a moral primordial public sphere, defined in terms of an ethnic group, within which relationships are seen in terms of duties.[61] The result is a failure to pay taxes and a disinclination to acknowledge the duty of citizens to create enduring and legitimate political institutions. Both Dia's and Enemuo's views are oversimplified: not only were precolonial authority and state structures varied and often contested, ethnicity was also (re)constructed by the colonial powers. Nevertheless, in many countries, traditional organizational and political systems do provide systems of social rule which continue to have moral and political authority. Some, sharing Dia's positive view, consider that they could be a resource for social stability in a mixed government system without abandoning democratic reforms,[62] while

---

61 Francis C. Enemuo, "Problems and Prospects of Local Governance," in *African Perspectives on Governance*, ed. Hyden et al., pp. 181–204.
62 See Richard L. Sklar, "The Significance of Mixed Government in Southern African Studies," in *African Democracy in the Era of Globalisation*, ed. Jonathan Hyslop (Johannesburg: Witwatersrand University Press, 1999), pp. 115–121.

others see them as a hindrance, encouraging resource allocation on an ethnic basis and allowing the state to twist traditional institutions to its own purpose.⁶³ Moreover, consideration of alternative sources of social rules for associational and political life should not be confined to the supposedly "traditional" bases for social organization.

Potential roles for traditional authorities and other forms of social organization in urban governance can be considered at both city and sub-city levels. Akin Mabogunje, for example, advocates that traditional associations such as neighborhoods or urban quarters and their chiefs be integrated into urban management.⁶⁴ The 1994 municipalities law in Mozambique provides for a limited role for the traditional authorities, which were not recognized by the previous Frelimo regime but had been used by Renamo as a basis for a rudimentary administrative system. However, views on this role are mixed, because of conflicts between chiefs and their failure to always represent the wider community.⁶⁵

All political experience introduces participants to rules for engagement. Even if systems change, therefore, the legacy of earlier systems both influences subsequent political practice and provides a potential basis for political and social relationships. This is illustrated in the African urban context by the experience of the one-party "democracies" of the 1970s (Zambia, Mozambique, Tanzania), where grassroots organization was associated with the attempts of the ruling party to secure support and exert control. That is not to say that residents did not benefit from the hierarchical party structures, which were used for delivery of infrastructure improvements in many of the informal settlement upgrading projects of the time and which often included separate organizations for "youth" and women. Nor does it mean that there was no scope for participation, although they tended to be fairly autocratic, top-down organizations, and groups that refused to join political organizations (such as the Jehovah's Witnesses) were often penalized. With the reintroduction of multiparty democracy, the discredited local organization of the former ruling party could no longer claim it represented communities as a whole. The extent to which elements of the system persist, constituting a store of social and political capital, has not been systematically researched. Ann Schlyter shows that in George, an informal

---

63 For example, Mahmood Mamdani, *Citizen and Subject: Contemporary Africa and the Legacy of Late Colonialism* (Princeton, N.J.: Princeton University Press, 1996); Hyden, "The Governance Challenge in Africa."

64 Akin L. Mabogunje, "Local Institutions and an Urban Agenda for the 1990s," in Richard Stren et al., *Perspectives on the City* (Toronto: University of Toronto, Centre for Urban and Community Studies, 1995), pp. 19–45; and *Perspective on Urban Land and Urban Management Policies in Sub-Saharan Africa*.

65 See Alexander, "The Local State in Post-war Mozambique."

settlement in Lusaka, eighteen months after the transition to multiparty democracy, the idea of the ruling party as the sole community organization had persisted. MMD leaders in the area regarded themselves as community leaders, even though no functional local organizational hierarchy similar to that previously maintained by UNIP had been established and they had lost the role played by UNIP leaders in dispute resolution. In addition, women's space for political engagement had narrowed.[66] Elsewhere, however, there is some evidence that the structures and leaders left over from the one-party era still form an important part (officially or otherwise) of the administrative system (e.g., in Mozambique and Tanzania) and still have legitimacy in the eyes of the population.[67]

The political rules of patron-clientelism are today well understood in Africa, even if accepted by beneficiaries and resented by those sidelined in equal measure. Moreover, there is a legacy of institutions, strong in some countries (e.g., Ghana) and weak in others (e.g., Kenya), inherited from traditional authority and kinship systems. In addition, successive and specific urban political and social organizational experience has given rise to new bases for associational and political activity. In this context, *transition* and *complexity* would be more appropriate terms than *chaos* to describe the evolving social and political relationships and practices of African cities.

Urban Land Development: Formal and Informal Rules Interacting   Inherited formal land administration systems and their successors are, in theory, governed by formal rules (those embedded in statutes and regulations). "Traditional" tenure systems, on the other hand, are regulated by "custom" (a series of embedded but fluid social norms and practices which constitute generally unwritten rules).

> Customary land tenure refers to a system of land relation in which the ownership of land is vested in a collective (whether a family, a lineage or a clan) while individuals enjoy virtually unrestricted rights of usage. The head of such a collective (whether a family head or a chief) is regarded as a symbol of the residuary, reversionary, and ultimate ownership of all land held by the collective.[68]

---

66 Ann Schlyter, "Township Organization, Democracy and Women's Rights in Zambia," in *Democratization in the Third World: Concrete Cases in Comparative and Theoretical Perspectives*, ed. Lars Rudebeck and Olle Törnquist, 2d ed. (London: Macmillan, 1998), pp. 258–282.

67 See Wilbard J. Kombe and Volker Kreibich, *Informal Land Management in Tanzania* (Dortmund: Faculty of Spatial Planning, University of Dortmund, 2000); Paul Jenkins, *Emerging Urban Residential Land Markets in Post-Socialist Mozambique*, Research Report 75 (Edinburgh: Edinburgh School of Planning and Housing, 2001).

68 Mabogunje, *Perspective on Urban Land and Urban Management Policies in Sub-Saharan Africa*, p. 3.

Donald Krueckeberg, in his critique of three so-called creation stories or myths about the nature of land ownership in Africa, notes that the portrayal of African ownership as communal served the interests of both the colonial powers (who used it to reinforce/establish authority structures beholden to them, i.e., chiefs) and Africans (to protect their rights against further expropriation or taxation rather than as a description of actual rights). In addition, although such tenure might express African cultural values, it also suppresses the rights of some, especially women. In practice, much land is individually acquired and held, and the process of adjusting the rules governing customary tenure to the process of buying and selling land began early in the 20th century, despite the hostility or indifference of the colonial government.[69]

In urban areas, land transactions and conflicts are structured by hybrid institutions which are neither strictly formal nor customary and will be referred to here as informal. In contrast to the failures of the formal land administration system discussed above, processes of informal land development have been successful in delivering large quantities of land for urban residential development (often between 50 and 70 percent).[70] This success can be attributed to the social legitimacy of these processes, but the institutions that regulate transactions in and the use of land (including trust) come under pressure during the process of urban development. The systems of formal, "customary," and informal rules exist in parallel, although views about the relationship between them vary. Some see them as conflictual. Alternatively, in an interactive or synergistic view, elements of each institutional form are used by actors as appropriate to minimize transaction costs. Elements of each are combined in the notion of societal noncompliance, which involves synergy, conflict, domination, and manipulation in the relations between actors.[71] "[It] is considered a form of 'protest,' albeit with its own 'rules of the game,' which may be used to contradict, pre-empt or control those of the state, but which also observes and upholds other state rules."[72] It exploits contradictions and areas of ambiguity. Of interest here are the characteristics of social, economic, and political relations between the actors involved;

---

69 Krueckeberg, "Private Property in Africa."
70 See Durand-Lasserve and Clerc, *Regulation and Integration of Irregular Settlements*.
71 See Omar M. Razzaz, "Examining Property Rights and Investment in Informal Settlements: The Case of Jordan," *Land Economics* 69, no. 4 (1993), pp. 341–355; *idem,* "Contestation and Mutual Adjustment: The Process of Controlling Land in Yajouz, Jordan," *Law and Society Review* 28, no. 1 (1994), pp. 7–39; *idem,* "Land Disputes in the Absence of Ownership Rights: Insights from Jordan," in *Illegal Cities: Law and Urban Change in Developing Countries*, ed. Edésio Fernandes and Ann Varley (London: Zed Books, 1998), pp. 69–88; Tripp, *Changing the Rules.*
72 R. C. Leduka, "The Law and Access to Urban Land for Housing in a Sub-Saharan African City: Experiences from Maseru, Lesotho," paper presented at the Nordic Africa Institute conference "The Formal and Informal City – What Happens at the Interface?," Copenhagen, June 15–18, 2000.

the relative functions of formal, informal, and customary rules in rendering acceptable the institutions governing transactions; and the circumstances in which these institutions break down. The discussion will be illustrated by research findings from Tanzania, Lesotho, and South Africa.

Dar es Salaam. In Dar es Salaam, the formal land administration system has had great difficulty coping with the demand for urban land and services, and today over 70 percent of residents are accommodated in informal settlements.[73] Before independence, land transactions in the rural areas beyond the urban boundary were based on verbal agreements between buyers and sellers, often witnessed by adjacent owners. Where land is still held by indigenous residents under customary or pseudo-customary law, intensification of the demand for subdivision is weakening the strength of customary practices in land (especially where economic pressure or family crisis forces sale). Thus, while land sales are widespread, because there is some social stigma attached to selling family land, it is done discreetly (meaning quietly without publicity, not one by one).

Beginning in the 1960s, the informal market devised its own quasi-legal procedures to authenticate ownership, transfer, and sale.[74] Land transactions were, and still are, authenticated by local politicians (elected Ten Cell and sub-ward or Mtaa leaders), despite such transactions being contrary to government policy, which prohibited transactions in unimproved land. Individual rights, which are ceded in perpetuity, are certified and the use of written sale agreements has gradually become common practice. Transactions are given greater legitimacy by the use of local witnesses, who can be relatives, close associates of the transacting parties, or neighbors. In the 1980s, with expansion of the city and further development of land markets, more robust instruments for enhancing individual rights in property were developed, including registration. In certain areas, local political leaders have, with the agreement of local residents, established a set of mandatory procedures that have to be followed by all parties. In some, administrative fees are levied by sub-ward offices and honoraria paid to witnesses. However, leaders in other areas doubt their ability and right to enforce the norms necessary to safeguard interests in land. In Rangi Tatu, one peri-urban study area, 40 percent of owners had informal sale agreements authenticating their purchases, less than 10 percent had acquired land through the formal process,

---

[73] See Wilbard J. Kombe, "The Demise of Public Urban Land Management and the Emergence of Informal Land Markets in Tanzania – A Case Study of Dar es Salaam City," *Habitat International* 18, no. 1 (1994), pp. 23–43; J. M. Lussuga Kironde, "Land Policy Options for Urban Tanzania," *Land Use Policy* 14, no. 2 (1997), pp. 99–117.

[74] See Kombe, "The Demise of Public Urban Land Management."

and nearly 50 percent did not have evidence to support their ownership but were increasingly trying to regularize it through the informal system, in which they placed considerable confidence. In addition to rights and transfers being authenticated at the local level, disputes are often arbitrated and resolved where possible at the sub-ward level, by a committee of elected local elders, and are only referred to the courts when the elders are unable to resolve the dispute.[75] Leaders also sometimes take the initiative to arrange housing plots in an orderly way, following existing features (e.g., tracks), allowing for access and circulation, and designating sites for public uses (school, market, cemetery). Their concepts of order, which seem to be acceptable to residents, are based on facilitating the routine activities of residents, providing security, and supporting social and cultural values. Efforts to provide services generally come last – they tend to be sporadic, sponsored by local leaders or private individuals, but often with community committees, e.g., construction of a primary school or improvements to water supply. Higher levels of the local administration (e.g., the ward) only occasionally get involved in providing social infrastructure. The shortcomings of this approach are evident: it results in uncoordinated and patchy provision, and becomes increasingly difficult as market pressures on land increase, especially where local organizations have poor links to the local authority.

As urbanization proceeds, the social recognition of land rights by leaders is vulnerable to the erosion of trust, pressure on land, and the increased power of the market. Research found that, while hybrid informal/formal institutions successfully regulate transactions in newly developing or partly consolidated residential settlements, they are unable to cope with the pressures in a consolidated inner city informal settlement.[76] In Keko Mwanga, access tracks were being encroached upon, there was no land for social facilities, and problems of trespass and multiple sales of the same plot had increased. Sub-ward leaders reported that, since the introduction of multiparty politics, they had been unable to restrain building activities, but this may also be because sub-ward leaders in this area are associated with the ruling party. In this area, Ten Cell leaders were no longer able to resolve disputes between neighbors and the aggrieved parties resorted to the formal legal system. Despite litigants' lack of formal title, in settling such disputes, state courts take into account only the merits of individual cases, without challenging or questioning the legal bases of transactions or the rights of disputing agents to transact in land.[77] Therefore

---

75 See Kombe and Kreibich, *Informal Land Management in Tanzania*.
76 See ibid.
77 See ibid.

in spite of the fact that informal housing land sub-division, transactions and development take place outside the formal or statutory urban land management processes, there have been initiatives to adapt some of the normative principles for the spatial organization and development of urban land.[78]

Maseru. A significant proportion of the recent population increase in Maseru has occurred in peri-urban settlements outside the formal urban boundaries, where agricultural land is privately subdivided for sale under the authority of the traditional leaders, the chiefs. The result is unplanned urban sprawl, with initially large (1,000 square meters plus), irregularly shaped plots which are inefficient to service. The Land Act of 1979 attempted to regularize the situation by nationalizing land and distinguishing between land leased from the state and rural arable land to which use rights were to be allocated in perpetuity by "democratically elected" land allocation committees. The Act also includes provision for the designation of Selected Development Areas to allow the acquisition of land within urban boundaries for new areas of urban use or upgrading of unplanned residential areas. The effect of the SDA declaration is to cancel existing rights and interests in land without compensation, pending the issue of leaseholds. The Act failed to streamline land delivery, reduce the loss of agricultural land to urban development, or promote "orderly" urban growth, because of various forms of subversion by the state itself, local chiefs, and owners of use rights to peri-urban cropland (field owners). The problem is defined officially not as inappropriate law but as the lawlessness of chiefs and their subjects.

Because of the difficulties faced, especially by middle- and low-income people, in accessing land through the formal system, for the majority the only feasible option has been to purchase directly from field owners. Whereas by custom, chiefs allocate land freely to their immediate subjects and to a small number of incomers from other areas, increasingly they are dealing with requests from unknown people. Under these conditions, a "moral economy" of custom, where access to free land was guaranteed by allegiance to a chief, has been supplanted to some degree by an "amoral economy" of impersonal market exchange. Popu-

---

[78] Wilbard J. Kombe, "Regularizing Housing Land Development during the Transition to Market-led Supply in Tanzania," *Habitat International* 24, no. 2 (2000), pp. 174–175. In Maputo, Grupos Dinamizadores, established in the socialist period, continue to allocate land rights on the periphery, some of which are accompanied by the issue of a document. Conflicts related to such land transactions are relatively low level, as the arrangements are underpinned by social acceptance of the role of GDs, so that agreements reached between neighbors, households, and the local GD have high legitimacy. However, these practices are under pressure from the commercialization of land and the transition to a market economy in the 1990s (see Jenkins, *Emerging Urban Residential Land Markets in Post-Socialist Mozambique*).

lar opinion is that individual field owners are encouraged by their chiefs to subdivide and sell their agricultural landholdings or face state appropriation without compensation. In turn, chiefs issue certificates of allocation to plot buyers (so-called Form Cs, backdated to before June 1980, when the 1979 Land Act came into force). While in the past, chiefs would have been expected to undertake this task free, today they charge a fee for issuing such certificates. Such land subdivision aims to avoid direct confrontation with state law enforcement machinery by occurring at night, over the weekend, or on holidays, copying official land parceling practice, and involving public officials in the process (buying and selling land, advising the chiefs and replenishing their supply of Form Cs, or advising prospective land buyers in return for cash "for lunch").

The role of chiefs and field owners in subdividing and selling land for urban development has been recognized *de facto* if not *de jure*, in part because of specific instances of noncompliance. Following the acquisition of land without compensation at Khutetsoana, on the outskirts of Maseru, for a World Bank–funded sites-and-services scheme, field owners in the adjacent area of Ha Mabote, who under the 1979 Act had only licenses issued by the state for agricultural land within urban boundaries, rushed to sell their land in case it was also expropriated without compensation.[79] The government moved in 1984 to declare Ha Mabote an SDA before it could be completely subdivided and developed. However, not only did subdivision continue apace, with the backing of the chiefs, but the latter also succeeded in preventing the demolition of "illegal" structures. With the connivance of officials, provided routes reserved for roads were respected, chiefs urged continued subdivision, while negotiating their acceptance of the project in return for recognition of existing use rights. Eventually (in 1986) they succeeded in getting the provision for licenses repealed and compensation payable for all land expropriated by the state. By exploiting their political position and inconsistencies in the land law and administration, in this instance chiefs were able to derive benefits for themselves, their subjects (the relatively low income field owners), state employees, and the purchasers of subdivided agricultural land, while enabling government to produce an urban extension broadly in accordance with the intended layout.[80]

Maseru therefore illustrates not only the operation of social rules but also how noncompliance as a political relationship between state and society has served to achieve the political objectives of reinforcing the efficacy and position

---

79 See Nick Devas, "The Evolution of Urban Housing Projects in Lesotho: The Tale of Five Schemes," *Land Use Policy* 6, no. 3 (1989), pp. 203–216; Leduka, "The Law and Access to Urban Land for Housing in a Sub-Saharan African City."
80 See Leduka, ibid.

of chiefs, to the greater satisfaction of many citizens than formal state decision making and land administration. The Dar es Salaam and Maseru examples illustrate the close links between urban politics and the rules governing land administration, and these are demonstrated even more graphically in our final case study of an area on the outskirts of Durban, which illustrates how the trajectory of an area of informal settlement and the well-being of its residents are determined by its changing relationships with the wider political system.[81]

Durban. The story of Besters Camp in Durban illustrates the interrelationship between informal rules for land development and electoral politics and also the way in which rules change over time.[82] The early settlement in this area on the far northern outskirts of the city consisted of illegal subdivision ("shack-farming") by legal Indian landowners. In the mid-1970s, Inkatha was reconstituted and began to assert political control by establishing committees in the area. In the second half of the 1980s, as the struggle between Inkatha and the UDF/COSATU heightened, there were widespread disturbances. Violence against the Indian owners caused them to flee, permitting Inkatha to assert control (and seize vacated property), with the state turning a blind eye to what was going on. For example, in the unsettled area of Ekutholeni, a series of invasions were organized by self-proclaimed Inkatha "councillors." Settlers were required to pay an Inkatha membership fee, a token payment for the site, and a fee to the warlord's functionaries who demarcated the plot. The warlord in this area established four wards, each with a chairman appointed by him. This formed the territorial base from which he controlled the politics of the area, using force, blackmail, and protection rackets to control land ownership and subdivision, businesses, water supply, taxis, and the social activities of residents. The warlords and their men acted as both police and judiciary in the absence of an effective state presence. In the adjacent areas of illegal subdivision, the warlords organized infill development, with non-Zulu residents sometimes being forced out. Because Inkatha was able to maintain control during these turbulent times, a symbiotic relationship between the movement and the national and Kwa Zulu

---

81 S. K. Gitau suggests that in Nairobi, uneven patterns of demolition and new settlement formation can be attributed to political factionalism and have intensified since the introduction of multiparty politics in 1992. Because political competition is defined in ethnic terms, she asserts, ethnic clustering at settlement level has increased. Moreover, a degree of illegality in land subdivision is permitted and accommodated by the state as a means of political patronage and source of corruption. The emergence and sustainability of informal settlements are therefore determined, she argues, by the extent to which they can negotiate political protection. See S. K. Gitau, "The Role of Politics in the Emergence and Expansion of the Informal City in Kenya," paper presented at the Nordic Africa Institute conference "The Formal and Informal City – What Happens at the Interface?," Copenhagen, June 15–18, 2000.

82 See Basil Van Horen, "The De Facto Rules: The Growth and Change of an Informal Settlement in Durban, South Africa," *Third World Planning Review* 21, no. 3 (1999), pp. 261–282.

governments developed, although not without conflict and tension, in return for which basic services (e.g., tanker water) were provided.

By the 1990s, Inkatha control was undermined by its reliance on force and inability to provide services. Residents switched their allegiance in the hope that the UDF/ANC would deliver services, with the result that some warlords were driven out and others changed their allegiance, even adopting leadership roles in the new regime. This period was marked by greater autonomy from the state, but also by a period of organizational turmoil marked by power struggles between criminal gangs, "youth," and women's groups. Excluded from mainstream civic politics and emerging from the control of warlords who had suppressed other forms of social organization, new forms of order developed, but these depended on the arbitrary exercise of power by youth and so-called people's courts. The emerging ANC and civic leadership therefore had to both assert control and try to deliver services.

In the 1990s, the area was the site of the first major upgrading project in South Africa, initiated by a private-sector NGO with city and IDT funding. This was made possible by the new legal framework, and adopted an innovative organizational approach in which there was a high degree of resident participation. A Community Development Trust (with resident representation) was established as the organization in charge, responsible for installing infrastructure and issuing freehold titles. However, some unregulated buying and selling of surveyed sites has continued, so it is expected that differences between registered and *de facto* ownership will emerge in time. With the CDT, elected councillors, and Ward Development Forums similar to those elsewhere in the city, the area is now integrated into the local political structures, but there are pressures because the settlement leaders are still dependent on political patronage, and power struggles over access to external resources have increased. Informal organization, especially the women-dominated Health and Welfare Committee, continues to be strong, reaching down to the household level. "Strong men," often ex-Inkatha leaders who have kept control over the key economic enterprises in the area, have benefited from the increased cash circulation which resulted from upgrading, especially the labor-based construction contracts which they won and on which they were able to employ their followers.

External political backing, with the support of these powerful informal networks, was important to ensure that the CDT and WDFs were able to secure upgrading, from which the informal networks benefited in turn. The settlement is now legally incorporated into the land administration system and urban management structures, but the informal internal sociopolitical fabric remains, in parallel with and often in support of the legally constituted structures. Political legitimation has not brought notable changes to the internal social fabric, leading to ongoing challenges to integrate formal/informal and *de facto/de jure* aspects of politics and land administration.

Recognition of the ability of informal urban land development processes to deliver large quantities of land relatively cheaply to meet urban demand does not deny their disadvantages: informal settlements are characterized by environmental degradation, public health hazards, and the use of unsuitable land for urban development. They give rise to water pollution, encroachment on public land, and additional costs of retrofitting services, especially when densities reach a high level. They cannot necessarily guarantee security of occupancy, protect against fraud, or resolve all disputes. Nevertheless, they result in residential development which, while far from orderly in conventional terms, is not chaotic.

Conclusion

In reaction to fears of uncontrolled urban growth and the political mobilization of urban mobs, as well as a desire to secure urban environments conducive to efficient enterprise and public health and responsive and accountable political systems, colonial and postcolonial regimes have tried to institute systems of political representation and land administration capable of dealing with the pressures of urban development. However, the consolidation of political systems based on conventional theories of liberal democracy has proved problematic in Africa at both the national and urban levels. Furthermore, formal land administration systems designed to protect individual property rights and regulate urban development have benefited fewer than half of all urban residents and have failed to cope with rapid demographic growth. This paper has argued that we need, therefore, to question the concepts of order and the formal rules on which these systems are based. Their colonial origins, theoretical assumptions, and specific organizational design together make them, to a considerable degree, inappropriate and unrealistic in contemporary Africa.

In practice, much political practice consists of patronage, exit, or noncompliance, and much land development is informal, in the sense that it does not comply in one or more respects with formal state law and regulations. These practices are in some respects disorderly, but they are far from chaotic. While the social rules of authoritarian, clientelist spoils politics are widely understood, they cannot be said to have a high degree of legitimacy or to be based on high levels of trust. In other respects, however, political and land development practices are governed by systems of social rules that are widely accepted. These are not drawn from an idealized and unchanging inheritance of traditional authority, social organization, and kinship. Although all of these institutions may be important, to a greater or lesser degree, in different societies, they have evolved in response to a long series of colonial and postcolonial changes, have not always successfully adapted to the demands of contemporary societies, and can be oppressive and exclusive. In addition to these sources of institutions, the urban experience of recent decades, especially since the postindependence state-led development model has been discredited, has spawned a variety of new associational forms. While most are ostensibly nonpolitical, many have gained legitimacy because of their success in supporting their members during periods of government incapacity, and some have challenged the political order or made political gains through practices of widespread noncompliance.

This is not to say that formal political and administrative systems should be abandoned: informal patronage practices have wasteful and inequitable outcomes, exit and noncompliance are essentially negative, and unplanned land development gives rise to insecurity and poor living environments. Moreover, even such informal institutions are not divorced from political and administrative systems based on formal rules. During periods of both democratic and authoritarian rule, informal practices have borrowed from formal rules systems and in some instances modified or transformed them in turn. Many aspects of informal and customary political and land development practices have wide social recognition – it is this familiarity, understanding, and legitimacy, this rootedness, that helps to explain their prevalence and their relative success. However, they also have dysfunctional and conservative aspects, while the formal rules on which liberal democratic political systems, private property rights, and planning and regulatory systems are based are becoming increasingly embedded and accepted. In addition, experiments designed to overcome some of the shortcomings of formal representative politics and land administration systems, such as democratic decentralization,[83] participatory and deliberative democracy,[84] regularization of informal tenure, and reforms of planning and building codes, are under way.

Future research needs to develop a better understanding of the characteristics of informal political practices, property rights, and land development processes, of the relationships between formal and informal systems, and of the outcomes of promising experiments. Such an analysis will enable the strengths and limitations of contemporary political practices, informal tenure and land development processes, and new approaches to be identified. It will provide a frame-

---

83 See Harry Blair, "Institutional Pluralism in Public Administration and Politics: Applications in Bolivia and Beyond," *Public Administration and Development* 21, no. 2 (2001), pp. 119–129.
84 See David Miller, "Deliberative Democracy and Social Choice," in *Prospects for Democracy*, ed. Held, pp. 74–92.

work both for the development of distinctive and locally appropriate rules frameworks and politico-administrative systems and for the transfer and adaptation of solutions from other societies within Africa and beyond. These might include forms of democratic engagement which complement representative democracy and mechanisms of accountability which can crosscut ethnic divisions and give voice to the poor, replacing particularistic patronage politics and majoritarian winner-takes-all elite politics with a more truly social democratic system.[85] They might also include forms of tenure and development regulation which are manageable in a context of demographic growth and limited resources, provide affordable land for development in appropriate locations, and ensure an acceptable level of security for urban residents and enterprises.[86]

That cities demonstrate multiple conflicts and contradictions (between wealth and poverty, tradition and modernity/postcolonialism, men and women, old and young, power and powerlessness, opportunity and marginalization) is not denied. That the attempts of formal urban political and land administration systems to manage these conflicts and contradictions have had serious shortcomings is evident. Clearly, aspects of urban political practices and land development processes are disorderly. However, the continued (if inadequate) functioning of electoral processes, city administrations, formal property rights systems and regulatory procedures, and the parallel operation of multiple sets of social rules that govern so-called informal political practices and land development processes bely the notion that cities are chaotic and contain promise that more appropriate conceptualizations of political and physical order can lead to improved urban governance arrangements in future.

---

[85] See Ján Bucek and Brian Smith, "New Approaches to Local Democracy: Direct Democracy, Participation and the 'Third Sector,'" *Government and Policy* 18, no. 1 (2000), pp. 3–16; Brian Smith, "The Concept of an 'Enabling' Local Authority," *Government and Policy* 18, no. 1 (2000), pp. 78–94; Blair, "Institutional Pluralism in Public Administration and Politics."

[86] See Durand-Lasserve and Clerc, *Regulation and Integration of Irregular Settlements*; Kombe and Kreibich, *Informal Land Management in Tanzania*.

Between Euphemism and Informalism: Inventing the City

Antoine Bouillon

The following reflections are grounded in a three-year experience of life and research in Durban, South Africa, of indissolubly associated lived experience and socio-anthropological investigation. I am still very much in the process of systematically processing the data, hence the hesitations, the clumsiness, the many unanswered questions the reader may notice in the following remarks.[1]

Into the Dialectical Reality of Citizenship

To get to the heart of the matter, let's plunge into the dialectical reality of citizenship, between transcendence and contingency, enunciation and inheritance, praxis and status.

The whole phenomenon of citizenship refers to a *dialectical reality* between the unconditional values that it embodies and the sociohistorical conditions of its appearance. It is, at the very same time, radically, absolutely unconditional and indissociable from universal human rights, *and* sociohistorically conditioned and engineered.

One will find this dialectic of the *given-granted versus* the *initiated*, in the opposition between citizenship as a given relationship to a national State (and territory) and citizenship as a self-legislating voluntary practice; between citizenship as a statutory body of inalienable rights and citizenship as praxis and

---

1 Focusing on residential and insertion strategies of foreign and national migrants, my work was undertaken in the framework of the "Three Cities Project" on "Governance, Urban Dynamics, and Economic Development: A Comparative Analysis of the Metropolitan Areas of Durban, Abidjan, and Marseilles." This program involves researchers in these three cities of France, Ivory Coast, and South Africa in investigating social and economic governance issues in the three metropolises. Let me express here my gratitude to my colleagues of the "socio-anthropological cluster" for their support and cooperation, and to all those officials, politicians, street people, community leaders, foreign African migrants and refugees, young adults from the townships, for their welcome and their open-minded collaboration. Thanks to them, the said "fieldwork" was a humanly very rewarding experience.

action; between the *possession* and the *exercise* of citizenship; between "passive" and "active" citizenship, etc.

Thus the experience of citizenship re-iterates the enigmatic process of our self-"production" or self-interpretation rooted in the original experience of our *self-body* as reconstructed in Maurice Merleau-Ponty's phenomenology of *le corps propre*:[2] as subjects, we are appearing in the world while being at the same time its very *source* or *limit*.

The South African experience of citizenship has been reflecting in a telling way this dialectical reality: against the disenfranchisement of the majority on the basis of so-called race differences, the call for equal political membership for all has been at the very root of the struggle against apartheid, through an ambivalent experience: the vast majority of the South African people experienced citizenship negatively, as something of which they were deprived, but also positively, *as something they were calling upon* – something they could call upon as belonging to themselves as to every human being – and there is no more powerful testimony of this than the Rivonia trial speech of Nelson Mandela. Mandela, and all the people fighting against apartheid in the name of universal human rights and democracy, were calling upon the people "as a whole," which did not yet exist, to come into existence. Eventually, it came about, in the performative act of the April 1994 elections whereby the South African people instituted itself as the unique sovereign, the only source of legitimacy, in the paradoxical act of a self-performative enunciation that is ahead of itself.

And which remains ahead of itself: citizenship has been a pivotal idea of the whole transition, being at the same time the *tool*, the *foundation*, and still the *objective* of the new democratic dispensation. If it has been efficient enough to provide the way in which apartheid could be abolished and a new, democratic and republican, regime instituted, it can do nothing more than lay the ground for democratic practices to come, thus leaving all of us with the question of the way in which this could and should be done. The legal reestablishment of the society on democratic republican citizenship is a foundation, and the implementation of these ideals, through institutional and procedural translations, citizens' practices and initiatives, remains open to question. To speak of the dialec-

---

2 "To be born is to be born of the world and to the world. The world is already constituted, but it is never completely constituted. In respect to the former, we are solicited; in respect to the latter, we are open to an infinity of possibilities. But this analysis remains abstract, for we exist in both respects at the same time. Never is there determinism nor absolute choice, never am I a thing and never a naked consciousness." Maurice Merleau-Ponty, *Phénoménologie de la perception* (Paris: Gallimard, 1945), p. 517 (my translation). This experience is reflected in the aporia of the "anchorage" of the subject of enunciation in generality and absolute singularity at the same time (any "I" or any "me" is at the same time a *type* and a *token* [C. S. Peirce]): the viewpoint of any talking subject is the limit of the world and not simply part of it.

tical reality of citizenship, then, is to speak of the historical responsibility that it establishes by opening it to historical action: *What does one do with it? How does one use it?*

But the dialectical reality of citizenship is not without revolutionary implications, inasmuch as it relies on the unconditional acknowledgment of the individual's freedom. The citizen is constituted as such by his/her possession of an irremovable and irreducibly equal part of the people's sovereignty, which is recognized as the only legitimate source of any democratic governmental power. His/her individual freedom exceeds citizenship itself, which cannot be legally forced upon him or her. As such, the power of the citizen "is not limited by any border," as James Tully says, "since it is the very source where players, rules and ways of playing are coming into being."[3] Sociopolitical membership as organized by citizenship relies on the individual's free and autonomous decision, on voluntariness. Citizenship is an "activity,"[4] representing the notion of democratic participation in public life and based on voluntary association, and consequently, the citizens first govern themselves and cannot then govern anyone else as subjects of their domination without exceeding or retreating from democracy.[5]

It follows that there can be no citizenship that is not conceived and enacted as such, that is to say, that is not a *statement* about each other's equal membership. Social production of citizenship is based on its *enunciation*, linguistically and practically speaking.[6] More precisely, citizenship comes in as a *performative act* – not only forming the reality but actively producing it – through protest, claim, demand, denial, etc. A striking demonstration of this is given by Judith Shklar who, after Rousseau, places at the core of citizenship the feeling of injustice and protest. I quote: "Protest is often the main activity of citizens"; "the citizen, as a subject who tends to be politically passive, is often only awakened by the experience of injustice"; and the "first injustice is exclusion, full or partial, from citizenship itself."[7] The liberation struggle of the South African people can indeed be qualified as an exemplary illustration of this rise of citizenship through the injustice of its suppression.

Thus, citizenship is a status that implies that it is first a praxis, a creative, institutionalizing, historicizing action, before being part of institutionalized sociohistorical procedures and practices. It is a tool for ever-questioning the dis-

---

3 James Tully, "The Agonic Freedom of Citizens," *Economy and Society* 78, no. 2 (May 1999), pp. 161–182.
4 Ibid.
5 Cf. Michael Walzer, *Pluralisme et démocratie* (Paris: Esprit, 1997), p. 25.
6 Michel de Certeau, *L'invention du quotidien*, vol. 1, *Arts de faire*, new ed. (Paris: Gallimard, 1990), p. 36.
7 Judith N. Shklar, "Justice et citoyenneté," in *Pluralisme et équité: La justice sociale dans les démocraties*, ed. Joëlle Affichard and Jean-Baptiste de Foucauld (Paris: Esprit, 1995), p. 94.

pensation, and we can say that citizenship represents a constant dis-location, dis-sonance, or dis-sensus, a kind of "revolutionary kit" at everyone's disposal, in order to reestablish a more inclusive, democratic, and just society.

The citizenship instituted by the 1996 Constitution of South Africa is a fully-fledged democratic and republican citizenship of that type flanked by the most advanced kinds of guarantees one can find in the world today for fundamental individual freedoms. As such, the South African case becomes a powerful demonstration of how the advent of democracy entails a "revolution" (as Claude Lefort says[8]), since, as part of the modern nation-state system and apparatus, it provides the member of citizenry with a social link of its own kind, differing from the preexisting, "primary" bonds of locality, ethnicity, common descent, common culture, and religion. It stands in meaningful and practical opposition to these other kinds of membership, as it implies the inversion of the most fundamental symbolism of the society by refounding the social order upon the social itself instead of an external, supra-societal, extra-mundane foundation (to which any substantial community difference pertains ultimately). Thus, its foundation is procedural – consensus on decisions, as Habermas says, "stems in the final instance from an identically and equally applied procedure recognized by all"[9] – and, as such, is antagonistic to any fundamentalism. What democratic citizenship means in practice and in theory is that political society has to be acknowledged as being based on itself, in other words on an ultimately undetermined and procedural foundation, which can always be called into question.

But precisely this insistence on the excess and radicalism of citizenship must not make us lose sight of the other side of the coin: unconditional as they are, the citizen's freedoms and rights must be acknowledged to become effective. Reciprocally, granted as they are, they have to be thoroughly (re)appropriated and exercised by the subject to become effective.

Nationality and Citizenship

There is one more aspect of this "dialectic" of citizenship that I would like to emphasize: the well-known couple of nationality and citizenship, often confused. Following Habermas, we are of the opinion that the notions of *nation* and *citizenship* pertain to quite different spheres of meaning and that, consequently, their relationship has to be "problematized." It is a fact that these two

---

8 Cf. Claude Lefort, *Essais sur le politique, XIXe–XXe siècles* (Paris: Seuill, 1986), p. 27 of the first part, "La question de la démocratie."
9 Jürgen Habermas, "Citizenship and National Identity," in *The Condition of Citizenship*, ed. Bart van Steenbergen (London: Sage, 1994), p. 24.

ideas have been historically in close association, but it does not detract from this other fact that citizenship does not refer *as such* to any substantial collective, be it the "nation," the "race," or any other collective that would owe its identity to a prior commonality of descent or culture. Not even, Habermas insists, has citizenship to be based on all citizens sharing the same language or ethnic and cultural origin, because it is rather the reverse: citizenship can be instrumental in the democratic transformation of the preexisting local political culture. Such a reversal of perspectives seems congruent with the democratic transformation of South Africa, which is on its way to showcase to the coming generations how citizenship can help build a nation – a "nation of citizens," deriving its identity "from the praxis of citizens."

But this very reversal of perspectives in fact is a clear demonstration that, if there is no conceptual linkage between the notion of nation and the notions of city and citizenship, the two notions are related through their difference in a mutually determining way. In practice, the membership of the political community cannot be completely divorced from the membership of historical, local, ethical, concrete communities, and it is certainly not by chance that citizenship, whatever its conceptual distinctiveness, has been closely articulated to, if not subsumed by, the idea(l) of the nation. Given its procedural nature, citizenship's strong limitation in terms of affectivity and emotion means that it may not be a sufficient condition for society to hold together. Intellectual adhesion has to be completed by emotional mobilization – the lack of which would mean that it leaves a clear field to the passions inspired by the other forms of community.[10]

Only the self-produced sociohistorical reality of a "nation of citizens" can provide citizenship with an emotional basis of its own in the longer term. Time (as *duration*) is therefore a key dimension of the issue, and in today's South Africa, the universal, human rights–based, open interpretation of citizenship, upheld by the most eminent institutions, singularly the Constitution and the Constitutional Court, conflicts with the resilience of so-called national or racial or cultural identities and the hegemony of socioeconomic segregation values.

Citizenship and the Relationship with the Center-City
Citizenship as a *praxis* implies a dialectical relationship between a sociohistorical and local implication on the one side, and the generality and universality produced by its procedural abstraction from contingency on the other. Conse-

---

10 See Dominique Schnapper, *La communauté des citoyens: Sur l'idée moderne de nation* (Paris: Gallimard, 1994); idem, *La relation à l'autre: Au coeur de la pensée sociologique* (Paris: Gallimard, 1998).

quently, it necessarily involves, among other things, the relation of the individual with a political community, a *local* "city" of some sort. This locality can be situated simultaneously at different levels of territorial identification (local / national / international / global), but in most cases, the local town in its physical and administrative reality is the first locality/local-city, as it occupies the bottom levels of procedurally concretized political communities. If one is not a citizen of the local city, where is it that one will exercise one's local but also national and possibly multinational, international, if not global, rights? Without citizenship, no human rights.

This link between the local city and citizenship takes on a particular relief in South Africa, given the ways in which the relationships between the people and the (local) city have been historically framed. This historical local city has been at the same time the local, concrete city (of Durban), and "The" City as such, symbolically opposed to the rural areas and to its townships or suburban periphery. South African black people have historically been denied access to *both* the *city* and *citizenship* at the same time, as the physical and the symbolic/legal sides of the same coin.

And the fact is that citizenship is still at stake in the ways in which people are able to practice the city or not and to "produce" it while they "produce" themselves before it. In the ways *city users* have access or not to *city spaces and services* (to streets and banks, to shops and bars, to flats and means of transport, to state personnel and elected representatives, etc.); in the ways they relate to each other and (re)produce social categorizations; in the ways the city identifying itself with *formality* implies and excludes "informal" practices and practitioners; in the politics of urban space, as applied by local urban planning, economic development, taxation, housing, welfare, policing, and other policies (including the historical exclusion of townships from local planning responsibilities); in every case, what is at stake is whether or not one can be a citizen if one is not recognized as a member of the city. It is this very link between the city and the citizen that is questioned when the national minister of police, lashing out at street traders who are "turning pavements into 'slums,'" declared that "many township people still viewed Durban as a 'white man's town' and therefore did not treat the city with respect."[11] It is again the same link that is mobilized and questioned when residents of the center-city talk of what to do with destitute and homeless people.

---

11 *Daily News* (Durban), October 1, 1999.

Local/Foreigners: A Differing Relationship   African migrants from outside southern Africa, those for whom there is no tradition of migrant labor connected to South Africa, tend to approach the center-city from the moment they arrive as the "obvious" place to be. Being in the center-city is for them just a matter of good sense if one is looking for services and markets. African townships have such a reputation of violence and criminality that the newcomers would not need any further warning against local xenophobia. They brave as well as they can exclusive, repressive, or aggressive gestures coming from officials, would-be employers, and ordinary people. Their relation to the city is therefore not immune from strong ambivalences, but most of them appear to remain convinced that, in their given conditions of life as refugees or foreign migrants, the center-city is the place to be, as long as they cannot envisage moving to a safer and more pleasant suburban area (which some of them do, who can afford it). They believe that they have the right to wage a "normal" life in the city, and this conviction helps them to cultivate and develop "normal" local friendly relations. Their extensive urban experience – since most of them have been living in other big cities on the continent or overseas – give them a solid ground to uphold such a conviction. It allows them to consider the local city (Durban) as one in a whole series of towns that they know outside South Africa as well as within the country itself, and to assess its value comparatively. Accordingly, they stand for a "revisited" understanding of citizenship, at a distance from the interpretations trying to legalize and legitimize different ways of excluding foreigners from social rights.

People from South (and to a large extent southern) Africa display an altogether different story in relation to the center-city, a relation that is problematic and sensitive. At least, this is the way it appeared to me in Durban, as opposed to Johannesburg, where I had been working previously. Why is this so? Perhaps it is an effect of the obvious differences in size and number of their inner cities, the radically different historical, economic, and socio-spatial conditions (like the proximity of rural areas in the case of Durban, as opposed to "Egoli," Johannesburg "the city of gold"), which have built up strongly differentiated urban individualities, impacting on the ways people relate to its reality.

The symbolic of the city/town of the past turned upon an axis opposing the center to its periphery and making of them contrary, "complementary" sides. To cut a long and painful story short, the basic rule was the exclusion of black people from the city, except under strictly limited and controlled conditions. Some black people have traveled up and down this township/city axis as the ordinary process of work and life, and all have experienced it, be it only in the imaginary, as a structuring dimension of the social power and value landscape. In the last three decades, and more than ever after the demise of the so-called influx control regulations (1986), more and more people began establishing themselves in the city, opening a new experience of it as a lifetime process. Also, more and more people experienced it as a strategic location in terms of economic survival – not necessarily a place where one has to settle, but certainly a place where one must reside for periods.

For today's black people born and raised in what were previously exclusive white urban areas, the center-periphery axis corresponds to an emerging generational process, those who cross the "border" from black to former "white" areas (by themselves or through their parents) being unlikely to make their way back. This new category of black young adults entertain a split imaginary and emotive relationship with their township background, and township dwellers label these mobile individuals "coconuts" – black outside, white inside. Similarly, local citizens feel betrayed when their representatives settle "in town."

With the center-periphery relationship, we then have a *spatial, temporal, axiological, and teleological axis in one*, according to which the town/city is something else than the "location," something of a different nature with a superior status. The location is only good for those who are excluded from the city/town because they are not worthy of it, looked down upon as poor people or informal users. That this axis is oriented and irreversible is attested by all those in-migrants for whom going back to the "location" represents such a failure that they cannot entertain such a prospect. Exactly as the foreign migrants fear being forced to come back to their country empty-handed, the local in-migrant is likely to go to extremes rather than return to the farm or the township with nothing.

The city/town that is imaginarily constructed in the process conforms to the ideology of its planners by being altogether a world of means, respect, status, order, and regularity, exactly the opposite of the disorder, noise, uncontrolled, crooked, and twisted ways of the "location." The town is the embodiment of cleanliness and visibility, order and regularity: of *formality*. "To come to town," as observed by one of the rare African refugees to have resided in a township, "you need a status." The ongoing agitation and noise characterizing parts of the center-city neighborhood of Albert Park is described by my interlocutors as transforming the area (back) into a "township" or "location." Thus the city is regarded with awe, all the more since its historical statutory confiscation was accompanied by unrelenting control and brutality, in such a systematic way that formality has been erected in the imaginary of all as a mass discrimination device and making civility and the law of the strongest two faces of the same coin. Formality has been first and foremost a tool for massive exclusion, a way of barring all those who have no presentable credentials, an instrument for qualifying citizenship and making it conditional.

Thus, the presence of black people in the center-city stands as a powerful historical and political statement – but it is so only inasmuch as this very city/town remains not theirs: a foreign territory, governed by formality, a "white man's thing." Today, they are there in the streets and buildings, each and every day, by their hundreds of thousands, transforming the ways of life in a number of areas, but the phenomenon is hegemonically perceived as a massive influx of informality, illegality, and criminality. Steps are taken to "protect" the beachfront and, less systematically, the city center (the former white Central Business District) as tourism enclaves. Wherever possible, sub-urbanization is the preferred counter-move.

Such characteristics render access to center-city urban areas a *split*, strongly ambivalent process, whereby former location practices have to be ignored or denounced and rejected as disqualifying practices for would-be "city-zens." Repressive "clean up" policies lend legitimacy to the claim for city exclusivity – as a formal, modern, European and "world-class," neat and ordered space – and to the branding of urban practices coming from township life as "uncivilized" or "undesirable," including those very practices that are all over the world considered representative of urban life: unrelenting agitation, congestion, light, noise, rubbish … The practices of inhabiting the street and talking, loitering, drinking in its public space like at home, are considered and declared unreceivable.

This "euphemismization" of the city goes hand in hand with the qualification of the suburban as the achievement of the urban, the consideration of the suburb as the quintessence, the perfection of city/town virtues – of order, neatness, calm, regularity, predictability. From this suburban point of view, symbolically adopted by all, the townships are encroaching on city life, and the ideal is to bypass the city/town altogether. Meanwhile, the city is, for the most part, left to black people and poor people, workers and employees, officials and politicians. It is still frequented by suburban people, but in specified, rather closed, spaces/times: particular clubs, specific administration buildings, sections of the beachfront, etc.

The symbolic division of the urban between the "urban" urban (the city/town and its values) and the "nonurban" urban (the "location"/township practices) is part of a set of operations that *relate* these opposite spaces as much as they *reproduce and confirm the gap* between them in all kinds of ways. Such *continuity* was well expressed by one of my interlocutors: "Town is not as bad as the township but it is not as good as the suburb, so if you can get the money, you'll go to the suburb." The center-city is perceived as problematic, security wise, housing wise, image wise: as one local official put it to me, "black people don't want to live in the city because it means that you are lower class." For all social groups, the center-city is identified with *flatlands* and *tenancy*, in contrast with the suburbs that embody the dream of access to *property*.

Irrespective of "racial" differences, the common mobility pattern involves residence in the city as a matter of an idealized social trajectory, where the center-city represents the middle ground between township and suburb, "squeezed" between its two peripheries. But if the suburbs integrated the imaginary and allowed the dream of bypassing the town, inaccessible as they are, the suburbs leave the town to be "invested." So, if "it is assumed that life in the suburbs is the right choice for a family and a better place to live," since it is "associated with status, pride and wealth,"[12] for the masses, the meaningful link remains between the two opposite worlds of the township and the center-city. In the setting of the vast metropolitan region, the center-city – associated with and distinguished from the locations as it is – is in continuity and rupture at the same time, the normal place aimed for in the search for survival, a convenient place to go in case of family or neighborhood problems in the township. It has *integrated people's multilocal "residential system"* and informal networks of places, people, and activities. While the black middle class in-the-making is converging in it, the poor, the migrant, the informal traders converge as well.

This split and contested ground provides a matrix for many a split life. The center-city and the township play respectively and mutually the role of stage and backstage, albeit in a different manner. In front of the city, the township embodies "communal life," it is where one comes back for a drink at the shebeen, for the Sunday service or to visit relatives and grandparents; the periphery network of places, with their different degree of extra-territoriality regarding the rule of law, provides a "backstage" where it can be practical to "disappear." Reciprocally, the center-city can also be a practical place to "disappear," because, in front of the township's "communal" social control, it embodies the freedom of individual life and sheer functionality: this is where the person is the most likely to experience his/her individual autonomy (and "young people, especially those who are employed, prefer living in flats and duplexes around the city"[13]), where he or she will have a network of temporary places, enjoy social times at a distance from the community, entertain extra-conjugal relations, etc. It is useful for *hiding* and *staging* life at the same time, as one does in front of "foreigners," a life which in time might begin to form a second life-society. It is also useful in allowing access to some degree of formality, if only by reputation or to better

---

12 Themba Nyathikazi, "The Great Trek from Township to Suburb," *Metro Beat*, March 15, 2000.
13 According to Themba Nyathikazi also, "men, to a greater extent than women, find it boring and very lonely in the suburbs" (ibid.). Practically speaking, the conclusions can differ a lot, like in the case of African migrants' wives, for example. While most Congolese wives seem to be restricted to their flats, only allowed to travel short distances and under supervision (they have to be accompanied, it has to be to visit female relatives, etc.), a number of Burundian and Rwandan couples will give a living account of how their refugee life has reshuffled the gender division of roles in a way that has the potential to set the woman on a more open trajectory of social mobility.

resort to informality. Something very similar can be said about its use by suburban people returning to town to experience a social life at some distance from their family and community, for example in the nightclubs that proliferate in the center-city. Because of the differing criteria for social control applied in the different communities (for example, and quite strongly, between the Indian and colored communities), the end result can be very different, but the center-city provides all communities with the convenience of a *distant* place with different norms, whether from the residential familial and communitarian world of the township or the suburb, where one will rush to form an extension in kind of the said "community."

Thus the city is a paramount embodiment of ambivalence, a distant, strongly attractive, and simultaneously repulsive middle and mixed ground. Suburb and township dwellers alike will tell you that they will never ever come to the city "to be mugged." Meanwhile, more and more middle-class and poor people as well are converging on it as the prime place to find opportunities for employment or some kind of economic activity, to further studies or launch a career. They also flock to it for shopping, for weekend "clubbing," for enjoying the beach, for visiting relatives, for having a drink with fellow (wo)men in a hotel lounge, and experiencing a different kind of social life.

The structural divide of the past between the modern and white-only center-city and the black-only periphery is still providing avenues to symbolization and "mythification" along "racial" lines: *eThekweni* (the Zulu name for the place and today's name for the metropolitan area) is the black city that provides *Durban*, the white city, with its lifeline and its workforce, but that has been forcefully separated and relocated at a good distance. As this divide keeps growing "day by day," eThekweni, one commentator says, will "more than ever haunt Durban."[14]

Such a symbolism does not budge from the "coconut" ideo-logic, based as it is on "racial" mythology. Therefore, not only is it part of the communitarian symbolic violence that goes with any individual interpretation denying its individuality since it would reflect a collective being, but it does not do justice to the ambivalence it is expressing by reducing it, apologetically, to "racial" and "functional" dimensions.

"Durban" is also part of the imaginary and the practice of "eThekweni," and "eThekweni" is today right in the middle of the city! The relationship is going both ways and the center-city is a fiercely contested ground between formality

---

14 See Yogin Devan, "Hurt eThekweni and Durban Will Die," *Sunday Tribune* (Durban), September 10, 2000, for one telling version of this thinking. The new "unicity" framework is seen as an opportunity for the coming together of the two cities: the task is presented as almost desperate ("… eThekweni will pursue its own agonizing destiny, Durban will continue to flourish …") but ultimately depending on "Durban" relinquishing its "intolerance and deep-seated prejudices."

and informality. What appears to be the hegemony of "white," "European," "Western," "modern," "world-class," "formal" values, complicates the configuration with a number of splits and paradoxes. Among other things, it seems to point in the direction of a seemingly insuperable gap, split, or conflict, between Africanity and urbanity/modernity, as long as the anti-urban suburban values are able to exclude African urban practices as anti-urban.

Contrary to what seems to imply the above "coconut" rhetoric, the powerful ambivalence of the center-city prevents those who have been historically excluded from it, as much as those who have identified exclusively with it, to proceed with its confiscation, and makes it precarious, conflictual, and unstable. But by so doing, it helps to maintain it *open to all*, and to make of it something that belongs to no one in particular but to everyone in general.

Alternative Enunciations of Citizenship

Foreign Migrants/Refugees and Locals   All African foreign migrants finding a friendly ear are quick to raise the issue of what they consider as their basic rights being threatened or denied by the attitude of policemen, civil servants, company and corporation officials, estate agencies, banks, etc., and ordinary people. There is clearly a confrontation, a strong antagonism going on, confirmed day after day by the ways in which foreign migrants and refugees call upon universal human rights in a *defensive reaction* to what they perceive, and indeed often experience, as local xenophobia.

Local people's attitude, as willingly aggressive as it is, is also *reactive* to the mere presence of these foreigners, which is deemed to be illegitimate in and of itself ("illegal immigrants" has become a tautology). It is remarkable that the South African national democratic identity should be performed by the marking (*amakwerekwere*) and exclusion of people on the basis of their foreignness in relation to the historical community of the people making up South Africa. The extent and emotional strength of this performance seem to have something to do with the deeply entrenched "multi-racial" and "multi-national" ideology.

On the city front-stage area, "racial" communities are in the foreground. At the national and local level, "race" language and concepts dominate public space. The democratic transition has certainly not affected the fundamental and unanimous belief in "race" – that is to say, in human "races." On the contrary, nation-building is largely conceived as requiring the exhibition of the "color" differences that make up the "rainbow-nation." In such a perspective, South African nationality is no more than a hollow container, only "groups" or "races" are real, and as the playwright Ronnie Govender says, "racial self-consciousness is given greater respectability."[15]

Since South Africa and South Africans could only find their common ground in the history that has thrown them together, as conflicting and antagonistic as it is, and the external borders they have inherited from it, citizenship is the tool for drawing a border that has to be constantly re-performed to give substance and effectiveness to national identity. In the way refugees and migrants are denied free exercise of a regular economic activity and barred from a number of other key urban life services, it appears to be used as a basis for a legitimate exclusion, the reverse side of the democratic legitimate inclusion of all South Africans as such. Consequently, all foreigners or "non-nationals," are put in the same bag, indiscriminately, and there is no point in distinguishing between migrant, immigrant, asylum seeker, and refugee status.

Confronted with repressive policies, formal and informal prohibitions, foreign African migrants call upon basic human rights in *an alternative enunciation of citizenship*, which they say must not be used to discriminate against foreigners, all the more when they are refugees, and deny them some of their most basic human rights. By this defensive argument, they try to protect themselves against the stigmatization and criminalization context that is suppressing the way they can actually exercise their rights, even at the level of common law. From a human rights perspective, South African refugee and immigration policy challenges at least three universal freedoms: of movement, of looking for decent means of survival, and of leading a normal individual and family life, a situation that was recently improved by the courts but has since been worsened by a new law depriving refugees of the right to work while their asylum application is in process.

In placing citizenship under the jurisdiction of universal human rights, the migrants have a point. Not only because their argument is the most convincing in a country that has based its political revolution on human rights substituting for apartheid; but because citizenship is indeed, theoretically and practically, a *sine qua non* for the exercise of all those universal rights that can only be fulfilled in the context of a national state. This constitutive citizenship dimension of human rights provides reciprocally citizenship with *a constituent human rights dimension* that renders the actual definitions and implementations of citizenship in local nation-state contexts forever questionable. By living in a foreign country, you cannot forfeit your basic rights, and national citizenship has then to be supplemented by a similar body of rights and duties for foreigners, in a way that does not infringe on their basic rights through undue discrimination.

If most migrants tend to use human rights discourse expediently, some individuals among them attest their open understanding of citizenship by con-

---

15 Ronnie Govender, *Daily News* (Durban), February 4, 2000.

tributing to local civic projects, asserting their citizenship while they are deprived of its recognition. A *positive* or *creative* performance of citizenship, we might say. If their great vulnerability prevents them from expressing their feelings and opinions and from reacting against unfair treatment at the hands of officials or the police, they tend not to give up easily but to mobilize all their capacities to devise regular or irregular ways of overcoming obstacles. Thus the vast majority, who are not involved in criminal activities, can indulge in irregularities that they do not see endangering their sense of morality or their loyalty toward the local society. A few individuals have initiated sustainable welfare and advocacy projects (shelters to start with, but also classes, language courses, etc.) targeting refugees, some with a strong human rights dimension; by setting up these organizations, they also want to send a message that they are willing to enter into formal exchanges with local authorities and civil society actors.

Residents/Homeless Coming now to the enunciations of citizenship in relation to homeless and destitute people, and the informal users of the city, we witness what we could call, in reference to a new and powerful South African writer, the production of a "euphemistic" city, based on a permanent, ever-going "clean up," like "these spaces called euphemisms, where arid Bantustans became homelands; where any criticism of Apartheid thinking became a threat to public morals."[16]

The values at stake in city life are meant to stand on their own as basic criteria of "urban," "modern," "civilized," "respectable" life in society, and to be acceptable by anyone irrespective of "racial" distinctions: in link with the specter of crime, represented as a frontal attack against the very possibility of society, they are considered constituent elements of any "civilized" social life, in a willingly exclusive interpretation of citizenship as *entitlement*,[17] supportive of stigmatization and expulsion procedures with respect to "unqualified" members. The divide of yesterday between the "urban," "modern," "European," "Western," etc., center-city and the "nonurban," "traditional," "communal," etc., locations is reproduced but in *racially connoted class terms*, and *within* the center-city and the urban order itself. In the absence of any alternative "African" model of urbanity and modernity, the appropriation of city life and uses "from below" appears to be read by many city residents, black or white, upper or middle class,

---

16 Phaswane Mpe, *Welcome to Our Hillbrow* (Pietermaritzburg: University of Natal Press, 2001), p. 57.
17 Like the so-called "Tebbit cricket test," where "citizenship is the ideological yardstick for measuring the entitlement of 'worthy' applicants to residence." Geoff Andrews, ed., *Citizenship* (London: Lawrence & Wishart, 1991), p. 13.

as its in-formalization, its de-naturation, its "de-moralization": in other words, its potential *destruction*. Is not the question, as it is said, repeated and not contested, to "save" the city center?

Confronted with the prospect of the relocation, into their area, of the biggest shelter in Durban for homeless and destitute people, the (mainly white) property owners of this inner-city area, called Albert Park, came up in arms against the authorities. Later, when the so-called revitalization of Albert Park began, opposition to the move was publicized as the definitive stand of "the community." In meetings and statements of the area Working Group set up to represent the community in the process, representatives speak as if it is understood and assumed that "the community" is, "of course," against the relocation of the shelter (called the Ark), even if no consultation had ever been organized on the issue, because no consultation is necessary. And the fact is that actors from nearly all social and ideological affiliations advocated, on the basis of what they consider a fundamental antagonism between "residents" and "street people," the expulsion of the destitute "out of the town," possibly on its outskirts where they would be kept at a safe distance and, possibly, reeducated so as to be "reintegrated" into society. Three years down the line, the motto is exactly the same.[18]

What is said, advocated, and, as much as possible, put into practice, is that those "street people" (alias "hobos," "broken people," "misfits," and the like) have fallen "out of the society" and that their correct place is therefore "out of the city." In the divide between "residents" and "street people," the whole society is performed as finding its constitutive limit. Meanwhile, the divide is turned into two different kinds of membership of the city for two opposite kinds of people, in such a way that poverty is not the issue, but the poor, who are not fit for city life.

"A good clean up is not only good for the house – it's also good for the soul," proclaims an advertisement in the press. A "well-organized" home is "a sign of being in control." As the director of a "psychological services" company from Texas says, "we don't have control over what happened on September 11 or in

---

18 We cannot expand here on the history of the "revitalization" process of Albert Park and the details about its actors, proceedings, vision, and achievements. The reader will be able to find such details in my "The Place of the Poor in the Central City: The Relocation of the 'Ark Shelter' as a Case Study of Citizenship Issues in a Mutating Durban (South Africa)," in *Three Cities Project: Governance, Urban Dynamics, and Economic Development: A Comparative Analysis of the Metropolitan Areas of Durban, Abidjan, and Marseilles*, ed. Antoine Bouillon, Bill Freund, Doug Hindson, and Benoit Lootvoet (Durban: Three Cities Project, Department of Economic History, University of Natal, 2002), pp. 103–140, in relation to the Ark's relocation issue, and in a forthcoming article on "Community Politics and Inner-City Revitalization: The Case of Albert Park (Durban Central City)," to serve as a basis for comparing the Albert Park case to the Warwick Junction case, as investigated by my "cluster" colleague of the Three Cities Project, Jeremy Grest.

Afghanistan, but it's really important to focus on things we do have control over." A clean home "can at least be a comfort amid the chaos outside. ... Being able to create that harbour in the storm, that personal safety net, can be comforting in terms of feeling as if your home environment is not chaotic."[19]

The holy war against crime is a convenient excuse – since its ardent obligation prevents it from ever being used as an excuse – for an ever-cleaning/cleansing, an ever-reordering of the city, that is to say, for pushing, wiping out of the city public space all those said to be "undesirable." In practice, different spaces are distinguished within the center-city itself and ordered in a hierarchy. Cornerstone of community, local government, and business partnership, the war against crime enrolls local communities in *divisive* and *exclusive* endeavors targeting the poor, the foreigner, and the informal, in order to "cleanse" the area of all *potential* criminals. ("There is positive feedback from the side of the community, people are reporting criminals/criminal activity in the area," summarizes a report of the Albert Park Working Group.[20]) The solution to the problem, be it illegal immigration, homelessness, criminality, is to get rid of the people who embody it: to eliminate crime, "eliminate criminals."[21] The problem is that, to do so, you must get rid of all those who "look like" and "behave like" criminals, who *might* be criminals, according to a set of criteria establishing a continuity between poor-informal-illegal-criminal, which makes of these qualifications as many qualities pertaining to the very same category of people, the un-qualified.[22]

I cannot here provide a detailed account of the ways in which the poor and the poorer immigrants in the center-city, foreigner or local, confront these exclusion practices and devices. I will simply highlight a few aspects of them to conclude.

---

19 *Daily News* (Durban), November 23, 2001.
20 Minutes of Albert Park Working Group meeting held on September 29, 1999.
21 "It has become unsafe for residents to live here" declares a councillor for one crime-ridden area of Chatsworth. "We have to eliminate the criminal elements." *Tribune Herald* (Durban), February 4, 2001.
22 Reflecting on his experience of public discussion of the issue, Sayed-Iqbal Mohamed, PR councillor and director of the Organisation of Civic Rights, emphasizes the point: "there is a great deal of incorrect information been filtered right to grassroot level saying: we cannot have the Ark, these are a bunch of criminals, hobos, this and that. ... So people who don't even know what the Ark does have that kind of impression. I have been in many meetings and some people have been diplomatic and they said: 'no, the Ark is doing a good work but ...' and a whole barrage of attack starts, that they are going to increase the crime level in the area and so on" (interview, May 22, 2000). According to the interviews conducted by the authors of the Social Impact Report on the relocation of the Ark, Albert Park's residents, businesses, and institutions alike consider that "residents of the Ark engage in criminal activities," even if no evidence is to be found of such a "fact." Another example among many others of this continuity: "the homeless people sleeping on land by the railway line had moved off. This had improved safety." Mr. Naas Rossouw, facilities manager at Metro Rail, talking of the Grey Street area renewal, *The Mercury* (Durban), January 30, 2001.

In terms of housing and accommodations, for example, budget considerations meet with security and safety concerns to form the key criteria in the search for a place, with ensuing practices of sorting spaces/social categories into a hierarchy of territorial self-exclusion. In choosing to get a flat in this building or that one, or to go to this or that shelter, or to sleep on the pavement here or there, one endorses a range of qualifications. But, be it in the street as the last resort, it is still a way to carve oneself a place in the local society.

If one can say that the opposition of the Albert Park "community" to the relocation of the Ark shelter corresponds to the willingness of residents to avoid being confused with the poorest section of the local city community, this exclusion/inclusion device is operated by marginalized people as well to perform, in their own environment, their membership of the community of respectable, euphemistic citizens, in opposition to "unqualified" intruders or pretenders. The fact is that such an exclusion is the most common tool at the disposal of any member of the local society to insert him or herself into the community of qualified citizens: the less means you have, the more likely you are to rely on this symbolic violence to be translated into physical exclusion, in order to concretely sanction the illegitimacy of the "pretender." Thus, for example, in the community of shelter users, it will appear critical to make people understand the difference between the poor and the destitute, the respectable citizens living a life of hardship and the social misfits who have fallen into irremediable hardship: you want them to understand that although you might be too poor to afford your share of a rental, you are still, like your shelter, "upperclass"[23] and not to be confused with the destitute and misfit.

Thus, the claim for "clean up" operations is shared down to the "bottom" of the social hierarchy by those who are likely to fall among its very victims, but, simultaneously, a number of them are involved in the creation of inclusive local communities, the institution of an inclusive local city, on a contractual basis. This is clearly the case with the shelters, which do not exist without a number of *rules* to which the applicant must subscribe, and which will in turn confer on him or her a membership status in the local community. All of them differ not only by their physical location and structure and what it allows or not, but by their set of rules that create different kinds of "atmosphere" and community. If needed, the actual payment for entry and the clear, redundant marking of the delineation between patrons and managers, will prevent the customer and the observer alike from falling into any romanticism in that respect. It remains that

---

23 In reference to "The Upperclass Shelter" opened by a couple of white "street people" in the center-city, whose name is supposed to make it clear that "it is not like the Ark, it is not for the destitute." See Bouillon, "The Place of the Poor in the Central City."

through the implementation of and respect for these rules (some go to the extent to claim that they are discussed and agreed upon between managers and patrons), marginalized people are inventing a *contractual social order* of their own as a prerequisite for any collective undertaking like sharing accommodations.

In the conditions of the center-city, such initiatives recall the powerful claim of township dwellers mobilized to fight the eviction of rent defaulters by the city: "We are not Indians, we are the poors."[24] In a unique performance, they attest that they cannot be reduced to their "race" identity (and dealt with, "accordingly," in a racist way), and they proclaim that they are members of the local society, albeit victimized: they are "the poors." Deprived as they are of everything, they reverse their un-quality of "poor" into a last form of entitlement: as "poor," they have nothing but their citizenship.

Such protests represent as many calls upon the *(local) city to exist, that will allow citizenship to be;* and in their less vocal and visible initiatives, the shelter/street people are also claiming and implementing at the same time their qualification for citizenship. They do not wait for the community to intervene; in the urgency of the situation, they initiate a city accommodative of all kinds of differences, a city that does not reject you, that still accommodates you when the rest are not, a city that acknowledges that the town is no longer exclusive, that it belongs to everyone – that it has to be shared. Between euphemism and informalism, these city dwellers are busy inventing a city that might go beyond "good" or "bad" morals to practically and legitimately re-question issues of city-life legitimacy and qualification.

---

24 Ashwin Desai, *The Poors of Chatsworth: Race, Class and Social Movements in Post-Apartheid South Africa* (Durban: Madiba Publishers, 2000), p. 53.

Figures of the Subject in Times of Crisis*

Achille Mbembe and Janet Roitman

"Moi, quand quelque chose me dépasse,
je ris seulement."
      Douala resident, August 1993

The following remarks are about subjectivities of "the crisis" and their corollary, the crisis of the subject. The first term refers to the crisis as a constitutive site of particular forms of subjectivity. The second term invokes the crisis of the very act of signifying this moment. These two instances, constitution and signification, are decisive elements in the generalized production of violence in the world today. They are also instances of its specificity.

The moment being considered, then, is not without date, place, or name. In fact, the object of our commentary is a precise phenomenon: contemporaneousness. Its real time can only be called the "immediate present." And it is the spirit (*esprit*), visibility, and profanity of this immediate present that is at the heart of our inquiry. This "immediate time" and "present duration" are defined by the acute economic depression, the chain of upheavals and tribulations, instabilities, fluctuations and ruptures of all sorts (wars, genocide, large-scale movements of populations, sudden devaluations of currencies, natural catastrophes, brutal collapses of prices, breaches in provisioning, diverse forms of exaction, coercion, and constraint) that make up the fundamental experiences of African societies over the last several years.[1] The specific conjuncture referred to here, this age

---

* First published in *Public Culture* 7, no. 2 (1995), pp. 323–352. © Duke University Press. All rights reserved. Reprinted with permission.
This article was translated from French by Janet Roitman with the assistance of Lisa McKean. The following study results from residence in Cameroon: from March 1992 to December 1993 (Janet Roitman) and June to August 1993 (Achille Mbembe). Roitman acknowledges the generous support provided by the SSRC-MacArthur Program on Peace and Security during this period. Mbembe acknowledges the support of the History Department, University of Pennsylvania. We benefited from the assistance, commentary, and criticism of Jean Marc Ela, Thierno Mouctar Bah, Vianney Ombe Ndzana, Sidonie Zoa, Hamidou Bouba, Amadou Inoua, Anatole Ayissi, and Adam Ashforth. Carol A. Breckenridge offered insightful remarks and encouragement.

1 For some examples of these events, see Stephen K. Commins et al., eds., *Africa's Agrarian Crisis: The Roots of Famine* (Boulder: Westview Press, 1986); Richard Sandbrook with Judith Barker, *The Politics of Africa's Economic Stagnation* (London: Macmillan, 1985); Thomas M. Callaghy and John Ravenhill, eds., *Hemmed In: Responses to Africa's Economic Decline* (New York: Columbia University Press, 1993); Christian Geffray, *La cause des armes au Mozambique: Anthropologie d'une guerre civile* (Paris: Karthala, 1990); Tim Allen, "Understanding Alice: Uganda's Holy Spirit Movement in Context," *Africa* 61 (1991), pp. 370–399.

that merges with immediate time, this contemporaneousness, is what Africans and others have called "the crisis." That is to say, and this is what we hope to demonstrate: the entanglement of a plurality of real and not wholly distinct transformations; the combining and packaging of experiences lived by people at all levels of society; and the physical and mental violence that issues from the lack of coincidence between the everyday practice of life (facticity) and the corpus of significations or meanings (ideality) available to explain and interpret what happens, to act efficaciously and, in so doing, attempt to overcome the specter of nothingness (*le néant:* in the double sense of nothingness and meaningless).

This inquiry responds to several questions, some theoretical, others less so, but all concern the general *problématique* of the constitution of specific regimes of subjectivity in the context and as a result of the specific conjuncture described below. By regime of subjectivity, we mean: a shared ensemble of imaginary configurations of "everyday life"[2] imaginaries which have a material basis; and, systems of intelligibility to which people refer in order to construct a more or less clear idea of the causes of phenomena and their effects, to determine the domain of what is possible and feasible, as well as the logics of efficacious action. More generally, a regime of subjectivity is an ensemble of ways of living, representing, and experiencing contemporaneousness while, at the same time, inscribing this experience in the mentality, understanding, and language of a historical time.

According to this formulation, we are not interested primarily in the *problématiques* of resistance, emancipation, or autonomy.[3] We distance ourselves from these questions in order to better apprehend, in today's context, the series of operations in and through which people weave their existence in incoherence, uncertainty, instability, and discontinuity; then, in the experience of the reversal of the material conditions of their societies, they recapture the possibility for self-constitution, thus instituting other "worlds of truth." By setting our sights on the domains of the unforeseen and the unexpected, the productive moments during which the incomplete nature of things coincides with the reversibility of that which has been acquired, and by attending to the stupor associated with terror, where individuals and societies are taken aback, defigured and without stable referents, we hope to apprehend an apparent paradox: in Africa today, becoming a "subject" involves a splitting of identities which fuels a certain pragmatics of subjection, both of which make up a simultaneous moment.

---

2 Michel de Certeau, *The Practice of Everyday Life*, trans. Steven F. Rendall (Berkeley: University of California Press, 1984); Fernand Braudel, *The Structures of Everyday Life: The Limits of the Possible*, trans. Miriam Kochan (London: Collins, 1979).

3 Cornelius Castoriadis, *Philosophy, Politics, Autonomy*, ed. and trans. David Ames Curtis (Oxford: Oxford University Press, 1991).

This approach, contrary to typical discourses on politics and the economy in Africa, does not reduce the crisis to an event whose meaning is exhausted once it has been analyzed and deciphered statistically, becoming then simply an object of proposed reform as in the framework of structural adjustment programs.[4] Against statistical representations, this is an attempt to treat the crisis as, above all, lived experience. Secondly, this suggests that it is in everyday life that the crisis as a limitless experience and a field of the dramatization of particular forms of subjectivity is authored, receives its translations, is institutionalized, loses its exceptional character, and in the end, as a "normal," ordinary and banal phenomenon, becomes an imperative to consciousness. Such "normalization," which is also the tautology involved in explaining the crisis by the crisis, results from a combination of repertoires. The very notion of the crisis widely serves as a structuring idiom. In this sense, it constitutes almost in-and-of-itself a singular mode of apprehending (and hence narrating, or living) immediate agonies. The crisis also operates as a figure of rationality and an existential device. In other words, by relegating the crisis to the realm of the inexplicable, people likewise simultaneously circumscribe a field of both constraints and possible, reasonable, and legitimate action. Through acting on the basis of these rationalities, in the midst of these entangled fields of action, they themselves end up participating in the very process of the production of the crisis: a self-referring chain.

Yet we do not wish to underestimate the weight of external factors and the role of global forces on the origins and course of what has been called the crisis. The nature of these constraints has largely been explored and documented, and their historical underpinnings brought to light,[5] even if their present mutations still essentially belie analysis.[6] The question for research is no longer simply measuring the impact of the crisis on society or measuring the disparities between prescribed reforms and their realization as in the case of classical analyses. Unlike readings of the crisis that are limited to socioeconomic indicators commonly used to describe, understand, and explain the current situation in Africa, the approach outlined here obliges the scholar to "return to the field."[7] Return to the field does not signify, however, a mechanical turn to "local knowl-

---

4 Cf. World Bank, *Sub-Saharan Africa: From Crisis to Sustainable Growth: A Long-Term Perspective Study* (Washington, D.C.: World Bank, 1989).

5 See, for example, Frederick Cooper, "Africa and the World Economy," *African Studies Review* 24, nos. 2–3 (1981). See also John Lonsdale, "States and Social Processes in Africa," *African Studies Review* 24, nos. 2–3 (1981).

6 See, however, Zaki Laïdi, *L'ordre mondial relâché* (Paris: Seuil, 1992); "Points de vue sur le système monde," special issue of *Cahier du GEMDEV* 20 (1993); Arjun Appadurai, "Disjuncture and Difference in the Global Cultural Economy," *Public Culture* 2, no. 2 (1990), pp. 1–24.

7 By "return to the field" we are not necessarily referring to anthropologists' debates on the construction of the object of study and their trenchant critique of the supposed objective character of that object. In our opinion, the point that the researcher is implicated in the demarcation and construc-

edge"; people themselves claim that they no longer understand what is happening to them, much less that they have mastered the ins-and-outs of the processes in which they are implicated. The problem is, indeed, that the determining forces of the societies we study are not located in the sites where inquiries founded on a static epistemology have until now sought to find them.[8] Thus, contrary to an approach based on linear perceptions of cause and effect, one must, in a self-reflective move, apprehend what the analyst defines in terms of the destructuring "effects" of the crisis as in fact *already there*, or in the process of being constituted in an uneven manner. Thus one approaches the crisis not as a system, but as a prosaic: the routinization of a *register of improvisations* lived as such by people and, in this sense, belonging at most to the domain of the obvious or self-evident, and at least to the banal or that which no longer evokes surprise.

This, then, is what we shall examine through examples taken, for the most part, from urban life in Cameroon. In the first part of this discussion, we will outline a geography of the crisis by detailing, from examples lived and known by a large number of people, the way in which the crisis is inscribed in the everyday urban landscape, in its material structures such as roads, residences, and office buildings, and in social interactions and relations of power, profit, and subsistence. This description serves two purposes. First, it gives a concrete indication of the living space of the subject, the forms of inscription of the crisis in public space, the body, and material life, in brief, its physicality.[9] It also serves as an introduction to the very field of representations of the time and imaginary of the crisis, paying heed to its supposed abrupt and sudden character. In the remaining part of the text, we underscore the relationship that exists between these representations and the destabilization of certain referents. And since in the present context, this relationship also opens the way for a remarkable proliferation of criteria for judgment, we will examine how this proliferation affects logics of efficacious action and renders recourse to paradoxical logics more likely.[10] Finally, we shall indicate how all of this leads to a crisis of the subject –

   tion of the object of study goes without saying. Cf. George E. Marcus and Michael M. J. Fischer, *Anthropology as Cultural Critique: An Experimental Moment in the Human Sciences* (Chicago: University of Chicago Press, 1986); James Clifford and George E. Marcus, *Writing Culture: The Poetics and Politics of Ethnography* (Berkeley: University of California Press, 1986).
8 This epistemological problem also concerns claims to knowledge based on founding oppositions, which impose order on, and preclude the legitimate status of, unrelatedness and unsystematicity, reversibility and surprise, inconclusiveness and the plurality of social time and space, which in turn leads to often problematic distinctions between levels of reality, everyday practices, and extraordinary experiences.
9 We are not describing havoc in Cameroon. We are trying to underline the materiality of the crisis in order to then look at its representational effects.

and thus of meaning – and produces conditions favorable to forms of violence that are specific to the present conjuncture.

The Crisis in Space and Matter   Of all African countries, Cameroon was considered and considered itself, until the mid-1980s, to be a land endowed with economic assets such as petroleum, lumber, cocoa, coffee, cotton. Its annual rates of growth were among the highest on the continent. The implementation of a series of five-year development plans led to numerous investments, expanded the mass of wealth, and accelerated the process of social stratification. A powerful urban middle class emerged. On the whole, however, this class depended on its incorporation in the state apparatus, and especially the army and civil service, for its reproduction. A private sector was developing and its dynamism varied according to regions and sectors of activity.[11] Furthermore, this relative prosperity had been made part and parcel of official and popular representations of national identity and Cameroonian singularity.

These representations were based on the idea that Cameroon was on a continuous and irreversible path of progress in a context in which the creation of wealth and material welfare seemed without limits. This context was translated for urban and rural families in concrete terms by the possibilities for investing in children's education, attaining health care, buying real estate or a car, building a house, or even engaging in entrepreneurial activities – in brief, of raising their standards of living.[12] This ensemble of virtual and real possibilities included both that which had been acquired, insofar as this involved specific possessions, and that which was assured, to the extent that one imagined the present and the future, and thus elaborated ideas about society and community on the basis of these possibilities. Moreover, a tacit pact, guaranteed by the single party and founded on the principle of the reciprocal assimilation of elites into the centers of power, allowed for the unequal redistribution of material and symbolic rents between different social strata and regions. This in turn assured a certain legitimacy for the ruling regime.[13] And it is this entire material and symbolic architecture that has crumbled under the weight of the crisis.

---

10 We are not asserting that this proliferation is without precedent. At this point in the discussion, we want to emphasize the relationship between the crisis in meaning and references, on the one hand, and the problem of criteria for efficacious action on the other.
11 On certain aspects of these processes, consult the cases in Peter Geschiere and Piet Konings, *Itinéraires d'accumulation au Cameroun/Paths of Accumulation in Cameroon* (Paris: Karthala, 1993).
12 Jean-Pierre Warnier, *L'esprit d'entreprise au Cameroun* (Paris: Karthala, 1993).
13 This process has been best described and interpreted by Jean-François Bayart, *L'État au Cameroun* (Paris: Presses de la Fondation Nationale des Sciences Politiques, 1979).

Its most physical and visible mark, that which captures the eye and is instantaneously frozen as a vision, what one might call its iconicity, is the image of abandonment and general decomposition which contrasts so starkly with the picture of affluence and prosperity that prevailed only a few years ago. The apparently abrupt nature of this rupture is most obvious in Yaoundé, where, as Cameroon's capital, the markers of modernity are supposed to be exhibited. Since the colonial period, roads have been one of the city's most distinctive signs of modernity. Today, Yaoundé's roads are in near total disrepair and dilapidation. Central avenues are as bad as streets in peripheral neighborhoods. Many roads that were paved a few years ago are now paths of beaten earth. They are broken up by sections that juxtapose efforts at resurfacing with potholes, crevices, and ditches which can be as wide as the road itself. Most traffic circles are nothing more than a heap of old tires or empty, rusted barrels.

The traffic lights no longer function. Some are still intact, but no longer give off any luminous signal. Due to the absence of maintenance, vandalism, or, more often, car accidents, others have either been torn out of the ground, exposing their massive cement base, or dangerously lean over the ad hoc sidewalk or road. Although they are all still there, sometimes in the very spot where they were erected, they are now masses of useless "traces," outliers of bygone days.

Such conditions incite a very particular economy of traffic circulation.[14] At first glance, its seems to lack rules or order. The chaos is undeniable even if it is sometimes misleading. In fact, drivers combine manners proper to the bush and those of the town, those of the military with the civil. These conditions produce deviations from recognized norms, such as the observance of specific rights of way, which of course, lead to accidents. The road is a disputed space, where private cars, taxis, public transportation, truck drivers, military jeeps, police cars, mopeds, bicycles, rickshaws, pedestrians, cattle, sheep, goats, and fowl intermingle and confront one another. Sudden stops and random parking, collisions that block traffic and cause congestion, the exchange of insults and physical abuse are par for the course. Furthermore, now that the automobile has entered the realm of increasingly rare objects, the figure of the pedestrian is again firmly rooted in the urban landscape. With every passing vehicle the partly beaten earth, partly paved roadway becomes a "whirlwind of red dust which suffocates the pedestrian and sticks to clothing, even becoming a sticky, thick muck with the least bit of intemperate if not infrequent rainfall."[15] The absence of traffic lights and thus explicit rules of circulation combined with this teeming, swarming atmosphere render the road a particularly productive disciplinary device.

---

14 For a purely geographic point of view on this subject, see the study by E. Tazo, "La circulation routière à Yaoundé," Master's thesis, Université de Yaoundé, 1980.

Experience on and familiarity with the road gives rise to an array of dispositions and arts of negotiation that are constitutive of subjectivities of conflict.[16]

The other attribute and metaphor of progress and modernity was, until recently, the automobile itself. Today, the passenger is never sure about arriving at the desired destination. This is partly due to the innumerable breakdowns resulting from the vehicle's age and problems such as sagging shock absorbers, missing windshields and doors, car bodies riddled with holes, faulty soldering and makeshift repairs leading to defective articulations as well as dead starters which require a car to be pushed to get it going. Factors as prosaic as lack of servicing, the artisanal mounting of spare parts,[17] and impossibility (when one is without a salary) of paying for gas must also be taken into account. In fact, most cars run on the reserve tank. Parsimony constrains drivers to turn off the engine and coast down hills in order to save gas. The wreckage of automobiles, bus cemeteries, passengers who strain behind a wheezing car: all of this has been from day to day so etched onto the urban landscape that it no longer creates a spectacle. It ceases to surprise. And so the physicality of the crisis reduces people to a precarious condition that affects the very way in which they define themselves.

The automobile, however, continues to "be useful for something." It is still an object of appropriation as a sign, belonging to a logic that is partly inspired by class affiliations.[18] This is evident from the attraction to, and fascination with, the most luxurious and expensive models. But, at the same time, because it is most often broken down and immobilized, the car no longer participates with the same intensity in the logic of ostentation, at least for the middle class. Its presence can be more of a monument than anything else: a broken utensil; a vestige of a shattered career; a once prosperous commerce now bankrupt; and a social status from which one was seemingly ejected. At most, then, it has become a figurative object.

Like roads and cars, the crisis has reconfigured another sign of modernity and economic progress – electric lighting. There are very few neighborhoods where all houses, buildings, and streets have electricity. With dusk, the city, now

---

15 "… un tourbillon de poussière rouge dont le piéton suffoque et qui colle aux vêtements, quitte à se transformer en une boue épaisse, plus collante encore, à la moindre pluie, intempérie plus que fréquente." Mongo Beti, *La France contre l'Afrique, retour au Cameroun* (Paris: La Découverte, 1993), p. 61, our translation.
16 For a technocratic reading of these practices, see Xavier Godard and Pierre Teurnier, *Les transports urbains en Afrique à l'heure de l'ajustement* (Paris: Karthala-INRETS, 1992).
17 The point is not that they are done improperly, but rather that they are done under certain circumstances and according to a particular level of infrastructure.
18 In the sense in which Jean Baudrillard speaks of a "sign function" (*fonction-signe*), a function that refers to a "class logic." See *Pour une critique de 1'économie politique du signe* (Paris: Gallimard, 1972).

dulled, spreads over its vast expanse of hills and valleys, gaping in places with black holes and shadows, brightened elsewhere with small concentrations of light, sometimes emanating from kerosene lamps. These pockets are magnets for various passersby who participate in the city's nocturnal life. On the edges of the ad hoc sidewalks, the commerce of the night proceeds. An entire urban food economy controlled by women selling foodstuffs like beans and fish provides subsistence to those on the margins and, increasingly, entire families struck by the irregularity of revenue and rarity of money. Public lighting and the lack of it also have other meanings. Associated with violent scenarios, the lack of public lighting and entry into a state of darkness throw into question the specificity of Cameroonian national identity. The idea of its specificity rested in part upon the notion that violent scenarios belonged to countries like Rwanda, Somalia, Chad, Zaire, or Liberia, and that such situations were not reproducible in Cameroon. The failure of public lighting and the plunge into darkness are now perceived as intimating that such violent scenarios are now on the order of the possible (*de l'ordre du possible*).[19]

The signs of dilapidation are not only visible in places where people move about. The landscape of decay is everywhere, unfolding and arranging itself like a fold in a fabric on the edge of the world; in the midst of an almost surreal decor, transformations are enveloped in quasi-magical effects. The city is laced with a string of litter and refuse that is rarely collected.[20] Masses of rubbish have become the capital's landmarks, replacing street names and main crossroads. When they spill over in all directions and infest the atmosphere with their stench, the garbage is set on fire. Its smoke rises from entire parts of the city and can be seen from miles away. It is testimony to this work of Sisyphus; this devouring and omnivorous force cannot be ensnared and becomes practically autonomous. Vegetation overruns not only the capital city, but also most of the secondary towns, which were once prosperous due to their integration in economic and transportation circuits. The following passage describes one of these towns:

---

19 At a meeting of public officials and merchants, one official commented, "SONEL [the national electricity company] is going to cut us off. It's shameful; the administrative center of the province in darkness. ... and SONEL always acts with its sister, SNEC [the national water company]. They will cut the water off. It's the lifeline of humanity, it's the life of the cattle, it's death, it's tragic." Later, he commented on the rise of vandalism, noting that "If SONEL cuts [the electricity], there will be theft, murders ... living in fear. You are the ones who will be living in insecurity." A merchant responded, "they'll be able to come into our houses to take what they want. So, you've seen Zaire. I'm asking you to pay [taxes] if you don't want problems like they have in Zaire, where famine is starting to threaten, and civil servants have started to make noise [the military being included as civil servants]." Janet Roitman, from notes of discussions in Maroua, Cameroon, April 15, 1993.

20 See the studies by Anne-Sidonie Zoa, "Les ordures à Yaoundé. Jalons pour une garbéologie africaine," Master's thesis, Université de Yaoundé, 1993; and T. Tang, "L'évacuation des eaux usées à Yaoundé," Master's thesis, Université de Yaoundé, 1990.

Today, what once was the river quay is now overrun with bushes of wild grass; the arrival of lumber by floating, a spectacle that always brought reveling schoolchildren, of which I was one, belongs to the past. A mysterious scourge chased away the white exploiters of the forest. The trading posts and general stores that swarmed with rustic and avid clients have disappeared, as have their light-skinned managers, always disdainful and never attentive. Mbalmayo is only a phantom of what it once was, a sort of dusty and flea-ridden Far West.[21]

The same is true for certain gigantic industrial projects dating from the era of abundance. This is notably the case for the Cellucam paper pulp factory at Edea, which is located in the very heart of the equatorial forest on a plateau overhanging the cutoff of the Sanaga River. The part of the forest granted to the company contained more than twenty-five species that are highly valued on the world market (*bubinga, doussié, sipo, sapelli, mahogany, iroko,* and *azobé*). Aside from the actual industrial infrastructure, the site includes a residential complex. The executive housing estate contains about fifty whitewashed villas surrounded by fir trees; the workers' housing development consists of about one hundred buildings. The encampment which was reserved for expatriate and bachelor workers who helped build the factory includes an impressive edifice over fifty meters tall. It towers majestically in the middle of a collection of other colossal constructions which covers over sixty hectares and is cordoned off by a practically insurmountable hedge.

Over this site, now engulfed by rampant grass, reigns the silence of a cemetery. It looks like a ghost town, completely deserted by its inhabitants. Luxurious vegetation has invaded up to the asphalt paths that once gave the encampment the look of a modern city. The buildings, with their dilapidated walls and rusted antitheft window coverings, have lost their fixtures and, for the most part, their electricity meters as well. All metal apparatus is heavily damaged; immense machines are now jammed and inoperable. The most gripping image of this "cannibalism" and spectacular destruction of wealth is the factory's parking lot. David Nouwou describes the debacle:

Imagine several hundred rotted vehicles (trucks, buses, personal cars, lumber haulers, tractors of all kinds) barely visible, buried in a tawny vegetation that has established its

---

21 "Aujord'hui, ce qui fut le quai aux grumes est envahi par les buissons d'herbes folles; l'arrivage du bois par flottage, spectacle dont venaient se repaître les écoliers de la ville, dont j'étais, appartient au passé. Un fléau mystérieux a chassé les exploitants forestiers blancs. Les comptoirs et les bazars grouillant de chalands rustiques et avides ont disparu ainsi que leurs gérants à peau claire, toujours dédaigneux, jamais empressés. Mbalmayo n'est plus que le fantôme de ce qu'il fut, sorte de Far-West poussiéreux et pouilleux." Beti, *La France contre l'Afrique*, pp. 56–57, our translation.

right to the city. When walking amongst them, one discovers that the vehicles were geometrically arranged, certainly being in perfect condition at the time. Today they are 100 percent deteriorated. Only the bodies upheld by the wheel rims attest to the car models. They say there are hundreds of vehicles thus abandoned in the different zones of the forest where companies operated; scores of others having been sold off or stolen.[22]

And the stock of over a thousand blocks of wood stored by the company before its closure was devoured, over a one-month period, by a gigantic brush fire, thus transforming the area into an immense Gehenna.

This state of decay and destitution can also be gleaned from the numerous construction sites that have been abandoned long before completion of their projects. The phenomenon is so extensive and so significant that it is worth introducing a few distinctions. First, some of these are public construction sites that were initiated by the government. These mostly include administrative office buildings; their construction began when the state had more or less stable sources of revenue. Today these work sites, which are in the city center, look as though the construction workers left one day for lunch and never returned. Tools are strewn about, often fixed in positions as if they were still in use.

Other buildings seem, from the outside, like modern skyscrapers. When night falls they are even lit up. Sometimes a security service prevents thieves from making off with the precious objects found within. However, these buildings are not at all operational. This is the case, for instance, with the edifice located on the Boulevard John Paul II, which was to be the headquarters of the Cameroonian Development Bank. Its cost was estimated at 5 billion francs CFA (or US$20 million).[23] In 1991, while this luxury building was being raised, the bank was dissolved by presidential decree. The bank had financed nonprofitable projects and various dignitaries of the regime had large outstanding credits with the bank.

Other similar buildings thrust massive cement columns into the sky. Ironwork, doors, shards of broken windows, even shredded curtains clutter these buildings, the rest of their contents such as doors, tiles, locks, sanitary material having been pillaged, sometimes right in front of passersby and public authorities. Some of these places, now used as squats, have been transformed into hideouts for all sorts of marginalized people. The Interministerial Building at the Central Post Office crossroads is one example. Work on this building was interrupted in the middle of the 1980s, even though it was nearly finished. Its cost was estimated at more than 20 billion francs CFA (US$80 million). It was being

22 See the narrative of David Nouwou, "Voyage au coeur d'un monstre économique mort," *La Nouvelle Expression* 56 (June–July 1992), p. 11.
23 All figures are based on exchange rates prior to the devaluation of the franc CFA in 1994.

financed with public funds and the work executed by a group of French and Cameroonian companies. Today, small-scale informal trade flourishes in front of this twenty-story uncompleted architectural undertaking. Countless street vendors have colonized this space and sell pedestrians an array of merchandise, from shoes, radios, cassettes, books, and diverse documents, pharmaceutical products, and beauty aids to trinkets and cheap kitsch. And besides serving as a refuge for marginals, the interior of the building is now a public urinal and depository for excrement.[24]

And, still under the rubric of official buildings, there are the homes and palaces of disinherited notables and historical figures of Cameroonian society. A particularly prominent example is the old presidential palace on the slopes of Mont Febe. The palace had been built by Ahmadou Ahidjo, who was head of state from 1958 to 1982 and died in exile in 1989 after having been condemned to death and then pardoned by the successor that he himself had selected.

Abandoned work sites include not only factories, offices, and residences but also places of worship. Two examples are the Catholic cathedral of Mvolye and the mosque at Tsinga. The cathedral seems hardly begun; its collection of icons, pillars, and columns might almost have been excavated from a Greco-Roman archaeological site. The mosque, which seems hardly finished, features a decapitated minaret. Both administrative and religious buildings, with their massive amounts of cement buried in the ground or rising into the sky, attest not only to a form of architecture entirely dedicated to the grandiloquence and baroque majesty adored by postcolonial power in Cameroon, but also to its corollary, an extravagant and unproductive economy of public and private expenditure. Central to this unproductive economy was a system of public contracting (*marché public*).

According to its generally accepted definition, a *marché public* is open to public bidding. It issues from a contract concluded between a public or private entity and a public establishment or collectivity, or even a parastatal body. By contract, the former makes a commitment to the latter to realize, either for their benefit or under their surveillance, work defined by a common accord, or to furnish goods and services. In principle, and at the level of regulation, an offer to tender was an obligatory procedure for all Cameroonian public contracts with costs exceeding 50 million francs CFA (US$200,000). For lesser amounts, a letter from the minister or head of the establishment sufficed, at least until recently. The open call to tender generally involved a public call for competitive bidding unless it was addressed to a limited number of candidates chosen for apparent economic or technical reasons. In this case, it was termed "limited" or "restrained."

---

24 Refer to the observations made by Daniel Atangana, "Des milliards enterrés," *Galaxie* 48 (June 1993), p. 6.

A central structure, the Direction Générale des Grands Travaux du Cameroun (DGTC), was charged with initiating invitations to tender on behalf of the administration and local collectivities, as well as public and parapublic firms. It was also responsible for consultative advice as to the ranking of the submitting parties during the period of examination. This was done upon completion of the work of a technical subcommission, composed of representatives of the DGTC and those of the ministry or other entity involved. This subcommission established a first ranking on the basis of ostensibly technical criteria. The portfolios were then submitted to the National Commission of Markets for scrutiny before passing for signature to the representative of the presidency. After this procedure for making a public contract was concluded, the DGTC was responsible for monitoring the project, providing technical assistance, and signing accounts and bills presented by the firm for reimbursement.

This bureaucratic framework for negotiating and monitoring contracts gave rise to an entire social commerce with forms of political exchange and modes of appropriating public goods that were widely known. The architectural text of unfinished edifices stands as a reminder of this political subtext. This commerce and these forms of exchange involved a diverse set of Cameroonian and foreign actors which includes businessmen, high-ranking officials, firms, French negotiators, and brokers. Together, and often in competition and conflict, they plotted a structure of interests and set in motion a regime of ownership and modalities for the realization of private revenues. The specificity of this regime was that it relied neither on imposing obligatory labor on subjects, nor on directly using the labor force itself. This mesh of predatory interests, brokers, and local agents rendered the state less a public good than a social relation of domination founded essentially on coercive exchange, plunder, and consumption. In other words, this manner of appropriating wealth created its social meaning through the very act of destroying and dissipating wealth.

This system allowed public contracts to be concluded with firms which had not presented any submission. Other contracts were offered without a call to tender; that is, without a call to competition and hence in violation of regulatory statutes which defined them as restrictive, and prescribed that their signing be authorized by the president of the Republic. Over-invoicing was also a common practice. This was the case for overhead and assignment costs, especially when they involved expenses accruing to so-called expatriate personnel.[25] To these practices must be added those involving large expenditures for standing

---

25 Until recently, the combined salaries of the six French directors of the DGTC amounted to 22.5 million francs CFA (US$90,000) per month. Cf. Jean de Dieu Sibafo, "Bâtiments et travaux publics: DGTC, l'édifice s'effondre inexorablement," *La Nouvelle Expression* 81 (July 1993), p. 8.

fleets of cars with the Land Cruiser, Renault 19, Peugeot 405 and 605 as the preferred models. In short, this was the nature of an array of officially acknowledged practices that were not, however, sanctioned and which were ultimately directed at circumventing regulation. In many ministries, one tactic involved the fragmentation of all contracts worth over 50 million francs (US$20,000) into packages with costs below this mark, thus bringing them under the jurisdiction of the letter of order. Other methods of circumventing regulation were invented under the guise of "privatization." Fictitious firms and warehouses were created to recycle gains and avoid customs. Resulting income and properties were converted into a certain number of ornamental and prestige goods and objects. These goods could be displayed. They were circulated on the market of symbols and used by those in power to dumbfound, stupefy, and politically subjugate their dependents, or simply to mark the glamour of their social position, especially via ceremonies and other forms of grandiose expenditure.[26]

To be sure, according to economic calculations of loss and profit, this capacity for waste and the spectacular destruction of wealth is, as Bataille would have it, of a purely excremental order.[27] However, the experience examined here also indicates that such an interpretation is in some ways insufficient. In fact, the very meaning of loss must be elucidated if one is to respond to the question posed at the beginning of this discussion. And, as we have seen, the loss in question implies enormous material and physical investments. Likewise, an important part of the life of private and public institutions, as well as the various networks that gravitate around them, are organized according to these very acts of dissipation. Furthermore, the country's integration in the world economy is based on these logics, which combine consumption and national debt. That this immense work of material, physical, and symbolic investment leads to the depository for excrement described above undoubtedly confirms some of Bataille's intuitions. And yet another aspect of this situation is that, through this evaporation of wealth, people also construct relations of cause and effect, thus circumscribing fields of possible action and elaborating forms of behavior that accentuate the crisis.[28]

---

26 Yamdeu, "Grande bamboula pour Tchouta Moussa," *Soleil d'Afrique* 24 (July 1993), pp. 6–8. The author describes ceremonies organized to "salute in grand pomp" the nomination of Tchouta Moussa to the head of the Office National des Ports du Cameroun. To celebrate this nomination "with éclat," Tchouta Moussa was able to mobilize members of the government, thirty-six traditional chiefs, and businessmen. In a more general sense, see Achille Mbembe, "Provisional Notes on the Postcolony," *Africa* 62, no. 1 (1992), pp. 3–37.
27 Georges Bataille, *La part maudite, précédé de la notion de dépense* (Paris: Éditions de Minuit, 1967), p. 29.
28 But one could also argue that, since this opens contradictory fields of potential action, certain forms might counter this tendency.

Public expenditures can also be interpreted as one of the registers of sovereignty. It provides the sites where the state endeavors to combine the monstrative exercise of physical violence and arbitrary symbolic acts. In this way, expenditure is part of an omnivorous political configuration, where public and private forces mingle; where spoils, salaries, exactions, fees, and monopolies are inseparable; and where the state apparatus and framework for extraction are one and the same. Hence, during the "forced recovery" (*recouvrement forcé*) or collection of taxes (automobile stickers, small merchant licenses, the headtax) the police, militia, and army set up barriers all along the national roads, through cities and villages, giving Cameroon the air of a country at war.[29] All these forces are charged with "closing establishments and firms, impounding vehicles and locking up thousands of young, unemployed youth who are incapable of attending to their basic needs let alone paying their taxes."[30]

Finally, the crisis seems to have seized people in the very interiors of their homes, becoming a part of their domesticity. Between 1984 and 1988, Cameroon witnessed a boom in the building industry. The years of relative affluence (1979–86) following the injection of a portion of oil revenues into the economy led to a frenzy in construction that was not limited to the state. And even though the conditions for accessing credit remained prohibitive, numerous executives, managers, and officials who once rented their houses decided to privilege investment in property. At the same time, large-scale urban renewal was initiated. This run on property was still underway when the crisis hit; and the crisis abruptly ended it. Every neighborhood in the city is now studded with half-built villas and abandoned houses, sometimes with belongings and furniture left inside or overrun with undergrowth that the rainy season sends to vertiginous heights. Families living in semi-constructed houses and villas have become so commonplace that one is regularly ushered into homes with, "Welcome to our construction site!" or "Excuse us, we live in a construction site." Obsolete and rundown furnishings and appliances have become a constitutive feature of home decor; often a telephone sits mutely on a pedestal, with service terminated due to unpaid bills.[31]

The sudden nature of this intrusion is well illustrated by popular expressions: "The crisis fell on our heads" (*La crise est tombé sur nos têtes*) and "I've got the crisis" (*J'ai la crise*).[32] This experience, which is at once intimate and dra-

---

29 Eyoum Ngangue, "Péage routier: Les limites d'un nouveau racket," *Le Messager* 326 (September 1993), p. 5.
30 A. C. Fomi, "Lettre ouverte au ministre des finances," *Dikalo* 82 (July 1993), p. 15.
31 H. L. Bateg, "Impayés du telephone: Qui va payer la note?" *Dikalo* 83 (July 1993), p. 7. Also, M. Waffo, "La SIC aux trousses des locataires indélicats," *Challenge Bi-Hebdo* 95 (July 1993), p. 8.
32 The latter being intoned in the same way one says, "I have a cold."

matic, gives rise to narratives that no longer locate the crisis in an evolutionary history; that is to say, in a causal description of an event that develops over a relatively long period of time. The experience and the imaginary of time that results are of a condensed, compressed, and abrupt nature. Because of this contraction, the transformations taking place are not necessarily correlated to precise factors and historical referents, even if one is aware that these elements do in fact exist. For lack of these referents, the crisis is exiled to the domain of the inexplicable.

Explanation by the Inexplicable When one asks people to explain the events described above, and to render "intelligible" the lived experiences these situations incite, people generally respond that they no longer understand what is happening. However, it would be wrong to regard this answer as a simple claim to ignorance. To the extent that this statement tends to become, for those involved, an answer which is valid in-and-of-itself and is hence legitimate, it deserves further consideration. On the one hand, it is important to retrace the path that leads to such a response (how does one arrive there?). On the other hand, if people "understand" their lived experiences as incomprehensible, what forms of (in)action does such an intelligibility or even such a mental disposition lead to? And to what extent can one say, at the same time, that this complex of dispositions and conduct itself contributes to the very aggravation of the crisis?

Without responding directly to these questions, insight can be gained by recalling the historical context and intellectual moment from which they arise. The historical context is that of a society knocked about and mistreated by a succession of instabilities, shortages, constraints, and blockages. Some of these phenomena are of external origin, others are from within, but all bring about several types of incoherence. As noted above, these discontinuities and contradictions (*incohésions*) are becoming more and more systematic, to the point where one can no longer locate what results from mere chance, or accident, and what results from the "normal" state of affairs. The examples outlined above also demonstrate that the conditions of the very material reproduction of society are being intensely modified. This movement appears to be taking place in a manner that is so unexpected and sudden, at least in people's consciousness, that it induces "surprise," "perplexity," and even a sort of "stupor." Because it is lived as an abrupt experience, this bundle of events incites recourse to other categories of reference, other systems of causality, or, in brief, other regimes of intelligibility. On the other hand, Cameroonian society's long-standing capacity to "imagine" itself in a certain manner – to mentally author and, from this, institute itself[33] – has been contradicted and seems now thrown into question. As indicated above, at the time when annual growth rates were on the order of six to seven percent, Cameroonians perceived themselves as a part of a rich nation, with infinite possibilities before them. This was, to be sure, part of a deliberate effort to imagine a national identity founded on economic attributes. Today's bankruptcy places this mode of imagining the nation in check, leaving in its wake certain forms of nostalgia. One is incessantly reminded: "Only a few years ago, things were not as they are now."[34] This attests to a sense of loss both in the material sense of waste and dilapidation as well as in the sense of existential deprivation and disorientation.

Indeed, from within this dislocation Cameroonians attempt to articulate new forms of rationality based on emergent understandings of efficacious action which often issue from ambiguous and contradictory situations. For example, consumers of electricity provided by the national company, sometimes with the complicity of the company's own agents, have their meters jammed so that they can consume as much electricity as desired for free. The same practice applies to water consumption. The rationing of water and the segmentation of its sale have also become widespread: the consumer of water, no longer able to pay for the service, is obliged to buy it from itinerant vendors or from private parties who subcontract it out. Furthermore, agents of the urban transport company have established parallel services for the sale of tickets. Similarly train passengers, instead of buying tickets at the normal price, "make arrangements" (*s'arrangent*) with conductors at much lower prices. In a like manner, during roadblock inspections, a common occurrence, police and militiamen pocket the fines for citations and "warnings."

Fraudulent identity cards; fake policemen dressed in official uniform; army troops complicit with gangs of thieves and bandits; forged enrollment for exams; illegal withdrawal of money orders; fake banknotes; the circulation and sale of falsified school reports, medical certificates, and damaged commodities: all of this is not only an expression of frenetic trafficking and "arranging." It is also a manifestation of the fact that, here, things no longer exist without their parallel. Every law enacted is submerged by an ensemble of techniques of avoidance, circumvention, and envelopment which, in the end, neutralize and invert the legislation.[35] There is hardly a reality here without its double. Hence acting efficaciously requires that one carefully cultivate an extraordinary capac-

---

33 Cornelius Castoriadis, *L'institution imaginaire de la société* (Paris: Seuil, 1972).
34 "Il y a seulement quelques années, les choses n'étaient pas comme maintenant."
35 Here we are referring to combinatory effects and, eventually, the production of another *kind* of system and not simply a *parallel* one.

ity to be simultaneously inside and outside, for and against, and to constantly introduce changes in the reading and usage of things, playing, in this way, with the structures and apparatuses, capturing them where possible and eluding them where necessary, and in any event, amputating them and almost always emptying them of their formal and designated functions so one can better restore them with those that correspond best to desired goals and expected gains.

Without denying the scattered and inchoate character of most of these acts, their ultimately unsystematic, chaotic, and inconclusive nature, it should be noted that they are repeated with such regularity at all levels of society that they are well known to almost everyone. They are widespread and are, in this sense, no longer simply isolated incidents or simple tinkerings with the system in order to survive.[36] Instead, they have become "ways of doing" which belong to the register of new forms of public knowledge: the constitution of a prosaic that is not specifically African, but is rather particular to all times of crisis in a general sense. Certainly, for now, the legitimation of such practices is an object of dispute. They are vehemently condemned by the public authorities (without leading to effective sanctions) as well as by the general public, even while they themselves continue to resort to such practices.

To a large extent, it is the daily negotiation with the absurd in order to subsist and survive that induces people to say they "no longer understand." The paradoxical situations in which they find themselves are thus qualified as "incredible," "unimaginable," and even "insane."[37] The density of the constraints that grip everyday life is no doubt such that one is never sure to get by, as the following narrative of a train ride demonstrates:

> It was the station at Belabo. We wanted two seats on the night train to Ngaoundere. The station teemed with people. Some were standing, others lay on the ground or sat on the edge of the rails, sometimes in the shadows. Itinerant vendors, legal and clandestine transporters, an entire mass of people came and went in indolence and numbness, punctuated by abrupt waves. A long line of travelers waited wearily; their wait would last an eternity. Finally, at 11 p.m., the ticket window opened. Yet the line remained as immobile as before; while purchasers advanced, other voyagers tacked on to the end so that the length of the line seemed always the same. The sale of a ticket took about fifteen minutes, including the identification of destination, the choice of

---

36 In this sense, it is fallacious to consider them purely and simply in terms of survival strategies or as acts of resistance, as does James C. Scott, *Domination and the Arts of Resistance: Hidden Transcripts* (New Haven: Yale University Press, 1990).

37 Conversations with Jean Marc Ela, Vianney Ombe Ndzana, Thierno Mouctar Bah, Yaoundé, July 1993.

seating, the unraveling of the tickets, unfurling of bank notes and coins, the search for change, calculating the difference, the manual inscription of the price and other information, and the inevitable rubber stamp officializing the document. From entry into the line to arrival at the ticket window, we spent over an hour. Upon leaving the window, it was evident that the train's estimated arrival time had long passed.

Hoping to have a minimum of comfort but not wanting to pay the price of a berth, we had twice requested access to the first class wagon. And the cashier twice responded favorably. We consequently paid the required fee. The train arrived at about 1:40 in the morning. We immediately sought out the first-class car. It was nowhere. The second-class car and bunk car were all that were to be found. The train had hardly come to a halt when the crowd, once nonchalant and dozing, suddenly arose. Unleashed, the mass took the second-class car literally by assault. People pushed, swore, hurled abuses, and tossed bags, packages, children, and animals through doorways and windows, in a tumultuous confusion.

We located the conductor and, with all required deference, noted that the agent of the rail company had sold us tickets for services that were nowhere to be found. We thus had no seats for a night voyage of over 400 kilometers. A first-class wagon for night trains? No such thing existed, he informed us, adding that we could have access to the berth for a sum. We could have discussed it all night, but the fact was that the agent had consciously sold us fake tickets for services that did not exist. We traveled standing up, caught between voyagers who, overcome with fatigue, were strewn along the aisles, knocking the knees of those who constantly flowed from one end of the car to the other, in a quest for what, we never knew.[38]

In this specific instance, a formalized agreement such as paying a precise sum for a precise service on the basis of information given by the railway employee resulted in a loss of money and frustration. But this is not because formal rules and conventional procedures are not publicized or not respected. One can very well respect them. Yet this in no way automatically implies that the prescribed results will be attained. To the contrary, those who scrupulously follow the rules sometimes find themselves in a snarl, facing figures of the real that have little correspondence to what is publicly alleged or prescribed at the point of departure. Whether this involves a bureaucratic or a purely private transaction, every step must be negotiated. Thus when people refer to "insanity," they are not referring to a state which defects from reason, but rather to the unbearable discrepancy that exists between publicly announced reality and that other constantly changing, unstable and uncertain, quasi-elliptic realm that is consistently

[38] The experience of the authors, Cameroon, July 1993.

pursued and always dissipates, often emerging only after a long and exhausting bargain. It follows that "the real" of the crisis is "ephemeral" since it is marked by and punctuated with false starts, hyperbolic and highly eccentric rules, all of which require not only a particular theory of uncertainty, but also of causality and error. Every step or effort made to follow the written rule is susceptible to lead not to the targeted goal, but to a situation of apparent contradiction and closure from which it is difficult to exit either by invoking the very same rules and authorities responsible for applying them, or by reclaiming theoretical rights supposed to protect those who respect official law.

Furthermore, even where contracts and engagements are made, they are almost never definitive; they are always liable to renegotiation. Thus every contract or negotiation constitutes in itself a vast field of ambiguity which, as such, leaves enormous potential for dispute, argument, and discord. This profoundly provisional and revisable character of things is at the origin of the proliferation of criteria for efficacious action. The ensuing conduct ranges from pure and simple infractions to violations, evasion, avoidance, deviation, figuration, use of circumlocutions, improvisation, tossing the dice, and turning things inside out. Sometimes one-and-the-same operation requires several levels and forms of negotiation with several kinds of authority. This is, in part, due to the absence of institutional and material infrastructure: the telephone is not working; the electricity is temporarily cut; the attendant is out or absent; money or a letter has not arrived; the schedule has changed or is broken; the chain of command is defective; the person responsible did not complete the required task; another document or official stamp is necessary.

Such conditions also relate to the extraordinary fragmentation and redundance of administrative services: for a single service, A can only give you certain information; B can only give you the application; C can give you advice about general formalities. D can sell you the stamp, but his services are located elsewhere and you must go in person. Only E can verify that the application has been properly filled out before transmitting it to F, who types it and sends it to G, who submits it to H, who is the supervisor. H then authorizes G to apply the rubber stamp. After the document is stamped, it is brought back to the supervisor, H, for signature. One must then return, often several times, before recovering it. Or, when it is not necessary to "come back tomorrow," one must stay and wait – "it's not ready yet."

These examples clearly demonstrate that extreme bureaucratization and specialization (Weber) do not necessarily lead to increased productivity.[39] With

---

[39] In an entirely different context, this point is also suggested by Darius M. Rejali, *Torture and Modernity: Self, Society and State in Modern Iran* (Boulder: Westview Press, 1994), pp. 42–44, 61.

respect to the context being considered here, this gives rise to a particular mode of managing "public goods," where users substitute themselves for agents who undertake tasks and services usually rendered by public power. When trying to obtain an official document in a police station or ministry, one must purchase the application, furnish paper and writing utensils, find stamps, photocopy documents, and gather exact change before presenting oneself to the cashier. The same process also applies to other public institutions. In hospitals, it is not unusual that, to "be served," the patient must obtain cotton and alcohol, furnish implements for surgery, and pay – beyond salaries – the doctors and nurses. And schoolchildren must often bring chalk, tables, and chairs to class; their parents also contribute in cash or kind to the salary of the teacher. This is what we have labeled "do-it-yourself bureaucracy." However, what we wish to underscore is not the extraordinary, but the routine. In constructing the frameworks of everyday life, these now common practices destabilize the referents once considered intrinsic to the constitution of order and hierarchy. One of the consequences of this is the corrosion of long-standing conceptions of causality and responsibility, or the dissolution of authority itself.

The Crisis of the Subject and Historical Violence The dissolution of authority and the unhinging of its associated hierarchy and order first take the form of a dispersal of the attributes of public power. This, however, does not mean that there are no longer mechanisms and agents of power. Soldiers, policemen, and militia continue to lead the "fiscal war," for example, they survey documents, extort goods, and confiscate commodities. But this kind of violence does not necessarily imply an opposition between a dissipating form of authority and an emergent one. As the following example shows, this is not the case since it proceeds from the monopolization and reinterpretation of roles in directions that were, in the past, either unthinkable, reprehensible, and reprimanded, or impracticable:

> After the inspection of documents, the police officer asks the taxi driver to put his foot on the brakes. If the brake lights fail, the poor driver falls through the trap. If not, the inspection continues. Everything is subject to it: tires, brakes, shock absorbers, headlights, blinkers, bumpers. Tired of insisting, the cops have recourse to their last card, the missing fire extinguisher and first-aid kit, before asking all of the passengers for their papers. The second device is simply to waste time. The policeman stops a taxi, asks for "the documents," and moves away from the vehicle. He talks with his colleagues without even deigning to glance at the papers. Hurried and tired of waiting, the passengers get out of the taxi one by one and hitch rides with other cars. … As soon as

the taxi driver gives "500," the policeman returns his documents and the pigeon is free to fly away and be plucked elsewhere.⁴⁰

The decline of public authority and its defection from responsibility has led to a situation of confusion and chaos which people impute not only to the crisis, but also to "democracy": "Now everyone does what they please." Such is the case when one considers the state of the garbage in Yaoundé. Common responses to the problem are: "It's uncontrollable," "it's ungovernable," "we don't know whom to address," "we no longer know who is responsible for what," "we don't know what to do any longer," "it's beyond us." Generally speaking, the expression "we no longer know what to do" implies that one has tried in vain to transform existing conditions to the point where the capacity to produce concrete effects has been exhausted. "We no longer know whom to address" implies that one can no longer identify pertinent authorities or, in any case, be heard by them. This also indicates that some sites of power now escape all control; that is, they are now endowed with immunities.

Such conditions structure forms of violence in daily transactions and relationships which include the transgression and forced alienation of rights, as well as purely physical abuse. Practices that are perhaps most likely to entail violent confiscation of goods and property are those involving the systematic sale of public services. Here, for example, is a description of an everyday scenario:

> In certain magistrates' courts, retrieval of official documents, such as form number 3 from the criminal record, requires one to respond to superfluous demands for stamps [which, once] applied, will be immediately recuperated and resold by administrators. [Among other requests, there are] so-called research expenses. Their costs multiply with the number of copies requested by the user. And this, without counting the eventual inflation of the final bill, is much influenced by the appearance of the client. Attempts at fraud are now assured at all levels. ... At the treasuries, the little swindlers continue to systematically apply a "commission" of 5 to 25 percent on bills and salaries to be paid. Furthermore, it is now difficult to mobilize the police for a problem under their jurisdiction if one has not "greased his palm." In all sectors of public service, there is always a slightly illegal way to "get by." Fewer and fewer bosses who have not maintained their small network of "fakes" have conserved their aura. ... Women try to sell their colleagues as many tidbits and trinkets as possible in order to make ends meet.⁴¹

---

40 Eyoum Ngangue, "Taximen contre policiers: Combat de rue ou guerre de tranchées?" *Le Messager* 315 (July 1993), p. 11.
41 Jean-Marc Soboth, "Fonctionnaires: La fin des patates," *La Nouvelle Expression* 87 (August 1993), p. 6.

In order to apprehend these developments in a manner which demonstrates clearly how they are implicated in the general enactment of power, and moreover, in the structuration of violence – thus contributing to the latter's specific content – analyses proceeding from normative concepts such as corruption are to be avoided. Indeed, state services and functions which are thus sold are, above all, a series of formalities. The user is constrained to carry out or fulfill these formalities each time he or she must retrieve a salary, pass an official examination, go before the courts, obtain a visa, or renew a license. In perfect colonial tradition, the maximal content of the formality is the signature, itself authenticated by the rubber stamp.[42] And here public power surely has the monopoly, at least in principle. In a sense, the formalities – the signature being the one that perhaps most efficiently reduces power to the sign – are what users must buy at public prices applicable to all. The purchase allows users access to formal "rights" or, even better, to "authorizations" corresponding to domains covered by the object bought.

For now, we will simply consider that which is exercised at the precise moment when agents of so-called public service sell formalities to users on behalf of the state. In this instance, various phenomena are brought together, each contributing to the specific character of the exercise of violence in a time of crisis. First, there is the generalization of favors and privileges: one wants access to officially prescribed rights and authorizations, but by circumventing required formalities. This can be accomplished in many ways. Private arrangements can be made with the agent responsible for the public service. Or, in a context where agents of public power are paid episodically and public power itself no longer disposes of the necessary infrastructure to exercise its command, the user is often forced to purchase the materials necessary for the functioning of an official institution. Thus, in a private capacity, one directly assures the financing of a public service. Also, in buying the formality, one directly compensates the public servant who is supposedly remunerated by the state. Otherwise, one pays stamp and other formal taxes, and sometimes even assumes the very task of the bureaucrat. What we termed *do-it-yourself bureaucracy* is a site where, on the one hand, functions devolved to public power are exercised by private users (a formal substitution) in an official capacity; and, on the other hand, the user is *de facto* no longer served, but pays to "self-serve." The formalities that are at the origin of these transactions continue, however, to be the property, so to speak, of public power and are not, strictly speaking, the object of an individual appro-

---

42 Janet Roitman, notes, Maroua, 1992–93. In a more general sense, cf. Béatrice Fraenkel, *La signature: Genèse d'un signe* (Paris: Gallimard, 1992). However, she considers the signature only in the sacred terms of a new conception of identity and recognition of the singularity of the human being.

priation or a definitive alienation. What is important for our argument is that, at the heart of such a structure of action, the existence of these formalities is neither disputed nor does it determine the nature of day-to-day violence in the public sphere. Governing the specific content of the violence of the crisis is the interpretation of formalities and the determination of where and when they must be fulfilled, for example, what papers one must have when one drives a car. This interpretation is sufficiently underdetermined so that substantial margins are open for the intensification of impositions or levies, as well as their generalization. The violence of the crisis emerges as much from the dissolution and dispersion of authority as from the possibilities that follow from conducting arrangements from within official sites themselves.

But this excess, this proliferation of legitimate interpretations and the attendant violence itself rests on specific material conditions and a singular political economy. To be sure, in the public mind, the state is no one's property, not even the autocrat's. It is an anonymous and vacant domain. By the discretionary path of "nomination" and "the decree" the autocrat can nonetheless cede a portion of this anonymous domain to obliged subjects. Nomination to a position of responsibility or command, that is, control of a part of the apparatus of authorizations and formalities, is lived as an allocation in kind from which one can, by being astute, organize levies and parallel fiscal mechanisms. The present circumstances, where the autocrat endowed with the power of nomination finds himself no longer able to settle accounts, are favorable for the emergence of a particular type of domination that might be described as "discharge" (*décharge*). Through discharge, operations once solely executed by the state are allotted to henchmen who generalize, in this manner, the extortion of dues and fees. Here, extortion seems to be a substitute for forced labor. It is based on the idea of the enactment of fiscal relationships in kind. But discharge in no way implies the permanent appropriation of state property, anonymous as it is. At most, this only involves a concession; at best, a benefaction. It does not, however, guarantee immunity to whomever profits in a precarious or provisional manner. These practices should then be interpreted more in terms of dispensation than privatization.[43]

But one of the most flagrant signs of the decline of public power is what surely appears to be "the end of the salary" and its substitution by occasional payments, the amounts of which are steadily declining. This state of affairs, never before known in the history of the country, extends beyond agents of pub-

---

43 Contrary to Nicolas van de Walle, in "The Politics of Nonreform in Cameroon," in *Hemmed In: Responses to Africa's Economic Decline*, ed. Thomas Callaghy and John Ravenhill (New York: Columbia University Press, 1993), pp. 357–397.

lic service. It includes the entire salaried population and is linked to the problems of disaccumulation and illiquidity that now sap the country. The shortage of money affects the urban centers as well as the rural areas, the latter having lived to the monetary rhythms of the specific seasonal cycles of cocoa, coffee, cotton. In order to discern the magnitude of the dislocations that followed and the ways in which they have structured the subjectivities of the crisis, two points must be made. The first is that a major part of Cameroonian economic and political life was, until recently, organized around the "end of the month." The regularity of salary payments allowed for the regulation not only of the lives of those who earned them, but also those who depended on them for their survival, according to the principles of redistribution, allocations, transfers, and reciprocity studied by François-Régis Mahieu in the case of the Ivory Coast.[44] The cycle of debts, contracts, and obligations was stimulated in this way, as was most formal and informal economic activity.

At the present time, the decrease in salary levels and irregularity of payments have introduced ruptures and discontinuities in these cycles, obliging people to negotiate forms of uncertainty and instability unknown heretofore. One of these is the date of salary payments. A large part of social life, particularly in cities, has been reorganized around this now unpredictable moment. Many live on the lookout, plunged in anxious, open-ended anticipation. They look for signs: a mob in front of the Treasury building or the bank, rumors and news of dates. People insist that they can no longer plan their lives or even make commitments. And this concerns events and phenomena as ordinary and vital as children starting the new school year, all sorts of ceremonies, health prevention and care, and even death and burial. All contracts become, of course, a risk. New forms of migration have appeared: every month, numerous government employees head for the capital from distant provinces in search of their salaries. From time to time soldiers and policemen, and even regular citizens, sequester bank managers and treasurers, retaining them as hostages, demanding to be paid on the spot. Because salaries allowed people to procure the necessities and even conveniences of life and assured subsistence for recipients and their dependents, allowing them to clothe and house themselves, and to prevent illness and hunger, this interruption leaves them exposed to the pressures of need and to the specific form of violence which is constituted by shortages and scarcity.

Because of the contradictory nature of subject positions and conduct (being inside and outside, for and against) described above, the response to this situation has not been uniform. Organized and silent protest alternates with accom-

---

[44] François-Régis Mahieu, "Principes économiques et société africaine," *Tiers-Monde* 30, no. 120 (1989), pp. 725–753.

modation and acceptance of a *fait accompli*. To understand the violence inherent in this atonic situation, it is important to remember that, in postcolonial Cameroon, besides being one of the privileged sites for the structuration of inequality and social stratification (because all remunerations are not equal), the relationship between salary, work, and wealth has led to a more or less legitimate form of domination, a particular form of civility that itself merits discussion.

For the general public, the equivalence between wealth and work understood as "toil and time, the working-day that at once patterns and uses up man's life,"[45] was unclear since, for Cameroonians, it was obvious that people could become rich without submitting to fatigue and hunger, and without being exposed to death. Thus, bureaucratic "work" was neither perceived nor lived as a specifically or necessarily productive activity. It was therefore not conceptualized as a commodity or ware that one sold to the state, which purchased it for the price of a salary. Consequently, the quantity and value of work as such was not what was remunerated by these payments.

In the pre-crisis system, the salary was, like public expenditures examined above, a positivity not reducible to remuneration for productivity or the formation of wealth. It was a resource of the state insofar as it served to purchase obedience and to settle the population in disciplinary mechanisms. The salary, then, legitimated subjection by establishing a particular type of civility: authoritarian civility.[46] In this sense, it constituted a purely ascriptive and juridical allocation, as well as an indispensable cog in the dynamics of the relationship between state and society, and the constitution of a particular type of citizenship. This type of citizenship was not, above all, founded on the principle of political equality and representations thereof. It was based on "claims" (the salary being the most significant) from which the state created social debts. The construction of the political relationship was thus enacted in redistribution and not on the basis of representations of equivalence between human beings endowed with their own natural and civil rights, and thus able to have an effect on political decisions. By transforming the salary into a claim and a formality, the state granted subsistence to its subjects. But these means did not sanction a conversion of energy into wealth; they resulted in a specific figure of obedience and domination. This is, moreover, why, in public discourse, these claims are sometimes represented as favors or, at least, privileges.[47]

---

45 Michel Foucault, *The Order of Things: An Archaeology of the Human Sciences* (New York: Vintage Books, 1973), p. 225.
46 Achille Mbembe, "Prosaics of Servitude and Authoritarian Civilities," *Public Culture* 5, no. 1 (1992), pp. 123–148.
47 This part of the discussion owes much to a series of conversations with Jean Marc Ela in Yaoundé during July and August 1993.

This is perhaps why the "end of the salary," and its replacement with occasional payments, has not provoked the kind of outright, contentious mobilization one might expect. Civil workers continue to go to their offices even though they are not paid. Certainly, their reasons for doing so are complex. Many still hope that their salaries will arrive, betting that they are simply "late." Fear of losing the little that one has is, no doubt, a persuasive factor, since large-scale layoffs have taken place and continue to be announced. From a strictly sociological point of view, it is important to note that the workplace is also a social site, not unlike a café or salon. One goes there to make phone calls, visit people, sell things, converse. It is also a place for *rendezvous*. It marks off, in this sense, the frontier between "life inside," with its familial pressures, and "life outside."

What has developed is a form of protest by inertia. Few people come to their offices on time. Many are almost never there, preoccupied with the salary-chase or out "getting by" to make up for what is lacking at the end of the month. The disorganization of schedules is such that being present at work does not necessarily mean that one actually works nor that one is actually there.[48] Here, the absence of a violent popular reaction relates to two factors. For one, there is a profound memory of fear and real trauma associated with the defeat of historical movements of insubordination.[49] Also, after the failure of the civil disobedience movements of 1992 (Opération Villes Mortes), all protest is now thought to be inefficacious. In this context but on another level, the idea of inefficaciousness results from a certain conceptualization of relations of cause and effect which is connected to the experience of dissipation and loss discussed above.

It is important to underscore that irregular payment of salaries is not the only visible dimension of this violence. The other aspect, which affects innumerable high school, university, and technical graduates, is the large-scale layoffs implemented in response to conditions set by international financial institutions such as the World Bank and the International Monetary Fund. This phenomenon is so massive that it has provoked an immense sense of anguish among an entire generation of young, educated persons. Those who still have a job live under the permanent threat of losing it. In response, a vast array of forms of protection have emerged, drawing from popular modes of Christianity and Islam–exorcism, purification and annointing, having offices blessed, wearing sacred objects and medications – as well as from the autochthonous world of the night and the invisible (*monde de la nuit et vie de l'invisible*).[50] This

---

48 Present practice involves signing a roll call at various times during the day to establish theoretical presence while not actually being physically in the office or workplace throughout the day.
49 Cf. Richard A. Joseph, *Radical Nationalism in Cameroon: Social Origins of the UPC Rebellion* (Oxford: Oxford University Press, 1977); Bayart, *L'État au Cameroun*; Achille Mbembe, *La naissance du maquis dans le Sud-Cameroun, 1920–1960* (Paris: Karthala, 1996).

atmosphere of insecurity and tension is not limited to public places; the rise in domestic conflict, the rapidity with which people resort to anger, verbal abuse, and physical violence are evident in intimate and daily interactions. And this is aggravated by new forms of urban violence, inspired either by the quest for subsistence or attempts to eradicate the very sources of perceived danger. Such violence includes the lynching of thieves and presumed bandits by the citizenry, the repression of protesters and murder of taxi drivers by the police, armed attacks, and highway robbery.[51] In sum, a situation marked by extraordinary tension and nervousness (*nervosité*) prevails: the proliferation of all kinds of rumors; the escalation of credulity; the unleashing of an imaginary of marvel (*le merveilleux*) and evil (*malheur*), bad luck and pain. This deployment of violence has plunged a large part of the population into a prolonged state of anxiety and perplexity.

All of this, however, goes hand-in-hand with an extraordinary capacity to turn violence, the absurd, and even terror itself into a source of derision.[52] In the context described above, laughter is inseparable from the fear inspired by the immediate present, populated, as we have shown, by "evil spirits," that is, those things which are out of control, such as automobile circulation, garbage, brushwood, construction sites, authorities, and people on the margins. The proliferation of criteria for judgment induces a state of uncertainty and contradictory or easily reversible forms of behavior which, in turn, lead to increased levels and new forms of violence. Fear, and the laughter it provokes, are often an effect of the ambiguity of lived experience: one is subject to this violence and yet, often in spite of oneself, one participates in its very production.

To the extent that, in a time of crisis, relations of domination conceal themselves behind figures of monstrosity, the absurd (*l'absurde*), and suffering, *to laugh* means not only to hypostasize domination, but also to mark the noncorrespondence between objectified violence and the fear that one endeavors to admit and avert. But as a magical imaginary and particular figure of superstition, laughter, derision, and mockery themselves harbor enormous possibilities for substitution, imitation, and falsification. They aim to travesty, avenge, scare the evil spirits and appease them, or to exercise reprisals on "the signs of the

---

50 Cf. Peter Geschiere, *Sorcellerie et politique en Afrique: La viande des autres* (Paris: Karthala, 1995); Eric de Rosny, *L'Afrique des guérisons* (Paris: Karthala, 1992).
51 See "Un macchabée calciné à Yaoundé," *Challenge Bi-Hebdo* 106 (August 1993), p. 9; or C. Yaho, "Gangstérisme urbain: La justice populaire comme réponse à l'insécurité," *La Nouvelle Expression* 81 (July 1993), p. 4.
52 Cf. the popular caricatures found in the weekly *Le Messager-Popoli: La version-image de l'actualité*. Also, Ferdinand Oyono, *Une vie de boy* (Paris: Julliard, 1956) and *Le vieux nègre et la médaille* (Paris: Julliard, 1956).

thing"[53] (*les signes de la chose*), which cannot be overcome otherwise. As rites of expiation, laughter, and derision give way to an imaginary well-being, they allow for distance between the subject who laughs and the object of mockery. The division thus realized is precisely what permits the laughing subject to regain possession of self and to wear the mask – that is, to become a stranger to this "thing" (*la chose*) that exercises domination – and then to deride torture, murder, and all other forms of wretchedness.

---

53 Martin Heidegger, *Qu'est-ce une chose?* (Paris: Gallimard, 1971).

**From Obsolescence to Dynamism:
Reinterpreting African Urban Futures**

Popular Shaping of Metropolitan Forms and Processes in Nigeria: Glimpses and Interpretations from an Informed Lagosian

Babatunde A. Ahonsi

This paper has been motivated by the proposition that understanding the processes that have shaped and are shaping the spatial and demographic transformation of Lagos (and its adverse concomitants) requires attention to two sets of conditions. First are the specific historical, geographical, and political factors that have driven the rapid emergence of Lagos as one of Africa's largest cities. Second is the role of the mass of people that have interacted with and responded to these sweeping conditions in modifying and mediating their consequences for the livability, productivity, serviceability, and manageability of Lagos. Such a rounded approach to the study of Lagos is especially called for if the derived conclusions are to serve as a basis for conceptualizing and planning effective responses to the key social, economic, environmental, and political problems that have earned Lagos so much notoriety since the early 1980s.

Yet, a quick reading of the fairly large and growing academic literature on Lagos reveals an almost exclusive preoccupation with the urban pathologies that are prevalent within the metropolis. There is virtually no difference between the titles of newspaper articles and video film productions about Lagos and those of research papers in academic texts and journals. Social science research on Lagos has been reduced to mechanistic accounts of spatial disorder, de-beautification, organized violence and crime, inter-ethnic strife, civil disorder, overcrowding, flooding, air and noise pollution, unemployment, widespread poverty, traffic chaos, and risk-bearing sexual practices among other problems.[1] While these constitute an important part of the Lagos reality, the puzzle that needs to be resolved via research and analysis is larger than and transcends these problems. This is because with cognizance of the ecology of Lagos and the clearly unmanageable rapidity with which it has grown in the last four decades, it should also

---

[1] See, for example, Adepoju G. Onibokun and Adetoye Faniran, *Urban Research in Nigeria* (Ibadan: French Institute for Research in Africa and CASSAD, 1995), and Tunde Agbola, *The Architecture of Fear: Urban Design and Construction Response to Urban Violence in Lagos, Nigeria* (Ibadan: IFRA/African Book Builders Ltd., 1997).

be of research interest to find out why the metropolis has not completely descended into a permanent state of chaos, illegal squatting, interpersonal-cum-inter-group strife, and blight. The now long-standing prediction that Lagos is about to implode as a result of its explosive growth seems to be blocking creative and critical assessment of where Lagos is, has been, and is heading.

This paper therefore interrogates the development and problems of Lagos through the lens of a deeply "doubly involved" social demographer. The claim to being a Lagosian derives from the fact of having resided in Lagos for most of the time since 1976, living in Isolo within the middle belt of the metropolis for four years, Ojota/Ogudu to the northeast for thirteen years, Shangisha/Magodo also to the northeast for four years, Yaba/Alagomeji to the east for two years, and finally Lekki/Ajah to the extreme southeast since January 1, 2000. This experiential knowledge of the city, together with my involvement in a series of sustained social scientific investigations of its growth and environmental problems undertaken during the mid-1990s and my continuing interest in investigating Lagos as a socio-demographic phenomenon, informs the rather arrogant claim to being an informed Lagosian. But social science is always hugely enriched by history, even recent history, especially if the quest is to understand patterns in the collective and entrepreneurial activities of a mass of people spread across space and time, as is the case in Lagos, with its poor, suffering but undaunted majority.

The rest of the paper draws on an inter-mixture of autobiography and conventional urban research evidence to: (1) provide a balanced reading of the metropolitanization of Lagos by giving greater visibility to the role of the poor majority in shaping the boundaries and population distribution of the city; (2) briefly discuss the scale and severity of some of the key problems of Lagos in relation to its exceptional rate of urbanization and the grossly inadequate expansion of formal employment opportunities, infrastructure, and services; and (3) examine the contributions of "everyday" Lagos residents to the prevention of environmental collapse and to the governability of Lagos. Done this way, the paper is able to conclude that properly harnessed, the productive, civic engagement, and sustainable livelihood activities of the urban majority can provide the basis for the transformation of Lagos into a more liveable and environmentally stable metropolis.

I. The Metropolitanization of Lagos: The Conventional and the Complete Story

The Standard Account of the Development of the Lagos Metropolitan Area There is general agreement among scholars and informed observers that the demographic growth and spatial expansion of Lagos has by all standards been spectacular.[2] In 1910, Lagos was limited to an area less than five square kilometers and inhabited by fewer than 50,000 persons. By the year 2000, it had grown both spatially and in population size by more than a factor of 100. Today, metropolitan Lagos, which encompasses less than 2.5 percent of Nigeria's land area of 923,768 square kilometers, accommodates at least 8 percent of Nigeria's total population of around 115 million. Relatedly, the population density of Lagos city 40 years ago is about 45 percent less than that of the urban sprawl of contemporary Lagos, which averages 8–10,000 persons per square kilometer, but reaches over 20,000 persons per square kilometer in several neighborhoods. This transformation is generally explained by the fact that the population has grown at a much faster rate than the land area, with in-migration estimated as contributing about 65 percent.

The resultant process of metropolitanization has been marked (especially since the early 1970s) by two trends: (a) increasing population density within existing built-up areas, and (b) population expansion into new land areas via the progressive incorporation of neighboring towns and outlying rural settlements – many of the latter had a long history of independent existence before becoming part of metropolitan Lagos. One obvious consequence has been the precipitously declining share of the Island areas in the population distribution (see panel 3 of Table 1). At least 90 percent of the population of contemporary Lagos resides outside these areas, which viewed together may be referred to as *Old Lagos* or *The Municipality*.

A close examination of Figure 1 showing the map of Greater Lagos around 1975 and around the year 2000 (with the latter being on a scale that is about half of the former) brings out vividly the exceptional rapidity of its metropolitanization. In twenty-five years, Lagos has so expanded horizontally, especially westward and northeastward, that it has at least tripled in areal extent and in density of active, fully built-up neighborhoods. Such a rapid spatial expansion and associated population growth and redistribution inevitably has far-reaching implications for the environment, economy, and society. It is a point that must be stressed and re-stressed in any discourse on Lagos.

Indeed, of the eight divisions into which Lagos State was once divided, only two fell within the municipality four decades ago, whereas today, only Epe and

---

2 See, e.g. Dele Olowu, *Lagos State: Governance, Society and Economy* (Lagos and Oxford: Malthouse Press, 1990); Tade Akin Aina, Florence E. Etta, and Cyril I. Obi, "The Search for Sustainable Urban Development in Metropolitan Lagos," *Third World Planning Review* 16, no. 2 (1994), pp. 201–219; Babatunde A. Ahonsi, "Population Growth, Urbanization and the Environment in Metropolitan Lagos," background paper for *The Environmental Problems of Lagos Project: 1993–'95* (Lagos: The Lagos Group for the Study of Human Settlements, 1995); Kunle Lawal, ed., *Urban Transition in Africa: Aspects of Urbanization and Change in Lagos* (Lagos: Pumark Nigeria, 1994).

Greater Lagos, circa 1975 (After A. L. Mabogunje, *Cities and African Development,* Ibadan: Oxford University Press, 1976)

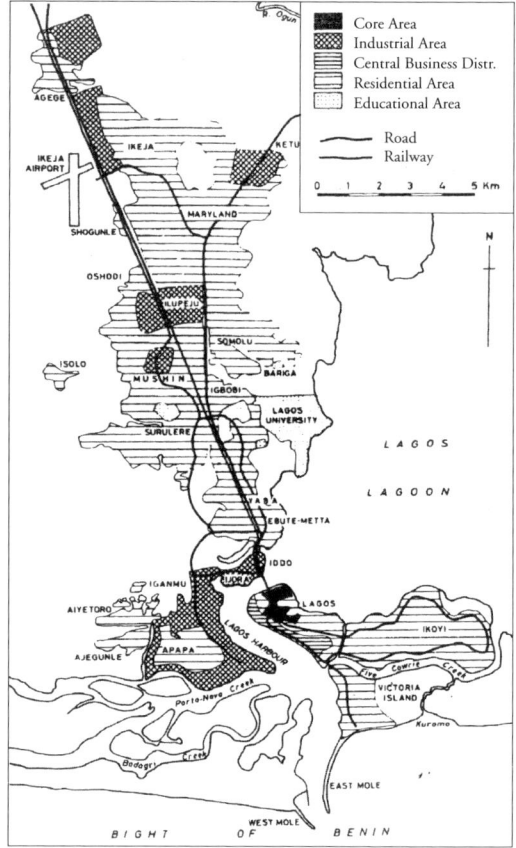

Greater Lagos, circa 2000 (After J. A. Babarinde, "Industrial Migration and Residential Relocation Decisions in Metropolitan Lagos," unpublished Ph.D. diss., University of Ibadan, 1995)

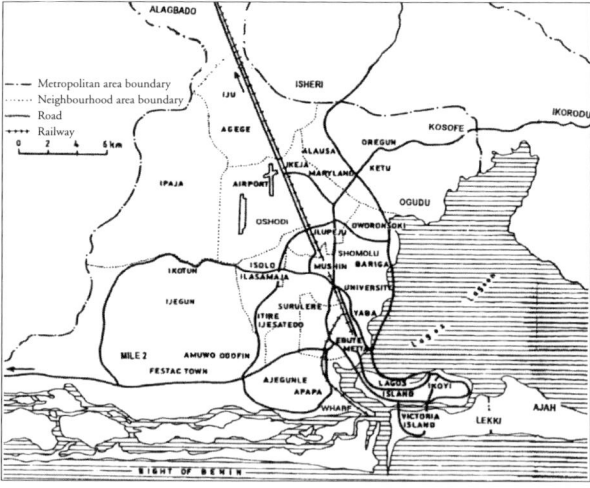

Figure 1. Metropolitanization of Lagos, circa 1975 and 2000

Badagry have some stretches of land that could be described as rural and lying outside the metropolis. Its metropolitanization has advanced so far that, following the classification by Olowu,[3] we can neatly divide contemporary Lagos into three distinct zones. These are (a) *the Municipality*, consisting of an area of 70 square kilometers and made up of Lagos Island, Ikoyi, Victoria Island, Iddo, and closely contiguous parts of the Mainland; here, there is virtually no remaining space for development although wetland conversions of swamps and filling of the lagoons have created new government-controlled settlements in Ikoyi and beyond Victoria Island in Lekki; (b) *the Inner Metropolitan Zone*, which consists of most of the continuously built-up parts of the Lagos Mainland including such areas as Mushin, Somolu, Ilupeju, Surulere, Oshodi, and Ikeja; again, extensive in-filling of depressions and land reclamation constitute the main processes of settlement formation therein; and (c) *the Outer Metropolitan Zone*, which consists of more distant centers of the metropolitan economy such as Agege, Ketu, Ojo, Ipaja, and Ajah as well as the fast industrializing towns in nearby Ogun State, namely Sango-Ota, Ota, and Agbara.

In terms of periodization, the key observation is that after the steady though somewhat uneven growth and expansion of Lagos up to the time of independence in 1960, the data (even after adjusting for gaps and quality problems) indicate that the population of Lagos doubled between around 1965 and 1975, and doubled again between 1975 and 1985. The rate of growth then declined to slightly below 5 percent per annum by the early 1990s after the city had already exceeded a population of 5 million. Indeed, it is noteworthy that whereas Lagos was only one of many medium-sized Yoruba towns up to the mid-1960s,[4] it was by the late 1990s the only urban center in West Africa that, by virtue of its population size, areal extent, and the cosmopolitan composition of many of its neighborhoods, qualified to be called a mega-city. There is perhaps no adult Nigerian today who has never visited or lived in Lagos or who has no close ties with a resident of Lagos. Current fertility and in-migration indices, however, suggest that although the population of Lagos will continue to grow for at least another twenty-five years, this would be at increasingly slower rates.

The unmanageability of the exceptional spatio-demographic transformation of Lagos is clearly revealed in the concomitant escalation of its housing, solid waste, and poverty problems as summarized in Table 1. The data indicate, for example, that the city's housing situation has worsened by more than tenfold since the early 1960s, while the proportion of residents living below the poverty line has tripled within the same period.

---

3 Olowu, *Lagos State: Governance, Society and Economy*.
4 Margaret Peil, *Lagos: The City Is the People* (London: Belhaven Press, 1991).

Table 1. Aspects of the Demography, Economy, and Environment of Urban Lagos, circa 1960–2000

Aspect	ca. 1960	ca. 1980	ca. 2000
Population size (in millions)	0.7	3.5	10.5
% Net migrants	56	65	88
% Resident on mainland	38	80	90
% National industrial employment	20	53	60
Incidence of poverty[a]	10	20	35
Housing stock deficit[b] (in millions)	0.1	0.7	1.2
Solid waste generated[c] (in '000 tonnes per week)	5	17	54
Actual land area[d] (in '000 hectares)	12	23	35

Sources: Indicative estimates drawn from various sources and based on numerous assumptions and statistical techniques especially in Ahonsi, Ayeni, Akintola-Arikawe, Olaore, Odumosu, Peil, NPC, and Odunaiya and Ugbe.[5]

a Indicative estimates based on national consumer, employment, and income survey data as analyzed by the World Bank.[6] The poverty line is set at N395 per person per annum at 1985 prices.
b Indicative of new dwelling units needed to absorb the poorly housed and unaccommodated population of Lagos during the relevant period given prevailing building efforts, estimated number of households, an average household size of 4–5, the estimated annual population growth rate of 5–6 percent, previous deficits in housing supply, and rate of physical deterioration of existing housing stock.
c Based on survey data indicating per capita generation of 0.5–1.0 kg per day; note that "000" refers to "in thousands."
d Refers to the actually developed land out of the estimated 47,000 hectares available for development.

5 Ahonsi, "Population Growth, Urbanization and the Environment in Metropolitan Lagos"; Bola Ayeni, "The Growth and Development of Metropolitan Lagos," paper prepared for a Seminar on *The Effect on Lagos of the Movement of the Federal Capital to Abuja* (November 21–22, 1991, Lagos); J. Olafioye Akintola-Arikawe, "The Rise of Industrialism in the Lagos Area," in *A History of the Peoples of Lagos State*, ed. Ade Adefuye, Babatunde Agiri, and Jide Osuntokun (Lagos: Lantern Books, 1987); G. O. Olaore, "Population Growth and Environmental Pollution," in *Population and Development in Nigeria*, ed. Israel O. Orubuloye and Olatunji Y. Oyeneye (Ibadan: Nigerian Institute of Social and Economic Research, 1983); Tayo Odumosu, "Housing and Land Use in Lagos State," in *Urban Transition in Africa*, ed. Lawal; Peil, *Lagos: The City Is the People*; National Population Commission, *1991 Population Census of the Federal Republic of Nigeria – Analytical Report at the National Level* (Abuja: NPC, 1998); and C. Odunaiya and U. Ugbe, *Participatory Rapid Assessment of Waste Management and Communities in Lagos: A Report Prepared for Development Initiatives Network* (Lagos, 2000).

In terms of explanation, the following factors, which are all acknowledged to have been mutually reinforcing, feature prominently in the urban research literature:

(1) The historical advantages that Lagos has enjoyed as a natural harbor within a colonial economy oriented to serving the raw materials needs of the British industrial economy, and its reinforcement by the postindependence import-substitution industrialization strategy. The pull of Lagos is presented as being clearly linked to the fact that Nigeria's air, road, and rail transport networks have been built to revolve around Lagos, which in turn ensured that it became the commercial and industrial nerve center of Nigeria. Lagos remains the single most important location of job opportunities and social amenities, and, until 1991, the locus of state power and its numerous attendant benefits.

(2) The construction of major railway lines, roads, and bridges which accelerated the integration of hitherto autonomous nearby towns and villages into the metropolis. In the post-1970 era, the construction of the Ikorodu Road, the Third Mainland bridge, and the Lagos-Badagry, Victoria Island–Epe, and Lagos-Abeokuta highways (financed largely from crude oil export earnings) have been widely noted to have sped up the metropolitanization of Lagos.

(3) The pressure of human numbers on the built-up areas in the context of the economic boom (1967–79) and bust (mid-1980s–late 1990s) effects (including the impact of the structural adjustment program) on land values and associated land use patterns. The emphasis is on how the identified economic trends have tended to squeeze more and more of the poor majority into outlying areas; and

(4) Federal and state government policies, strategies, and programs on land acquisition, land use regulation or zoning, infrastructure, and housing development have also helped to shape the dynamics of metropolitanization in Lagos. For example, dating back to the colonial period, the central government's land reclamation schemes have helped the core Island areas (the Municipality) and its periphery to absorb increasing population as well as reduce the physical gulf between it and the rest of the metropolis (that is, the mainland areas).

---

6 World Bank, *Nigeria: Poverty in the Midst of Plenty – The Challenge of Growth with Inclusion* (Washington, D.C.: World Bank, 1996).

The Missing Piece: The Poor as "Pioneers" in the Metropolitan Process   In much of the analysis summarized above, it has been difficult searching for the real human beings in the metropolitanization process and their place in it as agents, not just as beneficiaries or passive victims, as many scholars tend to imply. A resort to some autobiography, as a way of looking at the recent history of Lagos, therefore becomes necessary at this point.

In the mid-1970s, as an adolescent, I experienced Isolo and it was presented to me as being limited to the area around the palace of the traditional ruler (the Osolo of Isolo) as well as the main thoroughfare, Aina Street. Nearby settlements such as Oke-Afa, Egbe, and Ejigbo were viewed by Isolo's middle-class residents as havens for criminals and social misfits. In reality, these areas accommodated hundreds and, fairly soon, thousands of recent migrants. Some of them farmed lands leased from customary owners as well as land speculators, whose real interest was in securing their possession or ownership of these assets. For many others, these settlements were the locus of their productive activities as artisans and small-scale entrepreneurs, and for some others it was both home and place of work. Many therefore engaged in land clearing, various land improvement activities, and progressive housing development. By the mid-1980s, the foundational settlement activities of the mass of the early residents had pushed up the value of land throughout Isolo area. Its extensions consequently became progressively dissociated from criminality and marginality.

As an increasing number of the oil boom–created middle-income earners moved into these hitherto fringe neighborhoods, state-funded road, infrastructural, and housing developments and greater investments by the organized private sector followed. Consequently, the neighborhoods not only became fully absorbed into an expanded Isolo but transformed in status from being wholly blighted to differentiated neighborhoods with significant presence of middle/high-income earners and associated living conditions. In the interim, some of the poor early settlers were squeezed into small islands of deprivation and squalor, while most have become part of new urban frontier extension processes joined by more recent migrants.

The foregoing brief personal account on Isolo's development during the mid-1970s to the mid-1980s can be repeated for Ojota in relation to Ogudu during the early 1980s to the early 1990s based on my experience and observations as a resident there for much of this period. Such stories would also, in all likelihood, be told of many other neighborhoods by witnesses to their growth, including old Ikeja (the capital of Lagos state) in relation to such extensions as Opebi, Agidingbi, and Alausa. In fact, a similar interpretation can be made of the state coercion-aided extension of Victoria Island into Maroko, which forcibly displaced over 300,000 poor people in 1990.[7] This is made easier if we remember that although many people in Maroko lived in squalor, the larger community was made quite habitable through self-help initiatives and social amenities established by the government, including two banks, a public library, a police station, an area office for the Eti-Osa Local Government, eight primary schools, a secondary school, and 15,000 residential buildings. Today, the land once occupied by the Maroko community which was later parceled out to high-ranking military officers and private developers features huge mansions, an elite secondary school, and business offices, while less than 5 percent of former Maroko residents were resettled.

The point about the transformation of the social and economic status of hitherto marginal settlements into broadly middle-class, medium-density neighborhoods is brought out clearly via a reflective long-standing resident's examination and interpretation of Table 2. The table shows 42 settlements across the Lagos metropolis which were classified by the early 1980s by the Lagos state government as *blighted* on account of having the following features (among others):

- Flooding area / Environmental pollution
- Dirty environment / Uncontrolled waste
- Overcrowded area / Overcrowded househoulds
- Squatted area / Unauthorized construction
- Low-income people / Poor or bad building conditions
- Poor building materials / No ventilation space between buildings
- Unplanned road network / Traffic congestion / Difficult access
- No health clinics / Insufficient schools / No police station

The interesting observation to make is that these settlements as of 1980/81 were overwhelmingly the residential and work locations for the mass of recent migrants and the long-resident poor. Twenty years later, and partly because of the pioneering role of the poor majority in the transformation of these parts of the growing metropolis, several of these settlements would no longer qualify to be described as blighted. In fact, if the present writer's observational assessments are correct, at least one-fifth of the 42 settlements that were considered *blighted* during the early 1980s no longer qualified to be so described by the year 2000.

---

7 T. Akin Aina and O. Taiwo, "Public-Private Inputs into the Provision of Urban Facilities in Low Income Settlements: The Case of Metropolitan Lagos," *NAGARLOK: Journal of the Indian Institute of Public Administration* 32, no. 4 (1990), pp. 25–38; SERAC, *Expendable People: An Exploratory Report on Planned Forced Evictions in Lagos* (Lagos: Social and Economic Rights Action Centre, 1997).

Table 2. Increasing Differentiation in the *Blightedness* of Settlements in the Lagos Area

Column headers (left to right after Total Rating):
1. Unplanned area
2. Not in line regional plan
3. Uncontrolled land use
4. Squatted area
5. Unlandscaped
6. No trees
7. Flooding area
8. Environmental pollution
9. Dirty environment
10. Overcrowded area
11. Low-income people
12. Overcrowded households
13. No pipewater
14. No public taps
15. No sewer system
16. Roads – no drainage
17. No electricity
18. Uncontrolled waste
19. No public toilets
20. Bad roads
21. Unplanned road network
22. Difficult access
23. Traffic congestion
24. No sidewalks
25. Parking problems
26. Insufficient schools
27. No health clinics
28. No post office
29. No police station
30. Insufficient recreational facilities
31. Unplanned markets
32. Poor building conditions
33. No ventilation space between buildings
34. Insufficient setbacks
35. Unauthorized construction
36. Poor building materials

#	Settlement	Total Rating
1	Iju	21
2	Apapa	18
3	Orile-Agege	22
4	Agege	27
? 5	Ogba West	23
? 6	Agidingbi	26
? 7	Alausa Village	25
? 8	Oregun	23
9	Olushosun	23
10	Ipodo Area – Ikeja	29
? 11	Shogunle	25
? 12	Onigbongbo	20
13	Oshodi Mkt. Area	21
14	Egbe/Bolohun-Pelu	20
15	Iwaya	29
? 16	Abule-Ijesha	29
17	Makoko	30
18	3rd M/L Bridge-Oyingbo	25
19	Otto	28
20	Ilaje	30
21	Ijora Oloye	30
22	Sari-Iganmu	27
23	Amukoko	27
24	Ajegunle	28
25	Marine Beach	10
26	Obalende	13
27	Badia	30
28	Maroko	32
29	Idi-Araba/Mushin	26
30	Ijeshatedo-Itire	23
31	Lawanson-Ikate	21
32	Aiyetoro	25
33	Ali Oromoko Village	23
34	Shomolu	23
35	Bariga	23
? 36	Oworonsoki	23
? 37	Ogudu	20
38	Mile 12 Mkt. Area	22
39	Lagos Island	25
40	Olaleye-Iponri	31
41	Ikorodu	22
42	Ejigbo	22

Source: Unpublished survey, Department of Urban Renewal, Lagos State Ministry of Economic Planning and Land Matters, 1982. As cited in Aina et al., "The Search for Sustainable Urban Development in Metropolitan Lagos," p. 217.

Note: "?" indicates settlements that by 2002 *no longer* qualify to be classified as *blighted* according to the author's assessment of the quality of housing stock, the socioeconomic status of the majority of residents, and the presence of urban infrastructure, public utilities, and health/educational institutions.

Also noteworthy is the tendency for the "newer" areas of these now differentiated settlements, inhabited almost exclusively by poor recent migrants two decades ago, to become the abode of middle/high-income groups.

The Complete Story   The account provided in the preceding section suggests to us that an analysis of the development of Lagos as a metropolis and the associated problems would be incomplete without sufficient attention to the active role of the mass of people that helped and still helps to define the form and content of Lagos spatially, economically, and environmentally. Metropolitanization has demographic, structural, and behavioral dimensions. But the interconnections between them only become clear and meaningful when the activities and everyday situations of the majority of the human actors within the process are brought into focus. The lesson here is that urbanists must take due account of the *new frontiers* and the foundational and reconstructive role of the poor majority of residents in any interpretation of the rapid growth of Lagos into a mega-city and the associated problems.

II. The Problems Associated with the Rapid Metropolitanization of Lagos

The scale, range, and severity of the problems of contemporary Lagos are largely a consequence of the speed with which the city grew, which perhaps was inevitable given the interaction of history, geography, and politics. The list is long: housing shortage, environmental pollution, high incidence of crime and organized violence, transportation crisis, flooding, unemployment, etc., etc. But at the heart of these problems is weak macroeconomic performance, which makes it particularly difficult to finance the development and maintenance of urban infrastructure and services, as well as urban policy design and implementation failures, which compound the effects of a feeble economy.[8]

Metropolitanization without Sustained Economic Growth: Effects and Responses

Lagos acquired the status of a genuine mega-city at about the same time that Nigeria was beginning her fast-track transition from a lower-middle-income country (with GDP per capita of over $1,000) by the mid to late 1970s, to one of the world's poorest countries with a GDP per capita of less than $300 by the

---

8 Ahonsi, "Population Growth, Urbanization and the Environment in Metropolitan Lagos"; World Bank, *Restoring Urban Nigeria: A Strategy for Restoring Urban Infrastructure and Services in Nigeria* (Washington, D.C.: World Bank, 1995).

year 2000. Among the particularly threatening fallouts of this situation are widespread unemployment, an urban transport crisis, a crippling housing shortage, huge waste-management problems, and a grossly ill-equipped local urban administration. Indeed, the costs of ensuring acceptable standards of environmental management and urban services provision have clearly been beyond the resources of the state and local governments.

Moreover, it is the case that official responses to the national economic crisis via structural adjustment has worsened the breadth and depth of poverty among the residents of Lagos, with the incidence of relative poverty in the city roughly doubling from 17 percent in 1980 to over 30 percent by the late 1990s.[9] But one way that the poor majority has responded to these adverse trends has been to devise more creative ways of coping with and transcending the challenges posed by metropolitanization without economic expansion. This is best observed in the ongoing growth and differentiation of micro-enterpreneurship within the metropolitan economy.[10] Indeed, it is quite clear that with the imposition of structural adjustment, the metropolitan informal economy has greatly expanded, perhaps increasing by 20 percent to about 70 percent of the workforce between 1980 and the late 1990s.[11] This is in line with the argument that among the four categories of the poor across urban Nigeria, that is, the entrepreneurial poor, the self-employed poor, the laboring poor, and the vulnerable poor, the fastest growing sub-group throughout the 1990s was the entrepreneurial poor. This sub-group is estimated to have grown by 61 percent between 1992 and 1999 in the context of rising urban poverty levels.[12]

Evidence abounds of the increasing absorption of school leavers, university graduates, and retrenched public- and private-sector middle-level workers into the informal economy. And their absorption is not just into the traditional petty trading and artisanal activities, but increasingly into more value-creating and employment-generating lines of productive and commercial activities like printing, waste recycling, transportation, security service provision, secretarial and information technology services, and cottage industrial production. There is also some evidence of the increasing cooperativization of the sector as a strategy for raising additional capital and extending access to middle-to-high ends of the

---

9 Economic Policy Coordinating Committee, Office of the Vice-President, *Federal Republic of Nigeria: Interim Poverty Reduction Strategy Paper* (Abuja: EPCC, 2001).

10 Olanrewaju J. Fapohunda, *The Informal Sector of Lagos: An Inquiry into Urban Poverty and Employment* (Ibadan: University Press Limited, 1985); Seed Capital Development Fund, *Nigeria: Nascent Hope After a Generation of Decline* (Washington, D.C.: SCDF, 2000).

11 Kate Meagher and Mohammed-Bello Yunusa, *Passing the Buck: Structural Adjustment and the Nigerian Urban Informal Sector*, Discussion Paper 75 (Geneva: UNRISD, 1996).

12 SCDF, *Nigeria*.

market.¹³ However, state response to the challenge of growing this sector through credit, export market exploration, training, and technical support has been neither coordinated nor sustained. In fact, many operators within the sector report that they experience only harassment and sanctions from public officials in government's poor attempts at regularizing and formalizing the sector.¹⁴

The Urban Management Challenge Three obstacles bedevil official responses in terms of the management of the problems associated with the rapid metropolitanization of Lagos. These are:

(1) The lack of coordination (and conflicts over statutory responsibilities) between the three tiers of government, especially since the seat of the federal government moved to Abuja. This is illustrated by the frequent occurrence of disagreements between the federal government and the Lagos state government during the late 1990s about primary responsibility for the maintenance of so-called federal roads in Lagos, which resulted in most of them falling into a state of utter disrepair. The same problem has also been shown to be affecting the collection and disposal of solid waste.¹⁵ This is particularly so as regards the division of responsibilities for the control of industrial waste from cottage factories between the state and local government in Lagos.¹⁶ Even for waste from industrial and commercial firms, which is mostly dumped wherever convenient, the lack of coordination between the Federal Environmental Protection Agency, the Lagos State Waste Management Authority, and the local councils may be exacerbating the situation.¹⁷ A related dimension to this administrative quagmire is the lack of collaboration and functional interdependence between agencies providing related services, for example, the water utility, sanitation management, and traffic control agencies in relation to waste disposal.

---

13 Odunaiya and Ugbe, *Participatory Rapid Assessment of Waste Management and Communities in Lagos*; SCDF, *Nigeria*.
14 F. O. N. Roberts, "Garbage Crisis and Federalism in Nigeria: The Political Economy of Environmental Sanitation in Lagos State," *Annals of the Social Science Council of Nigeria*, no. 5 (1993), pp. 85–109; Ahonsi, "Population Growth, Urbanization and the Environment in Metropolitan Lagos"; Odunaiya and Ugbe, *Participatory Rapid Assessment of Waste Management and Communities in Lagos*.
15 Roberts, "Garbage Crisis and Federalism in Nigeria."
16 Odunaiya and Ugbe, *Participatory Rapid Assessment of Waste Management and Communities in Lagos*.
17 See relevant contributions in Pius O. Sada and F. O. Odemerho, eds., *Environmental Issues and Management in Nigerian Development* (Ibadan: Evans Brothers Publishers, 1988).

(2) The unhealthily top-down urban policy development and implementation in Lagos. For example, despite the knowledge that the huge urban housing problem of Nigeria cannot be solved by the federal and state governments building and delivering houses to the needy, this approach has remained dominant since the 1970s. Targets always turn out to be grossly ambitious and the houses often end up being too expensive and/or poorly located to be accessible and attractive to the poor.[18] In fact, the mass housing construction and delivery programs embarked upon between 1970 and the late 1990s by the two tiers of government all achieved success rates of less than 20 percent, with the rate for the Lagos metropolis being always lower at around 10–13 percent.[19]

Furthermore, the completed houses inevitably turn out to be unaffordable to the low income and lower-to-middle income groups for which they were planned due mainly to cost overruns associated with construction delays, hyperinflation, and reliance on high-import-content building materials. Margaret Peil cites the example of a middle-income housing estate in Ebute-Metta built in the late 1980s which ended up being offered at N140,000 for a three-bedroom flat at a time that the middle-income level was less than N20,000 per year.[20] Similarly, in 2002, the Lagos state government is offering dwelling units for sale which range in price from N2.8 million for a two-bedroom flat to N15.5 million for a four-bedroom terrace house.[21] This is in a context of a practically nonexistent mortgage finance sector and average annual household income of less than N30,000. Cooperative housing and upgrading of residential buildings of the poor which require partnership with the local organizations of poor people continue to be ignored in planning for and responding to the acute housing problem of the Lagos metropolis. The same point applies to the collection of waste through a central authority when many urban neighborhoods cannot be accessed by conventional waste collection trucks.

(3) The problem of technical and managerial capacity within the public sector for dealing with such problems as flooding, industrial waste manage-

---

18 Aina and Taiwo, "Public-Private Inputs into the Provision of Urban Facilities in Low Income Settlements"; Remi Adeyemo, *Access to Shelter by the Poor through Community Participation*, IFRA Occasional Publication No. 3 (Ibadan: French Institute for Research in Africa, 1994).
19 See also B. O. Achunine, "Housing and Urban Development," in *Nigeria: The First 25 Years*, ed. Uma Eleazu (Ibadan: Heinemann Educational Books, 1988), pp. 145–157.
20 Peil, *Lagos: The City Is the People*.
21 *The Guardian* (Lagos), Monday, February 18, 2002, p. 53.

ment, transport administration, financial management, and crime prevention/control has also been alluded to by many scholars.[22] This problem is further compounded by high turnover in the leadership of urban administration units and conflicting policy guidelines on such matters as transport and waste management.[23] For example, despite the progressive commercialization of its services since 1991, the Lagos State Waste Management Authority's operations have not improved significantly. It continues to suffer from internal inefficiencies associated with inadequate controls over stores and finances, suboptimal cost-recovery performance, and paucity of skilled technicians. The result is that less than 50 percent of its equipment is operational and it is only able to collect one-third of the metropolitan area's waste.[24]

III. Popular Engagement with the Challenges of Metropolitanization in Lagos: Two Examples

As suggested earlier, the poor majority's role in shaping the metropolitanization of Lagos has been two-sided. On the one hand, they have, as demonstrated above, driven the areal extension and population redistribution within the evolving metropolis in direct and significant ways. But on the other hand, they have also responded creatively to the challenges thrown up by the rapid growth of Lagos in ways that provide pointers to some opportunities that could be harnessed in planning and executing interventions for making the metropolis a more functional and hospitable city. We now turn to two case studies that help to substantiate the second point.

The Refuse Problem Example: Lessons from Lagos Dumpsites Given the population growth and land use patterns prevalent in Lagos, I have often wondered as a resident with a pair of demographic lenses why the refuse problem of Lagos is not worse than it is currently. This curiosity led me to dumpsites and their surrounding communities during the 1990s where I learned a lot about the various stakeholders in the waste collection, recycling, processing, and disposal chain as well as the opportunities that exist for wealth creation and environmental pro-

---

22 See e.g. Sada and Odemerho, eds., *Environmental Issues and Management in Nigerian Development*; Adebayo Adedeji and L. Rowland, eds., *Management Problems of Rapid Urbanisation in Nigeria* (Ile-Ife: University of Ife Press, 1973).
23 World Bank, *Restoring Urban Nigeria*.
24 Roberts, "Garbage Crisis and Federalism in Nigeria"; World Bank, *Restoring Urban Nigeria*.

tection through a poor people–centered approach to solid waste management in Lagos. This experience prompted my participation in a rapid assessment study on waste management and communities in Lagos, conducted in 2000.

The study led by Odunaiya and Ugbe entailed the use of individual interview schedules, in-depth discussion guides, site visit inventories, and site visit photography to elicit data on the practices and perspectives of a wide range of stakeholders in waste management in Lagos.[25] The focus was on the three official dumpsites, all on the mainland, that is, in Abule-Egba to the northwest, Olusosun (Ojota) in the north-central part of the metropolis, and Iyana-Ipaja, to the west-central axis. Interviewees included waste managers within the relevant Lagos state governmental agencies (the Ministry of Environment and Physical Planning, the Waste Management Authority – LAWMA – and the state Environmental Protection Agency), waste generators (residential/domestic, market areas/commercial, and industrial), waste collectors (cart pushers, government-appointed private-sector contracts, and LAWMA), waste processors, dumpsite neighborhood communities (voluntary settlers and others), and dumpsite service providers (scavengers, food sellers, and others). Some of the salient findings were:

(1) LAWMA has no facilities whatsoever for waste treatment at the dumpsites under its management and none of the local government authorities have a defined department with sole responsibility for waste management.
(2) Scavengers turn out in large numbers to sort and collect various items at dumpsites and are unwilling to quit the job because it is more financially rewarding than a salaried job. They sell their products to small-scale itinerant buyers on a cash-and-carry basis, and the latter in turn sell to the bigger buyers, usually waste recycling plant operators. But their livelihoods have become threatened by the phasing out of transfer loading systems and promotion of sealed bags for waste collection, following the introduction of private-sector participation by the state government.
(3) A huge amount of waste is sorted and processed daily at the dumpsites. The prominent items collected include used cartons, paper, plastics (except thermoses), metals, cans, bottles and broken glasses, disused tires, textiles, and a wide variety of nylons.
(4) The banning of cart pushers has adversely affected the operations of scavengers as it limits the range and size of waste they can collect and

---

25 Odunaiya and Ugbe, *Participatory Rapid Assessment of Waste Management and Communities in Lagos*.

transfer, and with the ban has come more harassment by local government officials.

(5) There is some degree of cooperativization among operators at the dumpsites. Particularly active were associations of scavengers and waste recycling cooperatives. They meet regularly to set negotiation terms, fix prices of their products, and provide social support to members. Some of the older scavengers have apprentices and expressed a strong willingness to work through their association to establish a waste recycling plant so as to reduce their dependence on middlemen and therefore expand their profit margins.

(6) Formal sector industrial and commercial firms routinely purchase waste products originating from the dumpsites such as ground plastic, copper, horns and bones from cow by-products. One plastics manufacturing firm which produces jerry cans, combs, baskets, cloth hangers, and cosmetics jars was observed to be heavily reliant on ground plastic supplied by local plastic grounders who obtain their raw materials from plastic scraps supplied by scavengers operating within the studied dumpsites.

(7) Health and safety risks abound in the waste-to-wealth business, especially injuries from sharp objects and respiratory problems from intense exposure to polluted air and stench.

(8) There are at least seven groups of actors (scavengers, cart pushers, waste sorters/cleaners/packers, suppliers of recyclable materials including waste converters, buyers including waste product exporters, dumpsite service providers like food sellers, and official waste managers) making a living out of the dumpsite-centered waste management chain. Given this multiplicity of stakeholders, a holistic approach is required to better handle the problem of waste management at Lagos dumpsites.

(9) Opportunities exist via partnership between government, the private sector, and scavenger/scrap collectors, waste processing, and recycling groups for scaling up waste-to-wealth businesses via capital injection, skills training, and simple machine procurement to process more waste and create more wealth out of waste. This can and should be a key weapon in the management of metropolitan Lagos given its very poor solid waste and unemployment situation.

Urban Local Governance: Insights from Two Poor Neighborhoods The literature on urban development in Africa clearly acknowledges the role of community organizations formed or dominated by residents of low-income settlements in the economic and social development of cities. The point is frequently made that the urban poor routinely intervene to compensate for the failure of formal governance structures to deliver services and provisions that meet their employment, land ownership, housing, health, and environmental protection needs. The reasons for this situation include increasing state withdrawal from the provision of social infrastructure and services associated with Africa's long-running economic crisis; the distance, policy indifference, and sometimes outright hostility of central and provincial governments to poor urban settlements; as well as the huge capacity deficits of municipal administrations across much of urban Africa.[26] This situation is however sometimes discussed in ways that seem to imply that the urban poor play a rather inconsequential role in urban politics, especially vis-à-vis their engagement with decision-making processes. Indeed, many studies of popular initiatives in Nigerian towns and cities essentially present poor people's community organizations as moderately effective vehicles for welfare provisioning, social development, and poverty alleviation.[27]

But if we adopt a less formalistic definition of politics as being about *who gets what, where, and when*, a different interpretation of the role of poor people's community-based organizations (CBOs) in urban political processes would begin to emerge. Central to city politics in this context is the issue of governance, defined as:

> relations between the state and other institutions, including private business and civil society. It represents the relationship between the government and the governed, encompassing issues of accountability and empowerment, particularly of those normally marginalized. … Governance can be defined as the means and processes through which a city … fulfils its functions effectively.[28]

Indeed, the data and insights that the present writer became familiar with as a member and later convenor of the Lagos Group for the Study of Human Settlements (LGSHS) from 1992 to 1997 seem to underline the significance of the role of popular initiatives in the relative orderly functioning of metropolitan

---

26 See, for example, various contributions in Arne Tostensen, Inge Tvedten, and Mariken Vaa, eds., *Associational Life in African Cities: Popular Responses to the Urban Crisis* (Uppsala: Nordiska Afrikainstitutet, 2001); Aina and Taiwo, "Public-Private Inputs into the Provision of Urban Facilities in Low Income Settlements"; African NGO Habitat II Caucus, *Citizenship and Urban Development in Africa: Popular Cities for Their Inhabitants* (Dakar: ENDA-ECOPOP, 1996).

27 Victor A. O. Adetula, *Welfare Associations and the Dynamics of City Politics in Nigeria: Jos Metropolis as a Case Study*, A Research Proposal submitted to the Multinational Working Group on Urban Processes and Change in Africa of the Council for the Development of Social Science Research in Africa (Dakar: CODESRIA, 1999); Adepoju G. Onibokun and Adetoye Faniran, *Community-Based Organizations in Nigerian Urban Centres: A Critical Evaluation of Their Achievements and Problems as Agents of Development* (Ibadan: Center for African Settlement Studies and Development, 1995); Tade Akin Aina, *Health, Habitat and Underdevelopment in Nigeria with Special Refer-*

Lagos despite the prevalence of all the ingredients required for it to be in a permanent state of social disorder, communal feuds, and inter-group conflict.

The LGSHS is a collective of sociologists, geographers, educators, economists, historians, and demographers founded at the beginning of the 1990s by academics based within higher education institutions in the Lagos metropolitan area. It works to promote greater understanding and the adoption of sustainable solutions to the key human settlement problems of the Lagos metropolis through research and technical assistance to CBOs struggling to overcome environmental and livelihood problems within their low-income unplanned settlements. The focus of much of its research and action work between 1990 and 1997 were six of the most blighted settlements in Lagos – Badia, Oluwa community in Ajegunle, Iwaya, Makoko, Olaleye-Iponri, and Wasimi. The research findings pertaining to the problems and the struggles for sustainable development in four of these settlements have been published in earlier studies.[29] The settlements that have not been highlighted so far are Wasimi and Oluwa community in Ajegunle. Both communities are located on the Lagos mainland – Wasimi to the north-central belt of the metropolis within five kilometers of Ikeja, the state capital, and Oluwa community in Ajegunle, to the southern end of the metropolis, about seven kilometers from the seaport of Apapa. Both are populated overwhelmingly by poor recent migrants and long-settled residents. But while Ajegunle residents are largely factory workers, casual laborers, and self-employed petty traders/artisans (and their families) serving the industrial and seaport sectors in nearby Apapa, Wasimi, being located on marshy land next to Iya-Alaro River, is populated mainly by fishermen, fishery products processors, natural resource–based artisans like basket weavers, and low-level clerical workers employed by establishments in and around Ikeja.

Between 1995 and 1997, the LGSHS conducted eight focus group discussions each, numerous site observational assessments, and many strategic informant interviews in Wasimi and Oluwa with a view to understanding the role of the community development associations (CDAs) in sustainable development struggles and in local governance. Numerous capacity-building workshops were also held for the leaders and select members of the CDAs on basic management

---

  ence to a Low Income Settlement in Metropolitan Lagos (London: International Institute for Environment and Development, 1990).

28 Panos Institute, *Governing Our Cities: Will People Power Work?* (London: Panos Institute, 2000), p. 9.

29 Florence E. Etta, *Gender in Urban Natural Resource Management: An Investigation of a Low Income Settlement in Lagos*, Mazingira Institute Research Report (Nairobi: Mazingira Institute, 1996); Aina and Taiwo, "Public-Private Inputs into the Provision of Urban Facilities in Low Income Settlements"; Aina, Etta, and Obi, "The Search for Sustainable Urban Development in Metropolitan Lagos."

techniques, conflict resolution, lobbying, and project planning and administration. The qualitative research and observational assessments threw up a number of interesting findings regarding the role of CDAs in urban local governance in metropolitan Lagos.

First, the CDAs in Wasimi and Oluwa community were both initiated by landowning early settlers in the late 1960s. But by the mid-1980s, they had fully transformed into officially registered (with the local government), broad-based membership grassroots organizations (having tenants as the majority) with a nonpartisan, nonreligious, not-for-profit, and nonethnic mission to work for the *general upliftment, security, and interests* of their communities. By the early 1990s, both had evolved a two-tier governance structure comprising the general assembly (that is, all dues-paying members), which meets quarterly, and an executive committee (a small group made up of the founding members and other persons elected to represent other interest groups within the community – youth, women, traditional/religious institutions, and vocational groups), which meets every month to assess and ensure the implementation of decisions sanctioned by the general assembly. In both CDAs, women are seriously under-represented, being disadvantaged by the dues-paying basis of membership and the time-demanding nature of their meetings. Nevertheless, as of 1997, Oluwa CDA had four women in its twelve-person executive committee and two women as opposed to four men on a sort of elders' council. Both CDAs also kept financial records and minutes of meetings, and maintained bank accounts. Overall, the LGSHS found in both communities a strong sense of acceptance of the CDA as the legitimate intermediary between the residents and the different tiers of government, powerful private external interests, other communities, and the traditional authority institutions.

Second, as found by Onibokun and Faniran in an extensive 1994 study of indigenous CBOs in towns and cities across the six geopolitical zones of Nigeria (excluding Lagos), the Oluwa and Wasimi CDAs were observed to be vanguards in infrastructural development, environmental services and sanitation improvement, and general socioeconomic progress of their communities.[30] In both places, and in spite of modest success in internally generating financial resources through dues, levies, and fund-raising campaigns, the CDAs successfully paved streets, constructed security gates, routinely cleared and cleaned their surroundings (including dealing with the aftermath of flooding), maintained public water pipes and taps, and devised vigilante security arrangements for dealing with the problem of armed robbery.

---

30 Onibokun and Faniran, *Community-Based Organizations in Nigerian Urban Centres.*

Third, and more striking, were the longer-term solutions that the CDAs had fashioned in response to the major problems of their communities deriving from their peculiar circumstances. In the case of Wasimi community, a portion of its land area had been under threat of acquisition by powerful individual and corporate interests because of its high value linked to its proximity to the state capital and several high-income, low-density residential neighborhoods. Led by its CDA, in the early 1980s the community began a primary and secondary school development project on the stretch of disputed land and attracted media interest to the issue as a way of securing use of the land. Subsequently, despite initial setbacks, including the illegal demolition of some of the structures that had been put up on the site, the state government, in response to lobbying from the CDA and pressure from other voluntary associations external to the community, took over the development of the school, equipped and staffed it, and got it running as a public school. This solution was what the community desired all along. The school provided its children easier access to the public education system, which was and remains tuition-free, and, moreover, it became a *natural barrier* against further incursion into the community's land. In addition, as a result of this experience, the Wasimi CDA was to later collaborate with CDAs of neighboring communities to establish the Maryland Community Bank, which continues to function profitably.

In the case of Oluwa community, on the other hand, the main problem was and remains that of security of lives and property as a result of the high incidence of violent crime, especially armed robbery in the larger Ajegunle area. So serious is the problem that both residents and nonresidents often refer to Ajegunle as the *jungle city*. The CDA's response was to go beyond a conventional vigilante security arrangement by recruiting community youth as paid security guards. These were then given basic security training, routinely provided arms for their night patrols, and worked with the CDA officials to gather information on persons suspected to be planning or engaged in criminal activities. With an unwritten agreement with the local police station to share this information, suspected criminals were regularly arrested, interrogated, and prosecuted when necessary without much fuss. By the second half of the 1990s, the system had developed to a point where police personnel routinely treated as reliable the intelligence data from the Oluwa CDA and tended to act promptly on it. In addition, the community became popular within the larger Ajegunle area as a safe haven, leading to a situation in which many residents of nearby communities resorted to parking their cars within Oluwa community at night in return for a fee in the assurance that their vehicles will not be stolen by armed robbers.

A key inference that has to be drawn from this discussion is that the community organizations of the urban poor do play a sufficiently significant role in local governance to be viewed as the fourth tier of government in Lagos metropolis. Judging by the findings from Wasimi and Oluwa, it can be said that organized efforts by the urban poor to engage with formal governance structures help to make their communities more liveable, secure, and governable. Strategic partnerships with other CBOs seem to have been perfected by the urban poor for leveraging resources for the better functioning of their communities. As observed in the activities of the two CDAs over a period of three years, grassroots organizations of the urban poor in Nigeria constitute a veritable vehicle for urban governance, especially since there are no specific statutory provisions for the administration of urban centers. This is a finding that has not been sufficiently highlighted within the urban research literature on Nigeria when compared to studies on other African cities like Accra, Harare, and Cairo.[31] It may well be that more sustained, extended, and deeper forms of social investigation of poor urban communities are required for the patterns reported here to be uncovered than has been done so far by previous studies.

Conclusion

The purpose of the foregoing discourse has not been to create the impression that life for the majority of Lagos residents is rosy and free of hardship. It is not and has never really been so. The social, economic, and environmental conditions within the metropolis make life for the majority a daily struggle. But the story is not all about coping or not coping in the face of overwhelming forces. As with other socioeconomic groups, the poor majority has and is creatively responding to the challenges of economic livelihood, waste management, asset-building, and local governance. While these efforts could be easily dismissed as being of low value using conventional cost-benefit analysis, they represent, in my opinion, the only genuine building blocks for truly transforming Lagos into a more liveable and manageable metropolis.

Spatio-demographic changes have occurred and are occurring at a pace that far outstrips the ability of government to respond adequately. Given the bleak prospects for economic growth and the weakness of existing urban management structures, Lagos can aspire to functioning sustainably only if the government, working with the organized private sector, actively collaborates with local organizations of the poor majority (that help to organize popular initiatives) on two fronts. First, to ascertain real needs, and second, to judiciously deploy available resources for the sustainable development of the component settlements of

---

31 See, for some examples, Tostensen et al., eds., *Associational Life in African Cities*.

Lagos. It is difficult to imagine how the enormous challenges of Lagos can be effectively addressed without involving and empowering those most affected and who everyday find ways to modify and moderate the impact of the problems.

Closure, Simulation, and "Making Do" in the Contemporary Johannesburg Landscape

Lindsay J. Bremner

In 1988, a student of architecture at the University of the Witwatersrand presented an undergraduate thesis entitled "A new architecture for a new people in a new city – a civic center in a post-apartheid quarter." This title encapsulates what we all naively believed at the time – that the post-apartheid world would be dramatically, radically different from the one in which we lived then and would be represented by new civic monuments.

Let me turn the clock forward to Johannesburg 2002. Will Smith and director Michael Mann have come to town for the South African premier of *Ali*, a gala event attended by the glitterati of the new South Africa, including Nelson Mandela and his daughter Zinzi. Where is it held? In the interiorized Tuscan twilight of our very own world-class casino complex, Montecasino, in the northern suburbs of Johannesburg, now firmly located at the center of the new democratic imagination.

The disjuncture between the undergraduate student's brave new world and Montecasino's simulated one is illustrative of the wholly unanticipated ways in which the apartheid city of Johannesburg has unraveled. It is most certainly different, but not in the ways we thought it would be.

From the late 1970s onward, Johannesburg's economic base,[1] along with its legislative and administrative apparatus, slowly came undone[2] and a new city

---

1 See Herman Pienaar, "Economic Study: Johannesburg/Central Wits," unpublished memo, Johannesburg City Council Urban Strategies Division, 1994; Christian M. Rogerson and Jayne M. Rogerson, "Intra-metropolitan Industrial Change in the Witwatersrand, 1980–1994," *Urban Forum* 8, no. 2 (1997), pp. 195–223. In ways typical of similar cities across the world, Johannesburg's economy has declined since 1980. Its traditional manufacturing base (clothing, printing, textiles, food, fabricated metals) lost activity across all sectors, declining from R3.4 billion in 1980 to R2.5 billion in 1994. At the same time, its financial and government sectors increased (finance from R3.2 to R4.8 billion, government from R0.8 to R1.2) while commercial activity remained stagnant at R3 billion (Pienaar, "Economic Study: Johannesburg/Central Wits").

2 See, for example, Richard Tomlinson, *Urbanisation in Post-apartheid South Africa* (London: Unwin Hyman, 1990); Jennifer Robinson, "Power, Space and the City: Historical Reflections on Apartheid and Post-apartheid Urban Orders," in *The Apartheid City and Beyond: Urbanisation and Social Change in South Africa*, ed. David M. Smith (London: Routledge, 1992); Ivan Turok, *Urban*

emerged. In a tangled network of transforming social and political orders, a stagnating economy, new political, technical, and professional discourses, and a host of unprecedented urban practices, many things have stayed the same,[3] while many things have changed quite fundamentally.

This paper does not claim a comprehensive analysis of these dynamics, which have been covered, in parts, elsewhere.[4] Rather, my aim is to identify and interpret certain socio-spatial figures that have emerged in the landscape of the contemporary city – a juxtaposition of closed spaces and fixed identities, simulated histories and the necessity, for most, of "making do."

My premise follows that of the American geographer Peirce Lewis,[5] that ordinary built landscapes are a reflection of the culture that has produced them, and that interpreting them is not possible from a single disciplinary perspective. Hence my methodology is eclectic, drawing from the fields of landscape studies,[6] cultural studies,[7] and urban studies.[8] From my own discipline, architecture, it acknowledges the growing field of interest and literature in the "architectural everyday" inspired by Henri Lefevbre's work.[9]

Planning in the Transition from Apartheid (Glasgow: University of Strathclyde, Centre for Planning, 1993).

3 As predicted by, for example, Keith S. O. Beavon, "The Post-apartheid City: Hopes, Possibilities, and Harsh Realities," in *The Apartheid City and Beyond*; Robinson, "Power, Space and the City."

4 See, for example, Mark Swilling et al., eds., *Apartheid City in Transition* (Cape Town: Oxford University Press, 1991); Alan Morris, *Bleakness and Light: Inner-city Transition in Hillbrow, Johannesburg* (Johannesburg: Witwatersrand University Press, 1999); The City of Johannesburg Council, *Johannesburg, an African City in Change* (Cape Town: Zebra, 2001).

5 Peirce F. Lewis, "Axioms for Reading the Landscape," in *The Interpretation of Ordinary Landscapes*, ed. Donald W. Meinig (New York: Oxford University Press, 1979).

6 See, for example, John Brinckerhoff Jackson, *Discovering the Vernacular Landscape* (New Haven: Yale University Press, 1984); idem, *A Sense of Place, a Sense of Time* (New Haven: Yale University Press, 1994); Lewis, "Axioms for Reading the Landscape."

7 See, for example, David Harvey, *The Condition of Postmodernity* (Oxford: Blackwell, 1989); Michel de Certeau, *The Practice of Everyday Life*, trans. Steven Rendall (Berkley: University of California Press, 1984); Luce Giard, ed., *The Practice of Everyday Life*, vol. 2, *Living and Cooking*, trans. Timothy J. Tomasik (Minneapolis: University of Minnesota Press, 1998); Sarah Nuttall and Cheryl-Ann Michael, eds., *Senses of Culture* (Oxford: Oxford University Press, 2000); Njabulo Ndebele, "Game Lodges and Leisure Colonists," in *blank——: Architecture, Apartheid and After*, ed. Hilton Judin and Ivan Vladislavic (Rotterdam: NAi, 1998).

8 See, for example, Michael Sorkin, ed., *Variations on a Theme Park: The New American City and the End of Public Space* (New York: Hill and Wang, 1992); Edward W. Soja, *Postmodern Geographies: The Reassertion of Space in Critical Social Theory* (London: Verso, 1989); Joel Garreau, *Edge City: Life on the New Frontier* (New York: Doubleday, 1991).

9 Henri Lefebvre, *The Production of Space*, trans. Donald Nicholson-Smith (Oxford: Blackwell, 1991), and *Critique of Everyday Life*, vol. 1, trans. John Moore (London: Verso, 1991); e.g. Steven Harris and Deborah Berke, eds., *Architecture of the Everyday* (New York: Princeton Architectural Press, 1997); Malcolm Miles, *The Uses of Decoration: Essays in the Architectural Everyday* (Chichester: Wiley, 2000).

Absa Head Office, downtown Johannesburg

Closure

When Audrey Zwambila, an energetic corporate consultant in her mid-thirties, realized that her new job with Absa, South Africa's fourth largest bank, would mean working in Johannesburg's city center, she was horrified. Says Zwambila, who lives in the upmarket northern suburb of Bryanston: "I didn't want to be in town and I was very nervous about driving to work." Two years on she is "pleasantly surprised" to find that she's happy to be there and feels safe enough to recommend downtown to her still skeptical friends.[10]

There's just one catch: the R450 million (US$40 million) award-winning prestige precinct housing Absa's 4,500 Head Office employees might as well be anywhere for all it has to do with the gritty city around it that had experienced high levels of capital flight since the early 1990s.[11] Its three linked office towers contain a number of internalized atria, between them boasting an art gallery,

---

10 Much of the research used in this paper was conducted by myself for the *Sunday Times* newspaper as part of the Bessie Head Fellowship, which I was awarded in 2001, on the basis of a proposal entitled "Contemporary Johannesburg: Spaces, Cultures, Identities." This was published as five articles in the newspaper between February 17 and March 17, 2002. This contribution is gratefully acknowledged.

11 Between 1982 and 1994, 17 of the 65 top 100 national public companies located in Johannesburg moved from the central business district (CBD) to decentralized locations. Similarly, of a total of 104 top national business enterprises located in Johannesburg, in 1994 only 27 percent were located in the CBD. Of the top ten retail companies in the country having their head offices in Johannesburg, only two remain in the CBD. In the area of accounting, all leading accounting firms in the country have retained their head offices in Johannesburg, but, whereas in 1982 all seven

mobile sculpture court, ponds, bridges, palm trees, and a miniature rain forest. They offer a comprehensive array of services. Staff can shop at a convenience or hardware store, visit the hairdresser, work out at the gym, take lunch in the staff canteen or a coffeeshop fronting the street – all within the Absa precinct. After work, taxis and buses stop outside the front door, freeway access is close by, and, should there be a problem, help is on hand from the Absa-sponsored satellite police station, also within the precinct. All of which is why Zwambila loves it.

> "Absa has created a self-sufficient environment that I never have to leave," she says. Yet though she enthuses that it's wonderful "when you realize you can walk down the street and not be mugged," she admits to having ventured outside Absa's patrolled, designer-perfect world just once in two years – to attend a meeting in the Carlton Centre, a block away.

Zwambila's relationship to her work environment captures the contradictory relationship many have with Johannesburg today. What has "grown on" her is not the city, but the reassurance of knowing that her corporate world is just the same as it would be anywhere else in the city or possibly anywhere else in the world – a secured, self-sufficient cocoon which she never has to leave. She can avoid altogether the chaotic – to her, threatening – multicultural muddle around it.

Absa, whose decision to stay in the city's downtown in the 1990s was applauded for its optimism and investment in the decaying center, is not alone in building on the idea of elegant isolation in the midst of unpredictability. It takes its cue from Sandton, the city's new financial and corporate hub, where Nedcor's new R850 million Head Office complex adopts a similar approach. Here too, boasts Derek van den Bergh, general manager of Nedcor's Property Services, "staff don't have to venture out." Everything they need – library, restaurant, convenience store, travel agent, bank, crèche – can be found on its secured, internal street.

> were located in the CBD, by 1994 only three remained. While these relocations can be attributed to many factors (infrastructure requirements, convenience, corporate restructuring, prestige, etc.), a clear picture emerges of capital flight from the CBD. While the Johannesburg area has maintained its national head office function, the central city has weakened for nearly all sectors, with the exception of retail. Remaining in the CBD are the major financial institutions that have sunk considerable investments into property over the last ninety years. Of these, life assurance companies (Old Mutual, Sage, and Sanlam), national banking institutions (Absa, Standard, First National, and Nedcor), mining houses, Anglo American, and the Johannesburg Chamber of Industry are dominant. With approximately 13 other owner occupiers, this group owns and controls the major landholdings in the CBD. See Richard Tomlinson et al., *Johannesburg Inner City Strategic Development Framework: Economic Analysis* (Johannesburg: Greater Johannesburg Transitional Metropolitan Council City Planning Department, 1995).

Fourways Gardens
nature reserve,
Fourways,
Johannesburg

Ten years before the construction of these corporate enclaves, when rumors of a "Norweto" being planned by the Transvaal Provincial administration shocked Johannesburg's northern suburban residents out of their peri-urban bliss, Anglo American Properties laid out a 420-stand, fenced, gated residential township, in what was then the far north of the city. Each of its curving streets was planted with a different indigenous tree and named after it – Wild Pear Crescent, Paperbark Road, Soetdoring Way. It boasted clipped verges, cobbled crossings, an immaculately maintained park along a watercourse, a clubhouse, and a nature reserve stocked with small buck, birds, and a breeding zebra couple.

Over the years, this tamed, suburban bushveld has become the model for Johannesburg's upmarket lifestyle. Jonathan and Paddy Best, Anglo American executive couple, have lived there for eight years. She loves it most of all "for its bird-life" and stocks feeders in her garden, where a number of species breed. Jane Matthews, an energetic optometrist in her mid-thirties with a large practice in Mellville, likes its "aesthetic appeal" as well as the social life it offers her and her three young children – walking clubs, running clubs, holiday events, etc. Mrs. Gulbun Quinlan, a Turkish American whose husband heads the international operations of an American trucking company in Africa and Australasia, tells me that she chose Fourways Gardens seven years ago because she "likes to live in places where the trees are already grown. I move so often," she adds, "that I hate planting trees for someone else to enjoy." She concedes, though, that Fourways Gardens is a bit of a "la-la land. It's a utopia. You forget what is out there and can easily let down your guard."

Buying into this precinct is not just purchasing a piece of land or a house. It is buying into an idealized image of suburban life in Africa – homogeneous,

Entrance porticoes to security estates, Fourways, Johannesburg

Road closure, Orange Grove, Johannesburg

tamed, the secured space in the bush, to where one can withdraw to enjoy the fruits of one's labor. In it, those with whom one comes into daily contact are more or less the same as oneself. Anyone unknown or different is shut out through an elaborate ritual of identification and approval. The comings and goings of domestic workers, plumbers, electricians, artisans, or guests are subjected to strict disciplinary codes. Whatever or whoever else is "out there" in the city is guaranteed to stay at bay.

This has become the way of life for most middle-class white Johannesburgers and the preferred locale for the new black bourgeoisie.[12] All over the city, walls, booms, and security personnel have transformed parks, offices, shops, suburbs, and entertainment areas into closed enclaves with controlled access. Citizens

Advertisement for razor wire, *Homemakers Fair* magazine, 1998

have closed off streets, walled off suburbs, excising whole neighborhoods from the public realm. For those living inside these barriers, a triumphant (or sometimes regretful) sense of security and communality is regained.

Those not so fortunate fortify their homes and businesses with walls, razor wire, electrified fencing, security gates, intercoms, concealed cameras, and the human shield offered by private security companies. Low walls are raised and topped with spikes or glass chips. Razor wire (a particularly cruel form of barbed wire developed in South Africa for counter-insurgency purposes) unfurls around perimeter fencing. Designed to shock when touched, live electrical wires are mounted on garden walls; security gates transform homes into prisons. Fortified against crime, their fear of the other contained, residents reconfigure their lost Eden. Life has returned to what it was when they were sure about things.

Visible boundaries and enclosures, designed to impose unity and order, have long been associated with the political organization of space.[13] In Johannesburg, as the powerful spatio-legal apparatus that kept apartheid in place lost its efficacy, as familiar institutions of urban management and government were dissolved and replaced by poorly functioning transitional arrangements, people invented new ways to manage and govern themselves. The walled enclosure became an

---

12 Recent research by Keith Beavon ("Northern Johannesburg: Part of the 'Rainbow' or Neo-apartheid City in the Making?," *Mots Pluriels*, no. 13 [April 2000], http://www.arts.uwa.edu.au/MotsPluriels/MP1300kb.html) and myself ("Living on the Edge," *Sunday Times Lifestyle*, February 17, 2002) indicates that only 2 percent of established white residential suburbs are black, and that middle-class blacks have a preference for select northern suburbs. For instance, at Kyalami Estates, an upmarket security suburb in Midrand, 17 percent of residents are black.

13 Jackson, *Discovering the Vernacular Landscape*; Michel Foucault, *Discipline and Punish: The Birth of the Prison*, trans. Alan Sheridan (New York: Pantheon, 1977); Miles, *The Uses of Decoration*.

Montecasino, Fourways, Johannesburg

effective means for restoring a sense of order and control, keeping the stranger out and preventing the overlapping of identities and the clashing of cultures.

These newly constructed frontiers, woven through and carving the city into a myriad of enclaves, have produced a new spatiality of fixed identities and logics of discrimination. As people retreat into the known, new rigidities in the definition of self and the other are constructed. While race is no longer privileged as the "master signifier" in these definitions,[14] increasingly homogeneous enclaves operationalize and render productive the fear of the other which haunts the South African psyche, or provide protection to those seeking assimilation into the middle class. Presented as crime deterrents, these spatial practices sooth the anxieties, uncertainties, and fears that the end of apartheid has brought to white South Africans.[15] When adopted by middle-class black South Africans, they facilitate easy identification with the dominant middle-class culture of conspicuous consumption and social indifference.[16] They also enable people to avoid confronting their former selves in the township world or urban streets.[17] A new homogeneity prevails.

---

14 Nuttall and Michael, eds., *Senses of Culture*, p. 12.
15 Jennifer Robinson, "(Im)mobilizing Space – Dreaming (of) Change," in *blank——: Architecture, Apartheid and After*.
16 Denis-Constant Martin, "Identity, Culture, Pride and Conflict," in *Identity? Theory, Politics, History*, ed. S. B. Bekker and Rachel Prinsloo (Pretoria: Human Sciences Research Council, 1999).
17 The space inhabited by many of Johannesburg's new black middle class is a contradictory one (cf. Ndebele, "Game Lodges and Leisure Colonists"). On the one hand, middle-class values and preoccupations – individual achievement, status, nuclear family life, space, security, and sport – are best satisfied within the infrastructure of the security suburb. On the other hand, a proud and

Montecasino, Fourways, Johannesburg

Simulation   Montecasino, the Tuscan gambling citadel in the northern suburbs, is an ungainly sprawl from the air. Inside, its authentically fake ornamental landscape wraps us in a fun-filled, never-ending twilit utopia, where the pigeons don't shit and the roofs cast shadows on the sky.

This gambler's paradise was built in the late 1990s by Tsogo Sun, Southern Sun's gaming division, backed by South African Breweries. At the time that its concept architects, Creative Kingdom, were working on it, Ken Rosevear, former CEO of Sun International, now development director of MGM Grand, which operates the casino, had just spent a holiday in Tuscany and loved it. He also knew that there was no other casino anywhere else in the world with a Tuscan theme, and thought its "earthy feel" would appeal to South Africans. "So Tuscan it was," says Edmund Batley of Bentel Abramson architects, who built the project. "It was not a big intellectual decision, it just happened because Rosevear thought it would work."

Montecasino is now rated one of the top ten casinos in the world, far outstripping its South African counterparts. And Rosevear still flies in regularly to advise on changes to the underwear hanging in its streets and to ensure that the flags draped in Piazza Duomo follow the fortunes of the Italian soccer teams. With people like Rosevear attending to the details of the simulation, our Tuscany is infinitely preferable to the real thing.

essential, yet nostalgic, relationship to the culture of township life is maintained. People often spend their leisure time (weekends or holidays) in the townships (Bremner, "Living on the Edge," *Sunday Times Lifestyle*, February 17, 2002, and "When Worlds Collide," *Sunday Times Lifestyle*, February 24, 2002).

Sandton Square, Sandton, Johannesburg

Montecasino is one of the glamour zones of the new city of Johannesburg, which is invested with meaning by being configured as a little bit of Italy. Elsewhere, sipping cocktails in the lounge of the Michelangelo Hotel, favorite haunt of South Africa's new black bourgeoisie, eating pizza in the piazza of Sandton Square, or returning to one's "Tuscan" townhouse, images of Italy proliferate.

Why Italy? one might ask. In a city with a very short past and an uncertain future, investing in images of Italy achieves a number of things.

First, it confers a sense of stability and timelessness on people's lives. It distances them from the real history, real place, and the uncertainty around them. The imported landscapes of Italy locate them in an illusion of a past and free them from the burden of having to be agents in the present. They are able to act out the everyday rituals of shopping, eating, television, sport, or travel with immunity.

Second, Italy, or Tuscany in particular, is constructed as *la dolce vita* in the popular imagination of Johannesburgers. Terracotta colors, garden courts, Florentine gazebos, Italian tiles bring a promise of romance, warmth, earthiness, and passion. *"Choose this sanctuary of elegant, old Tuscan architecture – reminiscent of the romantic Italian Renaissance, and, as a haven, the perfect foil for today's fast-paced lifestyle. Here you can sooth your soul in a harmony of earthy Tuscan style, excellent taste and a vibrant charm,"* or *"Imagine Siena, romantic heart of central Tuscany, where vine clad hills are dotted with farmhouses, villas and baronial castles. Siena, now brought to life here in Waverly"* people are promised in the promotional brochures for the Via Reggio and Via Siena housing estates. By living here, your lives will be soothed and become harmonious, vibrant, romantic, and

"Tuscany was never so perfect" billboard, Fourways, Johannesburg

in touch with the rhythms of Old World earthiness. Wrapped in the image of a timeless, unchanging world, you will be able to withdraw from and obliterate the relentlessly fast-paced, confrontational, aggressive, transforming world around you. Public space and private realm will be clearly delineated and separated.

Third, these Italianate enclaves are found in the northern parts of the city where, despite increased densities and a mushrooming of new corporate headquarters, a suburban character is still evident. In these suburbs desperately trying to become a real city, Italy represents the authentically urban. By borrowing its image, our city becomes a real city; it gains an urban identity. People become civilized, urbane, and cultured. Nagging insecurities, anxieties about being or being thought to be uncivilized or parochial are silenced.

This search for the authentic has recently taken a new shape at Melrose Arch, a still-under-construction development adjacent to the M1 motorway to Pretoria. This development ripped up one of the city's oldest, most established residential suburbs to create, in the first of six phases, a 52,000-square-meter premixed design package of corporate facilities, smaller offices, penthouses, shops, a hotel, health club, theater, car showroom, and public square, offering a total lifestyle package to the young cosmopolitan.

It has already attracted the attention of the international and local business community. One of its first tenants was Arthur Andersen and Associates, multinational accountants and auditors, who, at the end of 2001, moved their 450 employees from their former premises in a more conventional office park, attracted by the live/work/fun lifestyle it promoted. The results have been "sensationally successful," Daryll Jackson, Andersen's CEO, tells me. "Our staff love

Melrose Arch, Johannesburg

working here, productivity is up, and this environment promotes the teamwork we require." With open-plan offices furnished with imported Herman Miller plug-in workstations and Museum of Modern Art Aaron chairs, discrete meeting rooms named after every citrus fruit in the family, their own in-house Seattle Coffee Shop opening onto a bright, grassed internal courtyard, and special rates from the hairdresser downstairs, I am not surprised.

What initially attracted Andersen's global real estate group, which decides where the company's branches locate, is Melrose Arch's allusion to the traditional city – intimate streets, small-scale facades, a village square, designer signs, lampposts, bollards, trees, benches – familiar attributes of cities in many parts of the world. In fact, it is familiar to Johannesburgers, who will recognize its pattern in Parkview, Greenside, or even Yeoville – the mixed-use suburban Main Street. Here people live above where they work, have coffee and a roll at the local coffeeshop on the way to the office, all know and greet each other, and generally live like good neighbors, even greeting the local lumpen or homeless waif.

There is one irony. Whereas elsewhere in the city, Melrose Arch's model is falling apart – boarded up first-floor windows, cracking pavements, parking problems, poor people lying about, low-paying tenants – here clients are moving in before the paint is dry, desperate to be at the forefront of the trend. For this Main Street is a sanitized lifestyle package which conjures up an emotionally satisfying image of bygone times while offering the most high tech of services, including raised-access flooring, a 178-camera closed-circuit television network, and two levels of parking garage under the cobbles. It is the city as we wish it were (classy, secure, and homogeneous), represented as an idealized fragment of what it was (snug, human scaled, and neighborly).

Rockey Street, Yeoville, Johannesburg

View from the road, Montecasino, Fourways, Johannesburg

All of these scenic enclaves – Fourways Gardens' suburban bush, Montecasino's Tuscan hill town, Via Reggio, Via Siena, and Melrose Arch's suburban main street – do the same thing. They hollow out parts of the city and, on the basis of idealized images, construct urban places appealing to the desire, nostalgia, or paranoia of people who can pay to be there. None of these enclaves have much, if any, connection to the rest of the city or its history. The city is being remade as a collection of juxtaposed fragments. In between, the gritty, complex city (as opposed to its glitzy, idealized version), with its highways, crime, suburban sprawl, vacant office space, neglected buildings, traffic congestion, poor people, Big Mac and McDonald's, is upstaged and obscured. Simulated glimpses of what cities once were are celebrated as signs of develop-

Melrose Arch, Johannesburg

Hillbrow, Johannesburg

ment while, in between, the city they represent, or even copy, decays and disintegrates.

This reframing of urban reality is comforting in times of transition.[18] The repackaging of the city in enclaves of fantasy urbanism has the effect of calming anxieties brought about by change. It is taken as evidence that the city can be restored to being safe, clean, and humane. In bracketed moments, traffic, poverty, litter, smells, disorder, social inequality, crime – evidence of present-day failures – are erased. Progress and development are thereby metonymically signified to citizens struggling to make sense of their lives in a changing city.

Making Do Outside these fixed encampments lie ambiguous and ill-defined public spaces whose very fluidity and aterritoriality are providing the ground for an-other city to emerge. These spaces – streets, roads, parks, highways – released from the containment of apartheid, are becoming spaces where new livelihoods are being made and new experiences of the city lived. They are sites of conviviality, livelihood, and leisure, as individuals or groups try out or invent new social or economic roles in an attempt to make the city work for themselves.

Some of these spaces are brutal and terrifying – car hijackings and cash-in-transit heists turn roads and traffic intersections into places of violent contesta-

---

18 M. Christine Boyer, "Cities for Sale: Merchandising History at South Street Seaport," in *Variations on a Theme Park*.

Closure, Simulation, and "Making Do" in the Contemporary Johannesburg Landscape   167

Street restaurant, Woodmead, Johannesburg

Meeting of the Shembe people, Pieter Roos Park, Hillbrow, Johannesburg

tion.[19] But others make visible the highly complex networks of small-scale, informal, fluid social and economic associations upon which an increasing number of peoples' lives depend.[20] The very exclusivity of suburban enclaves, with their homogeneous, sanitized reconstructions of idealized citiness, operationalizes the metropolis without. Here people's survival depends on the ability

19 Lindsay J. Bremner, "Crime and the Emerging of Post-apartheid Johannesburg," in *blank—: Architecture, Apartheid and After*.
20 Robinson, "(Im)mobilizing Space – Dreaming of Change"; AbdouMaliq Simone, "Globalization and the Identity of African Urban Practices," in *blank—: Architecture, Apartheid and After*.

Informal meeting place, Killarney, Johannesburg

to move, select a location, network, group, regroup, and on the anonymity and chance encounter that metropolitan life offers.

> Magnus Mabaso was a domestic worker in Killarney until 1998 when her "old lady died. But I much prefer my new job," she says of the life she invented to replace domestic work. She sits, day in and day out, on the corner of Riviera and Main selling peanuts, cigarettes, and sweets to commuters or passing pedestrians. She makes R30 to R40 per day, from which she contributes to supporting all four of her adult children. An ironing board covered in plastic serves as her stall, newspapers on the ground as her carpet. She and her friends sit, at sundowner time, on orange crates eating unburned peanuts and drinking water from yoghurt containers. "Now I can sit and talk to my friends while I work," she explains, as she sells a cigarette for R1 to a man about to catch his taxi. Next to her, a man offering shoe repairs plays cards with his mates, while, across the road, veggie sellers mind each other's children.

These activities do not rely on fixed infrastructure, fixed locales, or fixed investment for their survival. They "make do" with what the urban realm offers – a garden wall, a shady tree, a busy intersection, an ironing board, claiming space for a while and, if necessary, moving on. A fine balance exists between stasis – staying in one place long enough to be recognized – and mobility, the ability to pack up and move on.

In this way, practices unfamiliar in the urban world have been introduced into the Johannesburg landscape. For instance, each year, between late October and May the following year, an intricate, colorful drama unfolds, as mealies, the staple diet of South Africa's rural people, are brought to town and traded on the

Informal urban infrastructure, Yeoville, Johannesburg

Traditional "muti" market, Faraday Station, downtown Johannesburg

city's streets. Rural women in colorful Shangaan cloth, coal smoke rising from vacant lots, braziers carried by young men around the city's streets, are visible signs of a complex configuration of informal urban-rural trade.

> Gladys Kubayi is in her late forties and lives in Chiawelo, Soweto. Each year since 1994, she has spent the summer months buying mealies from a farmer in Britz and getting up at 4h00 a.m. to journey to Noord Street, site of one of downtown's busiest taxi ranks. She arrives at 5h00 and makes the fire on which she will braai [barbecue] mealies all day, selling them for R3 each. On a good day, this can make her R200.
>
> Unlike Kubayi, who is self employed, Johanna Sibia, a young woman in her early twenties, sells for a man from Hammanskraal, north of Pretoria. During mealie season,

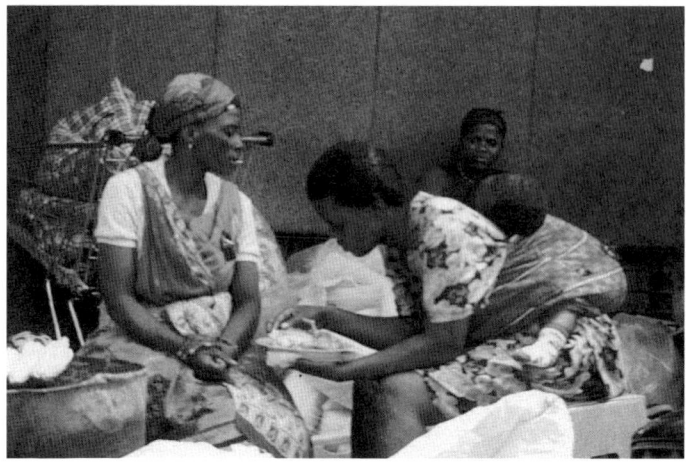

Mealie sellers, downtown Johannesburg

he provides food and lodging for her in Braamfisher, a shack settlement in Dobsonville, Soweto, as does another mealie boss from Kwa-mhlanga. "We are well looked after," she says, telling me that she earns between R120 and R500 per day, depending on how much she sells. "Our parents told our boss to treat us like children. They even told him to punish us if we misbehave. But he treats us right. He gives us money for food and there is someone to cook for us when we get back in the evening. We will go home for Christmas and come back in the New Year."

Others are not so lucky. Lena Skosana comes from Kwa-Ndable and has been selling mealies since 1992. She, like others she works with, is paid just R20 per day, irrespective of her sales. "Our boss treats us very badly," she says. "We sleep in the open next to the truck. Sometimes people steal our clothes and blankets. We do not have a place to bath or change our clothes."

Many of these women are not here by choice. Their occupation of the city's streets is both desperate and dignified. They have children to support and no way of doing so in their villages. By word of mouth they hear of farmers taking their stock to town and looking for sellers. Many end up on the city's streets for years, during which they build a solidarity and camaraderie. "Sometimes we gossip and fight," says Sibia, "but we do what we do because we don't want to be prostitutes or our children to become thieves."

These little tactics of survival,[21] in which ordinary people are reusing and remaking urban space, have transformed the city. Their livelihoods are depend-

---

21 De Certeau, *The Practice of Everyday Life*, p. xix.

Temporary trading stalls, Park Station, Johannesburg

ent on the solidarity of shared routines and the mobility of the road, anathema to middle-class notions of guarded space and fixed identity. In the spaces between corporatized communities and nostalgic enclaves, an-other city, a common ground for public life, is being lived.

Conclusion   This is the Johannesburg of today – a city retreating from itself into safe, sanitized encampments and corporate cocoons, or wrapping itself in the accoutrements of consumption. At the same time, it is being remade informally and unpredictably by the myriad of small, everyday, often survivalist practices of ordinary people who claim space in between. While the one comprises a series of well-defined, inward-looking spaces, whose symbols are the familiar ones of architecture and style, the other is made up of the intersections, verges, margins, the continuous, interconnected, outward-looking spaces that hold the landscape together. As people populate these public spaces, a new improvised spatiality emerges. While planners, developers, architects, and government officials rearrange the city into the sanitized fragments and idealized reflections of global capital, and fail abysmally to redraw the lines of the apartheid city, ordinary people, as they "mobilize" urban space,[22] transform the social and economic character of the city and connect its divided landscape. It is only in their fluid groupings and regroupings, in their reimagining and remaking of their lives on the streets and pavements of the modernist city, that apartheid spatiality

22 Robinson, "(Im)mobilizing Space – Dreaming (of) Change."

has been redrafted. Here a different city has been imagined and new sites of resistance identified.

It is important to narrate, map, and mark this territory and its relationships with the private enclaves it both encircles and penetrates, for these are the sources of the city's new urban imaginary and of its emerging postmodern, post-apartheid morphology. Increasingly unplanned and largely unmanaged, this is how the city's spatiality, sociability, and new urban vernacular are being thought out, negotiated, and configured. Somewhere between desire and paranoia, necessity and contingency, mobility and stasis, the new Johannesburg is taking shape.

Fragments of a Lecture on Lagos

Rem Koolhaas

For the past six years, I have been overseeing something called Project on the City with students from the Harvard Design School. We have been looking at a number of urban conditions, particularly when and where they change most intensely and most quickly. We have looked at the Pearl River Delta in China, which has witnessed the most rapid urbanization in the world. We have investigated the effects of shopping on the urban condition throughout the world, and, since 1999, we have been looking at Lagos. Taken together, these studies suggest that the notion of the city itself has mutated into something that is no longer Western.

This work is not inspired by the need to discover ever more exotic, violent, extreme urban thrills, but by the realization that the engrained vocabulary and values of architectural discourse are painfully inadequate to describe the current production of urban substance. They perpetuate an image of the city which is essentially Western, and subconsciously insist that all cities, wherever they are, be interpreted in that image; they systematically find wanting any urban form that does not conform. Ours words cannot describe our cities with any precision or pleasure.

Four years ago, from outside of Nigeria, it was incredibly difficult to get access to information about Lagos. The idea of traveling to Lagos was severely discouraged, officially by the US State Department and unofficially by European governments. Lagos was considered, universally, the most dangerous city in the world. There was almost no satellite evidence of Lagos' presence. Anything beyond a vague, schematic representation was impossible to find. Nigeria itself was imagined as simply an abstract country with a single, notorious city.

The study of Lagos was inspired by two central intentions: to understand and describe how an African metropolis works, and by the knowledge that Lagos will, in fifteen years, be the third largest city in the world. The combination of its huge size and apparently distressed urban conditions became a compelling reason to go.

There is a remarkably intense network of urban rumors about Lagos, about the dangers that it presents. They begin at the airport, continue along the highway, the bridges, the buses, into every neighborhood.

Our initial engagement with the city was from a mobile position. Partly out of fear, we stayed in the car. That meant, in essence, that we were preoccupied with the foreground, and, at that time, Lagos had an incredibly dense foreground. Viewed through the density of the foreground, the greater depth of the city took time to reveal itself.

Lagos seemed to be a city of burning edges. Hills, entire roads were paral-

leled with burning embankments. At first sight, the city had an aura of apocalyptic violence; entire sections of it seemed to be smoldering, as if it were one gigantic rubbish dump.

At first sight – and focusing exclusively on the foreground – it was difficult to distinguish to what extent this was a real disaster or a representation of disaster, and where the foreground ended and the background began.

We were not convinced that our initial impressions told the entire story, so we began to look more closely. On our second and third visits, we ventured out of our cars and discovered that what seemed a completely random and improvised world included a number of very elaborate organizational networks. Some of the places that, at first sight, seemed to be tragic manifestations of degraded urban life were actually intensely emancipatory zones, where the recent arrivals from outside were "processed" as citizens of Lagos.

On closer inspection, the apparent randomness of the garbage revealed heaps of similar materials and colors. The activity taking place was actually not a process of dumping, but more a process of sorting, dismantling, reassembling, and potentially recycling. Underneath the viaducts, there was a continuous effort to transform discarded garbage.

Certain elements were being picked out and designated for second lives as electronics and communication devices. It became clear that such apparently dilapidated zones were intensely used. In the end, we were able to precisely map all of the activities and performances that were taking place on what had seemed, at first sight, a prototype of the city-as-dump. Responsibilities were being distributed in areas that appeared to be abandoned, but were actually highly planned communities. We saw that an apparently chaotic city could organize incredibly efficient transformations of garbage in a highly structured way.

On our third visit, we were able to rent a helicopter, the helicopter of the President. We were finally able to go beyond the foreground and discover another Lagos, a much less improvised, much less chaotic Lagos. From the air, the apparently burning garbage heap turned out to be, in fact, a village, an urban phenomenon with a highly organized community living on its crust. Our preoccupation with the apparently "informal" had been premature, if not mistaken.

What was stunning, and visible only from above the city, was the fact that these processes were taking place at scales that were almost unimaginable in any other city. What seemed, on ground level, an accumulation of dysfunctional movements, seemed from above an impressive performance, evidence of how well Lagos might perform if it were the third largest city in the world.

Lagos is a city of processes: unfolding on the ground, uncontained by build-

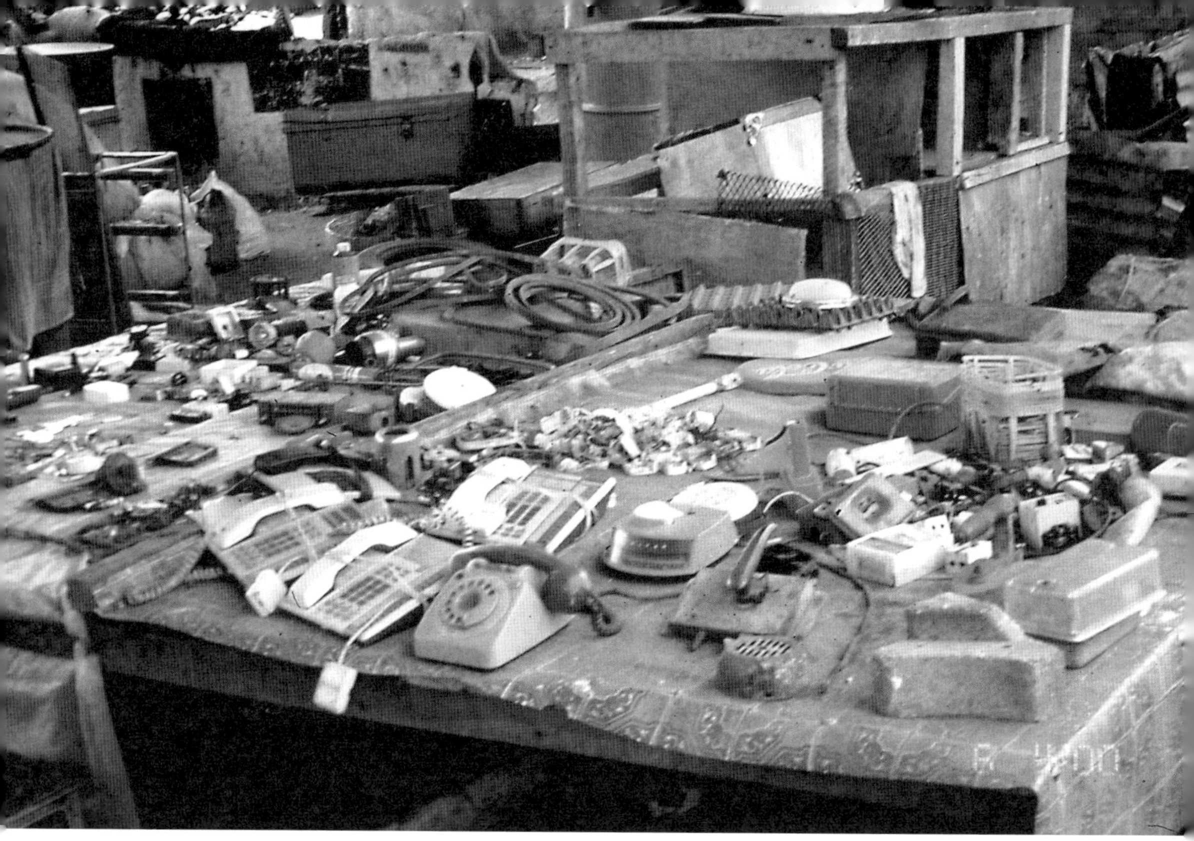

ings, but, for that reason, no less highly conceptualized or organized. Each of these entities (the garbage heaps, the railroad tracks, the connected cloverleafs, the burning village, etc.) was a self-administered enclave with strong rules and regulations that applied only within the parameter of those areas.

Flying over the city, Lagos reveals – at Oshodi Junction – the greatest density of both traffic and human beings ever known to man, literally unimaginable numbers of people. But here too what originally seemed to be simply a point of crisis, on closer inspection turned out to be a deliberately engineered situation.

It became obvious that the permanent "go-slow" of the traffic itself was functional in that it created a systematic interface between vendors – who filled every gap between stalled vehicles – and their captive cargos of consumers. A railway track that was still in occasional use was, after the train's passage, immediately inundated by a sea of human beings who resumed trading in a very efficient way. What seemed an improvisation proved to be a systematic layering where the enormous amount of minuscule transactions necessary to stay alive in Lagos – the endemic issue of poverty – were made possible through the arrangement, intersection, and mutual confrontation of people and infrastructure. A

traffic jam is a grid of static cars that comprise a momentary exchange mechanism between buyers, users, and sellers – an instant urbanism that emerges contrary to the intentions of its planners.

Apart from these large self-organized entities, Lagos is also a place of huge housing projects and architectural complexes of a scale rarely seen in the resistant West. They are the historical city's "gifts" from other states – Israel, Czechoslovakia – that donated entire city sectors as aid or to stake some kind of now-defunct claim on Nigeria's once fabled resources.

Misleadingly, Lagos presents a foreground of perpetual drama – product of a continuous friction between economy and politics – but beyond that exists large, coherent complexes that continue to function impassively, as characteristic of the city as the hysterical "friction zone." The first category, the urban donations, are silent reminders of Nigeria's potential just after independence, the second category of the waning of that original promise.

Nigeria became independent in 1960. We have to understand the 1960s and '70s in general to understand the '60s and '70s in Nigeria. It was the first time that oil became a critical issue. Huge amounts of money came in unfamiliar hands, sponsoring frenzied speculation, by both visionaries (Doxiadis, Buckminster Fuller, etc.) and corporate engineers, on how to change the world for the better. A macro-engineering movement proposed a number of interventions on the globe itself that would, in a drastic way, address persistent problems, with the ultimate goal of benefiting humankind. That same speculative frenzy looked at Africa as one of its potential subjects. Nigeria's economy was stronger than that of South Korea; Lagos became a target, visited by U.N. commissions, invited experts, planners.

Some of their visions were realized through the activities of the construction and engineering firm Julius Berger Nigeria, a subsidiary of the German-based firm which strove to be viewed as an African rather than a colonial firm. Berger proposed enormous extensions of Lagos island, huge extensions of the business core. The firm then used these territories for infrastructural interventions and traffic improvements of unusual complexity and intricacy. It also built the bridges that connect Lagos island with the mainland, producing a false vernacular propaganda showing contemporary infrastructure as integral to African life.

In the end, when Berger had finished with Lagos, the entire city was caught in a network of highways, motorways, and incredibly complex intersections – a model of '70s smoothness. It is no coincidence that the areas of Lagos' greatest "dysfunctionality" and greatest current density of informal exchange coincide exactly with that network.

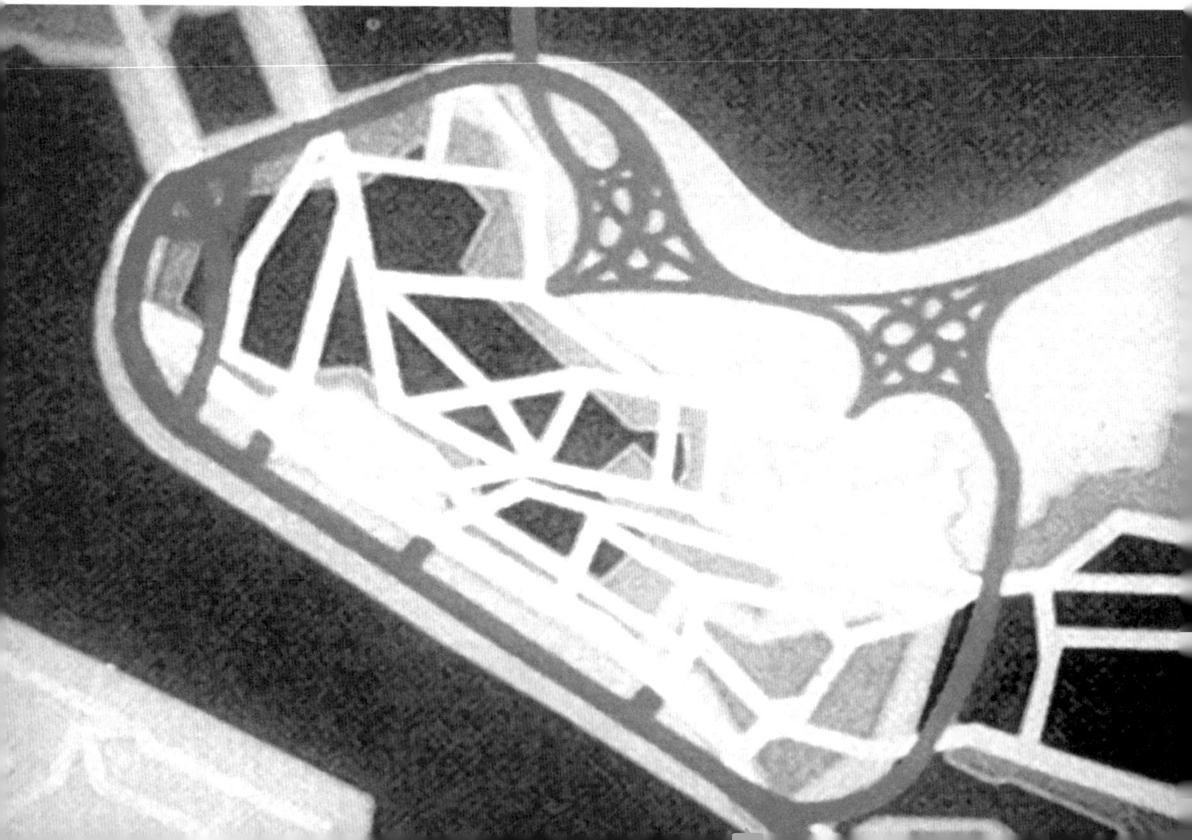

In 1977, during the height of the speculative frenzy, the Festac festival was organized. It marked a shift in Lagos' perception, a moment in which the development of Lagos as a modern city began to take on political implications. A spontaneous, free-wheeling African modernity – that had developed its own '70s glamour: scooters, Afros, birth-control – was marshaled into a political enterprise and confronted with "power." Through Festac, Lagos was turned into a representation of what an African city ought to be. The festival stands as one of the last moments of confident, deliberate modernity in Lagos.

The power systematically disappointed. A series of dictators plundered the country and the city. Lagos was left to its own devices, then abandoned. The city became ungovernable. From one day to the next, the government simply disappeared to Abuja.

The current status of Lagos is a hybrid – a patchwork of self-organization that has evaded the rigorous organization and certainties of '70s planners. Without their interventions, the current city could not exist or survive. Their own inadvertent contribution is perhaps the most anyone involved in the "professional" treatment of the city can hope for.

Kinshasa: Beyond Chaos

Thierry Nlandu

Being neither a sociologist nor a specialist in urban issues, I will explore the condition of modern life in Kinshasa from the perspective of an inhabitant caught prisoner of a distorted, dichotomized city. Here "la Ville," or "the urban," gains a status in itself and stands as superior to "the Cité," "the suburban." This tragic competition values the urban more than the suburban and makes the urban and the suburban forget that they are in reality interacting parts of the same whole, that is, the city.

The life narrative presented here is a translation of my perception of Kinshasa, a city very difficult to grasp, moving forward and backward with currents and undercurrents that merge into each other. A poor tourist guide, I refuse to reduce Kinshasa to a no man's land or a tragic space. Consequently, this narrative will selectively present different aspects of Kinshasa's life. It will be intuitively analytical, referring to facts, experiences, and accounts of facts. The thrust of this paper is to show how city dwellers in Kinshasa perceive and shape their individual and communal identities.

You will certainly notice many hesitations about the interpretation of the multifaceted image of Kinshasa. These limitations are part of this exploration conducted in a spirit of trying to understand rather than explain. Indeed, I want to *stand under:* to put myself in a lower position, a position of receiving, an attitude not of learning *about* but of learning *from* city dwellers in Kinshasa.

This stance is motivated by a desire to turn the present mental visit to Kinshasa into a real-life meeting with the "Kinois," the people in the capital of Congo. The intent is to share their perceptions of Kinshasa. I want to understand the forces that drive them in shaping their lives the way they do in a context not only of a deep sense of loss, but also of hope beyond pessimism. Indeed, there are city dwellers who maintain hope in Kinshasa simply because they can cope with the challenge of moving beyond dichotomized alternatives.

Let us now explore this city's ambivalence. Although indeed a tragic space and a no man's land, Kinshasa is also a healing environment constantly looking for ethical pillars, seeking to invest its social, political, and economic realities with meaning. It is no doubt the case that understanding this city life is intimately tied to the rediscovery of the necessity to integrate rather than separate these aspects of the city. This is possible in a process of selective reappropriation of the values and practices of both the "Cité" and the "Ville." In this search for the experience of wonder that is city life, the challenge remains the quest for a spirituality that unites rather than divides the urban and the suburban. A new art of living is developing in Kinshasa based on a simple lifestyle – love and concern for one's neighbor.

Kinshasa: A Tragic Space? Kinshasa is not the city of the dead, but a dead city. It is a city that has fallen apart. Nobody denies this, neither the Kinois nor the visitor who enters this space for the first time. City dwellers refer to Kinshasa as *kiima kinkaka*, a brewer's slogan for a bottled beer. Kinshasa is the sum of stories of physical and mental hardship.

Present-day Kinshasa is a large urban center in Central Africa. It is probably the largest and the ugliest in tropical Africa. Officially no one will admit this, but the Kinois is aware of it. Using his now legendary derision, he sings a verse in which *Kinshasa la belle* ("the beautiful") rhymes with *Kinshasa la poubelle* ("the dirty").

Kinshasa is a huge city encompassing the Ville and the Cité. It has one impressive street which dominates the center: Boulevard du 30 juin, the "Champs-Élysée" of Africa. The boulevard is eight lanes wide and runs almost the full length of the Ville. On it you will find major commercial stores and administrative offices, the main post office, and the city's number one landmark: the twenty-two-storey SOZACOM building (the mineral marketing company). About five kilometers from the center along the Congo River, you will come to Gombe, a chic residential district where is located the Hotel Intercontinental, the city's best hotel. The Ville includes the downtown area, with its places of employment, stores, and neatly planned neighborhoods where the privileged minority reside.

The pulse of the city is the Cité, the main artery being Avenue Kasa-Vubu. It runs perpendicular to the Boulevard du 30 juin, starting at the post office. When you arrive at Rond Point Victoire, four kilometers down Kasa-Vubu, you will be in the commune of Matonge. This is the vibrant heart of the Cité where you find cheap hotels, lively bars, Congolese foods, and the musical groups on which the country stakes its reputation. Matonge invites the visitor to *experience*, not just "see" the city. Kinshasa's nightlife is lively. In Matonge, almost any night of the week you can walk into a variety of colorful nightclubs and hear famous musical groups. It is said that no other city in Africa has as much live entertainment as Kinshasa.

The Cité covers more than three-quarters of the total area of the capital. This suburban area is where most Kinois live. One meets some of them in barely mapped-out older districts. The majority now live in newer, poorer zones, shantytowns of spontaneous peripheral expansion to the south, east, and west.[1]

The marginal neighborhoods or shantytowns on the fringes of the city arrogantly display their rudimentary shelters of two or three rooms in breezeblock wall and corrugated iron roofs. These, too, are Kinshasa, although concentrated in unplanned areas lacking basic urban services and infrastructure. Here people patiently await the moon, a better and more reliable supplier of light than the national electricity company.

The shanties, too, sing Kinshasa, thanks to the frenzied sounds of empty tomato tins drummed against Coca-Cola bottles, timing the creative advertisements of children selling kerosene. Unconsciously, the shanties are paving the ways of a city planned in smaller scale and in which inhabitants attempt to reestablish or reinvent their disrupted environment and communities.

Unexpectedly, the shanties become an alternative that is not a "backward culturalism." Like any other area of the city, the shanties need paved roads, sewage, and sanitary systems. But they also offer a chance for more social cohesion and solidarity, for here the Kinois ceases to be an object to be urbanized. Rather, he seeks to become the agent of his urbanization. He is the one who organizes his housing unit, introducing various changes to the shared spaces. Here he joins the pauperized functionary, the intellectual of the old districts.

People recognize the intellectual by his mastery of the French language, his nostalgia for French etiquette, his school education, and his petit bourgeois lifestyle. The intellectual still masters the language of his master, that is, French. He is a trained national, educated and bearing degrees from Cambridge, Oxford, the Catholic University of Louvain, Paris II or IV. However, he has lost what matters in present Kinshasa – financial power: "Français ny falanganyi!" "French is not money nor fortune!" Indeed, his knowledge of the master's language no longer guarantees high status, income, and other social privileges as it did in the past.

Torn between his old and new worlds, this collage of personalities redefines the intellectual's identity. This is the condition necessary to achieve a healing encounter with other city dwellers. He gradually becomes a city dweller among other city dwellers, no longer obliged to adapt his identity to the divided envi-

---

1 See René Devisch, "Frenzy, Violence, and Ethical Renewal in Kinshasa," *Public Culture* 7, no. 3 (1995), p. 598.

ronment like a chameleon. The intellectual is finally returning to a simpler lifestyle with less emphasis on material and academic success. He no longer considers himself a failure. He has faced the obvious: that his social climbing and his diploma were nothing but a mirage. Consequently, he is willing to reject the illusion that succeeds only in widening the gap between himself and his urban identity and mode of life.

Perhaps more than the city dwellers in the shanties, the old districts, and the Ville, the intellectual is nostalgic for their lost unity. He reacts against the feeling of incompleteness instilled in them for centuries. He invites the members of these different communities to turn their temporary material poverty into a symbol of dignity. Since materially poor persons do "not have" many things, they must concentrate on the strength of their inner "being" to restore and retain this sense of dignity.

Together with the inhabitants of the shanties and the Ville, the intellectuals are shaping the realities of a shared inhuman and divided city life. They are tapping their limited resources to inscribe new modes of being on older modes. Together they resist the antagonistic male-female or up-down division of the city. For many city dwellers, this division is a tragic and dramatic question of life against death, humanity versus exclusion.

For city dwellers, today's challenge is the ability to share the same social and physical space without erasing the trace of being rooted in their respective original space. Such a qualitative change does not imply a total rupture with the divided Kinshasa of the past. The shanties, the old districts, and the urban are not based in retrograde clan solidarity and will not simply disappear. They are not negative spaces to convert or abandon. On the contrary, they must blend into a new city characterized by adaptive transformation, that is, by continuity in change. New Kinshasa will move in a cyclical spiraling course, relating, relinking, reconnecting the suburban to the urban, reappearing in different but never entirely new environments.

What is the population of Kinshasa? No one knows except the white anthropologist, the specialist in demography and development issues, and probably Congolese political leaders when they claim for new seats in the Parliament. According to them, the population of Kinshasa is between five and seven million.

How do these millions survive the incoherent, miserable life of Kinshasa? City dwellers consider it a miracle! Indeed, many among them, if not the majority, are jobless. The pillages of September 1991 and January 1993 destroyed many jobs. If people happen to find a job, the salary is not regular. When one does get paid, it is very often a poor, miserable salary that does not cover a family's basic daily necessities. This paltry income is humorously referred to as

SIDA, an acronym for *Salaire Insuffisant Depuis des Années* (Insufficient Salary for Many Years).

How do people manage with the collapse of public transportation, the decaying infrastructure, the absence of roads, the breakdown of electricity and sewage systems? These are not questions to raise if one wants to remain sane.

What is the life expectancy of the Kinois? How do they provide education and health care to their children in this general state of material and ethical deficiency? Where do people go to solve the problems of infectious disease and nutritional health? Is decent housing a utopian ideal? God knows! No one invests time thinking about either these issues or the ruthless global economic order, the ceaseless inflation of the currency, and the collapse of public order and government institutions.

This is a city with a high birthrate where children suffer from malnutrition. Here the population grows rapidly even as people live on the edge of famine and are plunged into an existence marked above all by total uncertainty about the future.

People here simply live. There is no doubt they are living in extreme deprivation. However, they remain aware of the birth and death cycle that accompanies the life of Kinshasa and many other cities of the world. They respond by first attending to the immediately useful while struggling to safeguard their dignity. This period in the history of Kinshasa and its people is a step sideways. It enables all the inhabitants to explore new possibilities and combinations besides the familiar ones in the ongoing attempt to unite the urban and the suburban.

Kinshasa: A Big Bar   Kinshasa is a big bar. Characterized by an ambiance of uninterrupted feast. To paraphrase the song of Pepe Kalle, a famous Congolese musician, Kinshasa is a nightclub in which "those who want to drink, drink, and those who want to get drunk, get drunk." Every evening the bars and the discos transform the Cité into Kinshasa's hub. In these circumstances, hypnotized by light, music, colorful dress, and women, an individual can spend his daily earnings, even a month's salary, in a single night. *Mbongo eloko pamba*, money is nothing compared to what the bar can offer.

Songs like Papa Wemba's, Koffi's, Werrason's, erotic dances with evocative names like *ndombolo, Ko imbi ko, Kiri wa zenza Male ma mbwa*, games of seduction, beer, and mannerly speeches create the euphoric atmosphere that drowns out the frustrations of the day and the discriminations of age, income, class, and ethnic difference. Tangibly the city dwellers experience release and fulfillment in the bar. Throughout the night, affluent youngsters, married men, and unmarried women, along with the best singers and musicians, present a world hostile to continence, frugality, and sobriety as an ideal social model of openness.

City dwellers meet in the bar. Here they forget their social status. Fare-collectors from the taxi-buses, *pousse-pousseurs* (hand-driven carts), bootblacks, errand boys, motorcar guards come together in the bar to venerate the myth of elegance and money. In the recent past, the functionaries were monarchs in this arena. Nowadays, pocket money and style of dress buy a place in this space where money is the new master. Here people spend money as if it were peanuts. Money allows its owner to impose himself as the new king of this kingdom of perversion and illusion. Money buys beer, women, social relations, and probably redemption after a sinful night spent in the arms of many irresistible women! The accumulated money helps to accumulate women and social relations in the bar. In the bar, the slogan is "more-is-better."

The bar is the siege of those who have hands that spend easily, *maboko pete*. It rejects those who do not have money to consume beer and women. The pub is where people celebrate the cult of beauty, elegance, and the dandy look.[2] Here male and female achieve superiority and self-assurance through ostentatious or sumptuous behavior and frenetic exhibition.

The disco-bars and their musicians portray a society that vindicates the freedom and identity of the individual. They offer the illusion of an erotic world without structure or law.[3]

In this context, and from the male point of view, a woman is an object that is eaten. Her Christian name is *diamante*. Her family name is "money." Her surname is "wealth." The illusion created in the bar is that of men's superiority over women. Here, as in everyday life, women are asked and agree to be seductive, understanding, and caring. In reality, they feign respect for men's power over them because men often spend their daily pay or monthly salary in one night. That is the *Mushina* phenomenon.

Although men claim to control the female body, women constantly challenge men and refuse characterization as a mere body. Women in the bar take great pleasure in appropriating traditionally male roles. In the bar, the expected and accepted behavior of women becomes less and less clear. This space creates genuine confusion and overturns conventional perceptions of what it means "to be a man" or "to be a woman."

In the bar, women express their claims, although their voices are muffled by the volume of the music. Apparently, they are as good as men in this aggressive and violent win-win seductive game. Nevertheless, more than any member of

---

2 See ibid., p. 620.
3 See ibid.

the city, women know that life reduced to money and pleasure is nothing but deception.

The bar makes women aware that money generates both power and limits on their freedom. Consequently, although there may be no limits to male aggressive treatment of women in the bar, women very often succeed in drawing a line on what they will accept! In the bar, they subtly invite their partner on an interior journey toward the realization that they can regain their lost dignity only through common struggle. They have no choice. This recognition of oneness in their differences is vital for continuing to face and deal with the degrading forces of a city that separates them and finally destroys them. Without denying the presence of the oppressive man, women can adjust their priorities according to situations and moments of time inside the bar.

Therefore, in an arena where men seek "power over" them, women regularly maintain a balance between "power over" (control) and "power for" (service). In so doing, they refuse men's distorted image of women as passive receptacles. They invite men to move beyond gender disparities in an environment that is equally hostile to both men and women. In the bar, they remind men that they are all in the same boat, and they refuse the notion that a woman's honor should depend upon a man. In the bar, they ask men to recognize them not as the "dog that breaks the leash" (*mbwa bakata nsinga*), but as actors in their own right.

In the bar, drumming, passionate singing, and dance offer ludic and effervescent moments that reaffirm the ephemeral freedom and identity of the city dweller as a human being. The time for a beer, for a warm kiss and dance, the city dweller spends his money in search of a social status he knows the bar cannot truly provide. For beyond the show of fashion, and his spending and sexual behavior, the city dweller's strongest desire is to exist as a human being both in and outside of the bar.

The bar most definitely is not the locus in which the city dweller reconstructs his manhood. It is and will remain a temporary expiatory setting where the agonized city dweller laments the loss of unity with his environment and faces his permanent degradation. This process of introspection or revelation aims at filling the emptiness within the self. The passage to the bar becomes, then, a state of psychic illumination. The city dweller is induced to become aware of the deeper reasons for the disparities created by himself and by his divided city. He thereby avoids accusation, exclusion, and domination. Paradoxically, the bar initiates a process that begins with self-discovery and self-reflection. It ends with the recognition of the other human being and the city inside oneself. Since he cannot afford a psychoanalyst, the neurotic city dweller in Kinshasa goes to the bar and nightclub, paradoxically, to look for moderation and equilibrium.

Kinshasa: From Violence to Violence? Violence is everywhere in Kinshasa. Extreme deprivation due to the collapse of the formal economy and state institutions has created an underclass of demoralized and impoverished citizens. People in Kinshasa suffer from hunger. Children are starving from malnutrition or disease. Registration for secondary school and university is conducted by auction. The hospital detains some patients until they can pay the bill. The mentally ill, drug addicts, and alcoholics fight in the street over scraps of food. Small craftsmen, like their clients, receive only meager earnings and lead a life of misery. Rampant inflation continuously erodes the value of money. Neither wealthy nor poor have the means to avoid or deflect economic disaster. Life is a daily struggle to survive.

This state of perpetual violence induced by economic competition and the exclusion of urban dwellers from material progress foreshadows increasingly destructive behaviors. The adult loses his or her capacity to think clearly and to act according to conscience. The situation is no longer bearable and people are often unable to grasp the meaning of events or to distinguish between good and evil. The Ville and the Cité are victims of structural violence. They are victims of the dehumanizing principle "every man for himself" that deprives people of dignity and intensifies different forms of violence.

Violence, injustice, extortion, the systematic abuse of human rights, the extra-legal actions of police and private guards are entrenched features of life in Kinshasa. Military violence is difficult to contain in this urban setting, where weapons and military experts come from different countries and for various interests. In this world dominated by impunity, army and police violence, and abusive tribunals, hope for a better future becomes increasingly dim.

In Kinshasa, the forces of law and order are themselves one of the main agents of violence. The city's military police are plagued by corruption, entangled with organized crime and accustomed to using violent and illegal methods. In other words, violence, crime, abuse of human rights, and extra-legal actions on the part of police and military forces are increasingly widespread in Kinshasa. These practices are well known and include unsubstantiated arrests, torture, and battering. The military and police forces consider punishment and correction part of their duties.

The legal parameters of police work often shift, destabilizing the boundaries between legal and illegal and creating conditions for the continuation of routine abuse. In addition, police abuse has targeted the working classes in particular, and has frequently merged with political repression. Consequently, the poorer sectors of the population are routinely subjected to various forms of police violence and legal injustice.

Violence in Kinshasa marks the end of the era of conviviality between political leaders and the people. It occurs because rules governing the current military police include laws of exception that place them above civil justice and systems of accountability. This legal exception increases their impunity and their use of violence in dealing with civilians and assures them a wide margin of arbitrary behavior.

In Kinshasa, people lack the means to reestablish civil order. Most city dwellers have histories of police mistreatment and abuse to tell, and their narratives are full of indignation. Here apathy, irony, parody, derision, and violence have established themselves simply because the structures of law have failed or no longer exist. The majority of Kinois involved in any type of conflict do not call on the justice system to resolve their problems. The widespread feeling is that the system is extremely biased and does not offer poor people any possibility of justice. The people are under threat of dispossession, misappropriation, and dislocation. Permanently exposed to abuse and the deterioration of their city and communities, they have lost many of their illusions.

However, although exhausted, city dwellers refuse to turn against themselves. They reject self-victimization to avoid depression. In the immediate context, there are apparently no other strategies of resistance than violence. Uncontrolled, this violence is now breaking loose within the city. Constantly frustrated and deprived of hope, city dwellers frequently resort to pillages, reenacting the structural violence they have internalized. They attack the opulent, comfortable life represented by their targets, that is, luxury motor vehicles, symbols of a rapacious State and an ostentatious, self-indulgent privileged minority. City dwellers enter a cycle of violence in which the voiceless are always the losers. They destroy both enterprises and private properties and they lose their jobs. They violently react against a system characterized by institutionalized violence, extortion of the weak, arbitrary arrests, disastrous inflation, and a ruthless economy.

It would be wrong to interpret these revolts as reactions against modernity and the hopes that it awakened. City dwellers in Kinshasa do not refuse the material progress represented by factories, businesses, industrial complexes, warehouses, and dispensaries. They simply aspire to a system at the service of the majority, not the other way around. People need material progress that supports social bonds instead of destroying them. The burst of violence in Kinshasa has nothing to do with an inability to adapt to Western notions of material progress. Rather, it is a call for the redistribution of the goods produced by this material progress, a demand for social justice that says no to the law of the strongest and the brutal struggle for life based on the survival of the fittest.

Unfortunately, the victims have used the same weapons as their oppressors. Blinded by their anger and despair, they have missed the opportunity to introduce real change to the core of their existence. They have entered into the cycle of private and illegal vengeance that results in the spread and proliferation of violence.

The have-nots of urban and suburban Kinshasa have ceased to be passive beings. Indeed, exploitation, domination, exclusion have led them from resignation and despair to adjustment and resistance. Their violence constitutes a process of dual identification, with both the oppressor and the oppressed. As a result, they now refuse to validate the notion of violence as a banal and inevitable element in their struggle for survival. They seem ready for other victories, but this time over the civil that destroys the human being and establishes violence as inevitable in the process of deconstructing and reconstructing the fabric of Congolese society.

Kinshasa: An Economy of Resistance For the populations of the Ville and the Cité, most trade occurs within the so-called informal economy that functions as a survival strategy for the masses. The code that regulates the life of the growing dispossessed of Kinshasa is the now famous "Article 15" – "Fend for Yourself." This is the clause that the voiceless of Kinshasa would like to have seen in the Constitution of the wealthy minority. It stands for the economy of resistance, the various life and survival strategies that the excluded masses of urban dwellers use to manage difficult situations.

This economy of resistance takes various forms: self-managed workshops, food co-ops, soup kitchens, production workshops, small retail stores, junk collection and resale, taxi driving, small repairs, street vending, housing organizations, charity institutions, begging, drug smuggling, alcohol selling, and small theft. It concerns first the usufruct of "goods that one has displaced," such as tools, bricks, lumber, tires, piping, and other construction materials. In addition, it comprises acts of fraud and blackmail of all sorts. These often occur in a context of ruse and play. For example, the pedestrian or driver, simply by stopping in the anonymous public space, exposes himself to all kinds of extortionist games. For the oppressed, petty theft attains the status of a common mode of survival. It is a version of power for those who have little share in the material progress of the city.

The economy of resistance is the consequence of a dream of development that has turned sour for most urban dwellers, crushed under the weight of poverty. It is a soulless wasteland, characterized by the arrogance of the privileged, that spawned the informal economy. The intolerable and unsustainable degradation and acute misery of people in the Ville and the Cité are the root of this economic alternative.

Urban dwellers refer to the informal sector developing at the margins of the nation-economy and state with both self-conscious laughter and pride. This economy of resistance brings them honor where otherwise the logic of the market leads to total despair. Moreover, the informal economy provides greater benefits than regular employment. It is "informal" because it pays no heed to experts. The informal economy is neither irrational nor backward. It has its structure and does not need to be formalized or normalized with a view to accumulation. The experts qualify this economy with the term "informal" probably because they do not understand its mechanisms and its ethics.

As an intermediary place, the informal economy responds to a multiplicity of objectives that are simultaneously economic, social, and cultural. The informal world of crafty plunder and enterprise is the response of the voiceless to the collapse of political and economic life in Kinshasa. It is a state built on the fringes of the formal state, arrogantly challenging the privileged minority, who practice their own forms of plunder and extortion by exploiting the instruments of state for personal enrichment.

The informal economy is the space in which those who have no "civilization" – "the" underdeveloped, "the" black, "human garbage" – intend to reestablish the balance between "not-having" and "being." Here the individual – the subject who brings in the labor factor, his creativity, his potentialities, and his choices – organizes his market. He or she is the boss who hires workers from the local community or from his or her family. He or she steps into the informal economic space as an actor. He or she is at last the protagonist of an economic system in which cooperation and community play the central role.

As an active agent in this economy, the urban dweller ceases to be expelled from labor, that is, from productive activity. He or she organizes a market different from the world market, for it does not exclude him or her. The informal economy is the locus of the city dweller's renewal, where he or she begins again. Here people do not long for another America. They simply refuse to be the "beneficiaries" of an illusionary material progress promoted by a phantom State.

The above comments attest to the fact that informal activities constitute more than a roster of survival strategies. Indeed, in Kinshasa, these have evolved into a set of stable employment and revenue-generating economic organizations. Furthermore, people here reject the notion that the informal must be formalized to ensure the economic growth of the country. What is wrong is neither the existence of the formal nor of the informal economy. What is wrong is to claim that the formal economy alone is "economy." Just as man and woman make the "human," the formal and informal economies constitute "economy."

When the formal economy dominates, the informal does not disappear. It is still present, latent and patient. The same happens in a society dominated by the informal economy. The formal economy remains, although it no longer structures the economic life of society.

Taking the above considerations into account, we can see how tricky it is to ask the younger generation to be creative, economically speaking. There is no doubt that they are creative. Indeed, creativity is not the issue. What is at stake is the context of a formal economy that does not give them a chance at survival unless they become competitive, meaning that they "eat" each other. Obviously, adults are intelligent enough to avoid recognizing their responsibility in establishing the dominion of an aggressive formal economy in which only the "fittest" are winners.

Kinshasa: A Healing Parody Through parody, the urban dweller in Kinshasa writes a mock poem that allows him to overcome the manifold daily experiences of loss. Laughter, irony, mimicry are healing tools in the hands of the weak that enable them to stand as a moral critical instance of their fragmented city. In Kinshasa, people mock political leaders and their delusions of power over others. The church prophet and his arrogant pretension to liberate people are turned upside down. The priest and his fictive sanctity are caricatured. Jesus and the church he represents are not spared. They are also pillaged! The policeman and his corrupted sense of order are turned into derision. The married man who is always faithful until his partner finds him adulterous is ridiculed. Values embodied in the virgin are questioned. The white man and his illusory formal economy are ironically painted.

Things have fallen apart and the city dweller can exorcise the pain only through laughter, mimicry, irony, and parody. He laughs at himself as a member of this superficial and outmoded city. He ridicules his ability to live in this empty city. He mocks his reality and his dream of a better future or of salvation characterized by equality, equity, and solidarity. He reduces himself to an invisible man. He kneels down to rediscover the sense of humility that reveals his person as neither a *diplomé* nor an intellectual but simply as a human being.

This process requires tremendous strength and courage because the quest is for not only material progress but also ethical values. The issue for the urban dweller in Kinshasa is to attain a balance between the satisfaction of his need "to have" and "to be." To reach this goal, the city dweller must kill the false man and woman he or she has been thus far. He or she must get rid of the inhuman, unethical being he or she has been forced to become in order to have access to material progress. The city dweller can refuse to be reduced to his or her capacity for accumulating money and power. She or he can reject this world based on a perverse logic of growth, productivism, individualism, power over others, and profit maximization.

In this long pilgrimage, parody becomes the socio-drama that helps in these first moments of the city dweller's quest for political and economic activities that support social bonds. Thanks to this healing parody, the city dweller resists the failed recipes of Eurocentric modernity. For city dwellers in Kinshasa, economic and political activities are social activities. They do not conceive any personal betterment without social, political, and economic betterment, nor any social, political, and economic transformation without personal transformation. Individual political or economic profit is less important than the moral obligation to help others in need.

Parody is a means to put into question the idea of backwardness versus "being modern," the "joy" of accumulation without limits. Its goal is to transform both victim and agent of this violent and dehumanizing system. The purpose is to recreate unity through an act of reconciliation that requires respect of both man and woman, of oppressed and oppressor. Parody can lead to profound change, since it is the victim who initiates it and signals new ways of acting and being.

People are not against modernity per se, but against modernity that imposes the past of Euro-American societies as a future for our cities and countries. People are struggling for modernity on their own terms. Indeed, trying to be(come) like the other is not satisfactory. Parody is the first step in this long process. It begins with a deconstruction of the city dweller's self and leads to a search for an ethical order that will support modest and localized alternatives.

In present-day Kinshasa, people are not lacking in knowledge, but rather in wisdom. They frequently realize that their efforts to construct a sustainable and kind city require courage, or better, spiritual resources. To paraphrase T. S. Eliot, brave city dwellers will not cease their exploration because the end of all their exploring will be to arrive where they began and know the place for the first time.

Kinshasa: A Local Ethical Quest Kinshasa is a city visibly agitated. But this agitation goes together with a strong will to reshape the city and push it beyond dichotomies and the gospel of competitiveness. Strangely, it is here that urban dwellers learn to accept each other's limits and take responsibility for them. They seem aware that this is necessary to the city's revival or renewal. The visitor to Kinshasa who remains in the Ville will not notice this flame reshaping the city and its inhabitants. New Kinshasa is coming to life out of local communities (Christian or not), tontines, neo-lineage social clubs, and so on.

These local or communal organizations widen opportunities and reduce the risk of disaster generated by the dichotomous nature of the city. It is here at the local level, not the higher echelons of the city, that Kinshasa's people struggle against the entropy that created the divided city. Men and women from the Cité and the Ville face their human identities in crisis and realize that they are two wings of the same bird – that is, Kinshasa. Kinshasa can fly if both wings have the same motion. To be transformed, Kinshasa must move beyond the Cité/Ville divide.

The challenge in the local communities is to reach a balance in the appreciation of urban and suburban ways of perceiving life and shaping reality in Kinshasa. How do we reconcile the inhabitants of the urban and the suburban? How do we induce them to cross-fertilize, so to speak, rather than withdraw from each other?

Local communities are spaces in which people learn to tame all sorts of urban fears – innate or created, natural or cultural, existential or ideological – that otherwise lead to rejection of the other. Genuine change in the relationship between urban and suburban will occur only when urban dwellers face their deepest fears, of themselves and of the other. Local communities are initiating social changes generated by this interior journey to avoid backlashes, painful regressions that imply impoverishment for the city and its inhabitants. Here people from the urban and the suburban come together with their different worldviews and learn to communicate, to initiate an encounter that will not explode into violence.

As part of the history of groups of citizens living in the Cité and the Ville, these local communities are not static. They reflect and acknowledge a dynamic process of change. Indeed, it is at this level that social struggle, creativity, and solidarity are taking place. Here external and internal mutual influences, be they social, economic, political, ideological, or generational, continuously pose new challenges. New answers and new solutions are invented when the old ones are no longer satisfactory. Admittedly, these solutions are usually localized and modest. Still, they deserve our attention, even though no equally strong force of change in mentalities actually balances the force of change in practices. Will the Ville and the Cité one day be in a state of deep "interpenetration"? Will the dichotomy and the disparity between them one day vanish?

Examining these questions underlines the basic challenge all city dwellers face in Kinshasa, that is, establishing vital social networks that can offer assistance in times of need. It seems an endless and demanding process of gifts and counter-gifts. This process is ongoing, because of the evolution of the city dwellers themselves through different stages of life and because of broader changes in Kinshasa. The urban dweller's constant challenge is to reestablish or reinvent his or her disrupted communities and city. In this process, festivities, burials, and funeral wakes (*matanga*) play an important role. They are not wasteful but reasonable investments in social relations that may prove fruitful in the future.

Positive interaction between the Cité and the Ville will be possible only when the inhabitants of both are considered of equal value. City dwellers from the Ville and the Cité will move beyond this dichotomy only when they find new ethical and spiritual motivations. This is not pious sentiment or an unrealistic dream, but a concrete necessity for their future as city dwellers in Kinshasa.

Space, Culture, and Agency in Contemporary Freetown: The Making and Remaking of a Postcolonial City

Ibrahim Abdullah

The city, particularly the capital city in Africa, can best be understood within the context of the formation of the nation-state. That nation-state came dripping with blood, the result of the stitching together of several independent polities under the aegis of an external power – the colonial state. The capital city in Africa – a colonial creation founded on violence – was not built for Africans. Rather, it was built for the white man, the foreigner, the other! Its central and imposing architecture in the city center, its exclusive residential pattern, and its restrictions on the movement of specific social groups underline that violence. The colonial city was constructed on an exclusivist paradigm: it was the apartheid city par excellence. Exclusion was the major hallmark of the colonial capital city in Africa.[1]

This exclusion of particular social groups, subalterns, in my view did not come to an end with the formal attainment of flag independence. Put differently, the exclusive paradigm that informed the construction of the colonial city continued to reproduce itself in the postcolonial era. Exclusion denies citizenship rights to those excluded; their collective actions/voices are consequently criminalized; their honest and innovative strategies dubbed "informalization." I want to argue that the so-called informal sector, informal economy, informal settlement in African cities should be read as a counter-discourse. That is to say, a counter-discourse to the dominant and suffocating violence which induces an existential violence: the living conditions and ways of making a living of those who are collectively excluded. It is this counter-discourse that I here set out to capture.

The extreme centralization of political power, the devastating impact of World Bank structural adjustment policies, and the ten-year rebel war in Sierra

---

[1] On the making of the colonial city, see Frederick Cooper, ed., *Struggle for the City: Migrant Labor, Capital, and the State in Urban Africa* (Beverly Hills, Calif.: Sage Publications, 1983), and Michael P. Banton, *West African City: A Study of Tribal Life in Freetown* (London: Oxford University Press, 1957).

Leone have reconfigured the city of Freetown beyond the imagination of its city fathers or colonial planners.[2] School dropouts, erstwhile refugees, the mobile displaced population, or, better still, those without a visible source of income, congregate in the city center on a daily basis trying to make a living. In this quest, they have redefined working time and the marketplace: they work or ply their trade from sun up to sun down. And the market has become just about anywhere goods and services can be exchanged, while time has been stretched beyond the normally tolerable working hours. Too poor to afford the exorbitant dollar rent being demanded by exploitative landlords, these new citizens now live in numerous informal settlements in and around the city of Freetown.

Central to understanding this reconfiguring project is the role of subalterns as active agents carving a niche for themselves in a situation where the state or municipality is a fading reality. What we are witnessing here is not a case of a weak or collapsed state authority. Rather, it is one of total subversion of order. The irony here is that subalterns/lumpens constitute the very social group that the colonial state sought to exclude from the city – its altar of modernity – when it was constructed in the dying days of mercantile slavery. This group had its organic intellectual. It was Frantz Fanon who turned Karl Marx on his head by elevating the lumpenproletariat to the status of a revolutionary group.

This paper begins to explore aspects of subaltern existence in the city of Freetown. It argues that the reconfiguring of Freetown from below opens up the possibility of remaking the city within the framework of a more inclusive paradigm centered on social citizenship that would incorporate the interests of the different social groups. This radical alternative runs counter to the original Freetown project as an exclusive enclave for the realization of the notorious Cs: Christianity, Commerce, and Civilization. The paper is divided into three parts. The first section deals with the making of the colonial city; the second describes the remaking from below; while the third examines the impact of the war.

The Colonial Enclave   The modernist project that gave birth to the idea of Freetown was a product of the antislavery lobby in late 18th-century England. It was, arguably, the first major "humanitarian" project in modern history conceived as a way of compensating Africans for three-and-a-half centuries of European slavery. The original settlement was therefore designed as a "beacon of hope" for the people of Africa from where, it was argued, the blessings of the three Cs would flow to combat the deadly superstition, backwardness, and inhumanity that had

---

2 For Freetown, see Christopher Fyfe and Eldred Jones, eds., *Freetown: A Symposium* (Freetown: Sierra Leone University Press, 1968).

plagued the "dark continent." From 1787, when the first group of Africans from London and the so-called New World landed in Freetown, to 1893, when the city was constituted as a municipality, the settlement remained exclusive and discriminatory.[3] The returnees/settlers were not only favored in the day-to-day running of the settlement, but their descendants – who were later called Creoles – exerted enormous influence in the administration of the settlement from which the original inhabitants were excluded. Access to Western education and jobs ensured the dominance of the settlers in the social and commercial activities of the new enclave. This division between the indigenous peoples and the returnees/settlers – between citizens and subjects – would continue to shape political discourse and everyday life for the next two centuries.

The settlement in Freetown attracted people from the Sierra Leone hinterland, the West African sub-region, and the New World. The residential pattern in the city was ethnicized: each group was confined to a separate area in the city. Space, ethnicity, and Westernization were crucial variables in the making of the 19th-century city.[4] Thus, the settlers occupied the city center and its surroundings close to the business district and the seat of government together with the few European officials and administrators. The Europeans would vacate this central area in the late 19th century for the much more pleasant and amiable surroundings on the hilltop. The city center was dotted with impressive West Indian architecture complete with churches of the different Christian denominations – from mainstream Anglicans to dissenting Huntingdonians. The only ethnic group allowed to settle close to the city center were the Kru from neighboring Liberia – a seafaring group that was indispensable to British maritime commerce in the region. The original inhabitants were pushed to the fringes of the settlement, where they lived side by side with other immigrant groups like the Fullah, the Sosso, and the Mandingo, who were predominantly Muslim. These groups would establish their own mosques in their respective communities by the end of the 19th century. The existence of separate social and cultural groupings/communities was a key marker of Freetown in the 19th century. All these groups, without exception, were, however, subordinated to a higher authority: the crown colony state proclaimed in 1808 when the British Crown took control of the colony of Freetown from the Sierra Leone Company.[5]

---

3 See Christopher Fyfe, *A History of Sierra Leone* (London: Oxford University Press, 1962); John Peterson, *Province of Freedom* (London: Faber and Faber, 1965); Barbara E. Harrell-Bond, Allen M. Howard, and David E. Skinner, *Community Leadership and the Transformation of Freetown* (The Hague: Mouton, 1978).
4 Arthur T. Porter, *Creoledom: A Study of the Development of Freetown Society* (London: Oxford University Press, 1963).
5 For details on the administration of Freetown, see S. A. J. Pratt, "The Government of Freetown," in *Freetown: A Symposium*.

The most enduring legacy of the 19th century was undoubtedly the creation of two different types of administration for the two groups: the descendants of the settlers and the indigenous inhabitants.[6] Why did the British promote a discourse that facilitated the division of the city into citizens and subjects? What are the connections between the establishment of a city council in 1893 and the construction of a so-called "tribal" headman administration in the city at about the same time? What are the linkages between this laboratory of indirect rule in the city and the eventual imposition of indirect rule in the hinterland after the 1898 wars? Did this happen because the British "respected" the culture of the indigenous peoples in the hinterland, or was it a deliberate attempt to impose a botched modernist project? Are there any connections between the exclusionary nature of this modernist project and the exclusionary politics of the colonial and postcolonial states? Is there an archaeology of exclusion that runs through the colonial and postcolonial societies? These questions are crucial to understanding contemporary Freetown; they touch on the idea of the nation-state as it was imagined before independence, and they underline the obvious gaps in our knowledge of social citizenship, rights, and obligations.

That the British created two local government institutions – the city council and the system of "tribal" headman – for the two different categories of peoples they invented at a time when Creole identity was in the making suggests that the modernist project was exclusivist and discriminatory, designed solely for citizens. These two institutions, however, fall short of anything close to citizenship or subjecthood. The construction of these two categories was a convenient way for the British to manipulate two different symbols, two different systems of signification, to arrive at the same thing: domination and control.

The subjects in the city were ostensibly under the control of their respective "tribal" headman. The headman, who doubled as labor contractor and custodian of "tribal" culture, was responsible for the actions of his countrymen in the city. Yet he had no right to land nor was he in a position to determine what that "tribal" culture might be. He was therefore at the mercy of the British colonial official to determine what his real role was. Similarly, the construction of citizens supposedly gave members of the *civis* the right to govern themselves. Since they were, in theory, subjects of the British Crown, they were ipso facto accorded certain rights and privileges befitting their status as citizens. Their citizenship did not translate into making laws for themselves, nor did they exert considerable influence in the affairs of the city. Such rights and privileges – freedom of expression, of assembly, of the press, and so on – granted them were cir-

---

[6] Harrell-Bond et al., *Community Leadership and the Transformation of Freetown*.

cumscribed by the very colonial power which accorded them the right of citizenship. The inherent limitation of these two institutions became the subject of endless debate in the period prior to independence. The Freetown experiment would be extended to other parts of the country after the 1898 war against colonial taxation.

The city of Freetown did not change much between 1898, when it became the capital city of a much wider territorial area, and 1961, when Sierra Leone became independent. Freetown was more of an administrative center dependent on the hinterland and surrounding villages for its food supply. The colonial state was the largest employer of labor in the railways, the docks/port, and the state bureaucracy. The merchant class remained small and relied largely on import-export trade. The two world wars and the decision to abolish slavery in 1927 were the major developments that shaped the history of the city in the colonial period. The numerous construction projects during the wars created job opportunities for both skilled and unskilled labor. The boom in construction meant that more people left the hinterland for Freetown in search of jobs. Soldiers recruited from the hinterland opted to stay in Freetown after their discharge from active service. And when slavery was abolished in 1927, some ex-slaves, particularly those whose owners did not want to let go, migrated to Freetown in part to safeguard their newfound freedom but also to find other ways of making a living. By the end of the colonial period, the population of Freetown had doubled.

Remaking from Below   If the colonial city was palpably marked by its cultural and political divisions, the postcolonial city sought to mend those cracks by invoking the language of inclusion: the voice of the nation. Independence, in this reading, signified not only the end of colonial rule but also the beginning of prosperity for the citizens of the new nation-state. The bright lights of the city signified this new hope and aspiration; it was the place to go, the place to find jobs and the place to settle. The city of Freetown therefore became the dream destination of every citizen in search of the proverbial greener pasture – from the high school dropout to the college graduate, from the casual laborer to the skilled worker, from the rural migrant to the Sierra Leonean in the diaspora. And Freetown would be the place to go when a nasty rebel war broke out exactly thirty years after independence.

Key to understanding the postcolonial city is the extreme centralization of politics in the 1970s and the devastating consequences of the World Bank–sponsored structural adjustment programs of the 1980s. The centralization of politics/power under the All Peoples Congress (APC) from 1968 to 1992 made it impossible for any local government institution to function *qua* government. The Freetown city council that had functioned reasonably well, with regular free and fair elections, was converted into an arm of the ruling party patronage network. The outdated and backward system of "tribal" administration was subsequently reinvented and reintroduced to undermine the legitimacy of the municipality. Lacking any form of autonomy, the city council gradually ceased to play an important role in the running of the city. Consequently, all the municipal schools, the markets, the cemeteries, the City Park, and other revenue-yielding institutions directly under city control entered a long period of decline from which they have yet to recover. A management committee answerable only to itself has been in charge of the city administration for well over seventeen years. It is therefore not surprising that the city council was unable to function *qua* government when it was confronted with the devastating consequences of the World Bank–sponsored structural adjustment policies. By the time war broke out in 1991, the city's infrastructure was already in an advanced stage of decay. Incessant power cuts and erratic water supplies were part of the daily misery confronting Freetownians. Garbage piled up for months on the streets while corrupt officials at the Ministry of Lands, Housing, and Environment conspired to sell prized state land used as refuse collection points. The level of filth was so appalling in the mid-1990s that the government had to devote the last Saturday of every month to mass general cleaning of the city.

Cutbacks in education and social services, rampant corruption, dwindling revenue, galloping inflation, and chronic unemployment begin to describe the Sierra Leonean political economy in the 1980s. The most important development in the reconfiguration of Freetown was the ghettoization of the city and the intense struggle over space and housing. Unlike elsewhere on the continent, affordable housing, whether for the working class or the middle class, was never undertaken by the city or central government. High-ranking civil servants were encouraged through state grants to purchase and build their own houses in the 1960s and '70s, a result of the Africanization process in the era of decolonization. A modest attempt was later made to provide housing for people in the low-income bracket at Kissy, a location close to the industrial center on the outskirts of the city. This was not a city-sponsored project and it did not benefit the urban poor. A plan to continue the scheme in the late '70s had to be abandoned because of inadequate funding. The city's poor were to remain unhoused throughout the 1980s and '90s.[7]

---

7 Toma J. Makannah, ed., *Handbook of the Population of Sierra Leone* (Freetown: Toma Enterprises, 1996).

The lack of adequate housing is closely related to the increasing ghettoization of the city. And even though the discourse on ghettoization had entered the official mind in the post-1945 period, no attempt was made to arrest or reverse the situation. Overcrowding in the waterfront area of central Freetown, where families of three generations could be found living in abandoned warehouses, was to be reproduced tenfold in the East End area in the 1950s and '60s. Ask a Freetownian about the East End and he/she will immediately express his/her disapproval. The East End is not only the gateway to the city from the hinterland, it is also close to the industrial area and the city's major port – where many a migrant from the hinterland could easily get a job as a laborer. Migrants from the hinterland therefore make it their first port of call, a place to set up shop until they can find suitable accommodations. Close to 25 percent of the good houses in the East End were destroyed during the rebel occupation of Freetown in January 1999. The densely populated East End and its rough life contrast sharply with the sparsely populated central or West End and its posh hilltop suburbs of Wilberforce, Juba Hill, and Hill Station. The lack of affordable housing and the intense overcrowding in the East End opened up other avenues for those entering the city. "Illegal" structures or so-called informal settlements began to proliferate on the numerous hills surrounding Freetown.

More people entered Freetown during the 1980s and '90s than in any other period of its 200-year history. Unable to find a place they could call their own in an already crowded city, new Freetownians began to reclaim the hilltops in the east and central parts of the city. Informal settlements on state and private property began to emerge on the city's hilltop. Corrugated iron sheets – *pan bohdi* in Krio – held together by wooden pillars served the housing needs of Freetown's teeming population.[8] These *pan bohdi* are extremely hot in the dry season, when temperatures are high, and very uncomfortable in the rainy season, when it is wet and cold. Some inhabitants in these new settlements could access power supply through illegal channels, but in most cases these dwellings go without power or water. The inhabitants own some of these dwellings and they exploit informal networks to acquire legal documentation through the Ministry of Lands to legitimize their claim on their newfound property. Once constructed on state land, these structures are rarely taken down by officials.[9]

---

8 A *pan bohdi* dwelling consists of corrugated iron sheets held together by narrow wooden poles. These are the most popular dwellings among Freetown's urban poor. The materials are cheap and affordable but they are extremely uncomfortable in the tropical heat.
9 However, at the time this paper was being revised (July 2002), the Minister of Lands, Housing, and Environment had begun a demolition exercise of the so-called illegal structures in some of the informal settlements.

The struggle over space is so intense that Freetownians have encroached on land reserved for the dead: cemeteries. More than 50 percent of the land area of the Ropukur cemetery in the East End – a place where convicts and executed prisoners are laid to rest – has been illegally taken over by squatters and "legal" occupants. The Kingtom cemetery in the West End, the Circular Road cemetery in the central area, and the Kissy Road cemetery in the East End have all lost 10–25 percent of their space to informal settlements. The land grabbing or illegal occupation has occurred on both state and private property, so that more than 65 percent of lawsuits in Freetown involve land-related matters.[10] Whole new cities have sprung up within the city of Freetown. These cities of subalterns are expanding the frontiers of the ghetto from the East End to the west and central area. Every space in the city is under siege from subalterns: from open space in cemeteries to dangerously inaccessible areas under the city's numerous bridges and surrounding hilltops.

The culture in these informal settlements revolves around *potes*, the periodic masquerades, the video parlor, and the ever-present Pentecostal churches. The *pote* is a joint, a rendezvous, where young unemployed youth, mostly male, congregate to talk, do drugs, and just hang out. It is a space created by subalterns far away from the prying eyes of the law. It was in the *potes* of Freetown that subalterns and their student allies sat to discuss the insurgency alternative; it was to the *pote* that the rebel Revolutionary United Front (RUF) returned to recruit its cadres; and it was to the *pote* that they would turn for support when their short-lived regime was under siege in 1998.[11] The *pote* and the video parlor equipped with satellite dish rule the world in the numerous informal settlements. European soccer matches and Nigerian home video movies are the favorites. One can watch two European soccer matches in a day for just under one US dollar. The favorite teams are Manchester United and Liverpool, and it is not uncommon to see fanatic supporters arguing at the end of the game over what went wrong and why. Betting for one's team is also a common practice.

Home video movies and European soccer matches are the two most popular forms of leisure for the young in a city devoid of any common recreational space for its citizens. The collapse and eventual demise of the big cinema in the late 1970s and early '80s, the conversion of the only public park in the city center

---

10 Conversations with senior legal practitioners.
11 See the following for details: Ibrahim Abdullah, "Bush Path to Destruction: The Origin and Character of the Revolutionary United Front (RUF/SL)," *Journal of Modern African Studies* 36, no. 2 (1998), pp. 203–235; Ibrahim Abdullah and Patrick Muana, "The Revolutionary United Front: A Revolt of the Lumpenproletariat," in *African Guerrillas*, ed. Christopher Clapham (London: James Currey, 1998), pp. 172–193; Ibrahim Abdullah, ed., *The Sierra Leone War* (Dakar: CODESRIA, forthcoming 2003).

into a marketplace, and the appropriation of the few public spaces to resettle those displaced by the war have put paid to any form of recreational activity. The jogging culture, now a popular form of recreation, takes place on the streets. The street is currently being reclaimed in ways that were unthinkable in the past. Food vendors, kids playing soccer, and the ever-present mobile street hawker are all contesting for whatever little space they can claim on the city's narrow streets and pavements. Culture, leisure, and space are reconfiguring the city of Freetown in new and imaginative ways that continue to defy official logic.

There is a contradictory process going on here. On the one hand, there is ghettoization and an intense struggle over space; on the other hand, the establishment of many fancy restaurants in the city center and its posh beaches. These islands of plenty in a sea of filth cater exclusively to a foreign clientele – the expatriate worker and tourists with dollars to spend – with a menu featuring Asian, Middle Eastern, Indian, Mexican, and African cuisine. A new trend in this booming restaurant industry is the feminization of the workforce: the restaurants in the city center only employ female waiters, while those on the beachfront only have men. Whereas both women and men are to be found in the numerous security firms that have emerged in the city, the Internet cafés employ more women than men. There are more women working in the formal sector today than at any time in Freetown's history. The feminization of the workforce in the formal sector is partly a result of the war and partly due to the widespread poverty. Mostly young, single, and still living with parents or guardians, these women are compelled to earn a living to augment the household income constantly being eaten up by inflation and currency devaluation. The domestic pressure to earn a living, to subsidize the household budget, begins to explain the high number of sex workers, both male and female, in contemporary Freetown.

The traditional division of labor based on gender, which hitherto prevailed in the informal sector, has also disappeared. Women have moved from selling foodstuff and textiles to hawking all sorts of odds and ends in the city center. They now sell anything from razor blades to exercise books; from candles to matches; from safety pins to nail cutters and handkerchiefs. Hawking is now a full-time occupation for Freetown's teeming population of young men and women. Low overhead, aggressive marketing strategy, and mobility put the hawker in a better position compared to the stationary petty trader. But competition – too many hawkers selling the same item – makes one wonder how profitable this kind of trading is. The most common among this group are the men/boys selling coconut, the cigarette and kola boys, and the shoeshine boys from neighboring Guinea. Other groups worth mentioning are the dollar boys trading in foreign currency, the ever-present photographers in the city center, the newspaper vendors, and the audiocassette hawkers. Of all these groups, only the dollar boys and vendors are organized in the form of a union.

War and the City   Freetownians like to imagine that the current urban malaise is largely war induced. Overcrowded dwellings, the proliferation of sex workers, endless traffic jams, incessant power outages, and erratic water supply are some of the markers of everyday life in contemporary Freetown. But the ugly truth is that these developments predated the war. What the war did was to accelerate the rate and pace of decadence in a city with no visible governing structure, a city whose inhabitants do not pay taxes or elect those who run the affairs of its so-called management committee – an ad hoc body periodically appointed by the central government to guide the affairs of the city. Between 1991, when war broke out, to 1999, when Freetown was attacked and occupied by rebels, the city population trebled and living conditions deteriorated to an extent that people are to be found occupying any and every abandoned building. By 2000, the city could easily be described as congested, dilapidated, and abandoned. Its inhabitants living on top of each other: the rich at the top, the poor at the bottom. At the apex of this set-up, ironically, are those who had come to Sierra Leone because of the war: the UN personnel, both civilian and military.

The war in the hinterland remained a distant reality up to 1995. Before this period, the scars of war were visible only through the occasional mass recruitment drive in the city, the movement of large convoys of troops to the war front, and the trickling presence of displaced civilians seeking refuge. This was to change with the coming of mercenaries (the Gurkhas and the Executive Outcomes) and the multinational peacekeeping forces – the Economic Community of West African States Monitoring Group (ECOMOG) and the United Nations Mission in Sierra Leone (UNAMSIL).[12] The presence in the city of a substantial number of foreign troops and their civilian support staff put heavy strains on the already destroyed infrastructure, even as it brought in needed cash in a cash-strapped economy dependent on donor funding. Housing these newcomers in the city, their first port of call, drove up the price of rented space as landlords and fly-by-night estate agents hiked their rents a hundredfold. Instead of collecting rent in the local currency, landlords now demanded foreign currency and a minimum two-year lease. Stories abound of Sierra Leoneans who were evicted

---

12   The Economic Community of West African States (ECOWAS) deployed a multinational monitoring group with heavy Nigerian presence to keep the peace in Sierra Leone in 1998. The following year, 1999, the United Nations sent in a peacekeeping force – the UNAMSIL.

from their dwellings by their compatriots because they could not pay in dollars. Within two years of their arrival, the peacekeepers – ECOMOG and UNAMSIL – had taken over all the beautiful villas and bungalows in Freetown's posh suburbs. Their arrival in the city worsened the housing problem and pushed to the hilltops many who would otherwise have found a place with their kith and kin. Overcrowding, congestion, and over-stretched amenities describe the housing situation in the city.

War, it must be remembered, is a double-edged sword: it makes some people rich and others poor. The housing condition and the struggle over space constitute the most visible aspects of the state of abject poverty that predated the war years, 1991–2000. Every social group in Sierra Leone was hit by the war, beginning with the peasantry who lost their land, to workers who lost their jobs after the mines or factory folded up, and yet others who could not be paid because the money was just not available. A majority of those who lost out and could afford it traveled to Freetown hoping to begin a new life. Young teenage girls/women, forced by the war to fend for themselves or to augment meager household incomes, became involved in the sex trade. Their principal target clientele were United Nations personnel (UNAMSIL), who it is generally believed have more than enough dollars to spend. Armed with a cellular phone given to them by their UNAMSIL liaison and clad in tight jeans with outrageous wigs to match, these teenage girls/women could be seen on the beachfront, the main entertainment center and the UN headquarters, plying their trade from sun down to sun up. Most of them were displaced Sierra Leoneans from outside Freetown, or Liberian refugees who had come to the city to make a living. They could be seen every evening haggling with their prospective customers in their posh four-wheel-drive vehicles marked "UN." There are now more sex workers in Freetown than at any time in its history.

Freetown is what it is today not because of the war but because Sierra Leone is a one-city nation. To unmake Freetown, or even remake the city like its besieged inhabitants are currently doing, is to question received ideas and practices about who should be in the city and what rights they should have.

Mainstreaming Subalterns: By Way of Conclusion Contemporary Freetown is a city bursting at the seams with close to 2 million people crowded into a land space that has not seen any new network of roads for more than half a century. How do we begin to make sense of land grabbing ("encroachment" in local parlance), the proliferation of informal settlements, and the ghettoization of the city whose nominal administrators know nothing or care less about how its inhabitants live or even die? What tentative conclusions can we draw from the independent and single-minded action of its inhabitants to make life more comfortable for themselves? Do we dismiss these developments as a by-product of the war and therefore assume that they will vanish now that the war is over? Or do we fashion policies that will engage these multiple voices/actions from below and thereby arrive at a solution to some of these problems?

The citizen-subject dichotomy that characterized the colonial city may have disappeared, to be replaced by a new army of subalterns threatening to remake the city in ways that would be accommodative of their collective interests. This new army of subalterns defies subjecthood even as it strives toward the legitimate goal of social citizenship. After all, the city, the historical *civis*, was constituted as a place for citizens – people with full rights and obligations. The enormous energy being invested in this survivalist project, to live and to reproduce in the postcolonial city, could be channeled into more productive ways if only subalterns were accepted as citizens with full right and obligations. The lumpenproletariat may not be the revolutionary class that Fanon envisioned. And they may not have played the revolutionary role that he said they would. Yet their everyday action in the city of Freetown compels us to rethink the city and the role of its citizens in new ways that challenge our conception of urbanization, citizenship, and the role of the nation-state in the contemporary era.

Exploring the Rift/Shift in the African Urban Paradigm

"There's Space for Africa in the New South Africa (?)": African Migrants and Urban Governance in Johannesburg[1]

Maxine Reitzes

The title of this paper, borrowed from the headline (*sans* question mark) of an editorial on foreign migrants published in a South African Sunday newspaper, reflects the widespread ambiguity concerning the place of foreign migrants in South Africa, and the country's relationship to the continent. One of the dominant discourses concerning this relationship continues to divorce South Africa from "the rest of Africa." Anecdotal evidence abounds: for example, a black South African compere at a Johannesburg jazz club introduced a jazz band from Kenya as coming "all the way from Africa"; an academic presenting a paper on Uganda at a conference in Stellenbosch began with the telling introduction: "When I was in Africa..."

These ambiguities are illustrated in the attitudes and responses of South African policy makers and citizens living in Johannesburg to the influx of foreign African migrants.

There are two major discourses concerning South Africa's relation to the African continent, and to the rest of the world, which appear to be inherently contradictory. One is posited on legalistic and *realpolitik* notions of citizenship, nation-building, and territorial sovereignty. The project of forging a post-apartheid South African national identity tends to be informed by "othering" non–South Africans. This is perhaps one of the legacies of apartheid, in which diverse South African identities were constitutionally, territorially, and institutionally constituted primarily along the lines of race and ethnicity. Thus, with the advent of an inclusive, universal, and democratically constituted citizenship, South Africans had to forge a common national identity. Not really knowing who we were, as a cohesive nation with a coherent identity, the search for our own identity became largely predicated on who we were *not* – on an "othering" of non–South Africans. In addition, widespread antipathy developed toward foreigners, who were constructed as threats to hard-won inclusive citizenship

---

[1] This paper is primarily based on a large body of research which was conducted by the author at the Centre for Policy Studies, Johannesburg, and Cambridge University, from 1994 to 2001.

rights and entitlements from which the majority of South Africans had been excluded for decades.

The other discourse, characterized by the political polemic of "I am an African," notions of an "African Renaissance," and programs such as NEPAD (New Partnership for Africa's Development), suggest a transcendence of an exclusive South African identity based on a bounded, territorial sovereignty and citizenship, in favor of privileging an inclusive, African identity.

The major question which implicitly forms the backdrop to this paper concerns the apparent contradictions between these two discourses, and the attendant implications and challenges for migration policy and urban governance. The paradigm which continues to inform domestic policies relating to migration is haunted by *realpolitik*. It is therefore doubtful that initiatives such as NEPAD can be actualized: partnerships between South Africa and other African countries seem doomed when its citizens are openly hostile toward nationals of potential partners in continental development and poverty alleviation. Migration policy is informed by a perception that South Africa and its cities are besieged by foreign migrants.

To this end, and within the context of these discourses, this paper will explore South African government and citizen responses to non–South African Africans – so-called "foreign African migrants" in Johannesburg. It will investigate the contradictions between the legal "rules of the game" and the actual "state of play" concerning the presence of African migrants in Johannesburg; conflicts that arise between the "naming and claiming" of identities; and inconsistencies between a discourse which, casting its eyes to the West, calls for the transformation of Johannesburg into a "world-class city" and that which calls for Johannesburg to accept its identity as an African city, which will depend on the success of the renewal of relations with the people of the region. Based on extensive fieldwork, the paper ultimately attempts to give voice to the experience of foreign migrants and their relationships with South Africans.

The Existing Policy Framework   As there is no cross-border migration policy, migrants (as opposed to immigrants) in effect exist in a legal vacuum. No appropriate policy currently exists in terms of which they may legalize their status in South Africa. However, in practice, they are dealt with by government officials and citizens in terms of the legal framework of immigration policy, and deemed to be illegal, or undocumented, if they do not subscribe to the provisions of this policy, which is inappropriate for migrants. Thus, in terms of an inappropriate legal framework, they are "named" as "illegal immigrants," although the identities which they often claim contradict this nomenclature. Immigration policy is unenforceable for the purposes of managing, monitoring, or documenting migration to South Africa.

Subjective Challenges: Conceptual Contests   In order to represent the view from "the other side," and to understand the perspective of those perceived as "outsiders" and defined as "illegal," between 1995 and 2000 a number of interviews were conducted with foreign migrants residing in Johannesburg. The responses elicited from these interviews are not presented as definitive or generally representative. They are nevertheless important, as they begin to illustrate different perceptions held by "illegal" immigrants and migrants in South Africa of the concepts which inform immigration policy. As such, they send an important message to policy makers.

The interviews were conducted by a black South African researcher who spent a number of years in exile in Zimbabwe and Botswana. He is fluent in Shangaan, Shona, and seTswana. Some of the interviewees were accessed through Afrisaa (Affected Foreign Residents in South Africa Association), and also via networks tapped through casual conversation with people living in Kagiso (a black township outside Johannesburg) and those plying their trade on the streets of Johannesburg. Most interviewees can be categorized as unskilled and semi-skilled economic immigrants and migrants, as all claimed to be seeking improved economic opportunities.

For policy makers and urban planners, the most significant response from interviewees is that all of them expected their negative rights to be guaranteed and protected regardless of which state they happened to reside in. "Citizenship is a matter of choice of the individual," a Malawian respondent claimed, "and is not governed by legislation. One is free to choose where one wishes to reside, and the state must respect this choice. Although it does not distinguish between citizenship and human rights, this response seems to suggest an understanding of certain rights as portable, and of a responsibility of all states, at all levels of government, to protect them. By implication, this respondent regards himself as bearing a constant set of rights, regardless of which side of a national border he is on, and, by implication, in which urban location he is situated. Similarly, a Mozambican said, "I am not a 'grigamba,'"[2] but a human being, and, by implication, entitled to the guarantee of human rights. He does not accept the distinction between citizens and foreigners, and claims that everyone should be left

---

2 A derogatory term for foreigner.

alone to make his or her own way. For many, migration is a survival strategy related to a search for the guarantee of negative rights. In other words, what immigrants claim is participation in the normative, associational, and economic realm of society: "they should leave me to work."

Some respondents highlighted the racial exclusivity of the recognition of negative rights by the South African state. One pointed out that white foreigners, especially Portuguese from Portugal and Mozambique, are allowed to stay in South Africa. Another claimed that when he applied to the Department of Home Affairs for a residence permit, he was turned away by officials who told him that "we give it to whites who have better education."

Other respondents imposed a broader but still exclusive racial qualification on their claims to universal human rights. Although they did not perceive any differences between themselves and black South Africans – as a Mozambican said in Zulu, "People are the same, we are one type. We are black people." – their responses implied that claims for the protection of human rights are contingent on racial identity, and should therefore be limited to the region or the continent. This is in sharp contrast to some South Africans' perceptions, and a more limited politics of racial identity which seems to be developing. When asked why Zulus and Shangaans had mistakenly been targets of anti-immigrant attacks in Alexandra township, one respondent said it was thought that they were "too black to be South African."

Noting the existence of historical ties between most of the Ndebeles in Zimbabwe and the Khumalo people in South Africa, the chairperson of Afrisaa argued that most of the Khumalo people originated in Zimbabwe as victims of forced labor, which he called "semi-slavery. ... When the victims of forced labor tried to trek back [to Zimbabwe], the white men had by then introduced borders, thus inhibiting the free movement of people with the same historical ties," adding that, "Our forefathers built Jo'burg. No South African could mix sand and cement. They are lazy. Jo'burg is what it is today because of our forefathers, who were forced to work." The rights claims made by these respondents are directed particularly against the South African state, predicated as they are on specific historical understandings and constructions of ethnic and tribal identity.

Many immigrants, especially those from neighboring states, asserted that they had a right to be here. They would therefore continue to enter South Africa, regardless of the potential hazards. For many, economic, social, and political problems in their home countries had forced them to migrate. Some contended that apartheid South Africa, through its destabilization policy, was directly and/or indirectly responsible for these problems.

They also argued that they had been part of the South African national liberation struggle both while working here and through alliances between their own national liberation movements and South African counterparts, and the support their governments gave the South African national liberation movements, with negative consequences for their own countries (and citizens). They implied that it was treacherous for South African democrats to pursue policies and actions that resulted in closing doors on former political allies.

Many respondents moved beyond these explanations and invoked arguments about regional historical, economic, and cultural linkages. They claimed that the southern African region was one economic entity, and that southern Africans had worked in South Africa and contributed to the country's economic fortunes – "how can we now be regarded as foreigners?" A Zimbabwean explained that "South Africa is economically better off because some bosses started leaving countries in the region, due to war, for South Africa. Therefore job seekers had to follow job providers."

Some, especially Ndebele-speaking Zimbabweans, evoked the reign of King Shaka to reinforce their claims that historically and culturally they are South Africans. These historical-economic-cultural links have resulted in much social mixing, marriages, and children. They illustrated this point by describing family ties which sometimes straddled a few countries in the region. A Zimbabwean respondent told us:

> my father used to work here, but when he got too old, he went back home. My mother is originally from Zambia, and used to work in South Africa. My eldest brother was born here in 1949, during my father's working days. He then married a South African and lives with his wife and their children in Vosloorus.

Another Zimbabwean respondent pointed out that

> most Zimbabweans return and settle at home after long periods of working here. My [maternal] grandfather worked here in Jo'burg in the kitchens for ages, and then returned to Zimbabwe. My husband's father worked on the mines here and returned to Zimbabwe with a Tswana wife.

The separation of people on the basis of their present nationality results in the fragmentation of families, extended and multiple households, and dependency networks, all of which have had major social consequences for South Africa and the entire region. One respondent described the negative impact of such a policy as "causing social disintegration":

> Deportation causes family break-ups and emotional stress on those left behind, who sometimes have to cope on their own in a hostile and alien environment; the abandon-

ment of children, either because they are left behind, or because the sole breadwinner has been deported, and can no longer support them; increase in child abuse, delinquency, and street children (near Jo'burg station); abortions by abandoned women who cannot support themselves; prostitution and the spread of AIDS.

Furthermore, if one income earner is removed from a particular territorial "space," he loses his "place" in the network (usually male). The survival strategy is often to replace him with a number of others. This attests to the counterproductive and destabilizing impact of current policy responses, and ways in which they exacerbate the pressure to migrate.

In terms of the enforcement of immigration policy, many respondents claimed that officials discriminated against black foreigners. A typical sentiment was that

local blacks do not harass British whites or Chinese, but harass us from Africa. They also rob us because we do not know the place very well and are scared to report to the police because they also side with locals. Blacks should recognize that we are all Africans despite our language and cultural differences.

Other respondents went further, arguing that immigration itself is a racial issue: shop stewards of the National Union of Metalworkers of South Africa (NUMSA) suggested that the notion of "immigrant" was racially constructed, noting with concern that "immigrant" had racial connotations, and meant "black" or "African." They supported this contention by arguing that "foreigners of other race groups are not usually regarded as immigrants, or harassed like blacks and Africans in this country." Another respondent said, "Africans should be more welcome here than white foreigners. Anyway, not all whites bring capital to South Africa – there are also poor white foreigners, and workers, who are accepted here. Why not Africans from the region and the continent?"

Others feel that discrimination occurs on the basis of national origin, and that "only Mozambicans and Zimbabweans are harassed." Some respondents said they were disappointed that president Nelson Mandela's relationship with Graça Machel[3] had not improved relations between South Africans and Mozambicans: "Some South Africans are saying that Mr. Mandela is bringing immigrants into his own country because of his relationship with Mrs. Machel. We thought it would bring the two countries closer together, but the opposite happened."

---

3 Nelson Mandela was the first president of South Africa, post-1994; his wife, Graça Machel, is the widow of former Mozambican president Samora Machel.

A Mozambican trader claimed to have been so appalled by a particular means of enforcing immigration policy that he almost chose to go home: "There was a time in South Africa when the government promised a reward of R50 to South African citizens for every illegal immigrant that they could catch. That was the most inhuman experience I had in South Africa. I then thought of handing myself over to the police to be deported home."

Many respondents suggested that stricter immigration control to protect South Africans' jobs was not a viable solution. Instead, they advocated a framework for integrating the regional labor market. Unlike many South Africans who believe that their country can survive independently, migrants argued that no country in southern Africa could survive, let alone succeed, on its own. Many respondents suggested that the region should unite through the Southern African Development Community (SADC).

Many respondents are members of transnational communities and have what are, in effect, multiple national identities. One way in which these are constructed is through the institution of marriage. Many have at least two wives or partners; one in South Africa and one in their country of origin, often with children from both. For example Peter, a Zimbabwean respondent, is married in terms of traditional or customary law to three women – two South Africans and one Zimbabwean. He lives with one of his South African wives; the other lives in the Eastern Cape. He has three children with this wife, who stay with her. He also has children with his Zimbabwean wife. The wives in the Eastern Cape and Zimbabwe are subsistence farmers. The ease with which Peter can continually commute across borders facilitates these networks of dependency and multiple identities.

It is clear from the above that the "state of play" refutes the "rules of the game." Migrants' self-perceptions and identities, and their interpretations of the concepts which inform immigration policy are extremely varied, highly complex, and extraordinarily nuanced. The challenge for policy makers is whether to dismiss these understandings and constructions of identities as purely opportunistic, or whether to acknowledge them when formulating policy.

Experiences of Foreign Migrants in Johannesburg: A Case Study This section is based on an intensive eight-month study of the role played by "illegal immigrants" in South Africa's economy and society. The research was conducted mainly in the inner city of Johannesburg, from November 1996 to June 1997. The intention of the research was to challenge the pervasive demonization of foreign migrants and the perceptions on which it is based, and to begin to reformulate the image of migrants based on the research findings.

The influx of economic migrants into South Africa is a crucial issue – in terms of both human rights and social policy. However, it has become clear that the immigration policy debate will not be settled purely or even primarily by appealing to South Africans to respect the rights of migrants. Current immigration policies are repeatedly justified, most notably by Minister of Home Affairs Mangosuthu Buthelezi, on the grounds that recognizing the rights of transborder migrants would curtail those of South Africans, since migrants are perceived to threaten the viability of the country's new democracy by diminishing its citizens' access to scarce resources.

What follows is a collage of migrant/citizen experiences within various contexts in Johannesburg.

Given the vulnerable and insecure status of undocumented and illegal immigrants and migrants, as well as many South Africans' hostility toward and suspicion of them, they are a particularly difficult subject group to access. Based on their own and others' past experience, many feared being reported to Home Affairs officials and the police, and having their property confiscated. Establishing a relationship of trust and confidence in the field workers was a time-consuming process, demanding great patience and sensitivity on the part of the researchers. And, once they had agreed in principle to be interviewed, many migrants were unwilling to answer some of the more sensitive questions demanded by this study, such as those relating to their legal status and financial and personal circumstances.

Although we tried to make our sample broadly representative of different nationalities, the vast majority of foreigners interviewed were Zimbabweans. Language barriers made it difficult to interview foreigners from beyond southern Africa, especially those from West African francophone countries. Migrants from southern Africa were also generally more willing to speak to us. Historical, geopolitical, and linguistic ties with South Africa presumably played an important role in facilitating a better understanding among researchers and interviewees.

Immigrants in inner Johannesburg are a very diverse group. They do not constitute a community, but rather a number of communities. Thus, besides the general problems of trying to win their confidence, we encountered specific obstacles resulting from this diversity. It was necessary to identify different structures and/or personalities who could help us meet individuals and groups in different communities. Random sampling in hotels, bars, nightclubs, taxi ranks, street stalls, and markets was also undertaken.

Working in a crime-ridden context such as Johannesburg's inner city exacerbated the problems faced by field workers, and often placed them in dangerous situations. They encountered illegal immigrants who are members of drug syndicates, and who indicated that the researchers were not welcome in some areas unless they were there on "business." Such persons were unwilling to be interviewed, as they considered this to be a waste of time. On one occasion, the field workers narrowly missed a shoot-out in which a police informer who had been helping to uncover a drug ring was allegedly killed by Nigerian dealers.

Some nonmigrant informants also failed to cooperate. For example, taxi drivers claimed that the time spent speaking to field workers was money lost. There was an increasing tendency among research subjects to demand payment for being interviewed. Coach companies refused to divulge information on their operating costs, an apparent increase in migrants' demands for services, fare structures, and so on. Provincial and local government departments – such as education, health, and housing – which we believe might be most affected by an increase in migration to Gauteng either failed to respond to our requests for interviews and information, or were unable to identify the person responsible for immigrant issues.

The category of "illegal" is problematic, as many foreigners so defined are in fact undocumented;[4] and many so-called "immigrants" are in fact migrants, with no intention of settling in South Africa – the majority of the respondents in this study, regardless of their type of employment, can be categorized as such. For example, two self-employed Zimbabwean builders who regularly commute to and from Zimbabwe expressed no desire to settle permanently in South Africa: "Even if I was allowed to stay here for quite a long period, I would still return home – there is nothing better than home"; and "I do not intend applying for permanent residence here, because I am proud of being a Zimbabwean, and South Africa is not my ideal country. I am only here because there are financially greener pastures, unlike at home." Most of those who intend to settle here permanently are either married to South Africans or come from beyond the southern African region.

These findings are significant for the following reasons. First, they challenge the common assumption that *migrants* are specifically concentrated in the agricultural, mining, and informal trading sectors, and suggest that they operate in

---

4 Undocumented migrants are those people who oscillate regularly between their home countries and South Africa and who do not attempt to obtain temporary work and residence permits, usually because it is too difficult or impractical for them to do so. Most are citizens of SADC states, and were recently afforded the opportunity to apply for amnesty. The term "undocumented" was first used by critics of earlier South African immigration policy to denote those people who could not qualify for immigration to South Africa simply because they were black. As such, the term had a normative function; it is now used purely descriptively. For a more detailed discussion, see Maxine Reitzes and Nigel Crawhall, *Evaluating the 1996 SADC Exemption: Its Origins and Accessibility* (Cape Town: Idasa/SAMP, 1997). In a further development in terminology, the draft green paper on international migration refers to "unauthorized" rather than "illegal" immigrants or migrants, in an attempt to move away from the latter term's criminal connotations.

a wide range of economic sectors. Second, they attest to the economic interdependence of countries in the region. Third, migrants are likely to have a significantly different social and economic impact to that of immigrants. For example, those intending to settle permanently in South Africa are more likely to have their dependents with them and to make claims on social services, whereas the dependents of many migrants remain in their countries of origin and make no such claims. However, migrants are more likely to send South African goods and revenue out of the country. Fourth, the permanence or transience of settlement influences the extent to which foreigners are likely to integrate into the host community, which in turn affects their social impact. It is therefore necessary to formulate appropriate policies which acknowledge the differential needs and impact of these categories.

Thus the categories of people included in our sample are:
- immigrants and migrants who are either in the country illegally or have obtained their apparently legal status through illegal means;
- undocumented immigrants and migrants, who fulfill the criteria to be here but lack documentary evidence; and
- refugees.

1. Workplace Dynamics between Migrants and South Africans   *Migrants in higher-income jobs – such as telemarketing and switchboard operating – and very low-income jobs experienced less hostility from South Africans.* For example, a switchboard operator working with three other non–South Africans and a majority of white South Africans said there was a cooperative atmosphere, and employees "share facilities at the sports club." A self-employed Zimbabwean mechanic said other South African mechanics whom he knew were "very good. My car was bought and registered by one of them, and they always come to my rescue when I am harassed by the police." A Nigerian said he co-owned a nightclub with a black South African.

Conversely, a respondent who works as a messenger in a South African–dominated workplace said South Africans tolerated foreigners "as long as they do low-income work which South Africans are not interested in. I would like to remain in this kind of low-status job for my own safety, since South Africans don't want it." A Nigerian in the informal sector said: "I do not look for formal employment, because South Africans have an attitude problem towards Nigerians."

Black South African workers tend to be more xenophobic than white South African workers, and this xenophobia is largely justified by the pervasive perception that foreigners are responsible for the unemployment problem. Where black foreigners in the workplace are in a minority, they are disadvantaged both in relation to South African employers and employees, as they cannot effectively challenge xenophobia. Illegal migrants are even more vulnerable, as both employers and local workers intimidate and manipulate them and threaten to denounce them to the police. A Zimbabwean employed as a security guard claimed that, in a context where black South Africans outnumbered foreigners by a ratio of 10:1, the attitude of the former toward the latter was openly hostile: "The South Africans in charge try by all means to get rid of non–South Africans in order to replace them with South Africans. Damaging remarks are made to bosses in order to get them to dismiss foreigners." A Zimbabwean who was previously employed as a head security officer in a private hospital and had to oversee solely South African workers, said that "South Africans hated being under a non–South African, and were very disobedient. This led to serious chaos whereby the company sometimes lost contracts and workers lost their jobs. This was then blamed on me, and generated even more resentment towards me. They would threaten to kill me, saying I couldn't work while I made them lose their jobs. They would also be fired for stealing, and again blame this on me."[5]

Many of the migrant respondents volunteered their own explanations for the attitudes of South Africans, largely focusing on the perceived sense of superiority among South Africans and, paradoxically, their jealousy of foreigners; their lack of a work ethic and business acumen; their fear of competition; and their unreasonably high expectations – often created by the government, which now blames foreigners for its inability to deliver; and ignorance of the conditions which compel people to migrate. A significant number of respondents claimed that xenophobia was an expression of tribalism. A sample of these responses follows.

One respondent said that when he worked in a hotel,

> the South Africans were jealous of the Zimbabweans because of their hard-working character, versatility, and perfection in their job. The South Africans did not do their jobs properly, and stole crockery, cutlery, uniforms, and food, some of which they would sell. They justified this by saying that they were merely compensating themselves for low wages. They accused the Zimbabweans of being "the boss's spies," and

---

5 But another respondent perceives South Africans to be more obedient than Zimbabweans who exploit the "home-boy" factor, and band together in defiance of the orders of their superiors. Another exceptional response came from a Ghanaian hawker who sells fruit in Yeoville. He said that the majority of street vendors in the area are South Africans, and that "relations are okay – there is no talk of immigrants occupying space of South Africans, or competing unfairly." He does not belong to a hawkers' organization, and does not know of any. But he said that those in the area "do meet to discuss business-related issues, such as the cleanliness of the business spot."

threatened to kill a South African woman whom they accused of "selling out" because she fraternized with foreigners.

A Malawian businessman said that "doing business with South Africans is intolerable – they don't like foreign competition." A Malawian trader at one of the markets said:

> South Africans are very hostile towards us because they see that our business is thriving. They are not happy that we have a stand – they only want locals to have business, when they are not even good at it.
>
> There is no organization to tell us what prices we should sell our goods for. We foreigners agree amongst ourselves about the prices. It also depends on the kind of stuff you are selling. If we have the same kind of stuff like this woman next to me, we agree on the same price. We always compete with locals on prices. For example, when they sell baskets for R80, we sell them for R50. We do not run at a loss, because where we buy them they are cheap. It is a healthy competition. If locals want to reduce their prices below ours, they are free to do that. We travel a lot to get our goods at a lower price; they only buy from wholesalers here who are expensive. That is why they cannot tolerate our competition.

A Nigerian respondent echoed these sentiments:

> South Africans are very snobbish, yet they do not know how to do business – instead of trying to improve themselves, they complain about us taking their women and jobs. We from Nigeria are better educated than most South Africans, which is why, when we come here, we get better jobs and do business better.

Another migrant said: "black South Africans think white-collar jobs are naturally meant for them; they cannot do any other job, which they think is cheap and dirty. Many are unemployed because of this attitude." Another said: "people are expecting delivery, while very few are doing something to assist. There is a general unwillingness to do low jobs like selling in the street and domestic work. South Africans' wage and salary demands are also very high." A Zimbabwean builder said: "South Africans' hatred of foreigners comes from the government, because it cannot address the unemployment problem."

Migrants are subject to a complex web of pressures. Economic, social, and political difficulties in their own countries often force them to migrate to South Africa. Once here, one of their major concerns is to secure employment to maintain their dependents back home, who expect financial and material support. Migrants very often feel compelled to accept any possible means of earning a livelihood, regardless of the conditions of employment. Thus they are prepared to take dangerous, demanding, and low-paying jobs rather than remain unemployed. A Zimbabwean administrative worker said: "The South Africans where I work think that we are taking their jobs. They have told me that they would like to put their unemployed friends and relatives in my job. South Africans don't understand the socioeconomic difficulties due to drought, unemployment, and so on that drive us here. We are not the cause of unemployment: South Africans are responsible for this."

A significant number of respondents remarked on "tribalism," not only in the workplace but in South Africa generally. One Zimbabwean claimed that he had encountered hostility specifically from Pedis at two different workplaces, forcing him to resign from both jobs. When he worked at a bakery in a supervisory position, they refused to respect his authority, saying that they "couldn't be told what to do by a *kwerekwere*";[6] that he spoke "animals' language"; and when he spoke Ndebele, accused him "of being an Inkatha supporter."

Many respondents commented on the extent to which the isolation and ignorance of South Africans impacts negatively on foreigners. They also warned against tribalism: "South Africans should avoid tribalistic tendencies so that the new political dispensation can prosper." A Kenyan respondent argued that racial solidarity ought to transcend tribal differences: "Government should ensure that all tribes are treated equally, so that there is no quarrel or tribal hatred. We should unite as blacks." A Zimbabwean respondent noted the paradox of tribal ostracism compelling Ndebeles to migrate to South Africa, where they are now targets of xenophobic prejudice: "We Ndebeles are victims of tribalism; that's why we're here – they [the Shonas] killed us." She also alleged that "Xhosas are snobs who think they are better. If you are not Xhosa, you are considered to be an outsider. This tribalism means that whites continue to prosper while blacks remain divided."

Some respondents viewed xenophobia as an expression of tribalism, and urged South Africans to

> stop propagating tribal, ethnic, and regional politics. The South African economy should be opened up just like America during the migration era of the 18th century. Such an economic open-door policy would make South Africa economically strong just as it did America. We should build a united and integrated southern African regional economic bloc because southern Africa is already an integrated economic entity.

---

6 Another derogatory term for foreigner used by South Africans.

This argument was developed further by a Mozambican respondent:

> xenophobia is not a domestic phenomenon confined to national origin, but a regional and tribal phenomenon. Mozambique helped Zimbabwe during its liberation struggle, and Zimbabweans and Mozambicans were brothers in arms. But now they hate each other. Mozambicans go to Zimbabwe to steal cattle; Zimbabweans call Mozambicans all sorts of bad names, such as *makarushu*, which have the same reactionary content as *makwerekwere* and *magrigamba*.[7] Such terms are now used by Zimbabweans to describe all Mozambicans whether they are thieves or not, since Zimbabweans now regard all Mozambicans as criminals.
>
> South Africans also use certain terms towards Zimbabweans in a loose manner, for example *Kalanga*. Strictly speaking, *Kalanga* is a particular language, a mixture of Shona and Zulu/Ndebele; therefore Kalangas are of mixed descent of Zulus and Shonas. *Kalanga* is a type of Zimbabwean *fanakalo*,[8] yet South Africans simply call all Zimbabweans and Namibians *Kalangas*.

The apparently high levels of xenophobia is a post-1994 election phenomenon. Some migrant respondents believe that newly enfranchised South Africans have turned against black foreigners since 1994. For example, a Zimbabwean who had previously worked as a boilermaker claimed that

> relations with South Africans were very good. The anti-apartheid struggle forged solidarity among blacks, irrespective of countries of origin. There was no insulting terminology like *kwerekwere* or *grigamba* then. All this xenophobia is new, and came with the era of black rule. South Africans don't want to share the economic cake with foreigners.

Both white and black South African employers exploit foreign workers. One builder related the following story: "South Africans – both black and white – employ illegal migrants, and when payday approaches, they report them to the police, who then take them away, thus enabling the South Africans not to pay them – this is one way of how South Africans use the free labor of migrants." A South African respondent who worked as a carpenter claimed that the wage differential between locals and immigrants was as high as R130 a day, with migrants being paid R20 a day, black South Africans R100 a day, and "one colored guy

---

7 All derogatory terms for foreigner.
8 *Fanakalo* is a type of southern African "esperanto" – a pidgen language which is a mixture of numerous southern African languages and English. It was developed in the mines as a means of communication between migrant workers and mine managers.

R150 a day. As a result, the company threw out all the locals because it could pay migrants far less for the same job."

These claims illustrate how vulnerable foreign workers are, and the various ways in which they are abused: they work long hours; they derive no benefits, such as unemployment insurance, pension, and so on; they are not registered, so they have no legal recourse when their rights are abused; they are forced to accept such conditions or remain unemployed; they earn less than locals; they are subjected to unhealthy housing conditions, which can result in death; and they may be dismissed for voicing their grievances.

The allegations also demonstrate the extent to which employers are responsible for creating the conditions in which foreigners compete unfairly with locals, displace them from jobs, and depress wages and working conditions. Thus, while there is some truth to South African perceptions of migrant workers' negative economic impact, the causal explanations are often spurious.

While there is nothing wrong with competition for jobs and wages *per se*, the above quote seems to suggest that it is not the employment of foreigners as such which creates unfair competition, but rather employment practices in relation to foreigners, which depress wages and working conditions for all employees, both local and foreign. The insecure status of illegal workers – who may be illegal or undocumented immigrants or migrants – renders them more vulnerable to exploitative employment practices.

One union official remarked that foreigners had a differential impact on different classes of the economy – they "make a positive contribution to South Africa, as landlords and employers make huge profits by exploiting them. This is beneficial for landlords and employers, no matter how bad this is for South African workers and the poor. A lot of Mozambicans have building skills, and contractors exploit them heavily." Yet again, this seems to suggest that the problems often attributed to foreigners lie very much with how they are treated by locals.

Some foreigners contribute a range of skills to the market, and are very often multiskilled. Some migrant respondents pointed out that South Africans are not equipped to perform certain jobs, as a result of having been victims of bantu education. They therefore see themselves as making an economic contribution which many South Africans are unable to make. They do have a competitive advantage over locals, and may indeed displace them. A shop steward of the National Union of Metalworkers of South Africa (NUMSA) said that "due to their skills, immigrants can be very helpful to the South African economy. The South African government should arrange with other governments in the region to bring immigrants here in an orderly manner, to impart their skills to South Africans, but not to displace them."

The nature and extent of migrants' economic participation and contribution seems to suggest that current immigration policy is far too restrictive, and is depriving the South African economy of skills, experience, competition, and entrepreneurship.

2. Social Dynamics between Migrants and South Africans   Many migrants share accommodations and socialize with South Africans. Some also share with foreigners from the same country of origin as themselves, or from different countries. Some share with fellow country people with whom they also work.

Although foreigners' social relationships with locals vary, many foreigners who experience hostility from South Africans in the workplace have amicable social and living arrangements with them, as described by a Zimbabwean respondent: "in Yeoville [where I live], I mix with South Africans a lot, and there are no problems, like at work. I have many Zimbabwean friends living with, and married to, South Africans, and some even have children." A Zambian telemarketer offered a socioeconomic explanation for differential levels of xenophobia outside the workplace similar to that offered by a respondent for xenophobia in the workplace:

> South Africans are xenophobic; especially when they see a non–South African whom they consider to be economically and socially better off than them, they get jealous. I once shared a flat with two South African women who were jealous of my success. Hoping to steal my things, they called the police to arrest me and promised them their share. One of the police told me, and the plan collapsed.

A Zimbabwean respondent allegedly had a similar experience when he and his friend "had almost everything we owned stolen by South Africans we shared a flat with, and the police were involved. We now feel we cannot share living space with South Africans."

Conversely, a Zimbabwean who lives in a flat building inhabited by South Africans and foreigners said that

> relations between South Africans and non–South Africans are good; there are no inter-country tensions. There is good social interaction among residents, who eat and drink together. When someone has visitors staying over, and their flats are overcrowded, neighbors assist with accommodation. Interpersonal relationships such as marriage and friendship also cross national boundaries. Tensions are caused by bad behavior, irrespective of one's country of origin.

The profiles of South African/migrant relationships, in the work context and in the social context, suggest that South Africans and foreigners are more likely to come into conflict in situations of competition and perceived conflicts of interest, and are more likely to integrate in and through organizations which represent a perceived commonality of interests, such as religious institutions and sports clubs. This was endorsed by a number of respondents. For example, a Malawian businessman who is married to a South African said, "South Africans are very hospitable people. I have not experienced any problems with them. I attend the Methodist church, and frequent the township to visit friends." A Muslim respondent attends mosques where he experiences no problems with South Africans. One of the interviewees is a member of a predominantly South African band, and a Malawian trader plays for the Bruma Lake Football Club, which consists of foreigners and South Africans.

One of the factors which inhibits social integration is the transient and sometimes highly individualized nature of migrants' stay in South Africa. For instance, a Kenyan who rents a room in a hotel in Hillbrow said he had no problems with non–South Africans as "people just keep to themselves. I have my own small TV in my room, and thus avoid contact with South Africans – I don't have to watch the common one." He said it was difficult to organize social activities "such as football clubs, music groups, etc, because people don't stay here for long. Traders return home once the stuff they are selling is finished."

Many respondents cited language as an inhibitor of social interaction with South Africans, not only because of problems of communication but more importantly because it revealed one's foreign identity. This, they said, often elicited hostile responses from South Africans, acting on a range of assumptions which they harbored about foreigners. A Zimbabwean respondent explained that he had many South African friends, mostly Zulus, who "think I am South African because I speak Ndebele and Zulu. Once South Africans discover that one is not South African, they start distancing themselves from you. At best, they simply isolate you; at worst, they call the police to arrest or deport you." Another migrant explained that "people speak to you in their own language and you can't respond – then they know you are a foreigner, and foreigners do business and therefore have money. Then they harass you for money."

Speaking English is often likely to stigmatize a foreigner in the eyes of the locals: "If one can only speak English and not a South African language, you are immediately identified as a *kwerekwere*." Competency in a local African language seems to be a fundamental criterion for acceptance and integration of foreigners into black South African society.[9] A Zambian who works as a hotel receptionist said that "sometimes we receive locals who are hostile, especially if you cannot speak or understand a local language." A Malawian said, "South

Africa is a good place as long as you speak one of the local languages." A Zambian respondent explained how "bad situations develop when one is among South Africans and can't speak their languages. Resorting to English just worsens the situation. Even the police have a negative attitude towards a 'suspect' who responds in English. They immediately associate you with being a *kwerekwere*, and give you a hard time." This respondent has learnt seSotho, and a number of others are also learning South African languages: "It is socially necessary to do so, as well as being useful for work."

3. Foreigners and Crime Many respondents cited crime as one of South Africa's biggest problems, affecting both their personal safety and their business. They primarily blamed South African citizens and official corruption in the criminal justice system. A woman from Zambia said: "What is really bad about South Africa is the crime rate, especially crime against women, like rape. This shows that South African men do not have respect for their women." A Malawian trader commented on the negative impact which crime in Johannesburg has on his business:

> There are very few tourists here in Johannesburg because of crime. Many go to Cape Town and Durban. Yet everybody here is complaining that we are the people who commit crime and chase the tourists away. I believe many of us foreigners come here to earn a living decently, not by mugging, selling coke, or fraud. It is only a few who are involved and making life difficult for all of us. They also contribute to the bad attitudes locals have towards foreigners.

A Mozambican claimed that many South Africans justify their children's involvement in crime, arguing *bayaphanda* (crime as a survival tactic). However, identical allegations are made by South Africans against foreigners. A local respondent claimed that

> one finds that immigrants have got new electricity stoves, color television sets, and many utensils, yet they do not work. New cars are seen every three months in shacks inhabited by immigrants. When asked where do they get all these things, their reply is "bayaphanda."

---

9 A recent study has suggested that black South Africans themselves see English as an agent of access to and membership in the national bourgeoisie, and as an instrument of elite formation. See Maxine Reitzes and Nigel Crawhall, *Silenced by Nation-Building: African Immigrants and Language Policy in the New South Africa* (Cape Town: Idasa/SAMP, 1997).

And a new form of scapegoating may be developing in terms of which southern Africans criminalize foreigners from beyond the region: a Zimbabwean respondent said "non–southern Africans are criminals, for example drug dealers. The 'self-employed' ones are just using their 'self-employment' as a cover for drug dealing. Very few non–southern Africans are genuine job seekers." This could indicate a growing awareness of regionalism and the search for a regional identity through the construction of non-SADC state citizens as an adversarial "other." It may also be a response by citizens of SADC members states to their perceived victimization by South African authorities. A Zimbabwean respondent claimed that Zimbabweans were discriminated against, as "it is easy for the government to deport us, as [our country] is nearer to South Africa than Ghana and Nigeria."

4. Policing, Crime, and Foreigners in the Inner City   There are four stations policing inner-city Johannesburg: Hillbrow, Jeppe, Johannesburg Central, and Yeoville. Johannesburg Central is the largest police station in the country, with two sub-units, and services the central business district; Hillbrow station services Berea, Parktown, and Hillbrow; and Yeoville services parts of Observatory and Yeoville. The Hillbrow and Yeoville stations service areas with the highest population of immigrants.

From observations and informal discussions with the police, it seems there is no specific strategy for policing Hillbrow and Yeoville. With reference to "illegal aliens," the police cited as problematic the lack of mechanisms or data to indicate how many foreigners are living in these areas; the absence of entry points to the city to regulate the flow of people; and a lack of control centers from which the movements of migrants could be monitored. A spokesperson also said that "migrant networks (both criminal and noncriminal, documented and undocumented) are so sophisticated that it is difficult for the police to trace them. Often the police are paid protection money by undocumented migrants and criminals. Migrants often have no permanent abode, and very often are not documented as residents of certain addresses as the name of the person on the lease is not the same as that of the occupant(s)."

Research also revealed that police do not always distinguish between criminals and "unauthorized" foreigners. Both Yeoville and Hillbrow police stations have special units dealing with "illegal aliens," and twice a month they search buildings and check people's documents. However, crime prevention is based on operational analysis derived from monthly crime statistics from each station, and these statistics include foreigners who have been arrested solely because of their illegal status and not because they are criminals. This reflects a legal conflation of criminality and illegal status, which in turn informs inappropriate policies, confuses their implementation and the official functions of different line departments, and results in the misallocation of resources.

Even the National Crime Prevention Strategy (NCPS) reflects some confusion in distinguishing between illegal status and criminality: it raises the issue of "much of the popular concern over the role of ... illegals within the criminal sub-economy in South Africa," but then cautions in the very next sentence that "[t]here is a real danger that popular paranoia about this role of illegal immigrants will begin to generate ethnic-based xenophobia which could eventually manifest itself in serious social conflict and violence in the months and years ahead"; further on, it states that "[t]he impact of illegal immigration directly on crime is probably overrated, as illegal immigrants tend to be wary of attracting attention."[10] However, the conflation of criminality and illegal status, and the inclusion in general crime statistics of the number of arrests of unauthorized foreigners, are likely to have the exact effects against which the NCPS is warning: falsely representing foreigners as a particular criminal threat by exaggerating their impact on crime, thereby possibly exacerbating xenophobia.

Police contend that a high concentration of foreigners in the inner city resort to crime because

> Johannesburg is the economic heartland of South Africa, and has many incentives which attract people from across the borders. They migrate to the city with the hope of finding a job. The nearest place to find cheap accommodation close to the city is Hillbrow, Berea, and Yeoville. Many people's expectations are disappointed, and they fail to find economic opportunities. They then have to sustain themselves either by opening a shebeen, selling vegetables, prostitution, or selling drugs.

Hillbrow police also claim that certain nationalities are primarily involved in particular types of crime:

> most housebreaking in the area is done by Zimbabweans, drug trafficking by Nigerians and their local counterparts, and motor vehicle theft by South Africans and Zambians and Zimbabweans who have access to home markets. Zairians, Senegalese, and Ghanaians are primarily involved in fraud.

According to the police, the infrastructure of the area also contributes to the criminal environment. Many hotels, pubs, and nightclubs are havens for prosti-

---

10 Cited in Maxine Reitzes, *Government Speaks with Forked Tongue: The 1996 SADC Exemption and the Lack of a Coherent Policy Vision* (Cape Town: Idasa/SAMP, 1997).

tution and drug smuggling. Derelict and uninhabited municipal houses have become chop shops for stolen motor vehicles, and some flats house brothels. Street hawkers' stands are transit points for drug peddlers. Certain pharmacies and surgeries are used as covers for major drug and housebreaking syndicates, many of which include illegal immigrants.

We would argue that the relationship between migrants, unemployment, and crime is far more complex. Foreigners employ a range of survival strategies, both when they are employed and unemployed. Some of the respondents participated in credit societies at work, some of which were initiated by, and established exclusively for, foreigners. Others have their income supplemented or complemented by relatives, both here and outside the country – for example, a Ghanaian who earns an irregular income repairing shoes has a sister in Canada who used to send him money monthly when he was unemployed. She now assists him financially on request, but his brother in London continues to send him money every month.

A Zimbabwean respondent described how he survived unemployment for six months:

> I was given retrenchment pay of one month's wages by my previous employer. I used this money to buy goods in South Africa, and resold them in Zimbabwe. For example, a black and white television set for about R200 resold for about R450. I then bought two more of them in South Africa and resold them in Zimbabwe, and so the cycle continued, until I found a job again.

One unauthorized migrant explained that, during periods of unemployment, he would sell durable goods originally purchased for personal use, and which also served as a means of investment and a form of unemployment insurance: "Instead of saving money in [a] bank [which in any event is difficult without an identity document], I would buy things; and then when I was unemployed, I could sell them. Then, when I work again, I buy some more. We look after ourselves – we don't just resort to crime," he volunteered.

> However, there is little doubt that international criminal syndicates are increasingly penetrating South Africa. But members of such syndicates are often illegal because they are criminals, and therefore wish to remain undocumented. It does not therefore follow that undocumented foreigners are necessarily criminals. But a South African respondent inverted the causality of this argument: "Immigrants … easily get involved in criminal activities because they are not registered with the authorities and can therefore get away with crime because they have no fingerprints in the central database in Pretoria." However, Johannesburg police spokesperson Mark Reynolds conceded that "it was

difficult to say how much crime could be attributed to illegal immigrants," but many had been involved in criminal activities.[11]

The confusion between the categories is not exclusively a result of an inability to distinguish between criminality and illegal status, but is also sometimes used intentionally by various stakeholders to pursue their own political agendas. Police may consciously target foreigners and conflate two different sets of statistics in order to inflate the numbers of arrests, as a response to community and political pressure and to justify their demands for more resources.

Because of the high crime rate in the inner city, it is difficult to establish healthy community-police relations. Hotel and pub owners refuse to be involved in crime prevention activities because they are either involved in crime themselves or feel that by doing so their business will be affected, as many are patronized by known criminals, some of whom are also unauthorized migrants. As explained by a police spokesperson, "Participation in crime prevention against your own clients and customers will mean a closure of some businesses, as they move to more friendly areas."

Many foreigners – both legal and undocumented – also refuse to cooperate with the police, because they resent the xenophobia which makes them a scapegoat for high levels of crime. One respondent expressed the views of many:

> Policing is always equated with anti-immigrant sentiments. Why should [we] be involved in crime prevention when police make life uncomfortable for us? Why should we report crime when all crimes are blamed on us? We are always harassed by police who are involved in corruption, like when police evict us from our flats in favor of a local subtenant, and our belongings disappear with no trace of the subtenant or the police, or when police accept or demand bribes from us. Those of us arrested for our undocumented or illegal status can pay up to R300 for our "freedom." Those of us who do not have the money are thoroughly beaten and taken to Johannesburg prison or the detention center in Krugersdorp.

All the respondents condemned criminals, both South African and foreign. Some said that they would willingly collaborate with the South African Police Service (SAPS) in tackling crime, especially among foreigners, but cited corruption within the SAPS itself as the chief obstacle in the fight against crime. Since one of the main forms of this corruption is police harassment of immigrants by, *inter alia*, demanding bribes, unlawful arrest and deportation of immigrants,

---

11 *The Star*, May 1, 1997.

and dismissal of their cases against South Africans and the SAPS, immigrants have become alienated from the police. Zimbabweans in particular are so disgusted with this corruption that they have suggested "that the SAPS should go and learn from their Zimbabwean counterparts how to do their work professionally."

The majority of respondents had personally had negative experiences with the police, or knew someone who had. A trader explained that among the problems experienced by migrants as a result of police action is that "when the police arrest and deport you, your stuff is just left at the market. It's terrible if one has no friends; it means that one loses everything. Also, when raiding the homes of immigrants, police often 'confiscate' property, such as television sets."

Conclusion   To return to the beginning: South African migration policy and the sentiments of the majority of South Africans toward foreign migrants largely stand in direct contradiction to the NEPAD and newly formulated African Union initiatives. This also has far-reaching consequences for other member states.

If South Africa, as the champion of these initiatives, and other African states are to pursue political cooperation and joint socioeconomic development, implying some cessation of sovereignty, then the rights and entitlements of foreigners, the local siege mentality toward them, and xenophobia must be addressed and immigration policy revised accordingly. States must cease to view foreigners as threats to social security, and recast them as agents of socioeconomic security and development: the "D" in NEPAD stands for "development." Migrants are, arguably, agents of development. To this end, NEPAD and African Union member states need to take more cognizance of the implications of their principles and visions for guaranteeing and protecting the rights of foreigners. A commitment by individual states to uphold democracy, good governance, and the guarantee and protection of the rights of their own citizens, as well as voluntary submission to peer review, are necessary but not sufficient conditions for the success of these initiatives. What needs to be addressed is how these states intend to deal with the implications of the partial ceding of state sovereignty, and the extent to which this obliges them to guarantee and protect the rights of foreigners, resident both in their own states and in the countries of other member states.

This requires an immense and sustained exercise of political will across the entire continent.

Regenerating Downtown Lagos

Koku Konu

Lagos: Why all the Fuss? Nigeria, a former colony of Great Britain, is black Africa's most populous nation. According to a 1997 Transparency International report, it is also "the most corrupt nation in the world."[1] It has a land mass of 924,000 square kilometers (almost four times the size of Great Britain) and its rumored population of 110 million is projected to rise to 245 million by the year 2015. Lagos, so named by Portuguese explorers for its several inland waterways, has an unverified population of 11 million and is Nigeria's *de facto* capital.

Our Lagos Lagos, as many correctly assume, is a seething mass of fast-changing urban tissue. In the past, it has had the unenviable reputation of being the dirtiest capital in the world. Here the cruel juxtaposition of opposites is real and accepted, and it is thin yet decisive lines that hold the city together. Sometimes these lines are physical entities clearly identifiable on maps of the city – like the Ajegunle Canal, which divides the "haves" in Apapa, a desirable residential area, from the "have nots" in Ajegunle, Lagos' first real slum. Other lines are less tangible yet concrete and clearly understood by the city's inhabitants. For example, where does the CBD (Central Business District), the city's financial nerve center, become Isale-Eko, that den of urban squalor? Some lines – like those of the yellow privately owned transport vehicles that feature in every traffic jam – form, deform, and reform according to movement patterns. In similar fashion, so do the endless lines of containers at Tin Can Port, constructed in the 1970s to ease congestion at the nation's premier port. Some lines, like that of the outer marina flyover, which links Lagos Island to the mainland, have the collateral effect of causing irreparable slashes in the urban fabric. It is these and many other lines that make up the threads of the city's matrix.

---

1 *The Fight Against Corruption: Is the Tide Now Turning?*, Transparency International Annual Report 1997.

Fractures and fragments

Fractures and Dislocations   Lagos is fractured by the physical manifestations of rapid urbanization, e.g., the automobile, rising land values, limited horizontal expansion, inadequate infrastructure, overstretched communication networks, etc. Quite simply this city has grown from a well-planned colonial *polis* to one of "chaos" in the space of two decades. This disjunction has given credence to a number of pressure-releasing phenomena in the life of the citizens, ranging from corruption and other types of sleaze to overt religiosity. The container can no longer contain its contained and the heart of the city is dislocated, allowing life to proceed but at a sacrifice to the soul.

Against this backdrop, a group of architects, creative individuals, and students, living and working in Lagos under the acronym CIA (Creative Intelligence Agency), voluntarily prepared a scheme that would form the basis for any government-assisted regeneration initiative. The area of focus was the most volatile and spatially unresolved sector, i.e., where the CBD meets Isale-Eko, literally the "bottom of Lagos," or downtown Lagos. For those of us involved in prescribing solutions, the project allowed us to revisit our primary role, best typified in the words of Wolf Prix of Coop Himmelb(l)au: to "initiate, create, and invent." The schemes produced varied in approach and addressed a number of urban issues, including traffic problems, the creation of green spaces, establishing a processional route through the colonial legacy of streets and squares, the conversion of abandoned civic buildings, reactivating the neglected marina, and proposals for a land-air-sea terminal. However, the ones that relate to the role of contemporary artistic creation in the urban environment are best exemplified by three student schemes, all of which explore the issue of creating an environment conducive to the emergence of a positive, culturally based response to the rhythm of urban growth.

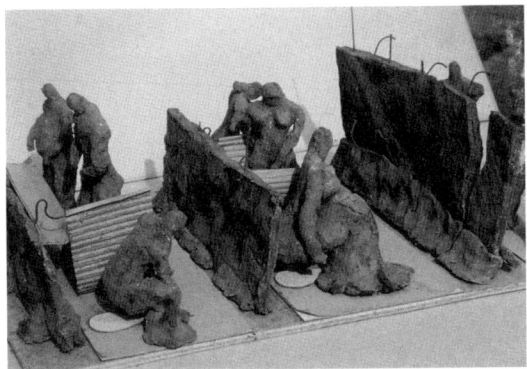

This is how we do

Same scene, different perspectives

Contemporary Problems, Cultural Solutions   In the first attempts to graphically denote the character of Lagos, we used a series of overlaid figure-ground drawings, techniques of abstraction, and fragmentation studies applied to an aerial ordnance survey map. The result is the representation of Lagos as a jagged city with a rough grain and coarse texture. The development of these exploratory drawings produces a moving travelator (powered by the negative energy of the city) positioned on designated sections of the main flyover, which makes it impossible for the infamous law-breaking yellow commercial buses to make illegal stops, the logic being that the buses may stop but other traffic along the road can keep moving.

The second uses the medium of collage to show the different views a driver and street trader have of the same spot in a traffic jam. This preemptive study proposes large-format information billboards designed to give motorists live pictures of the congestion ahead and therefore the opportunity to replan their route, en route. A kind of visual "sat-nav" without "sat." The validity of this proposal becomes all the more apparent bearing in mind that the vast majority of vehicles in Lagos are in poor states of repair, the roads potholed, and that any system designed to limit the amount of time spent in the vehicle on the road is ultimately better for the city and its citizens.

The third examines the cultural issue of personal hygiene and, through an initial study of the defecating and urinary positions of both sexes, results in an open public convenience constructed of simple mud walls of differing heights that allow one to *pee*, *poo*, and *scrub* modestly behind them. In light of the fact that the existing "modern" public conveniences under the flyover are disused and at variance with our cultural habits (since the colonizers of this no man's space generally prefer to do these things in the open), such a transitory convenience is indeed unique in its response to bridge the effects of urbanization.

Fledgling as these proposals may be, their ingenuity lies in the use of our culture, whether contemporary and technology-laden as in the first two, or low-tech and traditionally motivated as with the latter, to deal with the dilemma of rapid and uncontrolled urbanization. The appreciation and application of our culture in analyzing problems relating to our urban environment has in these instances given us the opportunity to scrutinize the sometimes imperceptible scalar quantities that generate the visible vector qualities of meaningful urban interventions.

Kinshasa: Tales of the "Invisible City" and the Second World

Filip De Boeck
*With photographs by Marie-Françoise Plissart**

> Kinshasa will never be New York. So much the better. Each city
> has its soul. Each city has its body, its skin, its intelligence, its
> its foolishness, its monstrous side, its poetry, its part of mystery.
> Sony Labou Tansi, "Kinshasa ne sera jamais"[1]

In 1997, while Brazzaville was busy bombing itself out of existence, and while rockets fired from the city's presidential palace in the direction of Kinshasa fell on Kintambo and other riverine neighborhoods, leaving tens of Kinois dead, historian Charles Didier Gondola published his *Villes miroirs: Migrations et identités urbaines à Kinshasa et Brazzaville, 1930–1970*. Gondola's book is a history of the twin cities of Kinshasa and Brazzaville, mirroring each other across the Congo River like an imperfect materialization of the city of Valdrada, which Italo Calvino describes in *Le città invisibili*.[2] This other book, *Invisible Cities*, tells the story of a Venetian traveler, Marco Polo, who diverts the aged Tartar emperor Kublai Khan with tales of the cities he has seen in his travels around the empire. Soon it becomes clear that each of the fantastic places that Marco Polo describes is really one and the same place, the city of Venice.

The Kinshasa described here resembles Calvino's invisible Venice, for it contains many cities in one as well. It is at once a city of memory, a city of desire, a hidden city, a trading city, a city of the dead, a city of signs, a city of words, an oneiric city, a city of utopia. And like Calvino's Venice and Gondola's twin cities, this Kinshasa too cannot be understood without reflecting upon reflection, upon reflecting realities, mirrors, images, imitation, imagination, and (self-)representation. This contribution presents Kinshasa as a vast mirror-hall. Starting from but drastically expanding Gondola's notion of mirroring cities, we seek to analyze the various levels of mirroring which fracture Kinshasa's urban world into a series of kaleidoscopic, multiple, but simultaneously existing worlds. Each of these "micro-cities" constantly reflects the others, though this reflection

---

* *Ed. note:* Filip De Boeck has conducted extensive field research in the Democratic Republic of Congo (formerly Zaire) since 1987. The present contribution on Kinshasa is part of a larger collaboration between De Boeck and photographer Marie-Françoise Plissart, which will result in a jointly produced volume on the city.
1 Sony Labou Tansi, "Kinshasa ne sera jamais," in his *L'autre monde: Écrits inédits* (Paris: Editions Revue Noire, 1997).
2 Italo Calvino, *Invisible Cities*, trans. William Weaver (New York: Harcourt Brace Jovanovich, 1974).

is not always symmetrical. Some of these cities, and some levels of mirroring between them, are more visible than others.

Above all, this contribution tries to capture Kinshasa's constant urge to move beyond the tarnish left upon the surface of its mirroring realities; the ways in which this city, sometimes playfully, sometimes desperately, but always with tremendous vitality, tries to break through the layers of dust and dirt, the palimpsests of colonization, de-, re-, and neocolonization that have settled upon its surface and have dulled, sometimes even destroyed, its luster. Living in an urban reality stained by a film of increasing poverty, by the tears and blood of physical and symbolic violence, as well as by a pervasive sense of societal crisis and loss, Kinshasa's inhabitants struggle to reach beyond the fractures inflicted by the postcolonial world and the disjunctions at play in the myths of modernity *and* tradition. This is also where the metaphor of the mirror is pushed to its limits. Kinshasa does not merely reflect. It is not merely represented in the mirrors held up by precolonial pasts, colonialist modernities, or nationalist myths. Certainly, to an important extent it is animated by the reflecting images of these imposed representations. Simultaneously, however, it resists, shatters, transforms, and moves beyond all of these in often unexpected and surprising ways.

Maisaf bar, Bandalungwa, May 2001

Paradigms of resistance against the hegemonies of state, money, and market fail to fully capture the complexities of the realities lived by many in Congo today, nor do they manage to seize the dynamics of subversion by means of which the metaphor of the mirror becomes alive in the urban world of Kinshasa. Both literally and figuratively, Congo's capital constantly smashes its own mirrors. At the same time, it never stops to piece itself back together. In ways that often leave the observer perplexed, the city constantly activates and undergoes the effervescent push and pull of destruction and regeneration. The incessant and chaotic crossing of the borders between these two forces somehow seems to generate the energetic source from which Kinshasa taps the power to embody, animate, and sustain its own *eidos*, its own ongoing attempts at societal creation. In its most essential form, this power is operated by a frontier logic of mutation. It is, in a way, the power of the fetish. Like the fetish, the

---

3 Ioan Davies, "Negotiating African Culture: Toward a Decolonization of the Fetish," in *The Cultures of Globalization*, ed. Fredric Jameson and Masao Miyoshi (Durham, N.C.: Duke University Press, 1998), p. 141. See also Patricia Spyer, ed., *Border Fetishisms: Material Objects in Unstable Places* (New York: Routledge, 1998).

city of Kinshasa is a constant border-crossing phenomenon, resisting fixture, refusing capture. And like the fetish itself, like the magic activated through the mirror in the bellies of Congo's power objects, the city's moving force of mutation is generated in "the slippage between the dominance and the subordination of the surface."[3] Mentally and materially, the city emerges in unstable space. It is a product of a profound mixture between different cultural itineraries and sites. Its content is composite and is generated through crossing various borders and mediating between different opposites. As such, it is also extremely well adapted to carry this mutant message, for it presents in and of itself a space of confrontation, mutation, and movement. Out of the breccia of broken glass, the debris of its own pasts, the city thus feverishly transforms and continues. In a sustained effort to recreate and institutionalize itself, the city tirelessly re-energizes an ever-growing web of plural meanings and social imaginary significations.

The following sections provide a summary of the different mirrors in which Kinshasa is captured and authored by external gazes and representations. More importantly, however, they also set the stage to move beyond such identity play which reduces Kinshasa to the mere role of "significant other," in an attempt to begin understanding Kinshasa's originality, its internal struggle to contemplate and author its own identity.

Mirrors and Models: The Colonial Speculum One level of reflection through which Kinshasa is made to exist is quite obvious: it takes place in the European mirror of colonialism which invented and created the primitivist idea of the Congo and its counter-image, the urban landscape. The history of the creation and evolution of the city that is called Kinshasa today, from its origins as a small trade station established by King Leopold's envoy Stanley upon his arrival in Ngaliema Bay on December 1, 1881, its subsequent rebirth as Léopoldville, capital of Belgian Congo, between 1908 and 1960, to the large city of at least 6 million people it has become now, is a trajectory that cannot be apprehended without taking into account the military, monetary, medical, and moral dynamics of the colonizing context in which it emerged.

1961. Lumumba murdered, Congo in crisis. I was born in 1961, a postcolonial subject. I was born not in Congo, but in Antwerp, in a street named Beschavingstraat, "Civilization Street." Standing in the shadow of the Church of Christ King, our house was one of many similar houses in a new suburban housing estate, erected after World War II. A couple of streets away, on a little square and opposite my grandparents' house, stood one of the only two houses that Le Corbusier

Statue of King Leopold II and the feet of a statue which represented Stanley, Limete, April 2000

built in Belgium. In 1961, this house, a 1926 realization, was still inhabited by its original principal, Mister Guiette, an Antwerp painter who, so my father tells me, also had two beautiful daughters. The house still exists, the daughters have gone. The postwar modernism of my childhood neighborhood, a modest reprise of Le Corbusier's architectural ideals, reflected the optimism of that period.

Our own street ended on the Tentoonstellingslaan, "Exhibition Avenue," close to what then was still the Kolonielaan, "Colony Avenue," which has undergone a name change since. The port of Antwerp was the umbilical cord connecting tiny Belgium to its giant baby of a colony. Yet, this was not the reason for all the colonial references in the street names of my early childhood neighborhood. Only recently did I realize why the streets were so full of colonial memories. Going through some of my grandmother's personal papers and documents after her death, I found some photos of the World Exhibition held in Antwerp in 1930. No doubt the photos had been made by my grandfather, who worked in a small photo shop in Antwerp in that period. An important section of the 1930 World Exhibition was dedicated to Flemish Art, appropriately housed in the Church of Christ King. On a plot next to this church, in the area where my childhood neighborhood would be erected two decades later, stood an imposing, resolutely modernist Congo pavilion in which Belgium's colonial oeuvre was proudly put on display. In line with a tradition that started with Universal Exhibitions at the end of the 19th century, including Tervuren's famous example of 1898, the 1930 Congo display also included a *village africain*, a "negro-village." This "African Village" consisted of an architecture that imitated the *style soudanais*, a vaguely Arabizing architectural style which never really existed as such in precolonial Congo, but which referred to a crucial element of the Leopoldian colonial mythology. In this mythological construction, the colonizing drive that was set in motion by King Leopold II and that swept through the Congo in the last decades of the 19th century was invariably legitimated as a humanitarian struggle against "Arab" slave traders such as the legendary Tippo Tip. The adobe style of the 1930 African Village provided an invented architectural commemoration of this era, which culminated in the *campagne arabe* of 1892–95 and similar events of the time, including that other, equally famous but slightly surreal colonial founding myth, Stanley's rescue of Emin Pasha. Throughout the colonial period, the Arabizing style remained popular in Belgian Congo as well. The architecture of the colonial prisons that the Belgians erected throughout the country and which continue to be used today still bear witness of this colonial orientalism.

The 1930 African Village conveys the complexities and ambiguities that are inherent in the notion of "place" as it existed in colonial discourse and imagination. The image of Congo that was created in this Antwerp display, next to a Le Corbusier house of the same period, calls into being a completely imaginary reconstruction of an equally imaginary traditional Africa. Within the exhibition display, this colonial reflection is mirrored in and juxtaposed by the "modern" imperialist Congo pavilion and the Flemish Art in the equally imperialist Church of Christ King. The Congo has, of course, always fascinated the Western imagination, from Conrad's *Heart of Darkness* to Naipaul's *A Bend in the River* and de Villiers' SAS pulp fiction airport literature, with titles such as *Panique au Zaïre* and *Zaïre adieu*, spectacularly racist cocktails of exoticism, sex, violence, intrigue, and betrayal, with an African pin-up girl on the cover.[4] In varying degrees, "Congo" appears in these works of fiction as a powerful negative image of the Western Self, in which the West projects all of its fears and fantasies. For example, in the wake of the 1995 Ebola outbreak in Kikwit, 500 kilometers southeast of Kinshasa, a leading Belgian newspaper characterized the

---

4 Joseph Conrad, *Heart of Darkness* (1902) (Harmondsworth: Penguin, 1983); V. S. Naipaul, *A Bend in the River* (Harmondsworth: Penguin, 1980); Gérard de Villiers, *Panique au Zaïre* (Paris: Plon, 1978) and *Zaïre adieu* (Paris: Editions G. de Villiers, 1997).

virus as symptomatic of a wild and undomesticated country. In the same way, Hollywood has associated the outbreak of AIDS with the Central African forest and phantasmagoric constructions of the ways in which the virus jumped from monkeys to Africans. The great discrepancy generated in the mirroring process between this topos, the Congo of the imagination, and the topicality of the physical Congo, which is rendered invisible by the strength of the imagined place, seems to go unnoticed by most. What the African Village of the 1930 World Exhibition reveals is precisely this rupture, this fault-line between representation and reality so characteristic of the problematic place of "place" in the colonial and postcolonial contexts.

It was not a coincidence that the World Exhibition of 1930 was organized in the same year that Belgium celebrated its hundredth anniversary as an independent nation-state. The works of colonial imperialism are intimately linked to the rise and consecration of the Western nation-state, of which the colony formed its external expansion. Within 18th- and 19th-century Europe, the changing nature of internal mechanisms of state control was based on processes of what Foucault has called "sequestration."[5] This term refers to the creation of new technologies of (state) supervision within new types of institutions: the prison, the asylum, the labor camp, the colony, the hospital, the *cité*... The genealogy of such spaces of social control illustrates changing conceptualizations of normality and deviance within Western society and within the expanding model of the modern nation-state as unifying moral project. These new institutions, as spaces of organized repression, thus became the depositories of new social categories of the "irrational," the "marginal," and the "deviant."

People who, in these emerging definitions, no longer occupied an unproblematic niche within society, who found themselves on the wrong side of the new lines of social acceptability, were readily subjected to the state technologies of power and control. As such, the nation-state, as panoptical, rationalizing project, developed new "geographies of perversion"[6] which "othered" the criminal, the madman, the beggar, the vagrant, the laborer, the prostitute, and the homosexual, and redefined these categories of people into readily identifiable targets for its programs of social engineering, education, civilization, and reeducation. Paradoxically, then, the state, as homogenizing project and as upholder of (the illusion of) unity, continuously produced difference as well, a difference

---

5 Michel Foucault, *Discipline and Punish: The Birth of the Prison*, trans. Alan Sheridan (New York: Pantheon, 1977).
6 Rudi Bleys, *The Geography of Perversion: Male-to-Male Sexual Behaviour Outside the West and the Ethnographic Imagination, 1750–1918* (New York: New York University Press, 1995).

which it simultaneously and systematically excluded, stigmatized, and pathologized. It is indeed interesting to see how, together with the rise of the European nation-state, new images and theories of atavism, degeneration (*dégénérescence*), and sociobiological decline emerged in European culture and politics.[7]

Within the hegemonic discourse of the state, the notion of degeneration was often linked to the *sociocultural* sites of those whom the state defined as deviant. Culture, in other words, became centrally implicated in forms of both physical and social disease. This also implies that medical intervention, at that point, became a form of *moral* sanitation. As a result, many of the techniques of state control did not hesitate to penetrate deeply into the lives and daily sociocultural locales of citizens. Very often, these techniques centered on the body, and aimed at imposing new norms of hygiene, at controlling sexual behavior, at changing the ways in which people were dressed and housed, and even at redefining kinship relations. As such, the structures of the working-class family, this basic building block of the nation-state, were thus reoriented toward a more acceptable nuclear form, which could then function as the nation-state's image on the local level.[8] The 19th-century proletarian was thus perceived to be a kind of Western "nigger" *avant la lettre*, the state's internal precursor of the later colonial subject.

The relations to the working and peasant classes which the colonial forces exported to their colonies differed greatly from one colonial context to the other. Consider the contrast between the British, who exported few workers, and the Italians, who used colonies for plantations to absorb excess peasants at home. In the Belgian colonial context, where an attempt was made at the creation of an indigenous working class, the formula used seemed to replicate many of the strategies and trajectories that the Belgian state applied at home vis-à-vis its own working classes and other "problematic" groups. Once that "internal other" was domesticated, his alterity defined, labeled, and then eradicated, the state embarked upon the same homogenizing sanitarian and environmental project in its colony.

In colonial Africa, writes Jean Comaroff, "as an object of European speculation, Africans personified suffering and degeneracy, their environment a hothouse of fever and affliction."[9] Although this statement, in its sweeping generalization, disregards the multiplicity of ideals that motivated missionaries and

---

7 See Sander L. Gilman, *Difference and Pathology: Stereotypes of Sexuality, Race, and Madness* (Ithaca, N.Y.: Cornell University Press, 1985); Daniel Pick, *Faces of Degeneration: A European Disorder, c. 1848–c. 1918* (Cambridge: Cambridge University Press, 1989).
8 Jacques Donzelot, *The Policing of Families*, trans. Robert Hurley (New York: Pantheon, 1979).
9 Jean Comaroff, "The Diseased Heart of Africa: Medicine, Colonialism, and the Black Body," in *Knowledge, Power, and Practice: The Anthropology of Medicine and Everyday Life*, ed. Shirley Lindenbaum and Margaret M. Lock (Berkeley: University of California Press, 1993), pp. 305–306.

other agents of colonialism, certainly when viewed in the Belgian colonial context, it undoubtedly also captures something of the Belgian sentiment with regard to its colony in the early decades of its colonial endeavor. Therefore, after a first period in which medicine aimed primarily at the protection of the expatriate colonial agents and military, the major imperialist interventions were often both medical and moral, in a joint venture between the cure and the cross.[10] They focused on issues such as disease control and, especially in the early mission medicine but also afterwards, on the regulation of the colonial subjects' unruly minds and bodies.[11] These bodies had to be clothed, educated, housed, and fed in drastically new ways. During the heyday of colonialism, nutritional studies in Africa, for example, were often prompted by colonial efforts to deal with the "problems of African native diet." As such, they were designed to provide ways of altering local attitudes to food production and consumption, in an attempt to reduce malnutrition, disease, and poor health, and heighten the "effective performance of individuals and communities."[12] More generally, and again for a variety of combined reasons ranging from moral and medical to economic, one of the major aims of colonial medicine was to control and diminish indigenous morbidity and mortality (and this while, at another level, the colony clearly functioned as an exploitative "space of death"; on that level, the colonial negrophile often turned out to be Africa's necrophile and necrophore). For the same reasons, the Belgian colonial administration interfered drastically in local modes of residence, sanitizing the spatial layout of villages, creating new types of settlement and housing, and controlling and restricting the movement of its colonial subjects.

Colonial medicine was also seen as "the greatest force for conceptual change, compelling Africans to abandon their unscientific worldview."[13] As such, colonialist modernity – of which medicine was an outspoken icon – intervened in the most intimate aspects of the colonized's culture, through its attempts at domesticating and controlling indigenous sexuality, imposing new concepts of

---

10 See Philip D. Curtin, *Disease and Empire: The Health of European Troops in the Conquest of Africa* (New York: Cambridge University Press, 1998).
11 See Maryinez Lyons, *The Colonial Disease: A Social History of Sleeping Sickness in Northern Zaïre, 1900–1940* (Cambridge: Cambridge University Press, 1992); Megan Vaughan, *Curing Their Ills: Colonial Power and African Illness* (Stanford: Stanford University Press, 1991); Jean Comaroff and John L. Comaroff, *Of Revelation and Revolution*, vol. 2, *The Dialectics of Modernity on a South African Frontier* (Chicago: University of Chicago Press, 1997), ch. 7.
12 J. Boyd, "Problems of African Native Diet," *Africa* 9 (1936), quoted in Filip De Boeck, "'When Hunger Goes Around the Land': Hunger and Food among the Aluund of Zaire," *Man: The Journal of the Royal Anthropological Institute* 29, no. 2 (June 1994), p. 258.
13 Terence O. Ranger, "Godly Medicine: The Ambiguities of Medical Mission in Southeastern Tanzania, 1900–1945," in *The Social Basis of Health and Healing in Africa*, ed. Steven Feierman and John M. Janzen (Berkeley: University of California Press, 1992), p. 256.

space, time, hygiene, causality, production, and accumulation upon the colonial subject in an attempt to reconfigure the colonial mind, and even genetically engineering a new race of ideal workers.[14]

Many studies of colonial medicine have taken the "medicine as social control" approach outlined above. In such approaches, the politics of the state, both at home and abroad, is perceived, in a very real sense, as (bio)social eugenics, a body politics, an "anatomy of power" which, as an implicit or explicit system of power, knowledge, and coercion, defined the relations between ruler and ruled: "Medicine and imperialism in nineteenth-century Africa are seen to be inseparably joined in practice and in concept. The evolving field of biomedicine, introduced by missionary healers, provided images of an ailing human body that would justify the intervention of a colonial state as it imposed its own order of domination."[15] As hegemonic discourse and practice closely related to the ideology of the state, or more generally as a "tool of empire," biomedicine was – and still is – centrally concerned with *difference*. As a metaphor for a more general colonial ideology and praxis, it is thus illustrative of many of the mechanisms that contributed in the creation and development of the urban colonial landscape, and of Léopoldville in particular.

Throughout its emergence and gradual development, Léopoldville, as colonial speculum and as large-scale project in social engineering, grafted upon its urban geography and ecology many of the evolutionist oppositions that also underpinned the cultural construction of difference in the medical colonial intervention. The difference between metropolitan Prospero and colonial Caliban, between Self and Other, Culture and Nature, Rationality and Irrationality, Man and Woman, writing and speech, knowledge and ignorance, modernity and tradition, or peace and war, is constantly generated in this European speculation. It is also the same mirror that gives birth to Léopoldville's two reflecting halves, the Western Ville and the indigenous Cité. In these complementary but

---

14 See Nancy R. Hunt, *A Colonial Lexicon of Birth Ritual, Medicalization, and Mobility in the Congo* (Durham, N.C.: Duke University Press, 1999); Jock McCulloch, *Colonial Psychiatry and "the African Mind"* (Cambridge: Cambridge University Press, 1995). On the colonial attempts at creating stronger and more productive laborers, the *tshanga-tshanga* race, in the labor camps of the Katangese Union Minière, see Bruno De Meulder, *De kampen van Kongo: Arbeid, kapitaal en rasveredeling in de koloniale planning* (Amsterdam and Antwerp: Meulenhoff and Kritak, 1996).

15 Shirley Lindenbaum and Margaret M. Lock, "Body Politics – Past and Present," in *Knowledge, Power, and Practice: The Anthropology of Medicine and Everyday Life*, ed. Lindenbaum and Lock (Berkeley: University of California Press, 1993), p. 303. See also David Arnold, ed., *Imperial Medicine and Indigenous Societies* (Manchester: Manchester University Press, 1988); Alexander Butchart, *The Anatomy of Power: European Constructions of the African Body* (London: Zed Books, 1998); Daniel R. Headrick, *The Tools of Empire: Technology and European Imperialism in the Nineteenth Century* (New York: Oxford University Press, 1981); Roy M. MacLeod and Milton J. Lewis, eds., *Disease, Medicine, and Empire: Perspectives on Western Medicine and the Experience of European Expansion* (London: Routledge, 1988).

opposing spaces, qualities such as "public" and "private" acquire radically different meanings.

The colonial triumvirate of sword, cross, and money, that is, of the colonial administration and its military arm, the church and its proselytizing activities, and the colony's powerful trade and industry circles, often had different and sometimes even contradictory agendas. They did not necessarily hold the same views on the development of the urban landscape and its inhabitants, and their actions were not always concerted. Nevertheless, these three pillars of Belgian colonialism in Congo shared the same underlying, although often vaguely defined, ideal of colonialist modernity as outlined above. It is this shared ideological configuration that underpinned to a large extent the ways in which the city was shaped and designed.

During the postwar period in which the modernist suburban housing estate of my childhood years was built, Belgian modernism was also given a second life in Congo. In 1940, Léopoldville was home to some 50,000 inhabitants. At the end of World War II, the number of inhabitants had doubled, to attain 200,000 in 1950, 400,000 at independence, and well over a million in 1970. In the early decades of the 20th century, Léopoldville developed along the axis Kintambo-Kalina. Kintambo developed out of Stanley's early trading post and consisted of the city's oldest industrial and residential sites. Kalina, currently Gombe, evolved into the capital's administrative area, housing the colonial administration's offices and residential villas. Gombe has very much kept that function today. Kintambo and Kalina were soon connected by a railroad. Around this axis gradually developed commercial centers and several *cités indigènes*, camps and settlements inhabited by Congolese workers. On the Kintambo side, the labor camps arose along the river, in proximity with the industrial activities of that part of the city, its shipyards, metallurgy, and other activities such as the confection industry of Utex Léo. On the Kalina side, a considerably larger space was set aside for the development of several indigenous neighborhoods, most notably Kinshasa, Barumbu, and Lingwala. Consisting of a large number of small *parcelles*, these neighborhoods were laid out according to a well-ordered grid which continued the original ground plan of an army camp that had been located there previously. These indigenous neighborhoods, camps, and, after World War II, *cités jardins* consisted of houses that were either individually constructed and owned (and there existed a Fonds d'Avance to encourage such individual ownership) or they were built by colonial employers and companies. Here, too, these neighborhoods existed in close proximity with the administrative and residential centers of Léopoldville. Yet they were consistently separated from these central areas by stretches of no man's land, by the main railroad (which also connected the city to the port of Matadi in the Lower Congo), as well as by a number of other *zones tampons*, such as the city's botanical gardens, commercial areas, an ethnographic museum displaying indigenous lifestyles, a zoological garden, mission posts, and army camps.

In terms of its spatial layout, the stretched-out booming urban conglomeration that Léopoldville was rapidly becoming thus emerged from the very beginning as a racially segregated city, with a strict demarcation line between a central white Ville, with its administrative and residential areas (Kintambo, Ngaliema, and the current Gombe, later expanded into the residential neighborhoods of Limete), and a "peripheral" African city, the *cité indigène*.

On top of the racial lines of segregation that structured the city of Léopoldville, or Lipopo as it was called by its Congolese inhabitants, the colonial economic demands and necessities also occasioned a demographic, strongly gendered segregation. In the early decades of the Belgian Congo's existence, the colonial population mainly consisted of men. It was only after World War II that families, wives, and children became an established fact of Léopoldville's urban social make-up. This demographic imbalance, however, was not a reality that characterized the lives of the white colonials alone. Before 1930, the male-female ratio in Léopoldville's indigenous neighborhoods was three to one. At the end of World War II, men still outnumbered women two to one, and special taxes were imposed on single women living in the *cités indigènes*. This reflected not only the colonial endeavor at controlling the city's growth rate, but also the simple fact that these indigenous *cités* mainly functioned as depots of cheap African labor, in which there was room neither for women nor the unemployed. Especially after the war, in a vain attempt to diminish and contain mounting social and political tensions in the city, the colonial administration developed a strict policy to clean up the streets. Those without jobs were rounded up by the Force Publique, the colonial armed forces, and sent back to the interior. Paralleling the city's segregated spatial and demographic development, the Force Publique, strategically located in army garrisons throughout Léopoldville, was built along equally strict segregated lines, with a superstructure of Belgian officers on the one hand, and a body of Congolese recruits, mostly Bangala from the Congo's Équateur province, on the other. It is mainly these soldiers who became the driving force behind the development of Lingala, their native language, as the city's major *lingua franca*.

Despite a vast array of far-reaching colonial measures aimed at restricting and controlling rural migration to the city, Léopoldville kept expanding. In 1949, faced with a demographic explosion and the increasing social unrest it engendered, the Belgian colonial administration began to implement a large urbanization program through the newly created Office de Cités Indigènes de Léopoldville (O.C.I.L.). One of the office's projects was the Renkin neighborhood (named after Belgium's first minister of colonial affairs), which later formed the heart of what would become Matonge, the vibrant core of Kinshasa's nightlife.

In 1952, the O.C.I.L. was succeeded by the Office de Cités Africaines (O.C.A.), created to better coordinate the government's response to the increasingly pressing needs of a rapidly growing city.[16] O.C.A.'s goal was ambitious: the construction of 40,000 new "quality homes" throughout the colony over the next ten years. Twenty thousand of these homes would be built in Léopoldville alone. Between 1952 and 1960, the city thus expanded drastically, giving birth to an impressive number of new "satellite" *cités* such as Bandalungwa, Yolo Nord and Yolo Sud, Matete, Lemba, Ndjili, and, finally, Kinkole.[17] Still, O.C.A.'s housing program and urban planning efforts, impres-

---

16 For a detailed history of colonial architecture in Léopoldville and Congo, see Bruno De Meulder, *Kuvuande Mbote: Een eeuw koloniale architectuur en stedenbouw in Kongo* (Antwerp: Uitgeverij Houtekiet, 2000). Personal reminiscences of a rapidly changing city are offered by Kolonga Molei, *Kinshasa, ce village d'hier* (Kinshasa: SODIMCA, 1979). See also Jean S. La Fontaine, *City Politics: A Study of Léopoldville, 1962–63* (Cambridge: Cambridge University Press, 1970).

17 See De Meulder, *Kuvuande Mbote*, ch. 14. See also Léon de Saint-Moulin, "Ndjili, première cité satellite de Kinshasa," *Cahiers Économiques et Sociaux* 8, no. 2 (1970), pp. 295–316; Léon de

sive as they may appear today, fell short of providing a satisfactory solution to the city's enormous demographic expansion and increasingly chaotic character. The colonial government concentrated all of its efforts at urban expansion in O.C.A., while barring all nongovernmental housing programs and initiatives. The government would refuse, for example, to sell land to private companies to construct new homes for their employees. And yet, the rate at which the much needed new houses were constructed within the O.C.A. program was far too slow to bear up against the population growth. Worse even, many of the new houses remained empty because they were too expensive for Kinshasa's commoners. As a result, shantytowns and *bidonvilles* began to spring up everywhere across the city. The situation worsened during the first years after independence. At first, O.C.A. plans continued to be implemented, though at a much slower pace. This effort at continued urban planning was coordinated by the Office National de Logement (O.N.L.) and financed by the Caisse National d'Épargne et de Crédit Immobilier. Gradually, however, the government aban-

Saint-Moulin and M. Ducreux, "Le phénomène urbain à Kinshasa: Évolution et perspectives," *Études Congolaises* 12, no. 4 (1969).

doned all efforts at urban planning. No longer restrained by government supervision, the shantytowns expanded into the endless and still growing sprawl of popular neighborhoods, the vast peripheral city, the *zones annexes* of which Kinshasa consists today. In the process, the capital grew far beyond its colonial borders: toward the Lower Congo in the western direction, and in the eastern and southern directions, over the hill range that once contained the city, toward the Bateke plateau and the Kwango. As a result, the city has grown away from its old colonial heart. This evolution was recently consolidated by Kabila Sr.'s decision to order the building of a new major market square in Masina, in an attempt to alleviate the pressure on the old central market area near the Rue du Commerce. Its construction confirms the fact that the colonial city center, which was also the geographic center during colonial times, long since ceased to be either, and had become peripheral in the daily experience of the majority of Kinshasa's population.

It is in Camp Luka, Masina, Kimbanseke, Kingasani, Kisenso, Ngaba, Makala, large parts of Mont Ngafula, and the many other similar *zones annexes* and *communes urbano-rurales* of postcolonial Kinshasa that the failure of modernist urban planning, as conceived by the colonial government and the early postcolonial state, was most clearly illustrated. It is here, also, that Kinshasa began to reinvent itself into the city that it has become today. The growth of this new Kinshasa has also marked a mental move away from the "place" of colonialism (and this place is both a spatial reality and a language, French). It has, in other words, moved away from the mimetic reproduction of an alienating model of colonialist modernity, imposed by the colonial and the Mobutist state upon the city's population through a wide-ranging arsenal of physical and symbolic forms of violence. For the past four decades, the city has also moved away from the secular "time of the (post)colonial nation" and the official "religious time" of the Catholic church which accompanied these efforts at nation-building. It is in these increasingly numerous informal urban areas, with its complex patchwork of multiple local ethnic identities, that the city's inhabitants have begun to reterritorialize the urban space, develop their own specific forms of what De Meulder has called "proto-urbanism," and infuse the city with their own praxis, values, moralities, and temporal dynamics. This process, which is perhaps better referred to as a form of "posturbanism," began at Kinshasa's margins and has now engulfed the city as a whole. Unhindered by any kind of formal industrialization or economic development, the city has bypassed, redefined, or smashed the (neo)colonial logics that were stamped onto its surface. It has done so spatially, in terms of its architectural and urban development, as well as in terms of its sociocultural and economic imprint. Reaching across the formation period of high colonialism and its modernist ideals, Kinshasa is, to some extent, rejoining its earlier rural roots. Today, aided by an unabating political and economic crisis, the city is undergoing a large-scale process of informal *villagization*, in which a new type of agrarian urbanity and even a new type of ethnicity is generated.[18]

For an external observer, it is not always easy to read this new urban landscape. Related to the Western failure to reach beyond its blurred vision of a largely fictitious Congo is the development of a second form of cataract, which is becoming increasingly apparent in the incapacity of much academic discourse to grasp fully and make visible the changing realities in contemporary Congo and Kinshasa. Faced with worlds and interactions that no longer correspond to the social interweave as we tend to conceptualize and experience it, one becomes acutely aware that it is futile to explain some of the processes currently taking place in Congolese society by means of the standard vocabularies used by social and political scientists, economists, demographers, and urban planners. Terms and concepts such as "state," "administration," "government," "governability," "democracy," "army," "citizenship," "law," "justice," or even "education" and "healthcare" no longer seem to apply unequivocally to the realities usually covered by those terms.

Why is a building called "national bank," "university," "state department," "hospital," or "school" when the activities that take place in it cannot be given the standard meanings and realities usually covered by those words? In January 1995, for example, Belgian newspapers reported that the national bank's total stock of foreign currency amounted to US$2,000 and a handful of Swiss francs. Similarly, university professors today earn US$200 a month – that is, if they are paid at all – and most departments of Kinshasa's national university have not bought books or produced a single doctoral dissertation since the Zaireanization in the early 1970s. What does it mean to be a city with an estimated 6 million inhabitants in which there is hardly any car traffic or public transportation, for the simple reason that, at frequent intervals, there is not a drop of fuel available for weeks or even months? Why continue the social convention of referring to a banknote as "money" when one is confronted daily with the fact that it is just a worthless slip of paper? The withdrawal, in November 1993, of the IMF and the World Bank from the country attested to the fact that Congo was no longer participating in the formal world economy. But what is the use of distinguishing between formal and informal or parallel economies when the informal has become the common and the formal has almost disappeared?

For years now, Congo's "second" or "shadow" economy has been the first and

---

18 On the notion of villagization, see René Devisch, "'Pillaging Jesus': Healing Churches and the Villagisation of Kinshasa," *Africa* 66, no. 4 (1996), pp. 555–586.

virtually only one. For Kinois, it has long since become a cliché to say that no economic model can explain how a city like Kinshasa survives. For the *poussepousseurs*, the *quados* (informal car mechanics), the *khaddafis* (illegal vendors of fuel), the *cambistes* (money changers), taxi drivers, shoe shiners, night watchmen, and *ligablos* (street vendors) who daily experience in the flesh the continuing deterioration of their standards of living, and whose lives unfold in *avenue misère*, the common discourses of political, economic, and other analysts and "experts" are therefore totally devoid of sense. To them, *Kinshasa la belle* has long since become *Kinshasa la poubelle*, referred to as *Koweit City rive gauche*, *Sarajevo*, or, more recently, *Kosovo* and *Tchetchénie*.

Mirroring the constant attempts of Kinshasa's inhabitants to rename and thereby reclaim their city, the colonial and postcolonial authorities invested a lot of energy in the construction of their vision of urban space. The colonizing dynamics of naming and renaming the city and its composite parts are typical of both the colonial and the Mobutist period. During colonial times, not only the city's name, Léopoldville, referred to the colonial master but so did the names of many a neighborhood: Belge I, Belge II, Bruxelles. Similarly, Mobutu stamped himself onto the city's map by renaming streets, buildings (Mama Yemo hospital, Stade Kamanyola), military camps, and neighborhoods (Cité Mama Mobutu, Camp Mobutu). These acts of name-giving illustrate the constant attempts at mastering the city, at producing domination, at defining place and encapsulating it in language. And yet, the names themselves immediately become sites of opposition against the official order.

The breakdown of the colonial city model and its local appropriation, transformation, and cultural reterritorialization had already started during the colonial period itself. In 1959, more than half of Léopoldville's population was under the age of eighteen, and of this large group, only half was schooled. In 1960, the capital, already overpopulated, was flooded by another wave of youngsters fleeing from the rebellion and warfare in the interior (a process that is currently repeating itself). It is against this background of a decade of rising insecurity and socioeconomic and political unrest that street gangs of youngsters without schooling or a salaried job began to make an appearance in the streets of Léopoldville.[19]

Between 1957 and 1959, in the same period in which the administrative reform took place, six movie theaters opened their doors: SIBIKA in the Kintambo neighborhood, and ASTRA, MBONGO-MPASI, MACAULEY,

---

19 Even before, between 1920 and 1940, small gangs of youngsters were a presence in Léopoldville. These gangs recruited members primarily among the children of policemen and soldiers of the Force Publique.

MOUSTAPHA, and SILUVANGI in the popular neighborhoods of Lingwala, Kinshasa, and Barumbu. These movie theaters, which flourished all over the city except for the "European" neighborhoods of Ngaliema, Léopoldville, and Limete, soon became a favorite meeting place of Léopoldville's youth, especially those youngsters at the margins of the colonial urban order, at risk of being expelled by the authorities. Hollywood westerns, in particular, had a tremendous impact on the way in which urban youth subcultures of that time chose to express themselves, and were a decisive factor in the creation of Billism. In particular, the image of the buffalo hunter and culture hero Buffalo Bill, alongside other cowboys such as Pecos Bill, left a deep impression.[20] These cowboys provided ideal role models for the young Kinois, who imitated the appearance (blue-jeans, checkered shirt, neckerchief, lasso) and the tics of the Hollywood

---

20 Charles Didier Gondola (*Villes miroirs: Migrations et identités urbaines à Kinshasa et Brazzaville, 1930–1970* [Paris: L'Harmattan, 1997], p. 310) mentions in particular two films that introduced Buffalo Bill to youthful Congolese audiences: the versions of Cecil B. DeMille (*The Plainsman*, 1937) and William Wellman (*Buffalo Bill*, 1944). Most popular, however, was *Pony Express* (translated as *Le triomphe de Buffalo Bill*), made by Jerry Hopper in 1953, in which Charlton Heston played the part of Buffalo Bill.

actors. After each movie, these young urban cowboys circulated on their "bicycle-horses" to announce the message of the western (*mofewana*, Lingala deformation of Far West), crying loudly *Bill oyee!*, upon which the bystanders would reply with *serumba!*

As such, Billism appropriated and transformed the image of the cowboy-hunter to make it its own. Most members of these ludic groups of young urban "terrorists," more generally known as "The Spongers of the Far West" (*Les Écumeurs du Far West*), lived on the margins of colonial society. The movement produced various competing gangs. Around 1957, most of these gangs, such as the "Yankees of Ngiri-Ngiri," shaped up around a few leaders. Among these early "ancestors," "priests" (*prêtres*), "sheriffs," or *grand maîtres* of the street gangs predominantly figured two persons known as William Booth and Gazin. Others soon followed: Grand Billy, Ross Samson, Néron (Monerona, author of a popular song, "Wele Kingo"), Tex Bill, Mive John, Mobarona, Khroutchev, Long Li Su, Azevedo, Eboma, Vieux Porain Zanga-Zanga, Libre, De Goum, Moruma, Demayo. Most of these were well-known local delinquents. Initially, the youngsters circling around these leaders lived together in houses (called "ranches" or "temples"). Later, groups hung out in what became known as *nganda*, a meeting place around a bar-restaurant. Well-known *ngandas* included Dynamic and Mofewana in Ngiri-Ngiri, or L'Enfer and Okinawa in Ndjili. These groups organized themselves into little territorial fiefdoms throughout the city (in Ngiri-Ngiri, Saint-Jean, Camp Luka, Bandal, Kintambo, Bandalungwa, Barumbu, Kinshasa, and later Lemba, Ndjili, Matete, Yolo) and, like sheriffs, they "made the law" (*kodondwa*) and "created order" (*tobongisa*, one of the Bills' slogans) in their neighborhood, while stealing for a living and fighting over territory with neighboring gangs.[21] Each territory, with its ranches and *ngandas*, thus had its chiefs and subchiefs, its ritual specialists known as *professeurs*, its own laws and rules, declared by the *maître* of each particular gang, its own systems of taxation (making other citizens pay for a safe passage through gang territory), and its own pass-time rituals, such as weight-lifting, gang-banging neighborhood girls, or smoking marijuana. Billism also strongly focused on music and guitars. As such, the movement was at the origin of the birth of multiple local orchestras, some of which later evolved into well-known bands, such as Zaiko. Thus, Billism, mobilizing and channeling social forces from the margin, greatly contributed to the establishment of one of the most powerful forms of expression in Kinshasa's flamboyant popular culture.

---

21 The fact that former rebel-leader Kabila, imposing his "law" throughout the country in 1997, was referred to as "Sheriff" (and dressed accordingly, wearing a Stetson hat) is an immediate echo of 1950s Billism.

Furthermore, each of these street groups had its own rituals of initiation. These usually consisted of a period of seclusion in the bush (thereby imitating the older rural model of the *mukanda* circumcision camp). There, one was trained into a specific style of ritualized combat, called *bilayi*, in which one had to learn how to butt one's head into a person during a fight. Overall, the Billies placed great value on violence, endurance, physical strength, and courage, qualities stressed in the nicknames the Bills bestowed upon each other such as *bois dur* or *bois fort*, "hard wood." The same stress recurs in popular slogans of Billism: *azongaka sima te*, "a Bill never retreats," or *tokende liboso*, "we go forward."[22]

What distinguished the Bills above all was the use of a particular argot, known as Hindubill, a mixture of French, Lingala, English, and local vernacular languages. In a counter-hegemonic inversion, "Hindu" refers to "Indian," the cowboy's natural enemy (that is, the state agent). It also makes reference to the "Indian" marijuana the Bills smoked. "Hindu" possibly also betrays the influence of Hindi movies shown in the theaters of Léopoldville during that period. This Indian cinematographic influence is partly responsible for the way in which the emerging figure of the Mami Wata – half woman and half fish, who promises access to wealth in return for human lives – began to dominate the city's imagination in the 1960s. In Kinshasa's popular paintings, Mami Wata invariably appears as a white-skinned "Indian" lady (and this in spite of the West African origin of the Mami Wata figure).

As the language of youth, Hindubill formed the hidden transcript of the youthful underdogs of Kinshasa who were excluded from education and salaried jobs and thus from the world of "adults." With Hindubill, the urban cowboys created their own modes of in- and exclusion. At the same time, the persona of the cowboy emerges as emancipatory figure, representing the spirit of the coming independence. The Bills played an important role in the lootings and the uprising that spread through Kinshasa in January 1959. They also reterritorialized the city in yet another way, by renaming various areas, markets, schools, bars, and other public spaces, upon which they bestowed names such as Texas, Dallas, Casamar, Godzilla. This reterritorialization implied an explicit criticism of the Belgians' insufficient and segregationist urbanization of a too rapidly expanding Léopoldville. Undoubtedly, the Billies' practice of reclaiming and renaming parodied the colonizer's imperialist obsession with mapping and labeling, while at the same time playfully commenting upon the claims of the emergent nationalist movement.

---

22 Today, *bana Lunda*, young diamond diggers from Kinshasa and other towns in southwestern Congo who go to dig diamonds in the Angolan province of Lunda Norte, describe themselves as *kuntwalistes*, "those who go forward" (from kiKoongo *kuntwala*), echoing the Billies' slogan *tokende liboso*.

From November 1960 onward, with the mounting "Congo crisis" and increasing unrest throughout the country, many new youth gangs appeared. These still made use of the vocabulary of the Bills, but at the same time increasingly shifted from the figure of the Cowboy to that of the Soldier, with references, for example, to the United Nations Blue Helmets, thereby reflecting in their vocabulary and organization the changing context of the period in which they emerged.

Billism laid the foundation for much contemporary urban youth culture. Kinshasa's movie theaters have long since disappeared. Instead, movies have become available through television, or they are watched in small neighborhood video-theaters, where one usually pays for a full evening program that includes clips of the latest Congolese hits and concerts, a movie à la Ninja or Rambo, some soccer, and, to top it off, a porn movie. Yet, the way in which western action movie hunters/warriors are captured and localized by Kinshasa's youth, and even more by the military, is reminiscent of the Billies in the 1950s. Zorro, Rambo, Superman, Terminator, Godzilla, and the Power Rangers have become common role models for Kabila's *kadogos* (child-soldiers) and for urban youth in general. Kinshasa's youth share with their forebears the same capacity to fracture and reinvent urban public space. Street children in Kinshasa sing: "It is said that water that sleeps does not move. The sleeping water only moves when one throws a stone into it." Often, Kinshasa's youngsters are like such a stone, shattering the water's reflecting surface and sending ripples and waves through the pool in which Kinshasa beholds itself. They inscribe themselves in new temporalities. They also recycle and generate surprising, oftentimes embodied, cultural vocabularies and aesthetics. Now, as in the past, these feverishly reflect Kinshasa's social history while providing a subversive comment upon the banalization of violence, the militarization of society, the apocalyptic gale-force sound and fury of the city's constant religious transfiguration, and the material hardships in today's urbanscape.

The Village and the Forest City The growing ruralization of Kinshasa is a strong reminder of the fact that the capital has not only looked into the mirror of modernity to design itself, but that it has always contained a second mirror as well. This mirror is provided by the Village, the rural hinterland that constitutes Kinshasa's demographic and ethnic make-up, the countryside that feeds Kinshasa, forms its natural backdrop, and exists in the city by way of contrast. It is this contrast that allowed the city to fashion itself as city, to define itself as *centre extra-coutumier* and, as marker of difference in opposition to the village, to place itself outside of the normative order of a rural and more traditional world that

was – and often is – considered to be backward and primitive. And yet, at the same time, the construction of Kinshasa's urban space and identity has always remained a contested and dislocating presence, a reminder of an artificial breach. In reality, this urban identity has constantly been invaded and formed by, blending with and depending on, the village's traditions, moralities, and pasts.

Three decades ago, someone like Henri Lefebvre, in his acclaimed work *The Production of Space*, could still, somewhat naively, write: "Much as they might like to, anthropologists cannot hide the fact that the space and tendencies of modernity (i.e. of modern capitalism) will never be discovered either in Kenya or among French or any other peasants."[23] Lefebvre thereby continued the same long modernist tradition which underpinned the creation of difference in the colonial period, and which is characterized by its conceptualization of the world within a polarized framework opposing, for example, modernity and tradition, city and countryside, center and periphery, "warm" and "cold" societies, culture and nature, male and female, the "hard rationality" of liberal capitalism gener-

---

23 Henri Lefebvre, *The Production of Space* (1974), trans. Donald Nicholson-Smith (Oxford: Blackwell, 1991), p. 123.

ated in the urban space and the "soft irrationality" of a rural "economy of affection," and so forth. However, the distinctions between urban and rural realities, between "modern" and "traditional" worlds, or between what is situated locally and what is considered to be global, can no longer be taken for granted. It is no doubt a perceptual error to concentrate exclusively on the center, or the city, in order to understand the production of modernity (or the construction of, for example, "modern" male African identity).[24] Rather than scrutinize the processes of modernity's construction from the metropole's perspective, it is also important to look at the fringes, at the periphery, at those sites, whether located in the rural countryside or in the city itself, where "modernity" has not solidified but is a fluid and negotiable reality, an unfinished hegemony.

In the postcolony, moreover, categories such as "center" and "periphery," or "city" and "village," and the string of qualities attached to them, have often themselves become states of mind rather than objective qualities of space. The way in which the urban and the rural are constantly deconstructed in the postcolony necessitates an imaginative theorizing of that reality. For example, whereas the space of the city has not only undergone a marked ruralization, it has also, and increasingly, become, in the collective social-instituting imaginary, the space of the forest. The hunter's landscape, which is a potentially dangerous, frontierlike margin, is thus constantly mapped onto the urban, and thus "central," landscape. Hence, Werrason, the current uncrowned king of Kinshasa's popular music scene, refers to himself as "the king of the forest" (*le roi de la forêt*) and the "chief of the animals" (*mokonzi ya banyama*). It is no coincidence that the bar, a most crucial site in the urban landscape, is often redefined as village, such as Village Syllo, with its pastoral setting, along the Avenue Lumumba, or Limete's Village Bercy. In the latter, the light bulbs are put inside Aladdin lamps, which function as *pars pro toto* for the local, conjuring up the rural and the village. At the same time, the notion of the village blends into an interesting palimpsest through a reference to an icon of the global Western world, the Stade de Bercy in Paris, where a number of Kinshasa's orchestras have given concerts in recent years. Often also, the bar is conceptualized as "forest." In the social imaginary, the nocturnal environment of the bar is no doubt one of the most important locales in which the city most fully displays its "urbanity" and modernity, and in which "diamond-hunters" and others who have access to dollars track down and capture, through ostensive consumption of beer, women, and consumer goods, their interpretation of the "good life" as promised by and defined in their notion of "modernity."

---

24 For an example of this tendency, see Tshikala K. Biaya, "Les paradoxes de la masculinité africaine moderne: Une histoire de violences, d'immigration et de crises," *Canadian Folklore Canadien* 19, no. 1 (1997), pp. 89–112.

Similarly, the city/forest has become the site of the hunter's female counterpart, the gatherer. Once a week, huge bus-trucks called CITY-TATA ("City-father") leave Kinshasa to transport passengers to Kikwit, 500 kilometers southeast of the capital, along a ravaged and dangerous road that once used to be a smoothly asphalted highway. Analogous to these trucks, the name CITY-MAMA has been bestowed upon small baskets that are used by an increasing number of urban women, the *mamas miteke*, who are without an income or a garden or field to till. These women take to the bush and swamps around the city to collect what little roots and grubs they can find there. Like the passengers in the CITY-TATA bus, the roots are then transported back to the city in the "basket-bus" on the women's heads. (Ironically, Kinshasa is being redefined in terms of the sylvan margin at a time when woods and forests around it are rapidly disappearing, a fact that has even changed its micro-climate.)

It thus seems that, in Kinshasa today, modernity as exemplified by the city is not only contested or unfinished at its fringes, that is, the rural hinterland, but also in its very heart, the polis, where the local logic of hunting and gathering has infused the urban world, both metaphorically and practically, with its own moralities, its own ethics of accumulation, expenditure, and redistribution, and its own specific pathways of self-realization. Especially for the urban young, the hunter provides a model of identification and a figure of success and eminence. It is no coincidence that it was precisely Buffalo Bill, a buffalo hunter, who became a culture hero for Kinshasa's youngsters. Even today, the image of the hunter continues to have a strongly epistemic power. It offers the possibility of remaking both identity and place, and generating – to some extent at least – a social environment in the midst of chaos and change. For the "children of Lunda" (*bana Lunda*) or "the children who work money" (*basali ya mbongo*), the numerous youngsters who leave Kinshasa and other urban centers to travel hundreds of kilometers to the Angolan diamond fields of Lunda Norte, "hunting" diamonds and dollars constitutes a crucial part of the active capturing of the urban space, for it allows them to refashion the city (and thereby "modernity," the West, the *mundele* or "white man") in their own terms, which are those of long-standing moralities, rooted in local rural pasts.[25]

---

25 See Filip De Boeck, "Domesticating Diamonds and Dollars: Identity, Expenditure and Sharing in Southwestern Zaïre (1984–1997)," in *Globalization and Identity: Dialectics of Flow and Closure*, ed. Birgit Meyer and Peter Geschiere (Oxford: Blackwell, 1999); Filip De Boeck, "'Dogs Breaking Their Leash': Globalization and Shifting Gender Categories in the Diamond Traffic Between Angola and DRCongo (1984–1997)," in *Changements au féminin en Afrique noire: Anthropologie et littérature*, vol. 1, ed. Danielle de Lame and Chantal Zabus (Paris: L'Harmattan, 1999); Filip De Boeck, "Le 'deuxième monde' et les 'enfants-sorciers' en République Démocratique du Congo," *Politique Africaine* 80 (December 2000), pp. 32–57.

Congolese youngsters' engagement in more global economies of diamond export and dollarization is thus often shaped from an utterly local perspective and out of a memory that is rooted in the *longue durée*. Although memory and history in the urban context are of a specific kind and have undergone some radical transformations over the past decades, the expanding peripheral city is thus not without history, unlike Koolhaas' notion of the "generic city."[26] To conquer the city and shape their own moral and social economies in this urban space, the urban young tap into sources and routes of rural identity formation, thereby negotiating and reinventing the content and architecture of the intermediate world in which they find themselves. As such, the passage into Angola is a contemporary version of a much older strategy of self-realization, as hunter and warrior, in that it constitutes a veritable rite of passage, modeled upon the old *mukanda* circumcision ritual which is still practiced in the countryside, and to which youngsters explicitly refer when they share and discuss their experiences in the Angolan diamond fields. It is important, however, to stress that the past (represented in the form of hunting logics, the village morality of capture and redistribution, the ultimately rural modes of self-making as hunter and/or warrior) which is thus carried into the urban present is *not* a static model. On the contrary, for urban youth the past becomes, if not reflexively at least in practice, a source for active engagement with the present, in ways that give shape to both very creative and outgoing forms of collective imagination and a constant invention of a future for tradition. (As imagined, for example, by Kinshasa's musicians in their video clips, in which the persona of the "traditional chief" is frequently reenacted as a potent icon of power. More generally, rural "folkloristic" music has been continuously recycled by urban bands such as Swede-Swede since the 1980s.)

At the same time, the rural periphery has (once again) gained in importance. As elsewhere in the world, where processes of globalization are played out in a context of frontier expansion,[27] the Congolese hinterland has become most central in capitalist dynamics and the dollarization of local economies, in particular, the little diamond boomtowns of Kahemba and Tembo, along the border between Congo's Bandundu province and the Angolan province of Lunda Norte. Whereas the city has become peripheral and in some respects village-like, the bush is the place where dollars are generated, where the "good life" is shaped, and where villages transform into booming diamond settlements, where

---

26 Rem Koolhaas, "La ville générique," *Architecture d'aujourd'hui*, no. 304 (April 1996), pp. 70–77.
27 On frontier urbanization and the creation of "rainforest cities" in the Brazilian Amazon, see John O. Browder and Brian J. Godfrey, *Rainforest Cities: Urbanization, Development, and Globalization of the Brazilian Amazon* (New York: Columbia University Press, 1997).

life focuses on money and the consumption of women and beer.[28] The diamond traffic, and the phenomenon of dollarization that has followed in its wake, are also emblematic of a return to the Léopoldian *comptoir* economy that has marked the origin of Kinshasa and so many other cities throughout Africa. The political economy of the *comptoir* has always been colonial in its very essence. In the past it contributed to the urbanization of the African material and mental landscape. The contemporary *comptoir* economy in Congo and Angola has continued to contribute a great deal to the frontier urbanization of places such as Mbuji-Mayi or Tshikapa (in the Kasai), Kahemba and Tembo, as well as the Kwango River diamond settlements in Angola, or the diamond "ranches" around Kisangani. These local sites have become, in certain ways, globalized spaces, the economic and cultural dynamics of which are linked to many other different places on the globe that play a role in a semi-formal world-economy, from Luanda, Kinshasa, Brazzaville, Bangui, and Bujumbura, to Antwerp, Bombay, Beirut, Dubai, Tel Aviv, and Johannesburg. At the same time, these locally generated "bush" dollars have also engendered the further development, revival, sometimes even gentrification, of certain areas in Kinshasa: Masina's *quartier Sans Fil*, Ndjili's *quartier sept*, and some parts of Lemba, such as the more residential areas of Salongo and Righini.

Diasporic Movement and the Mirroring of Modernity   The local creation of modernities leads us to a third mirror in which Kinshasa generates an image of itself, contemplates and reflects upon itself, and projects itself outward. This mirror is situated in the context of the diaspora. Effectively barred from traveling abroad during the colonial period, the Congolese were quick to inscribe themselves in processes of migration after independence. This mobility intensified and was accentuated by the gradual economic decline that began in the latter half of the 1970s and reached mind-boggling dimensions toward the end of Mobutu's long and disastrous reign. The breakdown of the Zairean state and the increasingly harsh living conditions in Kinshasa and the country at large prompted a huge exodus.

Almost invariably, the first stop along the often difficult path of diasporic existence was Belgium, and even today the focal point of Kinshasa's diasporic

---

28 The boomtowns of Tembo and Kahemba, in the administrative units of Kasongo-Lunda and Kahemba respectively, are a good example of these dynamics. In 1984, the *cité* of Kahemba officially counted 10,522 inhabitants (quartiers Kahemba, Mobutu, and Sukisa). Ten years later, the population of Kahemba had multiplied tenfold, with small aircraft flying in almost daily with goods and people from Kinshasa. Today the town of Kahemba is reducing in size again, due to the difficulties of accessing Angola since the end of 1998.

Rond Point Victoire, Matonge, April 2000

mirror remains the neighborhood of Matonge, situated in Brussels. This Belgian Matonge is named after one of Kinshasa's most vibrant neighborhoods, the fast-beating heart of the city's nightlife and popular music scene, with its effervescent central square, Rond Point Victoire, its nightclubs and open-air bars and *ngandas*, its West African *commerçants* in their suave *boubous*, the proud descendants of the Coastmen who arrived in Kinshasa in the 1930s, its freshly roasted *kamundele* goat meat, and its crowded Djakarta market lit by hundreds of little kerosene lamps at night.

The colonial mirror, the mirror offered by the village, and the mirror activated by the diasporic movement constantly echo a deeper level of speculation. This underlying mirror is often a broken and deforming one, a mirror that reflects Kinshasa's complex relationship with the outside and the beyond of a more global, transnational world, with the real and imagined qualities of "modernity" and of the wider, whiter world of the West. Driving along Kinshasa's Bypass, as the road which leads from the Rond Point Ngaba to the Échangeur of Limete is named, the observant eye might notice a dry cleaner – or *blanchisserie* ("whitener" in French) – named La Modernisation. On the facade of the house, stuck into the whitewashed cement, little shards of broken mirror form the

Dry cleaner "La Modernisation," Lemba, 1999 and 2001 (photo at left by Filip De Boeck)

letters of the word *Modernisation*. Not devoid of irony, mirroring modernity, assimilating to the West, and inscribing oneself in the project of what is, in the end, still a very colonialist modernity, is here shown for the whitewash operation that it has always been at heart. The colonial *évolué*, this prototype of Naipaul's *mimic man*, or Kinshasa's *mundele ndombe* (the "Black White"), or Fanon's *peau noir, masque blanc*,[29] or today's pale youngsters, whitened by disastrous "beauty" skin products – all of these figures illustrate the processes of imitation and the creation of image embedded in this mirroring. To some extent, the young diamond hunters of Kinshasa have moved beyond the mimetic. But it remains a complex process to break the spell of this image in the mirror, the image of this "African Europe" that colonial administrators, missionaries, expatriates, and the elites of the postcolonial state held up to Kinshasa as a model to aspire to.

In Congo, as elsewhere in Africa, the collective social imaginary concerning the West (referred to as Putu, Miguel, or Mikili) is rich in fairy-tale images that conjure up the world of modernity and the luxurious, almost paradisiacal lifestyle of the West. In Lingala, for example, Belgium is referred to as *lola*, "heaven." "The West," as a topos of the Congolese imaginary, where one enjoys the benefits of endless sources of wealth for free, sums up all the qualities of the "good life." The lifestyle of a local rich urban elite and of the expatriate confirms the reality of this Idea of the West. Also, rather than deconstructing this myth for the home front, people who themselves experience the often harsh realities of life in the diaspora usually go to great lengths to deny this grim picture and to confirm the exactitude of the collective imaginary. Admitting that life in the West is often a life of poverty does not invalidate the "topos of the Western Paradise" for those who remain behind on the home front. Instead, it is interpreted

---

29 Frantz Fanon, *Black Skin, White Masks* (1952), trans. Charles Lam Markmann (London: Pluto Press, 1986).

Matonge, Kinshasa (left); Matonge, Brussels (right)

as a sign of personal failure and weakness of the *mikiliste* who followed the trail of the diaspora. Rather than admitting that life in the diaspora is not that easy, Congolese living abroad therefore often prefer to send home pictures of themselves in front of a Mercedes, neglecting to mention that the Mercedes actually belongs to the neighbor. As such, Europe (and increasingly the United States, as the ultimate Land of Cocaigne, "the Putu of the *banoko*" [the Uncles, that is, the Belgians]) continues to be framed in these positive terms. Europe is *malili*, "cool," whereas Africa is *moto*, "hot," full of suffering. For most, the ideal of Putu conjures up a world without responsibilities: "Something is broke? Not to worry. Bring it to the white man and he will fix it" sang *feu* Pepe Kalle in one of his songs.

Nevertheless, this myth of the West has got the moth in it. Another phrase of Pepe Kalle's goes as follows: *bakende Putu, bakweyi na désert*, "they went to Europe, but landed in the desert." The phrase conveys the demythologization of the Idea of Europe: those who left for Europe and are now living in the diaspora have discovered that life in Putu is in reality a desert, a life of poverty filled with problems concerning money, housing, visa, and so forth. Simultaneously, the phrase also conveys a second meaning: "We Congolese started toward an insertion into a global ecumene of modernity, but we never attained our goal. Somewhere along the way we ran out of fuel and had to land in the desert." The world of modernity, with its tempting promises of boundless consumerism embedded in a vision of an expansive capitalism in the service of the nation-state, has become the fool's paradise in which the Congolese nation is no longer capable of living. It is out of reach for those who do not partake in the lottery of politics, have salaried jobs, know how to access international organizations and businesses, or have access to diamond dollars.

The blame for the impossibility of accessing this Western version of the "good life" is assigned not only to the excesses of the Mobutu era, but increasingly laid on the doorstep of the West itself. "When the Belgians left, they gave us independence, but at the same time they threw the key that opens the door to development into the ocean" is a frequently heard remark in Congo. The owner of a recently opened *magasin* painted the following motto above the shop entrance: *A qui la faute? Chez le blanc!* – "Who is to blame? The White Man!" As such, the motto translates a growing break from the world of modernity as defined by the metropole, a definition which reduces an increasing number of people in Congo to subaltern status as part of a swelling Third World proletariat.

For an ever growing number of "malcontents," the world of modernity as defined and propagated by the West and its agents – the state agent, the missionary, the development worker, the dwindling local urban elites – has indeed become an inaccessible chimera. Some observers have therefore interpreted *la grande fête de Kinshasa*, the wave of lethal and yet ludic lootings which swept through the city and demolished the country's economy in 1991 and 1993, as a radical break with the West. What was being demolished in the pillage were the icons of Western modernity: fancy restaurants, supermarkets, and industrial plants such as General Motors. Similarly, in 1997, Congo's new leaders, who to a large extent were recruited from the diaspora, were contemptuously nicknamed *occasions d'Europe* upon their arrival in Congo. In other words: the members of this new ruling elite were perceived to be like second-hand cars. No longer wanted in Europe and the States, where they could not obtain a steady position, they returned to Congo like *Bounties*, the brand name of a chocolate bar with a coconut filling: black on the surface and white at heart. This second-rate, hybridized version of the West is the best one can get, but is never quite the genuine article.

Although the tendency to turn away from the modernist position, in a true spirit of resistance against Western domination, is certainly there, this does not mean that people resist or reject modernity's promise of the good life itself. A painting by Chéri Samba, one of Kinshasa's most acclaimed artists, entitled *La femme et ses premiers désirs* (Woman and Her First Desires),[30] shows the painter's wife, Fifi, sitting in a bourgeois living room in Kinshasa, surrounded by the signs of her and her husband's status: refrigerator, television set, rotating fan, stereo chain, a cooking furnace... These are the fruits, the bourgeois contents of modernity that everybody, in the end, wishes for. What people increasingly object to, however, is the ideological hegemony of modernity, the fact that the West imposes upon them, from above and from outside, its own definition of

---

30 See Bogumil Jewsiewicki, *Chéri Samba: The Hybridity of Art* (Westmount, Quebec: Galerie Amrad African Art Publications, 1995), p. 56, pl. 13.

"the good life." Much of the cultural and political struggle in Congo today focuses on control over a politics of identity as self-representation, which implies that it is self-generated and self-constructed. To a large extent, the arguments of identity today center around the question of who represents whom, and to/for whom. Who is author, who is subject of representation? Recourse to colonial and postcolonial stereotypes is inevitable in situations where identities are at play.

A Secret City of Public Words   Behind the garden city, the forest city, and the village city lurks yet another city, an invisible but very audible city of whispers, of what Kinois call *les on dit*, of fleeting words, questions, harmful suspicions, and treacherous accusations. The powerful and relentless production of gossip and rumor constantly runs through the city. Shamelessly, leaving no subject untouched, it spreads like a bush fire through all of Kinshasa's communities. Often a weapon of the weak, it enters the scene from the margin and takes over the whole city, pumping its words like blood through the veins and arteries of this giant urban body. The motor of Kinshasa's public life, the capillary biopower of this *radio-trottoir* ("radio sidewalk") punctuates the city's heartbeat and constitutes its public eye.[31] Uniting and dividing the city through the force of words, it generates the capital's urban mythologies, its aesthetics of laughter, its cultural repertoires and collective imaginaries; it creates its heroes and damages the reputation of its most powerful and prominent citizens. It amplifies itself in the columns of the numerous newspapers that have proliferated since the end of Mobutu's one-party system and that daily are read and commented upon collectively at several points throughout the city by the *parlementaires debout*, the "politicians" of the street. Urban rumor solidifies in the paintings of Kinshasa's artists. It translates into the scripts of its popular street theater and locally produced TV soaps. It echoes in the lyrics of Kinshasa's urban troubadours. It is spelled out by actions such as the *radio tableau* ("radio blackboard"), where international radio news (RFI, BBC, Canal Afrique, Afrique No. Un) is written out and commented upon by the owners of small portable radios on a blackboard in the street while the whole neighborhood contributes batteries to keep the radio working, as a way of escaping and redirecting interpretations and representations imposed upon them from elsewhere.

In spite of its formidable creative force, Kinois rarely have anything good to say about their gossip mechanisms. Franco, the most prominent musician the

---

31 See Cornelis Nlandu-Tsasa, *La rumeur au Zaïre de Mobutu: Radio-trottoir à Kinshasa* (Paris: L'Harmattan, 1997).

city has ever produced, bitterly addresses *radio-trottoir* in one of his songs: "You sabotaged me, Radio Trottoir, You broke my marriage. With an information that you spread around but did not even bother to verify. You broke my marriage with your gossip!" In a similar vein his contemporary, Tabu Ley, complains in a song: "Gossip kills this city. Friends, you might hear something today, but try to see it with your own eyes before you start spreading illness for nothing." The invisible space of rumor and gossip constantly fractures and reshapes the composite anatomy of the city's public and private spaces.[32] It produces the awkward intimacy of a public secrecy, a crowded and promiscuous common living space, shared by all of the city's inhabitants. In colonial times, the qualities and characteristics of "private" and "public" held distinctly different connotations in the "white" city and the indigenous peripheries. At sunset a curfew banned the Congolese from the European areas of town, and both sides retreated into the privacy of their own living areas, ignorant of and often uninterested in each others' lives. The neighborhoods and houses where both worlds

---

32 On urban rumors, see also Hans Ulrich Obrist, "Urban Rumors," in Rem Koolhaas et al., *Mutations* (Barcelona and Bordeaux: ACTAR and Arc en rêve centre d'architecture, 2000).

touched each other geographically were often the literally intermediate and blended worlds of *métissage*, of those who did not firmly belong to either space or crossed the social or racial lines that pervaded colonial society and thus had no fixed place in it. Mixed African-European households, mostly set up by Portuguese or Greek traders and shop owners, formed a buffer zone between African and European neighborhoods. The colonials retreated into their residences, offices, clubs, and restaurants, and restricted their contact with indigenous worlds to a functional minimum, in ways not much different from the lifestyles of many expatriates in Kinshasa today.

Life in the African parts of town, on the other hand, was played out in the *parcelle* and in the street. The *parcelle* is a space that is typical of Kinshasa. Often surrounded by a wall and with an iron gate that demarcates its entrance, the *parcelle*, with its house or houses, and usually with its mango or palm tree and little garden of vegetables and crops, creates a small island of more or less private domesticity, in the shared intimacy of one's (extended) family and ethnic affiliations. In many areas of the city, though, the *parcelle* has been invaded by and lives in close proximity and symbiosis with the street. As such, many *parcelles* are rather "public" private spaces. Simultaneously, Kinshasa also generates "private" public spaces, such as the recreational and ludic places of the bar, the nightclub, the hotel, and the *nganda* (originally the retreat where fishermen rest after their work, but now the name given to "formally informal" restaurants, often in the backyards of private homes). Here men meet their friends, mistresses, and concubines in an atmosphere of privacy and secrecy, and yet invariably also in view of all, within reach of *radio-trottoir*'s tentacles and subjected to the gaze of the public eye. The *phonie* is another place where private and public become interchangeable. Every neighborhood has its small *phonie* enterprises, where one can enter into contact with otherwise unreachable friends and relatives in the interior of the country through radio-wave communication. Often the *phonie* is also a meeting point for people from the same regional or ethnic background. Money matters, love affairs, marriages, births, divorces, illnesses, deaths, and other private family matters are shouted into the microphone as well as into the ears of the neighborhood's and indeed the country's *trottoirs*. In Kinshasa, the private life of the individual and the moralities generated by the collective gaze live in a sometimes uneasy, often contradictory cohabitation.

Like many capitals around the world, Kinshasa has always been a narcissistic city, very much fascinated and preoccupied by the events of its own microcosmos. To an outsider unfamiliar with the city's inner argot, its signs and secrets, Kinshasa's urban codes therefore often appear difficult to crack. At the same time, Kinshasa constantly displays and puts itself on stage. Just like the city they live in, Kinois are extremely skillful at managing not just one but several individual identities at the same time. The constant negotiation between these individual and collective identities almost always takes place or is commented upon in the public sphere. Kinshasa exists in the public eye and through its public appearance. Nourished by the force of pretense, the *faire croire* and *faire semblant* that pervades the urban praxis, Kinshasa is essentially an exhibitionist city or, as Yoka says, *une ville-spectacle*, a spectacle city.[33] The urban aesthetics of display and public appearance are most clearly illustrated in the city's most private space, which is simultaneously also its most public theater: the body. Outdoing Proust's Paris, Kinshasa is a city of *flâneurs* and idle strollers, a proudly sensuous city where bodies, both male and female, are constantly dressing up and taking themselves out into the dusty streets and alleys of each neighborhood to be seen, to display themselves in feigned indifference to the public gaze; it is a city, also, where there are always eyes to see and behold, and where spectators constantly comment upon the outfit, the movement of hips and buttocks, the style of the hairdress, the whole bearing,

---

33 Lye M. Yoka, *Kinshasa, signes de vie* (Paris: L'Harmattan, 1999), p. 15.

Wedding, Foire Internationale de Kinshasa, April 2000

appearance, and *gabarit* of passersby, their social skin and social skill. In fact, the eyes of the beholders offer a mirror which constantly reflects one's own social strength. In spite of, or maybe precisely because of, its extreme poverty, Kinshasa's aesthetic regime of the body has turned into a veritable cult of elegance, culminating in the movement of the *Sape*, an acronym for *Société des ambianceurs et des personnes elegantes*, the Society of Fun Lovers and Elegant Persons. Begun in the early 1980s around "King of Sape" Papa Wemba, a popular musician, this movement escalated into real fashion contests and potlatches in which youngsters displayed their European designer clothes in an attempt to outdo each other. Recently, this spirit of elegance has found a second breath in the flourishing context of Pentecostalist and other Christian fundamentalist churches, in which the city's new figures of success, its most famed preachers such as Fernando Kutino or Soni Kafuta, show off their Armani and Versace suits to admiring and ecstatic followers, under the motto that "one has to appear clean before God" (*Il faut être propre devant Dieu*).

Pushing the mirror metaphor to the limit of reflection and beyond, the religious transformation which Congolese society is currently undergoing has contributed to a reconfiguration, if not an obliteration, of the dividing lines

between public and private space, as well as an increasing theatricalization of the city. This process goes hand in hand with an increasing star-ization of those who occupy the front stage, the *pasteurs* and musicians. The new *vedettariat* and *staromanie* in the popular music scene have given rise to new forms of violence. Not only does the music and its accompanying dance styles reflect, and reflect upon, the violence that pervades the city and Congolese society at large, but the frequent clashes between avid followers of rival bands have themselves become increasingly responsible for the mounting insecurity in Kinshasa's public spaces. Home to street children and military, Kinshasa's main arteries, crossroads, markets, sports stadia, and administrative sites have often become a social no man's land, governed by the predatory violence of the street. At the same time, the enchanting space of the church, with its new moral economies and its own forms of physical and symbolic violence, has swallowed and encompassed the space of popular culture. It has also claimed and drastically reconfigured public space as such. In all corners of the city, and at all times of the day and night, thousands upon thousands of Kinois gather to pray. In the process, the space of the church has become the city's main stage, a space of *témoignage* also, where people publicly bear witness of their sins and conversion, where they display and act out their poverty or wealth, their misery or blessing, leaving no stone of their personal lives unturned, no intimate detail unmentioned. In the process, the religious dynamics in these churches have also thoroughly impacted on private space and contribute to a radical restructuring of the social networks and moral and ethical matrixes that constitute the family, kin relations, and ethnic affiliations. Within the church context, the changed relations between the spaces of public and private are indicative of deeper changes in the relationship between subjectivity and intersubjectivity in Kinshasa today. While presenting a vast effort to recreate a new, all-inclusive intersubjectivity on a moral basis, the religious praxis pushes aside the intersubjective moral model which has always been provided by "the village," with its ethics of kin solidarity, reciprocity, and gift logic. Paradoxically, this effort thus contributes to an increasing diabolization of social life as it has been lived until now.

The First and Second Worlds of Kinshasa While taking into account these various levels which constitute Kinshasa's ecology today, there is yet another, and more fundamental, mirroring process that impacts on all the previous ones: that between the visible city of the "first world" and of the day, and an invisible Kinshasa that exists in what Kinois themselves refer to as the nocturnal "second world" or "second city," an occult city of the shadow, as it exists in the local mind and imagination. "If there can be a better way for the real world to include the one of images, it will require an ecology not only of real things but of images as well" wrote Susan Sontag.[34] The urbanscape of Kinshasa, its activities, its praxis, and its specific meaningful sites (the *parcelle* or compound, the bar, the church, the street) should be read not only as geographical, visible, and palpable urban realities but also, and primarily so, as a *mundus imaginalis*, a local mental landscape, a topography and historiography of the local Congolese imagination that is no less real than its physical counterpart, a "second world" that is collectively shared by all social layers in Kinshasa, uniting its *beau monde* and its demimonde.

In the autochthonous experience, daily life constantly uses the processes of mirroring and reflecting to make sense of itself. The activities of the day constantly include the world of the night, of the dream and of the shadow: to interpret the world of the living, a diviner opens up another space-time, another world, the world of ancestors, through a mirror, or by means of the unmoving surface of water in a gourd. Dreams are beacons in the night but they impact in

---

34 Susan Sontag, *On Photography* (London: Allen Lane, 1978), p. 180.

very tangible ways on decisions one has to make during the day: whether or not to travel today, whether to meet so-and-so, whether to set out on a hunt or postpone it. The material realness of the mask, as image, as double, and as dancing representation of the dead, does not make the existence of the dead any less real. Rather, the mask *becomes, is, posits* the ancestor while simultaneously being a mask made of raffia and wood. "To consider the obverse and the reverse of the world as opposed," writes Mbembe, "with the former partaking of a 'being there' (*real presence*) and the latter of a 'being elsewhere' or a 'non-being' (*irremediable absence*) – or, worse, of the order of unreality – would be to misunderstand. The reverse of the world and its obverse did not communicate with each other only through a tight interplay of correspondences and complex intertwined relations. They were also governed by relations of similarity, relations far from making the one a mere copy or model of the other. These links of similarity were thought to unite them, but also to distinguish them, according to the wholly autochthonous principle of *simultaneous multiplicities*."[35]

---

35 Achille Mbembe, *On the Postcolony* (Berkeley: University of California Press, 2001), pp. 144–145.

La ville de Kinshasa n'est elle pas envoutée? (Isn't the city of Kinshasa bewitched?), painting by painter-preacher Bodo, Kinshasa, May 2001

One of the main questions relates to the changes that seem to have appeared in the mechanisms operating this simultaneous multiplicity of the two different worlds that exist on each side of the mirror, and thus also in and through each other. In urban Congo, something seems to have changed in the slippage between visible and invisible, between reality and what we can call, for lack of better words, its double, its shadow, specter, reflection, image, or *elili*, as it is referred to in Lingala.

What is it, then, that has affected the praxis and rhetoric of the image in Kinshasa today? Within the local experiential frame, rendered in Kinois' accounts of their lives and of their city, the double, this other, nocturnal ghost of a city which lurks underneath the surface of the visible world, somehow seems to have taken the upper hand. Today, mirroring the way in which the second or "shadow" economy has taken over the first or formal economy, this other, "second world" (*deuxième monde*), "second city" (*deuxième cité*), "pandemonium world" (*monde pandemonium*), or "fourth dimension" (*quatrième dimension*, that is, one of the multiple "invisible" worlds of what is referred to as *kindokinisme*[36]) increasingly seems to push aside and take over the first world of daily reality. "The second world is the world of the invisible," says one inhabitant of Kinshasa, "and those who live in it and *know* are those who have four eyes, those who see clearly both during the day and during the night. Their eyes are a mirror. A man with two eyes only cannot know this world. The second world is a world that is superior to ours. The second world rules the first world." This and many similar accounts seem indicative of the widespread feeling that what you see is not what you see (unless you have four eyes), and what is there is not what is "really" there or, more important, is not what matters most. The seen and the unseen, it thus seems, no longer reflect, balance, and produce each other in equal and equally *real* ways. Somehow, the reverse has become more *ontological* than the obverse. It is no longer experienced as a similar but parallel reality, but, on the contrary, as the reality that has come to inhabit and overgrow its opposite. Symptomatic of this more general change is the invasion of the space of the living by the dead.[37] A term which is currently used in Lingala to describe this new quality of mounting *Unheimlichkeit* and elusiveness of the world is *mystique*. In the postcolonial *Afrique fantôme* that Congo seems to have become, it is increasingly common to designate people and situations as *mystique* – difficult to place, interpret, and attribute meaning to.

This changed nature of the point of inflection between different but simultaneously real worlds, the change in the mirroring mechanisms of reflection and retroflection that constitute the passage between the obverse and the reverse of the world, heavily impacts on daily life in Kinshasa. For example, it continuously transforms the qualities and realities of what constitutes life and death, as well as the ways in which they relate to each other. Similarly, the changed relationship between obverse and reverse constantly promotes a religious transfiguration of daily reality. The incessant reinvention of the Congolese urban lived-in environment is not at all marked by a Weberian *Entzauberung* (disenchantment). It is, on the contrary, enacted and produced most strongly, not only in the "enchanting" spaces of Christian fundamentalism that have taken over the city, but also in the frenzied and often obsessional production of discourses and practices surrounding witchcraft (and both are, of course, intimately related). In the process, the dynamics of witchcraft have undergone some dramatic changes. One of the most disconcerting phenomena that highlights this evolution is the central role that children are nowadays given in these newly developing witch-

---

36 *Kindokinisme* is derived from the Lingala term *kindoki*, "witchcraft." The use of the neologism is significant in that it illustrates how the unpredictable transformations of reality constantly seem to require new conceptual frameworks.

37 See Filip De Boeck, "Beyond the Grave: History, Memory and Death in Postcolonial Congo/Zaire," in *Memory and the Postcolony: African Anthropology and the Critique of Power*, ed. Richard P. Werbner (London: Zed Books, 1998).

craft discourses and practices. In contemporary Kinshasa, thousands of children are implicated in witchcraft accusations, and often end up in the street as a result. As such, they find themselves at the heart of one of the most disturbing transformations in the Congolese societal *multi-crise*, namely the changing relationship between the world of the visible and the invisible, between life and death, or between reality and its double. Commonly described as a "dead society" (*société morte*), Kinshasa's street children, who to a large extent live during the night and often sleep, eat, and live in places such as cemeteries, have come to embody the growing alienation of the order of the visible. They constitute a fulcrum between the processes of doubling and dedoubling and fully exemplify the permeability and interchangeableness of the borderlines between day and night, living and nonliving, public and private, or order and disorder.[38]

All of these changes are characteristic of some deeper alterations that Congolese society as a whole is undergoing. Without going into the historical roots of these changes here, this evolution may be summarized as a generalized crisis, situated in the Congolese capital's capacity at semiosis and semiotics, at observing and interpreting the syntaxis, semantics, and pragmatics of the sign *as sign*. Not that Kinshasa's inhabitants do not know how to work with signs, or have stopped doing so – quite on the contrary, one could even argue that Kinshasa is marked not by a lack but by a constant overproduction of leading sense, and that it is precisely this "overheating," this excess of the signifier, that leads to the crisis of meaningfulness. But it is also in the nature itself of the transcription of one reality into the other, and therefore in the nature of the representational, that the changes have ensconced themselves. In the process, something has happened to the relationship between image and reality. A change has occurred in the ways in which the representation and the represented reality relate to each other.

Applying a linguistic and sociological perspective to the daily scene in Kinshasa, one could say that the rupture between discourse, representation, action, and structure is total. The urban reality has gradually turned into a world in which fact and fiction are interchangeable. In Kinshasa today, it is no longer possible to forget or deny the Saussurian arbitrariness of the sign, or the facticity of the social fact. What Taussig has termed the "mimetic faculty,"[39] the capacity to pretend that one lives facts, not fictions, has often ceased to operate in an adequate way. To put it differently, there is a strong sense of what Baudrillard has termed the "precession of simulacra," thereby

---

38 See De Boeck, "Le 'deuxième monde' et les 'enfants-sorciers.'"
39 Michael Taussig, *Mimesis and Alterity: A Particular History of the Senses* (New York: Routledge, 1993).

pointing out the changing relations between the signifying "real" and the representational "imaginary," or the liquidation of all referentials.[40] The common links and paths of transfer between signifier and signified, or between predicate and subject, have imploded or are subverted: what I have previously called the *faire croire* and *faire semblant* have often taken over from reality. In Kinshasa, as a consequence, more than anywhere else, there is no reality that is strong enough to resist language. Often, the discrepancies between signifier and signified allow for the generation of a specific kind of Kinois humor, enabling, for example, the *locataire* of an old and decrepit shack to refer to his dwelling as the *palais du peuple*, "the people's palace," after the imposing parliamentary building of the same name which was constructed in the heart of Kinshasa by the Chinese. But in that specific Kinois language, the shifts are often less benign. Very often what poses as true is actually false, the lie becomes truth. As a result, to give but one example, the boundaries between legal and illegal are continuously shifting. Such shifts are operated by the widespread mechanism of reversibility that is constantly at work in the daily lives of most Kinois. Hence, also, as I noted earlier, the important place which this city attributes to appearance. Undoubtedly, this crisis of meaning that can be observed at all levels of Congolese society has profoundly alienating effects on both macro- and micro-levels of societal life.

But this sociological level only captures the more obvious effects of the crisis of meaningfulness that may be observed in Kinshasa. On another, deeper level, one could stand the argument on its head and say that Kinshasa's "image-repertoire" does not so much suffer from a lack but rather from an excess of overlap between the signifying and the signified, or between the structures of the symbolic, the "real" that resists language, and the level of the imaginary. On this level, the problem with notions such as "fact" and "fiction" is that they do not take into account the autochthonous experience of the realness of the double, but risk reducing it to something unreal, a mere "fantasy." But if, on the contrary, one takes seriously the reality of the thing and its double, one begins to see that the deeper crisis situates itself primarily in the changing functions and qualities of junction and disjunction (such as the disjunction between life and death), and hence of the role of the imaginary, which operates that disjunction or *dédoublement*. Much of the current Congolese societal crisis, the subjectivity of which is lived and experienced most strongly in precisely the urban locale, situates itself in this slippage. Put in a different way, the crisis in Congo essentially evolves around the containment of, the struggle to reestablish control over, an

---

40 Jean Baudrillard, *Simulations*, trans. Paul Foss, Paul Patton, and Philip Beitchman (New York: Semiotext(e), 1983).

increasingly overflowing imaginary. And at the heart of this struggle lies the ever more problematic possibility of the positing or "siting" of the double (for example, death as the double of the living, or the double as the living and familiar figure of death). What may be observed here is, in a way, the *liquidation* of the double, the unwholesome coalescence of the reflecting sides into one, or the gradual take-over of one by the other. As such, in its more extreme forms, this process of liquidation operates a killing, a destroying of reality, an annihilation or *néantisation* of the world in its most essential structure. And through this liquidation, which produces Kinshasa as idol and as *eidolon*, the imaginary ceaselessly creates its own level of autonomy, with all of its excesses, its witchcraft, its diabolization of social life. This new "siting" of the city's imaginary forms the undercurrent that reshapes the urban locale today.

Freetown: From the "Athens of West Africa" to a City Under Siege: The Rise and Fall of Sub-Saharan First Municipality

Alfred B. Zack-Williams

Between March 1991 and January 2002, Sierra Leone experienced a dreadful civil war. The war began when the Revolutionary United Front (RUF) invaded the southeastern corner of the country, close to the Liberian border. The insurgents were aided by an "international brigade,"[1] sponsored by the Liberian warlord Charles Taylor,[2] many of whom had fought in the Liberian civil war. In addition, a number of socially alienated local groups opposed to the authoritarian and kleptocratic policies of the All Peoples Congress (APC) used Liberia as a launching pad to try to unseat the APC government of President Joseph Momoh. The RUF's initial demand was a return to democratic pluralism, but this demand changed after the APC was toppled by a military coup in April 1992. The young officers who overthrew Momoh believed that the rebels could be defeated with good leadership at the center. However, as the conflict spread throughout the country, and as demand grew for a return to civilian rule, the National Provisional Revolutionary Council (NPRC), as this junta was called, sought a settlement with the rebel forces. Before a settlement could be reached, largely due to pressure from the international community and domestic democratic forces, in 1996 elections were held which saw the return to power of the Sierra Leone People's Party under the leadership of Ahmad Tejan Kabbah. While Kabbah sought a peaceful settlement with the leadership of the RUF, not all the major provisions of the 1996 Abidjan Accord were implemented. In particular, Kabbah refused to "reward" the rebels with a place in the government of national unity. Meanwhile, an undisciplined and restive army continued to plague the Kabbah administration. There were a number of reports of coup attempts, and by the time of the May 1997 coup which toppled the Kabbah government for the first time, several officers had been arrested and charged

---

1 Consisting mainly of Liberians, Bukinabese, and other Africans.
2 See William Reno, *Warlord Politics and African States* (Boulder, Colo.: Lynne Rienner, 1998), ch. 3 and 4; John L. Hirsch, *Sierra Leone: Diamonds and the Struggle for Democracy* (Boulder, Colo.: Lynne Rienner, 2001).

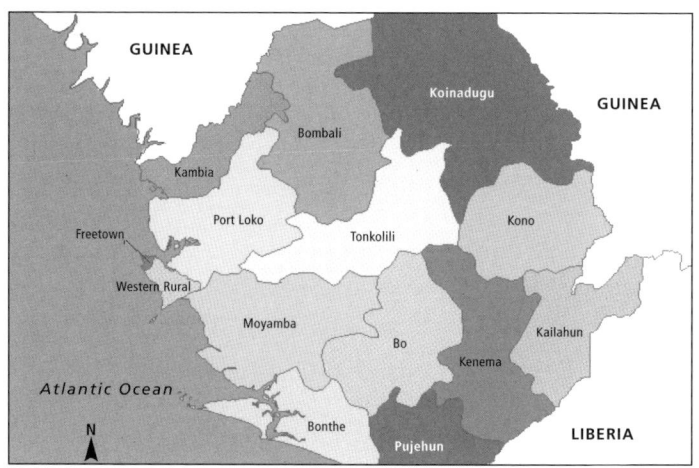

Administrative Districts of Sierra Leone

with treason. For the first time, Freetown, the capital, was under siege as the new military regime, calling itself the Armed Forces Revolutionary Council (AFRC) led by Major Johnny Paul Koroma, invited the RUF to enter the city in order to form a unified "people's army." The AFRC unleashed widespread violence – rape, arson, mutilation, murder – on the civilian population of the overcrowded capital. The junta, which had little or no support among Freetown's residents, encountered passive resistance from the civilian population, as well as strong opposition from the Kamajors and the Nigerian-led Economic Community of West African States Monitoring Group (ECOMOG), which was in Sierra Leone to help the government suppress the rebellion by pushing the junta and its allies out of the capital. In February 1998, Kabbah was restored to power by ECOMOG.

By Christmas 1998, Freetown was once again under siege. This time, RUF fighters threatened to breach the city's defenses. In January 1999, for the second time Foday Sankoh's forces entered the city at tremendous cost to the civilian population. The invaders were soon routed from the city, though a rump of the former AFRC (now calling themselves the West Side Boys) moved to the outskirts, where they engaged in acts of banditry. In July 1999, a peace accord was imposed on the Sierra Leone government by the United States and the United Kingdom, under which former rebel fighters received blanket immunity from prosecution for acts of atrocities against civilians. Furthermore, rebel leader Foday Sankoh was given the substantive positions of vice-president of the country and chairmanship of the Mineral Resources Commission; a number of his commanders were also appointed to cabinet posts in the civilian-led administration. Not satisfied with these gains, the RUF leadership hatched a plot aimed at

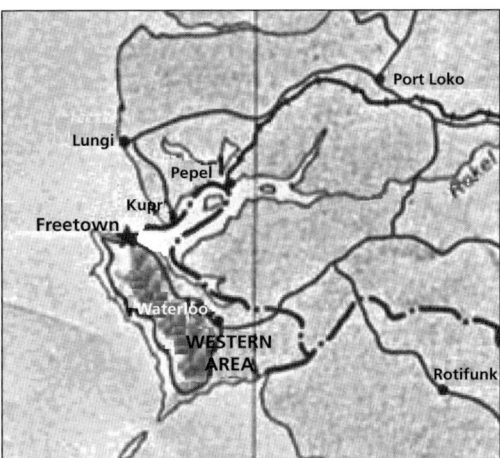

Map of the Western Area

unseating the civilian president, Ahmad Tejan Kabbah, in order to put the movement in total control of the country. The killings and other acts of violence following this attempted putsch led to British military intervention under the guise of evacuating British and Commonwealth citizens. This intervention restored calm and reassured the war-weary population, as well as paved the way for UN troops to consolidate their position in order to carry out the demobilization program.

In what follows, I will outline a brief history of Freetown, from its early beginnings as a province of freedom for former slaves and as the gateway in the British project of modernity. I shall draw attention to the city's rise to prominence in the last quarter of the 19th century, when it became known as the "Athens of West Africa," and how its fortunes diminished from the early 20th century century onward, reaching a nadir in the closing years of the millennium. Throughout its turbulent history, the fate of the city was very much tied to that of the country as a whole.

The Founding of Freetown   The capital of Sierra Leone, Freetown is situated on the northern seaboard of the Freetown Peninsula, overlooking some of the finest natural harbors in the world. Sierra Leone's first contact with the West came in 1462 when the Portuguese explorer Pedro da Cintra sailed down the West African coast in his quest to circumnavigate the world. He named the territory *Serra Lyoa*, meaning "lion mountains," after the terrain and the roar of thunder accompanying the rainy season, which was mistaken for the sound of lions. Other visitors to this territory that would soon become Britain's gateway to modernization[3] in West Africa included the Dutch admiral De Ruyter, who inscribed his name on a stone in the harbor; Sir John Hawkins, who made his fortune from slave trading in Sierra Leone, after which he embraced Christianity and wrote the celebratory hymn *Amazing Grace*; and Sir Francis Drake.[4] From this period onward, and throughout the 15th to 18th centuries, European ships made frequent stops at Freetown to obtain fresh water[5] and to purchase slaves. In the late 18th century, following the American War of Independence, many former slaves who had fought alongside the British and had been promised manumission, migrated to Britain.[6] These Black Poor, as the new migrants were called, soon attracted racist antipathy in Elizabethan England as resentment spread against the "Blackamores in the realm." Their plight attracted the attention of philanthropists such as Granville Sharpe and Henry Smeathman. In May 1787, some 411 of these Black Poor arrived in Sierra Leone and, following agreements with local chiefs, a settlement was established called Granville Town, in honor of their benefactor Granville Sharpe. The new settlement was also known as the Province of Freedom. In 1792, the Sierra Leone Company was formed, and soon took over the running of the settlement's affairs.[7] Captain Samuel Swan, a contemporary of Sharpe who traded with West Africa, has challenged the altruistic explanation usually asserted as the reason behind the founding of Sierra Leone during this time. In his view, trade was the primary incentive.[8]

According to Fryer, the "history of these settlers is one of disaster piled upon disaster. They died like flies. Some were sold to French slave-traders."[9] They faced harsh conditions, including starvation, as the seeds they brought with them from England would not grow in the tropical soil. The settlement was attacked and burned down by local rulers who had ordered them to leave, and only sixty of the original group survived four years after arriving in Sierra Leone. However, the population was increased by internal migration from the hinterland and beyond the Sierra Leone borders, as well as by slaves rescued on the

---

3 John Peterson has argued that "the foundations of the Sierra Leone colony are to be found in the thought of the 18th-century Enlightenment." See "The Enlightenment and the Founding of Freetown," in *Freetown: A Symposium*, ed. Christopher Fyfe and Eldred Jones (Freetown: Sierra Leone University Press, 1968), p. 10.
4 See J. McKay, "Freetown," in *Sierra Leone in Maps*, ed. John I. Clarke (London: University of London Press, 1966).
5 See Diane Frost, *Work and Community Among West African Migrant Workers Since the Nineteenth Century* (Liverpool: Liverpool University Press, 1999).
6 See Peter Fryer, *Staying Power: The History of Black People in Britain* (London: Pluto Press, 1984).
7 See Earl Conteh-Morgan and Mac Dixon-Fyle, *Sierra Leone at the End of the Twentieth Century: History, Politics, and Society* (New York: Peter Lang, 1999).
8 See G. S. Brooks, "A View of Sierra Leone ca. 1815," *Sierra Leone Studies*, no. 13–20 (1960–67).
9 Fryer, *Staying Power*, p. 201.

high seas by British antislavery naval vessels. The founders of the settlement were determined to rid the colony of slavery, although it continued in the hinterland. For example, E. Adeleye Ijagbemi has shown that during the 19th century, the growing demand for labor in nonagricultural sectors resulted in the intensification of slavery in the protectorate.

Following teething problems, such as the failure to "produce [a] prudent and right plan" (Fryer), in 1808 the territory was annexed as a crown colony by the British government. The population of Freetown increased from 2,500 in 1808 to around 6,000 in 1818. Migration into the colony continued as more slaves were captured and released in the Province of Freedom; many of these returnees were now Europeanized, including Africanus Horton (a banker), Sir Samuel Lewis (first African to be knighted), and Bishop Ajai Crowther (first African bishop). By 1870, the population had risen to 10,000 people, forming a cultural mosaic with several languages, African and European. The population rose to 33,000 in 1914 and stood at 55,000 in 1930.

Political and Cultural Development   Freetown became a municipality in 1799 through a charter granted to the Sierra Leone Company by the British Crown. The charter provided for a mayor, aldermen, and sheriff to be appointed by the governor and council;[10] however, by 1821 these officials lost their magisterial functions and the positions became merely honorific. The municipality was reconstituted in 1893, with powers to regulate trade, fire prevention, street trading, education, and rural planning. In this respect it was modeled on the British municipal system,[11] with administrative boundaries based on the ward system, and until 1945 voting was based on property qualification. This system, with its provision for coopted members and committees, remained in force until Siaka Stevens abrogated the system of local democracy in the 1980s, only to replace it with a management committee of appointed members.

Culturally, Freetown has been described as a city of "church and mosque,"[12] as both Christianity and Islam coexist peacefully. Religious intolerance has never been a source of conflict, perhaps because virtually every ethnic group contains Christians, Muslims, and those of African religious belief systems. Christian denominations include Catholic, Anglican, Methodist, Baptist, the Evangelical United Brethren (EUB) Church, Seventh-day Adventist, as well as

---

10 See S. A. J. Pratt, "The Government of Freetown," in *Freetown: A Symposium*. Christopher Fyfe dates the granting of municipal status to November 6, 1800. See his *A History of Sierra Leone* (London: Oxford University Press, 1962), p. 86.
11 Ibid.
12 Edward W. Fashole-Luke, "Religion in Freetown," in *Freetown: A Symposium*, p. 127.

African revivalist churches, such as the Church of the Lord Alladurah. The Muslim groups include Islamiya and Ahmaddiya. These religious networks played a major role in elementary and secondary school provision for most of the 19th and 20th centuries. The period 1815–27 has been described as memorable because of the great cooperation between the churches and the colonial state.[13] In 1827, the Church Missionary Society (CMS) founded Fourah Bay College as an institution for the training of priests and teachers; in 1876, it became an affiliated college of the University of Durham. This was followed in 1845 by the CMS Grammar School for boys; in 1849, the Annie Walsh Memorial School (CMS) was established for girls; the Catholic mission followed by setting up Saint Edward's School for boys in the mid-19th century, and Saint Joseph's Convent for girls in 1866. The Wesleyans set up the Methodist Boys High School and the Methodist Girls High School in 1874 and 1901 respectively; the Evangelical United Brethren established the Albert Academy in 1904; and in 1925 the city's first state secondary school was established when the Prince of Wales School was opened, following the visit of Edward, Prince of Wales, to the colony. Given this cultural renaissance,[14] which had been generated by the descendants of freed slaves in the Province of Freedom, it is not surprising that Sierra Leone at this time was described as the "Athens of West Africa," as Africans from the sub-region sought entry into the city's institutions. At the time, the name Freetown was associated with the dynamic of modernity, education, and progress, in marked contrast to the status of the city at the end of the millennium.

One important feature of life in Freetown has been its extreme heterogeneity, which was stratified along income and status lines, a society with the capacity to accept innovation, change, and social mobility.[15] Like Creole culture itself, Freetown was quite cosmopolitan, suited to "the enterprising and appeal[ing] to the upwardly mobile."[16] The limited physical space of Freetown impelled many to move to the hinterland to satisfy their ambitions. The city's leaders subscribed to British urban values: respectably orderly and respectful of the law. By the end of the 19th century, Krio had become the *lingua franca*, and many who had never been to Freetown soon learned to speak the language. By this time,

---

13 See G. Harding, "Education in Freetown," in ibid.
14 The literacy rate among Creoles was perhaps higher than among the subjects of the colonizing power.
15 See Christopher Fyfe, "The Founding of Freetown," in *Freetown: A Symposium*. See also Arthur T. Porter, *Creoledom: A Study of the Development of Freetown Society* (London: Oxford University Press, 1966).
16 Christopher Fyfe, "1787–1887–1987: Reflections on a Sierra Leone Bicentenary," in *Sierra Leone, 1787–1987: Two Centuries of Intellectual Life*, ed. Murray Last and Paul Richards (Manchester: Manchester University Press, 1987), p. 413.

the hybridized Freetown and Creole culture had become the embodiment of syncretic Afro-European cultural forms. For example, the same people who were members of the secret *Oje* society were also church stewards and members of exclusive Masonic lodges. Of the Creoles at this time, one commentator has observed:

> Successful in commerce and better educated as a whole than the British population at the time, Krio held many positions in British West African administration. They resisted domination by building up their own independent organizations, like churches and Masonic lodges, and by spreading across West Africa as traders and professionals. By the end of the nineteenth century their economic success and professional opportunities began to be undermined by Lebanese traders and racist attitudes among British colonials.[17]

Economic Development According to Cox-George, trading and agriculture remained the twin pillars of economic growth in the colony. In the 19th century, agricultural exports included sylvan culture, especially dyewood, ivory, and hides. Cox-George has noted three distinct phases of colonial rule in the period prior to the declaration of a protectorate in 1896: 1787–1790/91, the period of "virtual self-government or the proprietorship of Granville Sharpe"; 1790/91–1807, the period of Charter Company government; 1807 and after, the period of crown colony status.[18] In the first period, the major source of revenue was via direct taxation, particularly property taxation, including houses, land, horses and carriages, domestic animals, and roads. By this time Freetown could be described as a "model colony," as revenue for its administration was based on internal fiscal policy, as opposed to dependence on the metropolitan exchequer.[19] By contrast, from 1800 onward, it became clear that the company could not finance itself from trading profits, leading to the Crown's appropriation of the duties and responsibilities of the country. Thus, revenue in the crown colony era was based on parliamentary grants-in-aid for the running of the bureaucracy and defense.

In the 19th century, the returnees – who now described themselves as Creole or Krio – contributed immensely to Sierra Leone's economic and political life

---

17 Zachary Kingdon, "Sierra Leone," exhibit, forthcoming permanent exhibition at the Liverpool Museum, National Museums and Galleries on Merseyside, Liverpool.

18 N. A. Cox-George, "Direct Taxation in the Early History of Sierra Leone," *Sierra Leone Studies: The Journal of the Sierra Leone Society*, n.s., no. 5 (December 1955), pp. 20–35.

19 On the model colony thesis, see Geoffrey B. Kay, *The Political Economy of Colonialism in Ghana: A Collection of Documents and Statistics, 1900–1960* (Cambridge: Cambridge University Press, 1972).

and were instrumental in "opening up" the protectorate through commerce, particularly once the railway was constructed after 1898. They also worked in the colonial bureaucracy in other British territories in West Africa and were involved in commerce in such far-flung areas as Congo and Fernando Po. In the 19th century, Freetown's most important role was as an entrepôt for imports, exports, and storage facilities, and as an exchange center,[20] and after 1807, it became a naval station for antislave patrols as well as the headquarters of the newly formed West African squadron of the Royal Navy.[21] From this moment in Sierra Leone's history, Freetown became the major nerve center of the nation by supplying capital, labor, organizational skills, and specialized economic services, thus facilitating and coordinating commerce in an efficient way.[22] By the late 19th century, a variety of exports passed through Freetown harbor, including palm products, rubber, rice, kola nuts, and ground nuts. By the end of the century, larger ocean-going vessels began to use the city's ports, and its safe and commodious harbor was an added boost to the city's function as an entrepôt. Freetown merchants were prominent in the produce trade, stimulated by the railway, which helped to open up the interior.[23] Among the great African names in the trade were Williams Grant, Thompson Brothers, Abraham Hebron, and Malamah Thomas. In the first two decades of the 20th century, Freetown became pivotal to the development of the urban system in Sierra Leone.

However, it is important to note that Creole society was not a homogeneous one; indeed, Creole was not necessarily an ascriptive group, as people born outside of Creoledom can achieve Creole status. There were the commercial and administrative classes created out of the prosperous trading of the 1880s, and the professional bourgeoisie; there were the poor Creoles who were looked down upon by the rich Creoles; and there were also the lumpenproletariat elements in Creole society, who blamed the migrants from the interior for their deteriorating predicament. The differential outlook at this time is epitomized in an emerging class consciousness, which impelled the first labor strike in 1892. Nonetheless, there were widespread concerns among Creoles stemming from the arrival of new competitors, first the Lebanese/Syrian traders, and, in 1893, Indian commercial interests in the produce trade, beginning with J. T. Chanrai[24] and soon followed by K. Chellaram and T. Choitram, among others. Furthermore, following the crisis in the export market after 1875, the giant European trading houses began to

---

20 See A. Howard, "The Role of Freetown in the Commercial Life of Sierra Leone," in *Freetown: A Symposium*, pp. 38–64.
21 See Frost, *Work and Community*.
22 See Howard, "The Role of Freetown in the Commercial Life of Sierra Leone."
23 Ibid.
24 See J. McKay, "Commercial Life in Freetown," in *Freetown: A Symposium*.

deal directly with African producers, thus eroding the profits of the African middleman. And a new round of racism sweeping through the colonies – caused by the competition to defend profit margins in the depression, as well as the failure of the banks to grant Africans loans, while their deposits were promptly accepted – affected even those Creoles who belonged to the administrative class, which meant that many Creoles were now being pushed out of office.

As noted above, many of the Africans freed in Freetown were now highly Europeanized, and many accepted European standards as the basis upon which Africa should proceed and be judged.[25] While some among the educated elite such as Africanus Horton and Edward W. Blyden called for self-reliance and divorce from Europe, most were loyal to Britain and saw the complementary nature of the races.[26] We shall presently see that this "new modernizing elite," who took over the reigns of government from the departing colonialists, in practice deemphasized African self-reliance and failed to rupture the ties with the colonial power; instead, they settled for a subsidiary, rent-seeking role within the postcolonial state. By the late 19th century, there emerged out of Freetown's cultural mosaic a unique status group describing themselves as Creole and their language as Krio. This group soon came to play a major role in the economy and politics of the colony, which only popular franchise put pay to. Here is how Robert July described this group:

> They arrived in Freetown naked and abject, but after a few months of supervision were able to make substantial progress. They learned to read and write; they cultivated their own land and mastered a useful craft; they replaced ancient superstition with Christian worship; and they began to guide their actions towards each other on the basis of Christian ideas of justice, charity, fraternity and equality.[27]

As Fyfe noted, toward the end of the 19th century, the Creoles were "busy creating and diffusing a dynamic culture of their own."[28]

Freetown in the 20th Century The cultural and political zenith of Freetown can be traced to the last quarter of the 19th century. By the early 20th century, both Freetown and the Creoles had begun to lose what they had gained in the previ-

---

25 See Robert July, "Africanus Horton and the Idea of Independence in West Africa," *Sierra Leone Studies*, n.s., 13–20 (1960–67); Basil Davidson, *The Black Man's Burden: Africa and the Curse of the Nation-state* (New York: Times Books, 1992).
26 See July, "Africanus Horton and the Idea of Independence in West Africa."
27 Ibid., p. 5.
28 Fyfe, "1787–1887–1987: Reflections on a Sierra Leone Bicentenary."

ous century.²⁹ Nonetheless, the Creoles concentrated their efforts in obtaining a good education (particularly in the liberal professions) and administrative experience; at the same time, they were barred from office. As Fyfe observed: "After Sir Samuel Lewis died in 1903, the government paid little attention to what the Creole members of the Legislative Council said. Creole hopes of achieving self-government in the colony came to nothing."³⁰ The anti-Creole psychosis spread to other British West African territories; senior Creoles who entered government were discriminated against and thus denied seniority, as these openings were now reserved for Europeans.

The depression of the 1930s brought suffering to the people of Freetown, which was only ended by the boom of the war years. After the war, there was widespread agitation for greater participation by Sierra Leoneans and an end to racial discrimination. A new policy was implemented to end discrimination. But no sooner had the nation prepared itself for self-government than a schism erupted between the Creoles and the people of the protectorate. Mindful of the impact of majority rule on a once relatively privileged position and seeing themselves as the natural successors to the departing British, the Creole elite sought a judicial hearing on the Sierra Leone constitutional agreement laying the basis for political independence. They asked the House of Lords to declare the agreement *ultra vires*, hence, null and void. From this moment on, the decline of Freetown from its historic height in the 19th century mirrored the decline of the nation.

Colonial and Postcolonial Spatial Distribution in Freetown   In spite of the perceived intermediary role of the Creoles, the colonial situation in Freetown remained Manichaean.³¹ By the early years of the 20th century, a light railway had been constructed linking central Freetown with the cooler mountainous Government Reservation Area of Hill Station. This enclave of European colonial and business functionaries was fully self-sufficient, but for colonial domestic labor. It had its own very modern hospital as well as the famous Hill Station Club. Central Freetown constituted a series of ethnic settlements: to the east end of the city lay Foulah Town (Foulah), Fourah Bay (Muslim Creole), Kossoh Town (mixed), Magazine Court (Muslim Creole), Mountain Court (Muslim Creole), Kanike (Temne), Bambara Town (Mandingo and Su Su), and Gibraltar Town (Creole). Much of inner Freetown was inhabited by Creoles in the imme-

---

29 See Fyfe, *A Short History of Sierra Leone*.
30 Ibid, p. 162.
31 See Frantz Fanon, *The Wretched of the Earth*, trans. Constance Farrington (London: Penguin, 1965).

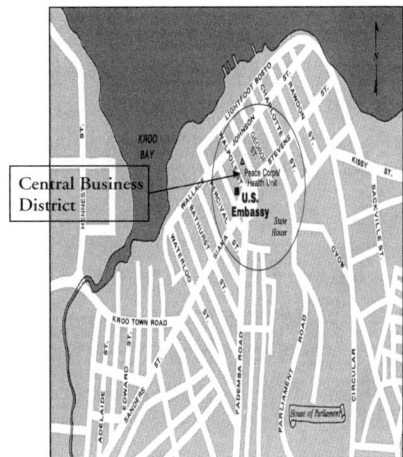

Freetown

diate east and west directions. West-central Freetown boasted such towns as Congo Town (Creole), Kroo Town (Kroo), Soldier Town (Creole), Ginger Hall (Limba), Portuguese Town (Creole), and Grassfield/Brookfields (Creole). The villages surrounding the city also reflected the ethnic constellation, with Creoles to be found in areas such as Leicester, Regent, and Gloucester, while the Lokko settled in parts of Regent and the Temne in Lumley village. This spatial dispersal reflected not just ethnicity, but also class, status, and privilege. The central business district consisted of European, Indian, Lebanese, and Sierra Leonean businesses.

Today, in post–civil war Freetown, many small foreign exchange bureaus dot the city, most located within the central business district. To the east of the city, through Sani Abacha Street and ECOWAS Street, are located the textile market and a series of kiosks run by African petty traders. Administrative buildings are situated to the south and west of the central business district, including the City Hotel (made famous by Graham Greene in his novel, *The Heart of the Matter*), the Secretariat Building, the Ministerial Building, the Law Courts, and the House of Representatives. To the west of the city, around Brookfields and New England, we also find loci of the administration, including the Yuyi Building and various ministries. The western half of the city is usually considered the more desirable. Land use patterns have changed as the population continues to expand, and more and more dwellings are being converted to commercial use, leading to further overcrowding.

The Politics of Patrimonialism, Social Exclusion, and the Origin of the War In order to understand the factors that impelled a group of "rebels" to attack the southeastern corner of Sierra Leone with the aim of toppling the APC government, we must look at the recent political-cum-economic history of the country. APC accession to power marked the beginnings of "the decline of politics and the politics of decline,"[32] as the economy began its long collapse in the midst of widespread corruption and rent-seeking activities.

The main causal factor behind the crisis and subsequent civil war can be traced to the corrosive effects of the personalized authoritarian rule of the APC under the leadership of Siaka Stevens, which led to the destruction of civil society, all forms of opposition, and any semblance of democratic accountability. This was paralleled by the introduction of a network of client-patron relationships, recently described as "the shadow state."[33] The activity of the shadow state and its reproduction were premised on state access to sufficient revenue in order to placate clients. Here lies the *force majeure* of "the politics of decline" in Sierra Leone. Now, by unleashing the full force of the oppressive state apparatus on civil society, as well as imposing forced savings on the peasantry (via the state-controlled Sierra Leone Marketing Board), the APC destroyed the enterprise and will of the people to be governed. The result is that peasant producers withdrew from the formal domestic market, and the educated classes and petit bourgeoisie migrated to greener pastures. Soon an informal economy and society were constructed, posing further threat to the legitimacy of the governing class. The latter's reaction was "to patrimonialize state offices and resources ... along ethno-clientelist and personalist lines,"[34] thus generating even more social and political discontent.[35] Economic decline and the destruction of democratic accountability occurred in tandem, and by 1984, the democratic mandate of Freetown, sub-Saharan Africa's oldest municipality, had been thoroughly undermined, as elected councillors were replaced by political appointments – Stevens' cronies.

---

32 Alfred B. Zack-Williams, "Sierra Leone, 1968–85: The Decline of Politics and the Politics of Decline in Sierra Leone," in *Sierra Leone Studies at Birmingham 1985*, ed. Adam Jones and Peter K. Mitchell (Birmingham: Centre of West African Studies, University of Birmingham, 1987).

33 William Reno, *Corruption and State Politics in Sierra Leone* (Cambridge: Cambridge University Press, 1995).

34 Jimmy D. Kandeh, "Sierra Leone: Contradictory Class Functionality of the 'Soft' State," *Review of African Political Economy* 20, no. 55 (November 1992), p. 30.

35 For a brief analysis of how the APC came to office and both democracy and the economy declined during its tenure in office, see Alfred B. Zack-Williams, *Coping with Complex Political Emergencies: An Aetiology of COPE in Sierra Leone 1991–98*, Centre for Development Studies, University of Leeds, Cope Working Paper, no. 17, April 1998; see also Alfred B. Zack-Williams, "Sierra Leone: The Political Economy of Civil War, 1991–98," *Third World Quarterly: Journal of Emerging Areas* 20 (1999), pp. 143–146.

One feature of this decline was the failure of the import-substitution strategy, launched in the late colonial and early postindependence period. Because of the high organic composition of capital in the capital-intensive technology, very little employment was provided. Moreover, the high-import content meant that no foreign exchange savings were realized; instead, the sector became a major drain on precious foreign exchange. The absence of forward or backward linkages between this and other sectors spelled the disarticulation of the economy. The situation was exacerbated by economic mismanagement and rampant corruption, with the result that unemployment became widespread, particularly among school leavers and graduates.

Sierra Leone at War with Itself   In 1984, an aging Siaka Stevens handed over power to his Force Commander, Major General Momoh. Recognizing the unpopularity of his predecessor, Momoh tried to distance himself from his sponsor's policies through what he called his New Order Regime. In November 1986, Momoh concluded a long-term structural adjustment agreement with the International Monetary Fund, as part of the new Economic Recovery Programme. In return for the usual macroeconomic conditionality (such as devaluation of the currency, reduction in the size of the bureaucracy, removal of subsidies on essential commodities, deregulation of rice importation, ending the state-controlled Marketing Board's monopoly on the importation of rice), the IMF provided the government with standby credit to the tune of SDR 40.53 million.[36] Structural adjustment programs added in no small measure to the political economic and social difficulties the country faced.

In 1987, Momoh declared a state of economic emergency under which the government assumed wide-ranging powers to crack down on corruption, gold and diamond smuggling, as well as the hoarding of essential commodities and the local currency. The aim of these policies was to counter the thriving parallel market, to which the formal banking sector had lost millions of leones. Momoh went further than his predecessor in applying the conditionality agreement.[37] Indeed, after the IMF had unilaterally abrogated the agreement in 1990 due to the government's inability to continue payment of arrears, Momoh embarked upon a "shadow program," i.e., conditionality without the loan to cushion the worst effects. Almost immediately these policies began to take their toll, as prices of basic commodities soared to astronomical heights and inflation ate

---

36 See Alfred B. Zack-Williams, "Sierra Leone: Crisis and Despair," *Review of African Political Economy* 17, no. 49 (Winter 1990), p. 29.

37 Stevens was always aware that full implementation might unleash social forces beyond his control.

into savings and wages. Momoh's position in the Congress was never as strong as Stevens'. He was an "imposed candidate" for the presidency and leadership of the party; he lacked a solid political base within the party; above all he was not as shrewd an operator as his predecessor. For many neutrals, Momoh was too phlegmatic, "a very indecisive, weak leader allowing ministers free reign to be corrupt,"[38] and it was not long before his image as a military strongman was transformed into that of an impotent civilian blabber. There were members of the "old brigade" who still saw him as an "ethnic upstart." Among these was his deputy and former SLPP stalwart Francis Minah, who allegedly used Momoh's growing unpopularity as the basis to organize a putsch, which resulted in Minah's execution for high treason. Earlier, he had been accused of highhandedness over the Ndogboyosi affair, a rural rebellion in which scores of peasants were killed.

Minah had been expected to succeed Momoh to the presidency and his execution incensed many people from the Southern Province, who felt that the entire episode was a plot by Northern zealots out to deprive them of power. In one fell swoop, Momoh became alienated from two of the most powerful ethnic groups in the country, the Temne in the northern and central areas and the Mende in the south. Together, these two groups account for about 60 percent of the total population. Momoh's insensitivity reached new heights when, over the Sierra Leone Broadcasting Service, he called for "ethnic corporatism," urging all of his subjects to organize themselves into ethnic cabals. Indeed, in this 1990 broadcast, to the Ekutay (a Northern ethnic cabal) annual convention at Binkolo, Bombali District, Momoh confirmed what many political pundits had by now often alluded to: mainly that power had shifted from Parliament and the Cabinet to the Ekutay.[39] The growing influence of the Ekutay in affairs of state would further erode ethnic relations and speed economic decline.[40] By 1991, the first UNDP index of human development put Sierra Leone at the very bottom of the list of 165 countries. Momoh's control of state affairs soon began to slip away, and the Eastern Province, Kono District in particular, maintained its notoriety as the "'Wild West of West Africa,' with a semi-permanent lawlessness in the diamond mining areas."[41]

---

38 Derek Partridge, former British High Commissioner to Sierra Leone, as quoted in Jane Knight, "Sierra Leone: Will Hope Triumph Over Experience?" *One World Link Newsletter*, June 1996, p. 7.
39 On the role of the Ekutay in bolstering Momoh's power, see Alfred B. Zack-Williams, "The Politics of Crisis and Ethnicity in Sierra Leone," paper presented at the Centre for African Studies, University of Liverpool, February 1991.
40 See Alfred B. Zack-Williams, "The Ekutay: Ethnic Cabal and Politics in Sierra Leone," in *The Issue of Political Ethnicity in Africa*, ed. E. Ike Udogu (Aldershot: Ashgate, 2001), pp. 125–148.
41 Stephen Riley and Max Sesay, "Sierra Leone: The Coming Anarchy?" *Review of African Political Economy* 22, no. 63 (March 1995), p. 122.

By the early 1990s, the "democratic winds of change" were now assuming gale-force proportions across the continent. Donors conditioned official loans on a return to democratic multiparty politics. Francophone Africa had popularized the system of National Convention as a *rite de passage* to democratic transformation. Yet, in Sierra Leone, the feeble leadership assumed an ostrichlike posture in the face of popular demands for democratic pluralism, led by the Sierra Leone Bar Association, the university community, as well as school children and the unemployed.[42] Momoh's response to demands for multiparty elections was to dispatch a warning via the hawkish secretary-general of Congress, E. T. Kamara, that any talk of multiparty democracy would be dealt with by the full force of the law, since all such discussions were illegal under the single-party state. The stage was now set for a bloody confrontation.

The Nihilism of the RUF   While Momoh was busy trying to preserve the *ancien régime*, civil war broke out in neighboring Liberia. The conflict soon engulfed much of Sierra Leone[43] when a group of Liberian "rebels" chose this moment to seek revenge against the Momoh regime. Stephen Ellis has argued that Charles Taylor, the Liberian warlord, felt aggrieved that the Economic Community of West African States Monitoring Group (ECOMOG) prevented him from taking control of Monrovia, the Liberian capital. In particular, Taylor was angry at Sierra Leone's double role as peacemaker and as a base from which ECOMOG bombed territories controlled by his faction. His National Patriotic Front of Liberia (NPFL) "swore to avenge the interference in Liberia's internal affairs ... Taylor's reaction was 'to do a RENAMO' on Sierra Leone,"[44] unleashing the RUF, under the leadership of Foday Sankoh, former corporal of the Republic of Sierra Leone Military Forces, on the country's Eastern Province, causing widespread destruction and terror.

Paul Richards, author of *Fighting for the Rain Forest*, has argued that the RUF were revolutionaries, inspired by Gadaffi's notion of a Third Way – between Soviet-style single-party rule and Western-style democracy – and determined to bring change to their country.[45] Richards also points out that the war

---

42 These would all be key social actors in the impending civil war.
43 For a chronology of the events leading up to the civil war in Liberia, see Stephen Ellis, "Liberia, 1989–1994: A Study of Ethnic and Spiritual Violence," *African Affairs* 94 (April 1995), pp. 165–197.
44 Alfred B. Zack-Williams and Stephen Riley, "Sierra Leone: The Coup and Its Consequences," *Review of African Political Economy* 20, no. 56 (March 1993), p. 93.
45 Paul Richards, "Understanding Insurgency in Sierra Leone (& Liberia)," paper presented at the Conference on Conflicts in Sierra Leone and Liberia, University College, London, December

was the culmination of the protracted, postcolonial crisis of patrimonialism. Ibrahim Abdullah takes up the theme of the "revolutionary vanguard" and the influence of Gadaffi's *Green Book* and Kim Il Sung's *Juche* ideas.[46] He notes the coming together of "town and gown" as the children of the petit bourgeoisie were drawn into prolonged discourse with lumpen elements in the Pote, where illegal drugs were used, cementing a strong counterculture. The RUF, which provided this link, appealed to socially excluded groups and all those other social elements who felt alienated by APC rule.

The National Provisional Revolutionary Council and the Demise of the APC Momoh was unable to bring peace to the country, and both government and rebel forces were accused of serious human rights abuse.[47] Momoh failed to exploit the opportunity for nationalist solidarity created by wanton rebel violence against civilians. By mid-1991 the economy took a nosedive, as agricultural production plummeted to an all-time low of US$10 million.[48] War casualties mounted and by early 1992 more than 10,000 people had been killed, 300,000 displaced, 200,000 forced into refugee camps in Guinea, and 400,000 trapped behind rebel lines. Meanwhile, Momoh tried to use the security situation as a pretext to delay calling a general election, which in turn infuriated opposition leaders. Troops dispatched to the front had to fight with obsolete weapons. More significantly, the cost of the war effort meant that the higher echelons of the military could no longer be protected from the worst effects of the economic crisis, which had engulfed the nation. In contrast to earlier periods, most of the spoils did not trickle down to junior officers, thus creating the conditions for a schism within the army officer corps. In addition, the policy of sending young and potentially rebellious officers to the front further alienated the younger ranks from those officers who were seen as occupying positions of opulence.

In April 1992, Momoh was removed by a group of young and relatively unknown officers led by army captain Valentine Strasser, who had escaped death after being severely injured in hand-to-hand combat with the RUF forces. In his first interview after the coup, Strasser described how he and his colleagues had

---

1995, p. 1. See also Paul Richards, *Fighting for the Rain Forest: War, Youth & Resources in Sierra Leone* (Portsmouth, N.H.: Heinemann, 1996).

46 Ibrahim Abdullah, "Bush Path to Destruction: The Origin and Character of the Revolutionary United Front (RUF/SL)," *Africa Development* 22, no. 3–4 (1997), pp. 45–76.

47 See Amnesty International, "Sierra Leone: The Extrajudicial Execution of Suspected Rebels and Collaborators," April 29, 1992; also, US Department of State, "Sierra Leone Country Report on Human Rights and Practices for 1997," Bureau of Democracy, Human Rights, and Labor, January 30, 1998.

48 See Zack-Williams and Riley, "Sierra Leone: The Coup and Its Consequences."

to fight the enemy with "obsolete guns that will not fire," and how his friend died by his side. He was brought to the capital with shrapnel in his leg to be operated on without anaesthesia, as none was available at the main city hospitals. To add insult to injury, the authorities refused to send Strasser and other injured soldiers overseas for treatment because the country could not afford it. This was the last straw for the young officers, who thereafter took decisive measures to remove Momoh and his decadent APC from office.

Strasser condemned the opulence and corruption of the Momoh administration and its inability to prosecute the war successfully. He promised to bring peace to the nation, although his tenure as leader saw growing rebel incursions all over the country. As part of its anticorruption crusade, the NPRC set up a number of commissions to inquire into the assets of ex-ministers and senior civil servants. In the aftermath of the coup, parallels were drawn with the first Rawlings intervention in Ghana in June 1979. The NPRC used the populist rhetoric of redemption, anticorruption, and personal sacrifice. Strasser was referred to as "the redeemer." As in Ghana, economic orthodoxy was combined with a limited politics of redistribution. After an initial period of "pariah status" following the execution of 28 civilians and military officers, an accord was struck with the IFIs, and in exchange for loans, Strasser implemented the programs negotiated by his predecessor with the IMF. This gave the green light to other donors, and loans and grants quickly followed from the European Union for infrastructure development, the International Labour Organisation, and the Africa Development Bank. The stabilization program produced widespread unemployment, as over 30,000 workers were made redundant, though the figure was ameliorated by the rapid expansion of the army, mainly through conscription of "street children." On the positive side, Strasser was able to reduce inflation from over 120 percent when he seized power in 1992, to below 50 percent by the end of 1994, as well as maintain the value of the currency.

Freetown: War, Peace, and Democracy Despite Strasser's success in stabilizing the economy (compared to his immediate predecessor), the popularity of the regime soon waned as domestic and international pressure for a return to civilian rule mounted. On the war front, rebels continued to hit targets in the interior of the country, including a brief occupation of the rich diamond fields of Kono District. The occupation of the Kono District marked a new phase in the war, as the RUF and dissidents from the Sierra Leone Army (SLA), the *sobels* (soldier/rebel), embarked on diamond mining. The RUF leadership was able to exchange diamonds for arms in order to prosecute their war against the government and people of Sierra Leone. On one occasion, rebel forces were reported to be only 45 kilometers from Freetown, preparing for a siege on the capital. By this time it had become clear that the Sierra Leone Army (SLA) was no match for the guerrilla rebels. In early 1995, the military government sought help from the British Army Gurkhas, who were soon embroiled in an ambush in which their Canadian commander, Colonel Robert Mackenzie, was killed.[49] Shortly after the Gurkhas left the country, they were replaced by the South African–based Executive Outcomes (EO),[50] who helped to shift the balance in favor of the NPRC by driving the rebels out of the diamond fields.[51] Nonetheless, EO was a major drain on the Sierra Leone exchequer at a cost of US$1.7 million a month.[52] Later, in 1996, after elections were held and a civilian government installed, scaled-down fighting as a result of a cease-fire and demands from the IMF to reduce payment to the organization led the government to negotiate EO's early departure. The resulting gap was filled by the emergence of a new fighting force, an adjunct of "civil society" called the Kamajors, or Mende traditional hunters.[53] The Kamajors formed the nucleus of the broader government-supported Civil Defence Force, which included the Kapras and Tamboros.

The Mende of the southeast constitute the largest ethnic group of Sierra Leone, accounting for some 30 percent of the population and traditionally providing the bulk of support for the Sierra Leone People's Party, the country's oldest political organization. The SLPP had been in the political wilderness since the 1967 elections, but won the 1996 elections. The Kamajors had distinguished themselves in 1994 in a series of encounters with RUF elements around Bo (the country's second largest town). In these clashes, the Kamajors succeeded in demystifying some of the rebels' claims of invincibility, at a time when the army had appeared incapable of confronting the RUF. As a result, the influence of the Kamajors grew, as they swapped "home-made rifles, machetes, and other crude weapons ... for more sophisticated weaponry."[54]

By early 1994, the shine had rubbed off "Strasser the redeemer." There was the scandal involving members of the junta engaged in diamond smuggling, which angered an already exasperated populace tired of the officers' youthful antics and their inability to end the war. Many saw the transition to civilian rule

---

49 See Stephen Riley, *Liberia and Sierra Leone: Anarchy or Peace in West Africa?*, Conflict Studies, no. 287 (London: Research Institute for the Study of Conflict and Terrorism, 1996).
50 See Jeremy Harding, "The Mercenary Business: 'Executive Outcomes,'" *Review of African Political Economy* 24, no. 71 (March 1997), pp. 87–97.
51 See Riley, *Liberia and Sierra Leone*.
52 See Stephen Riley, "Sierra Leone: The Militariat Strikes Again," *Review of African Political Economy* 24, no. 72 (1997), pp. 287–292.
53 Other ethnic fighters also joined forces against the rebels: the Kapras, Tamaboros, and *Badonsos*.
54 Riley, "Sierra Leone: The Militariat Strikes Again," p. 288.

as a prerequisite to ending the conflict. The immediate post-1994 period was marked by a much-contested debate concerning how to restore peace and democracy. On the one hand, the military and their sympathizers argued that peace must be negotiated before presidential and parliamentary elections were held, because free and fair elections would be impossible under war conditions. On the other hand, there were those led by civic organizations such as Women for a Morally Engaged Nation (WOMEN) as well as donors who held that a speedy return to democratic pluralism was a *sine qua non* for peace in the country. They argued that the military authorities were prevaricating on the issue of returning the country to democratic rule. In their view, Captain Strasser was trying to swap his military uniform for a civilian presidency à la President Rawlings of Ghana.

However, in January 1996, two months before the planned presidential and parliamentary elections, a schism emerged within the NPRC, which resulted in Strasser being replaced by his deputy, Brigadier Julius Maada Bio. This heightened public concerns about the intention of the junta. With civil war still raging, the transition to democratic rule reached its climax with the elections of February and March 1996. Ahmad Tejan Kabbah, leader of the Sierra Leone People's Party, was declared winner of the presidential election with almost 60 percent of the vote after a run-off with the leader of the United National Peoples' Party (UNPP), John Karefa Smart, who polled just over 40 percent. In Parliament, the SLPP won 27 of the 80 seats, and the main opposition the UNPP gained only 17 seats. Twelve seats were reserved for the Paramount Chiefs from the twelve districts. Although the SLPP did not have a majority, it could count on the support of the Paramount Chiefs.

The new government faced three major problems. First, to end the war and begin the task of national reconciliation. Second, to embark on policies of national reconstruction, including relocation of the population that had been displaced by the war. Finally, to secure discipline within the Armed Forces. In his inaugural speech, the new president referred to the three "Rs": reconstruction, reconciliation, and rehabilitation. In particular, Kabbah was very conscious of the politicized and undisciplined armed forces that he had inherited from the NPRC. Over the previous three decades, recruitment into the army had been based on ethnic and political patronage, and the army was regarded as an instrument of the ruling party, insulating it from the people. Thus, even if this party became unpopular, the army would ensure that it remained in power indefinitely.[55] Moreover, the April 1992 coup that brought down Momoh had destroyed the command structure of the army.

---

55 Ahmad Tejan Kabbah, "Restoration to Democratic Civilian Rule in Sierra Leone," Conference on Sierra Leone, London, October 20, 1997.

In order to achieve his stated goals, Kabbah formed a National Coalition Government to include the major parties in Parliament, as well as a rapprochement with Foday Sankoh, the rebel leader. Sankoh's reaction was to emphasize the point that he was willing to meet with Kabbah, not as president of Sierra Leone, but as leader of the SLPP. He called for power sharing with the new government and for "a people's budget" to include free and compulsory education, affordable housing, clean water, and a sewage system in every village. Finally, he demanded the withdrawal of all foreign troops, including those of Executive Outcomes and the Nigerian-led ECOMOG, and the absorption of some of his fighters into the national army. The government rejected Sankoh's demands, in particular his call for power sharing. Instead, the government set up the National Unity and Reconciliation Commission based on the model of South Africa's Truth Commission, to investigate and identify the causes of injustices against individuals and communities by the government. It also emphasized its determination to crack down on corrupt practices among public servants following the disappearance of 500 Sierra Leonean passports.

The government's immediate concern was to negotiate peace with the RUF, as well as to find funds (estimated at US$40 million) to facilitate the smooth demobilization and rehabilitation into civilian life of soldiers and ex-RUF fighters. The search for peace was now being conducted on two fronts: by the Organisation of African Unity (OAU) and by the Commonwealth, though the rapprochement with the RUF continued as both sides agreed to a cease-fire and the reciprocal release of prisoners.

Meanwhile, the economy continued to perform poorly, as the war brought agricultural and mining production to a standstill. Both the bauxite mines in Moyamba and the rutile mines in Sherbro were attacked and personnel seized by rebel forces. In September 1996, the poor economic performance prompted the IMF to demand a drastic cut in payment to Executive Outcomes before the country could receive US$200 million in foreign exchange funding for postwar reconstruction. This resulted in a new agreement with EO, and much-reduced fees for their services. In the same month, an attempted coup led to the retirement of 26 officers and 155 noncommissioned officers from the army. In December 1996, just a month after the conclusion of a peace accord with the RUF, 18 people were arrested after the revelation of another coup attempt. Despite this clear evidence of discontent within the army, in January 1997 the government cut subsidized rice supplies to the army, police, and prison services in response to demands made by the IFIs. In that same month, rice importation from South Asia alone cost the country some US$30 million; sold on the open market for Le23,000 a bag, the price of Le1,000 offered to military personnel indicates the generous subsidy this group enjoyed. Heavily subsidized rice had been the hallmark of military life since the days of Siaka Stevens. The cut in subsidies precipitated yet another coup attempt, as a result of which five officers were arrested, including Captain Paul Thomas, one of the leaders of the May 25 coup.

Growing undiscipline within the ranks of the army made the government more dependent on the Kamajors, who by now had assumed the status of an ethnic praetorian guard. This was particularly the case after the departure of Executive Outcomes and the failure of the United Nations to send peacekeeping troops to supervise the Peace Agreement.[56] Government dependence on the Kamajors worsened army-Kamajor relations, and this was reflected in the growing number of clashes between the two forces. The Kamajors saw the army as ineffective, corrupt, and unpatriotic, demonstrated by their inability to make any significant impact on the RUF and reflected in the rise of the sobels. Sobels were renegade elements of the national army who would loot private property and work the diamond fields by night, then return to soldiering by day. The army was accused of trying to undermine the first Southern-dominated government in thirty years, and was seen as an offshoot of both the APC and the NPRC. In short, the Kamajors considered the army a threat to the country's new democracy.

On the army's part, the Kamajors represented a major threat to national unity and a tool in the sectional divide, a group seeking to challenge the army's monopoly of the means of violence. For example, in March 1996, the civilian government ordered the Kamajors and the army to flush out rebels who had attacked civilians. The army felt that their role "as custodians of state security and defenders of the constitution"[57] was being challenged by the Kamajors. As such, the army saw the Kamajors as a danger to the state.

The chief link between the Kabbah administration and the Kamajors was Deputy Minister of Defence Samuel Hinga Norman, who was also leader of the Kamajors. Within a short period of time, the stature of the Kamajors rose from "ethnic hunters" to quasi-national army. Their growing confidence in dealing with rebels impelled the Kamajors to confront other civic associations, particularly in the North, but also in Bo, Kenema, and Zimmi. Corporal Gborie, who announced that the military had seized power in May 1997, accused the Kabbah administration of "crying down the army," and of "tribalism." Inevitably, one of the first acts of the junta was to outlaw the Kamajors, who in turn indicated their desire to mobilize 35,000 of their number for a march on

---

56 These were known as the Neutral Monitoring Group, under Article 11 of the Abidjan Accord.
57 Major Johnny Paul Koroma, dawn broadcast, Sierra Leone Broadcasting Service, May 25, 1997.

Freetown to oust the renegade soldiers. Until that moment, for much of the war, the citizens of Freetown had been relatively insulated from the excesses to which the RUF had been subjecting the people of the provinces, in particular, those to the east and south.

Kabbah was not the first to utilize an ethnic-based fighting force to govern the country. In the early 1970s, faced with a series of attempted coups, Stevens (with the help of Cuba) established the dread Internal Security Unit (ISU), later renamed the Special Security Division (SSD). This unit was used to put down demonstrations by students and trade unionists, as well as to confront rebellious elements within the army. The 1970s and '80s witnessed a number of clashes between the army and the SSD, including a potentially bloody confrontation in the National Stadium in 1976. Stevens' grip on both forces helped contain SSD-army conflicts so that these tensions and jealousies never became a major security concern. At this time, senior officers in both the army and the SSD were incorporated into the power structure of the Congress, as members of the ruling party. Not surprisingly, the threat of intervention came, generally, not from senior officers, but from military subaltern groups consisting of junior officers and noncommissioned officers, who felt a sense of exclusion and comradeship with the lumpen elements within the RUF and the sobels.

Freetown Under Siege A sense of economic and political insecurity among the population, the unresolved civil war, the Kamajor-army conflicts, the army's loss of privileges – all were major factors behind the military insurgency of May 25, 1997, which mounted a siege on Freetown. The rebels who had occupied a large portion of the country outside Freetown felt that their biggest prize would be the capital. Indeed, this analysis was correct, since despite the atrocities perpetuated on the rural population, there was little outcry from the government and the international community. It was only after rebels breached the defenses of the capital that the world press took notice of the horrors and widespread violation of human rights by both sides in the civil war.

As far as the May 1997 coup is concerned, it is important to note that in the last instance, the army would intervene in politics largely for military reasons.[58] While the charge of corruption against ousted regimes may be true, it is a rationalization central to all dawn broadcasts following a military take-over. In the end, the military tends to intervene to remove a civilian government when corporate interests are threatened. In the case of Sierra Leone, because of the

---

58 See Ruth First, *The Barrel of a Gun: Political Power in Africa and the Coup d'état* (London: Allen Lane, 1970).

clientelistic mode of accumulation and the breakdown of the command structure, junior officers developed a sense of political and economic marginalization welded in an esprit de corps with other marginalized groups and an exaggerated perception of support among the public in general.

Bad policy on the part of an ousted regime helps to create this illusion of a popular desire for military intervention. In the case of the Kabbah regime, there were quite a few poorly conceived policies, some of which we have already discussed. The first relate to security. The dependence on the Kamajors meant that the security of "Kamajor country" (Southern and Eastern Provinces) was guaranteed, but at the expense of the security of the capital. This lapse meant that for the first time, in May 1997, rebels were able to enter Freetown after members of the AFRC released prisoners and forged an alliance with the RUF to form a "People's Army." Similarly, Kabbah's failure to punish officers accused of plotting to overthrow his government reinforced his image as a weak and indecisive leader. This perception was not helped by the abrupt curtailment of the trial of an ex–foreign minister accused of selling the Sierra Leone passports to British–Hong Kong nationals. Furthermore, the generous terms and conditions that were offered to the disgraced former president Momoh astonished many Sierra Leoneans. These included a very generous pension of Le900,000, a house, servants, car, chauffeur, and bodyguards. Momoh's triumphalist manner and speeches helped to whip up antigovernment sentiment. He claimed that he had not been allowed to face the people in general elections before the army ousted him, and he used the opportunity to announce his return to active politics.

Despite good intentions for his country, Kabbah was neither a shrewd politician nor a war leader. Many Sierra Leoneans were disappointed at the composition of Kabbah's Cabinet and his style of government. It was hoped that he would appoint young, dynamic people who had not been contaminated by the politics of kleptocracy. Instead, the Cabinet consisted of discredited (recycled) SLPP politicians. While his personal honesty and integrity were not questioned, it was felt that he was "only paying lip-service to the welfare of the people; phlegmatic and carefree to the security and financial irregularities in Government."[59] He failed to utilize his advantageous position during the 1996 negotiation in Abidjan – when his fighters controlled most of the country – to impose stricter conditions on the rebel leadership. Many commentators felt that "the pluralist politics of democratic exchanges had deteriorated to an acrimonious and divisive process of exchanges and in division in Parliament."[60] This politics

---

59 *West Africa*, June 2–8, 1997, p. 868.
60 *West Africa*, July 14–20, 1997, p. 1118.

of attrition was symptomatic of the "character assassination by Government stalwarts of prominent and influential figures in opposition"[61] leading to the suspension from Parliament of John Karefa Smart, the opposition leader. Opposition parties blamed Kabbah in particular for not doing enough to prevent his suspension. Finally, there was growing undiscipline within the ruling party. By the time of the 1997 coup, there was much talk of Kabbah "the northern" being replaced by a Mende from the south.

This is not to suggest that this first period of Kabbah's rule was a total failure. The SLPP was able to reduce inflation from 40 percent in March 1996 to 6 percent at the time of the coup. Gross Domestic Product grew from −10 percent at the beginning of 1996 to 5.6 percent in December 1996. Kabbah was able to attract Western financial support for his five-year socioeconomic development program costing US$760 million. By the end of March 1997, donors had pledged US$640 million, or 84 percent of the fund. Much of this had been committed to infrastructure development, such as the construction of a sewage system in Freetown. These capital projects were abandoned following the coup, as many workers had been evacuated during the mayhem of the siege on the capital.[62]

In January 1999, cadres of the RUF were able once again to breach the city's defenses. Their entry into the capital saw some of the worst atrocities in the ten-year war. Civilians were mutilated, raped, and killed, private and government buildings destroyed, including much of the colonial architecture for which Freetown was renowned: the Secretariat Building, the famous City Hotel, the Central Police and Law Court Building (now restored), Holy Trinity Church, Saint George's Cathedral, and many private dwellings. In an ironic way, Foday Sankoh's infantile revolution aided the flight of skilled personnel out of the country by finishing the job begun a decade earlier by World Bank and IMF structural adjustment programs.

As noted above, one feature of the civil war is the prominent role that child combatants played. Many of these were abducted by both sides. In the case of the RUF, after a period of socialization into violence, including violence against their community and kin, these children were inducted into various areas of military life.[63] Children were considered expendable, since they did not have any dependents. In a gendered division of labor, girls and young women were used as sex slaves, while boys were used as fighters and miners in the diamond

---

61 Ibid.
62 See Zack-Williams, "The Political Economy of Civil War in Sierra Leone, 1991–98," pp. 143–146.
63 See Alfred B. Zack-Williams, "Child Soldiers in the Civil War in Sierra Leone," *Review of African Political Economy* 28, no. 87 (March 2001), pp. 73–82.

fields. Child soldiers were preferred because, it was argued, they are compliant and easy to manipulate. Moreover, their age and size render them ideal for gathering intelligence, as messengers and as spies on government positions, since they tend to attract little attention.[64] The AFRC/RUF coalition frequently pressed teenage boys into military service. Many were supplied with hallucinogenic drugs. They were forced to mingle with the crowd and hurl grenades at government soldiers. Gender and sexual victimization meant that girls were forced to become "soldiers' wives." The Women's Commission for Refugee Women and Children found that "as many as 80 percent of rebel soldiers are between the ages of seven and fourteen, and recent escapees from rebel camps have reported that the majority of camp members are young captive girls."[65] Furthermore, 60 percent of the 1,000 fighters recently screened by the Disarmament, Demobilisation and Resettlement Unit set up by the Kabbah regime before the May 1997 coup consisted of women. Between 1992 and 1996, the period of the most intensive fighting, both the government and the RUF forcibly recruited some 4,500 children. When children were not involved in fighting, the quiet moments in the camp would be spent cooking or transporting water, arms, ammunition, and other hardware.

Lome and After In July 1999, a peace accord was struck between the government and the leadership of the RUF. Under this agreement, the RUF leader Foday Sankoh became vice-president of Sierra Leone and took charge of the country's mineral resources, which the RUF had exploited to finance its war machine. In addition, a number of RUF field commanders were awarded cabinet positions. Perhaps the most disturbing aspect of the Lome Accord is the blanket immunity from prosecution granted to all RUF fighters. The accord was imposed upon the democratically elected president Ahmad Tejan Kabbah, who was summoned to Lome by Western leaders led by US Special Presidential Adviser on Africa, the Rev. Jesse Jackson, to sign the agreement. Western leaders who had become concerned about the bloodletting in Sierra Leone, but who had no intention of sending their troops into "Africa's futile wars" after the US debacle in Somalia, were ready to accept any deal that would bring peace to this troubled land. Furthermore, Kabbah had little room to maneuver in the negotiations, since at the time some two-thirds of the country was under rebel control.

64 See ibid.
65 Women's Commission for Refugee Women and Children, "The Children's War: Towards Peace in Sierra Leone," March 26–April 16, 1997, p. 1.

By 1999, the Disarmament, Demobilisation and Resettlement (DDR) program of ex-combatants had begun. However, the perceived lack of resolve by the international community to prosecute the rebel leadership for atrocities against the civilian population encouraged Foday Sankoh and his colleagues to seek total power in May 2000. As the last of the Nigerian ECOMOG troops departed, the RUF unleashed a putsch designed to unseat Kabbah and to install their leader as president of the country. Earlier, the RUF and its allies, the West Side Boys, had humiliated UN troops by capturing their weapons and armored vehicles, abducting them, stripping them naked, and killing a number of them. The attempted coup, in which Foday Sankoh himself was wounded and captured, caused both a humanitarian and a political emergency, which resulted in the British government sending troops to the country under the guise of evacuating British and Commonwealth citizens. The elite British Paratroops quickly secured Freetown against rebel incursions. Meanwhile, the gateway to the capital was still being menaced by banditry perpetrated by the rump of the former Sierra Leone Army/AFRC, which had staged the coup of 1997. The West Side Boys, as these thugs were called, captured and held hostage a platoon of British troops. In the ensuing battle to rescue the British soldiers, the West Side Boys were destroyed, thus heralding the true beginning of peace in Sierra Leone. The capture and destruction of their Okro Hill hideout opened the way for UN (UNAMSIL) troops to move into the interior, where they brought humanitarian supplies to the beleaguered civilian population and paved the way for government control in the area. For the first time in almost ten years, residents of Freetown felt a sense of security. Once British troops intervened, not only was the capital secured, thus ending the siege of Freetown, but as rebels surrendered to demobilization camps, it was possible for UNAMSIL to move in to fill the vacuum. By the end of the demobilization period in January 2002, over 46,000 fighters had been demobilized, more than half of them from the Civil Defence Force, the fighting arm of the government supporters; and several thousand were children who had been forced to fight on one or both sides of the divide.

The DDR experienced a host of problems: financial; a lack of confidence; repeat demobilizations; the negative attitude of parents to their returning children, many of whom had committed acts of violence. Demobilized ex-combatants were offered cash and promised training, including apprenticeship; former child combatants were promised education, which many had demanded. Many of the former fighters wanted to become skilled artisans as carpenters and joiners, masons and mechanics, and were apprenticed to artisans in urban areas and offered toolkits to boot. As the country's external trade had ground to a halt, and as agricultural land and diamond fields were occupied by rebel fighters, the cost of the demobilization and reintegration program was borne by donors, many of whom were now beginning to exhibit aid fatigue. Indeed, lack of finance delayed the demobilization process and brought it to a full stop on more than one occasion. Distrust between the government and the rebels also delayed the process. Both sides were suspicious of the other's intentions, and the establishment of the Special Court to try human rights abusers created additional tension, with many young fighters fearful of speaking to adults should they incriminate themselves. Many of the children who entered UNAMSIL's demobilization camps were highly traumatized, fearful of revenge attack and rejection by friends and relations as society labeled them "rebel children." Many refused to speak and were even prepared to return to the fighting forces that had been parent surrogates for so many years. There were also allegations of misappropriation of funds destined for demobilization. For example, the NGO Cause Canada is reported to have lost $27,000 through embezzlement of money allocated for skill training. In another case reported by the *Unity Now* tabloid, officials squandered Le94,000,000 destined for ex-combatants.[66] Poor infrastructure and lack of transportation have been major impediments to the disarmament, demobilization, and reintegration program.[67]

In January 2002, the Sierra Leone government established a protocol for the Special Courts to try those who have been accused of human rights abuses during the decade-long war. The chief accused is the leader of the RUF, Foday Sankoh, who is now incarcerated in the notorious Pademba Road Prison in Freetown. Others who may face trial include Norman Hingham, Deputy Minister of Defence and leader of the Kamajors; Johnny Paul Koroma, head of the government-sponsored Commission for the Consolidation of Peace, and former leader of the Armed Forces Revolutionary Council; and elements of the Sierra Leone Army, which ousted the elected government of Ahmad Tejan Kabbah and invited the RUF into a military coalition, in order to form a Peoples' Army. The junta and its ally caused widespread destruction in the city, including arson, rape, mutilation, looting, and murder. Clearly, while the victims need justice, the Special Court could pose major problems for the consolidation of peace in Sierra Leone, as many of these warlords still have followers and it is well known that not all weapons have been turned in at the demobilization camps. The issue is made more complex by the fact that many of the perpetrators were children who were not only acting under the instructions of adults, but many were under the influence of hallucinogenic narcotics. The problem becomes more acute as it is unclear how the new British-trained army, consisting mainly of former fighters, will behave in a political emergency: Will they remain neutral and fol-

---

66 *Unity Now*, August 27, 2001, p. 1.
67 See *Independent Observer*, August 27, 2001, p. 1.

low government directives, or will they follow the historic road of intervening directly in politics? The fact that former AFRC leader Johnny Paul Koroma is now a member of Parliament has further complicated the situation.

Presidential and parliamentary elections were held in May 2002 and were contested by nine political parties. The national Electoral Commission, which registered more than 2 million voters, was accused of favoritism toward the government by opposition politicians. The victorious SLPP government was accused of vote rigging and tampering with the ballot boxes, though the results were later accepted by all contesting parties.

In July 2002, British troops pulled out after two years of involvement in the country, which included providing security and training a new national army. The "loyal and royal" people of Sierra Leone felt a sense of gratitude to the British government for its part in bringing peace to the country.

Conclusion In this paper I have tried to situate the historic importance of Freetown within the developmental efforts of Sierra Leone as well as within Britain's project of modernity in West Africa. I have drawn attention to the fact that Freetown retained its prominence as the bastion of modernization from the inception of the colony until the early 20th century. By the late 19th century, largely because of the city's many institutions of learning, Freetown had become known as the Athens of West Africa. The fall in the nation's fortunes paralleled the demise of Freetown as an important commercial and intellectual center. The country's precarious position within the international division of labor, in addition to the rise of authoritarian and neopatrimonial politics in the postcolonial period, impelled the country's decline. Curative measures, through IFI adjustment policies, created further social and economic problems, forcing many skilled personnel to migrate to greener pastures. All of these factors provided the backdrop to the civil war, which laid a series of sieges on the inhabitants of Freetown. Thus, the optimism that accompanied the birth of Freetown at the dawn of the 19th century is in marked contrast to the pessimism surrounding the city's future as its citizens enter the new millennium.

Writing the Anxious City:
Images of Lagos in Nigerian Home Video Films

Onookome Okome

Theorizing the City and the Postcolonial   Chinua Achebe once wrote that the great problem of the continent of Africa is ANXIETY. In an extremely witty essay, "Africa and Her Writers,"[1] Achebe is concerned with literary writers and their works, not the medium of video film with which I am preoccupied in this essay. Yet, I think that both categories of writer – for the video producer does lay claim to that status – share this problem and also respond to the anxiety expressed in the cities where they live and practice their art. It is from this prism of commonality, then, that I recall an anecdote used by Achebe to illustrate a point about the crippling sense of futility which this anxious condition brings to bear upon the psychology of the postcolonial.

According to Achebe, the condition of the anxious African "is the source of our problem."[2] We are anxious because "Africa has had such a fate in the world that the very adjective *African* can still call up hideous fears of rejection." This fear is palpable, but he insists that "running away from myself seems to me a very inadequate way of dealing with an anxiety." He argues that "if writers should opt for such escapism, who is to meet the challenge?" To drive home his point, he relates a personal experience with a Nigerian poet "living and teaching in New York." This young man had sent Achebe a poem for publication in the literary magazine he edited in Nigeria. "It was a good poem," Achebe recounts, "but in one of his lines he used a plural Italian word as if it were singular." Finding no reason for "invoking poetic licence," Achebe made the "slightest alteration imaginable in the verb to correct this needless error" – which proved to be a grave mistake. The young man accused Achebe of being a "grammarian" and "contrasted the linguistic conservatism of those who live in the outposts of empire with the imaginative freedom of the dwellers of the metropolis." Here, then, is the heart of the matter: living in New York, the young Nigerian writer

---

1 Chinua Achebe, "Africa and Her Writers," in *Morning Yet On Creation Day: Essays* (London: Heinemann, 1982), pp. 19–29.
2 Ibid., p. 27 (here and following).

arrogates to himself the proprietorship of the metropolis and, by so doing, claims a place in the center, far removed from the outpost from which he was lately uprooted. The anxious need to claim this center clearly positions the Nigerian as the alienated one. With this single act, he relinquishes his homeland. He is the alienated African, searching for relevance in the New World, in the throes of "the *human condition* syndrome."[3] The anxiety behind this also compels him to call into service the Italian language, another signpost of his universalism which he assumes will demonstrate his complete immersion in the ethics of the metropolis. A false confidence arises from this. The young Nigerian writer now believes that the margin is worthless, or at best not noteworthy. Achebe returns to the crux of the matter: "this incident is really a neat parable of the predicament of the African writer in search of universality. He has been misled into thinking that the metropolis belongs to him."[4]

Since one characteristic of the postcolonial is the desire to live in the city, which is by its nature of coming into being nervous and anxious, how would the postcolonial write the nervous condition of the city? I have attempted to explain this anxiety in this paper. I am also interested in how anxiety is manifested in the producers of video film in Nigeria and in the city of the video film, Lagos. I want to examine how the nervous write the nervousness of the city. I am interested in the critique of this nervousness in a new kind of city literature, the video film. Is the anxiety expressed by the young Nigerian poet the same as that encountered in the characters of popular video films produced by and for the mass of toiling Nigerians? In other words, do perspectives differ in the articulation of the nervous city in the two types of narrative? These questions will be explored by examining the content of a number of video films, but first, let us see how the idea of the city is situated in the discourse of the anxiety of the postcolonial and the postcolonial city.

We live in the age of the city. The city is everything to us – it consumes us, and for that reason we glorify it. We may like it or hate it, but we must live in it. Sometimes we defeat the city and reshape it to suit our whims and caprices. We invent the city and it reinvents us. We are constantly fighting with and in the city. It is where everything happens. What is in this city? What constitutes a city in the way that Lagos, the mecca of video film in Africa, has defined itself in the last two centuries of its official existence?

---

3 Achebe uses this phrase, "the *human condition* syndrome" (ibid., p. 24), to mean a certain type of anxiety associated with the European philosophy that emphasizes man as an existential phenomenon. It is this belief that produces the so-called universal man that lacks a specific cultural locus. Achebe thinks this is reprehensible.
4 Ibid., p. 27. Franz Fanon also wrote about the anxiety of the postcolonial. While he expressed the opinion that this is a passing phase in the mental make-up of the colonial, he however linked it to the history of brainwashing, one of the colonial enterprises in Africa.

Jonathan Raban's *Soft City* offers clues to the issues at hand.[5] Cities, Raban tells us, are socially constructed. In many ways, they are like nation-states. They come and go. They are always in a state of flux, undergoing changes that – as Arjun Appadurai reminds us – are influenced by factors associated with the flow of "ideas and ideologies, people and goods, images and messages, technology and techniques."[6] Cities can be temporal. As a work in progress, cities are constantly fashioned and refashioned out of the needs and contingencies of this flow. Cities, like their inhabitants, are always on the move, being remade all along the way. Raban stresses the plastic nature of the city, its malleability. It is "like a theater, a series of stages upon which individuals … work their own distinctive magic while performing a multiplicity of roles."[7] But although the city offers individuals the freedom to act out preferences, they are also acted upon in significant ways. The city is open to all, but also leads actors to sites they may prefer to avoid. In the many theaters of the city, we confront head-on the various sites of hope and contestation. In the urban theater, with its "diverse network of social interactions, honeycombed and oriented towards diverse goals," there is no need to look back to some "longed-for community."[8] Social interactions are more or less defined, not by cultural, familial, or ethnic affiliations, as is the case in small communities, but by a network of personal goals and aspirations. Like a scrapbook filled with unintelligible messages, the relationship between one part of the city and another is never fully determined. In the modern city, Raban asserts, "personal identity has been rendered soft, fluid, endlessly open."[9] He rejects the notion that the city is structured according to some rationality based on class or occupation, "depicting instead a widespread individualism and entrepreneurialism in which the marks of social distinction [are] broadly conferred by possessions and appearances."[10]

Published in 1974, Raban's *Soft City* encapsulates the spirit of the postindustrial city of the Northern hemisphere. As ones reads his poetic prose, one cannot help feel the passion propelling the narrative. This passion is itself defined by the technological advances made by societies in this hemisphere, so that a proper understanding of the city in this light must also embrace within its critical province the debates around technology, information innovation, and the triumph of scientific reason. Raban's city emanates from this context. Using

---

5 Jonathan Raban, *Soft City* (London: Hamilton, 1974).
6 Arjun Appadurai, "Grassroots Globalization and the Research Imagination," *Public Culture* 12, no. 1 (2000), pp. 5–6.
7 David Harvey, *The Condition of Postmodernity: An Enquiry into the Origins of Cultural Change* (Oxford: Blackwell, 1989), pp. 3, 5, discussing Raban's book.
8 Ibid., p. 5.
9 Raban, *Soft City*, p. 61.
10 Harvey, *The Condition of Postmodernity*, p. 3.

London as the exalted example, Raban announces, "Cities, unlike villages and small towns, are plastic by nature. We mould them in our images: they, in turn, shape us by the resistance they offer when we try to impose our personal form on them. ... it seems to me that living in cities is an art, and we need the vocabulary of art, of style, to describe the peculiar relationship between man and material that exists in the continual creative play of urban living."[11] What Raban glosses over is the debate on those social and political dynamics that render the city as "art." For instance, are cities created out of the blues? Are they not part of a desperate system of political machinations?

Although Raban does not suggest a particular artistic vocabulary to be to employed in order to understand the city of his dream, it is important to note that he reversed the equation "art imitates life." For example, in juxtaposing the city and the village, he implies that the city can never be the village, that the city, unlike the village or any small town for that matter, offers itself to us, calling upon us to be part of it, to write over it, to mold it according to our desires and wants. The process of doing this, he tells us, is art and the relationship between material and persons can therefore exist in "a continual creative play." It follows, then, that city dwellers are artists – not by choice but of necessity. Once you live in the city, you are automatically living art. You *are* art. You are an *artist*. For Raban then, there is barely a distinction between life and art. In the city, they are one and the same. Art and living dissolve in the melting pot of the modern city.

Can this be said of all cities, everywhere in the world? I will return to this question shortly.

Raban also writes of two kinds of city: one is soft and pliable, the other, the hard city, the planners construct in the form of maps and concrete entities such as buildings. The suggestion is that the two exist simultaneously, each feeding into the other. But as David Harvey points out, Raban does not pretend that all is well with the modern city of his imagination. When "systems break down," Raban warns, "when we lose our grasp on the grammar of urban life," violence ensues. Beyond the poetic grandeur of the modern city, "the very plastic qualities which make the great city the liberator of human identity" can produce "psychosis and totalitarian nightmare."[12]

Like the concept of modernity itself, Raban's vision of the "soft city" is totalizing. He assumes that all cities conform to this vision, and neglects the social and political dynamics that influence the *real* city where illusions and aspira-

---

11 Raban, *Soft City*, p. 2.
12 Raban, quoted in Harvey, *The Condition of Postmodernity*, p. 6.

tions are played out on a daily basis. Can Raban's vision be applied to Lagos, the quintessential city of the postcolony on the West African coast? Do we find the same kinds of social and cultural anxieties in Lagos and London or New York? In other words, is the postcolonial city one and the same with the postmodern city that Raban describes? Can the anxiety expressed in both ever be the same?

Lagos: The Postcolonial City By every stretch of the imagination, Lagos is a postcolonial city. As a former outpost of the imperial empire controlled from London, it shares with other colonized cities of the world a history of intrusion in its formation. If the European metropolis develops from peasantry through the formation and dissolution of feudalism to a capitalist order, many African cities, including Lagos, did not follow this path of development. If the European city is a construction demanded by the needs of the industrial revolution and the movement toward a capitalist economy, this is not the case in Africa, where the city is a construction of the modernist dreams of colonizers who came to the continent to exploit its resources. According to David Simon, most African towns and cities "inherited a legacy of physical and socially structured inequality" but in spite of the deplorable consequences of Africa's involvement in Europe's modernity, Simon argues, "the modernization paradigm has persisted" and African town planners have only recently begun to reject its "narrowly conceived formalistic and procedural notion of urban order."[13]

The suggestion here is that the city in Africa is still intricately tied to what was inherited from the colonial past. Over the past three decades, after most African nations achieved independence, significant moves have been made by ordinary people to divest cities of these ties to colonialism. Simon asserts that the colonial agenda "began to wane, as a result of the sheer pressure of urban growth at one level but, more profoundly, also on account of ... internal conflicts and inappropriateness to local conditions."[14] And in the years following the structural adjustment programs, the "universalizing 'grand theory' or the meta-narrative concerned with defining a single 'best' or 'correct' economic and social strategy to a desired outcome"[15] fell face down. The result of the bottom-up rewriting of the inherited postcolonial city is that locals in African cities began to remap the shape of the city, redesigning desires and aspirations outside the order of the colonial city *and* outside the nation-state, which given its colo-

---

13 David Simon, "Rethinking Cities, Sustainability, and Development in Africa," in *Sacred Spaces and Public Quarrels: African Cultural and Economic Landscapes*, ed. Paul Tiyambe Zeleza and Ezekiel Kalipeni (Trenton, N.J.: Africa World Press, 1999), p. 20.
14 Ibid., p. 22.
15 Ibid., p. 24.

nial attachments is nothing but a "hollow pretence."[16] Appadurai gives a very lively description of a similar scenario of the local response to the global flow. The city is at the center of this local response: "a series of social forms have emerged to contest, interrogate, and reverse these developments and to create forms of knowledge transfer and social mobilization that proceeds independently of the notion of corporate capital and the nation-state system."[17] In other words, modes of interrogation and arenas of contestation operate beyond the watchful eye of the state, which has become, as Achille Mbembe describes it, nothing more than an "inflated ritual."[18] For Appadurai, the process itself is "undertaken on behalf of the people," and therefore rightly earns the appellation "grassroots globalization." This form of interrogation from below plays out the "saliency of the local," remapping areas of anxiety in a complex interplay of local utopia and dystopia. More than any other social formation, it is the postcolonial city so defined that harbors the cultural and social apparatus that engineers the many forms of local responses from the periphery. In the dialectics of these responses, we cannot fail to see the remaking of the colonial city. It is in part the subversion of the imported European modernity that gave rise to the postcolonial city. It is no longer the logic of Europe's modernity that is the deciding factor here, but the unfulfilled needs of the postcolonial subjects that determine how the city is constituted as a crucible of new experiences. As Simon correctly observes, this is a process of "reclaiming urban spaces" and remaking them in local images. One of the most revealing aspects of this contestation between the local and the flow from the global is found in the cultural productions that abound in Africa. It is the telling nature of these art forms that led Anthony Appiah to declare that "African cultural productivity grows apace"[19] in spite of the extreme conditions in which artists live. Karin Barber has drawn our attention to these forms in Nigeria, detailing how new forms of social imagining are derived from the interactions between the local and the global. The difference between the model of the modern city which Raban draws and the postcolonial city in Africa is that social imagining is heavily conditioned by "the politics of the belly"[20] undertaken by the common people as a means of negotiating postcolonial debilities. These cultural forms of expression offer profound insights into the debates that matter to ordinary people on the continent. As the crucible upon which all this happens, the African city positions itself as the local center

16 See Achille Mbembe, "Provisional Notes on the Postcolony," *Africa* 62, no. 1 (1997), pp. 3–38.
17 Appadurai, "Grassroots Globalization and the Research Imagination," p. 3.
18 Mbembe, "Provisional Notes on the Postcolony."
19 See Anthony Appiah, "Is the Post- in Postmodernism the Post- in Postcolonialism?," *Critical Inquiry* 17, no. 2 (1997), pp. 348–352.
20 Jean-François Bayart, *The State in Africa: The Politics of the Belly* (London: Longman, 1993).

of new ideas, inaugurating, as Appadurai has argued, a number of "global localities."

Home Video Film and the Anxieties of a Postcolonial Nation   In this, then, one can argue that Nigerian video film deals with "things that matter to the life of the common people"[21] in much the same way that popular Yoruba plays do. But it does so in a manner different from Yoruba traveling theater. While video film deals with things that matter to the common people, it does not exclude the things that matter to the elite class of Nigeria. Indeed, they form part of what matters to the common people. A genuine people's art, the video film in Nigeria shows how the city in which it is produced is tied to Raban's totalizing vision, but at the same time is different from it. One striking difference is the prevalence of the "economy of the occult" that rules the lives of all Lagos' inhabitants.

The video film made its debut in Nigeria in the 1970s. The phenomenon began in Lagos and still has a strong foothold there, where it has enjoyed tremendous patronage in the last ten to fifteen years. Coming from a complex interplay of economic and cultural needs, the video film in Nigeria is essentially an urban form. Like other forms of popular art in Africa, it responds to the "eccentric currents of modernity."[22] Produced mostly in the cities of Nigeria, it debates the city and relies primarily but not exclusively on information from the different theaters within it. Yet, the point ought to be made that the video film is not the first popular art form in Nigeria to take the city as the narrative verve of its system of signification. There were the pamphlets and novels of the 1960s that privileged the flamboyant discourses of the city in Nigeria as a location where the good, the bad, and the ugly is enacted. It is here, in the chimera of the city, much in the same way as Raban constructs the modern city, that individuals work out an elaborate map of pleasure. Thus, it was the Onitsha market literature that began the critique of *citiness* as opposed to *rurality*,[23] which became amplified in the city novels of Cyprian Ekwensi. Essentially, both forms initiated the narrative of the fractured society, calling attention to the place of the city in the scheme of things and to the sectors of this city in which the glam-

---

21 See Karin Barber and Christopher Waterman, "Traversing the Global and the Local: Fújì Music and Praise Poetry in the Production of Contemporary Yorùbá Popular Culture," in *Worlds Apart: Modernity Through the Prism of the Local*, ed. Daniel Miller (London: Routledge, 1995), pp. 240–262.
22 See Jean Comaroff and John L. Comaroff, "Millennial Capitalism: First Thoughts on a Second Coming," *Public Culture* 12, no. 2 (2000), pp. 291–343.
23 See Emmanuel N. Obiechina, ed., *Onitsha Market Literature* (London: Heinemann Educational Books, 1972), and *idem, An African Popular Literature: A Study of Onitsha Market Pamphlets* (Cambridge: Cambridge University Press, 1973).

orous is not so different from the devilish. By deflating the discourse of the city as something different and new, both forms privilege the city's *other* – the village.

Within a decade or so after the appearance of the Onitsha market literature, Cyprian Ekwensi repositioned the debate in his so-called city novels, giving minute and very interesting details about actors in the city and their places in it. His works lucidly reveal the emerging culture of the city, especially Lagos of the postindependence and oil-boom eras. A former crown colony of the British empire, Lagos has always known the influx of cultures and people, and has continuously invented itself as a city with pretensions to the imported modernity. By independence, it became the center of Nigeria's modern society, inviting all and sundry to partake in the modernity that was at best ill-defined in relation to existing local cultures. As a political and social center in the mid-20th century, Lagos witnessed considerable contestation between the local and the global. Forms of popular art evolved out of this chaos. Hanging onto its crown-colony moniker, the "Liverpool of West Africa,"[24] and touting its postcolonial reputation as a "center of excellence," Lagos quickly became known as the "mecca of the arts." In his landmark book *Victorian Lagos*, M. J. C. Echeruo describes the city as a place "where everything begins and ends,"[25] referring of course to the centrality of Lagos in Nigeria as well as the entire West Coast of Africa. Ekwensi's city novels originate from this context, although some of them are also set in Port Harcourt, another important colonial city located southwest of Lagos on the Atlantic coast.

Ekwensi's *People of the City* (1954) and *Jagua Nana* (1961) inscribe the city as place, as locality, for the first time. He shows that the culture of the city is tied to no one in particular, contending that everyone is free to act out his desires and aspirations. The flip side of this freedom is that the actor must negotiate life from diverse fronts. Ekwensi captures the "many contradictions"[26] of the city in his memorable, soulful, irrepressible, and vivacious character Jagua Nana, perceptively discussed by Ernest Emenyonu, who leads us into the soul of the new city by scrutinizing the aspirations and hopes of this city woman. Forced out of her village for not having a child after years of marriage, Jagua Nana comes to the city of Lagos to "make it," as the saying goes. The city provides a respite from the poverty and stifling moral codes of the village, but it is a temporary solace. Throughout the novel, the specter of the village hovers, until in the end

---

[24] Patrick Coleman, *Modern and Traditional Elites in the Politics of Lagos* (Cambridge: Cambridge University Press, 1993), p. 371.
[25] Michael J. C. Echeruo, *Victorian Lagos: Aspects of Nineteenth Century Lagos Life* (London: Macmillan Educational, 1977), p. 49.
[26] Ernest Emenyonu, *Cyprian Ekwensi* (London: Evans Bros., 1974), p. 81.

Jagua must return to it. As Emenyonu points out, Jagua may have "her own passion" but the changing faces of the city rule her life. In the city she is free to be herself, but this freedom is circumscribed by other factors operating in the daily life of those she meets. The commodification of her body as "she moves down the street ... wriggling her hips" in a seductive manner is one example of the imposition of the city's morality. She will be noticed only if she is shows something that others dare not reveal. And because the city gives her the space in which to act, she has no reason not to do so in a manner that will call attention to herself. But it is the same city in the person of her young boyfriend Freddy who rejects her because he will not be able to advance in life with a woman who has shown so much of herself to the world. Like any woman who comes to the city, Emenyonu tells us, Jagua is "imprisoned, entangled ... unable to extricate herself from the clutches of the city."[27] Yet the authorial voice of the novel is not satisfied to leave it at that. Jagua Nana is entitled to a moral cleansing, and so after ten years of unrewarded experiences in the city, she retreats to the village where she "makes her new discovery":[28] the city can indeed be all it pretends to be, but it can only be a site of adventure, never of the real life of the local. Emenyonu concludes: "the conflict in Jagua's life and ultimately the purpose of the novel must be found in something deeper than Jagua's promiscuous relationships with men in the city."[29] What else can this be but the irreconcilable difference between the village and the city and the daily struggle to survive in it?

I have devoted some time to the analysis of this character because she presages an important aspect of the new culture of the city, which in many ways reminds us of Raban's vision elaborated in *Soft City*. Yet Jagua Nana, the city woman, spells out in clear terms some of the anxieties of the postcolonial city. Although the authorial voice recognizes the city's active role in her life, it still manages to privilege the moral code of the village over the unfolding city culture. The city novels can be seen as the precursors of the video film in this and other respects. A 1960s character moving uncertainly into the turbulent 1970s, Jagua Nana, the postcolonial Renaissance woman, is caught in the arbitrary current of a postcolonial modernity that she barely understands. Many such characters are to be found in the Nigerian video film.

Rituals: A Critique of the Alternative Economy   The city determines the content and the characters of the Nigerian video film, which reinvents social conscious-

---

27 Ibid., p. 177.
28 Ibid., p. 88.
29 Ibid., p. 89.

ness by tapping the fears expressed in the city, reaffirming the content of rumor mills and other media, including newspapers and television.

Rituals is the prototypical city video film.[30] It is defined by a strange, ambiguous, and powerful attachment to the city as a whole and to the social dynamic expressed within the built environment. *Rituals* was produced by NEK Video Links in Lagos, and written and directed by Chief Kenneth Nnebue, a leading figure in the industry. An Igbo from the southeast, Nnebue is first and foremost a businessman who chanced upon videomaking and made fortunes with a number of video films. Even as a producer/director, he has maintained a close eye on the business aspect of his art.

In 1992, shortly after making his first series of video films in collaboration with Yoruba traveling theater directors, with Yoruba as the narrative language, Nnebue released *Living in Bondage*. It was an immediate hit, not least because it locates the essential core of the home video film – violence, superstition, sex, money, women, magic, fraudsters, and the dubious lives of the upwardly mobile – in the city of Lagos.[31] According to Okechukwu Ogunjifor, who describes himself as the "megastar of the video film,"[32] *Living in Bondage* also launched the phenomenon of the sequel as a format of the city video film. First made in the Igbo language, it was quickly dubbed in English, making it possible for the city's non-Igbo consumers to benefit from the social discourses that it privileges. The sequel, *Living in Bondage II*, also focuses exclusively on the city.[33]

The anxiety of the city, expressed in both parts of this video film, opens up a profound dimension of the city's confused modernity. Andy Okeke, chief protagonist and one of the city's many victims, becomes the typical man lost in what Raban describes as the "psychosis" of the city. Through him, a thorough and heart-rending critique is made of the city. In *Living in Bondage*, Lagos is rendered masculine. The elaborate narrative bridges bring the soft and hard parts of the city into close scrutiny. The built city, the hard city, is strong and towering. Its repeated visual occurrence between scenes evokes the power of the phallus, linking one scene (part) of the city to another in a menacing manner and defining for the viewer the city's inscrutability. Like the unconscious Freudian slip, *Living in Bondage* privileges the built up spaces of Lagos and insinuates the unequal relationship between the sexes in the city, enveloped in

---

30 *Rituals*, video (VHS), 120 min., color, English; script by Kenneth Nnebue, produced by NEK Video Links, Lagos, 1997.
31 See Onookome Okome, "The Treatment of Social Change: *Living in Bondage I* and *II*," *Ndunode* 2, no. 2 (1998).
32 Ibid., p. 49.
33 *Living in Bondage I*, 1992; *Living in Bondage II*, 1993; both: video (VHS), approx. 120 min., color, Igbo/English; script by Kenneth Nnebue, produced by NEK Video Links, Lagos.

the spirit of an inescapable masculinity. It is here that Andy Okeke lives out his anxieties. *Living in Bondage* tells the story of people caught in the bondage of the city, yet the plot moves back and forth from the city to the village.

Nnebue released another city video film, *Glamour Girls I* and *II*, in 1992–94.[34] If *Living in Bondage I/II* deal with a male protagonist who victimizes female antagonists, exemplified in Merit, the virtuous wife and one of the principal victims of the city's "economy of the occult," *Glamour Girls* significantly recasts the gender equation. Doris, Thelma, and Sandra, all women of the city, redraw the map of Lagos, consciously seeking to make victims of men who desire their sexuality. But unlike *Living in Bondage*, gender inequality is not so neatly drawn in *Glamour Girls*. Here the authorial intervention often calls attention to the implied fraud of the so-called glamour girls, who are nothing but city hustlers of no enduring relevance to society. If the overwhelming and cunning city is blamed for Andy Okeke's intransigence and travails, it is the intrinsic amorality of the glamour girls that is responsible for their deviance. The city is just a catalyst to what already exists. In *Glamour Girls*, the city women and their freedom is positioned against the backdrop of that other world, the village, with its different moral code.

Rituals, made in 1997, turns our attention to another part of the city's theater with a different tenor. It celebrates the "magic of despair" in the postcolonial city as described by Max Gluckman.[35] The tension inscribed in the built part of the city and in the intangible human factories of dreams reiterates what Jean and John Comaroff refer to as the "saliency of the locality, place and community in a way that often bypass[es] the state."[36] If *Living in Bondage* situates viewers/consumers within this locality, revealing the tensions and anxieties located in the sites of debate within this *civis*, *Rituals* zeros in on a number of these sites of debate. As in most video films, this sphere of debate is invested with a number of purposes and aims, some of which work at cross-purposes, others reinforcing social, political, and cultural anxieties at different social and political positions. While it is difficult to make rigid class differentiations, especially since the criminalization of the sphere of political action in Nigeria from the 1960s onward, it is still possible to recognize two, albeit nebulous, class categories: the ruling class, which can be represented by anything from the military to a private club of opportunistic people, and the large class of laborers, among whom we place those who are qualified but unemployed. Both classes generate

---

34 *Glamour Girls I*, video (VHS), 125 min., color, English, 1992; *Glamour Girls II: The Italian Connection*, video (VHS), 160 min., color, Igbo/English, 1994; both: script by Kenneth Nnebue, produced by NEK Video Links, Lagos.
35 Max Gluckman, "The Magic of Despair," *The Listener*, April 29, 1954.
36 Comaroff, "Millennial Capitalism," p. 305.

social meaning from their particular economic standpoints. Although different tensions may exist at either end of the spectrum, both determine how life is lived in this postcolonial city and in this form of popular expression, the video film.

Rituals, the city video film with its peculiar penchant for valorizing gangsterism, privileges two sites of debate – namely the character of the people of Lagos, and what Jean and John Comaroff call "the economy of the occult," an alternative form of expressing (not producing) wealth in the cities of Africa's postcolonies. It is the city that offers unparalleled freedom to engage in this "economy."

Rituals is about Lagos. Its narrative action revolves around it. It is at once a reaction and a response to city life. Sources of its narrative are as diverse as the filmic narrative itself. It could be argued that *Rituals* is a collage of events and actions culled from newspapers, television events, the rumor mills, and even the popular but incredibly contorted social pageants orchestrated by Sani Abacha's regime. Released during this regime, *Rituals* attempts to capture the many ways in which the people of Lagos make money and spend it. It situates characters within the dark and anxious city, but also highlights its positive aspects and insinuates the middle ground, the gray area between the two. In the three distinct parts of the city, the narrative of *Rituals* situates the characters of the exemplary postcolonial city.

Rituals is about a group of gangsters. Don Pedro is at the center. Wearing his chieftaincy title like a cloak, Don Pedro is reminiscent of another famous gangster, Don Corleone of Mario Puzo's novel, *The Godfather*. He organizes countless nefarious activities, causing mayhem about town. Although *Rituals* opens with a disclaimer, forcefully reminding viewers that the story is about no one in particular, once the credits begin to roll, it is not difficult to see that we are in Lagos, the "city by the Lagoon," as Odia Ofeimun describes it.[37] The characters are social types, the kind created by the incomplete city.

The narrative begins with a deathbed scene. The dying father of Richard and Ben is a member of several cults. His life is governed by cult activities and, as such, he believes that the only way to cure himself is through a sacrifice that requires a human head. Richard, a heart surgeon, insists that the father's ailment is medical, "a blocked artery in the heart," and is easily remedied. He has just come from the United States, where he practices medicine. The father rejects this diagnosis, insisting on the human head. Ben, the younger son who is wise to the ways of Lagos, answers his father's call. He goes into the street, finds one of the city's disposables, an Okada (d) rider (a motorcycle operative), kills and decapitates him, then brings the head to his father. The father takes the head to

---

37 See Odia Ofeimun, "Imagination and the City," *Glendora Review: African Quarterly of the Arts* 3, no. 2 (2001).

a cult meeting. After the usual abracadabra, he returns home and soon dies. The human sacrifice did not help.

A question of inheritance of the father's wealth soon arises. In the fracas that ensues, Ben, who is also a member of the dead father's cults, kills Richard. Enter Don Pedro. Ben is a member of Don Pedro's cabal and, through the established network of the gang, avoids punishment for killing his brother. The hoodlums unleash havoc on Lagos, leaving no doubt about who is in charge of the city. Their activities underscore the *absencing* of political authority. The ways by which the gangsters defy state authority are as mystical, superstitious, and corrupt as the ways employed by the nominal state itself to govern the *civis*.

As is the case with many video films, *Rituals* also foregrounds another crucial aspect of the city, the "occult economy that lacks logic."[38] The lives of Don Pedro, Richard, and Ben are governed by the freedom that the postcolonial city imposes upon its inhabitants. Their lives crisscross, leaving trails of disjointed and fragmentary stories, all woven around the inscrutability of the city. Ben favors the alternative diabolic political institutions of Don Pedro's gang and the cult of the dying father. Don Pedro also subscribes to cultic beliefs but recognizes the presence of an ineffectual political authority. He does not respect this authority. He deals with it, but on his own terms. The corruption of the local political authority becomes a vehicle to his own power and social leverage. He bribes officials and makes political authority a ridiculous show of ineffectuality. He creates a violent and distorted version of what David Hecht and Abdou-Maliq Simone call the "block association."[39] Don Pedro's actions restate the very absence of effective political governance. While institutions of governance are represented, we know that there is no strong political system. Desmond, one of Don Pedro's boys, is interested in the political position of governor of an unnamed state of the Nigerian federation. He is supported in this aspiration by the cabal, not by the popular will of the people. To attain this "political glory," he resorts to the occult, consulting soothsayers and aligning himself with the superstitions generated by the city out of its split character: divided between a tradition that looks back to the past and a modernity that identifies with progress and the benefits of globalization. This is the situation in *Rituals* that produces what Jean and John Comaroff classify as a "striking corollary of the damning age of millennial capitalism." It is this situation that has produced the "global proliferation of occult economies."[40] The "mass panic" inspired by the lawlessness which Don Pedro has orchestrated can be understood as the

---

38 Comaroff, "Millennial Capitalism," p. 310.
39 See David Hecht and Maliqalim Simone, *Invisible Governance: The Art of African Micropolitics* (Brooklyn, N.Y.: Autonomedia, 1994).

response of those who are "marooned by a rudderless ship of state" who must now "clamber aboard the good ship of Enterprise." As is the case with many postcolonial cities, hoodlums such as Don Pedro and his army of carpetbaggers captain the ship. Lagos, the fascinating yet fatally positioned city of Nigeria's postcolony, becomes, then, the opposite of what Odia Ofeimun refers to as the Good City. Characters in the physical Lagos work out their dreams in a postcolonial elixir of deceit and fraud, conjuring up "magical means for otherwise unattainable ends" even when some of them "vocalize a desire to sanction."[41] It is then a matter of art imitating life. But it is also a matter of life imitating art, as responses to video narratives testify. The dialectic of imitation goes both ways.

In *Rituals*, as in the real Lagos, the city is anxious. It is anxious about its status in the global flow of goods, services, and other kinds of exchange. Its inmates are insecure and anxious about their status within this anxious city. The concluding scenes of *Rituals* amplify the anxiety of the people of Lagos, the so-called city of excellence. At this point, Don Pedro's empire is crumbling. Desmond, his protégé, has lost the election. A number of Don Pedro's henchmen have been killed in the ritual of power, where those involved try to amass inordinate and superstitious powers via unknown spiritual forces. The discredited law is painfully fighting its way back to some reckoning. Faced with this backlash, Don Pedro prepares for combat: "The music has just begun ... we must start the war song to protect ourselves." The story closes. The vultures are besieged but only temporarily defeated. State authority remains weak. Corruption has not been dealt any hard blow and the anxieties of common people are fed constantly with superstitions about the invisible powers of the vultures. State agencies responsible for governance encourage these superstitions, leaving the common people whose lives are dispensable no recourse to seek solace and hope elsewhere.

Another prominent aspect of this film is its representation of the "economy of the occult" in the daily lives of the people. *Rituals* recreates the social and psychological map of the anxiety associated with this economy as an urban phenomenon where labor has been vigorously recast and consigned to the realm of superstitions. The city is anxious about the unknown but envied sources of wealth accrued by its nouveau riche.

Rituals expresses this aspect of the city's character in the actions of Don Pedro, Desmond, and Ben. Defined by the city, these characters understand that what matters in the short and long run is not how wealth and social position are acquired, but how these acquisitions are translated into power – power

---

40 Comaroff, "Millennial Capitalism," p. 310.
41 Ibid., p. 316.

to accumulate even more power and wealth for dubious reasons. Don Pedro "captures" a number of young girls and brings them to his house for ritual murder meant to generate more wealth. The house is palatial, stupendously furnished, fitted with an Olympic-sized swimming pool. Sumptuous parties are held by the pool. At one such party, a staggering amount of wealth is displayed, and a parody of the *absencing* of state authority is initiated by playing the national anthem. The party is held to honor Don Pedro, philanthropist and socialite. The viewers, of course, know that Don Pedro is anything but a patriot and that those he supports are social vultures preying on the innocents of the city. Don Pedro is described in the citation offered him as "one of the men of vision," an Oxford-trained businessman, "selfless," "a crime fighter." To play the national anthem that extolls the virtues of "our heroes past" and that pledges our allegiance to the nation of Nigeria, to a parade of people without the slightest commitment to neighborliness and good governance, is but a parody of the idea of nationhood. This is what happens when the State loses control over the city and its people. This is the city where "the problem is differentiating the philosophers from the fools, the witches from the Jehovah's witnesses, the police from the thieves."[42] This is the opposite of the Good City. This is Lagos, the epitome of all postcolonial cities.

Two scenes in *Rituals* stand out, as both reminders of its link to a global meta-narrative, and as depictions of the "economy of the occult," this "rupture expressed in the popular imagining in many peripheral economies."[43] Out of the "magic of despair" evolves an economy that "transgresses the conventional, the rational, the moral."[44] In *Rituals*, the sole means of producing wealth is ritual murder, handmaiden to the "economy of the occult." The proliferation of lurid visual representations of this phenomenon in *Rituals* and other video films testifies to its supreme position in popular imagination.

The first scene deals with Ben's father on his deathbed, described above. Wealthy and influential, we assume that he represents one of the new classes of the urban rich. He demands a human head. His belief in the efficacy of human sacrifice as a way of reinventing a tired body is symptomatic of the city's ailment. The ensuing events – the murder to acquire the head, the cult meeting, the squabble over the father's inheritance, Richard's murder – all signify the overthrow of logic, consigning to this city a different and dubious morality – the morality of the ritual of power. Against the tenuous apparatus of modernity is its antithesis, another logic that enervates the culture of liberal enterprise. In

---

42 Hecht and Simone, *Invisible Governance*, p. 20.
43 Comaroff, "Millennial Capitalism," p. 316.
44 Ibid.

this confused state of being, reflected in the characters of the city, is situated the consequences of an arrested path to the kind of modernity described by Jürgen Habermas,[45] the abrogation of that "project of modernity" characterized by the development of "objective science, universal morality and law, and autonomous art according to their inner logic."[46] The actions of the characters we meet in *Rituals*, located in the local/periphery, do not suggest sameness with the modernity of Habermas. These characters are, at best, part of modernity's "complex historical geography."[47] Their actions suggest another kind of modernity, implying that there are many different modernities existing within this "complex geography" of the modern.

The second memorable scene of the ritual of power occurs during the party set by the swimming pool. After Don Pedro and a number of "illustrious sons and daughters" of the community are invested with "national honors" for their "selfless service" to humanity, the party goes into full swing. A popular local musician, Bright Chimezie, sings one highlife tune after another. Meanwhile, in another part of the opulent house, the "economy of the occult" is enacted. The narrative suddenly shifts to this location, refocusing the source of wealth that makes such an elaborate party possible. Two women, looking terrified and helpless, are dragged into a room and stripped to their underwear. Their heads are clean-shaven, a sign of their preparedness as sacrificial objects. The rapid cutting back and forth between the party and the scene of ritual murder recalls a similar scene in *The Godfather* in which Michael Corleone kills a number of elders from rival families. Don Pedro appears, thoroughly examines the ritual "objects," and gives the go-ahead for the women to be murdered. He does not give a thought to the cries of these women, who are merely disposables. The act itself is simply a means to an end – the acquisition of wealth by ritual murder. The notion that blood *alchemizes* into money (wealth) in a ritual exercise of conjuration is an ancient one, probably originating in the traditional lore of many African societies, but Don Pedro's actions are precipitated by other, more immediate causes. The city has completely fractured village (rural) morality, even though its codes still lurk in the background. Living on the fringes of the liberal economy of the ex-colonial metropolis, the city's inhabitants are trapped in the web of a locality that is rapidly changing and a global world that is overbearing. In such a context, vestiges of traditional cultures are reinterpreted, producing what Jean and John Comaroff describe as a "rupture of the logic of modernism."[48]

---

45 Jürgen Habermas, *The Philosophical Discourse of Modernity: Twelve Lectures*, trans. Frederick G. Lawrence (Cambridge, Mass.: MIT Press, 1987).
46 Jürgen Habermas, "Modernity – An Incomplete Project," in *The Anti-Aesthetic: Essays on Postmodern Culture*, ed. Hal Foster (Port Townsend, Wash.: Bay Press, 1983), p. 95.
47 See Harvey, *The Condition of Postmodernity*.

Rituals is an example of this rupture in the Nigerian postcolonial city of Lagos. This social rupture defines the peculiar vernacular of local cultural technologies. The expert in this economy is no longer the scientist, the technocrat, the bureaucrat, or the administrator whose knowledge of human society derives from a planned economic framework. The expert is the *dibia* or the *babalawo*, whose skills include the ability to solicit assistance from the supernatural realm. In this sense, then, *Rituals* is a critique of the anxieties of the postcolonial city. Here, the "economy of the occult" hinted at in *Living in Bondage I/II* finally bursts forth. The sum total of the state's abdication and the institution of a blood economy is the grand ANXIETY of the continent to which Chinua Achebe refers. Only this time it is manifested in a popular form and not through the serious art of poetry. However, both originate from the same context – the Africa of the postcolonial era.

The intensity of the social and cultural anxiety may differ in degree from one video film to another. *Rituals*, a city video film, offers a stark and sometimes grotesque articulation. In other categories of video film, perspectives may differ as well as the means toward the amelioration (or total eradication) of the resulting psychosis. Several distinctions can be made between different types of video film, although these are not hard and fast. The city video film is set in the city and hegemonizes a psychology caught between a rural past and a muddied present looking toward a blurred, uncertain future. This same vision permeates the "epic" and "hallelujah" categories of video film. This is probably so because the city, which is the local grand narrative of the video phenomenon, is colored by an in-between(ness) of the city's soul.

Unlike the city video film, however, the narrative of the epic defines itself *in relation to* the city, not *as* the city. Epic video films are positioned as a glance backward to some rural past, usually made by video producers who are firmly rooted in the city. Their gaze is as much a nostalgic recall as it is a position of presumed superiority. The postcolonial city is often seen by the rural public as the place to be, the El Dorado of the postcolonies. The nostalgic perspective of the epic video film reproduces the periphery/center dichotomy in the postcolony, with the implication that the city is the undeniable center. The most important marker of the epic video film is the implied simplicity of rural people. The narrative is historical, set in some serene past, unspoiled and completely untouched by Western intrusion. One of the first video films of this type is *The Battle of Musanga I* and *II*, a naive and simplistic narrative of the battle that ensues when the first Christian missionaries set foot on Ohafia country in

---

48 Comaroff, "Millennial Capitalism," p. 310.

what is now Abia State in Nigeria. The naivete of the narrative perspective is unparalleled, with the closing remarks admonishing the "natives" as "heathen" for attacking the agents of civilization, the white missionaries. This kind of narrative reiterates the notion that the popular arts in Africa offer no critical platform from which to gauge Africa's processes of social and cultural negotiation. This is, of course, not the whole truth. Once one recognizes this gaze for what it is, that of Africa's confused modernity expressed from the city, a critical platform reveals itself. This is the vision of city people.

The most popular of the video films cast in the epic mode is *Igodo: Land of the Living Dead*, released in 1999.[49] *Igodo* has attracted a number of litigations. The story is lifted directly from *Langbodo*, a play by Yemi Ogunyemi which was Nigeria's theater entry for Festac 1977. *Igodo*'s screenwriter, Don Pedro Obaseki, denies having read *Langbodo*, but the similarity between the texts is obvious. This is a common occurrence in the video industry.

Igodo is set in an idyllic, pristine African village called Umo-oka. Shortly after this adamic paradise is introduced, we are launched into a social crisis: young people of the village are mysteriously dying. The Igwe, ruler of this village, must determine the source of this sudden calamity upon the land. The medicine man/soothsayer is called upon to sort out the problem. He in turn asks the council of the Igwe to look back into history to discover why the "gods are silent," explaining that the answer lies with an old man, Igodo, who lives in the forest. Igodo is brought before the Igwe and a new story begins. It is the story of Ihekwumere, a child who was to become the messenger of Amadioha, god of thunder, and who should have been the Igwe of Umo-oka. The village was divided on the matter. The victorious faction had Ihekwumere murdered after bribing the court priest to support them. Ihekwumere put a curse on the village before he died. The rest of the story is about how the seven selected sons of Umo-oka journey into the forest and the "hills of Amadioha" to find the tree under which Ihekwumere's cutlass lay buried. It is only by bringing home this mysterious cutlass that the village will be saved. Once this is done, a new Igwe is enthroned. Ihekwumere's story is a simple, naive tale about a past that is barely understood in the light of the present.

Conclusion: The Consequences of Anxiety The relationship between the city and the video film (by which I mean here the practice of video filmmaking and the industry that has grown up around it) is a symbiotic one. The city dictates the

---

49 *Igodo: Land of the Living Dead*, video (VHS), 102 min., color, English; OJ Productions, Lagos, 1999.

script of the video film, calling attention to a range of topical issues. Cast mostly in the combined form of television reportage and the soap opera/revision serial, the video film draws its themes and subject matter from the streets of the city. This is a point that Kenneth Nnebue emphasizes in an interview for a documentary on the development of Nigerian cinema made by Hyginus Ekwuazi. Asked why the video film is full of gory details about sexual murders, Nnebue stated simply: "we get these stories from the people and from the daily press."[50] Nnebue's video films are his response to the anxiety created by the city. The authorial voice questions the new morality of the city, knowing full well that the actions of the characters are determined by a capricious reality. If *Glamour Girls* tells us about "free" women in the "free" territory of the city, *Rituals* takes us to another theater in which the "occult economy" is glorified and consumed.

The moral subtext of the video film constructed around the spectacle of the city becomes a full-blown discourse in the hallelujah video film, which dramatizes the need for redemption of the lost souls of the city through a return to God and surreptitiously calls on the faithful to donate money and other forms of wealth in his service. Some scholars of new religions in Africa have called this the "prosperity gospel."[51] The principal actors in this drama are still confined to the city, most of them rich and able to dip into deep pockets for the worship of God. Unlike the free women of the city video, who are not much concerned with the Holy Book, characters of the hallelujah video are treated to vivid and frightening evocations of their spiritual vacuity and its consequences, in much the same way as hell and heaven are portrayed in *The Pilgrim's Progress*. Helen Ukpabio's *End of the Wicked* is an example of such a video film.[52] Nnebue investigates the "prosperity gospel" in a critical manner in *Endtime*, which questions the intentions of the new churches and, at various points in the narrative, exposes the shamanism of the enterprise.[53] By creating a critical space for the discussion of its own operation, the video film industry can claim to also be self-critical. Through this critical posture, the video film also provides a critical stop on the city, so that it would not be entirely true to say that it merely glamourizes the social life offered by the city.

50 *Pioneers*, a documentary film by Hyginus Ekwuazi, the managing director of the Nigerian Film Corporation, can be located in the Archives of the Nigerian Film School, Jos, Nigeria. In this interview, Nnebue is unequivocal about the *truthness* of the content of his video films vis-à-vis social reality in contemporary Nigeria. He is of the opinion that the audience primarily dictates the themes of the video film.
51 I first heard this phase from the scholar of religion Afe Adogame. This phenomenon is also referred to in Comaroff, "Millennial Capitalism."
52 *End of the Wicked*, video (VHS), 100 min., color, English; script by Helen Ukpabio, Liberty Foundation Gospel Church Production, Calabar, Nigeria, 1999.
53 *Endtime*, video (VHS), 120 min., color, English; script by Kenneth Nnebue, produced by NEK Video Links, Lagos, 1999.

On the other hand, the epic video film is a whimsical return to a past that is not fully represented because of inadequate knowledge. Overwhelmingly mediated by the power and influence of the city, this return can be uncritical, even conservative. But the epic's confused gaze is offset by the vivacity of its spectacular costume and locale, some of which recall the anthropological films of Africanists of the Herskovits generation. In the epic as well as the other types of video film considered in this essay, the confused vision of the postcolonial inscribes itself in the form and the narrative content, so that its discourse is not always a progressive one. *Igodo: Land of the Living Dead* is a typical example. The ultimate point in all three emerging genres of the video film is that the city sits heavily on their narrative and, for this reason, they all display attempts at the "grassroots globalization" that seeks to free the local from the incongruities of the global. These video films "intensify the presence, image and prospects of local actors"[54] by dramatizing postcolonial consciousness itself, to paraphrase Raymond Williams.[55]

From all of this, then, it is possible to see the video film as a complex flow of exchange and myth-making in which video filmmakers appropriate stories from social documents such as the newspaper, radio, television, and rumor mills and rewrite them into the peculiar art of the video film. Video narratives so produced then assume a life of their own, informing actions in the street. These actions are then recycled into the texts of new video films. Consumed in the domestic spaces and "video parlors" of rural and poor neighborhoods, the home video film places into circulation desires that go beyond the economics of the local poor. The role of the city, as I have shown, is crucial.

The Lagos of these video films is a city suffering the hardships peculiar to many postcolonies. The anxieties that it expresses through the actions of its inmates elaborately affirm the complex geography of this postcolony. Compelled by urban pressures and forced to engage in a frenzied global consumerism, video characters – like their real-life counterparts – simply flounder in the whirlpool of global tides.

The Nigerian home video phenomenon, one of the many cultural forms that have responded to these anxieties, forcefully calls our attention to the local and dramatizes its actions against the backdrop of the global. Lagos, like other cities in Africa, is still ANXIOUS. Video films merely replicate this condition. For this reason, the video film constitutes an important type of social chronicle of the city and its inhabitants.

---

54 Barber and Waterman, "Traversing the Global and the Local," p. 2.
55 See Raymond Williams, *Television: Technology and Cultural Form* (New York: Schocken, 1975).

Urban Processes and Change in Africa

The Production of the City and Urban Informalities: The Borough of Thiaroye-sur-mer in the City of Pikine, Senegal

Mohamadou Abdoul

The Concept-city is decaying. Does that mean that the illness afflicting both the rationality that founded it and its professionals afflicts the urban populations as well? Perhaps cities are deteriorating along with the procedures that organized them.

Michel de Certeau[1]

Informality and the Production of the City   In the many publications about the African city, the factors of ever-growing urbanization and ever-deepening poverty – indeed, a constantly accelerating pauperization – are often pinpointed to such a degree they begin to seem solely responsible for bringing the urban crisis to its current acute level.

There is no doubt that urbanization is one of the most remarkable revolutions Africa has witnessed in recent years. The phenomenon has been characterized as "out of control and anarchic." Most often paired with demographic growth, urbanization is considered to be the essential factor aggravating the urban crisis, which takes such forms as unemployment, lack of housing, rampant poverty, environmental degradation, weak – or absent – social services, and the inadequacies, negligence, or incompetence of the state and its organs.

True to this reading of the urban African context, a substantial number of studies have focused on the problem of sustainable development and the struggle against poverty.[2] These are in turn supported by an epistemology of normative action (on the part of governments and municipalities) or alternatives (on

---

1 Michel de Certeau, *The Practice of Everyday Life*, trans. Steven F. Randall (Berkeley: University of California Press, 1984), p. 95.
2 Within the formidable body of literature on the subject, some characteristic publications are: Richard E. Stren, Rodney R. White, and Michel Coquery, eds., *Villes africaines en crise: Gérer la croissance urbaine au sud du Sahara: Côte d'Ivoire, Kenya, Nigeria, Soudan, Sénégal, Tanzania, Zaïre* (Paris: L'Harmattan, 1993); Annick Osmont, *La Banque mondiale et les villes: Du développement à l'ajustement* (Paris: Karthala, 1995); ISTED (Institut des Sciences et des Techniques de l'Équipement et de l'Environnement pour le Développement), Working Group on the Mechanisms and Logic of Urbanization, *Dynamique de l'urbanisation de l'Afrique au sud du Sahara: Dans les pays du champ de la Coopération française*, presented to the French Ministry of Cooperation (Order Number 900373) on March 27, 1995. For cases specific to Senegal, this tendency is reflected in the following studies: A. Sané, *Étude monographique de Pikine* (Dakar: Enda–Programme Développement Social Urbain et Coopération Nord-Sud, September 1996); Salimata Wade, *La dynamique associative en milieu urbain ouest africain, synthèse régionale* (Dakar: Enda–Programme Régional de Formation et d'Appui aux Associations Locales et Initiatives de Base en Milieu Urban Ouest Africain, 1999); Momar Coumba Diop, *La lutte contre la pauvreté à Dakar: Vers la définition d'une politique municipale* (Accra: Programme de Gestion Urbaine, Bureau Régional pour l'Afrique, 1996).

the part of nongovernmental organizations [NGOs], community organizations, economic interest groups [EIGs], and so forth). A number of problems are analyzed according to this perspective. They are related to urban administration (citizenship, decentralization, participation, good governance); urban infrastructure and services (water, electricity, roads, sanitation, education, health, transportation, housing, and so on); and exclusions, marginalities, and forms of deviance (such as crime, violence, prostitution, drugs). Because of the gravity of the symptoms – whether or not they are actually linked to these causes – all are agreed that there is, indeed, an urban crisis and that action is urgently needed. Recommendations, when given, are mostly concerned with elaborating programs and projects of a strongly technocratic character. A few actors (the state, administrative services, associative structures, NGOs, and so forth) are called on to administer, either separately or together, the conception, elaboration, and implementation of whatever project or program is under discussion.

As a result, the elucidation of real processes and dynamics sometimes finds itself reduced or even conjured away. There is a failure to recognize the complexity of the transformations at work in African urban contexts, and particularly their historical depth. As René de Maximy has rightly remarked, the "urban crisis," or "poverty," type of analysis, whether structural or conceptual, is based, in effect, on a theoretical stance, one that is supported by an eminently normative and remedial course of action. Moreover, he writes (with much timeliness), "to speak of an urban crisis is not innocent. It suggests that the phenomenon is fleeting and therefore that the decisions required will be a function of this particular state of malaise or unhappiness."[3]

This crisis, as real and as deep as it is, is no less a crisis of theory and practice. As such, it is based on the problematic of regulating and/or regularizing those aspects of urban life that might be called informal, spontaneous, irregular, and illegal. The terminology of this regulating/regularizing discourse is generally shaped by the economist, the political scientist, the civil engineer, and the urban planner, all of whom find in it the explanation for the urban crisis and the justification for interventions that restrict or repress so-called informal activities.

Now, if such an approach to informality is reductive, it is indeed a sort of approach that envisions the dynamics of informality exclusively in the following terms: revenue generation; research into ways to better living conditions; the connections between the informal and so-called formal sectors, or between the informal sector and the state. But it is necessary to enlarge this perspective. To do so requires going beyond a normative and legalistic vision and embracing a

---

3 René de Maximy, *Le commun des lieux* (Sprimont, Belgium: Margada; Paris: Institut de Recherche pour le Développement, 2000), p. 47.

constellation of phenomena whose combined effects accelerate the changes shaping urban African contexts. To merely *describe* these phenomena is not to *explain* all of the dynamics involved. Their effects on populations and, above all, the reactions of the populations to their impact form an essential – and insufficiently analyzed – aspect. Anyone who wishes to elucidate the transformative processes at work in African urbanity must take them into account.

These changes clearly point to the notion of confluence between state regulations/controls and social dynamics, whether of a political, economic, land-related, or other nature. What we call "informality" is derived from the tension between these two poles, their coexistence and connections. Understood in this sense, the concept is one and the same with the process of urbanization. It is the lever by which the city is made. Urban transformations are conceived here as part of the evolution of this duality, of the combined course and interrelations of these two poles.

The category of informality is inscribed in Africa's political, economic, and social history – informal premises and characteristics were discernible in pre-colonial African cities, perpetuated and consolidated during the colonial period, and have developed – and finally exploded – in the postcolonial period, notably within the residential, social, and professional dimensions.[4] Seen from a historical perspective, the processes of urban change may be analyzed within the political order, that is, within social and cultural forms of organization. Informality is rooted, therefore, in the long-term. It translates, moreover, into a tension among phenomena that reveal what is regulated by a state entity and what escapes that regulation.

The concept of informality simultaneously reveals social frameworks, the construction of the state, and the regular changes taking place within the structures and natures of powers.[5] This makes it a pertinent category through which to examine urban transformations. It permits us to take into account the complexities of an evolving process, a set of interactions not only among actors, nature, and the object of their actions, but also the stakes and strategies that they employ in constructing a form of urbanity that is as animated by the formal sector as it is by the informal sector. Informality also presupposes an analysis of the articulations of this space through the ever-larger circles that influence it in one way or another. In sum, informality has an eminently political function. It is a relation to power that, through actors and structures, brings together

---

4 See Catherine Coquery-Vidrovitch, "L'informel dans les villes africaines: Essai d'analyse historique et sociale," in *Tiers-monde: L'informel en question?*, ed. Catherine Coquery-Vidrovitch and Serge Nédelec (Paris: L'Harmattan, 1991), pp. 171–196.

5 See René Gallissot, "Société formelle ou organique et société informelle," in ibid., p. 21.

registers and resources that provide individual or collective opportunities to give direction to lives.

This text proposes to study this interaction and these informalities. It is here that urban transformations reveal themselves in all their singularity. The problematic is based on an analysis of the modes of (re)configuring space, the social connections and networks of relations that ultimately regulate the process of politics and economics, and the appropriation and use of space. It takes into account the diversity and variety of initiatives and actions at the heart of the flows that traverse and animate the urban body. Social and institutional organs and corporations of complementary, or even contradictory, interest form the web of this flux according to constructions that are sometimes planned, organized, and negotiated but are just as often unpredictable and fortuitous. This approach conceives of urban establishments according to a double perspective: on the one hand, we examine the modes of production and decision makers and, on the other, we seek out the role of those local social actors who develop popular initiatives and strategies (individual or collective). For these, too, though they are certainly responses to multiple facets of the urban crisis, are also a mode of constructing and reproducing the city.

This study will emphasize the observation of urban changes in their spatial and economic dimensions and their connection to politics. This perspective is perfectly illustrated by the case of the Senegalese borough of Thiaroye-sur-mer and one of its neighborhoods, Santhiaba. Here one can see urban changes in correlation with the construction of space. Here one can observe how a condition of informality is connected to a process of urbanization as well as to the power relations between different authorities and different forms of legitimacy.

The Production of Space: Urbanization, the Stakes of Property, and the Stakes of Power Santhiaba is a neighborhood in the borough of Thiaroye-sur-mer, which itself is part of the city of Pikine. The latter was constituted in 1952 as part of the expanded zone of the national capital, Dakar.[6] Pikine was established as an autonomous city in September 1996 and consists of 16 boroughs

---

6 For more information on Dakar, see the descriptive summary in Roger Navarro, "'Irrégularité urbaine' et génèse d'africanité urbaine au Cap Vert (Sénégal, Pikine)," in ibid., pp. 215–237. See, in particular, the section entitled "Histoire de l'urbanisation du Cap Vert et genèse de l'urbanité africaine," in which the author highlights the different phases of this urbanization in relation to the incorporation of Lebou villages into the urban territory.
Today Dakar, capital of Senegal, covers less than one percent of the country's total area, which is 196,722 km². Located on Africa's westernmost point, Dakar's geopolitical position is strategic. Since September 1996, the capital region has consisted of four municipalities (Dakar, Pikine, Guédiawaye, and Rufisque). To facilitate administration based on proximity, these cities are subdivided

(*communes d'arrondisement*). Although it is still strongly linked to Dakar's urban agglomeration, this new city is also characterized by its own specific dynamics and problems. Several factors make Pikine a unique observatory for examining the current phenomenon of urban transformation: its strong rate of demographic growth, the overpopulation of its neighborhoods, the considerable rate of unemployment, several very specific environmental problems (such as pollution along the coast, periodic flooding in certain zones, and an inadequate sanitation system), and the recent increase in violence and security concerns. Equally interesting are the multiplicity of popular responses regarding the administration of public services, employment, the environment, and so forth.[7]

The territory of the borough of Thiaroye-sur-mer is estimated by the authorities to be about three square kilometers. It is a small area squeezed between the coast and National Route 1, which connects the Senegalese capital to the rest of the country. It is bordered by the boroughs of Tivaouane Diacksao and Guinaw Rail to the north; by Diamaguene-SICAP Mbao to the east; and by Daliford to the west. Thiaroye-sur-mer is bordered to the south by the Atlantic Ocean. Situated on Dakar's periphery along the southern coast of the Cape Verde peninsula, the community was originally a traditional village inhabited by Lebou farmer-fishermen.[8] Like other villages of the same type, Thiaroye-sur-mer was gradually integrated by the process of urbanization.

The borough's already reduced space is symbolic of the encroachment of urban territory onto the Cape Verde peninsula in general and the city of Pikine in particular. It illustrates increasing population density in the peripheral zones of Pikine. Due to natural growth as well as the progressive arrival of populations from rural areas, parts of Dakar, and other boroughs of Pikine, residential space in Thiaroye-sur-mer is disappearing. In 1998, the zone had an average density of 14,538 people per square kilometer. This gives a very precise sense of the tremendous demographic pressure on the space. According to the most recent census (1988), Thiaroye-sur-mer counted 30,290 inhabitants, distributed in

---

into boroughs (*communes d'arrondisement*). There are 19 in Dakar, 16 in Pikine, 5 in Guédiawaye, and 3 in Rufisque. Demographically, the population of Senegal was estimated in 1995 to be 7,884,257 inhabitants. The urban community of Dakar, including all four cities, has a population of 1,659,514 (21 percent of the total), of which 795,969 (48 percent) are men and 863,545 (52 percent) are women.

7 Pikine experienced two large-scale demographic influxes beginning in the 1970s: the arrival of populations that had been forced out – often by the military – of Dakar's working-class neighborhoods and shantytowns, and the arrival of people caught up in the rural exodus. The latter contributed considerably to the city's growth during the 1970s and '80s. Today the city of Pikine is said to have close to a million inhabitants, distributed over an area of about 80 km².

8 The Lebou people were the first occupants of Senegal's Cape Verde peninsula. The 14 villages they inhabited constituted the "Republic of Lebou."

1,934 compounds (called concessions),[9] or 3,181 households. There were 15,194 men and 15,096 women. A projection made in November 1998 based on these figures estimated a total of 40,700 inhabitants. This population growth has spurred a rapid expansion of built space imposed on grounds previously used for market gardening of vegetables *(maraîchage)*. This has greatly raised the stakes connected to issues of access to and control of real estate and buildings as well as the informal practices that support them.

In this district, the production of space is at the heart of the process of urban change. The gradual taking over of space shows a neighborhood in which the multiple uses of the terrain give it a texture characterized by a dynamic of complementary and antagonistic interactions among different actors. Most notable among the modalities of this dynamic are strategies to accumulate income from land and buildings. The stakes for control over a territory illuminate the forms of informality that support and, to a certain extent, dictate the management of land patrimony.

From an initial rural, village configuration, Thiaroye-sur-mer is taking on an increasingly urban, working-class character. The initial residential core, situated on a sandy elevation along the shore, still retains the characteristics of village spatial structure, even if the construction materials are more durable today than they once were. But the buildings in this original core are now considerably denser, without empty plots along the narrow winding roads. Dwellings are arranged according to concessions (or compounds), and extended families now live in extremely close quarters; the situation has changed from one in which a single family made up the concession to one in which some ten families (some of whom share no family ties whatsoever) live together within the same compound. Thus, urbanization – that is, the incorporation of Thiaroye-sur-mer in the urbanizing process – has modified the mode of inhabiting residential space and disarticulated traditional social and familial forms of organization.

Over the years, the inhabited area has grown increasingly dense. This has necessitated an acceleration of movement and extension northward to the neighborhood Santhiaba, where there is still some open space. But in fact, the process of expansion dates back to the colonial period, when the space of the city was extended in order to meet needs that were simultaneously residential, industrial, administrative, and related to social services.

---

9 Concessions are dwelling units characterized by the grouping of the extended family around the dwelling of the family chief. The chief directs the whole social and economic life of the family; he determines roles and tasks, and orders and assigns resources.

Spatial Expansion   The first encroachment of habitation on fields used for agriculture dates to around 1939. Since then, such expansions have taken place at closer and closer intervals. Thus, in 1953, 1955, and the years that followed, lands were broken up into smaller and smaller parcels in order for owners to set up family members or, under straitened circumstances, to sell to third parties, always called "foreigners." It was, in fact, only at the beginning of the 1980s that the expansion of Thiaroye-sur-mer began to attract inhabitants who came from zones beyond Thiaroye-sur-mer itself. Thus, at an ever-growing rate, areas often ill suited to habitation – low grounds, drained marshes, and agricultural lands – have been reclaimed. In Thiaroye-sur-mer, this mode of creating urban space is the form of informality par excellence in matters of building and real estate.

In addition to lands used for habitation, areas have been ceded to industry. Land transfers are executed by sale or by tacit contracts granting employment priority to the inhabitants of Thiaroye-sur-mer. Thus, a shoe factory was set up (SOFAC, sold to Lebanese nationals), along with industrial complexes for textiles (ICOTAF, SOTIMA), the conservation and processing of fish products (CAP VERT, later COTONNIERE), and a matchstick factory (CAFAL). A large number of people, today in retirement, have worked in these operations. The establishment of industries occurred after negotiations in which the residents of Thiaroye-sur-mer stipulated that they be given priority in recruitment of the workforce. This was granted in most cases. The workforce in the industrial complexes is largely furnished by the men of Thiaroye-sur-mer, who abandon market gardening at about the same rate as the space available for agriculture shrinks. Much like the spread of built space, salaried work has served as a mechanism for the urban integration of the community, which adopts the life rhythms required by the modern economic enterprise's model of organization (with its fixed hours and the monthly posting of salaries).

The production of space here also concerns the borough's relationship with the state, which has, since the colonial era, set up amenities and services on traditional familial lands. The progressive installation of amenities and social services in Thiaroye-sur-mer – for the most part in Santhiaba but serving the entire borough – is thus one element that integrates this space into the irreversible process of urbanization.

The national route, the principal, indeed sole, land mode of entry to the Cape Verde peninsula, reached Thiaroye-sur-mer in 1924. The route reinforces the borough's connection to the rest of the city. The first school was established there in 1927 near the fields of the Mbayène family. Thiaroye-sur-mer's first health clinic was set up within the school compound. It would later be moved onto land owned by a village family, the Diobènes, who consented after a certain amount of opposition. Electricity reached homes in 1953/54, along with public water pumps.

The effort to provide amenities and social services – synonymous with urbanization – did not, however, progress without a certain amount of conflict with the colonial administration. The latter pressured the customary local authorities to reduce social conflicts and facilitate negotiations between public powers and customary owners. Throughout the colonial period, there were violent conflicts in which control of lands was mixed with political competitions. These continue to nurture animosities among certain families even today.[10]

Generally, however, since the time that certain facilities were provided to the residents of Thiaroye-sur-mer, the objections of customary landowners were negotiated by the authorities and political figures who had some influence with residents. This process of dialogue and negotiation with customary landowners stemmed from a tacit recognition by the colonial powers of the rights of the Lebou people to the Cape Verde peninsula.[11] Moreover, during this time, the landowners still had some real estate reserves at their disposal. But as quickly as the population grew, the needs for residential space as well as for basic social services continued to make themselves felt.

The massive influx of rural peoples, pushed off their land toward Pikine by drought during the 1970s, threatened to fully saturate the area. This created a double movement in the adaptation of space. While public powers continued efforts to provide amenities, traditional landowners became active in selling and/or building on agricultural lands.

A health center was constructed in 1995, financed by the World Bank. A birth clinic, built in 1989, did not in fact begin operating until four years later, due to lack of personnel and sanitary equipment. In addition to a health infrastructure, during this period Santhiaba housed structures for public, private, and professional education: two public primary schools, a Franco-Arab school, a private school, and a technical training center for women. A youth and cultural center was built in 1981 on lands of the Démène family. It should also be noted

---

10 Residents are reluctant to describe the details of these land conflicts because they are connected to the political struggles that took place on the national level between Léopold Senghor and Lamine Guèye over representation in the National Assembly.

11 The colonizer required the relocation (with indemnification) of villages situated in areas affected by its urban plans. Thus, between 1858 and 1914, Dakar's first urban plan (known as the Pinet-Laprade plan) required the relocation of the villages of Kaye, Tann, N'Garaf, Thérigne, and Hock, among others, in order to create the area that today makes up the city center (Dakar Plateau). The Lebou people did not, in any case, fail to take advantage of the statute of citizens, which entitled them to residence in the four communes and preserved their customary land rights.

that Santhiaba[12] has a large mosque, a Muslim cemetery, and several public spaces that, though laid out, are not maintained and are therefore in an advanced state of disrepair.

The Assault of Built Space on Urban Market Gardening   This zone is also one in which market-scale vegetable farming had developed, with an essential economic function, even if today it only consists of a few hectares. The cultivated zone plays a role in provisioning legumes to a large portion of Thiaroye-sur-mer's population, along with that of the surrounding boroughs. Indeed, it ensures the existence of entire families. Roger Navarro, describing the perimeter of his area of study – Guinaw Rail, an irregular district of Pikine that joins Santhiaba to the north, across the national route – writes the following:

> On the southern coast of the Cape Verde isthmus, Genaw-Rails (which means "behind the Rails" in the Wolof language) faces the village of Thiaroye-Guej (Thiaroye-mer). From these heights, as far as the Rufisque route [the national route], one can easily see the quarter's southern edge. The area gives a double impression. First one sees the Cape Verde's great market garden, known as "the Niayes." These gardens, shaded by sparse stands of palm trees are tended by the Lébou of Thiaroye-mer, a people of fishermen who traditionally own the lands of the Cape Verde. Right next to this agricultural zone the terrain looks like a vast construction site. A number of buildings are being built here (in permanent materials). Masons are busy everywhere; piles of "bricks" (that is, bits of rubble made of sand mixed with cement and baked in the sun) mark the appropriation of parcels and clearly signal the projects of their owners for all to see.[13]

Since construction is, at this point, more profitable than agriculture, farmers are gradually losing their primary source of revenue and means of subsistence as houses are erected on spaces that they once used. In a dozen years, the total area devoted to vegetable farming has been cut in half. Based on the current pace of construction, urban market gardening will disappear entirely from the zone within a few years. Faced with this threat, the farmers took the collective initiative of forming an Economic Interest Group (EIG)[14] with the goal, first, of pre-

---

12 Santhiaba is one of twenty neighborhoods in the borough of Thiaroye-sur-mer. Its population is about 3,000 and is made up of several ethnic groups. The preponderant group is that of the Wolof/Lebou (66.66 percent). The population is 50.54 percent male and 49.46 percent female, and 99.99 percent Muslim. Women make up 27.34 percent of all heads of households.
13 Navarro, "Irrégularité urbaine," p. 216.
14 The Economic Interest Group (EIG), according to Law 85–40 of July 29, 1985, basically offers a legal framework that is very well suited to the exercise of economic activities of the association type, which is in any case one of its primary conditions. It entails the constitution of a group of

serving and maintaining their livelihoods and, second, of mutually reinforcing their opposition to the spread of the construction. The speed at which these activities have developed indicates the enormous stakes connected to the land, particularly to the bitter struggles (a dialogue of the deaf) taking place in the entire low-ground known as "the Niayes" among traditional proprietors, municipal authorities, representatives of the national lands, farmers, building developers, and so forth. These actors have all developed strategies for appropriating or conserving the property. Such strategies appear to be a consequence, according to the actors, of legal procedures, informal measures, or even a combination of both. Mamadou Diouf accurately sums up the situation:

> Urban morphology, in many situations, seems to be produced by an architecture in which the most dynamic element is a "recomposition" of one's identity or ethnicity in order to appropriate land. Such recompositions often entail plural forms of logic, which have, as their outcome, requests for different land-related systems. The resulting superposition of systems and extremely heterogeneous forms of appropriation have had consequences not only for urban morphology but also for social relations and networks of solidarity.[15]

The superimposition of rights (per Law 64–46 of June 17, 1964 regarding the national state territory[16] and the customary land rights of the initial occupants) and the designs of public powers in general and municipal authorities in particular incited the customary owners to construct on their lands and/or to sell parcels to third parties. Third parties come from other zones of Dakar's agglomeration in search of reasonably priced rents and real estate properties. At a distance of twelve kilometers from Dakar, Thiaroye-sur-mer is one of the city's closest peripheral zones. As Navarro describes it, "each day, construction gnaws away at more of the agricultural lands. This situation of rapid urbanization is typical of the entire zone of Pikine. Furthermore, in the other neighborhoods, the 'buildable' spaces are already saturated."[17]

Thus in this zone of expansion, in the neighborhood of Santhiaba, the construction of dwellings for rental use pleases the customary owners as well as

---

two or more (physical or moral) entities intended to facilitate or develop the economic activity of its members or to improve or increase the product of this activity.

15 Mamadou Diouf, "La société civile en Afrique: Histoire et actualité, notes provisoires," in *Proceedings of the Ninth General Assembly of CODESRIA: Globalization and Social Sciences in Africa, December 14–18, 1998* (Dakar: CODESRIA, 1998), pp. 19–20.

16 This law stipulates that unregistered lands and lands on which no clear proof of use (agriculture and construction) exists belong to the domain of the state.

17 Navarro, "Irrégularité urbaine, p. 216.

increasing numbers of "outside" proprietors. We are confronted here with an entirely new situation. The question of real estate is doubled by a booming construction economy.[18] The customary owner, once a territorial chief in charge of distributing land resources according to the family's needs for subsistence agriculture, has transformed himself into a real estate developer who sells parcels in exchange for cash.[19] We are far from the 1950s and the way customary authorities granted parcels of Thiaroye-sur-mer's old familial lands during that era.

This situation has engendered latent, occasionally open, conflict between customary owners and municipal officials. Beyond issues of land access and control of land-related resources, this involves a confrontation of two types of legitimacy and legality. The municipality wants to enhance the value of a portion of these lands in order to resell the parcels at a substantially higher price. It also wants to implant a socio-educational project: in one case, a high school and municipal sports complex. The customary landowners, farmers, and new residents of the zone tend, rather, to see this as a threat to their property and building rights. Numerous meetings between the different parties were cut short. The strong resistance of the inhabitants of Thiaroye-sur-mer eventually forced the city to seek another location for its high school. The customary landowners and the customary authorities – who are often one and the same – adopt different strategies according to the circumstances. They even mobilized Thiaroye-sur-mer's residents to petition for customary rights to portions of the Niayes zone that are in fact situated beyond the district's borders. To this end, a petition was circulated and the services of a lawyer (of Lebou ethnicity) were solicited.

But the most popular strategy is that of the fait accompli: a building is erected on the ground in question. Construction sites are constantly in progress. Some, though begun years ago, show no signs of reaching completion. In fact, a sizable portion of the built space in this zone is uninhabitable because of regular flooding in the rainy season and a very shallow water table. Stagnant waters invade the houses year round. Rather than habitation, the customary owners are aiming at a strategy of marking their territory. For it is this act of construction – more than a property title – that is the surest means of appropriating a space. At the time this text was prepared, these structures remained standing, in spite of a recent campaign to demolish illegal buildings in the urban areas of Cape Verde. It is unclear, however, whether they will escape demolition efforts in the future.

---

18 For a comparison with other situations, see Patrick Canel, Philippe Delis, and Christian Girard, *Construire la ville africaine: Chroniques du citadin promoteur* (Paris: Karthala, 1990). See the third chapter in particular: "Une appropriation conflictuelle du sol urbain," pp. 37–60.

19 See Michel Coquery, "Secteur informel et production de l'espace urbanisé en Afrique," in *Tiers-monde*, pp. 197–213.

The production of space and the phenomenon of urban expansion are, of course, normal to a city's evolution. However, to approach the phenomenon of urbanization through the conceptual framework of pure spatial geography – that is, the material configuration of space – yields very little and masks its complexity. To read this complexity requires putting into place a certain triptych consisting of perceived space, conceived space, and the lived spaces of representation.[20] In sum, it requires going beyond materiality and joining to it the different cultural, religious, and political imaginaries that shape one another.[21] Such a perspective permits us to clarify the behavior of actors in competition for an urban milieu in which contradictory interests carry the potential of enormous violence. But more fundamentally, it also shows the relationships of force that exist between legal and informal procedures that draw their legitimacy from historical and traditional points of reference. Such points of reference still have enormous influence within urban African contexts, even if – from a social, cultural, and economic point of view – they have undergone substantial change.

Beyond issues of access to and control of lands, there is the question of the confrontation of two political imaginaries, of two types of legitimate authority. This fundamental aspect of Thiaroye-sur-mer's life and relations is even more pronounced in the exercise of local power.

Local Power: Dual Forms of Territorial Legitimacy   The heritage of the traditional village survives in Thiaroye-sur-mer's forms of organization and traditional modes of decision making. These are specific to the Lebou people. Its sociopolitical organization is that of a gerontocracy; social, parental, and familial connections are very tight; and communal identity is strong. This structuring of political and social organization is the foundation of a vigorous political imaginary existing alongside communal authority.

Although Thiaroye-sur-mer has been completely integrated into the city of Pikine and has lost nearly all of its rural character, its inhabitants continue to consider it and to call it a village. Achille Mbembe calls this attitude the "re-

---

20 See Nick Oatley, "L'apparition de l'Edge (of) City: Quels mots pour les 'nouveaux' espaces urbains?" in *Nommer les nouveaux territoires urbains*, ed. Hélène Rivière d'Arc (Paris: UNESCO, Éditions de la Maison des Sciences de l'Homme, 2001), p. 19.
21 See the well-documented thesis by Cheikh Guèye on the holy city of Touba. This describes in great detail how the production of space by "urbanizing dervishes" shapes urbanization around the axis of symbolic representation. It also constructs a form of allegiance that includes the representatives of the state in religious powers. Cheikh Guèye, "L'organisation de l'espace dans une ville religieuse: Touba (Sénégal)," Doctoral thesis, Louis Pasteur University, Strasbourg, 1999.

enchantment of tradition,"[22] that is, the invention of a collective imaginary that constructs itself from the referents found in communitarian discourse, beginning with the two poles: on the one hand, the "rehabilitation of origins and of belonging," on the other, the reclaiming/appropriation of territory (upon which identity construction is founded and legitimates itself). This phenomenon of reinventing tradition finds its embodiment in Thiaroye-sur-mer in the constitution of a local political authority and an "administrative" net for the territory.

Thiaroye-sur-mer has a council of notables presided over by the village chief. Each council member carries a membership card. This authority installed a twenty-four–member executive organ, created in 1991, called the Association des Freys, which replaced another structure, the Até Togne (a type of tribunal). It also named five representatives and a neighborhood chief to each of the borough's twenty neighborhoods. The council of notables is influenced by the Collective of Imams and two dignitaries, the president of the Diambours and the representative of the Caliph of the Mourides.

The role of the council of notables is to manage "all the customary and religious problems of the village, in close collaboration with the borough." Its organs execute its decisions. It decides everything from the ordering of family ceremonies, the prohibition of music and tam-tam playing during the winter period, and neighborhood security, to the carrying out of measures concerning urban planning and renovation as well as other matters. The council has the right to seize "competent authorities" if its decisions are not respected.

In reality, the customary powers of Thiaroye-sur-mer dictate the whole life of relations in the community. The president of the Freys attests to this when he comments, "everything that enters Thiaroye-sur-mer passes before the Freys, and so does everything that leaves it." The decisions, initiatives, and actions of the customary authorities are irreversible.

The reified notion of the village is an eminently political category, a category that subsumes a space and its human and material components under a legitimate authority. Those who possess this authority "naturally" assume their role of administering the community's destiny. Thus, superimposed on an urban space, we see a territorial identity that legitimates a local particularism, even if the configuration of space shows the strong presence of "non-native populations" and a highly visible cosmopolitanism. This opens the way to exclusivist practices and/or attitudes that have obvious political and cultural foundations.

The customary and religious authorities have thus inherited the legacy of a political organization of the village type that, even if it is no longer what it once

---

22 Achille Mbembe, "À propos des écritures africaines de soi," *Bulletin du CODESRIA*, no. 1 (2000), p. 15.

was, continues to leave a marked impression on the decision-making process. Traditional political actors maintain their important roles while continuing to give themselves carefully structured powers of decision, in addition to efficient channels of communication and information. This situation is made possible by upholding a symbolic system of origins and belonging, and through identity construction that is manifested in territorial control. At the same time, it must be said that this authority adopts a modern vocabulary and positions itself theoretically as a structure that pressures municipal and administrative authorities; the council of notables meets as a "General Assembly," keeps "minutes" of its meetings, endows itself with an "Association," and furnishes its members with "membership cards."

On the other hand, the notables also declare their willingness to cooperate with the city and act as police for the population on behalf of "competent authorities." It is here that the ambiguity of the council's position becomes clear, not to mention the ambiguity of its relationship to the local administration. One example is the ban on festive noisemaking during the winter period. This law was devised by the notables, but it was the administrative authority – the prefect – who signed the measure. The example attests to the dominance of traditional authorities over the population but also their strong capacity to influence the decisions taken by local administrators. Control over the territory is real.[23] Following the example of urban processes instituted in the boroughs of Tivaouane and Guéoul,[24] Thiaroye-sur-mer's traditional leaders demonstrated a desire to exert more influence in matters of local government. The production of space is, in this framework, a political trump card that depends on the convocation of symbolic resources and history. These come together to legitimate and concretize the valorization of the ground.

Although it is a country with a long tradition of decentralization, Senegal in 1996 instituted a major reform in the name of regionalization. The reform created, among other things, the borough system. The lowest administrative sphere is thus set up as a local collectivity endowed with its own financial, human, and technical resources. By transferring a portion of its prerogatives to this sphere,

---

23 The central importance of controlling space as a means of influencing politics on the local level is abundantly illustrated in several studies. On Salé, Morocco, for example, see Abdelghani Abouhani, *Pouvoirs, villes et notabilités locales: Quant les notables font la ville* (Morocco: URBAMA [Urbanisation du Monde Arabe], n.d). But in contrast to Thiaroye-sur-mer and other Lebou territories on the Cape Verde peninsula, the situation in Salé, Morocco does not consist of a confrontation between local notables and municipal authorities. Rather, the municipal council is itself controlled by the notables, who take advantage of their positions to preserve and consolidate their own land interests and gain power.

24 See Oumar Sow, "Territorialités concurrentes et gouvernance des villes: Les enseignements des petits et moyennes villes du Vieux Bassin arachidier au Sénégal," unpublished paper, p. 3.

the central power of the state seeks to reinforce its powers of intervention, most notably concerning local needs such as the allocation of public services and the efficient, optimal regulation of space. Territorial control is exerted by a municipal council and its various organs. Its legitimacy stems from the devolution of authority from the central level (the state) to the local level (local collectivities). Its political base is a territory within which the bearers of this power – who are elected – enjoy the exercise of public power.

The borough of Thiaroye-sur-mer was created by the 1996 law on decentralization. Its municipal council consists of thirty-six members, six of whom are women. Its members come from three political parties: And Jëf/African Party for Democracy and Socialism (And Jëf PADS, two members), the Socialist Party (PS, six members), and the Senegalese Democratic Party (PDS, twenty-eight members). The mayor and his two deputies form the cabinet. The secretary general manages, in addition to the borough's secretariat, four services: markets and marketplaces; general administration and finance; patrimony and civil records; and youth, sports, and leisure. The borough has set up ten commissions: finance; culture; youth, sports, and leisure; markets and marketplaces; planning; environment and fish-related resources; administration and legal affairs; education; health, population, and social programs; and management of territory and housing.

The adopted model of organization is geared toward the territory's successful administrative and operational management. By classifying the municipality's areas of responsibility according to sectors of activity, the model seeks to give the necessary organizational means to its mission of local development, making it efficient and effective. But its financial means and qualifications must be up to its ambitions. The borough's budget is proposed by the mayor, voted in by the municipal council, and approved by the sub-prefect, a representative of the state. In 1997, the borough's budget was 59,100,000 CFA francs, but only 16,166,511 CFA francs of the projected budget were covered (that is 15.73 percent). In 1998, the projected budget was 63,145,538 CFA francs, but the sub-prefect approved it at 57,531,289 CFA francs. Only 27 million CFA francs were covered on December 31, 1998. The borough system is new, and the municipal team lacks sufficient experience. Moreover, its human, material, and financial resources are still extremely limited when one considers not only its prerogatives for local development but also the diversity and complexity of problems it must solve.

The establishment of boroughs thus created a new pole of power, which necessarily comes into conflict with the already established traditional and religious authorities. Two forms of logic for territorial administration thus confront one another at the same time that they pursue dialogue. They agree on some aspects of local administration and diverge on others. Moreover, instances of political divergence and competition between political groups affects the relationships of local decision makers. At the same time, spaces and channels of collaboration exist and are being developed. The stakes of power emanate from this political duality. Such stakes make themselves clear in the course of Thiaroye-sur-mer's social, economic, political, and cultural life. The coexisting powers can each take advantage of a certain legitimacy that has its source in totally different registers. These sources of legitimacy are the recognition and influence of the people for whom decisions are made and with whom the activities are carried out.

These different powers are necessarily caught up in a logic of tolerance, complementarity, instrumentality, and mutual competition. Their dynamics thus influence, consciously or unconsciously, a specific construction of this environment, with the primary stake being a strong presence in public space at the heart of which the play of actors seems to open new perspectives on urban government and new horizons on the exercise of power. Nothing short of the stark process of redefining the cadres who control local public space is underway. Associations and networks play a crucial role in this dynamic.

Associations and Networks: An Informal Model of Construction and Urban Economy
Decentralization reveals a failure of the model of the central state. Lat Soucabé Mbow describes it in these terms:

> With the political and economic changes that began in 1981, a rupture between the state and the city has emerged from the policies practiced in the past three decades. After dominating the urban sphere with the help of a suffocating legal arsenal and the massive use of capital in development programs conceived and realized through its organs, the central power, confronted by multiple challenges, took to its heels. In doing this, it returned to the local collectivities and to the population their portion of responsibility in urban administration, in order to better ensure its functions of orientation, coordination, and control.[25]

In fact, the loosening of state control, via the injunction of international financial institutions and bilateral sponsors, opened public space to a tremendous development: the trend of setting up associations. This signified an extremely high ability to adapt to social and institutional constraints of the environment,

---

25 Lat Soucabé Mbow, "Les politiques urbaines: Gestion et aménagement," in *Sénégal, trajectoires d'un État*, ed. Momar Coumba Diop (Dakar: CODESRIA, 1992), p. 205.

which is itself in constant evolution.[26] The activities of these associations provide for the individual and collective needs of their members. They also serve, to an increasing degree, the municipality in sharing its functions of administration and the allocation of social services. Due to the legitimacy that they have acquired through their capacity to mobilize, associations "organize resistance and impose on establishments and public powers collaboration on the occupation of space."[27]

What can be drawn from these developments is a process of *autonomizing* economic initiatives. On the one hand, these take the forms of modes of municipal regulation and, on the other, of the regulation of public space. This autonomizing process is illustrated by the extraordinary development of practices of self-organization and investment of public space carried out by people who negotiate and take different tacks with public powers. In doing this, the populations are in the process of constructing "new imaginaries and new arenas of power."[28] They create new forms of solidarity and construct forms of citizenship that enable them, in their own way, to expropriate territory. This liberation of popular initiatives is even clearer in the economic domain and can be noted from the 1980s onward.

Neoliberal reforms have in fact strongly marked African economies and have not resolved the economic crisis – far from it. This persistent crisis has had as a main consequence the progressive development of an "informalization" of the modes and mechanisms of generating revenue. This is a constantly evolving urban phenomenon that has become massive. In this regard, it is the clearest manifestation of a certain type of structuring of economic activity in African cities.

Forms of economic informality in Thiaroye-sur-mer are substantial. These consist of activities connected to the fishing industry (men engaged in small fishing establishments, women in processing and selling fish), urban market gardening, commerce, artisan production, carpentry, auto repair, private telephone (calling) centers, car and hardware sales, a garage for stationing heavy loads, and so forth. A kernel of industrialization exists in the hand-fabrication of flagstones. A whole range of related activities may be added to those listed here, throughout the communal territory: water pumps (allegedly public, though one must in fact pay to use them), several retail shops of the Mauritanian type (based on proximity), small markets for retail sales, and so forth.

---

26 See Abdoulaye Niang, "Les associations en milieu urbain dakarois: Classification et capacités développantes," *Afrique et Développement* 25, no. 1–2 (2000), pp. 99–159.
27 Diouf, "La société civile en Afrique," p. 23.
28 Salimata Wade, Mohamed Soumaré, and El Housseynou Ly, eds., *Organisations communautaires et associations de quartier en milieu urbain ouest-africain* (Dakar: Enda, 2002), p. 26.

Across the range of these economic activities, a significant number of Thiaroye-sur-mer's young people, men, and especially women are active participants. They participate not only for the survival of their households but also, perhaps even more so, for social intercourse. Women are particularly dynamic: they manage the water pumps, sell vegetables, are involved in food preparation and the restaurant sector, and make up the majority of members and participants in informal systems for accumulating money (such as tontine arrangements and mutual savings and loan organizations.) But above all, women process and sell local products in diverse settings and forms of organization. These settings have become the true elements structuring urban life, notably through their size, economic, social, and indeed, political weight. The authors of the summary commissioned by the French Ministry of Cooperation on urbanization in Africa have written:

> The informal economy has not only been a means of producing and selling, gradually integrating the elements of modernity into traditional structures. It has also been – above all – the centerpiece of a mode of effective sociopolitical regulation, largely determining urban forms and types of interventions on them.[29]

Among the forms of generating revenue outlined above, Economic Interest Groups (EIG) and larger groups such as unions and networks are being adopted with increasing frequency. This phenomenon has evolved significantly since the mid-1980s. This is the site of informality par excellence; the phenomenon has taken place on such a mass scale that its function and its role have become essential to social intercourse in the territory and to the construction of African urbanity.

These large groups and networks thus constitute a powerful instrument for the accumulation of capital that begins with informal activities. What we are effectively seeing is a switchover from tontine arrangements to mutual savings and loan organizations. A sliding is taking place; savings are being spent not only on subsistence and social and prestige expenses (like familial and religious ceremonies and feasts), but are also applied toward productive investments. This emerging phenomenon is at the same time accompanied by a movement of individualization of wealth through the enlargement of the scale of intervention or the nature of the activity. We are witnessing the birth of a new form of entrepreneurship in which women occupy the most powerful positions.[30]

---

29 ISTED, *Dynamique de l'urbanisation*, p. 78.
30 See Fatou Sarr, *L'entrepreneuriat féminin au Sénégal: La transformation des rapports de pouvoirs* (Paris: L'Harmattan, 1999), p. 218.

In the borough of Thiaroye-sur-mer, groups like Pencum Sénégal and Pencum Demba are active in the buying, processing, and marketing of fish products. They sell in Senegal and in a few other African countries. Pencum Sénégal is comprised of five EIGs and counts 290 members, both men and women. For their part, the Lebou guíi network is not insignificant. The network consists of sixteen women's groups and numbers 416 members. Groups are involved in various activities related to the processing and marketing of marine products, local products (such as juices from local fruits), tailoring, embroidery, and so forth. According to its president, the network has a turnover of 10 million CFA francs per semester.

The various structures working in fish processing in Thiaroye-sur-mer are grouped together in the Thiaroye-sur-mer Local Union of Fishing EIGs, which is the source of discussions and regulation of activities for processing and marketing fish products. This structure has an eminently political role. It is affiliated with national organizational cadres for this sector.

As we have shown, Thiaroye-sur-mer's economic associations, groups, networks, and unions are locally anchored structures that are at the same time open to the rest of the country. In the fish industry, for example, supplies come from numerous fish wholesalers who are also intermediaries between small fishermen and the economic operators for export circuits. The clientele consists of merchants (both male and female) from different markets in the capital, regions, and even certain countries in western sub-Saharan Africa.

Strategies of territorialization (having a local anchor) and deterritorialization (distributing their products beyond Thiaroye-sur-mer) in the revenue-generating activities of this new type of economic operation are linked to the requirements imposed by economic changes that have intervened in the past decade. Among these are the weakening of state regulation brought about by the liberalization of markets, the employment crisis, and unrestrained competitiveness. Regrouping and communalizing resources are one means of obtaining information about markets, as well as opportunities to gain knowledge and know-how without a concomitant obligation to share this information with other network members. Doing this, the operator multiplies and maximizes his or her business opportunities. The network is also a milieu of fierce competition over resources.

The economic network is in reality multifunctional. It follows a double logic: while other segments converge on it, others detach themselves from it. As a metaphor, the scales of a fish come to mind. The fish scales are woven together based on relations of family proximity, neighborhood, friendship, politics, and so on. According to common interest, certain knots consolidate and others fray or distend themselves. Thus, the network is the place for crystallizing heterogeneous urban identities through the formation of interest groups and a diversification of their social, economic, and political uses. The existence of such structures thus reveals the impressive capital of psycho-sociological resources of these actors, these animators of urban space.[31] The operators move within and among various types of relationships (familial, parental, religious, political, and so forth) and play on registers marked by extremely unstable modalities of construction. The registers are unstable because they make use, in a very unpredictable way, of opportunities for mobilization and/or access to economic, financial, or other resources.

The Pencum Sénégal coalition is a good example of how the network functions. The coalition is made up of two women's EIGs involved in the sale, processing, and marketing of fish products. Derived from a private initiative dating to 1962, Pencum Sénégal became an EIG in 1990, structuring itself in the form of a coalition of two EIGs: Bok Jom and Feek Beeg Jamm. The Pencum Sénégal coalition has regrouped 117 members of these EIGs. These women employ 56 other women and 43 men. Their annual turnover is about 200 million CFA francs, according to a representative from the departmental fishing service. They have clients in Senegal, in certain African countries, and the United States. This coalition has very quickly recognized its importance and sees a need to develop itself further. Furthermore, it has linked relations of partnership and exchange with other structures on the national as well as the international level. Its members have thus been able to benefit from professional and training sessions in areas such as smoking, salting, and drying fish; the financial potential of derivatives of primary materials (such as the air bladders of fish and shark fins); and the conservation of processed products, hygiene, and quality. Members have enjoyed courses in literacy and administration. In sum, the women of Pencum Sénégal have developed an expertise that has earned them consideration as among the best specialists in their realm of activity.[32] Their fame gained them entry to the International Fair in Dakar in addition to several other national forums. The coalition has also received financing that enables them to organize travel for exchange and study in certain countries in sub-Saharan Africa, such as Gambia and Ghana, and to participate in a meeting in Paris organized by an NGO.

The Pencum Sénégal coalition embodies the sort of informal activity that involves the highest level of professionalization and enlarges its scale of activity, notably through its strategy of anchoring itself in the local while connecting to the global.

---

31 See de Certeau, *The Practice of Everyday Life*.
32 The Pencum Sénégal coalition participated in the eighth annual competition for the Presidential Prize for the Advancement of Women. It won second place and was awarded a diploma, a check for one million CFA francs, and a mill valued at four million CFA francs.

This union for transformation and commercialization has become so important that the president of Pencum Sénégal has been obliged to accept political office, a replacement seat on Thiaroye-sur-mer's municipal council. Today, Pencum Sénégal's members play a crucial role in lobbying the municipality. They want to obtain a dock close to their site for unloading the catch of fishermen. They are also demanding the construction of a day-care center, since they already pay a municipal tax for the use of communal land for commercial purposes. This would allow the workers more time for their activities. They are simultaneously putting pressure on the customary authorities to help them win the case.

An analysis of the types of economic informality in the underprivileged urban milieu made from the perspective described here shows that actors have a tremendous capacity to adapt to this type of economy in an urban fabric that is in a state of perpetual decomposition and recomposition. The ability and fluidity of this economy can be explained by the close link of the informal economy to social and political processes and dynamics, notably by recourse to the services of networks. It is tightly enmeshed in a political and social environment at the heart of which the operators move within associations and networks based on various relationships (familial, parental, religious, tactical, political, and so forth) and play on registers whose modalities of construction are extremely mobile, since they weave themselves in a very unstable way, according to the opportunities for mobilization and/or access to economic, financial, or political resources.

Conclusion   In sum, the category of informality is simultaneously spatial, political, professional, and economic. It acts on a given political situation and has a deeply historical dimension. It is a mode of interaction between two logics of structuring space: the normative logic of the state, symbolized by municipal authorities; and the so-called informal logic, which is animated by the customary authorities. The functioning of politics, the occupation of space, and the flow of economic activity are determined according to them. It is in the convergence, divergence, and strategies of regulation on these two levels that the specificities of African urban contexts are constructed. Their relationships are the engines of production of the city and the levers of change.

The modes of informal regulation of the urban space of Thiaroye-sur-mer constitute the engine driving the current urban transformations. They are already inscribed in the urbanizing process, notably through strategies for the production of space. They organize economic activity and guarantee social intercourse. At the same time, they do not reestablish the prerogatives of the state. But state controls over issues ranging from the use, access, registration, and allocation of real estate resources, to financial drains on building properties and economic activities are marked by a culture of side-stepping, of negotiation, and of tolerance. The relationship between different actors is founded on postures, attitudes, and practices of accommodation.

From an economic point of view, Thiaroye-sur-mer's many Economic Interest Groups have become as important in terms of membership numbers as in terms of activities, financial accumulation, and the variety and diversity of their connections to other partners. Through a variety of individual or collective strategies for generating revenue, informality is the mechanism linking the local to the global. Associations and larger and larger networks allow for the development of economic activities through access to diverse resources. The accumulation of capital does not generally follow a capitalist logic. Revenues and benefits are more often invested in the reproduction of the system and in the preservation of a clientele and forms of political support. They fulfill a more social purpose, even if individual wealth is being created as well. But these benefits are beginning to be reinvested in production and distribution.

All in all, informality is the mode of regulating the life of relationships and the urban environment of contemporary Thiaroye-sur-mer. It structures the changes currently underway. In this respect, it is actually the sole mode by which Thiaroye-sur-mer is constructing itself. As such, informality should be viewed as an instance of the sort of urban transformation underway in many underprivileged urban contexts today.

Translated from the French by Miranda Robbins

Welfare Associations and the Dynamics of City Politics in Nigeria: Jos Metropolis as Case Study

Victor A. O. Adetula

The springboard for this research was my participation in a community-action project under the auspices of the African Centre for Democratic Governance, Jos (Nigeria), in 1997. This project involved 120 urban-based voluntary associations (called "welfare associations"). Between 2000 and 2001, with the support of the Council for the Development of Social Science Research in Africa (CODESRIA) through the Multinational Working Group on "Urban Social Process and Change in Africa," I was able to undertake a follow-up in-depth study of a selected few of the urban associations. The idea was to study the political dynamics through which members are mobilized within these associations, and to understand the ways through which urban welfare associations interact with the various tiers of the state. What influence do urban associational groups exert on the political system? What are the various coping strategies designed by urban welfare associations to help their members manage crises such as unemployment, insecurity, and the poor quality and distribution of public services and infrastructure? These questions guided the conduct of this study, which seeks to advance a new understanding of the operations of urban associational groups and the dynamics of city politics in Nigeria.

Background to the Study The majority of urban residents in Nigeria experience acute socioeconomic hardship and are consigned to poor housing and accommodations, as exemplified by ghetto settlements such as Ajegunle and Mushin in Lagos, Bere, Oje, and Inalende in Ibadan, and Angwan Rukuba, Angwan Rogo, and Dilimi in Jos. Social segregation is reflected in the concentration of the rich in the Government Reservations Areas (GRA), Senior Staff Quarters, and the "New Layout" and other such sparsely populated areas that dot the metropolitan landscape in many Nigerian cities. It is against this background of economic hardship experienced especially by poor city dwellers that one can understand the material and psychological basis for welfare associations. These associations in urban Nigeria exist in varied forms. Some are pan-ethnic umbrella organizations, while some are "development unions" concerned with members' home of origin. Others engage in mutual support for members. Some welfare associations seek to project the culture of origin and, in some cases, the political interests of their home of origin. Many of these associational groups now flourish in many cities in Nigeria, as observed by Björn Beckman:

> The country [Nigeria] bristles with organized interests at all levels of society, from village and community associations to specialized professional groups, including the associations of old-boys (and girls) from the most prestigious professional schools of the world, numerous and prosperous enough to rent luxury hotels for their annual conventions. Trade unions and employers associations, lawyers, doctors, teachers and students keep intervening dramatically in the public arena, contesting government regulations and policies and pursuing the demands of their members. An average market-place is criss-crossed by associations of traders, craftsmen, transporters and labourers enforcing prices and rules of competition, negotiating with police, the tax collectors and other agents of the state, occasionally engaging in violent battles. ... There is no doubt about the civic spirit of much of these associations, engaging in development projects, contributing to good causes, and even offering to supervise and enforce traffic regulations.[1]

In many African countries, the economic crisis of the 1980s aggravated the decline of already crumbling services and infrastructure in many cities. Coupled with this is the problem of inadequate local government structures and the shortage of housing and jobs.[2] It has been argued that the crises in many African cities resulted from the failure of government to provide a modicum of public services, that "local authorities have not been able to devise new regulatory frameworks which would serve urban residents better in their pursuit of livelihoods, shelter and services." Urban residents have responded by challenging "the monopoly of state institutions" with a proliferation of urban-based associations.[3] This in turn has intensified the expression of ethnic identity in African cities. It could be argued that many present-day welfare associations are indeed offshoots of the ethnic associations formed in the context of socioeconomic hardship and anxiety that characterized colonial rule in Nigeria. During this period, these associations mitigated the difficulties of urban life for their mem-

---

1 Björn Beckman, "Interest Groups and the Construction of Democratic Space," in *Expanding Democratic Space in Nigeria*, ed. Jibrin Ibrahim (Dakar: CODESRIA National Studies Series, 1997), p. 25.
2 Arne Tostensen et al., "The Urban Crisis, Governance and Associational Life," in *Associational Life in African Cities: Popular Responses to the Urban Crisis*, ed. Arne Tostensen, Inge Tvedten, and Mariken Vaa (Uppsala: Nordiska Afrikainstitutet, 2001), p. 10.
3 Ibid, p. 11.

bers. In the postcolonial period, they have continued this work, while also helping their members adjust to life in the cities. The economic crisis of the 1980s, and indeed the structural adjustment programs to which Nigerians have been subjected, gave these urban associations a new prominence. Consequently, today, in virtually all urban centers of Nigeria, there exist varied forms of welfare associations – ethnic unions, cultural associations, and development associations – with diverse and diffuse goals and objectives.

Statement of the Problem   African cities are in crisis. The various tiers of the state have failed to provide institutional and legal frameworks for the overall development of cities.[4] Local government structures are incapable of meeting the crisis, and social services have failed in the face of an acute shortage of housing and jobs, severe environmental problems, rampant poverty, and increasing inequality.[5] All of this has implications for the discourse on urban crisis in Africa. Theories about the explosive urban growth and adverse economic circumstances as reasons for the crisis have been expanded to include issues of urban governance. In this regard, analysis of urban crisis in Africa notes the failure of government in many African cities, which in turn has enhanced the visibility of welfare associations that are challenging the erstwhile monopoly of state institutions.

What is the relationship between urban welfare associations and civil society in Nigeria? And what are the implications of this relationship for urban politics? In what ways do urban associations represent "social capital" – the networks and norms of civil society? What are the political dynamics that condition their operations in the city? What role do they play in urban politics? For instance, do welfare associations exercise any pressure or place demands on the various tiers of the state on behalf of urban residents? In Nigeria (with Jos as our case study), in what ways have urban welfare associations contributed to the process of urban change? In many Nigerian urban centers, these associations engage in a range of activities, including provision of social services and infrastructure, credit and loans, and religious and social events. It is possible that, in the course of their work, these organizations have deepened the content of their activities to the level of promoting the empowerment of members. Beyond direct benefits to members, what is the extent of their participation in urban governance? In

---

4 Ibid.
5 See Richard E. Stren and Rodney R. White, eds., *African Cities in Crisis: Managing Rapid Urban Growth* (Boulder: Westview Press, 1989); and Carole Rakodi, ed., *The Urban Challenge in Africa: Growth and Management of Its Large Cities* (Tokyo: United Nations University Press, 1997).

what ways have urban associations participated in the political process? What are the political dynamics through which members of associations are mobilized for participation in urban governance? What kind of political strategies do these urban associations adopt in dealing with various tiers of the state? For instance, how do they organize to bring demands and pressures on the city administration to provide vital social services and infrastructure to ease the burden of life in the cities?

Jos metropolis enjoys a thriving associational life, and many associations are ethnic-based. Notable examples are the Jasawa Development Association, for Hausa-speaking settlers;[6] the Berom Educational and Cultural Organization, for the Berom; the Yoruba Community, for the pan-Yoruba group; the Igbo Cultural Association, for the Igbo people; the Igala Cultural Development Association, for the Igala; and the Tiv Development and Cultural Association (TDCA) or Mzoughu Tiv, for the Tiv. The activities of these associations range from mutual self-help and assistance during burials, weddings, and other ceremonies, to development of "home" communities. In other words, the primary focus of their activities is helping members cope with the difficulties of urban life. What is the relationship between these associations and civil society? What is the relationship of these associations with the state? Are these associations capable of providing a countervailing force to the state's domination of civil life, thereby forcing concessions in favor of the welfare needs of the masses? These associations have devised specific modes of operation and coping strategies to address the needs of their constituencies. How adequate are these coping strategies for protecting their members against the vicissitudes of urban life? What forms of social networks are built within these associations for resource mobilization to alleviate urban poverty, and also encourage participation in urban governance?

The expansion of space in the public realm, and also the question of power relations within these associations, are of primary concern. Both have implications for the internal capacity of urban welfare associations to, first, fulfill their obligations to members, and second, to serve as the vanguard of civil society. How often do they become involved in political dialogue, political actions, and protest on behalf of their members? What are the material and social resources available to the associations, and how have these – especially social resources such as social networks – been deployed to promote the general well-being of members? Why are urban welfare associations generally perceived to be too exclusive and parochial? They are often accused of promoting an "ethnic

---

6 "Jasawa" is a term used to describe the Hausa community in Jos.

agenda" and of being indifferent to "national issues" except when they are losing out in the invisible but potent "zero-sum-game" that defines their relationship with other communities.

Conceptual Discussion: Welfare Associations as Civil Society   The concept of civil society is central to the main issues in this study. However, the larger question is how to conceptualize civil society. The prevailing definition of civil society has been expanded to cover more and more forms of association. Mahmood Mamdani has drawn our attention to the serious task involved in conceptualizing civil society in a series of questions:

> What is civil society? Does it exist or is it emerging? Is it confined to the "modern sphere," whose organizations are predicated on a differentiation between the political and the social, the social and the economic? Or does it include the "traditional" sphere where the organization of life process proceeds on the basis of a diffusion, and not differentiation, between the economic, the social and the political? Is the problem solved by making a distinction between "modern civil society," and "traditional civil society"… Or is it thereby simply shelved? On the other hand, does the notion of a "civil society" as a modern construct lead at best to a one-eyed vision of social and political processes?[7]

Mark Robinson and Gordon White warn against the tendency to invoke the "virtuous stereotype" of civil society:

> Actual civil societies are complex associational universes involving a vast array of specific organizational forms and a wide diversity of institutional motivations. They contain repression as well as democracy, conflict as well as cooperation, vice as well as virtue; they can be motivated by sectional greed as much as social interest. Thus any attempt to compress the ideas of civil society into a homogenous and virtuous stereotype is doomed to fail. It is also intellectually harmful not only because it misrepresents the reality of civil societies, but also because it distorts development discourse more broadly by encouraging simplified but overwhelmingly negative conceptions of other societal agencies whether state or market.[8]

---

7   Mahmood Mamdani,"Introduction," in *African Studies in Social Movements and Democracy*, ed. Mahmood Mamdani and Ernest Wamba-dia-Wamba (Dakar: CODESRIA, 1995), p. 3.
8   Mark Robinson and Gordon White, *The Role of Civic Organizations in the Provision of Social Services: Towards Synergy*, Research for Action 37 (Helsinki: UNU World Institute for Development Economics Research, 1997), p. 3.

The expectation of some is that civil society can help tame the state in Africa. Also some in North America have advocated the substitution of state services with civil society. However, Mamdani's critique of state-centrist and society-centrist perspectives is very instructive. He further questions the universalistic pretensions of civil society–governed perspectives and rejects the conventional simplistic state–civil society dichotomy, the prescriptive modernization perspective, and also the denial of the existence of civil society in Africa.[9] Mamdani is not alone in his rejection of the claim that Africa lacks a civil society.

Peter Ekeh has observed that limiting civil society to civic organizations "points up the danger of transposing the raw notion of civil society in the West in its entirety to African circumstances and it raises the important question of what types of associations qualify for inclusion in the conception of civil society in Africa."[10] The dilemma of applying the notion of civil society to urban associations that unite individuals on the basis of ascribed identity (such as ethnicity and kinship) rather than shared professional or political interests confronts urban researchers in Nigeria, where most urban associations are ethnically based. Claude Ake rightly notes that the "ideal" of civil society is a phenomenon of industrial capitalism and its application to developing countries with limited penetration of capitalism is problematic. However, he acknowledges that there is a sense in which the concept of civil society can be applied to societies in which the development of commodity relations is still at a rudimentary stage. In such societies, "the elements of civil society are a mixture of secondary and primary groups." He explains further that primary groups "especially, ethnicities, nationalities, kinship groups, communal groups, language groups and religious sects tend to be very influential in such societies."[11]

The difficulties associated with defining civil society in Africa were considered at a CODESRIA-sponsored forum. Three related conceptualizations of civil society in Africa emerged at this meeting, and they are of relevance here. First, that "Civil society is made up of social movements that act in the public realm, and is located between the family and the State and serves the concerns of a well-defined group whose members are mobilised to reach more or less clearly-

---

9 See Mahmood Mamdani, "A Critique of the State and Civil Society Paradigm in Africanist Studies" in *African Studies in Social Movements and Democracy*, ed. Mamdani and Wamba-dia-Wamba, pp. 602–616.

10 Peter Ekeh, "The Constitution of Civil Society in African History and Politics," in *Proceedings of the Symposium on Democratic Transition in Africa, Ibadan, June 16–19, 1992*, ed. Bernard Caron, Ajibade Gboyega, and Eghosa E. Osaghae (Ibadan: CREDU, Institute of Development Studies, 1992), p. 194.

11 Claude Ake, *Why Humanitarian Emergencies Occur: Insights from the Interface of State, Democracy, and Civil Society*, Research for Action 31 (Helsinki: UNU World Institute for Development Economics Research, 1997), p. 6.

defined objectives." Second, that civil society could also refer to "A wide range of associative voluntary organizations – structured or unstructured – that occupy the space outside the state and which seek to influence the process by which state rules are made and applied in society. These may range from opposition political parties, professional associations, trade unions, NGOs, ethnic associations, cooperatives etc." And third, that civil society can refer to "the whole range of voluntary organizations and institutions outside/and independent from the State's political apparatus, and which aim at the improvement of members and the general welfare of the people with or without partnership with the State."[12]

Keeping in mind these strands of thought, we subscribe to the definition of civil society as given by Arne Tostensen and colleagues that civil society is "the public realm of organized social activity located between the state and the private household (or family) – regardless of normative orientations."[13] Thus, social interaction comprising family relationships, associational groups, and other "forms of public communication operating in the arena of the organized non-state, non-market sector with origins in both the modern and traditional bases of society."[14] In this sense, civil society is not homogeneous, nor does a single ideology or common vision of the political order guide it. It should be noted, however, that the nature of the relationship between civil society and the state may have either a legitimizing or delegitimizing effect on the exercise of state power.[15]

The extent of "pressures and anxieties" in developing societies, which are largely the consequence of "state building and the push of development," create a strong tendency among the people to focus on holistic identities, which provide "the requisite solidarity for dealing with t[h]reats that are cultural, ubiquitous, and multifaceted."[16] As our study has shown, identity solidarities dominate associational life in Nigerian urban centers. Over the years, these groups have performed within the confines of their particularistic concerns and ethnic/clannish orientations. In Western political thought, this would be considered a limitation. However, in Africa, "the ordinary individual" has always "sought to attain his security and welfare needs" from "kinship organizations which have accordingly grown bigger and bolder in African history, experienc-

---

12 See *Civic Agenda*, nos. 2–3 (September 3, 1999), p. 19.
13 Tostensen et al., "The Urban Crisis, Governance and Associational Life," p. 13.
14 T. Akin Aina, "The State and Civil Society: Politics, Government and Social Organisation in African Cities," in *The Urban Challenge in Africa: Growth and Management of Its Large Cities*, ed. Carole Rakodi (Tokyo: United Nations University Press, 1997), p. 418.
15 Tostensen et al., "The Urban Crisis, Governance and Associational Life," p. 14.
16 Ake, *Why Humanitarian Emergencies Occur*, p. 6.

ing a path of development directly opposed to that in European history."[17] In the cities, ethnic and clan associations replace the principle and practice of extended family – the tradition of social cooperation under which urban residents were raised in the rural areas (the hometowns) – and are now expressed in the association's function of ensuring the socioeconomic and psychological wellbeing of fellow kinsmen. A new entrant into the extratribal community of the urban environment through the kinship associations is provided with traditional social support to facilitate his adjustment. In this regard, the association creates a new solidarity with which the entrant can identify. Peter Ekeh has shown that every Nigerian seems to be relating to two different publics.[18] One public is the primordial community, for which he has tremendous respect and to which he relates with integrity and moral uprightness. The second public is the Nigerian State, for which he has no such regard nor any moral commitment, and is always ready to plunder. This relationship is succinctly described by Akin Mabogunje:

> The popular reaction to existing local government councils everywhere in the country is for most people to feel that they owe them no civic obligation, to try as much as possible to pay them no taxes or rates, but rather to encourage or condone local councillors to misappropriate the funds meant for local services. On the other hand, the same citizens who would pay no tax to the local government would strain themselves to pay levies and contribute or donate generously to the coffers of their community development associations.[19]

Tribal loyalty is still very strong in Nigeria. Testimony to its potential for social mobilization is seen in the historical records of pan-ethnic tribal unions such as Egbe Omo Oduduwa and the Igbo Cultural Association, for the Yoruba and Igbo respectively.

The expression of associational life on the basis of ascribed identity was characteristic of rural areas,[20] where forms of voluntary association were very visible particularly in activities such as burial, marriage, and other religious events. In the urban context, although they generally take the form of kinship organiza-

---

17 Ekeh, "The Constitution of Civil Society in African History and Politics," p. 191.
18 See Peter Ekeh, "Colonialism and Two Republics in Africa: A Theoretical Statement," *Comparative Studies in Society and History* 32, no. 4 (1975), pp. 660–700.
19 Akin Mabogunje, "Institutional Radicalisation, Local Governance and the Democratisation Process in Nigeria," in *Governance and Democratisation in Nigeria*, ed. Dele Olowu, Kayode Soremekun, and Adebayo Williams (Ibadan: Spectrum Books, 1995), p. 3.
20 See, for instance, K. Little, "Voluntary Associations and Social Mobility Among West African Women," *Canadian Journal of African Studies* 6, no. 2 (1972), pp. 278–288.

tions, reinforcing traditional social values as well as legitimizing community social structures, there are far more variants of welfare associations in the urban areas than are available in the rural areas. This is because the city harbors different ethnic-cultural groups that are in competition over scarce resources. In the face of these competitions, the urban ethnic-welfare associations function as adaptive mechanisms for individuals who have migrated from the rural areas to the unfamiliar urban centers. Although supporting kinsmen through a host of welfare activities is the trademark of virtually all ethnic-based welfare associations in urban Nigeria, they also serve as links to the "hometown" for "development" purposes.

Methodology A survey of urban welfare associations in Jos metropolis was undertaken in 1997. In 2001, five associations were selected for close observation and informal interviews to collect qualitative data on modes of operation as well as activities. Key association officials (such as president and secretary) were contacted especially for the informal interviews. However, it turned out that members were willing to provide information far more readily than the officials. A field team made up of four field workers with previous experience in data collection and interviewing were appointed and trained. The fieldwork lasted for about six months. Since all the field assistants were familiar with Jos, it was not difficult to enlist the participation of most of the associations.

The constitution, charter, and other documents and publications of some of the associations provided useful information. For example, some of the associations record minutes of their meetings to support their claims. Also, a few local government officials were interviewed, but they chose to remain anonymous.

Case histories of several welfare associations were undertaken to explore the operations of associational groups in the political life of Jos metropolis. These include the Berom Educational and Cultural Organization, Igbo Cultural Association, and Tiv Women's Association. Additional qualitative data was collected through informal interactions with stakeholders on such issues as social solidarity, political attitudes, and the influence of group pressure.

The violent ethno-religious conflict that erupted in Jos in September 2001 disturbed fieldwork as many of our prospective respondents fled the area. Those who remained refused to talk because of the sensitivity of the various ethno-religious groups around that time. Participatory observation helped to fill in the gaps caused by these unanticipated developments.

The Case Study: Jos Metropolis   Jos, the capital of Plateau State, is a cosmopolitan city. Jos metropolis includes Bukuru and encompasses the three Local Government Areas – Jos North, Jos South, and Jos East. Jos originally comprised the Berom, Jasawa, and Anaguta settlements. The 1990 provisional census puts its population at 496,409.[21] It is a microcosm of Nigeria with respect to the composition of its population. Virtually all the major ethnic groups in the country are present in Jos. As noted by Leonard Plotnicov, "almost everyone is a stranger to Jos."[22] This perhaps explains the plethora of ethnic-based urban associations in the city.

Jos was officially founded in 1915. From its inception, when the administrative headquarters moved from Naraguta to its present location, its economy was associated with colonial tin mining. The quest for labor power for the colonial tin-mining economy in Jos and its environs spurred an influx of migrants from Niger Republic, Borno Province, Chad, Kano, Western Niger, Benue Province, Bauchi Province, and other areas of southern Nigeria. Over time, this led to the concentration of people of diverse ethnic and cultural backgrounds that eventually culminated in the growth and development of migrant communities in Jos. The city's status as administrative headquarters facilitated urbanization. In response to the difficulties of urban life, the people formed welfare associations along ethnic and cultural lines.

The Berom, Afizere, and Anaguta, who claim to be the original "owners" of Jos, are mainly subsistence farmers, with some involvement in activities such as blacksmithing and pottery making. Few of those employed in local or state government agencies come from the lower cadre. Other major cultural groups in Jos include the Hausa-Fulani, the Yoruba, and the Igbo. The Yoruba migrated from southwestern Nigeria and other parts of the Middle Belt like Kwara State. They are engaged in commercial activities, especially wholesale and retail trade, which they dominated along with the Hausa until the coming of the Igbo people from eastern Nigeria.

A small percentage of peasants of the Hausa-Fulani group are involved in small-scale year-round farming and cattle grazing. The Hausa-Fulani middle class is largely engaged in retail trading, while the wealthy are involved mostly in speculative businesses, transport, estate ownership, and petroleum distribution. The activities of the Hausa-Fulani peasants, especially as these relate to land use,

---

21 Since the move of the federal capital to Abuja, and the recent introduction of *sharīʿa* in some states in northern Nigeria, Jos has continued to experience an influx of people. This has implications for available land space as well as available public infrastructure and services.

22 Leonard Plotnicov, *Strangers to the City: Urban Man in Jos, Nigeria* (Pittsburgh: University of Pittsburgh Press, 1967), p. 4.

have always brought their group into conflict with the Berom, Anaguta, and Afizere, whose livelihood depends essentially on accessibility to land and its natural resources. Such conflicts over resources have often served to bring up accumulated grievances and rivalry over political and economic power. As in most Nigerian urban centers, the economic hardship experienced by most city dwellers provides the material and psychological basis of ethnic and welfare associations. This kind of associational life has survived into the postcolonial period.

A significant proportion of the population is engaged in the public sector alongside a strong representation in the informal sector. The bulk of the former is employed in the state bureaucracies – federal, state, and local government, including such parastatals as the University of Jos and the Steel Rolling Mill, to cite just two. The organized private sector remains relatively weak, except for small-scale commercial activities such as in the hospitality industry (hotels, restaurants, etc.) and the sale of spare parts and building materials. Commercial activities, ranging from the traditional vending of items such as chickens, vegetables, and yams, to used clothes, electrical appliances, and the most sophisticated trade forms dot the city's economic landscape. The majority of residents in Jos live in substandard housing in densely populated areas such as Angwan Rukuba, Nasarawa Gwong, Angwan Rogo, and Dilimi. The rich are concentrated in high-income areas such as Ray Field, Liberty Dam ("millionaire quarter"), Government Reservation Areas (GRAs), and other sparsely populated zones.

Ideally, local government administration should impact the life of urban residents, especially the poor, through the effective and efficient provision of services and infrastructure. However, a tour of some settlements in Jos such as Nasarawa Gwong, Dilimi, and Angwan Rogo, which harbor close to 80 percent of the population, reveals the misery in which these people live. Social services such as pipe-borne water, public conveniences, or motorable roads hardly exist, and where they do, are barely functional or at most more expensive than efficient. A visit to public parks, where close to 75 percent of traffic into and out of the city converges, exposes one to a chaotic scene of epic proportion. Yet the people – individually and collectively – pay taxes and other levies. They know the purpose for which these taxes and levies are paid, i.e., to provide social services; they know that local governments are obligated to provide these services. But the glaring evidence of urban deterioration has not provoked responses from urban welfare associations, either in the form of civic action or otherwise geared toward pressuring authorities in Jos city and its environs to improve the provision of social services and infrastructure. Many urban associations are apathetic on the performance of local government administration. They focus their efforts on helping members cope with the effects of hardship, which may of course be the result of the ineptitude of municipal authorities.

Typologies and Characteristics of Urban Associations

Table 1. Types of Urban Welfare Associations in Jos Metropolis

Type of Association	No.	Percentage of Total
Town/village/cultural associations and unions	80	80%
Trade unions, cooperatives, craft associations	10	10%
Women's organizations, women's sections	10	10%

The survey shows that associations operating in Jos metropolis take various forms. It appears that town/ethnic/cultural associations (crudely referred to as "tribal" associations) are the most popular forms of welfare association in the city. A cursory look at the mandates of these associations reveals marked similarities in their goals and objectives that center on such claims as "promoting the welfare of members" and "development in the hometowns." Apart from cultural associations, there are others based on common economic/commercial interests. Occupational groups, it should be said, have a more stable structure. This may be linked to their specific experience as a form of workers' association, and by implication the skills of "unionizing" and "solidarizing." Also, these associations usually cut across different cultural groups. However, their interests are generally restricted to the commercial and professional spheres. These associations are often indifferent to political developments in the larger society within which their interests are being pursued.

The operations of these urban associations are based essentially on the voluntary involvement of their members as provided for in their constitutions and charters. Less than 30 percent of the associations surveyed had formally registered with either the local government or state agencies. While about half do not consider this necessary, the other half resent formal registration with governmental agencies. They claim it may involve the imposition of taxes and levies. For associations whose source of revenue is mainly through membership dues, levies, fines, and donations, the payment of taxes and levies imposed by the state is considered too burdensome.

A majority of the associations are locally based (i.e., operate within Jos metropolis). However, a few among them, mostly old boys/girls associations, have national (or international) coverage. Where this exists, the one in Jos metropolis represents only one branch of such associations. The survey reveals that many of the associations have been in existence for a long time. However, only a handful have reliable systems of administration and accountability. In most cases, the constitution provides for an organizational structure that typically consists of "the House," the Executive Committee, the Finance Committee, the Development Project Committee, and the Audit Committee; the affairs of the association are usually in the hands of a small group of "founding fathers." The latter often are free to operate undemocratically, since these associations are rarely properly registered as corporate entities.

There is a clear domination of executive positions by men in many urban associations. It would seem that in virtually all the urban associations with male and female membership, exclusion of women from leadership positions is an accepted norm. Some women explained that to vie with men for such positions is, in some cases, culturally unacceptable. And where a few women have ventured to challenge this culture, they have done so at the risk of being stigmatized. It was in response to this that some women established women's sections of the male-dominated associations.

Associational Life as Social Network A relatively rich associational life has emerged in Jos since the colonial period, with formal and informal social networks, uniting people around ethnic, cultural, and religious identities, performing a number of survival tasks in the face of urban hardship. Such tasks include ceremonial and religious functions, savings and credit, etc. Our survey reveals that there are as many as 200 such associations in Jos, but very few of these have the capacity for serious civic engagement. Here, the social networks of urban welfare associations in Jos is discussed, focusing largely on the experience of the Berom Educational and Cultural Organization, (BECO), Jasawa Development Association, Tiv Women's Association, the Yoruba Community, and the Igbo Cultural Association (ICA).

The Berom Educational and Cultural Organization is an umbrella organization for all the Berom cultural groups, such as the Berom Youth Movement (BYM), Berom Intellectual Revived Organizational Movement Club (BIROMC), Berom Elders Council, and the Berom Women's Association (BWA). The Tiv Development and Cultural Association (TDCA) became very active in Jos in 1967 following the creation of Benue-Plateau State, when most Tiv people previously in government service in the defunct Northern Region left for Jos, the new capital of Benue-Plateau State. TDCA was formed in Jos essentially to help the Tiv adjust to the realities of urban life. The organization is open to all sons and daughters of Tiv in and around Jos. After many years of partial exclusion from the activities of TDCA, Tiv women came together to form the Tiv Women's Association (TWA), "to protect the interest of Tiv women in Jos." The TWA still operates under the umbrella of TDCA as one of its "women's sections" spread all over urban centers in Nigeria.[23] Both the Igbo Cultural Association and the Yoruba Community are umbrella organizations for the several urban associations serving Igbo and Yoruba communities in Jos.

Concerns for the material survival of kinsmen and women is a major consideration for urban associations in the city. This, in effect, has narrowed the activities of many urban associations – notably "hometown" organizations such as the Tiv Women's Association – to the material and psychological support of members. Our study reveals that women's associations in Jos, though engaged in many collective activities, have rarely shown an interest in pursuing more generalized goals. Their activities are centered on savings and credit, which essentially support members' involvement in the urban informal sector. The Tiv Women's Association in Jos has a relatively developed savings and loan scheme called "Bam." This is a monthly savings or "contribution" by all members to a common fund that is made available to any member in need, usually as a loan to address such common but serious needs as payment of children's school fees, settlement of hospital bills, or initial capital for small-scale business. A similar practice is found among members of the Berom Women's Association (BWA), which is made up largely of Berom women in Jos. They meet regularly and contribute money, which is made available to "fellow sisters" as loans to help the latter start a small business. This practice is an adaptation of the rural tradition of communal work parties among the Berom, whereby "wives of the same clan" move from one farm to another on a rotational basis to provide labor.

The Igbo Cultural Association has long-established structures and patterns of operation. The Igbo originally came to Jos as part of the influx of migrant labor for the colonial mining economy. Up to about World War II, the Igbo were mainly in mining, government, and related activities. But with the war came opportunity for the diversification of the economy and the Igbo found themselves in such activities as transportation, lorry repairs, and trade in consumer goods. Today the Igbo population in Jos is primarily engaged in commerce, including the importation of consumer and intermediate goods, estate ownership, transport (small and large-scale), service sector, spare-parts dealing,

---

23 Nancy Ityavyar, "The Welfare Content of Ethnic Associations in the Jos Metropolis: The Case of the Tiv Development and Cultural Association in Jos," paper presented at the National Workshop on Community-Based Organisations in Jos Metropolis, organized by the African Centre for Democratic Governance, June 9–11, 1997.

retail trading, etc. The Igbo's increased involvement in commerce exacerbated competition with the Hausa and the Yoruba who, prior to the coming of the Igbo, were indisputably the African entrepreneurs in Jos. It was not long before the ethnic groups clashed, as in the 1945 Hausa-Igbo riot.[24]

Whatever the immediate cause of the 1945 riot, it is plausible to argue that competition, frustration, and status insecurity were responsible for the clash.[25] Competition for economic opportunities among the three ethnic groups – Hausa, Igbo, and Yoruba – was a factor, just as the Hausa-Fulani supporters of the NPC were increasingly suspicious of the political activities of the Igbo-dominated NCNC, which was also suspected of having links to the Igbo tribal unions. Throughout the period of the crisis, the Igbo State Union (now Igbo Cultural Association) provided a rallying point and instrument of mobilization as well as security for the Igbo in Jos.

Furthermore, the experience of the Nigerian civil war has taught the Igbo the necessity of collective efforts, which they have successfully applied to secure their economic interests in urban Nigeria. In Jos metropolis, the Igbo dominate particular types of business interests, such as motor parts, electrical supplies, clothing and shoes, and long-distance transportation services. There is the sense in which it can be said that the Igbo Cultural Association has promoted personal and informal networks among members to help in such areas as raising capital to start or expand business ventures. This form of support for the Igbo, the majority of whom are traders, is generally highly valued among the people, who have managed to dominate some business sectors in Jos. This type of informal network of mutual support comes in handy for Igbo traders who may have recorded losses during ethno-religious conflicts. Similarly, the ICA's influence has penetrated the public sector such as the University of Jos and other public agencies, where Igbo elites are now adopting the strategies of the ICA to advance their sectoral interests.

The relative stability enjoyed by the ICA is partly the result of its established institutions and social structures set up to pursue their objectives. For example, the Igbo Cultural Association in Jos has the Eze-Igbo, whose functions – as the traditional head of the Igbo – include acting as the custodian of Igbo culture, customs, and traditions in Jos, as well as mediating and settling disputes between the individuals and organizations that comprise the ICA. The Yoruba Community has not developed its structures to a comparable degree. While the office of the Eze-Igbo is fully integrated into the organizational structure of the ICA, the office of the Oba of Yoruba, which is considerably more recent in Jos,

---

24 Leonard Plotnicov, "An Early Nigerian Civil Disturbance: The 1945 Hausa-Ibo Riot in Jos," *Journal of Modern African Studies* 9, no. 2 (1971), p. 301.
25 Ibid., p. 305.

is less visible in the organizational structure of the Yoruba Community. Apart from these institutions, the involvement of welfare associations in specific benefit-yielding activities such as the establishment of schools, the building of halls and shops, as well as other forms of investment have enhanced identity formation and contributed significantly to the welfare of members.

The Yoruba have the greatest number of "hometown associations" and "development unions" in Jos. These exist at both town and village levels. There are development associations for all the Yoruba-speaking states – Lagos, Ogun, Ondo Oyo, Osun, and Kwara. Town-based organizations include associations such as the Owo Progressive Union (OPU). The Yoruba Community in Jos serves as the umbrella for all these associations. Besides helping to provide their kinsmen and women the necessary coping and survival strategies, the town associations and unions function as well-established links with the hometowns usually in the rural areas of origin. Serving as the intermediary between the communal and stable system of the hometown and the individualistic and crisis-ridden city, these town associations provide succor for their kinsmen in Jos. In addition, through them development is channeled back to the rural hometowns in the form of development assistance, scholarships, special projects, etc. The gains of these rural-urban linkages and social networks grounded in tribal consciousness can be the basis of the democratization of rural power, and also for the evolution and growth of a vital civil society. As Mahmood Mamdani observes: "So long as the rural is not reformed, the perversion of civil society is inevitable."[26]

Urban associations provide other forms of nonmaterial support to their members. The deep involvement of urban associations in religious ceremonies, burial rituals and rites, wedding ceremonies, cultural festivals, recreational activities, and sports events proves the essence of these nonmaterial coping strategies against urban vulnerability. Part of the welfare activities of the Tiv Women's Association is assisting the sick and bereaved. Members of the association are expected to stand by other members during illness, to provide psychological comfort and relief.

> Visits are usually paid to the sick member whether in the hospitals or at home. They [members of TWA] go in groups and individually. Many people confess their appreciation. … A good number say it is a thing of pride to them when many people came to see them, especially in the hospital before the watching eyes of other patients.[27]

---

26 Mahmood Mamdani, *Citizen and Subject: Contemporary Africa and the Legacy of Late Colonialism* (Princeton, N.J.: Princeton University Press, 1996), p. 297.
27 Ityavyar, "The Welfare Content of Ethnic Associations in the Jos Metropolis."

Also, the solidarity of TWA members becomes stronger during bereavement, exemplified in the following testimony of a TWA member on the association's policy on "burying its members":

> The policy is that whether the deceased member is [sic] employed or not, the association should make available a coffin and transport [for] both members of the association and the bereaved family to the burial ground – usually to Tivland. The extent of the association's involvement in the funeral arrangements depends on the financial strength of the bereaved family; sometimes, where the group stops, individual members take over as the situation demands. At such times of bereavement, every Tiv person can be contacted to contribute towards this need. For some members, this is equal to life insurance.[28]

Through their cultural associations, the various communities in Jos have devised events and activities to encourage interaction among kinsmen and women, and promote shared cultural values and identities. Virtually all the associational groups in Jos sponsor a "Cultural Day." Celebrations take the form of socioreligious festivals and rituals. There are numerous such festivals and rituals in Jos.

The Berom Educational and Cultural Organization sponsors the annual festival of Nzem Berom in Jos. This celebration provides the platform for flamboyant display of the richness of Berom culture. But more importantly, on this occasion, as recorded by Sen Luka Gwom, "the whole of the traditional past is recalled, and images of one's passed [sic] relations and events are recollected. It is then one would not know when his head would begin to nod like a lizard in appreciation and thanksgiving to almighty DAGWI (Almighty God)."[29] For the Berom community in Jos, the celebration of Nzem Berom is more than cultural entertainment; recently, it has become a political tool in the hands of Berom political elites, who have introduced political communications into the cultural festival. During the robust and extravagant celebration of Berom cultural values, the whole social order of the Berom as a cultural group is collectively acted out. The occasion provides opportunities and license for Berom elites to manipulate cultural resources such as oral literature (songs, praise poems, proverbs, slogans) and humor in the political sphere.

The Hausa-Fulani community, through its organizational structures – the Jasawa Development Association and the Jasawa Youth Association, but more

---

28 Ibid.
29 Sen Luka Gwom, *The Berom Tribe of Plateau State of Nigeria* (Jos: Fab Education Books, 1992), p. 144.

regularly the religion of Islam – has been able to mobilize its members toward political activism in urban politics in Jos. Friday Jumat prayer meetings in central mosques have dovetailed into political discussions especially on perceived marginalization by other cultural or religious groups. This mode of politics has found its way into some Christian churches in Jos, especially those with a high concentration of Berom, Anaguta, and Afizere who, after the violent riots of September 7–13, 2001, felt the time had come to introduce "liberation theology" to the Christian community in Jos.

Urban Associations and Political Space   Politics at any level is concerned with conflict and cooperation over questions such as who gets what, how power and resources should be distributed, and how decisions should be made. Thus, politics is about the struggle for power among constituents within a political system. Urban politics in this regard includes rivalry and competition among various ethnic groups or communities within the city over the "trinity of political goals" – deference, income, safety. When an action is labeled "political" or "politically motivated," what is always meant is that interests in the distribution, maintenance, or transfer of power are the underlying considerations spurring the said action.

The city of Jos, like most urban centers in Nigeria, is a microcosm of Nigerian society in terms of settlement patterns, socioeconomic characteristics, ethnic composition, vibrancy of associational life, and the nature and character of its politics. Indeed, the latter determines the scope and content of a city's associational life. City politics in Jos has revolved around the struggle for political and economic control. The struggle over power and resources has been between the Berom, Afizere, and Anaguta, on the one hand, and the Hausa's Jasawa community, which is predominantly Muslim, on the other. At different times, this struggle has involved land access and use, the creation and control of Local Government Areas in Jos, and political appointments by the various tiers of government. Associative groups have provided the rallying points for the articulation of their members' demands and protests.

The mandate of the Berom Educational and Cultural Organization, which serves as the umbrella organization for all the Berom welfare associations, is to cultivate "unity, love, progress and understanding among Berom people."[30] However, among other things, this mandate has been interpreted to include addressing the land question and, by implication, the ownership of Jos. The

30 Ibid., p. 244.

question of land has drawn the Berom into constant conflicts with other cultural groups, especially the Hausa-Fulani. The mandates of the Anaguta Youth Movement and Afizere Youth Movement are not in any fundamental way different from BECO's, especially on the land question. The Hausa-Fulani, who are routinely referred to as "the settlers" in disputes with the Berom, Anaguta, and Afizere communities, in response formed the Jasawa Development Association, which has since provided the Hausa-Fulani community with a forum from which to articulate its positions and mobilize members.

The land question remains fundamental to political conflicts in Jos. In addition, the issue of who controls Jos local administration historically has always pitted the Hausa-Fulani against the Berom, Anaguta, and Afizere. The dominance of the Hausa-Fulani in the local administration dates back to the colonial period. Between 1902 and 1947, the Hausa-Fulani were rulers in Jos, with the title of Sarkin Jos. Alhaji Garba Baka-zuwa-Jere was the first elected representative of Jos in the Northern Regional Assembly, and Alhaji Isa Haruna, a Hausa, represented Jos in the Pre-Independence Conference of Nigeria. During the Second Republic, three prominent members of the Jasawa Development Association represented Jos in the Plateau State House of Assembly, while the Federal House of Representatives had Alhaji Inuwa and Baba Akawu, who are also members of Jasawa. Moreover, the Jasawa provided the leadership of the old Jos Local Government. In 1991, in the Jos North Local Government elections, a member of the Jasawa group emerged as executive chairman, while eight out of the fourteen elected councillors were also members of Jasawa. It would seem that the Jasawa have always dominated the process of governance in Jos metropolis. Consider, for instance, that it was not until 1950 that a Berom man, D. B. Zangs, was nominated to the Northern Regional Assembly. The other early settler groups, the Anaguta, Berom, and Afizere, with some support from the Yoruba and Igbo, have always resisted the political domination of Jos by the Jasawa. In the 1990s, this resistance intensified, and even escalated into violent confrontation, as in the disturbances of April 12, 1994.

The appointment of Mallam Ibrahim Mato, a Hausa-Fulani, as chairman of the Caretaker Management Committee of Jos North LGA, and the reaction of the various ethnic groups, precipitated the April 12, 1994 riot. The Berom, Anaguta, and Afizere groups demonstrated their outright rejection of Mato's appointment in a peaceful protest on April 5, 1994. Tension mounted when the new chairman could not immediately take over the management of local government affairs after he was sworn in. The government intervened by suspending his appointment. While this action placated the Berom, Afizere, and Anaguta, for the Hausa-Fulani group, it was time for action. On April 11, Hausa-Fulani butchers slaughtered cows and other animals on the highway near the abattoir to protest the government's suspension of Mato's appointment. On April 12, the Hausa-Fulani community, led by youths of the Jasawa Development Association, embarked on a demonstration that culminated in a large-scale riot that spread through the city. The report of the panel set up by the government to investigate the causes of the riot is yet to be released, but subsequent actions of the government have shown some sensitivity to the issue of imbalance in political and economic power among the various cultural groups in Jos.

As noted above, the April 1994 riot was not the first of its kind in Jos. There was the 1945 Hausa-Igbo riot, which was essentially a struggle over control of commerce in the city. On September 7–13, 2001, Jos witnessed one of the most violent ethno-religious clashes in the history of modern Nigeria. The government has set up a judicial panel of enquiry to investigate the immediate and remote causes of the Jos crisis. The findings have not yet been publicized, but it is sufficient to note that violent conflict erupted when the federal government appointed a member of the Jasawa community as the poverty alleviation coordinator for Jos North Local Government. Before the appointment, there had been allegations and counter-allegations among the various ethnic communities of marginalization and oppression.

Conclusions and Policy Issues The activities of welfare associations in Jos demonstrate the resolve of urban residents in Nigeria, and to some extent city dwellers in African countries, to survive in spite of the failure of the state. This is evident in the way the people themselves have evolved institutions and structures to enhance their accessibility to basic human needs. The various welfare associations in Jos, in the form of community development associations, cooperative societies, and town unions, have demonstrated a commitment to grassroots welfare, cultural, development-oriented, and in some cases income-generating activities.

On local governance, ethnic umbrella associations like Berom Educational and Cultural Organization, the various youth leagues of the "indigene" organizations, and Jasawa Development Association appear to be paying much attention to participation in local governance – the actual process of rendering collective decisions on the management of a locality. However, these associations have not been part of the associative movement in Nigeria that "rediscovered" its vitality in the mid-1980s. It could be that the major constraint on these associations is their inadequate capacity to cope with the greater task and challenges of organizations that transcend narrow ethnic, cultural, and regional boundaries. Experience from elsewhere has shown, however, that the development of such forms of associational life takes a long time.

In Nigeria, civil society discourse is still largely dominated by the big pro-democracy and good governance organizations, leaving little or no space for the rest of association life represented by urban welfare associations such as those in Jos. Since the heyday of Generals Ibrahim Babangida and Sani Abacha, the number of pro-democracy and human rights organizations and other related NGOs has increased dramatically. These organizations notably have continued to receive support and assistance from international donor agencies and development partners whose assistance programs to Nigeria target democracy and good governance. Without any prejudice to these grant-aided organizations whose formal structures meet the conditions of the donor community, the question is whether the kind of associational relationship they represent can promote civic engagement down the line to include issues of interest to grassroots associational life. As international development agencies embark on the new development strategy of promoting partnership between NGOs and the state in Africa, there is much that can be accomplished in terms of urban transformation if the various welfare associations are brought in as partners in the development process. Within this framework, the various tiers of the state have the responsibility to legitimize urban social networks and also restructure them with the view to making them partners in development.

Housing in Marrakech:
The Contradictions of Public Interventions

Mohammed Gheris

The cities of Morocco have endured tremendous pressure due to demographic growth and rural exodus. Between 1960 and 1994, the Kingdom of Morocco's annual rate of population growth was 3.5 percent. Its urban populations grew by 5.9 percent.

This pressure has meant an urban housing deficit, officially estimated at over 700,000 units.

The housing crisis in the city of Marrakech is particularly acute. Demand greatly surpasses supply. As a response to this crisis, the national campaign to provide 200,000 homes (about 4,700 of which are located in Marrakech) has done nothing to remedy the city's anarchic urbanization. (See section I.)

Although the housing crisis in Morocco is a structural problem, the response of public authorities has only accentuated the country's inequalities and dysfunctions. (See section II.) In Marrakech, the official production of housing continues to be dominated by essentially one actor, ERAC-Tensift, the state land developer and property agent.[1] Because it lacks coordination, however, the state's activities have neglected several dimensions of the problem, notably the question of how to finance housing. However, creative responses to the problem (though rarely officially recognized) have been devised by the population. (See section III.)

With the establishment of the French protectorate in 1912, the urban tissue of Marrakech began to undergo profound transformations. These can be summarized as follows:

First, the rending of the urban fabric with the creation of the European city, which would later become Marrakech's principal business center. The willing-

---

[1] ERAC-Tensift, the Etablissement Régional d'Aménagement et de Construction de la Région de Tensift (Regional Agency for Development and Construction for the Tensift Region) was created by Dahir Number 172-438 on May 21, 1974. This public agency is endowed with financial autonomy and placed under the supervision of the Ministry of Housing. Its activities concern the development and sale of construction lands and the sale of individual and collective housing for itself or on the part of a third party.

ness of planners to intervene in the city's urban fabric was an expression of General Lyautey's desire to separate the medina – the core of Marrakech – from the modern city. This policy was intended not only to preserve the identities of the so-called autochthons who lived there but also to show the "civilizational superiority" of European Christian society over Muslim society.[2] As Abderrahmane Rachik has rightly pointed out,

> the urban planning recommended by "Lyautey" was based on the sort of relatively precise social project that occasionally takes on the allure of utopian ideology. If Lyautey considered this policy a way of respecting the customs of "indigenous peoples," objectively such a social practice is founded on preoccupations with hygiene, on feelings of fear and disdain with regard to the "indigenous," and consequently on a profound wish to regroup this "dangerous" population (hygienically speaking) and to distance it spatially from the city reserved for Europeans, in order to assure ease of control.[3]

On the other hand, the authorities of the French protectorate also created the industrial quarter, which would contain factories for processing the region's agricultural production.[4]

Second, the "informal" work sector[5] has exploded, and the unemployment rate is particularly high, both a consequence of the lack of industrialization in the urban economy, which continues to be dominated by artisan, commercial, and a handful of food- and agriculture-related industries. The city's economic fabric today has seen no important developments when compared to that of the past (with the exception, perhaps, of the leisure and tourism industry).

Third, poverty has spread,[6] accompanied by a notable spatial marginalization marked by strong segregation. This is exemplified by the "slumification" of

---

2 General Lyautey, the French colonial administrator in Morocco between 1912 and 1925, would see his ideas about planning in Moroccan cities expressed in the work of the great urbanist Henri Prost. The latter sought to apply the following principles to the work: (1) the creation of new cities alongside traditional ones; (2) the separation of these cities through the use of open space; and (3) the "preservation" of the traditional and original aspects of the existing urban fabric.

3 Abderrahmane Rachik, *Ville et pouvoirs au Maroc* (Casablanca: Éditions Afrique Orient, 1995), p. 27.

4 Paradoxically, the factories for processing agricultural products from the hinterland sparked a rural exodus and attracted a rural workforce to Marrakech. With this came the flourishing of makeshift residential quarters, many of them unsanitary.

5 According to recent estimates, informal employment represents some 60 percent of the total. For the least favored socio-professional categories, informal employment is even more important (approximately 90 percent for children). See "Diagnostic de la pauvreté urbaine à Marrakech," a document assembled by the PNUD/Ministry of Social Development, Solidarity, Employment, and Professional Training, March–August 1998, p. 10.

6 See Mohammed Gheris, "Espaces de la pauvreté et régulation étatique," paper presented at the Colloque International de Perpignan, France, October 20–22, 1999.

the medina and the proliferation of unhealthy *douars* (villages), which coexist with luxurious properties and villas (each of which extends over many hectares within the urban perimeter). The Tensift region (of which Marrakech represents 70 percent of the urban population) is the second poorest of the Kingdom's seven regions.[7] A few statistics confirm this situation:

- School-age children in Marrakech are less educated than the national average.
- The rate of child labor is highest in Marrakech, as is the number of single women.
- The total rate of employment is higher (since the poor are often obliged to hold down at least two jobs in order to survive).

Fourth, Marrakech has experienced a relatively modest rate of demographic growth compared to that of cities along the coast, but in keeping with the city's horizontal extension (as exemplified in ERAC-Tensift's new public housing developments such as those in Massira I, II, II, Laskar *douar*, etc.). Between the two census periods (1960–71 and 1971–82), the city's rate of annual growth went from 2.9 to 2.6 percent, while that of similar cities was on average 4 percent and 3.3 percent for the two periods respectively. Between 1982 and 1994, the city welcomed 232,778 new residents, that is, an average of 19,398 new residents per year, which is equivalent to 3,966 households.[8]

I. Anarchic Urbanization and the Housing Crisis in Marrakech

Because it lacks an industrial complex, which would promote progress and enrich both the population and the city, Marrakech is prone to suffer the vicissitudes affecting the hinterland (where, depending on the land's aridity, the pastoral and agrarian systems often experience sub-productivity). The result of this is an anarchic and unstructured urbanism, of which the primary manifestations are:

---

7 Per the old administrative division of the kingdom into seven regions, compared to the current provision of sixteen regions.

8 A comparison of the distribution of households according to the latest regional division (into sixteen regions) shows that in 1982, the region of Marrakech–Tensift–El Haouz represented 10.8 percent of total households, as compared to 10.2 percent in 1994. It thus holds the second highest number of households, after Casablanca (with 12.7 percent). In terms of urban households, out of a total of 2,519,685 households, the Marrakech–Tensift–El Haouz region has 177,753 households, or 7.05 percent. On the other hand, in 1994, 39.3 percent of this region's households were urban, compared to 29.2 percent in 1982. (Source: Department of Statistics.)

- Heterogeneous housing types.
- The absence of planning and urban controls (and, consequently, a high degree of urban speculation and lack of respect for the environment, among other things).
- A housing crisis in general and a social housing crisis in particular, to which public authorities have not responded adequately.

The Heterogeneity of Housing Types   As previous scholarship has stressed, the urban fabric of Marrakech is characterized by heterogeneity and diversity. Ahmed Bellaoui notes that:

> Marrakech thus represents the type of city in which general evolution is far from being linear and for which a prestigious past symbolized by a coherent and uniform Medina flagrantly contradicts that of its present, which is characterized, among other things, by the overly heterogeneous urban landscape. Far from constituting an element of grandeur, and by consequence, of dynamism, the medina could be seen as constituting, along with the peripheral *douars* [villages], the source of nearly all the problems that today are causing the greatest and the most prestigious of Morocco's cities to suffer.[9]

The city is structured by four types of housing:

- The historic medina, made up of houses with patios, apparently without a high degree of social segregation.[10]
- The new city, Guéliz, made up of sub-areas with diversified functions (zones for commerce and service, an industrial zone, a residential and hotel zone, and so forth).
- The state's private developments. Due to the medina's high density and degree of "ruralization," the public authorities have launched campaigns for development and inexpensive housing, as well as to improve sanitation networks and provide resettlement lots (Unit III), new neighborhoods for auto-construction (built by the residents themselves) (Massira I, II, II, Asli, etc.), and, lastly, the buildings that are part of the national project to construct 200,000 homes.
- Spontaneous urban *douars*.[11] According to the most recent census of makeshift habitats (1998), 156 *douars* were noted in Marrakech's urban

---

9 Ahmed Bellaoui, "Marrakech, des villes dans la ville," *Atlas Marrakech*, no. 2 (1994), p. 6.
10 Ibid.

community, compared to a mere 61 in 1991. This represents some 150,000 persons, or 22 percent of the total population of the greater urban agglomeration.[12]

The Absence of Planning and Urban Controls The proliferation of unsanitary housing conditions alone would suffice to demonstrate the weakness of city planning in Marrakech. This failure is even more puzzling when one takes into account the fact that the city's property structure is characterized by a predominance of private estates (35 percent of the total). But the availability of considerable numbers of private estates only weakly favors urban planning, for the following reasons: first, the existence of several constraints (*non aedificandi* [nonbuilding] zones and *non altius-tollendi* [nonremoval] zones), and second, an insufficient number of zones open to urbanization (such as Méchouar and the Kasbah).

Instead of urban *planning*, it might be said that there are presently only urban *renovations*.[13] Indeed, a proper urban policy would have to be based on the resolution of several problems.[14] For instance, such a policy would have to presume the existence of particular goals and means.[15] It would have to resolve the conflicts residing at the heart of the principal entity that implements it, namely, the central state. As it happens, this entity pursues several policies rather

---

11 The SDAU (Schéma Directeur d'Aménagement et d'Urbanisme) for Marrakech outlines three generations of spontaneous *douars*: the oldest (from the 1920s), which encircle the *nouvelle ville* (new city), with the exception of the neighborhood of Sidi Youssef Ben Ali (SYBA); the second generation (from the 1940s) along the industrial zone and the perimeter of the colonization to the west of the *nouvelle ville*; and the third generation (established after independence), which lies alongside and joins the Wadi Issil to the east and the Medina. The case of SYBA is an illustration. In 1955, this *douar* contained 2,821 unfinished houses and 1,768 completed ones, occupied by 2,013 *foyers*, that is, close to 10,000 people. In 1994, the population was estimated at 120,000. A decade ago, this district became a prefecture and has been able to benefit from important renovation work and beautification. For a complete historical analysis of the district, see M. de Leenheer, "L'habitat précaire à Marrakech et dans la zone périphérique," *Revue de Géographie du Maroc* (Rabat) no. 17 (1970).

12 See M. Mouradi, "Les douars d'habitat insalubre à Marrakech," in *Mémoire de D.E.S. en sciences économiques* (Marrakech: Université Cadi Ayyad, 1998), p. 85. The author notes that from 1982 to 1998, the population of the *douars* had multiplied by 3.6, or from 42,000 to 150,000 inhabitants. This represents a growth rate of 8 percent.

13 See Mohammed Gheris, "État, marché et financement du logement au Maroc: Contradiction des interventions publiques," paper presented at the colloquium "Europe-Méditerranée, vers quel développement?" 14th Meeting of the Association Tiers Monde CRERI, Université de Toulon et du Var, Île de Bendor, May 27–29, 1998.

14 See Mohammed Naciri, "Les politiques urbaines au Maghreb et au Machrek," Round Table IRMAC+ERA 1036/VA/913 of the CNRS, University of Lyon, 1982.

15 It seems that the "absurd" question, What kind of housing do Moroccans want?, is still being posed within the ministry in Rabat.

than a single policy, and these vary according to political, geographic, historical, and a variety of other circumstances. It would have to presume the existence of a convergence between global planning (the allocation of resources) and urban planning (the allocation of space),[16] as well as between the state and the region (decentralization), and the state and the private sector (a system of contracts).

In regard to the latter, the SDAU of Marrakech (Directive Plan for Urban Development) notes that "the voluntary activity of the large public developers – for whom the choice of sites is determined more by real estate opportunities than by the desire to occupy the site in a harmonious way – risks in the short term derailing the natural system of extension of the urbanized zone. Already, the strong westward push of the district of Massira has created elements that strain the fabric."[17]

The Housing Crisis in General and of Public Housing in Particular   Table 1 gives the SDAU's projections of the estimated number of households in Marrakech in 2010, based on an average household size of 5.5 persons between the years 1982 and 1990, 5.2 between the years 1990 and 2000, and 5.1 since 2000.[18] If we were to hypothesize a zero deficit of housing, 3,800 new homes would need to be built each year until 2010. As for actual supply, Table 2 gives an idea of the progress of authorized housing units in Marrakech.[19] The comparison between the level of housing need and number of officially authorized constructions shows a considerable deficit, close to 50 percent (at least for the years in which the production of housing units is considerable, in this case, 1997).[20] How, then, have the public authorities responded in order to meet these enormous needs?

---

16 See Mekki Bentahar, "Vie quotidienne banlieue marocain," in *La ville et l'espace urbain, Bulletin économique et social du Maroc,* nos. 147–148 (Rabat: SMER, 1981), p. 52.
17 Michael Pinseau, *Evidentiary Report of the SDAU of Marrakech* (Marrakech: Ministry of Interior, 1991), p. 20.
18 Ibid, p. 35.
19 These numbers are approximate in the sense that it is enormously difficult to arrive at an exact estimate of the number of constructed homes. On this matter, see a very interesting study that tried to evaluate critically the data-collecting system and the way results are analyzed relative to building permits. For the year 1994, this study achieved, on the one hand, an exhaustive census of building permits and, further, verified that registers of urban communes conformed to reality throughout a representative sample of chosen projects and research of construction sites. See the two-volume study by TEAM Morocco for Ministry of Housing, Direction of Building Promotion, *Étude relative à la détermination des flux de production de logements et l'évaluation du système de collecte des données des autorisations de construire,* 3d ed. (Rabat: Ministry of Housing, July 1996).
20 The population responds to this deficit in a number of ways, among them unauthorized construction, a high level of cohabitation among families, and increased numbers of persons per household.

Table 1. Projected Growth of Households

	Population	Number of Households	Persons per Household
1990	590,000	114,000	5.2
2000	750,000	147,000	5.1
2010	950,000	186,000	5.1

Source: SDAU of Marrakech, 1991

Table 2. Growth of Authorized Housing Units in Marrakech

Year	Number of Building Permits	Number of Authorized Housing Units
1982	1,075	1,699
1984	1,292	2,135
1986	1,551	2,668
1988	1,425	2,089
1990	1,251	1,867
1992	1,204	1,741
1994	613	987*
1996	–NA–	–NA–
1997	1,240	2,187*

Source: annual regional statistics
* Department of Statistics

II. Morocco's Housing Crisis and the Government's Response to It

Schematically, the action of the state takes several forms:

- The creation of laws and ordinances concerning urban development.
- Property development in the urban area.
- The reduction of unhealthy housing conditions.

- The production of social housing, notably through the national project to construct 200,000 homes. For the most part, this has been undertaken by various organs supervised by the Ministry of Housing (ERAC, ANHI, SNEC, and so forth).[21] These groups are known as *organismes sous tutelle* (OSTs).
- The granting of fiscal advantages to promoters and interest discounts to buyers, in particular for the category of housing known as the Habitat Bon Marché (HBM, or affordably priced home).
- The financing of development and acquisition by banks with a majority of public capital, such as the Credit Immobilier et Hôtelier (CIH) and the Banque Central Populaire (BCP).

It is, therefore, a multidimensional policy: statutory, institutional, and financial, among other things. Here I will focus on two areas of the government's housing policy in Marrakech: first, the project to build 200,000 units of housing nationally in response to the housing crisis, and second, modes of financing (for postfinancing in particular).

The Project to Build 200,000 Homes The year 1994 marked a turning point in the Kingdom of Morocco's housing policy. Before that date, the government's policy aimed at combating unsanitary habitats (such as shantytowns and unregistered/clandestine dwellings) by restructuring under-equipped neighborhoods and providing ready-for-construction lots. The various OSTs (supervised by the Ministry of Housing) conceived and brought about this policy. The provision of such lots, however, addresses only the destitute fringes of the urban population and the well-to-do (since lots for villas and larger buildings are also created). This policy excluded the middle social category – those unable to purchase a lot, for whom the sole remaining recourse is to rent (often in unhealthy neighborhoods). This middle-income class (or, rather, the lower middle class, since income levels do not exceed 3,600 dirhams a month) thus had very real needs. The royal speech of March 3, 1994 recommended the construction, with considerable support from the state and on very advantageous conditions, of a first program of 200,000 homes destined for this population.[22]

---

21 SNEC = Société Nationale d'Équipement et de Construction; ANHI = Agence Nationale de Lutte contre l'Habitat Insalubre.

22 Given the source of financing for the 200,000-unit campaign and the very severe degree of conditionality of the CIH, the households that participated in the program came essentially from the private sector affiliated with the CNSS (Caisse Nationale de Sécurité Sociale), that is, the employees of the local collectivities and agents of the public administration.

The measures taken to bring about this project were financial, fiscal, land-related, and connected to urban planning:

- The Affordably Priced Home (HBM) is defined as a dwelling that costs less than 200,000 Dhs (150,000 French francs) and has an area of less than 100 square meters.
- Credit will be given for a maximum of 25 years with an interest rate set by the state, of less than 6 percent.[23]
- Duties and taxes affecting the HBM are waived.
- Rights and taxes related to property taxes, building rights, permission to create lots, the intervention of agencies, of the National Office of Electricity (ONE), and the National Office of Potable Water (ONEP) are reduced.
- The creation of a mortgage market (May 2000).[24]
- The transfer – at nominal prices – of lands from the public land reserve to various construction companies, as well as the establishment of a conservation measure to set aside public lands that have been identified as potential supports for the realization of programs for social housing.
- The institution of permanent commissions, central and local, to select the sites designated for this program.
- The simplification and acceleration of transfer procedures for communal, collective, and state lands that are open to urbanization.

By 1999, barely a sliver of the project had been carried out – 48,000 units nationally – a large portion of which has not found buyers.[25]

The Limitations of the Project to Build 200,000 Homes   Apart from the inadequacy of the program's 200,000 units, compared to the size of the demand, several other criticisms may be made about the project:[26]

---

23 Buyers must pay an advance to the selling entity of at least 30,000 Dhs. Further on we shall see that future buyers meet this condition only with difficulty and that it in fact causes many buyers to pull out.

24 See Mohammed Gheris, "Financement du logement et titrisation hypothécaire au Maroc," paper presented at the UNIMED-FORUM seminar, "Politique et coopération économique," November 29–December 3, 1999, Aix-en-Provence.

25 See *Vie Économique* (Casablanca), December 17, 1999, p. 17. The newspaper notes, "In analyzing the non-sales of certain ERACs, it can be confirmed that this total quantity contains homes that are part of the project to build 200,000 homes. In other words, housing, even social housing (costing not more than 200,000 Dhs), turns out to be difficult to buy."

26 See "Étude relative aux aspects financiers et fiscaux," Group Algoe-Promoconsult, on behalf of the Ministry of Housing, 1997.

- In terms of needs, the program essentially targets only public and para-public employees.
- In terms of choice of residence, it offers the same solution and perpetuates only minimally differentiated choices.
- In terms of methods of financing, it maintains the existing system of rebates, which is very costly for the state's budget and is hardly an effective means of encouraging access to the properties.
- In terms of reforming the system of financing, it makes no contribution to improving the system but in fact worsens the administrated mobilization of resources[27] to the advantage of the bank (CIH). This reinforces the latter's monopoly and prevents the emergence of competition, which would enable the cost of credit to be lowered and expand the accessibility of credit.
- In terms of production, the program increases the role of the developers of social housing, without, however, providing an adequate solution for the housing sector.[28]

To conclude, the project to build 200,000 homes has exposed all the incongruities of the system for financing housing in Morocco. It is characterized by a condition of near-monopoly, in which a sole lending institution (the CIH)[29] provides close to 75 percent of the credit.[30] A discriminatory legal and legislative environment, long-standing privileges granted to the CIH,[31] and credit practices based on rationed resources (such as differentiated rates of interest) are the factors that permit this situation to be maintained. As a result, the conditions acquiring credit are very restrictive, access to credit for housing is discriminatory, and the fixed price of these credits generates a uselessly high profitability (with the exception of recent years).[32]

---

27 See, later in this text, the discussion of developments devoted to the system of financing housing in Morocco.

28 The current financing situation of the OSTs, notably of the ERACs, is critical. Because of their excessive indebtedness to the CIH, they are all more or less unable to pay back the loans that have been contracted with the latter. CIH has therefore suspended all prefinancing for the OSTs until their financial situation has been stabilized.

29 Social housing is in fact also financed by the BCP (Banque Central Populaire), which also benefits (as has the CIH since 1998) from the the authorization of the public powers to finance social housing. This possibility is accorded to other commercial banks, but to date, none of them have shown an interest.

30 This percentage is valid for the years prior to 1998. Since then, in the face of the general decline of CIH's activity, this part has considerably regressed. It must also be emphasized that several commercial banks (such as Wafabank, and notably BCP) are increasingly interested in financing buildings, although entirely for luxury developments.

31 For example, the CIH has a monopoly on financing the project to build 200,000 units of housing.

For Marrakech, the state acts directly through the construction of about 4,700 housing units within the framework of the national program for 200,000 homes.

III. The Government's Activities in Marrakech and Their Impact

Real estate development in the city of Marrakech is dominated by the activities of the OSTs such as ERAC-Tensift. The latter assigns the roles of the various players in the overall real estate development scheme. It is difficult to ascertain the exact position of the OSTs in the development process. Private building promotion is still largely unstructured and has far less breadth, although a number of groups (Chaâbi and Chkili, for example) are gaining a foothold. Furthermore, the social housing sector, long ignored by private promoters, is beginning to interest them, especially with the fiscal advantages now being granted through the launch of the 200,000-unit campaign.

One should, in fact, distinguish between two types of building promotion, both of which are dominated by public actors:

- Land development, which generally has involved small areas and has mobilized few financial means. Though OSTs are largely dominant in this segment, the private sector has also been active in it for some time, through the realization of lots for the construction of both inexpensive and luxury housing.
- Building development (the construction and sale of housing units), which, properly speaking, is the exclusive domain of the OSTs in general and of ERAC-Tensift in particular. These entities carry out the large projects while private building developers specialize in small ones (those with a few dozen units).

It must be emphasized that auto-construction (that is, people building their own homes) is extremely pronounced and meets more than three-quarters of the need for housing in the city. This route is symptomatic of the nonindustrial character of the production of housing in Marrakech.

For the most part, building development is therefore dominated by the OSTs, and by ERAC-Tensift in particular.

---

32 Comparative studies concerning Moroccan banks have shown that the net banking profit of the CIH was for the most part higher than those of the other banks (in the mid-1990s).

ERAC-Tensift, the Leading Building Developer in Marrakech   By the end of 1998, ERAC-Tensift had completed a total of 16,042 homes, 43,029 lots, 3,538 businesses, 76 offices, and 5,937 transfers to new housing. From this we can infer a total of some 130,000 homes housing around 720,000 people, which is roughly equivalent to half of the region's urban population.[33] Table 3 shows the accumulated physical achievements at the end of 1998.[34]

Table 3. ERAC-Tensift's Physical Achievements

Date Collected	Number	Percentage
December 31, 1989	25,953	41%
1990	4,448	7%
1991	3,441	5%
1992	4,787	8%
1993	5,638	9%
1994	6,016	10%
1995	4,578	7%
1996	415	1%
1997	2,381	4%
1998	5,470	9%
Total	63,127	100%

Source: ERAC-Tensift Activity Report, 1998

ERAC-Tensift's activities are diverse, even heterogeneous. It fights unhealthy housing conditions, outfits industrial zones, and prepares transportation routes, among other things. This heterogeneity contributes to damaging its profitability, which is already in poor shape. This is also true for the other ERACs of the Kingdom.[35]

---

33 Nearly three-quarters of ERAC-Tensift's activities have taken place within the city of Marrakech proper. For the latest figures, see ERAC's 1998 Activity Report, pp. 7, 26, and 32. The totals under construction since January 1999 consist of 1,182 housing units, 8,122 lots, 374 businesses, and the renovation of 2,265 units.
34 ERAC-Tensift's production, classified by type of product, consists of collective housing (11 percent), individual homes (13 percent), and finally, a predominance of lots on which individual homes are to be built (58 percent).
35 See *Vie Économique*, December 17, 1999, p. 17. Under the heading of works that do not enter

Because of its juridical nature (as a public establishment), because of the general context of the country's economy (the still strong presence of a state sector despite the fact that economic liberalism has been declared the strategy of choice), because of the fundamental nature of need – housing – to which it responds, and because of its position on the housing market (as dominant operator, especially for the national 200,000-unit project), ERAC is a "budgetivorous" operation. That is, its budget functions disproportionately. It concerns itself very little with market demand because the means of mobilizing funds to finance the project and the products it offers its clientele (the HBMs, or affordably priced homes, in particular) do not actually satisfy the clientele's needs. In 1997, ERAC's operational budget was 25.65 million Dhs for a turnover of 86 million Dhs, that is, about 29 percent. For 1999, this budget was estimated at 27.35 million Dhs for a team of 174 agents.

Several factors account for damage to the profitability of the investment:

- The reserve of federal lands is being exhausted. ERAC-Tensift is thus increasingly obliged to buy lands at market rates.
- Commercial competitiveness is weak. Stocks in late 1998 had a value of 1,730 million Dhs.
- Financial management is lax. ERAC-Tensift is overly indebted, particularly to CIH. At the end of 1998, its debt to CIH was 510 million Dhs, of which 150 million was due for payment.
- Negative profitability: in 1997, losses due to operational costs were close to 190 million Dhs.
- Of a total number of paid reimbursements concerning 45 loans for 683 million Dhs, ERAC paid 199 million Dhs in financial fees alone – an obvious sign of its disastrous financial management. These financial fees affect the cost of the dwelling and are consequently passed on to the buyers. In the opinion of the agency's director, "this situation may be explained on the one hand by the raised interest rate put into place by CIH, and on the other by the failure to pay back loans related to the entirely commercial operations."[36]

It is, however, the project for 200,000 housing units that most clearly reveals the agency's structural difficulties.

---

directly into ERAC-Tensift's competence, we must note that the latter enlarged National Route 1 Marrakech-Agadir by 2.7 km (2 x 9 m) and completed corresponding renewal projects, as well as other works, with a total value of 11.3 million Dhs (in addition to a main sewer outside the site of renewal at a cost of 10 million Dhs).

36 See ERAC-Tensift's 1998 Activity Report, p. 11.

A Supply That Does Not Meet Demand   The consideration of a triad of factors – district, type of housing, and mode of financing – enables an analysis of the disconnect between supply and demand for social housing:

The District. In Marrakech, the most important part of the government program to build 200,000 units was carried out by ERAC-Tensift in the district of HAM. This district consists of three sub-districts covering an area totaling 294 hectares:

- HAM I: 107 hectares, with a density of 3,060 lots: 1985
- HAM II: 92 hectares, with a density of 3,044 lots: 1986
- HAM III: 95 hectares, with a density of 2,241 lots: 1991

In terms of buildings, the area of HAM is divided into three zones: collective housing, low-priced individual housing, and residential housing (villas). Table 4 provides a projection of amenities required in the district of HAM. The surface areas reserved for necessary amenities were calculated based on national norms, although not all the amenities were carried out. However, Marrakech's portion of the national 200,000-unit campaign – almost entirely situated in the HAM district and covering a surface of 41 hectares built on unprepared land that lacked the required amenities (4,764 homes) – was incorporated "by force," one might say, in this space. It infringed vigorously on urban norms.[37]

Furthermore, the amenities did not grow in response to the district's heightened population density.[38] This is confirmed in our study of 75 households that were part of the program. Table 5 shows that the degree of satisfaction with HAM is medium (54 percent), due essentially to the lack of amenities and an unreasonably high number of annoyances. Considerable disparities exist within the district. The sub-district of HAM I (built in 1985) does not suffer so keen a lack of amenities as the sub-district of HAM III (currently under construction).

Financing. It must first be noted that the question of financing is of great importance, considering the nature of housing property, which cannot (or can

---

37 From our interviews with those responsible for urbanism in Marrakech and members of the Marrakech Urban Agency (l'Agence Urbaine de Marrakech), we learned of special dispensations accorded to ERAC-Tensift to enable the achievement of population densities and building heights that do not conform to the standards outlined in the city's urbanization charter.

38 Moreover, ERAC-Tensift recognizes that "the urgent nature of the program in terms of studies and projects launched has not been without negative repercussions on the regular progress of the construction sites and in terms of delays of execution." These remarks were made during a roundtable held on the social program of the HAM (district of Marrakech), ERAC-Tensift, July 2, 1999 (unpublished). It should also be noted that the urgent nature of the program led to the projects being launched without any synchronization with other ministries.

Table 4. Surface Area of Amenities, Broken Down by Activity Type and Sub-District (Areas in m²)

Activity	HAM I	HAM II	HAM III	Total
Education	42,876	33,396	45,451	121,723
Youth and sport	32,717	1,005	742	34,464
Health	8,259	5,128	699	14,086
Administration	9,327	12,166	106,339	127,932
National promotion	984	1,375	848	3,207
Culture	4,886	—	1,117	6,003
Religious institutions with property (*habous*) and neighborhood amenities	23,651	4,906	8,532	37,089
Total	122,700	58,076	163,728	344,504

Source: ERAC-Tensift, 1999

Table 5. Level of Satisfaction in the District

Level of Satisfaction	Number of Households Investigated	Percentage
High	27	36%
Medium	41	54%
Low	5	7%
No response	2	3%
Total	75	100%

Source: author's survey, March–April 2000

only rarely) be paid for in cash. Rather, housing requires long-term loans. All participants in the 200,000-unit program have turned to financing through the CIH.[39]

---

[39] This study is not directly interested in the problems of prefinancing faced by promoters of the campaign for the 200,000 units of housing. Rather, we have focused on the problems of post-financing (buyer credits).

For those surveyed, the question of financing their homes was summed up in two problems: first, the inadequacy of bank financing in terms of the financial situations of households, and second, the high cost of credit. Table 6 shows that 56 percent of those surveyed believe that bank financing is ill suited to their needs (the period of the loan is too short, the interest rates too high, the CIH too bureaucratic, and so forth).

It is interesting to consider the "financial" route taken by buyers. Before purchasing their homes, many turned either to the tontine[40] arrangement (Table 7) or to the pseudo-mortgage (Table 8) in order to accumulate savings, which would be needed as an advance (of about 30,000 Dhs) paid to ERAC-Tensift. Forty-one percent of buyers had recourse to the tontine scheme, while 34 percent turned to the pseudo-mortgage. These are considered informal financing practices – "informal" in the sense that they are not officially recognized.

The mechanism of the pseudo-mortgage is simple. A homeowner borrows a sum of money from someone and gives him the dwelling as security for the duration of the loan. A (relatively) moderate rent is paid to the owner, though this agreement is not indicated on the loan contract. The pseudo-mortgage thus allows for the dwelling's occupant to accumulate a "forced" savings, which will later serve as the initial advance on the purchase of a home.[41] The practice enables a balancing out of the tensions that exist on the urban housing market in several of the Kingdom's cities. Since renting a decent dwelling is out of the price range of the majority of Marrakech's urban households,[42] recourse to the pseudo-mortgage is an important phase along the path to financing a home. Furthermore, most of those surveyed (60 percent) continue to believe that the level of the pseudo-mortgage (generally between 30,000 and 60,000 Dhs) is reasonable (Table 9). As Table 10 shows, 72 percent of those surveyed consider the practice of the pseudo-mortgage to be well suited to their needs.

Highlighting the informal methods used to finance housing shows that several modes coexist. Paradoxically, the practices that dominate the system are not officially recognized. The official system of housing in Morocco conceives of the country's economy as a smoothly working banking economy, one in which the

---

40 *Tontine* is defined by *Webster's* as "an annuity scheme in which subscribers share a common fund with the benefit of survivorship, the survivors' shares being increased as the subscribers die, until the whole goes to the last survivor."
41 Most of those surveyed acknowledged that recourse to the system of pseudo-mortgaging over several years enabled them to amass some savings.
42 The archaic legislation concerning leasing of housing in Morocco discourages investment in this segment. Laxness on the part of the administration and the judicial authorities dissuades all property owners from renting their dwellings out of fear, quite simply, of losing them. It is for this reason that considerable guarantees (such as payment of several months' rent in advance) are required.

Table 6. Buyers' Assessment of Bank Financing

Assessment	Number	Percentage
Adapted to buyers' needs	26	38%
Moderately adapted	3	6%
Not adapted	38	56%
Total	67	100%

Table 7. Recourse to the Tontine

Question: Have you used a tontine?	Number	Percentage
Yes	31	41%
No	44	59%
Total	75	100%

Table 8. Status Prior to Purchasing Housing

	Number	Percentage
Renter	24	32%
Owner	4	5%
Pseudo-mortgage	26	34%
Lived with family	18	24%
"Pas de porte"*	1	2%
Other	2	3%
Total	75	100%

* A new occupant pays a right of entry to the dwelling's former renter before taking over the lease himself.
Source for Tables 6–8: author's survey, March–April 2000

Table 9. Opinion about the Level of the Pseudo-Mortgage

	Number	Percentage
High	29	39%
Medium	30	40%
Weak	14	18%
No response	2	3%
Total	75	100%

Table 10. Assessment of the Pseudo-Mortgage's Suitability

	Number	Percentage
Well-suited	54	72%
Moderately well-suited	7	9%
Not well-suited	11	15%
No response	3	4%
Total	75	100%

Source for Tables 9–10: author's survey, March–April 2000

correct administrative machinery and well-lubricated mechanisms are at work. In fact, two major points must be acknowledged. First, the provision of banking facilities for the economy is very weak, which has an undeniable impact on the mobilization of savings.[43] Second, the banking system contributes only 14 percent of the financing of constructed housing units.

The official system of financing housing is thus a marginal system and ignores the existence of other "decentralized" or informal financing arrangements.[44] These could in fact coexist with the official system quite well and might even help it to restructure itself. Efficient economic policies (both macro and micro) must take into account the articulation of various informal and formal circuits.

[43] See Philippe Hugon, "Incertitude, précarité et financement local, le cas des économies africaines," *Revue Tiers Monde* (January–March 1996), p. 145.

Conclusion

Several principles may be drawn from this investigation. First, the anarchic urbanization of Marrakech can only be controlled on condition that it acts on the system of production, according to a rigorous system of urban planning.

Second, Morocco's housing crisis is a structural problem. It is nothing short of an expression of the country's dynamic of underdevelopment. Without the engagement of a progressive dynamic based on the search for increased work productivity and capital, we will see the perpetuation of a vicious circle affecting its inhabitants (poverty → lack of skills → precarious work → unsanitary housing → and back again to poverty). Even in the realm of housing production, the dominant process of auto-production remains archaic and fails to set a productive dynamic into motion. As far as the public authorities are concerned (in the project to build 200,000 homes), instead of placing the problem in its larger context, the policy remains isolated and fails, therefore, to bring about structural change.

Third, the laws for the intervention of public authorities in the area of housing production are themselves problematic. Instead of distributing tasks between the public and private sectors, the public sector enjoys hegemony – in terms of producing laws and regulations, in terms of the production of lots and housing, in terms of restructuring unsanitary spaces, and so on. As a result, there is confusion on the level of responsibilities and a harmful inefficiency in terms of interventions. All of this translates into added costs, waste of scarce resources, and a supply that fails to meet demand, among other things.

Finally, in addition to the obstacle of real estate and the absence of a construction industry, the question of financing housing has in recent years been posed with great acuity. Instead of providing a response that takes account of the natural coexistence of official and "informal" systems of financing, the public authorities continue to operate as if the latter forms of financing did not exist. Here, too, the community loses.

The question of housing is a matter of social equity. To respond to it correctly requires not only technical and bureaucratic solutions but political courage and audacity as well. These alone can mobilize and engage the social resources required.

Translated from the French by Miranda Robbins

---

44 Institutional savings, which, for example, represented 70,755 million Dhs in 1997 compared to 56,962 in 1995, does not exceed 20 percent of the total investments by nonfinancial institutions. In contrast, liquid advances and short-term investments exceed 75 percent of the investments by nonfinancial agents. (Source: Report from the Bank Al Maghrib, 1997.)

Kisangani and the Curve of Destiny

Jean Omasombo Tshonda

The city of Kisangani lies in the northeast of Democratic Republic of Congo, the vast country in sub-Saharan Africa formerly known as Zaire. Dominating the region's large swampy basin, the city enjoys a monopolistic position. The Belgian colonial authority granted it municipal status in January 1959,[1] and it was called Stanleyville until 1966. In 1970, Zaire's head of state, Mobuto Sese Seko, designated Kisangani the capital of Congo/Zaire's third most important economic region. It is the third largest city, after the capital, Kinshasa, and the city of Lubumbashi.

By 2001, Kisangani's economic situation was deplorable. The city's largest enterprise, a textile factory called Sotexki, once employed 2,500 workers. It now has fewer than a hundred employees.[2] Brassicole Unibra, a brewery and soft-drink company, closed in 1996. Bralima, another brewery which in 1990 had almost a thousand agents, was functioning at 4 percent capacity; that is, producing only 1,250 hectoliters per day instead of 35,000 hectoliters. The Penaco paint factory now operates with two instead of twenty-five agents.[3] The Sorgerie soap factory does not manage to sell a fourth of its output. The population no longer has the financial means to buy its products and turns instead to handmade substitutes. These, though they are certainly of poorer quality, are less expensive. The river port (fourth largest in the country) has been completely devastated. The railroad does not have a single working locomotive. Of the three Tshopo River dam platforms that supply hydroelectricity to the city, only one continues to operate. This city of almost half a million inhabitants no longer has a public mode of transportation,[4] and there are fewer than ten taxis

---

1 After the cities of Kinshasa and Lubumbashi in 1941, and Likasi in 1943.
2 It is worth mentioning that half of these employees are watchmen hired to guard the empty buildings as they await the return of their usual occupants, who are presently unemployed.
3 See *Le Solidaire*, November 27, 1999. This biweekly newspaper is published in Kisangani and owned by Mokeni Ekopi Kane, the provincial president of the Federation of Congolese Enterprises.
4 In 1974, the public communal transportation enterprises STK and OTCZ had a force of eighteen vehicles.

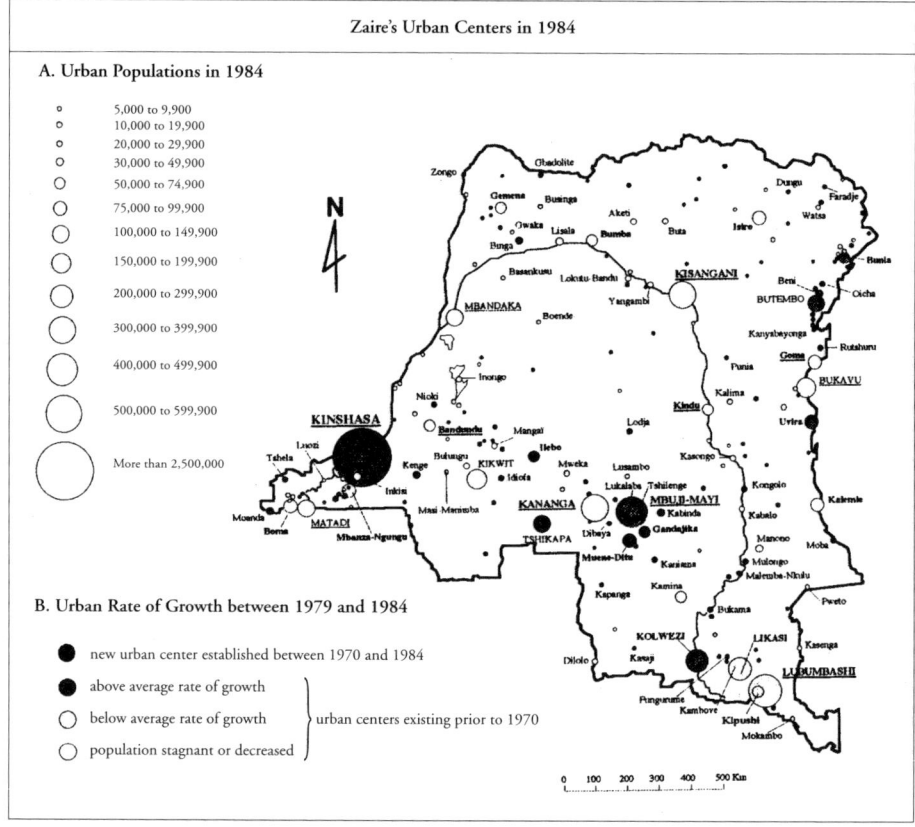

Urban Centers of Democratic Republic of Congo

Source: Jean-Claude Bruneau, "Crise et déclin de la croissance des villes au Zaïre. Une image actualisée," *Revue belge de géographie* 119, nos. 1–2 (1995), p. 107.

in circulation. Toleko bicycles, which began to invade the streets in 1993, are now the only functioning mode of transport.

Everything here is being dislocated and wasting away, to Kisangani's detriment. The city embodies the condition of decline now affecting all the cities of Congo/Zaire. Indeed, it is among the country's most devastated urban centers. Kisangani is a victim both of its riches and of the course of its development, which was inspired by its natural environment and history. Its history is marked by violence and predation. Its natural resources, so easy to exploit, have been "gathered" with the assistance of its own population, made up of farmers, hunters, fishermen, craftsmen, and merchants, who had to produce, exchange, and carry in order to survive. As one porter recounts:

I'm 32 years old. On my bicycle I haul two large sacks of charcoal, destined for sale, along with a small basket for my own household, pondu (cassava leaf), cassava, and firewood. Altogether, this weighs 232.5 kilograms. On certain days I make two, sometimes three, rounds. This is why my friends have given me the nickname "Machine."

Another adds:

I've been transporting supplies on my bicycle for six years. My baggage carrier has been improved – that is, it's reinforced with iron bars, sticks actually, which make it strong enough to take huge loads. I can easily take two sacks of charcoal on it, and I can manage all the hills even though I don't have any brakes. By putting the sole of my foot on the back tire I get the same results I would get with a good pair of brakes. So buying brakes is an unnecessary expense! Besides, brakes wear out the tires.

A third recounts:

My name is Mbole and I've lived in the commune of Lubunga for almost thirty years. I started this job at age 13 in 1968, when I was in the fourth primary class. At that time, I used my uncle's bicycle. He had become my guardian after the death of my parents, and when this man died, he left me four young children. I myself have a wife and three children. I carry pondu, sacks of charcoal, and cassava, which my wife sells in the market on the outskirts of the city. I do everything I can so that all of them can eat and study in schools I can afford. On weekends and holidays I drive the whole family out to the fields. But I have to say: if I've managed so far, it is thanks to the [protection of] fetishes. Despite the difficulty of working as a porter, I'm still healthy. A few of my neighbors are jealous of all that I have, compared to them. They seek to do me harm, but until now they haven't touched me.

It is not surprising that, in Kisangani's case, many of the various survival strategies developed by its population over a hundred years ago are still very much in place. The so-called informal activities[5] that can be seen here constitute neither a miraculous contemporary innovation nor a by-product of the Western economic model,[6] even if the economic environment in which they are practiced is,

---

5 In a country like Congo/Zaire in 2002, "informality," understood in both a narrow sense (as non-regulated activities) and in its larger sense (activities that escape forms instituted by laws, customs, institutions, and cultural models), characterizes the whole of the city's economic life (as well as different spheres of social practice). In other words, it is more than just the economy of "making do" to which the poor generally have recourse.

6 See Valdo Pons, *Stanleyville: An African Urban Community under Belgian Administration* (London: Oxford University Press, 1969).

of course, completely different. As a result of constant, vigorous exploitation, the population has lost "all" power of control over the use of its surplus. Despite the presence of a tiny bourgeois class, which was born at the end of the colonial period, Kisangani's ability to maneuver is persistently weak and limited.

But the survival practices of today have become poorer and poorer[7] and may well show the limits of creativity and inventiveness. Today, the city is marked by a deep sense of anomie. The crisis is partly due to the administrative apparatus of the state as well as the increasing scarcity of goods and services produced by the "modern" (capitalist) economy. The informal economy exploits the opportunities offered by poverty, introducing alternative or substitute products and services to the market. The population sees a rise of misery accompanied by a loss of its moral bearings and falls prey to forms of "deviance." There is most certainly the pursuit of "making do," but in the context of a societal crisis so general, so global, and so dramatic as the one that has taken hold in Congo/Zaire, the phenomena of anomie, accompanied by worsening social relations, dominate.

Kisangani under Arab and Colonial Domination

In 1875, when the explorer Henry Morton Stanley arrived on the actual site of Kisangani, he found a fairly large population base and organized forms of economic activity. He was just a few weeks ahead of the Arab-Swahili slave trader Muhammad bin Hamad (known as Tippu Tib). Until recently, it was thought that the Arabs (or, rather, the Arabized peoples who had come from the southeast) were the city's founders. It is now known that their role was more modest. "Rather," they "amplified and reorganized the previously existing economic networks to their advantage."[8]

Before the arrival of Arabized peoples in the region, Kisangani was already a gateway for considerable commercial activity. The populations located close to the river and its islands (Lokele and Wagenia) exchanged fish with the farmers and hunters of the area: primarily the Bakumu people, but also Bamanga, Topoke, Bambole, Turumbu, and Foma peoples.[9] Stanley relates that about a

---

7 Some rare exceptions to this rule are the airline Air Boyoma, the property of an ethnic Nande; the Palos company, which imports motorcycle and bicycle parts as well as household products (also owned by ethnic Nandes); and Atoul, which is owned by a Lebanese national. The latter dominates the import-export of manufactured products. But here, too, the activities operate on the brink of illegality and exploit products that are of pathetic quality. As far as the airline is concerned, the planes are old Atonovs long since out of use in the eastern countries. As for manufactured products, these come for the most part from Dubai, India, Singapore, and Taiwan, as well as Nigeria.
8 Léon de Saint Moulin, "La formation de la population," in *Kisangani 1876–1976: Histoire d'une ville*, ed. Benoît Verhaegen (Kinshasa: Presses Universitaires du Zaïre, 1975), p. 31.
9 These are the Lokele farmers.

thousand fish, ranging from two to twenty kilograms in size, were caught each day and that the Wagenia fishermen held impressive reserves of smoked fish, which they would sell. Nor was trade limited to provisions. *Pirogues* (wooden canoes), pottery, wooden utensils, fish filets, and metal objects were produced by specialized craftsmen. These artisans generally belonged to specific ethnic groups, such as the Bamanga people, who were renowned as makers of *pirogues* and wooden furniture.

In addition to local trade between the forest and river populations, communication routes enabled medium-range contact and exchange, either via the Congo and its main tributaries or via trails connecting Kisangani with the Uélé to the north, the l'Ituri to the east, and the Opala to the south. Neither the Arabs nor the Europeans created these trails, which attest to a degree of medium-distance traffic prior to their arrival. These groups, however, intensified traffic and diversified the merchandise carried along the routes; to handicrafts and food supplies were added ivory, slaves, arms, and provisions for military troops. Improved routes enabled long-distance commerce, toward Zanzibar and the eastern coasts for the Arabized traders and toward Kinshasa and the western ports for the Europeans. These ports were the destinations for products leaving the region or arriving from Asia and Europe, respectively.

The Arab occupation of Kisangani and the region lasted eighteen years (1875–93). Ivory and slaves were its essential economic objectives. The slave trade was not in itself considerable but was mainly connected to the necessities of ivory transport. Since Arab and Arabized merchants were not numerous in Kisangani, they needed to maintain good relations with local populations. Gilles Bibeau writes that "in Kisangani, Arab residents cultivated fields and raised chickens, sheep, and goats on a small scale"[10] They developed merchant connections to local populations in order to obtain ivory and provisions and used violence only if villagers refused to sell to them. The installation of the first Europeans in 1883 took place without difficulties and with the assistance of the Arabs. Relations began to deteriorate beginning in February 1886 with the arrival of a new representative of the Congo Free State (CFS). Calm was restored fairly quickly in June 1887 when Stanley appointed Tippu Tib governor on behalf of the CFS. On an economic level, the Europeans took control of commercial activity and ivory trade.

Tippu Tib recounts the details of the new European economic dominance:

---

10 Gilles Bibeau, "La communauté musulmane," in *Kisangani 1876–1976*, pp. 181–240.

> They loaded ivory every month, even if they could not always take away the whole stock. Stanley Falls [today, Boyoma Falls] was populated with Europeans, and you could find anything you wanted to buy there. Stanley Falls became a great port where you could get whatever you desired. Both Belgian and French companies established themselves there, and factories were springing up everywhere. ... Every steamboat that arrived would leave with a full load of ivory.[11]

Collaboration between Europeans and the Arabized traders disintegrated definitively with Tippu Tib's departure in April 1890. The competition over ivory gathering became more and more grim and finally degenerated into open conflict in 1892. The defeated Arabized traders eventually ceded the terrain to the Europeans, but for almost twenty years, Kisangani and its hinterland had been the theater of intense commercial activity. Tons of ivory were collected, transported, and resold; thousands of foreign men (as soldiers, auxiliaries, and porters) passed through the region and hundreds stayed on; caravans of many hundreds, sometimes thousands, of men traversed the region in search of ivory or engaged in military occupation of the country. These men had to be fed, their merchandise had to be carried, and trade products were exchanged with them. Tippu Tib writes in his autobiography that he arrived in Stanley Falls in 1883 accompanied by "three thousand men armed with rifles and six thousand unarmed men" and that after his arrival he organized some twenty caravans of several hundred men each.

In 1891, the new European occupier (the Congo Free State) claimed its right to all products derived from land owned by the state, thereby gaining control of the lucrative trade in rubber and ivory. This situation put the population of Kisangani at a profound disadvantage. As Bogumil Jewsiewicki affirms, it "put the city's economic position back into question" and "the economy of the Stanley Falls hinterland was condemned to stagnation by the concessionary system. Payment in kind replaced Swahili commerce, bringing about a slide back into subsistence for the local people."[12]

By 1897, it had lost its role as economic capital to the Swahili zone and as point of transit between the Arabized east and the European western part of the Congo. Officially it became capital of the entire eastern part of the country, even encompassing the provinces of Katanga (for a few years) and Kivu (until 1933). In fact, it was only a minimally developed administrative center surrounded by a few Congolese villages. "According to the witnesses of the period," Jewsiewicki continues,

---

11 Ibid, p. 212.
12 Bogumil Jewsiewicki, "Histoire d'une ville coloniale: Kisangani 1877–1960," *Les Cahiers du Cedaf* 5 (1978), p. 4.

the Arabized village of Kisangani-Singitini and the villages of Wagenia and Lokele, near the Falls, seemed prosperous enough. But their integration into the city, much like this city's integration into the monetary economy, was never actually achieved. The trade between these villages and the soldiers in the city was reduced to provisions in exchange for indigo; that of the Wagenia villagers was limited to fish in exchange for fabrics brought by the administration and its agents. The city, which did not in fact really exist yet, consisted merely of the administrative seats of the district commissariat and of European judges, beginning in 1908. Apart from the "boys," and soldiers of the Force Publique who lived in the field near the station, Africans did not actually live there; the city was a very small center for employment and was, above all, an administrative center.[13]

The population's condition improved with the introduction of tax reforms in 1910[14] and the remuneration of workers engaged mainly in the railroads (CFL, constructed between 1903 and 1906) and the workshops connected to them.[15] Commercial activities began to develop in 1912. The principal products bought from the local population or provided by way of taxes and obligatory agricultural requisitions were rubber, ivory, rice, and palm oil. In 1913, Kisangani had a biweekly and a daily market. Commerce between the city and its hinterland was regulated in that same year by the governor general. Among the diverse products on the market were household utensils, textiles, salt, and petroleum. Traveling peddlers would load up at Belgian as well as Greek and Asian firms. Until 1930, this was one of the rare sectors in which the role of Congolese subjects was sizeable.

After World War I (1914–18), agricultural products like rice, coffee, and palm oil gained importance over such "spontaneous" resources as ivory and rubber, for which the colonial power had a buying monopoly. Between 1922 and the economic crisis of 1930–33, Kisangani saw a rapid development of its commercial and transport activities. The 36 commercial firms counted in Kisangani in 1919 grew to 90 in 1922 and 144 in 1925. According to Jewsiewicki, the Congolese population in the city in 1920 was 4,000, to which one should add the inhabitants of the Arabized village and the village of Wagenia – about 2,000 people. Léon de Saint Moulin suggests a figure of 6,000 in 1921 for the three cities that would ten years later make up the Centre Extra Coutumier,[16] or Extra-Customary Zone, a territory outside the jurisdiction of the customary

---

13 Ibid, p. 10
14 The introduction of a monetary economy involved a switch from taxation in kind (rubber, ivory, nuts, etc.) to the payment of taxes in cash.
15 The estimate is somewhere between 500 and 700 workers.
16 Saint Moulin, "La formation de la population," p. 34.

(traditional) African chiefs. Blacks living in work camps, for example, were subject to colonial authority alone. The term made it possible to distinguish spaces such as work camps from traditional villages. The *cités* of the Extra-Customary Zone were, of course, strictly segregated from the *ville* and its exclusively white population.

The overwhelming majority of inhabitants at this time were workers whom the employers wanted to situate as close to the workplace as possible.[17] They came in part from the "licensed" villages and old military outposts around Kisangani. The colonial administration concentrated workers in three *cités*, or districts (known as Belges 1, Belges 2, and Bruxelles, and later renamed Mangobo, Lubunga, and Kabondo) in order to control them more effectively.

The Extra-Customary Zone in Kisangani was created in 1932 based on a decree of 1931 and was situated on the periphery of the European city. The district of Lubunga lies on the left bank of the river, and Mangobo and Kabondo are on the right bank. At the time of its creation, the area's population was estimated at about 10,000. In 1934, a first rigorous census produced the figure of 10,856. Ten years later, in 1943, the population, at 14,268, was only slightly higher.

How is it that Kisangani's urban population was so weak, although it was already the third largest city in the Congo and the capital of a rapidly growing region? The answer to this question reveals a great deal about the nature of a colonial city in this period. It was, in fact, much more of a work camp than an urban agglomeration. The African population was allowed entry exclusively for the purpose of meeting the demand for labor. It was driven out again upon the completion of work contracts and, more generally, in times of downturn. This mode of controlling the city was made easier by the fact that no black owned the land on which his home was built. Under these circumstances, Jewsiewicki concludes,

> The city was merely an administrative center, above all in its absence of a native bourgeoisie. The stabilization of an African population in the city, beginning with the creation of the Extra-Customary Zone in 1932, only touched the workforce of the colonial economic sector. Neither African trade nor African artisan production had a place in this context, to say nothing of industry. It was marked by the very absence of individual land property for Africans.[18]

---

17 Within this population, it is probable that the number of independents was very weak compared to the number of salaried employees hired by the colonizer. African economic actors were still based in the villages and chiefdoms close to Kisangani or its hinterland, where they independently assured the bulk of quick-growing agricultural production (rice, palm oil, provisions).

18 Jewsiewicki, "Histoire d'une ville coloniale," p. 26.

It was the war effort that, beginning in 1942, relaunched African commerce and crafts and thus marks the beginning of a genuine urban African economy. In Kisangani, the growth of demand for goods and services, the mobilization of a portion of Europeans in the war, the influx of rural people toward the city (bringing with them the necessary agricultural means) all combined to create conditions of social and professional improvement and new activities for an upward-moving portion of the Congolese population.[19]

After World War II, the zone's population swelled because of economic reprise, the arrival of new European colonials, the new projects outlined in the first ten-year plan of 1949, and the economic boom brought on by the Korean War. It grew from 13,500 in 1942 to 38,000 in 1950 and 91,000 in 1959.[20] This growth was accompanied by changes in the economic and social structures. To the administrative and economic responsibilities, concentrated in European hands, were added the economic and social activities necessary for running an urban center: wholesale and retail commerce, crafts, repair workshops, transport, leisure activities, and social services. The local population occupied an increasingly important position in these realms. The Congolese residents of Kisangani created and controlled small businesses catering to the African consumer.[21]

Within ten years, the face of Kisangani and its level of comfort were completely transformed. Although colonial segregation between the white and black cities was maintained, the pre-1940 "work camps" had made way to genuine urban neighborhoods, and the majority of residents owned their own houses.

Kisangani became a center of African economic life, in the proper sense of the word, and this gave birth to a new social class. In January 1959, the colonial authority granted it municipal status. One month later, the city created a motto, *Cuncti gens una* (One nation, together) and a coat of arms, which has been described as a green shield with a silver-colored wavy line running horizontally across the middle, between a golden letter "S" at the top of the shield and a pair of fish, also of gold, placed back-to-back at the shield's point.[22]

---

19 Regarding the social dynamic engendered by the war on the African population, see Benoît Verhaegen, "La guerre vécue au Centre extra coutumier de Stanleyville," in *Le Congo belge durant la Seconde Guerre mondiale: Recueil d'études* (Brussels: ARSOM, 1983).
20 The journal *Congo-Afrique* gives a figure of 109,607 inhabitants for this same year. See *Congo-Afrique* 47 (August–September 1970), p. 377 and passim.
21 Although African-owned firms represented only about 4 percent of the total number in 1949, they made up more than 50 percent of the total in 1956. Toward the end of the 1950s, Africans began to gain a foothold in transport along routes that were rapidly developing at the time.
22 See Roger Depoorter, *Elle est loin l'étoile: Petite chronique congolaise* (Antwerp, 1983), pp. 118–119.

From Independence to the Present

Congo achieved independence in 1960, but this was quickly followed by political crises. The country's small businessmen were utterly unprepared for what would happen. Kisangani, in particular, gradually sank into anarchy. This fragile city regularly served as the theater of war between armed, belligerent factions who coveted state power at the central level.[23]

The First Two Decades The first decade (1960–70) was marked above all by the disintegration of the colonial legacy, which took place long before attempts to reconstruct the city began. The few businesses that were still based in the city moved away during the conflicts, and only a few of them were able to reconstitute themselves after calm was reestablished. It was not until the middle of the 1970s that a few projects in the city were realized. Among these were the construction of the Sotexki textile factory in 1975 and the international airport in 1977.[24] The country's deep economic and political crisis, however, favored few other projects. On the contrary, it was no longer possible to maintain existing infrastructure.

In 1973, Kisangani had a population of 307,971. Overall employment city-wide was only 17 percent, with rates of 37 percent for men and 4 percent for women. If in 1956 the port of Kisangani had fourteen cranes, there were but seven in 1975. The number of packing and loading machines, which had been 86 in 1956, had declined to 72; the number of rickshaws and hand trucks had not changed, nor had the total amount of space occupied by stores along the quay; the number of palettes was dramatically lower, from 2,050 to 848. Even the total tonnage transported attests to a leap backward: 169,292 in 1954 and 203,010 in 1956, compared to 134,607 in 1973 and 99,414 in 1975.

The city had a mere 14.4 kilometers of passable roads, most made of dirt and in terrible condition because of the heavy rainfall that is characteristic of the equatorial region. In 1975, there were 7,472 vehicles in circulation, compared to 3,768 in 1969.

---

23 Between 1960 and 1962, Kisangani became the capital of the revolts let by Antoine Gizenga, whose government there rivaled that of the central government based in Kinshasa. Between 1963 and 1964, it was the base of the followers of (the assassinated prime minister) Patrice Lumumba; in 1966 and 1967, it harbored short-lived revolts against the central government by the ex-officers of the Katanga secession. More recently, in 1996–97, it was invaded by the Rwandan and Ugandan troops who had helped to bring Lawrence Kabila to power; after August 1998, these same troops reoccupied the city, bringing on a new rebellion and fiercely battling each other for control of the city's resources.

24 As soon as this airport opened, however, fraud connected to the export of ivory – a stock of which was seized in 1978 – led the state authorities in Kinshasa to suppress all international flights from the city.

The number of wholesale stores rose from 18 in 1970 to 36 in 1974, while that of retail stores only rose from 129 to 135 for the same period. What dominated the working-class neighborhoods of the city were small shops and redistribution workshops.

The Effects of National Decline on the City   Kisangani's political and economic importance has always been linked to the control of communications and to the transshipment of merchandise because of its geographic position at the terminus of river transport for loads traveling along the Congo. This city is a link in a chain of exploitation favoring the exterior. As such, it has always influenced its hinterland more as an administrative center than as a center of economic attraction.[25] Thus, in the postindependence period, the crisis of public powers quickly had a negative effect on the city's dynamic.

After a series of measures taken to nationalize businesses that had belonged to foreigners, a policy determined by the state authority in 1973–74, Congo/Zaire sank into a prolonged economic crisis, quickly followed by a political one. It has emerged from neither. The state's formal institutions, already much broken up in the 1980s, continued to disintegrate, crumbling in 1993 under the simultaneous battering of army pillage, monetary collapse, and political anarchy. The "complete" disappearance of public administration followed.[26] Today a battered Kisangani bears many of the same traits that marked it at its founding, over a century ago.

The degradation that has characterized Kisangani's history since the late 1970s has progressively and almost entirely wiped out whatever capitalist organization had been installed there in the course of previous periods: coffee plantations are now abandoned; commercial trade has been curtailed due to the deterioration of roads; the ivory trade has been halted (by international agreement); businesses have closed. The city has been deprived of many of the activities that had allowed it to procure a few resources. In 1986, however, diamond reserves were discovered in the city's immediate hinterland. As easily accessible as ivory

---

25 In the early 1970s, Kinshasa alone harbored 90 of the country's 126 industrial businesses, followed by the city of Lubumbashi. These disparities are the legacy of the colonizer, who aimed to achieve maximum profit from invested capital. As a result, capital was concentrated in certain centers to the advantage of the existing infrastructure of external economies, themselves furnished with other enterprises.

26 Today nothing is left but a collection of institutional ornaments, clothed in whatever legal and administrative packaging is still formally in place. Public entities have sprouted from the rubble of this fragmented, trompe l'oeil administration and judicial apparatus. These include the presidency, the ministerial cabinets, security services, offices, and other public establishments and operations of the state. All are more or less autonomous of one another.

had once been, diamonds immediately attracted numerous foreign predators from West Africa (Mali, Senegal, Guinea[27]), Lebanon, and other parts of the Congo. By 1997, the Rwandan and Ugandan occupiers of the region had also gained control of commercial administration. Indeed, the diamond trade provoked wars between the two occupying military forces, struggles similar to the ones that took place between the Arabized traders and Europeans in the late 19th century. Various intermediaries (once known as commissioners) have of course been able to open their own diamond-buying counters (*comptoirs*). Since its victory over the Ugandans, however, the Rwandan occupier has conferred the export monopoly on a Lebanese subject, Kalhil Hamed (known as Bakayoko); all other local merchants must henceforth sell him their purchases at a rate he has fixed.

In fact, the city's situation today, under Rwandan occupation, barely differs from its condition under the domination of Congolese authorities. In 1989, during Mobutu's reign, state authorities had declared that production would be left to small-scale exploitation. Since their discovery, diamonds have been extracted from Kisangani without any investment in return. The collected stones (including the large portion of fakes that slip through) are quickly rebought by independent diggers or by intermediaries. There is considerable turnover. In the course of the first trimester of 1994, for example, 1,123,950.37 carats of diamonds (with an estimated value of US$13,021,402.15) were bought through the *comptoirs* in Kisangani.[28] Combined, the *comptoirs* do not employ more than 200 agents. They are set up in the rooms of old colonial mansions, rented for ludicrously low prices. Compared to the large sums that the diamond trade generates abroad, the prices paid for diamonds in Kisangani are very weak. The buyer's equipment consists of a calculator, a scale for weighing the diamond, a magnifying loupe to discern any defects (such as breaks or holes), and an expert's manual to determine its color.[29]

Official businesses take care of taxes in Kinshasa with the aid of the national bank, which repatriates currency. Expatriates also purchase their residence per-

---

[27] In addition to new refugees, there are the descendants of the Arabized Muslims who did not take part in the conflict between the European and Arab chieftains in the late 19th century. These people continue to live, isolated and withdrawn, on the peninsula of Kisangani.

[28] Of the 43 dealerships (*comptoirs*) installed in March 1994, 36 are controlled by Lebanese.

[29] Since the latest war, which began in August 1998, the Rwandan occupier has brought in a few tractors to dig ditches and rapidly extract the diamonds from certain veins that were thought to be rich in minerals – such as those dispossessed from an old landowner named Pikoro. But the operation yielded nothing, and people in the area have begun to speak of the effects of sorcery. See Jean Omasombo Tshonda, "Diamonds of Kisangani: De nouveaux seigneurs se taillent des fiefs sur le modèle de l'État zaïrois de Mobuto," in *Chasse au diamont au Congo/Zaïre*, ed. Laurent Monnier, Bogumil Jewsiewicki, and Gauthier de Villers (Tervuren, Belgium: Institut Africain-CEDAF; Paris: L'Harmattan, 2001), pp. 79–126.

mits for Kisangani in Kinshasa, and no portion of the proceeds is remitted to the city. Also made in the capital are arrangements connected to obtaining approval for *comptoirs* (US$150,000), the purchase of annual projected license fees (US$100,000), and the payment of 15 percent of the export tax (in American dollars).[30] Even when Kisangani was authorized to sell wholesaler's permits, in 1995, the sharing remained heavily weighted in Kinshasa's favor. Permits cost about US$50 for a digger and US$100 for a wholesaler, but 80 percent of these receipts had to be given over to the national treasury. Only 20 percent was left over for the city and the rest of the province.

Since the late 1990s, instead of producing wealth for the city, Kisangani's diamonds have been exploited more in the spirit of the ruthless Congo Free State. Moreover, the diamond economy has brought about a situation of anarchy for the population. Everybody wants a piece of it. Each decision taken by the authorities is accompanied by a strategy of making demands and setting up detours. Both the general population and the powerful elite are implicated in the procurement and selling of contraband and the looting of public property.

In 1996, there were more than 300 diamond and gold quarries around Kisangani. A massive coming and going of migrant workers toward and away from the pits took place. The activity now occupies most of the local workforce and touches all social categories, including functionaries, business agents, small independents, nurses, ministers, soldiers, and athletes, among others. All hurry toward the pits, where they work as diggers, shopkeepers, dealers, porters, traffickers, intermediaries, and guards. At first, it seems that the initial capital each man brings with him will determine the way he will insert himself into the economy. But in practice, this insertion is largely open and depends on the play of each worker's resources and skills. And in the course of a single year, a worker can pass from one quarry to another in addition to changing jobs. The actors themselves confirm this when they say that each must take his chance everywhere.

The situation is quite clearly dominated by an ethic of fast money, often earned under dangerous and degrading conditions. The values of hard work and perseverance have suffered as a result. Success in school and university, agricultural pursuits, and, in a general way, all activities requiring long-term investment or a process of apprenticeship, have lost their appeal. Moreover, with the diamond stampede, numerous fetishists have gained a foothold in the city, even advertising on the local radio. The straw huts set up in front of their houses

---

30 In 1998, before the new war, the new minister of mines, Frederic Kibassa, arrived in Kisangani at the head of a political-military delegation and ordered the confiscation of all quarries from their former owners, who were accused of being enemy spies.

serve as waiting rooms, and they receive sick people who are too poor to pay a doctor. In this milieu, sorcery appeals to the Congolese population as well as to the Arabized families who have lived in the region since the late 19th century.

The system of small-time exploitation of diamonds on the lowest levels has not changed fundamentally in spite of the enormous political changes that have taken place since Mobuto's fall. These include the rise to power in 1997 of Lawrence Kabila, the Rwando-Ugandan occupation of the city from August 1998 onward, and, most recently, the Rwandan dominance. Rather, it is only the actors at the top and the dominant political-commercial networks who have experienced change based on the various political junctures.

Conclusion

The city of Kisangani remains a reservoir of precious resources and, as such, continues to attract predators. Yesterday they sought ivory. Today they exploit diamonds, gold, coltan (Columbite-Tantalite, an ore that when refined becomes metallic tantalum), and, as always, tropical hardwoods. Throughout its history, Kisangani has never been able to free itself from the course on which it was set during the European-Arab occupation in the late 19th century. Over time, the city saw a certain amount of development and less brutal but always efficient forms of domination, but it continued to play an auxiliary role, and its space was regularly despoiled. Repeatedly confronted by crises, the city withdrew into itself, and its activities were marked neither by durable technical progress nor by the formation of a stable social class. Unable to dispose of the surplus of its activities, the Congolese population was, *a fortiori*, unable to accumulate through productive investment. It was prevented from growing into a center that would attract and dominate the surrounding area and was forced instead, as a primary condition of its survival, to submit to economic pressures placed on it by successive dominators, their administrative rules, and their values.

Kisangani continues to function as a center for commercial exchange in the region. Manufactured products are still brought to it from many countries in Africa and Asia (Dubai) and redistributed through high numbers of small retailers. Private agencies arrange to grant visas on behalf of certain countries. Since 2000, a Somalian national has operated a private telephone network connected to his country's telephone code (00252), which allows the city to enter into contact with the rest of the world. The small traveling peddlers who once plied the routes around the villages on their bicycles have almost disappeared; they have either become diamond diggers in the quarries or operate as sellers close to the quarries.

Today, Kisangani's population subsists increasingly on the cassava-based *chikwange*, vegetables, cassava, banana caterpillars, and so forth. In other words, it depends for its survival more and more on the forest that surrounds the city and less and less on the capitalist economy. As a general rule, the city's population burns wood and charcoal for fuel despite the presence of a dam on the Tshopo River, which is little used,[31] and a hydroelectric center, which was built in 1974 but never in operation. The lack of automobiles means most loads are carried by bicycle, rickshaw, *pirogues*, and on the heads and backs of people. These have once again become the main modes of transport.

The problematic of this paper was inspired by the failure or disappearance of many of the African cities that were once capitals of famous empires and kingdoms. Kisangani was once known to tourists for the waterfalls that lie at the city's entrance and the Wagenia who fish there. It was known for the diversity of its population and as the popular base of the first Congolese prime minister Patrice Lumumba (assassinated in 1961), who became the city's symbol. It was known for the beauty of its women and enjoyed a reputation as a "city of free women."[32] Today most of the signs of its former glory lie in ruin. We face a striking case of perversion; the markers of urbanism are being effaced.[33] Failing businesses are repeatedly pillaged by the political and military-civil authorities, and the traces of modernity are disappearing. The wars to which Kisangani has been almost continually subjected since the fall of Mobutu have driven from the city whatever small investments had once been made there and have destroyed houses dating to the colonial period.

And so, after more than a century of history, Kisangani is indeed experiencing a revolution, but it is a revolution in the original sense of the word. The meteor has made a complete round and returns to its point of departure.

Translated from the French by Miranda Robbins

---

31 This hydroelectric center, constructed between 1950 and 1956, has a potential of 18,000 kWh, but daily use has never exceeded 1,000 kWh.
32 Benoît Verhaegen, *Les femmes zaïroises de Kisangani: Combats pour la survie* (Paris: L'Harmattan, 1990).
33 As AIDS gains ground, it affects prostitutes in particular; Rwandan and Congolese military forces have destroyed the scaffoldings alongside the Boyoma waterfalls (Stanley Falls) that were built by Wagenia fishermen for their traditional fishing techniques; since 1992, there has been a considerable increase in negative sentiment among native residents against outsiders.

Environment and Inhabitants of an Unplanned Area of Zaria, Nigeria

Mohammed-Bello Yunusa

The growth and expansion of towns and cities in Nigeria, particularly from 1900 to the present, brought to the fore problems of livelihood, survival, and environmental maintenance in these places of population agglomeration. The towns and cities have two sectors, each of which represents affluence and deprivation. The affluent sectors are planned and provided with a wide range of urban services, utilities, and facilities, and therefore glitter with the good life. Such sectors are mainly the former colonial European Reservation Areas (where the British administrators once resided) and now Government Reservation Areas (GRAs), occupied by top bureaucrats and businessmen. The GRAs, as enclaves of the rich and powerful, are sparsely populated.

By contrast, and sometimes existing side by side with the GRAs, are the many sections of towns and cities that are densely populated, unplanned, and poorly provided with urban services, facilities, and utilities. In these areas live the poor, the powerless, and the marginalized. These areas are commonly referred to as slums, blighted areas, or high-density areas, and they comprise a substantial proportion of towns and cities in developing countries, Nigeria inclusive. These areas are characterized by poor housing quality and quantity, unsanitary conditions, high illiteracy, and unemployment.[1] Due to the planlessness of these areas, it is almost impossible to effectively provide them with drainage and sewage systems or connection lines to urban facilities, utilities, and services. These areas constitute a sea of poverty at the periphery of African towns and cities. They present urban management problems in terms of food supply and distribution, land allocation and infrastructure, education, housing, transport, and health care (due to, for instance, poor ventilation and accumulated garbage), and pose a challenge to the ability of urban systems to generate employment and income for inhabitants.[2]

---

1 See William J. Hanna and Judith L. Hanna, *Urban Dynamics in Black Africa: An Interdisciplinary Approach* (Chicago: Aldine, Atherton, 1971).
2 See *The Urban Edge: Issues and Innovations* 9, no. 9 (1985) and 11, no. 7 (1987); Andrew G.

It is in the context of these challenges that this paper seeks to document the activity and environmental structure of inhabitants of such an area, using Anguwar Mai Gwado of Zaria metropolis as a case study. Based on the known characteristics of urban unplanned sectors, and in the context of urban development policies, it is important to understand the socioeconomic profile, practices, and welfare of people living in them. This facilitates the implementation of policy measures aimed at enhancing the capacity of the urban poor. The extent to which this can be achieved determines the ability of the poor to pay for urban infrastructure and contribute to municipal revenue that is needed for provision and maintenance of urban services.[3]

The purpose of this paper therefore is to detail the conditions of habitation and livelihood among the urban poor. Objectives include characterization of the living environment of the urban poor in unplanned areas, and an evaluation of how people in such areas organize and manage economic deprivation to meet social responsibilities. Thus the paper highlights the types of activities of individuals and their roles in household maintenance and sustenance. Based on these objectives, the paper concludes by highlighting policy implications and suggests ways of improving slum life and empowering poor individuals to cope with urban life.

A description of the physical state and economic activities of the Mai Gwado ward is important to understanding the behavior of the city. As V. F. Costello notes, "Besides being a social entity the city is a physical entity with physical problems, which is formed and structured by the society living in it."[4] To achieve the aims and objectives of this paper, discussions were held with men, women, and youth groups of the ward. The discussions focused on types of employment, housing conditions, major problems of the area, roles of the state and local councils in the development and management of the ward, as well as what can be done to make the place liveable socioeconomically. Further to the discussions, secondary data were also sourced from books, reports, and government publications.

Economic and Urban Development Policies in Nigeria

Towns and cities in Nigeria are subject to changes in economic and urban development policies. While rural-to-urban migration increases employment prob-

---

Onokerhoraye and Gideon E. D. Omuta, *Regional Development and Planning for Africa* (Benin City, Nigeria: Editorial Committee, Geography and Planning Series, University of Benin, 1986).
3 See *The Urban Edge: Issues and Innovations* 9, no. 9 (1985).
4 V. F. Costello, *Urbanization in the Middle East* (Cambridge: Cambridge University Press, 1977), p. 84.

lems, macroeconomic policies have implications for urban living. It should be noted that macroeconomic policies from the mid-1980s were tailored toward managing Nigeria's huge public debt. From the mid-1970s, Nigeria began to experience shortfalls in revenue, increased deficit financing, and accumulated domestic and international debt. The public debt increased annually.

These policies had a crushing effect on the urban poor. In 1970, the public debt stood at 3.4 percent of gross domestic product (GDP). By 1980, it was 3.7 percent, and by 1990 101.4 percent. By 1997, it had declined to 19.1 percent. However, an independent source estimates Nigeria's debt to be far higher: US$36.1 billion, which represents 133 percent of GDP.[5]

Economic Policies The policies directed at managing public debt include commercialization and or privatization of urban services, utilities, and facilities; devaluation of the naira against the US dollar; and appropriate pricing measures in both private and public sectors. Economic deregulation and commercialization policies that were fashioned to manage this situation drove up the unemployment rate, undermined purchasing power, and increased the cost of living.

The employment situation was aggravated by retrenchments in the public and private sectors of the economy. According to the Federal Ministry of Labor, in 1986 there were 85,158 registered unemployed lower grade workers. In the same year, 13,050 vacancies were declared for that category of workers but only 2,139 were placed or employed. In 1996, there were marginal improvements in the situation. There were a total of 83,411 registered unemployed, 8,940 vacancies, and 3,927 placements. Unemployment among professionals was very high in 1996 during which there were 30,467 registered unemployed, 3,694 vacancies, and only 72 placements.[6] These unemployment rates are mere indicators: millions of unemployed and underemployed Nigerians do not register with the labor office. In 1991, it was noted that 70 percent of secondary school graduates were unemployed.[7]

Urban poverty is exacerbated by the ever-rising cost of living. According to the Central Bank of Nigeria (CBN), the consumer price index for housing, fuel, and electricity was 1056.7 in 1994, 2525.6 in 1997, and 4945.5 in 1999. To put it differently, the composite price index for all items in urban areas was 25.2 in 1976, 110.1 in 1986, and 2771 in 1996. The consequence of this high cost

---

5 See S. Ibi Ajayi, "Nigeria: A Profile of Debt," *IDRC Reports* 20, no. 3 (October 1992), pp. 11–12.
6 See Central Bank of Nigeria, *Statistical Bulletin* 9, no. 1 (June 1998).
7 See Federal Office of Statistics, *A Statistical Profile of Nigerian Women* (Lagos, 1995).

of living is increased economic deprivation and an inability to meet basic needs, particularly among the poor.

Urban Development Policies Rapid urbanization places stress on urban services, infrastructure, water, waste disposal, housing, health, and transportation. To contain these problems, certain measures were needed particularly with an urbanization rate that far outstrips national population growth.[8]

Urban development policies were first formulated in Nigeria in 1861 in Lagos colony. Between 1861 and 1927, policies focused on solving health and hygiene problems, the control and prevention of hazards (particularly the spread of fire and disease), the development of sectors occupied by colonial administrators and protection of these sectors from the indigenous population, the creation of housing and road regulations, defining hierarchies and classes of towns and cities, and processes of land acquisition. In 1946, the Nigerian Town and Country Planning ordinance was enacted.

The 1946 ordinance provided the basis for replanning, improving, and developing towns and cities in Nigeria. The northern region within which Zaria is located adopted the ordinance in 1963. Yet, the Mai Gwado ward is still not indicated on the map of Zaria metropolis.

The urban development law of 1963, which is still operational, provided support for the creation and establishment of the Kaduna State Urban Planning and Development Authority (KASUPDA), the main urban development agency in Kaduna State. Currently, KASUPDA, the Sabon-Gari Local Government Council, and the Kaduna state government administer Anguwar Mai Gwado. KASUPDA enforces and monitors development control measures and overall physical development patterns in the ward, as it does in other towns and cities in Kaduna State.

In addition to KASUPDA's activities, the Local Government Council has statutory responsibilities to provide certain services, utilities, and facilities to citizens in both urban and rural areas. The local government reform of 1976 makes it the responsibility of local councils to provide sanitation inspection, sewerage, refuse and night soil disposal, public conveniences, community and recreation centers, parks, gardens, and open spaces, the naming of roads and streets, rural and semi-urban water supply, pollution control, public utilities (particularly transport), and town and country planning, among many other duties.

---

8 See André McNicoll, "The Ills of Urbanization: India Looks for a Solution," *IDRC Reports* 14, no. 3–4 (October 1985), p. 39.

The 1992 Urban and Regional Planning Law mandated that the council prepare and adopt local, subject, and town plans.⁹ Discussions with council officials reveal that they implement reforms in areas deemed favorable and ignore areas of low political and economic reward. Moreover, officials demonstrate a lack of awareness of these latter areas. Thus, over time, the councils have failed to build capacities for executing their responsibilities effectively.¹⁰ Adepoju Onibokun notes that the town and country planning law is not implemented in Nigeria because the responsible institutions are unaware of their planning and development obligations.¹¹ Those who *are* aware do not have the capacity (manpower, equipment, and finance) to execute their programs.

The Place: Anguwar Mai Gwado

Size and History   Anguwar Mai Gwado is in the Sabon-Gari local government area (SLGA) of Kaduna State. The ward has a population of 12,343 in the 1991 national population census. While the SLGA has a population of 224,067, Kaduna State has a population of about 4 million.

Mai Gwado is part of the Sabon-Gari district of Zaria metropolis. Zaria is an ancient city and the capital of one of the seven Hausa states, the Zauzzau kingdom. Zaria city (*Birnin Zariya*) was the headquarters of the Zauzzau kingdom administered by the emirate council headed by the emir.¹² Zaria metropolis is made up of Zaria city, inhabited by the indigenous people; Tudun-Wada, inhabited by the Hausa and Fulani migrants; and Sabon-Gari, inhabited by non–Hausa-Fulani and non-Muslim migrants. The town of Zaria has expanded over time to encompass other settlements such as Chikaji, Muchiya, Samaru, Palladan, Bassawa, Kwangila, Jemaa, and Dogon-Bauchi. These settlements are now wards in the Zaria urban system.

---

9 Local and town plans are physical development proposals out of which a subject plan is derived to provide details on specific aspects such as water supply, residential layout, health facility development, etc., for implementation.

10 It takes international institutions like the World Bank and the United Nations Development Programme (UNDP) to sensitize local councils on their responsibilities and appropriate policies for raising the standard of living of the urban poor in high-density areas. This is similar to the experience of Ma'aruf Sani working with the UNCHS in Kauru, a high-density area around Abuja, Nigeria's capital.

11 Adepoju G. Onibokun, "Nigerian Cities in the Twenty-first Century," paper presented at the 1997 World Habitat Day Celebration, October 6, 1997, Abuja, Nigeria.

12 See Sule Bello, "Birnin Zaria," *Nigeria Magazine: Cities of the Savannah* (Lagos: Federal Ministry of Information, n.d.).

Physical Characteristics Houses in Mai Gwado are built of mud or cement. A few zinc houses were noticed during a visit to the area. Most floors of buildings are of mud and cement. All houses are roofed with corrugated iron sheets. About a third of the inhabitants are tenants, who pay between 200 and 250 naira[13] per month in mud houses and between 300 and 350 naira per month in cement houses. The houses in the area are highly vulnerable to storm water. According to community members, many houses collapse during the rainy season due to weak structures. Houses are prone to waterlogging and being washed away by heavy rain floods. Storm water from neighboring wards accumulates in the area and causes houses to collapse during the rainy season. In addition, domestic wastewater drains into access ways and paths, making travel difficult. Local council staff occasionally visit the area to assess the damage but offer no solutions to the problems.

Physical inspection of the ward revealed that most houses can be reached on foot, bicycle, or motorcycle. There is only one motorable access way in the area. The access ways or paths are irregular and rough, and also serve as drainage for storm water during the rains as there are no drainage systems.

Anguwar Mai Gwado was originally a small settlement of farmers who migrated from Kofar Doko in old Zaria city. Its current site, on marshy land behind the walls of the military depot, was settled in 1945–46. Subsequent settlers were attracted by the available agricultural land adjacent to the ward, which they converted to residential use.

At this time, Mai Gwado was still a small village, and government or planning services were yet to take control of the growth and development of the ward. Thus, the area developed organically without a plan. The return of World War II veterans reinforced the unplanned pattern of development and growth in the settlement. From about 1950, the ward grew with squatter settlers (*yan shara guri zoana*), who were drawn by the fact that land was not sold – the ward head simply allocated land to individuals willing to settle there. (Today, land is a commodity in the ward. A plot of land that cost 20 to 70 naira in the 1970s currently sells for about 150,000 naira.) Most of the newcomers built houses on any available land. The first squatters were mainly railway workers, followed by workers from the Nigerian Tobacco Company and Ahmadu Bello University, in addition to war veterans from Chad Republic and Niger Republic who fought on the same side with Nigerians in the British army. Thus, new settlers, mainly non-indigenes of Zaria made up of railway workers and ex-servicemen and their families, moved into the area and built their own houses on free or cheap plots

---

13 118 naira = about US$1.

of land. It is estimated that about a third of Mai Gwado's current population are retired military men and their families.

Housing and Facilities   Between the late 1970s and early '80s, facilities and services were extended to the area by the government. Water supply lines were extended to the ward in 1979–80. The Local Government Council (LGC) began construction of culverts and minor pathway maintenance in 1991. A primary school was established for the community in 1981. Approval of development plans by urban planning agencies began in 1990. Since that time, buildings are never erected without a certificate of occupancy and an approved development plan.

The ward has taps without water, lacks a drainage system, and has a weak electricity supply. Heaps of accumulated garbage and human waste are common sights in the area. To control run-off erosion, people use sandbags, which appear too few and small in size to be effective.

Most of the houses are said to have all household facilities (kitchen, bathroom or bath place, and toilet). However, the ward head stated that most people defecate in the open, indicating that not all houses have toilets. During the rains, human waste is washed into the River Galma, which is a major source of domestic water in the area. This is a characteristic feature of areas inhabited by the urban poor. André McNicoll noted that in an Indian slum, "raw human waste floats in the streets contaminating already scarce fresh water supplies."[14]

Sources of domestic water in the area include streams, shallow wells, and sometimes tapwater. Some households in the ward go to the city center to fetch drinking water from the taps. Although Mai Gwado has a pipewater network, water does not flow from the taps. The ward head attributes this to the population size and the inability of the waterworks to pump adequate water to the ward. The women are bitter about the lack of water in the area as it impinges on their household chores and economic activities, which include preparing snacks and drinks for sale. Some houses have wells but many do not. In any case, at the peak of the dry season, the wells dry up and the community resorts to collecting water from the military depot, other parts of Sabon-Gari, and the River Galma. According to the ward head, the river is unhealthy:

> During the rains, the river is flooded by storm water from many parts of Sabon-Gari. In addition to this, people bathe, wash, and fish in the river. Yet people collect water from the river for household consumption.

14 McNicoll, "The Ills of Urbanization."

The area's electricity network receives a weak current, if any. According to the people, this is so because there is only one transformer, which serves both Anguwar Mai Gwado and Anguwar Mallam Sule. There are no health facilities in the area. People go to other wards like Sabon-Gari, Anguwar Fulani, and the military depot to obtain health care services. A local council clinic that opened in Mai Gwado was moved to another ward for unexplained reasons. This is an indication of the weak capacity of the inhabitants to negotiate for welfare improvements.

Administration of the Ward Anguwar Mai Gwado is administered by the Sabon-Gari Local Government Council and traditional administrative structures. Together with Anguwar Mallam Sule, the ward has an elected councillor. There is a Sarkin Juchi and Mai Gwado (i.e., the Hakimi) who operate under the Zaria Emirate Council. Under the Hakimi is the Mai Anguwar (ward head), who attends to the day-to-day affairs of the ward. He reports issues beyond his jurisdiction to the Hakimi, who transmits reports to the Local Government Council or the Emirate Council for attention.

One interviewee, a resident of the ward, described the leaders as corrupt, weak, and incapable of representing the interests of Mai Gwado. According to the interviewee, this explains the level of decadence observed there.

The traditional authorities in the area mobilize people for environmental sanitation. This is often done in conjunction with the Mai Gwado Development Association. These activities include sweeping and cleaning blocked "drains" and roads in the area.

Occupation and Income of Residents

Occupation The original settlers were mainly fishermen, hunters, and farmers, the latter engaged in both upland and *fadama* (lowland) farming in wet and dry seasons. Proceeds from these activities were either sold for cash or consumed in the household.

Women in present-day Mai Gwado are engaged in local snack preparation for sale. Food items include groundnut cake (*kulikuli*), drinks (*kunu, zobo,* etc.), bean-cake (*kosai*), rice, beans, cassava, yams, and maize. In addition, women knit, weave, and tailor clothing. They also engage in wet and dry grinding, and the sale of fuel wood and palm oil. The involvement of women in low-income forms of livelihood was earlier documented by Kate Meagher and me:

Women accounted for 41 per cent of enterprise heads and 45 per cent of informal sector labor. Owing to the omission of some of the more invisible activities from the study, this is likely to understate the real level of female participation. ... there is an overwhelming concentration of female participation at the low end of the informal sector.[15]

Earnings from these activities enable women to support themselves, their children, and sometimes other family members. In the women's discussion group, it was strongly asserted that their income is critical to households in which the male head has no regular income. The men's discussion group did not contradict this.

According to the elder population, youths are not taking up fishing, hunting, and farming as modes of livelihood. Rather, they learn bricklaying, carpentry, shoe mending, haircutting, and repair of electrical equipment. This was confirmed by discussions with women, who also assert that the youths have no work. While many girls are involved in sex work, the boys are into drunkenness and drug abuse, with a few youth operating motorcycle taxis, working in barber shops or hair salons, tailoring, shopkeeping, load-carrying using wheelbarrows, and such other economic activities. Few young people in Mai Gwado attend school up to university level, which would provide entry into the organized private and public sectors of the economy. There is a high level of unemployment and underemployment in the community, particularly among secondary school graduates.[16] Occupation wise, while older members of Mai Gwado are engaged in primary production, young people, when employed, work mainly in the informal sector providing services to meet urban demands.

Income The mean monthly income of a sample of household heads in the ward is 27,710 naira, that is, four times the 1998 minimum wage in the public sector (5,996 naira).[17] This income is in addition to cash gifts from friends, parents, other relatives, and patrons. Those who receive cash gifts get about 3,000 naira a month.

Among other members of households, which include grown children and women, the mean income per month from various economic activities is esti-

---

15 Kate Meagher, with Mohammed-Bello Yunusa, *Passing The Buck: Structural Adjustment and the Nigerian Urban Informal Sector* (Geneva: UNRISD Discussion Paper 75, 1996), p. 8.
16 See Mohammed-Bello Yunusa, "Life in an Urban High Density Area: The Case of Anguwar Mai Gwado in Zaria, Kaduna State, Nigeria," draft research report submitted to CODESRIA, Dakar, as a contribution to the Urban Process and Change in Africa Research Programme, February 2002.
17 Ibid.

mated to be about 19,000 naira, which is about three times the minimum wage of 1998. This is also in addition to monthly cash gifts of between 60 and 5,000 naira.[18] The cash gifts represent remittances from friends and relatives to support welfare and other activities.

Participants in the discussion groups indicated that much of their income is spent on food, school fees, health bills, house maintenance, electricity, and water. Indeed, 80 percent of sampled household heads in the ward spend one-half to three-quarters of their income on household food.[19] This is supported by other members of households, who report spending almost two-thirds of their income on household food. Overall, food expenditure consumes a hefty proportion of people's earnings.

Major Problems of Mai Gwado

All the discussion groups were asked to identify factors inhibiting a decent livelihood and existence in Mai Gwado. The responses are revealing. According to residents, problems include the lack of paved roads, a drainage system, a police post, a health center, and policies that would stimulate economic activities and provide employment for young people.

Efforts to develop paved roads have been resisted by property owners. The lack of roads inhibits such economic activities as sale of fuel wood by women. Delivery vehicles are only able to offload at convenient points for further transport to the compounds. This adds to the cost of transport and reduces profit levels. Furthermore, the lack of roads virtually precludes the construction of a drainage system in the area.

The need for a police post is based on the level of crime and drug abuse in the area. The ward head illustrated this by pointing to a large compound inhabited by prostitutes, thieves, and drunks who are sometimes protected by retired military personnel in the ward and the former Hakimi who owns the property. As one respondent put it:

> Kids in this area are undisciplined. They and their friends from outside this ward perpetrate criminal activities here. They use the army depot as a shield such that the ward is a breeding place for criminals. It is important to therefore clear all drinking joints and put a police post in this area to control the situation.

18 Ibid.
19 Ibid.

Discussions revealed that the ward head is constantly engaged in settling disputes. One that was witnessed during a discussion session had to do with a prostitute who bought some sticks of cigarettes and could not pay. The case was settled when an onlooker paid the trader 20 naira for the cigarettes. The high level of crime in the area is attributed to youth unemployment. Thus the discussants suggested the formulation and adoption of favorable policies that would:

- support agricultural activities through provision and availability of farm inputs, particularly fertilizer for both wet and dry season farming;
- make it possible for those in primary and secondary schools to learn various manual trades for self-employment upon graduation; currently people attend schools only to learn how to read and write without learning any skills, a situation that is not helping young people acquire jobs;
- enable the local councils and regional (state) governments to set up training workshops in various trades in the ward and other parts of the city for young people; this was stressed to be of particular benefit to the existing unemployed youth.

As for the women, the biggest problem is unviable economic activities. The activities are unviable due to small capital base. Household demands tend to deplete such capital and this leads to the collapse of the economic venture. Women in purdah (secluded in the household buildings or compounds) engage in food and snack preparation for sale, tailoring, knitting, petty trade, and sale of fuel wood. The men's discussion group agreed that women in purdah should be aided to acquire sewing, knitting, and machines for extracting groundnut oil. All of these economic activities are conducted inside the compounds. Children hawk food and snacks prepared by the women. Some women do not have children to hawk for them and this inhibits their income-earning capacity. It was noted at a discussion that schooling has taken children away from home and such activities as hawking.

The elder women are freer to move about than the younger ones, who are in purdah most of the time. Thus the elder women engage in buying and selling outside their homes. These women move between cities, buying and selling various wares, particularly used cloth. They go to Kano, Kaduna, and even Cotonou in Benin Republic for trading activities. The biggest problem for these women is lack of adequate funds to expand their trade. Efforts to resolve the problem of inadequate capital through small-scale soft loan institutions have not been fruitful.

Under the structural adjustment program, small-scale soft loan institutions such as the Community Bank, Peoples Bank, National Directorate for Employment, Family Support Program, Family Economic Advancement Program, and Poverty Alleviation Program were created. These institutions have the mandate to mobilize resources and provide soft loans for small-scale income-earning activities in rural and urban areas to alleviate the harsh effects of structural adjustment on poor households.[20] In small units of ten to twenty persons, organized as cooperatives or credit unions, women have approached these institutions for loans. They have received promises that were never fulfilled. Efforts to secure the aid of an elected councillor from the ward were unsuccessful, as the councillor refused to listen to them. The community, particularly women and youth, felt the councillor should have approached the loan institutions as their advocate. The noncooperation of the councillor was the end of the road. Without loan assistance, the women's income-earning activities remain at the lowest ebb.

This explains in part why so much of women's time is spent on childcare, household chores, and other non-income-generating activities. From a study in the ward (Table 1), it was found that most women devote their time to recreation, domestic duties, and social support networks.[21] As revealed in the discussion groups, women generate income from petty trade and petty commodity production, the products of which are hawked or sold from their homes. These are essentially informal-sector activities.

Women carry much of the burden of household chores. Men devote a greater number of hours per week than women on most other activities. It is normal for men to be more involved in social networks and support than women since the latter's movements are restricted.

From their earnings, women are able to support homes in which the man is unemployed. However, a good proportion of their earnings goes into funding daughters' marriages. Proceeds from women's various economic activities are invested in buying plates, bowls, cupboards, and clothing for female children in preparation for their wedding. This can take years of saving, buying, and accumulation. Much of the funds from rotating credit unions (*adashi*) are put into this. Women who have no female children or have wedded them all out often feel relieved to have escaped the traditional burden.

Most young people who were interviewed had attended and finished secondary schools and hoped to proceed to university. The youths constitute the bulk of the Mai Gwado Youth Association, which was formed with the aim of promoting the physical development and healthy environment of the ward. Fur-

---

20 Federal Government of Nigeria, Guidelines for the Implementation of Poverty Alleviation Programme.
21 See Yunusa, "Life in an Urban High Density Area."

Table 1. Mean Hours Spent on Various Activities in Mai Gwado per Week by Gender

Activity	Mean Hours per Week	
	Male	Female
Formal employment	10.9	3.8
Recreation	37.4	38.9
Social network	34.3	28.9
Farmwork	8.0	0.6
Other employment	23.1	21.4
Household chores	14.3	28.6
Worship	5.9	1.7
School attendance	2.6	2.9

thermore, the association is involved in promoting education of members to improve their welfare. The association mobilizes community members to carry out road maintenance and clear burial grounds, among other activities. When students are on vacation, it organizes revision classes to keep them busy. There are two centers in the ward for such classes.

Young people claimed that the level of unemployment among youth of the indigenous population is low, as this category is usually engaged in some form of economic activity. However, they acknowledged the fact that drunkenness, crime, and drug abuse among youth in the area is very high. Friends of young people in Mai Gwado come to the area and together they drink, smoke, take drugs, and commit crimes. They attributed this to idleness.

Young people who are self-employed in the informal sector have difficulty funding the expansion of their businesses. Like the women of Mai Gwado, their visits to small-scale soft loan providers have not yielded any positive results. Normally, the youth – again like the women – complete the required loan forms, attach their passport-size photos, and submit the materials to the relevant loan institution. After repeated visits to the institution and no loan is forthcoming, the applicants simply give up.

Social Network and Support

Issues were raised with inhabitants on their membership in various civil society associations and the type of assistance offered by these organizations at the individual and household level. Social organizations among the people of Mai Gwado include rotating credit institutions (*adashi*), town/regional or ethnic unions, and religious groups.

According to those who belong to such associations, they help them to organize naming and marriage ceremonies (as do relatives). None of the associations provide assistance with household supplies and maintenance. Through the credit associations, people are able to mobilize funds for various small-scale economic activities and household responsibilities such as wedding and naming ceremonies and even building repair. On the whole, although people are members of various unions, family and interpersonal networks are said to be more critical to survival and everyday life in urban areas.

Conclusion

Anguwar Mai Gwado is highly cosmopolitan, drawing its population from various parts of the country and outside. The incomes of the inhabitants are relatively high compared with Nigeria's national public-sector minimum wage. A large proportion of earned income is spent on food. The food expenditure is supplemented by income earned by other household members.

The community and household infrastructure is rather poor. The ward lacks roads, drainage systems, and efficient water and electricity supply. The lack of infrastructure is one of the major problems indicated by both men and women. People are members of cooperative, ethnic, and religious associations and credit societies. Membership is a way of identifying with ethnic origin and the aspirations of the community, or seeking economic and social advancement. Membership in associations is said to be helpful in arranging marriage and naming ceremonies.

Options offered by the people for improving the livelihood of residents in unplanned areas need serious consideration. The suggested policies would economically empower the residents. Improving the economic base of the area is crucial to empowering the people to increase their earning capacity and enable them to maintain their environment, redevelop their houses, and pay for urban services and utilities as a basis for improved services and utilities provisioning.

Furthermore, it is pertinent to build and strengthen the capacity of institutions responsible for the management of urban areas to make them relevant to the needs and aspirations of inhabitants. In pursuing this, it is imperative to establish communication lines between the institutions and urban communities to render urban governance more responsive, democratic, and participatory.

The City Center:
A Shifting Concept in the History of Addis Ababa[1]

Bahru Zewde

Historically, towns have grown around political, religious, or commercial centers. The palace or castle, the church/cathedral or mosque, and the market have generally served as the nucleus for urban settlements that have ultimately produced some of the major cities known today. In more recent times, railway terminals have served as centers of bustling urban life. Yet, as towns evolve into cities, they tend to assume a polycentric character. It is difficult to think of only one center for a metropolis. Old centers diminish in importance and new ones emerge. Commercial and cultural centers tend to overshadow political and religious ones. Thus, the West End has come to overshadow The City in London, and Times Square and Broadway likewise outshine Wall Street and its environs in New York.

Most cities of sub-Saharan Africa trace their origin to the colonial period. As such, they were influenced by the segregationist character of colonial urban policy. In effect, two towns have grown, one for the Europeans and another for the Africans. This pattern has become even more accentuated in situations where there is a sizable white settler community. Ethiopia differs from this pattern in some significant ways. By and large, urban development has been autochthonous. Two exceptions in Ethiopia are the railway town of Dire Dawa in the east and the inland port of Gambella in the west. The former long served as a sanatorium for the French community in Djibouti, who migrated in large numbers during summer to avoid the torrid climate of their colony. Eventually, they came to acquire a quarter of the town distinct from the area of Ethiopian settlement. In the case of Gambella, the British rulers of the Sudan converted the enclave they had acquired into a distinctive settlement opposite the Ethiopian village. In both cases, the two quarters were conveniently divided by a stream.

Addis Ababa falls into the pattern of autochthonous development referred to above. With the exception of the brief intervention of the Italians in the second

---

[1] The research for this essay was conducted as part of the CODESRIA-sponsored network on "Urban Processes and Change in Africa."

half of the 1930s, its evolution had an internal dynamic. Brief though it was, the Italian occupation did leave behind some enduring features of the urban landscape, however. Nor is this to deny completely the pertinence of other external factors in the evolution of Addis Ababa. As we will see in more detail below, the railway and air transport have played an important role in shaping settlement patterns. The advent of the railway in 1917 was the single most important factor in the gradual and still perceptible southward shift of the city center. This impact of the railway is consistent with its role in urban growth elsewhere in Africa. Indeed, cities like Nairobi owe their very genesis to the railway.[2] Addis Ababa's two airports, which were constructed after the introduction of air transport into the country in 1946, have successively attracted settlement by the affluent classes of society. Ironic as it may seem, Ethiopians have invariably rushed to settle near airports, not run away from them.

Precursors As an imperial capital, Addis Ababa has two illustrious predecessors: Aksum in ancient times (ca. 1st to 8th century A.D.) and Gondar in the 17th and 18th centuries. Of the two, it is the latter that provides instructive parallels (and some important points of difference) with the evolution pattern of Addis Ababa. French travelers of the early 19th century were ecstatic about this once glorious city, dubbing it "the Paris of Abyssinia."[3] In his study of Gondar and other precursors of Addis Ababa, Donald Crummey made the following observation: "Three major institutions shaped Ethiopian towns during our period: palace, market, and church. These institutions played three roles: political, economic, and cultural. The institutions and roles intertwined."[4] Indeed, one can say that Gondar had its genesis as a market town before it became a political and religious center.[5]

This fact constitutes the first major point of difference with the genesis of Addis Ababa. The site where Addis Ababa emerged had no commercial importance before the foundation of the town. The town of Rogge, an important stag-

---

2 See William John Hanna and Judith Lynne Hanna, *Urban Dynamics in Black Africa: An Interdisciplinary Approach* (New York: Aldine Publishing, 1981), p. 20.
3 Pierre Victor Ferret and Joseph Germain Galinier, *Voyage en Abyssinie, II* (Paris: Paulin, 1847), p. 240.
4 Donald Crummey, "Some Precursors of Addis Ababa: Towns in Christian Ethiopia in the Eighteenth and Nineteenth Centuries," in *Proceedings of the International Symposium on the Centenary of Addis Ababa, November 24–25, 1986*, ed. Ahmed Zekaria, Bahru Zewde, and Taddese Beyene (Addis Ababa: Institute of Ethiopian Studies, 1987), p. 21.
5 See Merid Wolde Aregay, "Gondar and Adwa: A Tale of Two Cities," in *Proceedings of the Eighth International Conference of Ethiopian Studies*, ed. Taddese Beyene (Addis Ababa: Institute of Ethiopian Studies, 1989), vol. 2, p. 61.

ing point on the long-distance trade route from southwestern Ethiopia to the Somali coast, lay some ten kilometers to the southeast. On the other hand, like Gondar, Addis Ababa grew on the slopes of hills overlooking a panoramic expanse of plains leading to Lake Tana in the case of the former and the hills on the edge of the Rift Valley in the case of the latter. As two other French travelers observed: "Gondar is built on a patchwork of isolated hills; it is a broken town. The town proper is located on the summit of a hill: on the slope and at the foot of the hill are found the different quarters."6

More importantly, Gondar, like Addis Ababa, grew around the political and religious centers, the famous castle complex and the renowned "forty-four" churches respectively. Of the latter, the churches associated with the *abun*, the expatriate head of the Ethiopian Orthodox Church and that of his Ethiopian subordinate (the *echage*), were of particular importance. The spontaneous and unplanned growth of Gondar is another feature shared with Addis Ababa. To European eyes, Gondar presented a rather confused picture of "an agglomeration of badly constructed houses, sprouting here and there without order and without plan. The routes of circulation were serpentine paths rather than roads in the strict sense of the word."7

Foundation and Early Years Addis Ababa, which means "New Flower" in Amharic, the lingua franca of Ethiopia, has had a life of just over a century. It was founded in 1886 by Empress Taytu, spouse of Emperor Menilek II (r. 1889–1913), who also gave the name to the new settlement. A major attraction of the site was the hot springs (Fel Weha) whose curative quality had invested it with special value to both royalty and nobility. The area was originally known by the onomatopoeic Oromo term, *Finfine*, expressive of the bubbling hot springs. Royalty and nobility had been shuttling there from their camps on the hills of Entotto to the north before they finally decided to move south for good. On the other hand, the move to the plains to the south was a natural outcome of the greater sense of security and confidence that Menilek and his entourage felt after they had subdued the surrounding population. Yet, not all was plain ground in Addis Ababa. The hills that dotted the landscape became natural nuclei of settlement for the nobility, the highest hill being naturally appropriated by the emperor. It was on this latter hill, not very far from the hot springs, that the imperial palace, the Gebbi, was constructed, forming the first major node of urban settlement.

6 Edmond Combes and Maurice Tamisier, *Voyage en Abyssinie* (Paris: Louis Desessarp, 1838), p. 341.
7 Ferret and Galinier, *Voyage en Abyssinie, II*, p. 236.

But it took a while before the imperial couple and their entourage finally decided to settle on the new site. For some six years, they continued to shuttle between the hilly stronghold at Entotto and the new, more relaxed abode. Letters of Emperor Menilek continued to bear the name of Entotto as the place of writing. It was with the construction of a more permanent structure (a palace) that the shift to the new capital was sealed. That palace has endured up to the present time as the preferred seat of real power, despite attempts by Emperor Hayla-Sellase to shift it to other, more sumptuous locations – one to the north of Menilek's Gebbi in 1934 and another to the south in 1955, the latter on the occasion of the Silver Jubilee of the emperor's coronation. Both the Darg and its strongman Mangestu, and the current leader, Meles, have preferred to barricade themselves in the strategically commanding palace of Menilek rather than the more vulnerable palaces of Hayla-Sellase. Indeed, it is a clear illustration of the reality of power that the prime minister, who heads the government and exercises real power, prefers to reside in Menilek's palace, whereas the president, who is essentially a figurehead, is considered sufficiently dispensable to be quartered in Hayla-Sellase's Jubilee Palace, renamed the National Palace after the 1974 Revolution that overthrew the emperor.

Although not to the same degree as in Gondar, the churches have served as foci of urban settlement, not to mention the fact that a number of neighborhoods (*safar*) derive their names from them. Of the churches, the most important in the early years of Addis Ababa, though not the first to be established, was Saint George Cathedral, located to the northwest of the imperial Gebbi. It arose on the site of a former Capuchin mission in an Oromo village called Birbirsa. The church attained particular prominence in the course of and subsequent to the Battle of Adwa (March 1, 1896), when Ethiopian forces led by Emperor Menilek decisively defeated Italian troops and thereby guaranteed the independence of the country. The battle took place on the day of Saint George in the Ethiopian calendar and there was an apocryphal story that, at the height of the battle, the saint was seen riding his famous white horse goading the Ethiopians on to final victory. The coronation of Emperor Hayla-Sellase in November 1930 in the same church and on the same day of the month enhanced even further the symbolic significance of the church. Appropriately enough, on the occasion of that coronation, an equestrian statue of Menilek came to be placed on the square facing the church.

The ultimate importance of the Saint George area was not only as a religious center, however. Soon, an important market grew up on the slope immediately to the southeast of the church. It came to be known by the term *Arada*, so called according to a prevalent version because of the sloppy nature of the ground. The church is also commonly referred to as "Arada Giyorgis" ("Saint George of

Arada"). Foreign observers who visited the market in its early days were impressed by its vitality and diversity. A British traveler of the early 20th century called it "the commercial pulse of Abyssinia," adding: "In the palpitating life and varied scenes of the market, one might see more of the people and their way of life in one morning than in a week's wandering about the capital."[8] This coupling of religious and commercial functions demonstrated by the Saint George neighborhood was replicated in more recent times, if only to a lesser degree, by the Qirqos church, located in the southern part of the city behind the railway station. Another church that came to have rival status with Saint George as regards to an important religious holiday is the Estifanos (Saint Stephen) church, located across the river from the Economic Commission for Africa (ECA). This church, characteristically built on top of a small hill, overlooks what in the pre-1974 period was known as Masqal ("Cross") Square, because it was there that the highly colorful ceremony commemorating the Finding of the True Cross by Saint Helena (mother of Emperor Constantine) was held. In the revolutionary period (1974–91), the square was expanded and renamed Revolution Square and the Masqal ceremony was transferred back to Saint George Square, where it was held in earlier years. But since the change of regime in 1991, the old Masqal Square has regained both its name and its functions. An additional factor for the growing importance of this square after the 1960s was that it became the entry point into the city of the main road from the international airport at Bole.

The Gebbi and Arada were thus the two nodes around which Addis Ababa emerged in the early 20th century. In the following pages, we shall examine how the centrality of these two points came to be challenged as the town expanded in all directions. For the sake of convenience, we shall divide our treatment of the subject into four distinct periods, more or less coinciding with the major chapters of the country's history in the 20th century. These are: the period up to the Fascist Italian invasion in 1935; the period of Fascist Occupation, 1936–41; the period from Liberation to Revolution, 1941–74; and the revolutionary period, 1974–91.

Developments Up to 1935 The overall impression that the town gave to early visitors was one of "a gigantic camp."[9] Over a half century later, someone who had studied the evolution of the city from a more expert angle could also conclude with the following words: "Addis Ababa was born around the royal tent of

---

8 P. H. G. Powell-Cotton, *A Sporting Trip through Abyssinia* (London: R. Ward, 1902), pp. 116, 168.
9 Count Gleichen, *With the Mission to Menelik 1897* (London: Edward Arnold, 1898), p. 157.

the Shawan king (i.e. Menilek, who hailed from the region by that name in south central Ethiopia), on a hill overlooking a thermal spring. The *Gebbi* was created around the tent, and the camp around the *Gebbi*."[10] Yet, a closer look would reveal that Addis Ababa in these early days was a collection of different camps rather than one camp. Much more apposite, therefore, is the summing up of another study of the city: "a settlement pattern clustered around a series of small nodes which are in turn clustered around larger main nodes; ... a series of radiating paths and routes connecting these nodes as well as exterior areas; ... the entire settlement ... scattered in a series of clusters that were situated outward to a radius of well over one mile in every direction from the Palace."[11]

Addis, in short, was in these early years a conglomeration of interspersed *safars*. The term *safar*, meaning "camp," is especially apt. For what were visible at the outset were a series of more or less self-contained camps. At the center of them all was the royal camp, immediately surrounded not by settlements of the nobility but by the various servants and attendants of the palace. This gave rise to a situation that has not substantially changed to this day, namely that the imperial Gebbi came to be surrounded by veritable slums, as the palace servants could not afford to erect imposing structures and their descendants have continued to live in these hovels. Yet, these plebeian settlements were sufficiently important to give their names to a genre of *safar*, what we may call the occupational *safar*, each *safar* reflecting the specific function of the inhabitants in the imperial palace (workers, saddlers, guards, etc.).

This pattern was duplicated around the other hills or elevated areas of the city, as various members of the nobility erected their dwellings on top of them and these in turn came to be surrounded by the much more modest habitations of their dependents. Understandably, as we have seen in the case of the churches, these various "camps" gave rise to another distinctive genre of *safar*, named after the particular member of nobility whose dwelling served as nucleus (e.g., Ras Tasamma Safar, Ras Berru Safar, Fitawrari Habta-Giyorgis Safar, etc.). A third genre of *safar* – the community *safar* – evolved corresponding with groups who came and settled from different parts of the country, such as Gojjam Safar, Gondar Safar, Gejja Safar, Dorze Safar.[12]

It is possible to identify certain landmarks that gave this rather fluid original settlement a more permanent shape and character. The first, around 1902–03,

---

10 See Édouard Berlan, *Addis Abeba, la plus haute ville d'Afrique: Étude géographique* (Grenoble: Imprimerie Allier, 1963).
11 Martin Eric Johnson, "The Evolution of the Morphology of Addis Ababa, Ethiopia," Ph.D. dissertation, University of California, Los Angeles, 1974, p. 85.
12 See Bahru Zewde, *A History of Modern Ethiopia, 1855–1991* (London: James Currey, 2001), pp. 46–47.

was the importation of eucalyptus trees from Australia. This development was of double significance. First, it gave the city its distinctive foliage. Early travelers commented on the scent of the highly fragrant tree that beckoned them as they approached the city. To this day, Addis Ababa remains a eucalyptus city. More importantly, the importation saved it from the fate of so many other capitals in the Ethiopian past that had to be abandoned as the perennial quest for wood forced a shift to another center. A culture that was voraciously keen on deforestation but not particularly adept at reforestation could only think of moving on when forest resources were depleted. Indeed, Menilek had seriously considered moving his capital to Addis Alam, some sixty kilometers to the west, and had even built an alternative palace there. It was the protest of the legations, who had invested in more permanent structures in Addis Ababa, and the propitious arrival of the eucalyptus that persuaded the emperor to reverse his decision.[13] The legations were particularly fond of this savior of Addis and their compounds are to this day adorned by old specimens of the exotic tree. Ethiopians also embraced it, as it greatly facilitated construction, initiating an important change of style from round to rectangular houses.[14]

The second major landmark was the beginning of the issuance of land charters in 1907. This gave property holders greater security and a stake in the fate of the city. Not only did the land charter become the most prized certificate of any urban household, but it also contributed to activating the urban economy through sales and mortgages. It was on the whole a novel experience and the Amharic lexicon initially had no equivalent for it, preferring to describe it as "the engineer's painting." Later, presumably during the Italian occupation, the Italian term *carta* came to be used and is still in vogue. It is also of interest that the basic geographical frame of reference for the charters was the parish (*atbya*) rather than the *safar*, reinforcing the importance of the churches of Addis Ababa as settlement nodes. The measurement of land also gave a graphic image of the incredible feats of landgrabbing that some members of the nobility had performed. There were at least three known instances of aggregate possessions of over half a million square meters. The value of land also indicated the centrality or otherwise of a location, Arada land understandably fetching the highest price.

A third important landmark in this period was the arrival of the Djibouti–Addis Ababa railway in 1917. One scholarly analyst of the evolution of Addis Ababa has underscored the importance of modes of transportation in the city's evolution – first human and animal transport, followed successively by

---

13 See ibid., p. 71.
14 See Berlan, *Addis Abeba, la plus haute ville d'Afrique*, pp. 67ff.

rail, motor, and air transport.[15] It had taken exactly twenty years to finish construction of the troubled line. But once it reached its final destination, its impact on national life in general and that of the capital in particular was immediate and palpable. Although the imposing building that now graces the station was not erected until about a decade later, the terminal formed an important nucleus and point of reference. By accident or by design, the station was almost exactly due south of Saint George Church and Arada, the commercial center. What came to be known as the Station Road linked the two nodal points. As Martin Johnson has observed: "the railroad focus was, and is, a different type of node than the two earlier nodes that had so much influence on city structure. Instead of being a focus of routes from many directions, it was a node that served the market by a single well-used road."[16]

Thus, the railway station gave the city a major artery that is still a dominant feature of its road network. Its primacy can be seen from the fact that, during the Italian Occupation, it was baptized Viale Mussolini (Mussolini Avenue) after the Fascist dictator who had launched the invasion. Subsequent to the end of Fascist Italian rule in 1941, it was rechristened Churchill Road (a name it carries to this day), in gratitude to the British World War II hero who helped launch the expeditionary force that terminated Fascist rule in northeast Africa. The construction of the City Hall in the early 1960s gave this artery a faint resemblance to the Champs-Élysées. The Hall, "with the symmetrical arrangement of its office wings, and the slender tower in the middle – looking out towards the monumental axis – seems to open up in a symbolic manner to embrace the city."[17] A French master plan drawn up in 1965 found the parallel and symbolism so irresistible that it envisaged a replication of the famed French avenue.[18] Unfortunately, like almost all master plans of the city to date, this one too came to naught.

The Station Road had an added significance for the future development of the city's road network. It gave rise to another important intersection, now known as Adwa Square, linking the Station Road with the Jimma Road, so called because it led to the coffee-rich town of that name in southwestern Ethiopia. After the construction of the Haile Sellassie I Theatre (rebaptized National Theatre after the 1974 Revolution), Adwa Square became a major cultural and entertainment center, competing with and eventually surpassing the

---

15 See Johnson, "The Evolution of the Morphology of Addis Ababa, Ethiopia," p. xvi.
16 Ibid., p. 280.
17 Dejene H. Mariam, "Architecture in Addis Ababa," in *Proceedings of the International Symposium on the Centenary of Addis Ababa*, pp. 207–208.
18 See Techeste Ahderom, "Basic Planning Principles and Objectives Taken in the Preparation of the Addis Ababa Master Plan: Past and Present," in *Proceedings of the International Symposium on the Centenary of Addis Ababa*, p. 256.

old Arada (known as Piazza after the Italian Occupation). A southern branch of the Jimma Road came to pass directly in front of the station toward Masqal/Revolution Square.[19] With the subsequent extension of this branch to what became Asmara Road, that square developed as the most important nodal point in southwest Addis Ababa.

The Jimma Road formed the southern lateral of a quadrangle, within which the pre-1935 city was primarily enclosed. The northern lateral was constituted by the road linking Saint George Cathedral to the *gebbi* of Ras Makonnen (Menilek's cousin and righthand man, and father of Emperor Hayla-Sellase) at what came to be known as Seddest Kilo. It is worth noting that this *gebbi* formed the site of the first of the two palaces alluded to earlier to have been built by Hayla-Sellase, subsequently turned into the main campus of Haile Sellassie I University (now Addis Ababa University). The road linking Makonnen's *gebbi* to the imperial *gebbi* (Seddest Kilo to Arat Kilo) formed another major artery roughly parallel to Station Road. In the middle of the two (northern and southern) laterals was the most important thoroughfare linking Arada to Arat Kilo. Along this winding artery, later to be famous as Haile Sellassie I Avenue, were constructed the modern buildings housing the major expatriate firms. The architecture in this period was predominantly Indian-Arab in style.[20]

The coronation of Emperor Hayla-Sellase in 1930 forms another landmark of this period. As Johnson has aptly observed, it introduced the tradition of renovating the city on special occasions and erecting facades to cover the old and ugly.[21] In addition to Menilek's equestrian statue cited above, the occasion gave rise to three other monuments. One of these was the statue of the Lion of Judah erected in the square in front of the railway station. The Italians, who did not particularly like this symbol of Ethiopian invincibility, removed it during the Occupation. It has now been restored to its original place. The second was a monument at Arat Kilo, a square that also reflected the shifting fortunes of the country as the symbol of conquest and liberation (both conveniently falling on May 5, the first in 1936 and the second in 1941). The third could be described as the epicenter of pre-1935 Addis, located in the southeastern corner of Arada. As was to be expected, it was called Haile Sellassie I Square, until changed to De Gaulle Square on the occasion of the French president's visit to Ethiopia in 1966. Such a dramatic act of self-sacrifice was perhaps explicable by Ethiopian flirtation with France in view of the imminent decolonization of its colony of Djibouti, an important outlet for Ethiopia.

19 See Johnson, "The Evolution of the Morphology of Addis Ababa, Ethiopia," p. 288.
20 Dejene, "Architecture in Addis Ababa," p. 202.
21 See Johnson, "The Evolution of the Morphology of Addis Ababa, Ethiopia," p. 290.

The Italian Occupation, 1936–41   With the inauguration of the Fascist Italian Occupation in May 1936, Addis Ababa was transformed from being the capital of Ethiopia to that of the new colonial empire of Italian East Africa (Africa orientale italiana, in its Italian rendering). This new entity was formed by the Italians through the merger of their newly acquired prize with the old colonies of Eritrea and Somaliland. The new colonial empire was divided into five ethno-linguistic regions (Eritrea, Somalia, Amhara, Harar, and Galla & Sidama) and a sixth metropolitan region centered in and designated Addis Ababa. In due course, however, Addis Ababa was changed to Scioa (Shawa). For some time, the Fascists had toyed with the idea of abandoning Addis Ababa as the capital and moving it either to the west or east. Factors that militated against the old capital were its altitude (which the new Mediterranean residents found exhausting), the population concentration that hindered new planning, and the dense foliage that provided cover to insurgents against Fascist rule. In the end, however, consideration of prestige tipped the balance and Mussolini decided to retain Addis Ababa as the capital.[22]

À propos the issue of the city center that is the theme of this paper, the Fascists introduced to the capital the quintessentially Italian concept of the piazza (square). In a small Italian town, the piazza is *the* center where people converge to relax and chat. It is also where the main shops are located. But the bigger the town, the more piazze there are, giving Italian cities their polycentric character. Addis Ababa being a relatively big town at the time of its conquest by the Italians, it also came to have more than one piazza. The old city center, Arada, was christened Piazza Littorio. To the north, the square facing Saint George Cathedral where the equestrian statue of Emperor Menilek had formerly stood was named Piazza Impero ("Empire Square"). The two nodes of the major eastern vertical route (the political axis – as it were – stretching from the new *gebbi* to the old one) were rechristened: Seddest Kilo became Piazza Roma ("Rome Square") and Arat Kilo Piazza 5 Maggio ("May 5 Square"). The former was a tribute to the imperial capital, the latter commemorated the fall of Addis Ababa in 1936. As already indicated, after 1941, May 5 Square became Miyazya 27 Square (Miyazya 27 being the Ethiopian equivalent of May 5) and came to commemorate Emperor Hayla-Sellase's triumphal entry into Addis Ababa on the very same day. Rome Square was changed to Yakatit 12 (February 19) Square, commemorating the thousands of Ethiopians brutally murdered in retaliation for the attempt on the life of the Italian viceroy Rodolfo Graziani.

---

22 See Richard Pankhurst, "Development in Addis Ababa during the Italian Fascist Occupation (1936–1941)," in *Proceedings of the International Symposium on the Centenary of Addis Ababa*, pp. 119–120.

Interestingly enough, after the departure of the Italians, while all the other piazze disappeared, Piazza Littorio has endured to this day as *the* "Piazza," the center. Until it came to be challenged by other centers that grew up in subsequent decades, it was the center of fashion and elegance. With its three cinema halls, it was also the major entertainment center. All three were built during the Italian period. The names of the first two had been appropriately changed after 1941 from Marconi to Adwa and from Italia to Ethiopia; the third was neutral enough to be merely translated from Impero to Empire. Piazza was where people went to wine and dine. The best Italian restaurant in the city, the Castelli, is still located there. It was where the young and trendy went to see and be seen, to show their new acquisitions, be it girlfriends (or boyfriends) and deluxe cars. In the 1960s, in particular, youngsters perambulating to and fro in the evening along the Haile Sellassie I Avenue (Corso Vittorio Emmanuele during the Italian Occupation) was a common enough sight, in somewhat the same way that the thoroughfares leading to the piazza of small Italian towns attract evening crowds.

As a commercial center, however, Piazza came to be challenged and ultimately overtaken by a new entrepôt in the western part of town. This was another outcome of the Fascist Occupation. In line with the colonial policy of segregation, reinforced by the racist ethos that permeated the Fascist order, the Italians embarked on an ambitious progam of restructuring the capital. Using the Kurtume River as a natural divide, the eastern part – which constituted most of the old city – was reserved for the Italians, ironically designated "nationals," while the western part was to develop as a separate town for the Ethiopians, *gli indigeni* ("the indigenous population"). To cater for the commercial needs of the Ethiopians, a new market was set up. Named *mercato indigeno* ("the indigenous market"), it later shed its ascriptive epithet and has come to be an enduring feature of Addis life as Mercato.

Mercato has two distinctive components: the open market and the shops, a number of the latter owing their origin to the Italian period. The former is reputed to be the largest open market on the continent. It is a scene of a dogged struggle for survival and of remarkable ingenuity and improvisation. The term *Arada*, initially associated with the pre-1935 market, was trans-located to the new commercial center. In its new context, it denoted not only commercial transaction but also inner-city smartness. The shops, expanded in the post-Liberation period, offer a mixture of locally manufactured and imported goods. Both the open market and the shops have come to be dominated by the Gurage, known for their drive and enterprise. Mercato also became the center around which a new urban settlement rose, inhabited mostly by the Gurage at the initial stage but eventually drawing other groups as well. Interestingly enough, the major settlement of the Gurage, located to the west of Mercato, came to be called Addis Katama ("New Town").

Of the other settlements that emerged in the quarter reserved for the Italians, the most notable was probably Casanchis. The name arose from a corruption of "Case INCIS," the acronym standing for the Italian parastatal entrusted with constructing residential blocks for state officials (Istituto nazionale per le case degli impiegati dello stato). Relics of these buildings still house one of the city's police stations, the Ministry of Agriculture, and the Ministry of Labor and Social Affairs. Otherwise, the quarter has come to distinguish itself – more than anything else – as one of the city's major night-life districts. The emergence and growth of Casanchis has had the effect of pulling the city southeastward and filling the gap, as it were, between the old Gebbi and Urael, one of the city's earliest churches, now probably the most popular place of worship for the Orthodox laity.

A final important legacy of the Italian period was in the sphere of architecture. The Italians built a number of buildings that still form visible landmarks in the city, particularly in the Piazza area, along the Churchill Road (Viale Mussolini during the Italian period), and in the residential quarters of Casanchis and Case Popolare (the more plebeian counterpart of Case INCIS). With their solid and rectangular shape, these buildings brought a new style so different from the conical and largely wooden structures of the pre-1935 period. Not least of the value of these Italian-built edifices was their use for government offices and business enterprises as well as entertainment centers in the post-1941 period.

From Liberation to Revolution, 1941–74 If the railway station could be said to have played a decisive role in pulling the city southward, the airports had an equally significant contribution in consolidating and deepening this process. In effect, they pulled the city first southwestward and then southeastward. In the process, what Johnson has dubbed "the Modernizing South"[23] was born. Two major nodes were created as points of entry into the city center: Mexico Square (formerly Maychaw Square) in the southwest and Masqal/Revolution Square in the southeast.

The first airplanes had made their appearance in 1929–30. But they pertained to the age of amateur rather than civil aviation. At the time, the race course at Seddest Kilo known as Janmeda (an ellipsis of Janhoy Meda, or "the Field of the Emperor") was deemed sufficient for landings and take-offs. With

---

23 Johnson, "The Evolution of the Morphology of Addis Ababa, Ethiopia," p. 383.

the inauguration of Ethiopian Airlines and the launching of the first international passenger service in 1946, it became necessary for a more open airfield and a terminal building. An airfield in the southwestern outskirts of the city, yet another relic of the Italian period, was converted into the first international airport.

Contrary to experience elsewhere in the world, where people equate airports with noise pollution, airports have exercised a strange magnetic pull on Addis Ababa residents. It is also true that, again unlike the situation in most countries, both airports in Addis Ababa's history have been located within a few minutes' drive from the city center. The opening of the old airport resulted in a dramatic rise in land values in the neighborhood, more specifically the area to the west and south of the airport. This became the site for the residential buildings of the affluent members of society and the growing expatriate community. The road leading from the airport also gained prominence and stimulated construction. Of the buildings that came to line the road, the most important are the former Princess Tsehay Hospital (named after Emperor Hayla-Sellase's favorite daughter) and the Building College. Two other major buildings, the Soviet-sponsored Balcha Hospital and the Technical School, seem to be relics of the Italian period in their architectural style.[24] The nodal point of the airport route was designated Maychaw Square, after the major battle of the Italo-Ethiopian War of 1935–36. Later, presumably at the height of Ethio-Mexican friendship, it was changed to Mexico Square.

In 1963, as Ethiopian Airlines entered the Jet Age, a new airport to accommodate the new aircraft was opened in the southeastern outskirts of the city. At the time, this was deemed sufficiently far from the city center. But it is now only ten to fifteen minutes' drive. Following the same curious logic that we have seen in the case of the old airport, the new airport also attracted large-scale settlement of the affluent and the expatriate. Bole, the name of the new district (and also of the airport), indeed remains to this day a symbol of affluence and class. There were two stages of this development. The first was marked by construction along the main road leading from the airport to Masqal Square – a process that is not yet completed, especially in the vicinity of the airport. The second involved construction in depth off the main road.

The Silver Jubilee of Emperor Hayla-Selasse's coronation in November 1955 was an event marked by considerable pomp and pageantry. It was as if the emperor wanted to show the world that Ethiopia had indeed finally joined the Modern Age. A grand exhibition showing the diversity of Ethiopian life and the

---

24 See ibid., p. 381; Berlan, *Addis Abeba, la plus haute ville d'Afrique*, p. 165.

notable achievements of the regime was staged, appropriately enough not far from the airport. More significantly for the theme of discussion here, some important buildings were constructed that contributed to accentuating two of the nodal points discussed above. The first building was the Haile Sellassie I Theatre (National Theatre after 1974), more grandiloquently dubbed the Opera. This building enhanced the nodal importance of Adwa Square by creating an entertainment center rivaling and ultimately surpassing the triple-cinema complex of Piazza. With the opening of the Ambassador Theatre less than a hundred meters to the northeast, the cultural preeminence of Adwa Square was assured.

A second major building activity involved the Jubilee Palace and the adjacent Ghion Hotel. The former contributed to the southward pull of the politico-administrative axis that had hitherto stopped at Arat Kilo. This in turn ensured the nodal importance of Masqal Square. Ghion remained the luxury hotel until superseded by the Hilton in the second half of the 1960s. On the other hand, the building of the Hilton, the Ministry of Foreign Affairs opposite, and the headquarters of the ECA, opened in 1958 across the park from the Jubilee Palace, completed the process of building up the stretch of ground between the old Gebbi and Masqal Square, the major southeastern node of Addis Ababa.[25]

The 1963 summit of African heads of state that led to the founding of the OAU could only reinforce the above trends. The elevation of the status of Addis Ababa from a national capital to a continental metropolis enhanced the importance of the above quadrangle – marked by Africa Hall, the Hilton, the Foreign Ministry, and the Jubilee Palace – and the importance of the Bole airport and Masqal Square. At the same time, it boosted the construction of upper-class residential buildings in the vicinity of both airports, old and new.

The Period of the Revolution, 1974–91 As is to be expected, the 1974 Revolution in Ethiopia had a profound impact on Addis Ababa, as it did on the country as a whole. If anything, the impact on the capital was bound to be most pronounced, as it was the center not only of national life but also of political contestation. The most decisive and bitter struggles for power were fought out not only in secret chambers of the palace but also in the streets of the capital. Addis Ababa also became the ultimate prized target of the guerrillas who in 1991 toppled the military regime known as the Darg that had appropriated the mantle of revolutionary leadership.

---

25 See Johnson, "The Evolution of the Morphology of Addis Ababa, Ethiopia," p. 381.

The first revolutionary measure that affected life in the city in a fundamental and enduring way was the nationalization of urban property and extra houses in July 1975. This was the second major blow to the ruling establishment, the first being the nationalization of rural land that was proclaimed in March of the same year. This measure had a number of ramifications. First and foremost, it stripped the rentier class of an important source of revenue. Secondly, the transfer of ownership of extra houses to neighborhood associations (if their rent was below Eth Birr 100 or US$50 at the prevailing rate) or the parastatal set up for the purpose (if their rent was above that figure) contributed significantly to the atmosphere of drabness and dereliction that has marked the city's buildings. Unlike private owners, these extraneous organs were not keen on repair and maintenance. The continuation of the same administrative regime after the change of system in 1991 has meant that there has not been any appreciable amelioration of the situation. If anything, things have gone from bad to worse. The sterility of architectural style in the revolutionary period – as opposed to the dynamism and innovation of the pre-revolutionary period[26] – has only tended to enhance the drabness.

Most importantly, the July 1975 proclamation was accompanied by the setting up of a new administrative structure. The lowest but most important unit of this new administration was the neighborhood association (the *qabale*), followed in ascending order of hierarchy by the "Higher" (*kaftañña*), the zone (*qatana*), and the city council.[27] The *qabale* became not only the administrator of the smaller houses (in many instances, sheer hovels), but also the battleground between the military regime and its civilian opponents, notably the members of the militant Ethiopian People's Revolutionary Party (EPRP). Many members of the former *qabale* administration, particularly those of the much-dreaded Revolutionary Defense Squad, are still in jail, undergoing trial for their role in the perpetration of the so-called Red Terror – the name given to legitimize the summary execution of suspected members of EPRP, as opposed to the "White Terror" committed by armed squads of EPRP.

But once the bloody shoot-out was over and the regime had consolidated absolute power, the *qabale* began to acquire some of the attributes of neighborhood associations, even if election of officials was always strictly controlled by the government. This became the situation in the 1980s and has more or less continued to this day. Their shops supplied – albeit rationed – much-needed and scarce commodities at reasonable prices. The more affluent *qabale* in the

---

26 See Dejene, "Architecture in Addis Ababa," pp. 212–213.
27 See Christopher Clapham, *Transformation and Continuity in Revolutionary Ethiopia* (Cambridge: Cambridge University Press, 1988), pp. 130–136.

Bole area developed into entertainment and leisure centers – some of them complete with tennis courts. In effect, some of these *qabale* have come to replace the old city centers as focal points of social interaction and entertainment.

As far as construction was concerned, the revolutionary period understandably resulted in what amounted to a freeze. This was particularly the case with regard to private construction. Few would be keen on building at a time when nationalization was the dominant ethos. This began to change only in the mid-1980s when, encouraged by the state, a number of housing cooperatives sprang up. This resulted in the growth of new residential quarters, almost entirely in the southern and southeastern parts of the city. Because of the small plots of land allowed, these buildings were highly economical in nature (*qutaba*, denoting frugality, is the Amharic term for them) and tended to give the new quarters a crowded look.

But the further pull of the city south and southeastward accentuated the polycentrism that had become a perceptible feature even before 1974. Shopping areas and refreshment centers sprang up to cater to the new constituencies. It is true that these new residential areas had no cinema halls. But under the spartan regime that prevailed, the old cinema halls had ceased to attract clientele because they could show only old and dated films. On the other hand, the phenomenal growth of video rental had rendered even the old cinema halls irrelevant and fostered an in-house entertainment culture throughout the city.

The forced shift from a command to mixed economy in the twilight hours of the military regime contributed to another boom in construction, this time in business enterprises, principally hotels. But most of these hotels were not completed until after the fall of the Darg in 1991. Once completed, however, they provided an alternative to the old established ones in the traditional center in the provision not only of accommodation but also of refreshment and social intercourse. This in turn accentuated the city's polycentrism.

The 1980s were also memorable for yet another effort to streamline the city's chaotic and spontaneous growth with the adumbration of yet another master plan. This plan took for granted the polycentric character of the city and envisaged the development of "a continuous urban system organized around six major sub-centers (*qatana* centers), and with limited and gradual expansion in the peripheral fringes and along the three main communication axes in the east, south, and west."[28] The southern edge of the city was to serve as the main location for industry and transport infrastructure. The plan also provided for a

---

28 Techeste, "Basic Planning Principles and Objectives Taken in the Preparation of the Addis Ababa Master Plan," p. 263.

greenbelt around the city with the twin purpose of peri-urban agriculture and recreation.

Like all earlier plans, this one too was not implemented on the ground, partly for lack of the necessary legal mechanism.[29] It is currently undergoing revision. In a similar manner, a master plan drawn up in 1956 by a British architect, Sir Patrick Abercombie, had been designed to "foster a richer and more intimate community life" and provided for six satellite towns around the city.[30] In a way, although it was sinister in its design and incomplete in its realization, the Fascist Italian master plan was more successful than all its successors. At the very least, it has given the city the permanent fixture of Mercato and foreshadowed the major artery (Viale Imperiale, as it was christened by the Italians) that extended the political axis to Masqal/Revolution Square.

Concluding Remarks Like many of its Ethiopian precursors, Addis Ababa owed its genesis to the twin pillars of church and state. These two institutions served as the nodes around which the city developed in its early years. The religious center, Saint George, had the added significance of evolving as the commercial center, Arada. For something like half a century, Arada was the social and cultural as well as the commercial center of the city. The Italian Occupation enhanced this role both by adding new buildings and by introducing the concept of the piazza. On the other hand, it contributed to the birth of a new commercial center, Mercato, which eventually appropriated the name Arada.

But more than anything else, the expansion of the city can be credited to the two universal indices of modern transport – the railway and the airline. Both developments, separated by something like three decades, were instrumental in drawing the city southward and creating new centers – going from west to east, Mexico Square, Lagahar (as the railway station area was known, through a corruption of the French term *la gare*), and Masqal/Revolution Square. These emerged in the second half of the 20th century as the nodes from which the southern extension of the city radiated.

A distinctive feature of the city's evolution has been its spontaneous, not to say chaotic, growth. The city has consistently defied planning. The many master plans drawn from the 1930s to the 1980s have been confined to the shelf. In the 1950s, the idea of moving the capital to the young and still planable town of Bahr Dar (on Lake Tana) was seriously considered. The idea was akin to the considerations that led to the birth of such new capitals as Brasilia (in Brazil)

---

29 See Tajebe Beyene, *Addis Ababa Tenagar* (Let Addis Ababa Speak) (Addis Ababa, 1968), p. 112.
30 "Sir Patrick Abercombie's Town Plan," *Ethiopia Observer* 1, no. 2 (March 1957), p. 35.

and Abuja (in Nigeria). But, in the Ethiopian case, the shift did not materialize. Even if it had, it is doubtful that it would have meant the eclipse of Addis Ababa, just as Rio de Janeiro and Lagos have not lost their vitality despite the shift to new capitals. Moreover, just as the eucalyptus saved Addis Ababa at the turn of the last century, the city's emergence as an African metropolis (as headquarters of ECA and OAU) ensured its permanence and centrality. As the century wore on, the city, chaotic and unmanageable, surged on, turning its back to the historic north and sprawling inexorably toward the resource-rich south.

Contributors

Mohamadou Abdoul is a member of CODESRIA (Council for the Development of Social Science Research in Africa) and a researcher in its Multinational Working Group, "Urban Processes and Change in Africa." He has produced studies on democratization and urbanization, and between 1992 and 2002 organized the media program of the Panos Institute West Africa. He is presently a program officer at Enda Tiers Monde (Environment and Development Action in the Third World) on the team "Prospectives Dialogues Politiques."

Ibrahim Abdullah is a professor in the Department of History, University of the Western Cape. He has taught at universities in Africa and North America and has published widely in the area of African social and labor history. His current research project, "Subalternity, Insurgency, and Post-conflict Strategy: An Alternative Reading of the Sierra Leonean Conflict," is being funded by the Social Science Research Council in New York. Abdullah is a member of the Scientific Panel of CODESRIA (Council for the Development of Social Science Research in Africa) and the South African History Project, a ministerial committee of historians tasked with rewriting South African history.

Victor A. O. Adetula holds teaching/research positions at the University of Jos, and served as the director of the Centre for Development Studies, University of Jos, 1998–2001. He has researched and published in the areas of Africa's international relations, the politics of development, democracy and governance in Africa, and human rights issues. His most recent publication is a co-edited book, *Border Crime and Community Insecurity in Nigeria* (2002). Adetula is an active member of the Nigerian Political Science Association, the Nigerian Society of International Affairs, and the Council for the Development of Social Science Research in Africa (CODESRIA). He has a history of active involvement in the Nigerian NGO/development community and is currently on leave of absence from his position as Senior Program Manager in the Democracy and Governance Office of USAID/Nigeria.

Babatunde A. Ahonsi is Senior Program Officer of the Human Development and Reproductive Health program in the Ford Foundation's Office for West Africa, Lagos. Prior to his appointment at Ford in 1997, he taught courses in sociology and demography at the University of Lagos and was involved in research and technical assistance to a number of Nigerian NGOs working on gender equity, reproductive health, environmental sustainability, and youth development. He has published numerous essays in scholarly journals and books, and is co-editor of *Widowhood in Nigeria* (1997). Among other professional engagements, he is currently a member of the Gender Advisory Panel of WHO's Department of Reproductive Health and Research.

For the past three years, **Antoine Bouillon** has co-supervised a comparative study on economic development, democracy, and governance in the cities of Abidjan, Durban, and Marseille for the Institut de Recherche pour le Développement (IRD) based in Paris. He is a co-founder of the French Anti-Apartheid Movement and the OFAS, a "Platform for Cooperation" between French and South African NGOs. He has taught philosophy and social sciences in France and Madagascar, and as a freelance journalist has published widely in many southern African–focused anti-apartheid publications. He is the co-editor of *African Immigration to South Africa* (2001) and *Governance, Urban Dynamics and Economic Development: A Comparative Analysis of the Metropolitan Areas of Durban, Abidjan and Marseilles* (2002).

Lindsay J. Bremner is currently chairperson of the architecture department at the University of the Witwatersrand, Johannesburg. From 1993 to 1997, she served on the Executive Committee of the Greater Johannesburg Metropolitan Council, during which time she chaired committees on planning, housing, urbanization, and environmental management. Bremner has published widely in books and journals, and is co-editor of *Freedom Square* (1998) and *Emerging Johannesburg* (forthcoming).

Filip De Boeck is professor of anthropology at the Catholic University of Leuven, where he co-directs the Africa Research Centre. In 2002, he was a visiting professor in the Department of Sociology, University of California, San Diego. Since 1987, he has conducted extensive research in Democratic Republic of Congo. De Boeck's current research interests include children and youth as emerging categories in postcolonial Africa. He is collaborating with photographer Marie-Françoise Plissart on a book about Kinshasa.

Mohammed Gheris is a researcher in the Multinational Working Group "Urban Processes and Change in Africa" organized by CODESRIA (Council for the Development of Social Science Research in Africa) and teaches in the law and economics program at the Université Cadi Ayyad in Marrakech. He is currently preparing a doctoral thesis in economics on the politics of financing housing in the Maghreb at Mohammed V University in Rabat and is a member of CEDIMES (Centre d'Études sur les Mouvements Économiques et Sociaux), which is based in Paris.

Koku Konu of the Lagos Urbanist Group is director of dkr associates–architects and designers, Lagos, and the director-general of the Creative Intelligence Agency (CIA), Lagos, which promotes creative solutions in the fields of architecture and urbanism. His recent activities include collaborative projects for Lagos 2000, an urban regeneration proposal for downtown Lagos; "What Is All the Fuss About?," an art and architecture tour through six European countries as part of Eurotour 2000; and Barcelona Debate 2001, which searched for a response to the premise that African cities grow through destruction and are organized through chaos.

Initially a journalist and screenwriter, **Rem Koolhaas** has worked as an architect since 1975, when he created the Office of Metropolitan Architecture (OMA). OMA has created master plans and designs for commissions around the globe, most recently, the Museum of Korean Art and the Seoul National University Museum, Universal Studios in Los Angeles, the city center in Almere, Netherlands, and Hanoi's New Town. Koolhaas and the OMA have been the subject of numerous publications, films, and exhibitions. Since 1995, Koolhaas has been a professor at Harvard University, where he has directed a series of research initiatives under the title "Project on the City," including one in Lagos. He is the author of the classic *Delirious New York* (1978) and *S, M, L, XL* (1995).

Achille Mbembe is a senior researcher at the Institute for Social and Economic Research, University of the Witwatersrand, Johannesburg. From 1996 to 2000, he was executive director of CODESRIA (Council for the Development of Social Science Research in Africa), and has held professorships and visiting scholar status at many universities, including Columbia and Berkeley. His most recent work, *On the Postcolony* (2000), is at the forefront of international debate about Africa's postcolonial predicament. Mbembe's many publications include *La naissance du maquis dans le Sud-Cameroun* (1996) and *On Private Indirect Government* (2000).

Thierry Nlandu teaches Anglo-American literature at the University of Kinshasa. He is the scientific advisor to the Congolese Association of Moralists, a Program Officer at the International Human Rights Law Group in Kinshasa, and a consultant in organizational development. A dramatist, he is known for his activities as a political activist and is a member of Groupe Amos in Kinshasa. He is particularly interested in issues relating to violence against women and collaborates actively with NGOs in Democratic Republic of Congo that promote women's rights through popular education.

Poet and film historian, **Onookome Okome** is currently the Alexander von Humboldt Research Fellow at the University of Bayreuth, Germany, and has taught at the University of Calabar since 1989. Widely traveled, Okome has given lectures in Brazil, Switzerland, Ireland, the UK, the US, and Israel. His publications include *Cinema and Social Change in West Africa* (with Jonathan Haynes, 1995), *Before I Am Hanged: Ken Saro-Wiwa, Literature, Politics and Dissent* (2000), *Ogun's Children: The Literature and Politics of Wole Soyinka Since the Nobel* (2002), and *Writing the Homeland: The Poetry and Politics of Tanure Ojaide* (2002). He is currently researching popular video films in Africa.

Carole Rakodi is professor of international urban development in the School of Public Policy, University of Birmingham. A geographer and urban planner, she worked for many years at the Department of City and Regional Planning, Cardiff University. She has professional and research experience in Zambia, Zimbabwe, Kenya, Ghana, and India, and has published numerous books and articles on urban planning and management, land and housing markets, and poverty. Her recent publications include *The Urban Challenge in Africa: Growth and Management of Its Large Cities* (1997), and *Urban Livelihoods: A People-centred Approach to Reducing Poverty* (2002).

Maxine Reitzes currently directs research in the Democracy and Governance Program of the Human Sciences Research Council, South Africa. She began her career as an academic, lecturing at universities in South Africa and overseas. After the 1994 democratic elections, she joined the policy community, and focused on policy research, evaluation, and formulation. She has worked for many NGOs and managed projects funded by a range of foreign political donors. Her numerous policy papers and studies include *The Migrant Challenge to Realpolitik: Towards a Human Rights–based Approach to Immigration Policy in South and Southern Africa* (1997) and *Funding Freedom? Synthesis Report on the Impact of Foreign Political Aid to Civil Society Organisations in South Africa* (with Steven Friedman, 2001).

Janet Roitman is a research fellow with the CNRS (Centre National de la Recherche Scientifique) in Paris. She has conducted extensive fieldwork in northern Cameroon and Chad on emergent forms of economic regulation. Her recent publications include "New Sovereigns? Regulatory Authority in the Chad Basin," in *Intervention and Transnationalism in Africa*, ed. Thomas Callaghy et al. (2001), and "A Mode of Governing in the Chad Basin," in *Blackwell Companion to Global Anthropology*, ed. Aihwa Ong and Stephen J. Collier (forthcoming). Her forthcoming book is entitled *Incivisme fiscale: Une anthropologie de la regulation économique*.

AbdouMaliq Simone presently holds joint academic appointments at the Graduate Program in International Affairs, New School University, New York, and the Institute of Social and Economic Research, University of the Witwatersrand, Johannesburg. He has worked for several African NGOs and regional institutions, including CODESRIA (Council for the Development of Social Science Research in Africa), the United Nations Economic Commission for Africa, and the United Nations Centre for Human Settlements. His publications include "Straddling the Divides: Remaking Associational Life in the Informal African City," *International Journal of Urban and Regional Research* (2001), and the forthcoming book, *For the City Yet to Come: Changing Urban Life in Africa*.

Jean Omasombo Tshonda is a member of the Multinational Working Group "Urban Processes and Change in Africa," operating under the auspices of CODESRIA (Council for the Development of Social Science Research in Africa). He is a professor of political science at the University of Kinshasa, where he directs the Center for Political Studies, and co-author of *Patrice Lumumba, jeunesse et apprentissage politique* (1998), and *République démocratique du Congo: Chronique politique d'un pays en guerre et des trente derniers mois de Laurent Désiré Kabila* (2001), among numerous other publications.

Mohammed-Bello Yunusa is head of the Department of Urban and Regional Planning and deputy dean of the Faculty of Environmental Design, Ahmadu Bello University, Samaru-Zaria, Nigeria. He has conducted numerous studies on nongovernmental organizations, rural and urban livelihood strategies, poverty, and infrastructure, and published in a number of books and journals in these areas of research. He is a member of the Multinational Working Group "Urban Processes and Change in Africa," organized by CODESRIA (Council for the Development of Social Science Research in Africa).

Alfred B. Zack-Williams is professor of sociology at the University of Central Lancashire, Preston, UK, and a member of the Editorial Working Group of the *Review of African Political Economy*. He has authored many articles and books on the political economy of underdevelopment in Africa, including *Tributors, Supporters and Merchant Capital: Mining and Underdevelopment in Sierra Leone* (1995), and *Structural Adjustment: Theory, Practice and Impacts* (with Ed Brown and Giles Mohan, 2000), and is the co-editor of *Africa in Crisis: New Challenges and Possibilities* (2001).

Bahru Zewde is professor of history at the University of Addis Ababa and a member of the Multinational Working Group "Urban Processes and Change in Africa," working under the auspices of CODESRIA (Council for the Development of Social Science Research in Africa). He is the author of *A History of Modern Ethiopia, 1855–1991* (2d ed., 2001), and *Pioneers of Change in Ethiopia: The Reformist Intellectuals of the Early Twentieth Century* (2002). Zewde is on the executive committee of the Organization for Social Science Research in Eastern and Southern Africa (OSSREA). His recent work concerns the historical roots and causes of the Ethiopia-Eritrea conflict.